Lecture Notes in Computer Science 14421

The series Lecture Notes in Computer Science (LNCS), including its subseries Lecture Notes in Artificial Intelligence (LNAI) and Lecture Notes in Bioinformatics (LNBI), has established itself as a medium for the publication of new developments in computer science and information technology research, teaching, and education.

LNCS enjoys close cooperation with the computer science R & D community, the series counts many renowned academics among its volume editors and paper authors, and collaborates with prestigious societies. Its mission is to serve this international community by providing an invaluable service, mainly focused on the publication of conference and workshop proceedings and postproceedings. LNCS commenced publication in 1973.

Elizabeth A. Quaglia
Editor

Cryptography and Coding

19th IMA International Conference, IMACC 2023
London, UK, December 12–14, 2023
Proceedings

 Springer

Editor
Elizabeth A. Quaglia 🆔
University of London
Egham, UK

ISSN 0302-9743   ISSN 1611-3349 (electronic)
Lecture Notes in Computer Science
ISBN 978-3-031-47817-8   ISBN 978-3-031-47818-5 (eBook)
https://doi.org/10.1007/978-3-031-47818-5

This Springer imprint is published by the registered company Springer Nature Switzerland AG
The registered company address is: Gewerbestrasse 11, 6330 Cham, Switzerland

Paper in this product is recyclable.

Preface

The International Conference on Cryptography and Coding is the biennial conference of the Institute of Mathematics and its Applications (IMA) on cryptography and coding theory. The conference series was established in 1995 and its 19th edition was held on December 12–14, 2023, at Royal Holloway, University of London.

The Program Committee for the conference, consisting of 21 international experts in cryptography and coding, selected 14 full papers from 36 submissions for presentation at the conference and inclusion in these proceedings. The review process was double-blind and rigorous. Each submission was reviewed independently by at least two reviewers in an individual review phase, and subsequently considered by the Program Committee in a discussion phase. Feedback from the reviews and discussions was provided to the authors and their revised submissions are included in these proceedings.

The papers accepted at IMACC23, which appear in this book, present cutting-edge results in a variety of areas, including coding theory, symmetric cryptography, zero-knowledge protocols, digital signature schemes and extensions, post-quantum cryptography and cryptography in practice.

The conference's program included invited talks from prominent researchers in the area, namely Dario Fiore (IMDEA Software Institute) and Carla Ràfols (Pompeu Fabra University), as well as the presentation of posters showcasing recent advances in coding theory and cryptography.

It was a pleasure to chair IMACC23, and I would like to thank in particular the Organizing Committee for their support, the Program Committee for their time, energy and very helpful work, and the IMA for their help in running the conference.

December 2023   Elizabeth A. Quaglia

Organization

General Chair

Elizabeth A. Quaglia   Royal Holloway, University of London, UK

Steering Committee

Martin Albrecht   King's College London, UK
Liqun Chen   University of Surrey, UK
Christopher Mitchell   Royal Holloway, University of London, UK
Máire O'Neill   Queen's University Belfast, UK
Maura B. Paterson   Birkbeck, University of London, UK

Organizing Committee

Angelo De Caro   IBM, Switzerland
Christopher Mitchell   Royal Holloway, University of London, UK
Maura B. Paterson   Birkbeck, University of London, UK

Program Committee

Olivier Blazy   École polytechnique, France
Xavier Bultel   INSA CVL, France
Liqun Chen   University of Surrey, UK
Elizabeth Crites   University of Edinburgh, UK
Alex Davidson   Universidade Nova de Lisboa, Portugal
Gareth Davies   NXP, Belgium
Angelo De Caro   IBM, Switzerland
Jean Paul Degabriele   Technology Innovation Institute, UAE
Itai Dinur   Ben-Gurion University, Israel
Benjamin Dowling   University of Sheffield, UK
Ashley Fraser   University of Surrey, UK
Lydia Garms   Keyless Technologies Limited, UK
Aurore Guillevic   Inria, France
Christian Janson   TU Darmstadt, Germany

Siaw-Lynn Ng	Royal Holloway, University of London, UK
Martha Norberg Hovd	Simula UiB, Norway
Maura B. Paterson	Birkbeck, University of London, UK
Thomas Prest	PQShield Ltd., UK
Elizabeth A. Quaglia (Chair)	Royal Holloway, University of London
Benjamin Smith	Inria and École polytechnique, Frances
Gaven J. Watson	Meta, USA

Additional Reviewers

Carsten Baum
Arghya Bhattacharjee
Gianluca Brian
Cyprien Delpech de Saint Guilhem
Scott Griffy
Jodie Knapp
Francois Morain
Christopher Newton
Morten Oygarden
Edoardo Persichetti
Wrenna Robson
Miruna Rosca
Yifan Song

Contents

Coding Theory

An Upper-Bound on the Decoding Failure Probability of the LRPC Decoder

Étienne Burle and Ayoub Otmani[✉]

Univ Rouen Normandie, INSA Rouen Normandie, Université Le Havre Normandie, Normandie Univ, LITIS UR 4108, F-76000 Rouen, France
{Etienne.Burle,Ayoub.Otmani}@univ-rouen.fr

Abstract. Low Rank Parity Check (LRPC) codes form a class of rank-metric error-correcting codes that was purposely introduced to design public-key encryption schemes. An LRPC code is defined from a parity check matrix whose entries belong to a relatively low dimensional vector subspace of a large finite field. This particular algebraic feature can then be exploited to correct with high probability rank errors when the parameters are appropriately chosen. In this paper, we present theoretical upper-bounds on the probability that the LRPC decoding algorithm fails.

Keywords: Rank metric · Decoding problem · LRPC code · Homogeneous matrix

1 Introduction

Rank-metric cryptography has attracted a relative interest over the last years mainly thanks to the recent trend that appeared with the goal of standardizing quantum-safe public-key algorithms. ROLLO [3] and RQC [1] are two examples of rank-metric public-key encryption schemes that were submitted to the NIST call for standardizing quantum-resistant public-key cryptographic algorithms. The theory of codes endowed with the rank-metric was first studied in [6] where a Singleton-type bound was proved and a class of codes reaching the bound was given. A few years later, Gabidulin constructed [7] the first example of rank-metric error-correcting codes which can be seen as the counterparts of generalized Reed-Solomon (GRS) codes. The so-called Gabidulin codes are defined from the evaluation of non-commutative linearized polynomials [12]. They can be efficiently decoded by an equivalent of the Euclidean algorithm [13] while achieving the rank-Singleton upper-bound. Not long after, the first rank-metric public-key encryption scheme called the GPT cryptosystem appeared in [8]. It bore strong similarities with the famous McEliece cryptosystem [11]. The GPT scheme is indeed an analogue of the McEliece cryptosystem but based on Gabidulin codes. Not surprisingly, this strong resemblance to GRS codes is the reason why their use in the GPT cryptosystem has been subject to several attacks [9,10], as well as the different reparations that were subsequently cryptanalysed [14–16]. These

© The Author(s), under exclusive license to Springer Nature Switzerland AG 2024
E. A. Quaglia (Ed.): IMACC 2023, LNCS 14421, pp. 3–16, 2024.
https://doi.org/10.1007/978-3-031-47818-5_1

flaws in the design do not mean that the rank-metric is not viable in cryptography. Indeed, the famous decoding problem has naturally its rank version which is also believed to be intractable both in a classical and quantum setting.

ROLLO replaces Gabidulin codes with the class of (Ideal) Low Rank Parity Check (LRPC) codes introduced in [4]. An LRPC code is defined by means of an homogeneous $(n-k) \times n$ parity-check matrix $\mathbf{H} = [h_{i,j}]$ where each entry $h_{i,j}$ lies in a linear subspace $W \subsetneq \mathbb{F}_{q^m}$ over $\mathbb{F}_q$ of relatively low dimension w. This property can then be exploited to design a probabilistic decoding algorithm that can recover any error vector $\mathbf{e} \in \mathbb{F}_{q^m}^n$ of rank weight $t \leqslant (n-k)/w$.

The principle behind the LRPC decoder [4] is to view the syndrome $\mathbf{s} = \mathbf{eH}^\mathsf{T}$ as a sample of a uniformly distributed random variable taking values on $(\mathcal{E} \cdot W)^{n-k}$ where $\mathcal{E} \subsetneq \mathbb{F}_{q^m}$ is the t-dimensional linear space generated over $\mathbb{F}_q$ by the coordinates of $\mathbf{e}$. Under the assumption that the linear space over $\mathbb{F}_q$ spanned by the entries of $\mathbf{s}$ denoted by $\mathcal{S} \subset \mathbb{F}_{q^m}$ is equal to $\mathcal{E} \cdot W$, the decoding algorithm first recovers a basis $\varepsilon_1, \ldots, \varepsilon_t$ of $\mathcal{E}$ by computing the intersection $\bigcap_{i=1}^{w} f_i^{-1} \cdot \mathcal{S}$ where $\{f_1, \cdots, f_w\}$ is an arbitrary (known) basis of W. The success of this step lies in the fact that with high probability this intersection is equal to $\mathcal{E}$. The last step then consists in computing the coordinates $e_1, \ldots, e_n$ of $\mathbf{e}$ by writing that $e_j = \sum_{d=1}^{t} x_{j,d}\varepsilon_d$ where each $x_{j,d} \in \mathbb{F}_q$ is unknown. One can then solve the linear system $\mathbf{s} = \mathbf{eH}^\mathsf{T}$ and expect to find a unique solution when $w \geqslant n/(n-k)$ because in that case the number of unknowns nt is at most the number $(n-k)wt$ of linear equations.

Recently, an encryption scheme based on LRPC codes has been proposed in [2] where the decoder receives a matrix of syndromes $\mathbf{S} = \mathbf{EH}^\mathsf{T}$ where $\mathbf{E}$ is an homogeneous matrix so that the probability that the entries of $\mathbf{S}$ span $\mathcal{E} \cdot W$ is increased. Another work [5] gives a new construction of error-correcting codes that can be decoded by the same techniques but relies on a generalization of the notion of homogeneous matrices. It introduced the concept of *semi-homogenous* parity-check matrices which are matrices such that the coordinates of each row span a different low-dimensional linear subspace of $\mathbb{F}_{q^m}$. This enables the authors to build a public-key encryption scheme where the public key is statistically close to a random matrix. Note that the security of ROLLO relies on the difficulty of the (Ideal) LRPC code *indistinguishability problem* which asserts that it is computationally hard to distinguish a randomly drawn parity-check matrix of an Ideal LRPC code from a random parity-check matrix of an Ideal code.

All these schemes have to deal with the decryption failures that inherently come from the LRPC decoding algorithm. As an adversary could shatter the security of these schemes if he manages to exploit decryption failures, it is therefore of paramount importance to lower the decoding failure probability below the desired security threshold. The best existing bounds on the decoding failure probability are given in [3,4]. It is stated in [4] that the decoding failure probability behaves essentially as $q^{-(n-k)+tw}$ which comes from an approximation of the probability that the entries of the syndrome vector $\mathbf{s}$ does not span $\mathcal{E} \cdot W$. Another analysis is given in [3] resulting to the expression $q^{-(n-k)+tw-1} + q^{-(w-1)(m-tw-t)}$. The first term corresponds to a tighter approximation of the one given in [4], and the quantity $q^{-(w-1)(m-tw-t)}$ reflects the probability that the intersection of random linear subspaces $\mathcal{R}_1, \ldots, \mathcal{R}_w$ all containing $\mathcal{E}$ is different from $\mathcal{E}$. Several works [2–4] assumed that $f_i^{-1} \cdot \mathcal{S}$ behaves as a random linear space $\mathcal{R}_i$ containing $\mathcal{E}$. But this hypothesis cannot be realistic because of the existence of the elements $f_1, \ldots, f_w$ in $\mathbb{F}_{q^m}$ such that $f_i \cdot \mathcal{R}_i = f_j \cdot \mathcal{R}_j$ for every $i \neq j$ when $\mathcal{R}_i = f_i^{-1} \cdot \mathcal{S}$. Although the validity of the approximation $q^{-(w-1)(m-tw-t)}$ is verified by simulations in [3], it does not necessarily predict the asymptotic behavior.

Our Contribution and Main Results

We revisit the analysis of the LRPC decoder with the main goal to establish provable theoretical bounds. Although we do not reach the best existing heuristic approximations, our work manages to close a little bit further the gap between the theoretical bounds and the practical approximations. We provide in Table 1 a comparison between existing bounds and the bounds we obtain in this work.

As we have seen, there are several reasons that make the LRPC decoder fail. The first one comes from the fact that the entries of $\mathbf{s}$ might not span $\mathcal{E} \cdot \mathcal{W}$. In [4, Proposition 4.3], the authors state that the coordinates of $\mathbf{s}$ are independently and uniformly distributed over $\mathcal{E} \cdot \mathcal{W}$ leading them to upper-bound the probability[1] by $q^{-(n-k)+tw}$. We provide in Proposition 1 a simple argument that explains why the coordinates of $\mathbf{s}$ are independent and uniform random variables over the random choices over $\mathbf{H}$ and $\mathbf{e}$. This enables us to use the closed-form expression of the probability that random vectors belonging to the same linear subspace span it. We apply this result to the coordinates of the syndrome vector $\mathbf{s}$ and we show in Proposition 5 that this probability is lower than $q^{-(n-k)+tw}/(q-1)$. We notice that when $\dim(\mathcal{E} \cdot \mathcal{W}) = tw$ the probability is equivalent to this term (see Remark 2). As a consequence, the upper-bound $q^{-(n-k)+tw-1}$ given in [3] cannot hold.

Next, the second reason why the LRPC decoder might not decode correctly comes from the fact that we do not obtain $\mathcal{E}$ when computing $\bigcap_{i=1}^{w} f_i^{-1} \cdot \mathcal{S}$. In the literature there exists essentially two ways to upper-bound the probability of occurrence of this event. One approach is described in [4] where two upper-bounds are given: in [4, Proposition 3.5] the probability is at most $tq^{tw(w+1)/2-m}$ and in [4, Proposition 3.8] it is at most $tq^{(2w-1)t-m}$. The other path followed in [3, Proposition 2.4.2] and [2, Proposition 3] consists in assuming as explained previously that $f_i^{-1} \cdot \mathcal{S}$ behaves as a random linear space $\mathcal{R}_i$ containing $\mathcal{E}$. This enables the authors to prove that the probability is at most $q^{-(w-1)(m-tw-t)}$. In this work, we depart from this assumption and we prove in Theorem 2 that this probability is at most $q^{(2w-1)t}/(q^m - q^{t-1})$. Although our bound is less interesting than $q^{-(w-1)(m-tw-t)}$, it is however better than the theoretical ones given in [4].

Finally the last situation that induces a decoding failure is when the unknown coordinates of $\mathbf{e}$ cannot be recovered because the linear system inferred from

---

[1] We can also get this result by using directly Theorem 2 from [2].

$\mathbf{s} = \mathbf{eH}^\mathsf{T}$ is not of full rank. This happens when the dimension of $\mathcal{E} \cdot \mathcal{W}$ is strictly less than $\dim_{\mathbb{F}_q} \mathcal{E} \dim_{\mathbb{F}_q} \mathcal{W} = tw$. The paper [4] shows in Proposition 3.3 that this case happens with probability at most tq^{tw-m} over the random choice of $\mathcal{E}$ and for a given set $\mathcal{W}$. In Proposition 4 we improve this bound by showing that this probability is at most $q^{tw}/\left(q^m - q^{t-1}\right)$.

Theorem 1 summarizes all our theoretical analysis which allows us to prove that when $twq^{-(n-k)+tw} \leqslant 1$, $tw = \omega(1)$ and $k = \Theta(n)$, we obtain an upper-bound asymptotically equivalent to $q^{-(n-k)+tw}/(q-1) + q^{2tw-m}$ as n tends to $+\infty$ (Corollary 1).

Table 1. Comparison with previous theoretical bounds

Case of error	Previous bound [4]	Our bound
$\mathbb{P}\left\{\langle\mathbf{eH}^\mathsf{T}\rangle_{\mathbb{F}_q} \neq \mathcal{E} \cdot \mathcal{W}\right\}$	$q^{-(n-k)+tw}$	$1 - \prod_{i=0}^{tw-1}\left(1 - q^{i-(n-k)}\right) < \frac{q^{-(n-k)+tw}}{q-1}$
$\mathbb{P}\left\{\mathcal{E} \neq \bigcap_{i=1}^{w} f_i^{-1} \cdot \mathcal{W} \cdot \mathcal{E}\right\}$	$tq^{(2w-1)t-m}$	$q^{(2w-1)t}/(q^m - q^{t-1})$
$\mathbb{P}\left\{\dim \mathcal{E} \cdot \mathcal{W} \neq tw\right\}$	tq^{tw-m}	$q^{tw}/\left(q^m - q^{t-1}\right)$

2 Preliminaries

2.1 Notation

The symbol $\triangleq$ will be used to define the left-hand side object. $|\mathcal{S}|$ denotes the cardinality of a set $\mathcal{S}$. We shall write $x \xleftarrow{\$} \mathcal{S}$ to express that x is sampled according to the uniform distribution over a set $\mathcal{S}$. We will use the notation $\mathbb{P}\{E(x) \mid x \xleftarrow{\$} \mathcal{S}\}$ to give the probability that an event $E(x)$ occurs under the constraint that $x \xleftarrow{\$} \mathcal{S}$. The finite field with q elements where q is a power of a prime number is written as $\mathbb{F}_q$. All vectors will be regarded by default as row vectors and denoted by boldface letters like $\mathbf{a} = (a_1, \dots, a_n)$. The linear space over a field $\mathbb{F}$ spanned by vectors $\mathbf{b}_1, \dots, \mathbf{b}_k$ is written as $\langle \mathbf{b}_1, \dots, \mathbf{b}_k \rangle_{\mathbb{F}}$. For $f \in \mathbb{F}$ and $\mathcal{U} \subseteq \mathbb{F}$, the set $\{fu \mid u \in \mathcal{U}\}$ is denoted by $f \cdot \mathcal{U}$. Given two arbitrary sets $\mathcal{A}$, $\mathcal{B}$ included in $\mathbb{F}_{q^m}$ where $m \geqslant 1$, we let $\mathcal{A} \cdot \mathcal{B} \triangleq \langle ab \mid a \in \mathcal{A}, b \in \mathcal{B} \rangle_{\mathbb{F}_q}$. The set of $r \times n$ matrices with entries in a set $\mathcal{V} \subseteq \mathbb{F}$ is denoted by $\mathcal{V}^{r \times n}$. The transpose is denoted by $^\mathsf{T}$. For matrices $\mathbf{A}$ and $\mathbf{B}$ having the same number of rows, $[\mathbf{A} \mid \mathbf{B}]$ represents the matrix obtained by concatenating the columns of $\mathbf{A}$ followed by the columns of $\mathbf{B}$.

2.2 Rank Metric

We consider a finite field extension $\mathbb{F}_{q^m}/\mathbb{F}_q$ of degree $m \geqslant 1$ where q is a power of a prime number. The *support* of a vector $\mathbf{x} \in \mathbb{F}_{q^m}^L$ denoted by $\langle \mathbf{x} \rangle_{\mathbb{F}_q}$ is the vector space over $\mathbb{F}_q$ spanned by its entries, namely

$$\langle \mathbf{x} \rangle_{\mathbb{F}_q} \triangleq \langle x_1, \dots, x_L \rangle_{\mathbb{F}_q} \subseteq \mathbb{F}_{q^m}.$$

The *rank weight* of $\mathbf{x}$ is then $\dim\langle\mathbf{x}\rangle_{\mathbb{F}_q}$. We let $\mathbf{Gr}_t(q,m)$ be the set of all t-dimensional linear subspaces over $\mathbb{F}_q$ included in $\mathbb{F}_{q^m}$. The cardinality of $\mathbf{Gr}_t(q,m)$ is given by the Gaussian coefficient:

$$\left|\mathbf{Gr}_t(q,m)\right| = \prod_{i=0}^{t-1} \frac{q^m - q^i}{q^t - q^i}. \tag{1}$$

The *sphere* in $\mathbb{F}_{q^m}^L$ of radius w centered at $\mathbf{0}$ is denoted by $\mathbb{S}_t\left(\mathbb{F}_{q^m}^L\right)$. Notice that if $(\beta_1,\ldots,\beta_t)$ is a basis of $\mathcal{E} \triangleq \langle\mathbf{x}\rangle_{\mathbb{F}_q}$ where $\mathbf{x} \in \mathbb{S}_t\left(\mathbb{F}_{q^m}^L\right)$ then there exists $\mathbf{M} \in \mathbb{F}_q^{t\times L}$ such that $\mathbf{x} = (\beta_1,\ldots,\beta_t)\mathbf{M}$.

2.3   Auxiliary Results

We gather in this part some results that will be useful in the next sections.

Proposition 1. *Let N, L, r be natural numbers, and consider two independent and uniformly distributed random matrices $\mathbf{U} \xleftarrow{\$} \mathbb{F}_q^{N\times(L+r)}$ and $\mathbf{V} \xleftarrow{\$} \mathbb{F}_q^{(L+r)\times r}$ with the assumption that $\mathbf{V}$ has rank r. Then the entries of $\mathbf{UV}$ are independent and uniformly distributed random variables.*

Proof. Let us write $\mathbf{UV} = \mathbf{U}_1\mathbf{V}_1 + \mathbf{U}_2\mathbf{V}_2$ where $\mathbf{U} = [\mathbf{U}_1 \mid \mathbf{U}_2]$ with $\mathbf{U}_1 \in \mathbb{F}_q^{N\times r}$, $\mathbf{U}_2 \in \mathbb{F}_q^{N\times L}$, and $\mathbf{V} = \begin{bmatrix}\mathbf{V}_1\\\mathbf{V}_2\end{bmatrix}$ with $\mathbf{V}_1 \in \mathbb{F}_q^{r\times r}$, $\mathbf{V}_2 \in \mathbb{F}_q^{L\times r}$. Without loss of generality we can assume that $\mathbf{V}_1$ is non-singular and because $\mathbf{U}_1$ is a uniform random matrix, $\mathbf{U}_1\mathbf{V}_1$ is consequently a uniformly distributed random matrix. The fact that $\mathbf{UV}$ is a uniform random matrix can be inferred from the uniform randomness of $\mathbf{U}_1\mathbf{V}_1$ and the independence between $\mathbf{U}_2\mathbf{V}_2$ from $\mathbf{U}_1\mathbf{V}_1$. □

Proposition 2. *Let $\mathcal{U}$ be a vector space of dimension at most d over $\mathbb{F}_q$ and consider an integer $n \geqslant d$. The probability that n vectors drawn independently and uniformly at random $\mathbf{u}_1 \xleftarrow{\$} \mathcal{U},\ldots,\mathbf{u}_n \xleftarrow{\$} \mathcal{U}$ span $\mathcal{U}$ over $\mathbb{F}_q$ is at least*

$$\prod_{i=0}^{d-1} \left(1 - q^{i-n}\right).$$

Proof. Let a be the dimension of $\mathcal{U}$. The probability that $\mathbf{u}_1,\ldots,\mathbf{u}_n$ span $\mathcal{U}$ is equal to the probability that an $n\times a$ random matrix with entries in $\mathbb{F}_q$ has rank a. This probability is then given by

$$\frac{(q^n-1)}{q^n} \times \cdots \times \frac{\left(q^n - q^{a-1}\right)}{q^n} \geqslant \frac{(q^n-1)}{q^n} \times \cdots \times \frac{\left(q^n - q^{d-1}\right)}{q^n}$$

where the inequality is derived from the hypothesis that $a \leqslant d$. □

Remark 1. The inequality in Proposition 2 is an equality if the dimension of $\mathcal{U}$ equals d.

Lemma 1. *Consider $\mathcal{A} \subseteq \langle g_1, \ldots, g_r \rangle_{\mathbb{F}_q} \subset \mathbb{F}_{q^m}$ with $0 < r \leqslant m$, and let us assume that $\mathcal{A}$ contains a linear space over $\mathbb{F}_q$ of dimension at least $d \leqslant r$. For randomly drawn elements $e_1, \ldots, e_t$ from $\mathbb{F}_{q^m}$ such that $\langle e_1, \ldots, e_t \rangle_{\mathbb{F}_q} \in \mathbf{Gr}_t(q, m)$, there exists $\mathbf{a}$ in $\mathcal{A}^t \setminus \{\mathbf{0}\}$ such that $\sum_{j=1}^t a_j e_j = 0$ with probability at most*

$$\frac{q^{tr+1} - (q^d - 1)(q^t - 1)}{q^{m+1} - q^t} \tag{2}$$

Proof. Let us fix an arbitrary t-tuple $\mathbf{a} = (a_1, \ldots, a_t)$ from $\mathcal{A}^t \setminus \{\mathbf{0}\}$. There exists then $i \in \{1, \ldots, t\}$ such that $a_i \neq 0$. The condition $\sum_{j=1}^t a_j e_j = 0$ is equivalent to writing that

$$e_i = -a_i^{-1} \sum_{j \neq i} a_j e_j. \tag{3}$$

Knowing that $e_1, \ldots, e_t$ are random elements picked from $\mathbb{F}_{q^m}$ that are linearly independent, we can see that we would have a contradiction if $a_j a_i^{-1}$ lies within $\mathbb{F}_q$ for every j different from i. Consequently, we introduce the set $\mathcal{T} \subsetneq \mathcal{A}^t \setminus \{\mathbf{0}\}$ that *does not* contain t-tuples $\mathbf{a}$ such that there exist $i \in \{1, \ldots, t\}$ and scalars λ_j from $\mathbb{F}_q$ so that we have both $a_i \neq 0$ and $a_j = \lambda_j a_i$ for every j in $\{1, \ldots, t\} \setminus \{i\}$. We can remark that the number of t-tuples is least[2] $(q^d - 1)(q^t - 1)/(q - 1)$ and therefore the cardinality of $\mathcal{T}$ is at most $q^{rt} - 1 - (q^d - 1)(q^t - 1)/(q - 1)$. From the whole previous discussion, and after applying the Union bound, the probability that we are looking for can be upper-bounded as follows

$$\mathbb{P}\left\{\exists \mathbf{a} \in \mathcal{A}^t \setminus \{\mathbf{0}\}, \ \sum_{i=1}^t a_i e_i = 0\right\} = \mathbb{P}\left\{\exists \mathbf{a} \in \mathcal{T}, \ \sum_{i=1}^t a_i e_i = 0\right\}$$

$$\leqslant \sum_{\mathbf{a} \in \mathcal{T}} \mathbb{P}\left\{\sum_{i=1}^t a_i e_i = 0\right\}.$$

Furthermore, because of (3), the probability that $\sum_{i=1}^t a_i e_i = 0$ given that $(a_1, \ldots, a_t) \in \mathcal{T}$, is at most the ratio between the number of $(t-1)$-tuples that are linearly independent over the number of linearly independent t-tuples, that is

$$\mathbb{P}\left\{\sum_{i=1}^t a_i e_i = 0\right\} \leqslant \frac{\prod_{j=0}^{t-2}(q^m - q^j)}{\prod_{j=0}^{t-1}(q^m - q^j)} = \frac{1}{q^m - q^{t-1}}.$$

---

[2] Such t-tuples $\mathbf{a}$ are of the form $(0, \ldots, 0, a_i, \lambda_{i+1} a_i, \ldots, \lambda_t a_i)$ where i can take any value in $\{1, \ldots, t\}$, a_i is any non-zero element in $\mathcal{A}$, and $\lambda_{i+1}, \ldots, \lambda_t$ have arbitrary values in $\mathbb{F}_q$. The number of such tuples is therefore at least $(q^d - 1)\sum_{u=0}^{t-1} q^u$ because the choice over a_i can be restricted to the linear space of dimension d contained in the set $\mathcal{A}$.

The conclusion then follows as we have

$$
\sum_{\mathbf{a} \in \mathcal{T}} \mathbb{P} \left\{ \sum_{i=1}^{t} a_i e_i = 0 \right\} \leqslant \left(q^{rt} - 1 - (q^d - 1) \sum_{u=0}^{t-1} q^u \right) \frac{1}{q^m - q^{t-1}}
$$

$$
\leqslant \frac{q^{rt} - (q^d - 1) \frac{q^t - 1}{q-1}}{q^m - q^{t-1}} \leqslant \frac{q^{rt} - (q^d - 1) \frac{q^t - 1}{q}}{q^m - q^{t-1}}
$$

which provides the claimed bound (2). □

3 Decoding of LRPC Codes

This section is devoted to explaining how to solve efficiently the Rank decoding problem with an homogeneous matrix, or stated otherwise, we will explain how LRPC codes can be efficiently decoded. We first recall the definition of the *Rank decoding* problem and then introduce the family of LRPC codes through the notion of homogeneous matrix.

Definition 1 (Rank decoding problem). *Let q, m, n, k, t be a natural numbers such that $k < n$ and $t < n$. The* Rank decoding *problem consists in finding* $\mathbf{e}$ *from the input* $(\mathbf{R}, \mathbf{eR}^{\mathsf{T}})$ *assuming that* $\mathbf{R} \in \mathbb{F}_{q^m}^{(n-k) \times n}$ *and* $\mathbf{e} \xleftarrow{\$} \mathbb{S}_t(\mathbb{F}_{q^m}^n)$.

Definition 2 (Homogeneous matrix & LRPC code). *An $r \times n$ matrix* $\mathbf{M}$ *is* homogeneous of weight w and support $\mathcal{W} \in \mathbf{Gr}_w(q,m)$ *if* $\mathbf{M} \in \mathcal{W}^{r \times n}$. *A linear code defined by an homogeneous parity-check matrix is named a* Low Rank Parity Check (LRPC) *code.*

Throughout this section we consider $\mathbf{s} \in \mathbb{F}_{q^m}^{n-k}$, an homogeneous parity-check matrix $\mathbf{H} \in \mathbb{F}_{q^m}^{(n-k) \times n}$ of weight w and support $\mathcal{W}$ and an integer t. The goal is then to find a vector $\mathbf{e} \in \mathbb{F}_{q^m}^n$ such that $\mathbf{s} = \mathbf{eH}^{\mathsf{T}}$ and $\langle \mathbf{e} \rangle_{\mathbb{F}_q} \in \mathbf{Gr}_t(q,m)$. Throughout this section we assume that an arbitrary basis $\{f_1, \dots, f_w\}$ of $\mathcal{W}$ was picked, and the parameters satisfy the following constraints,

$$
\begin{cases} tw & \leqslant n - k, \\ n & \leqslant (n-k)w. \end{cases} \tag{4}
$$

3.1 Description

We aim here to give a full description of the LRPC decoder. It consists of two steps that will be described below. We will also give in Theorem 1 an upper-bound on the probability that the LRPC decoder fails. But before that, we first explain how from an input $(\mathbf{H}, \mathbf{eH}^{\mathsf{T}})$ the algorithm first recovers the support $\langle \mathbf{e} \rangle_{\mathbb{F}_q}$, and then all the entries of $\mathbf{e}$.

The first step is given in Algorithm 1. The goal here is to compute a basis $\varepsilon_1, \dots, \varepsilon_t$ of $\langle \mathbf{e} \rangle_{\mathbb{F}_q}$. One can observe that the algorithm fails at this stage if one of the following events occurs:

Algorithm 1. Step I – Support Recovering $(\mathbf{H}, \mathbf{s}, t)$

1: $\mathcal{B} \leftarrow \emptyset$

2: **if** dim $\bigcap\limits_{i=1}^{w} f_i^{-1} \cdot \langle \mathbf{s} \rangle_{\mathbb{F}_q} = t$ **then**

3:    $\mathcal{B} \leftarrow \{\varepsilon_1, \ldots, \varepsilon_t\}$ where $\varepsilon_1, \ldots, \varepsilon_t$ is a basis of $\bigcap\limits_{i=1}^{w} f_i^{-1} \cdot \langle \mathbf{s} \rangle_{\mathbb{F}_q}$

4: **end if**

5: **return** $\mathcal{B}$

---

1. $\langle \mathbf{s} \rangle_{\mathbb{F}_q} \neq \mathcal{E} \cdot \mathcal{W}$ which will in particular always occur if $n - k < tw$,
2. Or $\langle \mathbf{s} \rangle_{\mathbb{F}_q} = \mathcal{E} \cdot \mathcal{W}$ holds but yet the strict inclusion $\mathcal{E} \subsetneqq \bigcap_{i=1}^{w} f_i^{-1} \cdot \langle \mathbf{s} \rangle_{\mathbb{F}_q}$ happens.

In the following, we elaborate more on these cases. The second step then starts once a basis $\varepsilon_1, \ldots, \varepsilon_t$ of $\mathcal{E}$ is successfully recovered. Next, it checks whether the dimension of $\mathcal{E} \cdot \mathcal{W}$ is equal to tw. Note that in this case, a basis of $\mathcal{E} \cdot \mathcal{W}$ is given by

$$\left\{ f_i \varepsilon_j \mid i \in \{1, \ldots, w\}, \; j \in \{1, \ldots, t\} \right\}.$$

Each entry of $\mathbf{s} = [s_r]$ is written as $s_r = \sum_{i,j} \sigma_{i,j}^{(r)} f_i \varepsilon_j$ where $\sigma_{i,j}^{(r)}$ lies in $\mathbb{F}_q$. Similarly each entry of $\mathbf{H} = [h_{r,d}]$ with $d \in \{1, \ldots, n\}$ is decomposed as $h_{r,d} = \sum_i \nu_i^{(r,d)} f_i$ with $\nu_i^{(r,d)}$ in $\mathbb{F}_q$. Lastly each entry e_d of the unknown vector $\mathbf{e}$ is written as $e_d = \sum_j x_j^{(d)} \varepsilon_j$ where $x_j^{(d)}$ are unknowns that are sought in $\mathbb{F}_q$ so that we have

$$s_r = \sum_{d=1}^{n} h_{r,d} e_d = \sum_{d=1}^{n} \left(\sum_{i=1}^{w} \nu_i^{(r,d)} f_i \right) \left(\sum_{j=1}^{t} x_j^{(d)} \varepsilon_j \right)$$

$$= \sum_{i=1}^{w} \sum_{j=1}^{t} \left(\sum_{d=1}^{n} \nu_i^{(r,d)} x_j^{(d)} \right) f_i \varepsilon_j.$$

The latter equality implies that we have a system of $(n - k)tw$ linear equations involving tn unknowns composed of the linear relations

$$\sigma_{i,j}^{(r)} = \sum_{d=1}^{n} \nu_i^{(r,d)} x_j^{(d)}$$

where (r, i, j) runs through $\{1, \ldots, n - k\} \times \{1, \ldots, w\} \times \{1, \ldots, t\}$. As we have taken $(n-k)w \geqslant n$ and since $\dim \mathcal{E} \cdot \mathcal{W} = tw$ we are sure to get a unique solution. We see in particular that this second step always fails if the dimension of $\mathcal{E} \cdot \mathcal{W}$ is not equal to tw.

3.2   Decoding Failure Probability

In this part, we focus on the question of estimating the probability that the LRPC decoder fails on a random input $(\mathbf{H}, \mathbf{e}\mathbf{H}^{\mathsf{T}})$. Henceforth we denote it by

$\mathbb{P}\left\{ \Phi(\mathbf{H}, \mathbf{eH}^{\mathsf{T}}) \neq \mathbf{e} \right\}$ where Φ denotes the LRPC decoder. We also define the probability that Φ fails at the first and second step by $\mathbb{P}_{\mathrm{I}}$ and $\mathbb{P}_{\mathrm{II}}$ respectively. We then clearly have $\mathbb{P}\left\{ \Phi(\mathbf{H}, \mathbf{eH}^{\mathsf{T}}) \neq \mathbf{e} \right\} = \mathbb{P}_{\mathrm{I}} + (1 - \mathbb{P}_{\mathrm{I}}) \mathbb{P}_{\mathrm{II}}$ which implies that

$$\mathbb{P}\left\{ \Phi(\mathbf{H}, \mathbf{eH}^{\mathsf{T}}) \neq \mathbf{e} \right\} \leqslant \mathbb{P}_{\mathrm{I}} + \mathbb{P}_{\mathrm{II}} . \tag{5}$$

We now state our main result.

Theorem 1. *Consider natural numbers w, t, m, k, n such that $tw \leqslant n-k$, $n \leqslant (n-k)w$ and $2(w-1)t < m$. Assume that $\mathcal{W} \xleftarrow{\$} \mathbf{Gr}_w(q, m)$ and $\mathcal{E} \xleftarrow{\$} \mathbf{Gr}_t(q, m)$. For $\mathbf{H} \xleftarrow{\$} \mathcal{W}^{(n-k) \times n}$ and $\mathbf{e} \xleftarrow{\$} \mathcal{E}^n$, the probability $\mathbb{P}\left\{ \Phi(\mathbf{H}, \mathbf{eH}^{\mathsf{T}}) \neq \mathbf{e} \right\}$ is at most $\mathbb{P}_{\mathrm{I}} + \mathbb{P}_{\mathrm{II}}$ where*

$$
\begin{cases}
\mathbb{P}_{\mathrm{I}} & \leqslant \; 1 - \displaystyle\prod_{i=0}^{tw-1} \left(1 - q^{i-(n-k)}\right) + \dfrac{q^{(2w-1)t+1} - (q^w - 1)(q^t - 1)}{q^{m+1} - q^t}, \\[2ex]
\mathbb{P}_{\mathrm{II}} & \leqslant \; \dfrac{q^{tw}}{q^m - q^{t-1}}.
\end{cases}
$$

The rest of this section is devoted to proving this theorem.

3.3   An Upper-Bound on $\mathbb{P}_{\mathrm{I}}$

The algorithm Φ fails during the first step if either $\langle \mathbf{s} \rangle_{\mathbb{F}_q} \neq \mathcal{E} \cdot \mathcal{W}$, or $\langle \mathbf{s} \rangle_{\mathbb{F}_q} = \mathcal{E} \cdot \mathcal{W}$ holds but we have $\mathcal{E} \neq \bigcap_{i=1}^{w} f_i^{-1} \cdot \langle \mathbf{s} \rangle_{\mathbb{F}_q}$. Consequently the probability $\mathbb{P}_{\mathrm{I}}$ is at most

$$\mathbb{P}\left\{ \langle \mathbf{s} \rangle_{\mathbb{F}_q} \neq \mathcal{E} \cdot \mathcal{W} \right\} + \mathbb{P}\left\{ \mathcal{E} \neq \bigcap_{i=1}^{w} f_i^{-1} \cdot \langle \mathbf{s} \rangle_{\mathbb{F}_q} \;\middle|\; \langle \mathbf{s} \rangle_{\mathbb{F}_q} = \mathcal{E} \cdot \mathcal{W} \right\}.$$

In order to give an upper-bound on $\mathbb{P}\left\{ \langle \mathbf{s} \rangle_{\mathbb{F}_q} \neq \mathcal{E} \cdot \mathcal{W} \right\}$ we use Proposition 1 to claim that the entries of $\mathbf{s}$ are independent and uniformly distributed random variables taking values on $\mathcal{E} \cdot \mathcal{W}$, and then we use Proposition 2 to bound the probability that randomly drawn vectors from a finite-dimensional vector space over $\mathbb{F}_q$ form a set of maximum dimension.

Proposition 3. *For $\mathbf{e} \xleftarrow{\$} \mathcal{E}^n$ and $\mathbf{H} \xleftarrow{\$} \mathcal{W}^{(n-k) \times n}$ where $\mathcal{E} \in \mathbf{Gr}_t(q, m)$ and $\mathcal{W} \in \mathbf{Gr}_w(q, m)$, the probability that $\langle \mathbf{eH}^{\mathsf{T}} \rangle_{\mathbb{F}_q}$ is different from $\mathcal{E} \cdot \mathcal{W}$ is*

$$\mathbb{P}\left\{ \langle \mathbf{eH}^{\mathsf{T}} \rangle_{\mathbb{F}_q} \neq \mathcal{E} \cdot \mathcal{W} \right\} \;\leqslant\; 1 - \prod_{i=0}^{tw-1} \left(1 - q^{i-(n-k)}\right).$$

Proof. Let $\mathbf{h}_1, \ldots, \mathbf{h}_{n-k}$ be the rows of $\mathbf{H}$. Consider a basis ε of $\mathcal{E}$, and similarly fix an arbitrary basis β of $\mathcal{W}$. Let us define $\mathbf{E} \in \mathbb{F}_q^{t \times n}$, and $\mathbf{M}_1 \in \mathbb{F}_q^{w \times n}, \ldots, \mathbf{M}_{n-k} \in \mathbb{F}_q^{w \times n}$ such that $\mathbf{e} = \varepsilon \mathbf{E}$ and $\mathbf{h}_i = \beta \mathbf{M}_i$ for each $i \in \{1, \ldots, n-k\}$. Clearly the entries of the matrices $\mathbf{E}$ and $\mathbf{M}^\mathsf{T} \triangleq [\mathbf{M}_1^\mathsf{T} \mid \cdots \mid \mathbf{M}_{n-k}^\mathsf{T}] \in \mathbb{F}_q^{n \times w(n-k)}$ are independent and uniformly distributed random variables over $\mathbb{F}_q$, and additionally, we have

$$\mathbf{e}\mathbf{H}^\mathsf{T} = \varepsilon \mathbf{E} \left[(\beta \mathbf{M}_1)^\mathsf{T} \cdots (\beta \mathbf{M}_{n-k})^\mathsf{T} \right] = \varepsilon \mathbf{E}\mathbf{M}^\mathsf{T} \begin{bmatrix} \beta^\mathsf{T} & & 0 \\ & \ddots & \\ 0 & & \beta^\mathsf{T} \end{bmatrix}.$$

We know from Proposition 1 that $\mathbf{M}\mathbf{E}^\mathsf{T}$ is uniformly distributed matrix over $\mathbb{F}_q^{w(n-k) \times t}$ which therefore implies that the entries of $\mathbf{e}\mathbf{H}^\mathsf{T}$ are independent and uniformly distributed random variables over $\mathcal{E} \cdot \mathcal{W}$. We then use Proposition 2 to conclude. □

We now focus on the second reason why Φ fails in step one, namely we would like to upper bound $\mathbb{P}\left\{ \mathcal{E} \neq \bigcap_{i=1}^w f_i^{-1} \cdot \langle \mathbf{s} \rangle_{\mathbb{F}_q} \mid \langle \mathbf{s} \rangle_{\mathbb{F}_q} = \mathcal{E} \cdot \mathcal{W} \right\}$. This will be done in Theorem 2 whose proof requires Lemma 1 which will also be useful as we will see for establishing the probability of failure in the second step.

Theorem 2. *Let $\mathcal{U} \triangleq \mathcal{E} \cdot \mathcal{W}$ where $\mathcal{W} \in \mathbf{Gr}_w(q, m)$ and $\mathcal{E} \xleftarrow{\$} \mathbf{Gr}_t(q, m)$ with $(2w-1)t < m$. Then for an arbitrary basis $f_1, \ldots, f_w$ of $\mathcal{W}$, we have*

$$\mathbb{P}\left\{ \mathcal{E} = \bigcap_{i=1}^w f_i^{-1} \cdot \mathcal{U} \;\middle|\; \mathcal{E} \xleftarrow{\$} \mathbf{Gr}_t(q, m) \right\} \geqslant 1 - \frac{q^{(2w-1)t+1} - (q^w - 1)(q^t - 1)}{q^{m+1} - q^t}.$$

Proof. We know that $\mathcal{E} \neq \bigcap_{i=1}^w f_i^{-1} \cdot \mathcal{U}$ is actually equivalent to the strict inclusion $\mathcal{E} \subsetneq \bigcap_{i=1}^w f_i^{-1} \cdot \mathcal{U}$, which in particular implies $\mathcal{E} \subsetneq f_1^{-1} \cdot \mathcal{U} \cap f_2^{-1} \cdot \mathcal{U}$. Given a basis $e_1, \ldots, e_t$ of $\mathcal{E}$ and for every $j \in \{1, \ldots, w\}$, a generating set of $f_j^{-1} \cdot \mathcal{U}$ as an $\mathbb{F}_q$-linear subspace of $\mathbb{F}_{q^m}$ is given by

$$\{e_1, \ldots, e_t\} \bigcup \left\{ e_k f_\ell f_j^{-1} \mid \ell \in \{1, \ldots, w\} \setminus \{j\}, \; k \in \{1, \ldots, t\} \right\}. \quad (6)$$

So the existence of a non-zero element in $f_1^{-1} \cdot \mathcal{U} \cap f_2^{-1} \cdot \mathcal{U}$ means that there exist scalars $\lambda_k, \gamma_k, \alpha_{k,\ell}, \beta_{k,j}$ in $\mathbb{F}_q$ not all zero such that

$$\sum_{k=1}^t \lambda_k e_k + \sum_{k=1}^t \sum_{\ell=2}^w \alpha_{k,\ell} f_1^{-1} f_\ell e_k = \sum_{k=1}^t \gamma_k e_k + \sum_{k=1}^t \sum_{j=1, j\neq 2}^w \beta_{k,j} f_2^{-1} f_j e_k. \quad (7)$$

In order to have this element not in $\mathcal{E}$, we must have in particular $\alpha_{k,\ell}$ and $\beta_{k,j}$ not all zero. In other words, by defining $\mathcal{A}$ as the subset of $\mathbb{F}_{q^m}$ such that

$$\mathcal{A} \triangleq \left\{ \lambda + \sum_{\ell=2}^w \alpha_\ell f_1^{-1} f_\ell + \sum_{j=1, j\neq 2}^w \beta_j f_2^{-1} f_j \;\middle|\; \lambda \in \mathbb{F}_q, \; (\alpha_\ell, \beta_j) \in \mathbb{F}_q^{2w-2} \setminus \{0\} \right\}$$

we see that (7) entails that there exist $a_1, \ldots, a_t$ in $\mathcal{A}$ such that $\sum_{k=1}^t e_k a_k = 0$. Notice also that $\mathcal{A}$ is included inside a linear space of dimension $2w - 1$

and contains the linear space of dimension w that is generated by the linearly independent elements $1, f_1^{-1} f_2, \ldots, f_1^{-1} f_w$. Consequently from Lemma 1 we can write that

$$\mathbb{P}\left\{ \mathcal{E} \neq \bigcap_{i=1}^{w} f_i^{-1} \cdot \mathcal{U} \ \Big| \ \mathcal{E} \xleftarrow{\$} \mathbf{Gr}_t(q,m) \right\} \leqslant \mathbb{P}\left\{ \mathcal{E} \subsetneq f_1^{-1} \cdot \mathcal{U} \cap f_2^{-1} \cdot \mathcal{U} \right\}$$

$$\leqslant \frac{q^{(2w-1)t+1} - (q^w - 1)(q^t - 1)}{q^{m+1} - q^t}$$

which concludes the proof.   □

3.4   An Upper-Bound on $\mathbb{P}_{\mathrm{II}}$

We have seen that the second step of Φ fails if the dimension of $\mathcal{E} \cdot \mathcal{W}$ is not equal to tw, that is to say we have

$$\mathbb{P}_{\mathrm{II}} = \mathbb{P}\left\{ \dim \mathcal{E} \cdot \mathcal{W} \neq tw \right\}. \tag{8}$$

Then the bound given in Theorem 1 follows from the following result that can be proved thanks to Lemma 1.

Proposition 4. *For* $\mathcal{W} \in \mathbf{Gr}_w(q,m)$ *and assuming that* $wt < m$, *we have*

$$\mathbb{P}\left\{ \dim \mathcal{E} \cdot \mathcal{W} = tw \ \Big| \ \mathcal{E} \xleftarrow{\$} \mathbf{Gr}_t(q,m) \right\} \geqslant 1 - \frac{q^{tw}}{q^m - q^{t-1}}. \tag{9}$$

Proof. $\mathcal{E} \cdot \mathcal{W}$ is generated by $\{e_i f_j \mid 1 \leqslant i \leqslant t, \ 1 \leqslant j \leqslant w\}$ where $\{f_j \mid 1 \leqslant j \leqslant w\}$ is a basis for $\mathcal{W}$ and $\{e_i \mid 1 \leqslant i \leqslant t\}$ is a basis for $\mathcal{E}$. Furthermore, the dimension of $\mathcal{E} \cdot \mathcal{W}$ is different from tw means that there exist scalars $\gamma_{i,j}$ in $\mathbb{F}_q$ such that

$$\sum_{i=1}^{t} \left(\sum_{j=1}^{w} \gamma_{i,j} f_j \right) e_i = 0.$$

We can then apply Lemma 1 in order to obtain the following lower-bound

$$\mathbb{P}\left\{ \dim \mathcal{E} \cdot \mathcal{W} \neq tw \ \Big| \ \mathcal{E} \xleftarrow{\$} \mathbf{Gr}_t(q,m) \right\} \leqslant \frac{q^{tw}}{q^m - q^{t-1}}.$$

This clearly is equivalent to (9) and terminates the proof.   □

4   Asymptotic Analysis

We recall from Proposition 3 that the probability that the coordinates of $\mathbf{e}\mathbf{H}^{\mathsf{T}}$ do not span $\mathcal{E} \cdot \mathcal{W}$ is given

$$\mathbb{P}\left\{ \langle \mathbf{e}\mathbf{H}^{\mathsf{T}} \rangle_{\mathbb{F}_q} \neq \mathcal{E} \cdot \mathcal{W} \right\} \leqslant 1 - \prod_{i=0}^{tw-1} \left(1 - q^{i-(n-k)} \right). \tag{10}$$

The goal here is to upper-bound the term $1 - \prod_{i=0}^{tw-1} \left(1 - q^{i-(n-k)} \right)$.

Proposition 5. *Let us define* $T(q,t,w) \triangleq 1 - \prod_{i=0}^{tw-1}\left(1 - q^{i-(n-k)}\right)$. *Then under the condition that* $twq^{-(n-k)+tw} \leqslant 1$, *we have*

$$0 \leqslant \frac{q^{-(n-k)+tw}}{q-1} - T(q,t,w) \leqslant \frac{q^{-(n-k)}}{q-1} + \frac{1}{q+1}\left(\frac{q^{-(n-k)+tw}}{q-1}\right)^2$$

In particular, with $tw = \omega(1)$ *and* $k = \Theta(n)$, *it entails that* $T(q,t,w) \sim \frac{q^{-(n-k)+tw}}{q-1}$ *as* n *tends to* $+\infty$.

Remark 2. We know by Remark 1 that if $\dim(\mathcal{E} \cdot \mathcal{W}) = tw$, then (10) is an equality. Hence $\mathbb{P}\left\{\langle \mathbf{eH}^\mathsf{T}\rangle_{\mathbb{F}_q} \neq \mathcal{E} \cdot \mathcal{W}\right\}$ is equivalent to $q^{-(n-k)+tw}/(q-1)$.

Proof. Note that by expanding the expression of $1 - \prod_{i=0}^{tw-1}\left(1 - q^{i-(n-k)}\right)$ we have

$$T(q,t,w) = 1 - \prod_{i=0}^{tw-1}\left(1 - q^{i-(n-k)}\right) = \sum_{i=1}^{tw}(-1)^{i+1}u_i \tag{11}$$

where

$$u_i \triangleq \sum_{\substack{\{k_1,\dots,k_i\} \subseteq \{0,\dots,tw-1\} \\ |\{k_1,\dots,k_i\}|=i}} q^{\sum_{j=1}^{i}k_j - i(n-k)}.$$

We will prove that the sequence $(u_i)_{0 \leqslant i \leqslant tw-1}$ is decreasing. Let us suppose for the moment that it is true. Then the whole sum $\sum_{i=1}^{tw}(-1)^{i+1}u_i$ satisfies the inequalities

$$u_1 - u_2 \leqslant \sum_{i=1}^{tw}(-1)^{i+1}u_i \leqslant u_1 \tag{12}$$

with $u_1 = q^{-(n-k)}\sum_{j=0}^{tw-1}q^j = q^{-(n-k)}(q^{tw}-1)/(q-1)$ and $u_2 \leqslant \frac{q^{-2(n-k)+2tw}}{(q-1)^2}$ because of the following series of inequalities,

$$u_2 = q^{-2(n-k)}\sum_{k_1=0}^{tw-2}q^{k_1}\sum_{k_2=k_1+1}^{tw-1}q^{k_2} = \frac{q^{-2(n-k)}}{q-1}\sum_{k_1=0}^{tw-2}q^{k_1}\left(q^{tw}-q^{k_1+1}\right)$$

$$= \frac{q^{-2(n-k)}}{(q-1)^2}\left(q^{2tw-1} - q^{tw} - \frac{q^{2tw-1}-q}{q+1}\right)$$

$$= \frac{q^{-2(n-k)}}{(q+1)(q-1)^2}\left(q^{2tw} - (q+1)q^{tw} + q\right)$$

$$\leqslant \frac{q^{-2(n-k)+2tw}}{(q+1)(q-1)^2}$$

Gathering this last inequality with (11) and (12), we obtain then

$$\frac{q^{-(n-k)}}{q-1}\left(q^{tw}-1\right) - \frac{q^{-2(n-k)+2tw}}{(q+1)(q-1)^2} \leqslant T(q,t,w) \leqslant \frac{q^{-(n-k)}}{q-1}\left(q^{tw}-1\right)$$

To finish the proof, it only remains to prove that $u_1, \ldots, u_{tw}$ is a decreasing sequence. Let us choose i in $\{1, \ldots, tw-1\}$. We have then

$$
\begin{aligned}
u_{i+1} &= q^{-(i+1)(n-k)} \sum_{\substack{\{k_1, \ldots, k_{i+1}\} \subseteq \{0, \ldots, tw-1\} \\ |\{k_1, \ldots, k_{i+1}\}| = i+1}} q^{\sum_{j=1}^{i+1} k_j} \\
&= q^{-i(n-k)} q^{-(n-k)+tw} \sum_{\substack{\{k_1, \ldots, k_{i+1}\} \subseteq \{0, \ldots, tw-1\} \\ |\{k_1, \ldots, k_{i+1}\}| = i+1}} q^{k_{i+1} - tw + \sum_{j=1}^{i} k_j} \\
&\leqslant q^{-(n-k)+tw} q^{-i(n-k)} \sum_{\substack{\{k_1, \ldots, k_{i+1}\} \subseteq \{0, \ldots, tw-1\} \\ |\{k_1, \ldots, k_{i+1}\}| = i+1}} q^{\sum_{j=1}^{i} k_j} \\
&\leqslant q^{-(n-k)+tw} q^{-i(n-k)} \sum_{\ell=0}^{tw-1} \sum_{\substack{\{k_1, \ldots, k_i\} \subseteq \{0, \ldots, tw-1\} \setminus \{\ell\} \\ |\{k_1, \ldots, k_i\}| = i}} q^{\sum_{j=1}^{i} k_j} \\
&\leqslant tw q^{-(n-k)+tw} u_i.
\end{aligned}
$$

By assumption we have $tw q^{-(n-k)+tw} \leqslant 1$ which shows that $u_{i+1} \leqslant u_i$. $\qquad\square$

Corollary 1. *With* $tw q^{-(n-k)+tw} \leqslant 1$, $tw = \omega(1)$ *and* $k = \Theta(n)$, *we have when* $n \to \infty$

$$
\mathbb{P}\left\{ \Phi(\mathbf{H}, \mathbf{e}\mathbf{H}^{\mathsf{T}}) \neq \mathbf{e} \right\} \leqslant \frac{q^{-(n-k)+tw}}{q-1} + q^{2tw-m}.
$$

Proof. It follows from Theorem 1 and Proposition 5.

5   Conclusion

The LRPC decoding algorithm is becoming more and more a predominant tool in rank-metric cryptography as it is the main ingredient that serves to invert encryption functions in [2,3,5]. It is therefore of great importance to establish well-grounded bounds on the decoding failure probability to ensure a trust on the parameters provided for those schemes. Yet all existing bounds are either too loose for being interesting in concrete cryptographic applications, or are tight according to experimental observations but are not supported by realistic model. This work partially fill this gap by improving existing theoretical bounds. Our upper-bound behaves asymptotically as $q^{-(n-k)+tw}/(q-1) + q^{2tw-m}$.

However, there is still a large gap with the experimental bound given in [2,3] that comes from the second case of failure in the first step of the decoding algorithm. That is why a finer analysis of this event could result to a better bound. Lastly, our analysis applies specifically to "unstructured" LRPC codes and it would be interesting to study the decoding failure probability of *ideal* LRPC codes.

Acknowledgments. E. Burle is supported by RIN100 program funded by Région Normandie. A. Otmani is supported by the grant ANR-22-PETQ-0008 PQ-TLS funded by Agence Nationale de la Recherche within France 2030 program, and by FAVPQC (EIG CONCERT-Japan & CNRS).

References

1. Melchor, C.A., et al.: Rank quasi cyclic (RQC). Second round submission to the NIST post-quantum cryptography call, April 2019
2. Melchor, C.A., Aragon, N., Dyseryn, V., Gaborit, P., Zémor, G.: LRPC codes with multiple syndromes: near ideal-size KEMs without ideals. ArXiv, abs/2206.11961 (2022)
3. Aragon, N., et al.: ROLLO (merger of Rank-Ouroboros, LAKE and LOCKER). Second round submission to the NIST post-quantum cryptography call, March 2019
4. Aragon, N., Gaborit, P., Hauteville, A., Ruatta, O., Zémor, G.: Low rank parity check codes: new decoding algorithms and applications to cryptography. IEEE Trans. Inform. Theory **65**(12), 7697–7717 (2019)
5. Burle, É., Gaborit, P., Hatri, Y., Otmani, A.: Rank metric trapdoor functions with homogeneous errors. In: AlTawy, R., Hülsing, A. (eds.) Selected Areas in Cryptography - SAC. LNCS. Springer, Cham (2022). https://doi.org/10.1007/978-3-030-99277-4
6. Delsarte, P.: Bilinear forms over a finite field, with applications to coding theory. J. Comb. Theory Ser. A **25**(3), 226–241 (1978)
7. Gabidulin, E.M.: Theory of codes with maximum rank distance. Problemy Peredachi Informatsii **21**(1), 3–16 (1985)
8. Gabidulin, E.M., Paramonov, A.V., Tretjakov, O.V.: Ideals over a non-commutative ring and their application in cryptology. In: Davies, D.W. (ed.) EUROCRYPT 1991. LNCS, vol. 547, pp. 482–489. Springer, Heidelberg (1991). https://doi.org/10.1007/3-540-46416-6_41
9. Gibson, K.: Severely denting the Gabidulin version of the McEliece public key cryptosystem. Des. Codes Cryptogr. **6**(1), 37–45 (1995)
10. Gibson, K.: The security of the Gabidulin public key cryptosystem. In: Maurer, U. (ed.) EUROCRYPT 1996. LNCS, vol. 1070, pp. 212–223. Springer, Heidelberg (1996). https://doi.org/10.1007/3-540-68339-9_19
11. McEliece, R.J.: A Public-Key System Based on Algebraic Coding Theory, pp. 114–116. Jet Propulsion Lab. DSN Progress Report 44 (1978)
12. Ore, Ø.: On a special class of polynomials. Trans. Amer. Math. Soc. **35**(3), 559–584 (1933)
13. Ore, Ø.: Theory of non-commutative polynomials. Ann. Math. **34**, 480 (1933)
14. Overbeck, R.: Extending Gibson's attacks on the GPT cryptosystem. In: Ytrehus, Ø. (ed.) WCC 2005. LNCS, vol. 3969, pp. 178–188. Springer, Heidelberg (2006). https://doi.org/10.1007/11779360_15
15. Overbeck, R.: A new structural attack for GPT and variants. In: Dawson, E., Vaudenay, S. (eds.) Mycrypt 2005. LNCS, vol. 3715, pp. 50–63. Springer, Heidelberg (2005). https://doi.org/10.1007/11554868_5
16. Overbeck, R.: Structural attacks for public key cryptosystems based on Gabidulin codes. J. Cryptology **21**(2), 280–301 (2008)

Coset Leaders of the First Order Reed-Muller Codes in the Classes of Niho Functions and Threshold Functions

Claude Carlet[1,2], Serge Feukoua[3(✉)], and Ana Sălăgean[3]

[1] LAGA, Department of Mathematics, University of Paris 8 (and Paris 13 and CNRS),
Saint–Denis Cedex 02, France
[2] University of Bergen, Bergen, Norway
[3] Department of Computer Science, University of Loughborough, Loughborough, UK
S.C.Feukoua-Jonzo@lboro.ac.uk, A.M.Salagean@lboro.ac.uk

Abstract. The notion of coset leader has applications in coding theory and cryptography. It has been studied in several papers. In this paper, we extend a recent study, made on the coset leaders of the first order Reed-Muller codes, to two classes of Boolean functions which have played an important role in diverse domains of Boolean functions, and whose study was missing in this context. We characterize the coset leaders that belong to the classes of Niho functions and threshold functions (this second class being a generalization of the class of majority functions).

Keywords: Boolean functions · coset leader · Walsh transform

1 Introduction

A coset leader of the first order Reed-Muller code (denoted by $RM(1, n)$; the Reed-Muller code, of length 2^n and order r being denoted by $RM(r, n)$, see [2,11] for more details on Reed-Muller codes) is a Boolean function $f : \mathbb{F}_2^n \mapsto \mathbb{F}_2$ whose Hamming weight $w_H(f)$ is the minimum in the coset of $RM(1, n)$ containing it: $w_H(f) = \min\{w_H(f + \ell) : \ell \in RM(1, n)\}$.

Coset leaders play a role in coding theory and present an interest from the cryptographic viewpoint. Indeed, as mentioned in [4], they can be used in maximum likelihood decoding analysis (see [1], [9] for more details). Concerning cryptography, if $f + \ell$ is a coset leader (located in the $RM(1, n)$-coset including f), then ℓ is a best affine approximation of f. Finding such ℓ is the crucial step in cryptanalyses based on affine approximations, such as the fast correlation attack [12]. Furthermore, the Hamming weight of a coset leader of $RM(1, n)$ is equal to its nonlinearity, an important notion in cryptography, see [2].

The study of coset leaders of $RM(1, n)$ was commenced in [4]. After characterizing the coset leaders in the well known classes of direct sums of monomial functions and

The research of the first author is partly supported by the Norwegian Research Council and the two other authors are partly supported by EPSRC, UK (EPSRC grant EP/W03378X/1).

© The Author(s), under exclusive license to Springer Nature Switzerland AG 2024
E. A. Quaglia (Ed.): IMACC 2023, LNCS 14421, pp. 17–33, 2024.
https://doi.org/10.1007/978-3-031-47818-5_2

Maiorana-McFarland functions, this reference left open the characterization of coset leaders in the class of Niho functions (which provide under certain conditions functions with optimal nonlinearity called bent functions, see [2,13]) the class of Carlet-Feng functions and the class of symmetric functions. Symmetric functions are of interest for cryptography, as they allow to implement in an efficient way non linear functions on large numbers of variables, see [2]. An important subclass of symmetric functions are the threshold functions; majority functions are particular cases of threshold functions. The majority functions and the Carlet-Feng functions are known for having an optimal algebraic immunity, another important parameter in cryptography, see [2,3,8].

As already observed in [4] (and straightforward), determining the coset leaders in a given coset $f + RM(1, n)$ is closely related to determining the Walsh transform of f (see its definition in Sect. 2). Note that many cryptographic properties (such as nonlinearity and balancedness) can be characterized by means of the Walsh transform (see [2,6]).

In [7,15], the Walsh spectrum of rotation symmetric functions (that is, functions which output the same value at all the inputs obtained by applying a circular permutation on the coordinates of a given input) is computed for degrees 3 and 2 respectively. In [8], the Walsh spectrum of the majority function is given.

This paper aims to study the coset leaders in the class of Niho functions and in an infinite class of symmetric Boolean functions called the threshold functions which generalize the class of majority functions. Note that, as mentioned in [4], when a class is not a union of cosets of $RM(1, n)$, it is not sufficient to determine the coset leaders which belong to the class; we need to extend this determination to the class equal to the union of the cosets $f + RM(1, n)$ when f ranges in the class.

The paper is organized as follows: Section 2 recalls the background on Boolean functions and the properties of coset leaders useful for our characterizations. Section 3 is devoted to the characterization of coset leaders in the class of Niho functions and in Sect. 4 the characterization is made for the class of threshold functions.

2 Preliminaries

In this document $\mathbb{F}_2^n$ denotes the vector space over the finite field with 2 elements $\mathbb{F}_2$. A function from $\mathbb{F}_2^n$ to $\mathbb{F}_2$ is called a Boolean function on $\mathbb{F}_2^n$, or an n-variable Boolean function, or a Boolean function in dimension n. There are different ways to express Boolean functions, each ensuring uniqueness. Among them, we have the multi-variate polynomial expression called the algebraic normal form (in brief, ANF), belonging to $\mathbb{F}_2[x_1, \ldots, x_n]/(x_1^2 + x_1, \ldots, x_n^2 + x_n)$ and defined as follows:

$$f(x) = \sum_{I \subseteq \{1,2,\ldots,n\}} a_I \left(\prod_{j \in I} x_j \right) = \sum_{I \subseteq \{1,2,\ldots,n\}} a_I \, x^I \text{ where } a_I \in \mathbb{F}_2.$$

We also have the possibility of representing Boolean functions by their trace representation. In such representation, the vector space $\mathbb{F}_2^n$ is identified with the field $\mathbb{F}_{2^n}$ (thanks to the choice of a basis of $\mathbb{F}_{2^n}$, which is an n-dimensional vector space, decomposing any element in $\mathbb{F}_{2^n}$ on the fixed basis). Every Boolean function f can then be written in the form $f(x) = \text{tr}_n(F(x))$ where F is a mapping from $\mathbb{F}_{2^n}$ to $\mathbb{F}_{2^n}$ and where tr_n is the trace function from $\mathbb{F}_{2^n}$ to $\mathbb{F}_2$, defined by $\text{tr}_n(x) = x + x^2 + x^{2^2} + \ldots + x^{2^{n-1}}$ (more generally, for any $m > 1$ dividing n, the trace function from $\mathbb{F}_{2^n}$ to the subfield $\mathbb{F}_{2^m}$ is denoted by tr^n_m and defined by $\mathrm{tr}^n_m(x) = x + x^{2^m} + x^{2^{2m}} + ... + x^{2^{n-m}})$.

The *algebraic degree* of a Boolean function f, denoted by $\deg(f)$, is the degree of its ANF (see [10]). For every binary vector $x \in \mathbb{F}_2^n$, the Hamming weight $w_H(x)$ of x is the number of its non zero coordinates (*i.e.* the size of the set $\{i \in \{1, ..., n\} : x_i \neq 0\}$, called the support of x). The *Hamming weight* $w_H(f)$ of a Boolean function f on $\mathbb{F}_2^n$ is also the size of the support of the function, denoted by $\mathrm{supp}(f)$, *i.e.* of the set $\{x \in \mathbb{F}_2^n / f(x) = 1\}$. The *Hamming distance* between two Boolean functions f and g denoted by $d_H(f, h)$, equals the Hamming weight of their sum, that is, $|\{x \in \mathbb{F}_2^n; f(x) \neq g(x)\}|$.

We define in what follows the notions of affine equivalence and of affine invariance which lead to the first trivial property of coset leader in [4].

Definition 1. *Two Boolean functions f and g are said affinely equivalent, and we write then $f \sim g$, if there exists L, an affine automorphism of $\mathbb{F}_2^n$, such that $f = g \circ L$, where '$\circ$' is the operation of composition. If L is a simple permutation of the input bits, then f and g are called permutation-equivalent.*

A parameter associated to a function is called an affine invariant if it is preserved by affine equivalence. For instance, the Hamming weight and the algebraic degree are affine invariants.

Let us recall the coset leader definition.

Definition 2. *An n-variable Boolean function f with $n \geq 2$ is called a* coset leader *of the first order Reed-Muller code $RM(1, n)$ if for all $\ell \in RM(1, n)$, we have $w_H(f + \ell) \geq w_H(f)$. By abuse of language, given any Boolean function f, we shall call "coset leaders of f" the coset leaders in the coset $f + RM(1, n)$.*

The property of being a coset leader is of course also an affine invariant:

Lemma 3. *[4] Let n be a positive integer, and let f and g be two n-variable Boolean functions with $n \geq 2$ such that $f \sim g$. Then, f is a coset leader of $RM(1, n)$ if and only if g is also a coset leader of $RM(1, n)$.*

We shall use the notion of Fourier and Walsh transform defined as follows:

Definition 4. *Let f be a Boolean function in n variables. The Fourier transform of f, valued in $\mathbb{Z}$, is denoted by $\widehat{f}$ and defined as:*

$$\widehat{f}(u) = \sum_{x \in \mathbb{F}_2^n} f(x)(-1)^{u \cdot x}, \text{ for all } u \in \mathbb{F}_2^n,$$

where "$\cdot$" is some chosen inner product, that is, where $x \cdot y$ is a bilinear form such that $x \cdot y = 0$ for every $y \in \mathbb{F}_2^n$ if and only if $x = 0$ (i.e. the only element orthogonal to $\mathbb{F}_2^n$ is 0). Note that in this expression, f is treated as valued in $\{0, 1\} \subset \mathbb{Z}$ and not in $\mathbb{F}_2$. Equivalently, we have $\widehat{f}(u) = \sum_{x \in \mathrm{supp}(f)} (-1)^{u \cdot x}$.
The Walsh transform of f, denoted by W_f, is the Fourier transform of the sign function $f_\chi(x) = (-1)^{f(x)}$:

$$W_f(u) = \sum_{x \in \mathbb{F}_2^n} (-1)^{f(x) + u \cdot x} \text{ for all } u \in \mathbb{F}_2^n.$$

The Walsh transform satisfies the so-called *Parseval relation* $\sum_{u \in \mathbb{F}_2^n} W_f^2(u) = 2^{2n}$.
In the following, given a Boolean function f in n variables, the Walsh spectrum $\{W_f(a), a \in \mathbb{F}_2^n\}$ of f is denoted by $WS(f)$.

Let f be an n-variable Boolean function. It is clear that $(-1)^{f(x)} = 1 - 2f(x)$ which implies $\widehat{f}(u) = 2^{n-1}\delta_0(u) - \frac{1}{2}W_f(u)$, where δ_0 is the Kronecker symbol defined by $\delta_0(u) = 1$ if u is the null vector and $\delta_0(u) = 0$ otherwise. In particular, $u = 0$ yields

$$w_H(f) = 2^{n-1} - \frac{1}{2}W_f(0).$$

The nonlinearity $\mathrm{nl}(f)$ of a Boolean function f over $\mathbb{F}_2^n$ is the minimum Hamming distance $d_H(f, h) = |\{x \in \mathbb{F}_2^n; f(x) \neq h(x)\}|$ between f and affine functions h (in other words, the distance from f to $RM(1, n)$). We have:

$$\mathrm{nl}(f) = 2^{n-1} - \frac{1}{2}\max_{a \in \mathbb{F}_2^n} |W_f(a)|. \tag{1}$$

Thanks to the Parseval Relation, the maximum of $W_f^2(a)$ is larger than or equal to its arithmetic mean $\frac{2^{2n}}{2^n} = 2^n$, and we have then the so-called covering radius bound:

$$\mathrm{nl}(f) \leq 2^{n-1} - 2^{n/2-1}.$$

We have also the following easy result from [4]:

Lemma 5. *[4] An n variable Boolean function f is a coset leader of the first order Reed-Muller code $RM(1, n)$ if and only if $\mathrm{nl}(f) = w_H(f)$, that is, $W_f(0) = \max_{a \in \mathbb{F}_2^n} | W_f(a) |$, or equivalently, $W_f(0) \geq |W_f(a)|$ for all $a \in \mathbb{F}_2^n$, or still equivalently $\widehat{f}(0) \leq 2^{n-1} - \max_{a \neq 0} |\widehat{f}(a)|$.*

Given a Boolean function f and a vector a, denoting the function $a \cdot x$ by $\ell_a(x)$, we have $W_{f+\ell_a}(0) = W_f(a)$ and $W_{f+\ell_a+1}(0) = -W_f(a)$; then we have:

Lemma 6. *[4] For every n-variable Boolean function f, every vector a and every bit ϵ, the function $f + \ell_a + \epsilon$ is a coset leader if and only if $|W_f(a)|$ is maximal over $\mathbb{F}_2^n$ and either $W_f(a) > 0$ and $\epsilon = 0$, or $W_f(a) < 0$ and $\epsilon = 1$.*

Since the threshold functions and the majority functions (see the definition in Sect. 4) are symmetric functions, we recall now some properties of symmetric functions useful in the sequel. Note that a function is called symmetric if it is invariant under any permutation of the variables, i.e., if $f(x_1, \ldots, x_n) = f(x_{\pi(1)}, \ldots, x_{\pi(n)})$ for any permutation π on $\{1, \ldots, n\}$. For Boolean functions, this is equivalent to the fact that f outputs the same value for all the inputs having the same Hamming weight. Further, when a symmetric Boolean function contains a degree r monomial, then it contains all the other degree r monomials (see [8]), i.e. its ANF is also symmetric. One can represent an n-variable symmetric Boolean function $f(x_1, \ldots, x_n)$ in a reduced form by the $(n + 1)$-bit string $(\mathrm{re}_f(i))_{i=0,1,\ldots,n}$ where:

$$\mathrm{re}_f(i) = f(x), \text{ where } w_H(x) = i.$$

The Walsh spectra of symmetric Boolean functions have very nice combinatorial properties related to the Krawtchouk polynomials [14]. The Krawtchouk polynomial of degree i is given by

$$K_i(x, n) = \sum_{j=0}^{i} (-1)^j \binom{x}{j}\binom{n-x}{i-j}, \quad i = 0, 1, ..., n. \tag{2}$$

For a fixed vector a such that $w_H(a) = k$, we have that $K_i(k, n) = \sum_{w_H(x)=i}(-1)^{a \cdot x}$, and we can easily check that $W_f(a) = \sum_{i=0}^{n}(-1)^{r_{ef}(i)}K_i(k, n)$. Since any symmetric function f satisfies $W_f(a) = W_f(b)$ for all a, b such that $w_H(a) = w_H(b)$, we will denote by $W_f(k)$ the value of the Walsh transform of the symmetric function f at any point a with $w_H(a) = k$.

We shall need the following result which is a part of Proposition 4 in [8]:

Proposition 7. *[8, Proposition 4]*

1. $K_0(k, n) = 1$, $K_1(k, n) = n - 2k$.
2. $K_i(k, n) = (-1)^k K_{n-i}(k, n)$ *(for n even and k odd, $K_{\frac{n}{2}}(k, n) = 0$)*
3. $K_i(k, n) = (-1)^i K_i(n - k, n)$

Some proofs in Sect. 4 will rely on the following two results:

Proposition 8. *[8, Proposition 5]*

$$\textit{For } n \textit{ even}, K_i\left(\frac{n}{2}, n\right) = \begin{cases} 0 \textit{ for odd } i \\ \binom{\frac{n}{2}}{\frac{i}{2}} \textit{ for even } i \end{cases}.$$

For any $\alpha \in \mathbb{R}$ we use the usual notation whereby $\lfloor \alpha \rfloor$ denotes the integer part of α ($\lceil \alpha \rceil$ denoting the smallest integer greater than or equal to α).

Lemma 9 *[8, Lemma 4]. Let f be the majority function in n variables.*

1. For k even, $W_f(k) = \begin{cases} K_{\frac{n}{2}}(k, n) \textit{ for even } n \\ 0 \textit{ for odd } n \end{cases}$,

2. For odd k, $W_f(k) = 2 \sum_{i=0}^{\lfloor \frac{n-1}{2} \rfloor} K_i(k, n)$,

3. $W_f(1) = 2\binom{n-1}{\lfloor \frac{n}{2} \rfloor}$,

4. $W_f(n) = \begin{cases} (-1)^{\frac{n}{2}}\binom{n}{\frac{n}{2}} \textit{ for even } n \\ (-1)^{\frac{n-1}{2}}2\binom{n-1}{\frac{n-1}{2}} \textit{ for odd } n \end{cases}$,

5. for even n, $W_f\left(\frac{n}{2}\right) = \begin{cases} (-1)^{\frac{n}{4}}\binom{\frac{n}{2}}{\frac{n}{4}} \textit{ for even } \frac{n}{2} \\ 2\sum_{i=0}^{\frac{n-2}{4}}(-1)^i\binom{\frac{n}{2}}{i} \textit{ for odd } \frac{n}{2} \end{cases}.$

3   Coset Leaders in the Class of the Niho Functions

We address here the well known class of Niho functions. To define the functions in this class, we identify $\mathbb{F}_2^n$ with $\mathbb{F}_{2^n}$ (the finite field of order 2^n) and we use the so-called polar decomposition of the elements of $\mathbb{F}_{2^n}$ into the product of an element of the subfield $\mathbb{F}_{2^{\frac{n}{2}}}$ (meaning that n must be even) and of an element of the multiplicative subgroup of $\mathbb{F}_{2^n}^*$ of order $2^{\frac{n}{2}} + 1$ (see [13] and [2, Subsect. 5.1.2] for more details).

Definition 10. *Let n be an even positive integer and $m = \frac{n}{2}$. A Niho function f is a Boolean function whose restriction to the set $\mu \mathbb{F}_{2^m}^*$ is linear for any $\mu \in \mathbb{F}_{2^n}^*$ (where μ can without loss of generality be taken in the multiplicative subgroup U of $\mathbb{F}_{2^n}^*$ of order $2^m + 1$). In other words f is a function defined as:*

$$f(\mu y) = \mathrm{tr}_m(y \phi(\mu)); \; \mu \in U, \; y \in \mathbb{F}_{2^m}^*, \tag{3}$$

where tr_m is the trace function from $\mathbb{F}_{2^m}$ to $\mathbb{F}_2$, and ϕ is a function from U to $\mathbb{F}_{2^m}$.

From e.g. [2], for all functions f given by Relation (3), and denoting by tr_m^n the trace function from $\mathbb{F}_{2^n}$ to $\mathbb{F}_{2^m}$, we have, for every $u \in \mathbb{F}_{2^n}$:

$$W_f(u) = (-1)^{f(0)} + \sum_{\mu \in U, \, y \in \mathbb{F}_{2^m}^*} (-1)^{\mathrm{tr}_m(y \phi(\mu)) + \mathrm{tr}_n(\mu y u)])}$$

$$= (-1)^{f(0)} + \sum_{\mu \in U, \, y \in \mathbb{F}_{2^m}^*} (-1)^{\mathrm{tr}_m(y [\phi(\mu) + \mathrm{tr}_m^n(\mu u)])}$$

$$= (-1)^{f(0)} - (2^m + 1) + 2^m \, \mathrm{card}(\{\mu \in U, \phi(\mu) + \mathrm{tr}_m^n(\mu u) = 0\}) \tag{4}$$

$$w_H(f) = 2^{n-1} - \frac{1}{2}\big((-1)^{f(0)} - (2^m + 1) + 2^m \, \mathrm{card}(\{\mu \in U, \phi(\mu) = 0\})\big)$$

and

$$\mathrm{nl}(f) = 2^{n-1} - \frac{1}{2} \max_{u \in \mathbb{F}_2^n} \left|(-1)^{f(0)} - (2^m + 1) + 2^m \, \mathrm{card}(\{\mu \in U, \phi(\mu) + \mathrm{tr}_m^n(\mu u) = 0\})\right|.$$

Note that if $f(0) = 0$, then from Relation (4), f is bent (that is, f has maximal non-linearity $2^{n-1} - 2^{m-1}$; equivalently $W_f(u) \in \{\pm 2^m\}$ for every u) if and only if for all u, $\mathrm{card}(\{\mu \in U, \phi(\mu) + \mathrm{tr}_m^n(\mu u) = 0\}) \in \{0, 2\}$.

Remark 11. *From Lemma 6, we have that, given a Niho function f defined by Relation (3), the functions $f(\mu y) + \mathrm{tr}_n(u \mu y)) + \epsilon$ in the coset $f + RM(1, n)$ are coset leaders of $RM(1, n)$ if and only if*

$$\max_{u \in \mathbb{F}_2^n} \left|(-1)^{f(0)} - (2^m + 1) + 2^m \, \mathrm{card}(\{\mu \in U, \phi(\mu) + \mathrm{tr}_m^n(\mu u) = 0\})\right| =$$

$$(-1)^{\epsilon}\big((-1)^{f(0)} - (2^m + 1) + 2^m \, \mathrm{card}(\{\mu \in U, \phi(\mu) = 0\})\big).$$

The class of Niho functions is not a union of cosets of the first order Reed-Muller code. As we mentioned in the introduction, we need then not only to characterize the coset leaders of $RM(1, n)$ among all functions in this class, but more generally those belonging to the $RM(1, n)$-cosets having non-empty intersection with the class. Note that if $m = 1$ (that is, $n = 2$), the Niho function is in fact a Boolean function in 2 variables and its coset leaders are easy to determine. Indeed, there are only 16 functions (whether Niho or not) in 2 variables: the 8 affine functions and the 8 functions of the form $x_1 x_2 + a(x)$ with $a(x)$ affine. The zero function is the unique coset leader of each of the 8 affine functions and for the others 8 functions, the unique coset leader of each of them is the function $x_1 x_2$.

This is why, in the following result, we assume $m \geq 2$:

Theorem 12. *Let n and $m \geq 2$ be two positive integers with $n = 2m$. Let f be a Niho function defined by Relation (3). For all $u \in \mathbb{F}_{2^n}$, we set $N(u) = \text{card}(\{\mu \in U, \phi(\mu) + \text{tr}_m^n(\mu u) = 0\})$ and $N_U = \max_{u \in \mathbb{F}_{2^n}} N(u)$. According to the two possible values of f at 0, we have:*

1. *If $f(0) = 0$, then the coset leaders of f are:*
   - *the functions $f(\mu y) + \text{tr}_m(y\, tr_m^n(\mu u))$ where $N(u) = N_U \geq 2$;*
   - *the functions $f(\mu y) + \text{tr}_m(y\, tr_m^n(\mu u)) + 1$ where $N(u) = 0$, $N_U \leq 2$.*
2. *If $f(0) = 1$, by distinguishing the following two cases, we have:*
   a) *For $m = 2$, the coset leaders of f are:*
      - *the functions $f(\mu y) + \text{tr}_m(y\, \text{tr}_m^n(\mu u))$ where $N(u) = N_U \in \{3, 4, 5\}$;*
      - *the functions $f(\mu y) + \text{tr}_m(y\, \text{tr}_m^n(\mu u)) + 1$ where $N(u) = 0$ and $N_U \leq 3$.*
   b) *For $m \geq 3$, the coset leaders of f are:*
      - *the functions $f(\mu y) + \text{tr}_m(y\, \text{tr}_m^n(\mu u))$ where $N(u) = N_U \geq 3$;*
      - *the functions $f(\mu y) + \text{tr}_m(y\, \text{tr}_m^n(\mu u))$ with $N(u) = N_U = 2$ when $N(v) \neq 0$, $\forall v \in \mathbb{F}_{2^n}$;*
      - *the functions $f(\mu y) + \text{tr}_m(y\, \text{tr}_m^n(\mu u)) + 1$ with $N(u) = 0$; $N_U \leq 2$.*

Proof. Note that the expression $\ell_a(x) = a \cdot x$ of Lemma 6 is replaced here by $u \cdot (\mu y) = \text{tr}_m(y\, \text{tr}_m^n(\mu u))$.

Since we have $\text{card}(U) = 2^m + 1$, then the possible values of $N(u)$ are $0, 1, 2, ..., 2^m + 1$ and according to Relation (4), we have $W_f(u) = (-1)^{f(0)} - (2^m + 1) + 2^m N(u)$ which means:

1. If $f(0) = 0$, then the values $0, 1, 2, ..., 2^m + 1$ of $N(u)$ yield the following possible values of the Walsh transform of f: $-2^m, 0, 2^m, 2^{m+1}, 3 \cdot 2^m, ..., 2^{2m}$. We can therefore write $WS(f) \subseteq \{-2^m, 0, 2^m, 2^{m+1}, 3 \cdot 2^m, ..., 2^{2m}\} = A \cup B$ where $A = \{-2^m, 0, 2^m\}$ (whose elements correspond respectively to the values $N(u) = 0, 1, 2$) and $B = \{2^{m+1}, 3 \cdot 2^m, ..., 2^{2m}\}$ (whose elements correspond respectively to the values $N(u) = 3, 4, ..., 2^m + 1$) and since $m \geq 1$, then for all $k \in B$ and $l \in A$, we have $k > |l|$. Hence, the inequality $N_U \geq 3$ implies there exists u such that $W_f(u) \in B$ meaning that the maximal value of $|W_f(u)|$ is obtained in B and corresponds to the maximal value of $N(u)$ which is N_U, and the inequality $N_U \leq 2$ implies that $WS(f) \subseteq A$. Thus, we distinguish the two cases:
   - $WS(f) \cap B \neq \emptyset$, that is, $N_U \geq 3$
   - $WS(f) \subseteq A = \{-2^m, 0, 2^m\}$, that is, $N_U \leq 2$, in which case there exists u such that $W_f(u) = -2^m$ that is, $N(u) = 0$ or there exists u such that $W_f(u) = 2^m$ that is, $N(u) = 2$ (note that the case $W_f(u) = 0$ can not yield a coset leader of f since by the Parseval relation, we have $\max_{a \in \mathbb{F}_2^n} | W_f(a) | \neq 0$ for all f),
   and the result follows from Lemma 6.

2. If $f(0) = 1$, then the values $0, 1, 2, ..., 2^m + 1$ of $N(u)$ yield the values $-2^m - 2, -2, 2^m - 2, 2^{m+1} - 2, 3 \cdot 2^m - 2, ..., 2^{2m} - 2$ as the possible values of the Walsh transform of f. We can therefore write $WS(f) \subseteq \{-2^m - 2, -2, 2^m - 2, 2^{m+1} - 2, 3 \cdot 2^m - 2, ..., 2^{2m} - 2\} = C \cup D$ where $C = \{-2^m - 2, -2, 2^m - 2\}$ (whose elements correspond respectively to the values $N(u) = 0, 1, 2$) and $D = \{2^{m+1} - 2, 3 \cdot 2^m - 2, ..., 2^{2m} - 2\}$ (whose elements correspond respectively to the values $N(u) = 3, 4, ..., 2^m + 1$) and we have:

a) If $m = 2$, then $C = \{-6, -2, 2\}$ corresponding respectively to $N(u) = 0, 1, 2$ and $D = \{6, 10, 14\}$ corresponding to $N(u) = 3, 4, 5$. The result follows from Lemma 6 by distinguishing the following three cases:
   - $W_f(u) \in \{10, 14\}$ for some u with $N(u) = N_U = 4, 5$
   - $W_f(u) \in \{-6, 6\}$ for some u when $N_U \leq 3$ and where $W_f(u) = -6$ means $N(u) = 0$ and $W_f(u) = 6$ means $N(u) = 3$.
   - $W_f(u) \in \{-2, 2\}$ for all u when $N(u) \in \{1, 2\}$ for all u (but this last case is impossible because by the Parseval Relation, the Walsh spectrum of f can not be contained in $\{-2, 2\}$ when $m \geq 2$).

b) If $m \geq 3$, then the element $2^{m+1} - 2$, which is the minimum of D, is such that, for all $s \in C = \{-2^m - 2, -2, 2^m - 2\}$, we have $2^{m+1} - 2 > |s|$, implying that for all $r \in D$ and $s \in C$, we have $r > |s|$.
   If $N_U \geq 3$, then there exists u such that $W_f(u) \in D$, and the maximal value of $|W_f(u)|$ is obtained in D and corresponds to $N(u) = N_U$.
   If $N_U \leq 2$ then $WS(f) \subseteq C$. This case yields the subcases:

   * $N(v) \neq 0$ for all v and $W_f(u) = 2^m - 2$ for some u with $N(u) = 2$ (note that by using again the Parseval relation, the case $W_f(u) = -2$ can not yield a coset leader of f);
   * $W_f(u) = -2^m - 2$ for some u that is, $N(u) = 0$.

□

4   Coset Leaders in the Class of Threshold Functions

We address now the class of threshold functions, which is a particular class of symmetric Boolean functions.

Definition 13. *[5] Let n and d be two positive integers with $d \leq n + 1$. The threshold function of parameters d, n is the Boolean function in n variables denoted by $T_{d,n}$ and defined by:*

$$T_{d,n}(x) = \begin{cases} 0 & \text{if } w_H(x) < d \\ 1 & \text{otherwise} \end{cases},$$

Definition 14. *[5] For any positive integer n, the majority function in n variables is the Boolean function f defined by:*

$$f(x) = \begin{cases} 0 & \text{if } w_H(x) \leq \lfloor \frac{n}{2} \rfloor \\ 1 & \text{otherwise} \end{cases},$$

Note that if f is the majority function in n variables, then $f = T_{\lceil \frac{n+1}{2} \rceil, n}$ meaning that the family of threshold functions is a super-class of that of majority functions. Note also that the majority function is balanced when n is odd (see [8]).

The nonlinearity of threshold functions is given in [5] as follows:

$$
\mathrm{nl}(T_{d,n}) = \begin{cases} 2^{n-1} - \binom{n-1}{\frac{n-1}{2}} & \text{if } d = \frac{n+1}{2} \\ \sum_{k=d}^{n} \binom{n}{k} = w_H(T_{d,n}) & \text{if } d > \frac{n+1}{2} \\ \sum_{k=0}^{d-1} \binom{n}{k} = 2^n - w_H(T_{d,n}) & \text{if } d < \frac{n+1}{2} \end{cases},
$$

Hence, from Lemma 5 and Lemma 6, we have the obvious:

Corollary 15. *For any integers $d \le n + 1$, we have:*

- *if $d = \frac{n+1}{2}$, the coset leaders of $T_{d,n}$ are all the functions $T_{d,n}(x) + a \cdot x + \epsilon$ where $a \in \mathbb{F}_2^n$ and $\epsilon \in \{0, 1\}$ are such that*

$$
W_{T_{d,n}}(a) = 2(-1)^\epsilon \binom{n-1}{(n-1)/2}.
$$

- *if $d > \frac{n+1}{2}$, then $T_{d,n}$ is a coset leader and the other coset leaders of $T_{d,n}$ are all the functions $T_{d,n}(x) + a \cdot x + \epsilon$, where $a \in \mathbb{F}_2^n$ and $\epsilon \in \{0, 1\}$ are such that $W_{T_{d,n}}(a) = (-1)^\epsilon (2^n - 2w_H(T_{d,n}))$.*
- *if $d < \frac{n+1}{2}$, the coset leaders of $T_{d,n}$ are all the functions $T_{d,n}(x) + a \cdot x + \epsilon$, where $a \in \mathbb{F}_2^n$ and $\epsilon \in \{0, 1\}$ are such that*

$$
W_{T_{d,n}}(a) = (-1)^\epsilon \left(2^n - 2 \sum_{k=0}^{d-1} \binom{n}{k} \right).
$$

Since the class of threshold functions is not a union of cosets of $RM(1, n)$, we have to characterize the coset leaders of each functions in this class.

The following two results from [8], in which $K_i(x, n)$ denotes the Krawtchouk polynomial of degree i defined in Relation (2), are also useful:

Lemma 16 *[8, Lemma 5]. For all $1 \le k \le \lfloor \frac{n-1}{2} \rfloor$ and $0 \le i \le \lfloor \frac{n-1}{2} \rfloor$, $K_i(1, n) \ge |K_i(k, n)|$.*

Corollary 17 *[8, Corollary 1]*

1. *For odd n, $|K_i(1, n)| \ge |K_i(k, n)|$ for all $0 \le i \le n$, and $1 \le k \le n - 1$.*
2. *For even n, $|K_i(1, n)| \ge |K_i(k, n)|$ for all $0 \le i \le n$, and $1 \le k \le n - 1$ except $i = \frac{n}{2}$ or $k = \frac{n}{2}$.*

From Lemma 16, $K_i(1, n) \ge 0$ for all $0 \le i \le \lfloor \frac{n-1}{2} \rfloor$ and then Corollary 17 yields:

Corollary 18. *We have*

1. *For odd n, $K_i(1, n) \ge |K_i(k, n)|$ for all $0 \le i \le \lfloor \frac{n-1}{2} \rfloor$, and $1 \le k \le n - 1$.*
2. *For even n, $K_i(1, n) \ge |K_i(k, n)|$ for all $0 \le i \le \lfloor \frac{n-1}{2} \rfloor$, and $1 \le k \le n - 1$ except $k = \frac{n}{2}$.*

By recalling that $W_f(k)$ denotes the Walsh transform of a symmetric function f at any vector of weight k, we have the following result (in which nothing is said for the case $k = 0$ in the second item but we will address this case in the proof of the next theorem):

Proposition 19. *Let $n \geq 3$ be a positive integer and let f be the majority function in n variables.*

1. *For odd $n \geq 3$, $W_f(1) > |W_f(k)|$ for all $2 \leq k \leq n - 1$ and for $k = 0$.*
2. *For even $n \geq 4$, $W_f(1) > |W_f(k)|$ for all $2 \leq k \leq n - 1$.*

Proof

1. Let n be odd. According to the first item of Lemma 9, for all even k, $0 \leq k \leq n-1$, we have $W_f(k) = 0$ meaning clearly that $W_f(k) < W_f(1)$ by the third item of Lemma 9. Moreover, from the first item of Proposition 7, for all $k = 2, ..., n - 2$ we have $|K_1(k,n)| = |n - 2k| \leq n - 4 < n - 2 = K_1(1, n)$. So, from the first item of Corollary 18 and the second item of Lemma 9, for all odd k, we have

$$W_f(1) = 2\left(1 + K_1(1, n) + \sum_{i=2}^{\lfloor \frac{n-1}{2} \rfloor} K_i(1, n)\right) > 2\left(1 + |K_1(k, n)| + \sum_{i=2}^{\lfloor \frac{n-1}{2} \rfloor} |K_i(k, n)|\right)$$

$$\geq \left|2 \sum_{i=0}^{\lfloor \frac{n-1}{2} \rfloor} K_i(k, n)\right| = |W_f(k)|,$$

   and the result follows.

2. Let n be even. For all odd k, $2 \leq k \leq n - 2$ and $k \neq \frac{n}{2}$, by using again the second item of Lemma 9 and the second item of Corollary 18 the proof is similar to the case of k odd in the proof of the first item.

   For $k = \frac{n}{2}$ odd, according to Lemma 9 (item 5), we have $|W_f(\frac{n}{2})| = \left|2 \sum_{i=0}^{\frac{n-2}{4}} (-1)^i \binom{\frac{n}{2}}{i}\right| \leq 2 \sum_{i=0}^{\frac{n-2}{4}} \binom{\frac{n}{2}}{i} = 2^{\frac{n}{2}}$. By induction on $n \geq 4$ (n even), it is easy to check that $2^{\frac{n}{2}} < 2\binom{n-1}{\frac{n}{2}} = W_f(1)$.

   Now for k even, $2 \leq k \leq n - 2$, the first item of Lemma 9 and Relation (2) yields

$$W_f(k) = K_{\frac{n}{2}}(k, n) = \sum_{j=0}^{\frac{n}{2}} (-1)^j \binom{k}{j}\binom{n-k}{\frac{n}{2}-j} =$$

$$\sum_{\substack{j=2p \\ j \leq \frac{n}{2}}} \binom{k}{j}\binom{n-k}{\frac{n}{2}-j} - \sum_{\substack{j=2p+1 \\ j \leq \frac{n}{2}}} \binom{k}{j}\binom{n-k}{\frac{n}{2}-j} = a - b$$

   where we can easily check that $a = \sum_{\substack{j=2p \\ j \leq \frac{n}{2}}} \binom{k}{j}\binom{n-k}{\frac{n}{2}-j} > 0$ and $b = \sum_{\substack{j=2p+1 \\ j \leq \frac{n}{2}}} \binom{k}{j}\binom{n-k}{\frac{n}{2}-j} > 0$ for all $2 \leq k \leq n-2$. According to Lemma 9, $W_f(1) = 2\binom{n-1}{\frac{n}{2}} = \binom{n}{\frac{n}{2}} = \sum_{j=0}^{\frac{n}{2}} \binom{k}{j}\binom{n-k}{\frac{n}{2}-j} = a + b > |a - b| = |W_f(k)|$.

For the last case $k = n - 1$ which is odd, Lemma 9 (item 2) and Proposition 7 (item 3) yield:

$$W_f(n - 1) = 2 \sum_{i=0}^{\lfloor \frac{n-1}{2} \rfloor} K_i(n - 1, n) = 2 \sum_{i=0}^{\lfloor \frac{n-1}{2} \rfloor} (-1)^i K_i(1, n).$$

By Relation (2), we have clearly $K_i(1, n) = \binom{n-1}{i} - \binom{n-1}{i-1} > 0$ for all $0 \le i \le \lfloor \frac{n-1}{2} \rfloor$ and since $n \ge 4$ (meaning that, $\lfloor \frac{n-1}{2} \rfloor \ge 1$ and then the sum in $W_f(n - 1)$ above is a sum of at least two elements), we obtain (by recalling that if $a_0, ..., a_{p-1}$ are $p \ge 2$ positive numbers, we have clearly $\sum_{i=0}^{p-1} a_i = |\sum_{i=0}^{p-1} a_i| > |\sum_{i=0}^{p-1} (-1)^i a_i|$):

$$\left| W_f(n - 1) \right| = \left| 2 \sum_{i=0}^{\lfloor \frac{n-1}{2} \rfloor} (-1)^i K_i(1, n) \right| < 2 \sum_{i=0}^{\lfloor \frac{n-1}{2} \rfloor} K_i(1, n) = W_f(1),$$

which ends the proof.

$\square$

We have then the following result:

Theorem 20. *Let $n \ge 3$ be a positive integer and f the majority function in n variables.*

1. *For n odd, the coset leaders of f are the functions:*
   a) $f + x_j$ *for all $j = 1, ..., n$,*
   b) $f + \sum_{j=1}^{n} x_j + \frac{1}{2}(1 - (-1)^{\frac{n-1}{2}})$.
2. *For n even, f is a coset leader and the other coset leaders of f are the functions:*
   a) $f + x_j$ *for all $j = 1, ..., n$,*
   b) $f + \sum_{j=1}^{n} x_j + \frac{1}{2}(1 - (-1)^{\frac{n}{2}})$.

Proof. According to Lemma 9 and to [8, Theorem 3], the Walsh transform of the majority function f at any vector of weight 1 denoted by $W_f(1)$, is positive and has maximal absolute value. Hence, items 1.a and 2.a follow from Lemma 6.

1.b) Let n be odd. According to Lemma 9 (item 4), $\left| W_f(n) \right| = \left| 2(-1)^{\frac{n-1}{2}} \binom{n-1}{\frac{n-1}{2}} \right| = 2\binom{n-1}{\frac{n-1}{2}} = W_f(1)$ that is, $W_f(n) = W_f(1)$ if $n = 4k + 1$ and $W_f(n) = -W_f(1)$ if $n = 4k + 3$. Thus, $\left| W_f(n) \right|$ is maximal and the results follows from Lemma 6.

2.b) Let n be even. According to Lemma 9 (item 1) and Relation (2), $W_f(0) = K_{\frac{n}{2}}(0, n) = \binom{n}{\frac{n}{2}} = 2\binom{n-1}{\frac{n}{2}} = W_f(1)$ meaning that f is a coset leader. According to Lemma 9 (item 4) again, $\left| W_f(n) \right| = \left| (-1)^{\frac{n}{2}} \binom{n}{\frac{n}{2}} \right| = \binom{n}{\frac{n}{2}} = 2\binom{n-1}{\frac{n}{2}} = W_f(1)$ that is, $W_f(n) = W_f(1)$ if $n = 4k$ and $W_f(n) = -W_f(1)$ if $n = 4k + 2$. Thus, $\left| W_f(n) \right|$ is maximal and then the result follows from Lemma 6 again.

By Proposition 19 there are no other coset leaders, which ends the proof. $\square$

We address now the characterization of coset leaders in the class of threshold functions. The next result is for n odd; the case $d = \frac{n+1}{2}$, which corresponds to the majority function was addressed in Theorem 20 and will therefore not be considered in the following.

Theorem 21. *Let $n \geq 3$ be an odd integer and d a positive integer such that $d \leq \frac{n-1}{2}$. Then $T_{d,n} + 1$ is the unique coset leader of the threshold function $T_{d,n}$.*

Proof

- For k even, since $K_i(k,n) = (-1)^k K_{n-i}(k,n) = K_{n-i}(k,n)$ then we have

$$W_{T_{d,n}}(k) = \sum_{i=0}^{d-1} K_i(k,n) - \sum_{i=n-d+1}^{n} K_i(k,n) - \sum_{i=d}^{n-d} K_i(k,n) = -\sum_{i=d}^{n-d} K_i(k,n) = -2\sum_{i=d}^{\frac{n-1}{2}} K_i(k,n)$$

and the fact that for all integer $i = 0, 1, ..., n$, $\binom{n}{i} = \binom{n}{n-i}$ yields $W_{T_{d,n}}(0) = -2\sum_{i=d}^{\frac{n-1}{2}} \binom{n}{i}$. It remains to show that $\left|W_{T_{d,n}}(0)\right| > \left|W_{T_{d,n}}(k)\right|$ for all k even, $k = 2, ..., n$. Note that for all a with $w_H(a) = k$ and $i \geq 1$, we have $K_i(k,n) = \sum_{w_H(x)=i}(-1)^{a \cdot x} = \sum_{1 \leq t_1 < t_2 < ... < t_i \leq n}(-1)^{a_{t_1} + ... + a_{t_i}}$ and the fact that $1 \leq k < n$ implies there exist $1 \leq t_1 < t_2 < ... < t_i \leq n$ with $a_{t_1} + ... + a_{t_i} = 1$ and there also exist $1 \leq t_1 < t_2 < ... < t_i \leq n$ such that $a_{t_1} + ... + a_{t_i} = 0$ meaning that $|K_i(k,n)| = \left|\sum_{1 \leq t_1 < t_2 < ... < t_i \leq n}(-1)^{a_{t_1} + ... + a_{t_i}}\right| < \binom{n}{i}$ and since $K_i(k,n) = K_{n-i}(k,n)$ (k being even), then we have:

$$\left|W_{T_{d,n}}(k)\right| \leq 2\sum_{i=d}^{\frac{n-1}{2}} |K_i(k,n)| < 2\sum_{i=d}^{\frac{n-1}{2}} \binom{n}{i} = \left|W_{T_{d,n}}(0)\right|.$$

- For k odd, since $K_i(k,n) = -K_{n-i}(k,n)$, then we have $W_{T_{d,n}}(k) = 2\sum_{i=0}^{d-1} K_i(k,n)$ meaning for $k = 1$ that, $W_{T_{d,n}}(1) = 2\sum_{i=0}^{d-1} K_i(1,n) = 2\sum_{i=0}^{d-1}\left(\binom{n-1}{i} - \binom{n-1}{i-1}\right) = 2\binom{n-1}{d-1}$. Using the well known fact that $\binom{n}{d} \leq \binom{n}{\lfloor \frac{n}{2} \rfloor}$ and the fact that $\binom{n-1}{d-1} < \binom{n}{d}$ (a consequence of the well-known formula $\binom{n-1}{d-1} + \binom{n-1}{d} = \binom{n}{d}$) we have

$$W_{T_{d,n}}(1) = 2\binom{n-1}{d-1} < 2\binom{n}{d} \leq 2\binom{n}{\frac{n-1}{2}} \leq 2\sum_{i=d}^{\frac{n-1}{2}} \binom{n}{i} = |W_{d,n}(0)|.$$

For k odd with $2 \leq k \leq n-1$, then according to Corollary 18, $|K_i(k,n)| \leq K_i(1,n)$, for all $i = 1, ..., \frac{n-2}{2}$ meaning that

$$\left|W_{T_{d,n}}(k)\right| = 2\left|\sum_{i=0}^{d-1} K_i(k,n)\right| \leq 2\sum_{i=0}^{d-1} |K_i(k,n)| \leq 2\sum_{i=0}^{d-1} K_i(1,n) = W_{T_{d,n}}(1) < \left|W_{d,n}(0)\right|.$$

Now for the last case $k = n$ which is odd, according to Proposition 7 and using the fact that for all $d < n$, $\sum_{i=0}^{d-1}(-1)^i\binom{n}{i} = (-1)^{d-1}\binom{n-1}{d-1}$ (which can be easily proven using $\binom{n-1}{i-1} + \binom{n-1}{i} = \binom{n}{i}$) we have

$$\left|W_{T_{d,n}}(n)\right| = 2\left|\sum_{i=0}^{d-1} K_i(n,n)\right| = 2\left|\sum_{i=0}^{d-1}(-1)^i K_i(0,n)\right| = 2\left|\sum_{i=0}^{d-1}(-1)^i\binom{n}{i}\right| =$$

$$2\binom{n-1}{d-1} < |W_{d,n}(0)|.$$

The proof is completed by Lemma 6.   □

Note that for n odd and for all $d = 1, 2, ..., \frac{n-1}{2}$, the inequality $\frac{n+3}{2} \leq n - d + 1 \leq n$ holds and we have $W_{T_{n-d+1,n}}(k) = -W_{T_{d,n}}(k)$ when k is even (meaning that $W_{T_{n-d+1,n}}(0)$ is positive) and $W_{T_{n-d+1,n}}(k) = W_{T_{d,n}}(k)$ when k is odd. Then, according to the proof of Theorem 21 we have the obvious:

Corollary 22. *Let* $n \geq 3$ *be an odd integer and* d *a positive integer such that* $d \geq \frac{n+3}{2}$. *Then* $T_{d,n}$ *is the unique coset leader of the threshold function* $T_{d,n}$.

The following results give the coset leaders of $T_{d,n}$ when n is even. We start with $d = \frac{n}{2}$.

Theorem 23. *Let* $n \geq 4$ *be an even integer. Then the coset leaders of* $T_{\frac{n}{2},n}$ *are the functions:*

a) $T_{\frac{n}{2},n} + 1$
b) $T_{\frac{n}{2},n} + x_j$ *for all* $j = 1, 2, ..., n$.
c) $T_{\frac{n}{2},n} + \sum_{i=1}^{n} x_j + \frac{1}{2}(1 + (-1)^{\frac{n}{2}})$

Proof

- For k even, by using the fact that for all integer $i = 0, 1, ..., n$, $K_i(k, n) = K_{n-i}(k, n)$, we have:

$$W_{T_{\frac{n}{2},n}}(k) = \sum_{i=0}^{\frac{n-2}{2}} K_i(k, n) - \sum_{i=\frac{n+2}{2}}^{n} K_i(k, n) - K_{\frac{n}{2}}(k, n) = -K_{\frac{n}{2}}(k, n),$$

meaning that $W_{T_{\frac{n}{2},n}}(0) = -K_{\frac{n}{2}}(0, n) = -\binom{n}{\frac{n}{2}}$ and $W_{T_{\frac{n}{2},n}}(n) = -K_{\frac{n}{2}}(n, n) = (-1)^{\frac{n}{2}+1}\binom{n}{\frac{n}{2}}$. Now let us show that for all $k = 2, ..., n - 2$ even, we have $\left|W_{T_{\frac{n}{2},n}}(k)\right| < \binom{n}{\frac{n}{2}} = \left|W_{T_{\frac{n}{2},n}}(0)\right|$. Note that for all a with $w_H(a) = k$,

$$K_{\frac{n}{2}}(k, n) = \sum_{w_H(x)=\frac{n}{2}} (-1)^{a \cdot x} = \sum_{1 \leq i_1 < i_2 < ... < i_{\frac{n}{2}} \leq n} (-1)^{a_{i_1} + ... + a_{i_{\frac{n}{2}}}}$$

the fact that $1 \leq k < n$ implies that there exist $1 \leq i_1 < i_2 < ... < i_{\frac{n}{2}} \leq n$ with $a_{i_1} + ... + a_{i_{\frac{n}{2}}} = 1$ and there also exist $1 \leq i_1 < i_2 < ... < i_{\frac{n}{2}} \leq n$ such that $a_{i_1} + ... + a_{i_{\frac{n}{2}}} = 0$ meaning that $\left|K_{\frac{n}{2}}(k, n)\right| = \left|\sum_{1 \leq i_1 < i_2 < ... < i_{\frac{n}{2}} \leq n} (-1)^{a_{i_1} + ... + a_{i_{\frac{n}{2}}}}\right| < \binom{n}{\frac{n}{2}}$ and therefore for k even we have:

$$\left|W_{T_{\frac{n}{2},n}}(k)\right| = \left|K_{\frac{n}{2}}(k, n)\right| < \binom{n}{\frac{n}{2}} = \left|W_{T_{\frac{n}{2},n}}(0)\right|.$$

- For k odd, since $K_i(k, n) = -K_{n-i}(k, n)$ and $K_{\frac{n}{2}}(k, n) = 0$, we have

$$W_{T_{\frac{n}{2},n}}(k) = \sum_{i=0}^{\frac{n-2}{2}} K_i(k, n) - \sum_{i=\frac{n+2}{2}}^{n} K_i(k, n) - K_{\frac{n}{2}}(k, n) = 2\sum_{i=0}^{\frac{n-2}{2}} K_i(k, n)$$

meaning that for $k = 1$,

$$W_{T_{\frac{n}{2},n}}(1) = 2\sum_{i=0}^{\frac{n-2}{2}} K_i(1,n) = 2\sum_{i=0}^{\frac{n-2}{2}}\left(\binom{n-1}{i} - \binom{n-1}{i-1}\right) = 2\binom{n-1}{\frac{n-2}{2}} = \left|W_{T_{\frac{n}{2},n}}(0)\right|.$$

According to Corollary 18, for all $i = 1, \ldots, \frac{n-2}{2}$, for all $2 \le k \le n-2$ with $k \ne \frac{n}{2}$, we have $|K_i(k,n)| \le K_i(1,n) = \binom{n-1}{i} - \binom{n-1}{i-1}$ and $|K_1(k,n)| = |n - 2k| < n - 2 = K_1(1,n)$. Thus,

$$\left|2\sum_{i=0}^{\frac{n-2}{2}} K_i(k,n)\right| \le 2\sum_{i=0}^{\frac{n-2}{2}} |K_i(k,n)| < 2\sum_{i=0}^{\frac{n-2}{2}} |K_i(1,n)| = 2\binom{n-1}{\frac{n-2}{2}} = \binom{n}{\frac{n}{2}} = \left|W_{T_{\frac{n}{2},n}}(0)\right|$$

For the case $k = \frac{n}{2}$ odd, from Proposition 8, we have $K_i(\frac{n}{2},n) = (-1)^{\frac{i}{2}}\binom{\frac{n}{2}}{\frac{i}{2}}$, Meaning that

$$\left|W_{T_{\frac{n}{2},n}}(\frac{n}{2})\right| = \left|2\sum_{i=0}^{\frac{n-2}{2}}(-1)^{\frac{i}{2}}\binom{\frac{n}{2}}{\frac{i}{2}}\right| \le 2\sum_{i=0}^{\frac{n-2}{2}}\binom{\frac{n}{2}}{\frac{i}{2}} = 2\sum_{i=0}^{\frac{n-2}{4}}\binom{\frac{n}{2}}{i} = 2^{\frac{n}{2}} < \binom{n}{\frac{n}{2}} = \left|W_{T_{\frac{n}{2},n}}(0)\right|.$$

For the last case $k = n - 1$ which is odd, the third item of Proposition 7 yields:

$$W_{T_{\frac{n}{2},n}}(n-1) = 2\sum_{i=0}^{\lfloor\frac{n-2}{2}\rfloor} K_i(n-1,n) = 2\sum_{i=0}^{\lfloor\frac{n-2}{2}\rfloor}(-1)^i K_i(1,n),$$

since $K_i(1,n) = \binom{n-1}{i} - \binom{n-1}{i-1} > 0$ for all $0 \le i \le \lfloor\frac{n-1}{2}\rfloor$, then we have:

$$\left|W_{T_{\frac{n}{2},n}}(n-1)\right| = \left|2\sum_{i=0}^{\lfloor\frac{n-1}{2}\rfloor}(-1)^i K_i(1,n)\right| < 2\sum_{i=0}^{\lfloor\frac{n-1}{2}\rfloor} K_i(1,n) = W_{T_{\frac{n}{2},n}}(1).$$

Thanks to Lemma 6, a) and c) follow from the case k even and b) follows from the case k odd. $\qquad\square$

The result is different for $d \le \frac{n-2}{2}$.

Theorem 24. *Let $n \ge 4$ be an even integer and d a positive integer such that $d \le \frac{n-2}{2}$. Then $T_{d,n} + 1$ is the unique coset leader of $T_{d,n}$.*

Proof

- For k even, $1 \le k < n$, since $K_i(k,n) = (-1)^k K_{n-i}(k,n) = K_{n-i}(k,n)$, then we have

$$W_{T_{d,n}}(k) = \sum_{i=0}^{d-1} K_i(k,n) - \sum_{i=d}^{n} K_i(k,n) = \sum_{i=0}^{d-1} K_i(k,n) - \sum_{i=d}^{n-d} K_i(k,n) - \sum_{i=n-d+1}^{n} K_i(k,n) =$$

$$- \sum_{i=d}^{n-d} K_i(k,n) = -2\sum_{i=d}^{\frac{n-2}{2}} K_i(k,n) - K_{\frac{n}{2}}(k,n).$$

Hence, $W_{T_{d,n}}(0) = -2 \sum_{i=d}^{\frac{n-2}{2}} \binom{n}{i} - \binom{n}{\frac{n}{2}}$.

Since for all k such that $1 \leq k < n$, we have $|K_i(k,n)| < \binom{n}{i}$, then for $k \neq 0$ even, this implies

$$\left| W_{T_{d,n}}(k) \right| = \left| -2 \sum_{i=d}^{\frac{n-2}{2}} K_i(k,n) - K_{\frac{n}{2}}(k,n) \right| \leq 2 \sum_{i=d}^{\frac{n-2}{2}} |K_i(k,n)| + \left| K_{\frac{n}{2}}(k,n) \right| <$$

$$2 \sum_{i=d}^{\frac{n-2}{2}} \binom{n}{i} + \binom{n}{\frac{n}{2}} = \left| W_{T_{d,n}}(0) \right|.$$

For $k = n$ which is even, $W_{T_{d,n}}(n) = -2 \sum_{i=d}^{\frac{n-2}{2}} K_i(n,n) - K_{\frac{n}{2}}(n,n) = 2 \sum_{i=d}^{\frac{n-2}{2}} (-1)^i \binom{n}{i} - (-1)^{\frac{n}{2}} \binom{n}{\frac{n}{2}}$ and we have clearly $\left| 2 \sum_{i=d}^{\frac{n-2}{2}} (-1)^i \binom{n}{i} - (-1)^{\frac{n}{2}} \binom{n}{\frac{n}{2}} \right| < 2 \sum_{i=d}^{\frac{n-2}{2}} \binom{n}{i} + \binom{n}{\frac{n}{2}} = \left| W_{T_{d,n}}(0) \right|$.

- For k odd, since $K_i(k,n) = -K_{n-i}(k,n)$ and $K_{\frac{n}{2}}(k,n) = 0$, then we have

$$W_{T_{d,n}}(k) = \sum_{i=0}^{d-1} K_i(k,n) - \sum_{i=d}^{n-d} K_i(k,n) - \sum_{i=n-d+1}^{n} K_i(k,n) = 2 \sum_{i=0}^{d-1} K_i(k,n).$$

According to Corollary 18, for all $i = 1, ..., \frac{n-2}{2}$, for all $2 \leq k \leq n-2$ with $k \neq \frac{n}{2}$, we have $|K_i(k,n)| \leq K_i(1,n) = \binom{n-1}{i} - \binom{n-1}{i-1}$ and $|K_1(k,n)| = n - 2k < n - 2 = K_1(1,n)$. So for $2 \leq k \leq n-2$ with $k \neq \frac{n}{2}$,

$$\left| W_{T_{d,n}}(k) \right| = \left| 2 \sum_{i=0}^{d-1} K_i(k,n) \right| \leq 2 \sum_{i=0}^{d-1} |K_i(k,n)| < 2 \sum_{i=0}^{d-1} K_i(1,n) = W_{T_{d,n}}(1) <$$

$$2 \sum_{i=0}^{\frac{n-2}{2}} K_i(1,n) = 2 \binom{n-1}{\frac{n-2}{2}} = \binom{n}{\frac{n}{2}} < \left| W_{T_{\frac{n}{2},n}}(0) \right|$$

For $k = \frac{n}{2}$ odd, from the proof of Theorem 23,

$$\left| W_{T_{d,n}}(\frac{n}{2}) \right| \leq 2 \sum_{i=0}^{d-1} \left| K_i(\frac{n}{2}, n) \right| < 2 \sum_{i=0}^{\frac{n-2}{2}} \left| K_i(\frac{n}{2}, n) \right| < \binom{n}{\frac{n}{2}} < \left| W_{T_{\frac{n}{2},n}}(0) \right|$$

For $k = n - 1$, which is odd, the third item of Proposition 7 yields:

$$\left| W_{T_{d,n}}(n-1) \right| = \left| 2 \sum_{i=0}^{d-1} K_i(n-1,n) \right| = \left| 2 \sum_{i=0}^{d-1} (-1)^i K_i(1,n) \right| \leq$$

$$2 \sum_{i=0}^{d-1} K_i(1,n) < 2 \sum_{i=0}^{\frac{n-2}{2}} K_i(1,n) = \binom{n}{\frac{n}{2}} < \left| W_{T_{\frac{n}{2},n}}(0) \right|.$$

The proof is completed by Lemma 6.   □

Note also that for n even and for all $d = 1, 2, ..., \frac{n-2}{2}$, the inequality $\frac{n+4}{2} \leq n-d+1 \leq n$ holds and we have $W_{T_{n-d+1,n}}(k) = -W_{T_{d,n}}(k)$ when k is even (meaning that $W_{T_{n-d+1,n}}(0)$ is positive) and $W_{T_{n-d+1,n}}(k) = W_{T_{d,n}}(k)$ when k is odd. Then, according to the proof of Theorem 24 we have the obvious:

Corollary 25. *Let $n \geq 4$ be an even integer and d a positive integer such that $\frac{n+4}{2} \leq d \leq n$. Then $T_{d,n}$ is the unique coset leader of $T_{d,n}$.*

Remark 26. *Note that Helleseth and Klove defined in [9] the notion of false neighbor of a codeword $h \in C$ which is a nonzero codeword $g \in C$ such that $w_H(h - g) \leq w_H(h)$. They showed that an error e has no false neighbor if and only if it is the unique coset leader in its coset. Thanks to the above characterizations, the threshold function $T_{d,n}$, with n even (resp. odd) and $d \neq \frac{n}{2}, \frac{n}{2} + 1$ (resp. $d \neq \frac{n+1}{2}$), has a unique coset leader in its coset, meaning in the coding point of view that it has no false neighbor.*

Conclusion

In this paper, we answered some of the open problems raised in a recent study. We characterized the coset leaders in the class of Niho functions, majority functions and in general in the class of threshold functions. Many questions are still to be addressed. For instance, the general structure of coset leaders is still to be investigated. Moreover, the characterization of coset leaders in the whole class of symmetric Boolean functions is not yet completed and in many other classes of Boolean functions (such as the class of Carlet-Feng functions whose Walsh spectrum is unknown), this characterization remains to be determined.

References

1. Barg, A.: Complexity issues in coding theory. In: Handbook of Coding Theory, vol. I, II, pp. 649–724. North Holland, Amsterdam (1998)
2. Carlet, C.: Boolean Functions for Cryptography and Error Correcting Codes, 562 p. Cambridge University Press (2021)
3. Carlet, C., Feng, K.: An infinite class of balanced functions with optimal algebraic immunity, good immunity to fast algebraic attacks and good nonlinearity. In: Pieprzyk, J. (ed.) ASIACRYPT 2008. LNCS, vol. 5350, pp. 425–440. Springer, Heidelberg (2008). https://doi.org/10.1007/978-3-540-89255-7_26
4. Carlet, C., Feukoua, S.: On those Boolean functions that are coset leaders of first order Reed-Muller codes. Ann. Math. Artif. Intell. (2023). https://doi.org/10.1007/s10472-023-09842-5
5. Carlet, C., Méaux, P.: A complete study of two classes of Boolean functions: direct sums of monomials and threshold functions. IEEE Trans. Inf. Theory **68**(5), 3404–30425 (2021)
6. Carlet, C., Mesnager, S.: Four decades of research on bent functions. Spec. Jubilee Issue Des. Codes Cryptogr. **78**, 5–50 (2016)
7. Cusick, T.W., Stănică, P.: Fast evaluation, weights and nonlinearity of rotation-symmetric functions. Discret. Math. **258**, 289–301 (2002)
8. Dalai, D.K., Maitra, S., Sarkar, S.: Basic theory in construction of Boolean functions with maximum possible annihilator immunity. Des. Codes Crypt. **40**, 41–58 (2006)

9. Helleseth, T., Kloeve, T.: The Newton radius of codes. IEEE Trans. Inf. Theory **43**(6), 1820–1831 (1997)

10. Langevin, P., Solé, P.: Kernels and defaults. In: Proceedings of the Conference Finite Fields and Applications Fq4, Contemporary Mathematics, vol. 225, pp. 77–85 (1999)

11. MacWilliams, F.J., Sloane, N.J.: The Theory of Error-Correcting Codes. North Holland (1983)

12. Meier, W., Staffelbach, O.: Fast correlation attacks on stream ciphers. In: Barstow, D., et al. (eds.) EUROCRYPT 1988. LNCS, vol. 330, pp. 301–314. Springer, Heidelberg (1988). https://doi.org/10.1007/3-540-45961-8_28

13. Niho, Y.: Multi-valued cross-correlation functions between two maximal linear recursive sequences. PhD. dissertation, University of Southern California, Los Angeles (1972)

14. Savicky, P.: On the bent Boolean functions that are symmetric. Eur. J. Comb. **15**, 407–410 (1994)

15. Zhang, X., Guo, H., Feng, R., Li, Y.: Proof of a conjecture about rotation symmetric functions. Discrete Math. **311**, 1281–1289 (2011)

Revisiting Nearest-Neighbor-Based Information Set Decoding

Andre Esser[✉][iD]

Technology Innovation Institute, Masdar, UAE
`andre.esser@tii.ae`

Abstract. The syndrome decoding problem lies at the heart of code-based cryptographic constructions. Information Set Decoding (ISD) algorithms are commonly used to assess the security of these systems. The most efficient ISD algorithms rely heavily on nearest neighbor search techniques. However, the runtime result of the fastest known ISD algorithm by Both-May (PQCrypto '18) was recently challenged by Carrier et al. (Asiacrypt '22), which introduce themselves a new technique called RLPN decoding which yields improvements over ISD for codes with small rates $\frac{k}{n} \leq 0.3$.

In this work we first revisit the Both-May algorithm, by giving a clean exposition and a corrected analysis. In this context we confirm the result by Carrier et al. that the initial analysis is flawed and conclude with the same runtime exponent. Our work aims at fully substantiating the corrected runtime exponent by a detailed analysis. Furthermore, we show that the Both-May algorithm significantly improves on memory complexity over previous algorithms. Our main contribution is therefore to give the correct perspective on the significance of the Both-May algorithm and to clarify any remaining doubts on the corrected baseline.

Further, we outline a potential strategy for enhancing the Both-May algorithm by merging two of its subroutines, by introducing a fixed-weight nearest neighbor variant. Although we do not obtain immediate improvements, the nearest neighbor variant has already found novel applications in recent research. This initiated study of algorithms to solve the fixed-weight variant could potentially lead to future improvements through our construction.

Keywords: representation technique · syndrome decoding · nearest neighbor search · code-based cryptography

1 Introduction

Cryptography based on the hardness of the decoding problem, known as code-based cryptography, is a promising candidate for post quantum secure systems.

Supported by the Deutsche Forschungsgemeinschaft (DFG, German Research Foundation) - Project-ID MA 2536/12.

E. A. Quaglia (Ed.): IMACC 2023, LNCS 14421, pp. 34–54, 2024.
https://doi.org/10.1007/978-3-031-47818-5_3

The ongoing fourth round standardisation effort of NIST includes three candidates, all of them being code-based constructions. Therefore it is certain that after the end of this round at least one code-based scheme will be selected for standardisation. This makes analysis of those schemes, their security and especially strengthening our understanding of the hardness of the underlying problem an important task.

The *binary syndrome decoding problem* can be formulated as given the parity-check matrix $\mathbf{H}$ of a binary linear code of length n and dimension k as well as a syndrome $\mathbf{s} = \mathbf{He}$, recover the low Hamming weight vector $\mathbf{e}$. The fastest known algorithms for solving generic instances of this problem are usually Information Set Decoding (ISD) algorithms, pioneered by the original work of Prange in 1962 [21]. Since then there have been numerous improvements on Prange's algorithm [1,2,4,5,9,18–20,22], mostly by extending the initial algorithm by an enumeration step. These works usually improve the asymptotic runtime exponent as long as the error-weight, i.e., the Hamming weight of $\mathbf{e}$, is as high as $\Omega(n)$. In this case the asymptotic running time is of the form 2^{cn}, where the constant c depends on the precise code parameters and the ISD algorithm. However, most code-based constructions do not fall into this regime by using an error-weight as small as $o(n)$. Moreover, it has been shown that the asymptotic advantage of all ISD improvements vanishes for a sublinear choice of the error weight [23]. And yet, the best known algorithms for attacking those code-based schemes are exactly these ISD extension of Prange's algorithm, still improving second order terms or polynomial factors in this regime.

Usually, the theoretical study of algorithmic improvements in the constant or high weight regime serves as an indicator which variations lead to practical improvements in the cryptographic setting. Just recently the ISD algorithms by May-Meurer-Thomae (MMT) [19] and the one by Becker-Joux-May-Meurer (BJMM) [1], both initially studied and proposed in the constant weight regime, were used to obtain new computational records in the cryptographic setting [13]. In their work, Esser, May and Zweydinger [13] identify the memory consumption of these algorithms as one of the major bottlenecks for practical applications. Further, the memory consumption, or more precisely the slowdown emerging from the *memory access cost* that goes along with accessing large amounts of random access memory (RAM), is essential for currently proposed parameter sets to reach the necessary security goals [8,11,13]. Therefore, for the security of code-based constructions as well as for the practical adaptation of advanced ISD techniques it is important to understand how and if this memory usage can be reduced. Recently, first time-memory trade-offs to achieve this goal were introduced [14], but those techniques always come at the cost of an increased time complexity.

The most recent ISD algorithms speed up the enumeration step by the use of nearest neighbor search techniques [4,5,20]. The fastest of these algorithms by Both and May [5] claims significant improvements on the time and memory complexity of previous proposals. However, in a recent work, Carrier, Debris-Alazard, Meyer-Hilfiger and Tillich [7] challenge the result of Both and May, by pointing out a flaw in the analysis of its time complexity. Note that (a later revision of) [7] includes the corrected time complexity exponent together with a correction of necessary parts of the original analysis. However, considering the significance of the Both-May algorithm a self-contained corrected analysis providing full details is of major importance for the field. Note that the significance of the Both-May algorithm stems from the fact that the corrected time exponent still slightly improves previous ISD, and the algorithm hence remains the baseline for new improvements.

This baseline is of utmost importance to classify the gain of new ISD and other decoding algorithms, as for instance the newly proposed RLPN technique of Carrier et al. [7], which achieves runtime improvements over ISD in some regimes. In this work we clarify any left doubts by giving a corrected and simplified analysis of the Both-May algorithm confirming the exponent stated in the revision of [7]. Furthermore, our analysis also reveals *significant* gains in the memory complexity of the Both-May algorithm over previous works, contradicting the perception that the algorithm after all constitutes only as a slight improvement over previous ISD. Overall, this result is in line with the results from Esser and Bellini [11] who performed a more practical study of the algorithm also observing mostly memory rather than time improvements.

Furthermore, we extend the algorithm by Both and May by detailing a possible strategy for future improvements. Our idea combines two steps which are usually performed sequentially in the enumeration part of the algorithm – the nearest neighbor search and a subsequent filtering of the found solutions according to some criterion. Therefore we treat the nearest neighbor search in non-blackbox fashion which allows us to directly embed the filtering into the procedure.

Our Contribution. We provide a clean description of the most recent ISD algorithm by Both and May and a corrected analysis. Our main contribution is therefore to provide the correct baseline for further improvements. In this context, we confirm the result of Carrier et al. [7] that the initial analysis of the algorithm is flawed and confirm the corrected runtime exponent (delivered previously in a revision of [7]). Concentrating solely on the minor improvement in the runtime exponent gives the impression that the Both-May algorithm and with it the broader research on extensive nearest neighbor search in the ISD context are of low significance. However, in our analysis we find that the Both-May algorithm significantly lowers the memory consumption of previous ISD algorithms. Considering the importance of the memory-usage observed by multiple recent works, this strongly supports the significance of the algorithm and, more broadly, its research field.

More precisely, we confirm that the Both-May algorithm reduces the worst-case runtime in the full distance decoding setting from $2^{0.0953n}$ down-to $2^{0.0951n}$. On the other hand, we observe that the memory consumption is lowered from $2^{0.092n}$ to $2^{0.076n}$, yielding the largest memory improvement made by any ISD algorithm so far.

A second contribution lies in detailing a possible strategy for future improvements of the algorithm by Both and May. Our strategy relies on a novel combination of the nearest neighbor search and a subsequently applied filtering step. We therefore treat the nearest neighbor search in a non-blackbox fashion to embed the filtering, such that a single application of the adapted algorithm yields the already filtered lists. In this context, we introduce a variation of the nearest neighbor problem, the *fixed-weight* nearest neighbor problem and propose a first algorithm solving the problem.

We note that our current analysis does not yield an improvement in the time or memory complexity of the Both-May algorithm. However, we outline further future directions for improvements. Furthermore, our definition of the fixed-weight nearest neighbor problem might be of independent interest, as it already found application in the recent SievingISD algorithm by Guo, Johansson and Nguyen [16]. This initiated study might lead to future improvements on algorithms for solving the fixed-weight nearest neighbor problem, and in turn lead to an improved decoding procedure via our construction.

All used optimization code is available at https://github.com/Memphisd/Revisiting-NN-ISD.

Outline. In Sect. 2 we cover necessary basics on nearest neighbor search, the syndrome decoding problem and the general technique of ISD. Subsequently, in Sect. 3 we recall the Both-May algorithm and give a corrected analysis. Finally, in Sect. 4 we give a high-level description of our potential improvement strategy, while for the full technical details, we refer to the full version of this work [10].

2   Preliminaries

We denote vectors by bold lower case and matrices by bold upper case letters. All logarithms are base two. We use standard landau notation for complexity statements. We denote by $H(x) := -x\log(x) - (1-x)\log(1-x)$ the binary entropy function. To approximate binomial coefficients, we make use of the well known approximation

$$\binom{n}{k} = \tilde{\Theta}\left(2^{nH(k/n)}\right). \tag{1}$$

For a vector $\mathbf{v}$ we denote by v_i the projection to the i-th coordinate of $\mathbf{v}$. We extend this notation to sets of coordinates, i.e., for a set $I \subseteq \{1, \dots, n\}$, where n is the length of $\mathbf{v}$ we denote by $\mathbf{v}_I$ the projection of $\mathbf{v}$ to the coordinates indexed by I. For a binary vector $\mathbf{x} \in \mathbb{F}_2^n$, we let $\mathrm{wt}(\mathbf{x}) := |\{i \mid x_i = 1\}|$ be its Hamming weight. We refer to the set of vectors of length n and Hamming weight w as $\mathcal{B}(n, w) := \{\mathbf{x} \in \mathbb{F}_2^n \mid \mathrm{wt}(\mathbf{x}) = w\}$.

Nearest Neighbor Search. Most recent ISD techniques rely on subroutines to solve a specific kind of nearest neighbor search problem. Informally, given two lists of binary vectors and a distance ε the problem asks to find all pairs with distance ε between the two lists. In our analysis we use the algorithm by May and Ozerov [20] to solve this problem, which achieves the best known time complexity. More precisely, we use a recent adaptation of the algorithm by Esser, Kübler and Zweydinger [12], which generalizes May-Ozerov's result to arbitrary list sizes and distances. The following lemma (compare to [12, Theorem 1]) states the time complexity of the algorithm.

Lemma 2.1 (May-Ozerov Nearest Neighbor [12,20]). *Let $\varepsilon \in [\![0, \frac{1}{2}]\!]$ and $\lambda \in [\![0, 1]\!]$, $n \in \mathbb{N}$. Given two lists L_1, L_2 of size $|L_i| = 2^{\lambda n}$ containing uniformly at random drawn elements from $\mathbb{F}_2^n$, there is an algorithm that returns all pairs $(\mathbf{x}_1, \mathbf{x}_2), \mathbf{x}_i \in L_i$ with $\mathrm{wt}(\mathbf{x}_1 + \mathbf{x}_2) = \varepsilon n$ in expected time $2^{\vartheta n (1+o(1))}$, where*

$$
\vartheta = \begin{cases} (1-\varepsilon)\left(1 - H\left(\frac{\delta^\star - \frac{\varepsilon}{2}}{1-\varepsilon}\right)\right) & \text{for } \varepsilon \leq \varepsilon^\star \\ 2\lambda + H(\varepsilon) - 1 & \text{for } \varepsilon > \varepsilon^\star , \end{cases}
$$

with $\delta^\star := H^{-1}(1 - \lambda)$ and $\varepsilon^\star := 2\delta^\star (1 - \delta^\star)$ using memory $|L_i|^{(1+o(1))}$.

We encounter a slightly different setting where the vectors contained in the lists are of length $\ell \cdot n$ for some constant $\ell \in [\![0, 1]\!]$ instead of length n. It is easy to see that by normalizing ε and λ to ℓ we can still make use of Lemma 2.1 in this case.

Corollary 2.1. *Let $\varepsilon' \in [\![0, \frac{1}{2}]\!]$ and $\lambda', \ell \in [\![0, 1]\!]$, $n \in \mathbb{N}$. Given two lists L_1, L_2 of size $|L_i| = 2^{\lambda n}$ containing uniformly at random drawn elements from $\mathbb{F}_2^{\ell n}$. Then there is an algorithm that returns all pairs $(\mathbf{x}_1, \mathbf{x}_2), \mathbf{x}_i \in L_i$ with $\mathrm{wt}(\mathbf{x}_1 + \mathbf{x}_2) = \varepsilon' n$ in expected time $2^{\vartheta \cdot \ell n (1+o(1))}$, where ϑ is as in Lemma 2.1 for $\varepsilon := \frac{\varepsilon'}{\ell}$ and $\lambda := \frac{\lambda'}{\ell}$.*

Decoding. A binary linear code $\mathcal{C}$ of length n and dimension k is a k-dimensional subspace of $\mathbb{F}_2^n$. Such a code can be represented via the kernel of a *parity-check matrix* $\mathbf{H} \in \mathbb{F}_2^{(n-k) \times n}$, i.e. $\mathcal{C} = \{\mathbf{c} \in \mathbb{F}_2^n \mid \mathbf{Hc} = \mathbf{0}\}$. The task of recovering a codeword $\mathbf{c} \in \mathcal{C}$ from a given faulty version $\mathbf{c}' = \mathbf{c} + \mathbf{e}$ is known as the *decoding problem*. This problem is polynomial-time equivalent to the *syndrome decoding problem*, which asks to recover the error term $\mathbf{e}$ from the given syndrome $\mathbf{Hc}' = \mathbf{H}(\mathbf{c} + \mathbf{e}) = \mathbf{He}$.

Definition 2.1 (Syndrome Decoding Problem). *Let $\mathcal{C} \subseteq \mathbb{F}_2^n$ be a random linear code of dimension k with constant rate $\frac{k}{n}$ and parity-check matrix $\mathbf{H}$. Given a syndrome $\mathbf{s} \in \mathbb{F}_2^{n-k}$ and an integer $\omega < n$ the syndrome decoding problem asks to find a vector $\mathbf{e} \in \mathbb{F}_2^n$ of Hamming weight $\mathrm{wt}(\mathbf{e}) = \omega$ that satisfies $\mathbf{He} = \mathbf{s}$. We call $\mathbf{e}$ the solution and $(\mathbf{H}, \mathbf{s})$ an instance of the problem.*

Note that ω is usually rather small and that without this restriction on the Hamming weight the problem could easily be solved by Gaussian elimination. The most commonly considered setting is the *full* distance decoding setting, which bounds ω by the minimum distance of the code. The minimum distance d of a code $\mathcal{C}$ is the minimal weight of the sum of two codewords of $\mathcal{C}$, i.e., $d := \min_{c_1, c_2 \in \mathcal{C}} \text{wt}(c_1 + c_2) = \min_{c \in \mathcal{C}} \text{wt}(c)$. Random linear codes are known to asymptotically achieve a minimum distance of $d = H^{-1}(1 - k/n)n$ [15,24]. Now, the *full distance decoding* setting bounds $\omega \leq d$, which implies that for each uniformly random choice of $(\mathbf{H}, \mathbf{s})$ there exists one solution in expectation.

Information Set Decoding (ISD). The best known strategy to solve generic instances of the syndrome decoding problem is ISD. Given an instance $(\mathbf{H}, \mathbf{s}')$ of the syndrome decoding problem, ISD algorithms first apply a random permutation $\mathbf{P}$ to the columns of $\mathbf{H}$ to obtain a permuted instance $(\mathbf{HP}, \mathbf{s}')$ with solution $\mathbf{P}^{-1}\mathbf{e}$. Then $\mathbf{HP}$ is transformed into systematic-form by multiplication with an invertible matrix $\mathbf{Q}$, which yields the identity

$$(\mathbf{QHP})(\mathbf{P}^{-1}\mathbf{e}) = (\mathbf{I}_{n-k} \mid \mathbf{H}_1)(\mathbf{e}_1, \mathbf{e}_2) = \mathbf{e}_1 + \mathbf{H}_1\mathbf{e}_2 = \mathbf{Q}\mathbf{s}' =: \mathbf{s},$$

where $\mathbf{P}^{-1}\mathbf{e} = (\mathbf{e}_1, \mathbf{e}_2)$. The permutation step aims at distributing the weight on $\mathbf{P}^{-1}\mathbf{e}$ such that $\text{wt}(\mathbf{e}_1) = \omega - p$ and $\text{wt}(\mathbf{e}_2) = p$, where p has to be optimized.

In a last step the algorithm then recovers $\mathbf{e}_2$ and $\mathbf{e}_1$ from the identity $\mathbf{H}_1\mathbf{e}_2 + \mathbf{s} = \mathbf{e}_1$. The subroutines to accomplish this last step differ between ISD algorithms, but commonly they rely on enumeration of the weight-p vector $\mathbf{e}_2$ and try to identify those for which $\mathbf{H}_1\mathbf{e}_2 + \mathbf{s}$ is of small weight $\omega - p$. If this does not lead to a solution the weight was not distributed as desired and the algorithm starts over with a new random permutation.

ISD and nearest neighbor. The identity $\mathbf{H}_1\mathbf{e}_2 + \mathbf{s} = \mathbf{e}_1$ defines a nearest neighbor problem. Therefore let $\mathbf{e}_2 = (\mathbf{e}_{21}, \mathbf{e}_{22})$ and rewrite the identity as

$$\mathbf{H}_1(\mathbf{e}_{21}, \mathbf{0}) = \mathbf{H}_1(\mathbf{0}, \mathbf{e}_{22}) + \mathbf{s} + \mathbf{e}_1.$$

Since $\mathbf{e}_1$ is not known, but of small Hamming weight $\omega - p$ we have

$$\mathbf{H}_1(\mathbf{e}_{21}, \mathbf{0}) \approx \mathbf{H}_1(\mathbf{0}, \mathbf{e}_{22}) + \mathbf{s}.$$

We can solve this identity directly by applying Lemma 2.1. Therefore, enumerate all $\mathbf{e}_{2i}$ and store the left (resp. right) side of the above identity in list L_i, and let the target distance be $\varepsilon = \omega - p$.

However, prior to the result of Both and May, ISD algorithms solve the identity mostly by guessing (or enumerating) the bits of $\mathbf{e}_1$ on some projection π of its coordinates. This leads to an exact identity $\pi(\mathbf{H}_1\mathbf{e}_2) = \pi(\mathbf{s} + \mathbf{e}_1)$ where the value of $\pi(\mathbf{s} + \mathbf{e}_1)$ is known. Now the algorithms solve the problem on the projection π after which they check if they fulfill the identity on all coordinates.

Modern ISD algorithms split $\mathbf{e}_2$ in multiple addends and then solve the exact identity in a binary tree fashion, where at the leaves candidates for the summands are enumerated (similar to the two list example above).

3 The Both-May Algorithm

The algorithm by Both and May differs from previous works in how it solves the nearest neighbor identity

$$\mathbf{H}_1\mathbf{e}_2 + \mathbf{s} = \mathbf{e}_1 \qquad (2)$$

In contrast to previous works the algorithm does not enumerate coordinates of $\mathbf{e}_1$ to obtain an exact identity. Instead it solves the nearest neighbor identity directly by using the May-Ozerov nearest neighbor search algorithm.

The algorithm still relies on a search-tree to construct $\mathbf{e}_2$. Therefore it splits $\mathbf{e}_2 = \mathbf{z}_1 + \mathbf{z}_2$ in the sum of two addends. From Eq. (2) it follows that $\mathbf{H}_1\mathbf{z}_1$ and $\mathbf{H}_1\mathbf{z}_2 + \mathbf{s}$ are wt$(\mathbf{e}_1)$ close, since $\mathbf{e}_1$ is of small weight this implies

$$\mathbf{H}\mathbf{z}_1 \approx \mathbf{H}\mathbf{z}_2 + \mathbf{s}. \qquad (3)$$

Now the algorithm makes the bet that both sides of the equation are itself small on some projection π of the coordinates, i.e., that wt$(\pi(\mathbf{H}\mathbf{z}_1)) = \omega_a^{(1)}$ and wt$(\pi(\mathbf{H}\mathbf{z}_2 + \mathbf{s})) = \omega_a^{(1)}$ for some small $\omega_a^{(1)}$. Then it splits $\mathbf{z}_1 = \mathbf{y}_1 + \mathbf{y}_2$ and $\mathbf{z}_2 = \mathbf{y}_3 + \mathbf{y}_4$ again in the sum of two addends. Assuming both sides of Eq. (3) are indeed small on the projection π, we obtain the two nearest neighbor identities

$$\pi(\mathbf{H}\mathbf{y}_1) \approx \pi(\mathbf{H}\mathbf{y}_2) \text{ and } \pi(\mathbf{H}\mathbf{y}_3) \approx \pi(\mathbf{H}\mathbf{y}_4 + \mathbf{s}). \qquad (4)$$

3.1 Depth-2 Variant

For didactic reasons let us start with the algorithm using a search tree in depth two to construct the solution $\mathbf{e}_2$. Therefore, in the base lists L_i, $i = 1, \dots, 4$ all possible values for the $\mathbf{y}_i$ are enumerated. Then L_1, L_2 and L_3, L_4 are combined by solving the respective nearest neighbor identities from Eq. (4). This yields two new lists $L_1^{(1)}$ and $L_1^{(2)}$ containing candidates for $\mathbf{z}_1$ and $\mathbf{z}_2$ respectively. In a final step the lists $L_1^{(1)}$ and $L_1^{(2)}$ are combined by solving the nearest neighbor identity from Eq. (3) to find $\mathbf{e}_2$. This process is illustrated in Fig. 1. A pseudocode description of the algorithm is given by Algorithm 1. In the graphic as well as in the algorithmic description the projection π is chosen to map to the first ℓ_a bits of the given vector.

Finding a Representation of the Solution. Let the permutation induce a weight distribution, such that wt$(\mathbf{e}_2) = p$ and wt$(\pi(\mathbf{e}_1)) = \omega_a$, where π is, as defined in Algorithm 1, the projection to the first ℓ_a coordinates of $\mathbf{e}_1$, while p, ω_a and ℓ_a have to be optimized. Also let $\mathbf{z}_i \in \mathcal{B}(k, p_1)$, $i = 1, 2$, for some p_1 that has to be optimized. Observe that this implies multiple *representations* of $\mathbf{e}_2$, i.e. multiple different pairs $(\mathbf{z}_1, \mathbf{z}_2)$ that sum to $\mathbf{e}_2$. Precisely there are

$$\mathcal{R}_1 = \binom{p}{p/2}\binom{k-p}{p_1 - p/2}$$

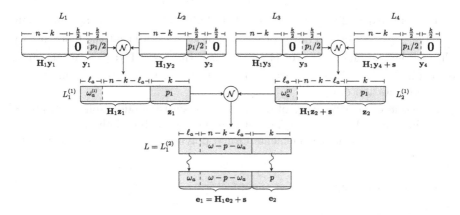

Fig. 1. Both-May algorithm in depth-2. Weight in gray regions differs from weight of uniformly random vectors. Numbers inside gray areas indicate regions of fixed weight. Curly arrows illustrate final check for contained solution, $\mathcal{N}$ indicates nearest neighbor search. (Color figure online)

such representations, where $\mathbf{z}_1, \mathbf{z}_2$ have both weight p_1. Here the first term counts the possibilities to distribute $p/2$ out of the p one-entries of $\mathbf{e}_2$ on $\mathbf{z}_1$, while the remaining $p/2$ ones must be set in $\mathbf{z}_2$. The second factor then counts how the remaining $p_1 - p/2$ one entries in $\mathbf{z}_1$ and $\mathbf{z}_2$ can cancel out. The goal of the algorithm is to enumerate only an $1/\mathcal{R}_1$ fraction of these representations, as any representation leads to $\mathbf{e}_2$. To achieve this, a constraint on the space of representations is enforced via the weight-guess $\omega_a^{(1)}$ made on the projection π of both sides of Eq. (3). The parameter $\omega_a^{(1)}$ has to be optimized as well.

On the base level all possible $\mathbf{y}_i$ are enumerated in list L_i, where we let $\mathbf{y}_1, \mathbf{y}_3 \in \mathcal{B}(k/2, p_1/2) \times 0^{k/2}$ and $\mathbf{y}_2, \mathbf{y}_4 \in 0^{k/2} \times \mathcal{B}(k/2, p_1/2)$, i.e., we perform a meet-in-the-middle split of $\mathbf{z}_1$ and $\mathbf{z}_2$. The lists L_1 and L_2 are then combined by searching those pairs $\mathbf{y}_1, \mathbf{y}_2$ with $\mathrm{wt}(\pi(\mathbf{H}_1(\mathbf{y}_1 + \mathbf{y}_2))) = \omega_a^{(1)}$. The lists L_3 and L_4 are combined analogously by previously adding $\mathbf{s}$.

Let us analyze the probability that any representation of the solution fulfills the weight-guess $\omega_a^{(1)}$ on the projection. More precisely, let the probability that for any representation $(\mathbf{z}_1, \mathbf{z}_2)$ of $\mathbf{e}_2$ we have $\mathrm{wt}(\pi(\mathbf{H}_1\mathbf{z}_1)) = \mathrm{wt}(\pi(\mathbf{H}_1\mathbf{z}_2 + \mathbf{s})) = \omega_a^{(1)}$ be q. Then we have

$$q := \Pr\left[\mathrm{wt}(\pi(\mathbf{H}_1\mathbf{z}_1)) = \mathrm{wt}(\pi(\mathbf{H}_1\mathbf{z}_2 + \mathbf{s})) = \omega_a^{(1)} \mid \mathbf{e}_2 = \mathbf{z}_1 + \mathbf{z}_2, \mathrm{wt}(\pi(\mathbf{e}_1)) = \omega_a\right]$$

$$= \Pr\left[\mathrm{wt}(\mathbf{a}_1) = \mathrm{wt}(\mathbf{a}_2) = \omega_a^{(1)} \mid \mathbf{e}_1' = \mathbf{a}_1 + \mathbf{a}_2, \mathrm{wt}(\mathbf{e}_1') = \omega_a, \mathbf{e}_1' \in \mathbb{F}_2^{\ell_a}\right] \quad (5)$$

$$= \frac{\binom{\omega_a}{\omega_a/2}\binom{\ell_a - \omega_a}{\omega_a^{(1)} - \omega_a/2}}{2^{\ell_a}},$$

since there exist 2^{ℓ_a} pairs $\mathbf{a}_1, \mathbf{a}_2$ that fulfill $\mathbf{e}'_1 = \mathbf{a}_1 + \mathbf{a}_2$, but only $\binom{\omega_a}{\omega_a/2}\binom{\ell_a - \omega_a}{\omega_a^{(1)} - \omega_a/2}$ of them have correct weight $\omega_a^{(1)}$.[1] Note that the first equality follows from the randomness of $\mathbf{H}$ and the fact that $\mathbf{e}_1 = \mathbf{H}_1\mathbf{e}_2 + \mathbf{s}$. Concluding, as long as $q \cdot \mathcal{R}_1 \geq 1$, we expect the two lists $L_1^{(1)}$ and $L_1^{(2)}$ to contain at least one representation of $\mathbf{e}_2$.

Note that our construction of $L_i^{(1)}$ (via a meet-in-the-middle split) only allows to obtain balanced $\mathbf{z}_i$, i.e., elements with weight $p_1/2$ on both halves of their coordinates. However, balanced elements form a polynomial fraction of all elements, since using Eq. (1) we obtain $\frac{\binom{k/2}{p_1/2}^2}{\binom{k}{p_1}} = \tilde{\Theta}(1)$. Therefore we still can construct $\mathcal{R}_1$ representations up to a polynomial factor.

Algorithm 1: BOTH-MAY DEPTH-2

Input : $\mathbf{H} \in \mathbb{F}_2^{(n-k) \times n}, \mathbf{s}' \in \mathbb{F}_2^{n-k}, \omega \in \mathbb{N}$
Output: $\mathbf{e} \in \mathbb{F}_2^n, \mathbf{H}\mathbf{e} = \mathbf{s}'$ with $\mathrm{wt}(\mathbf{e}) = \omega$

1 Choose optimal $p, p_1, \ell_a, \omega_a, \omega_a^{(1)}$ and define

$$\pi \colon \mathbb{F}_2^{n-k} \to \mathbb{F}_2^{\ell_a} \qquad , \pi(x_1, \ldots, x_{n-k}) = \{x_1, \ldots, x_{\ell_a}\}$$
$$\bar{\pi} \colon \mathbb{F}_2^{n-k} \to \mathbb{F}_2^{n-k-\ell_a}, \bar{\pi}(x_1, \ldots, x_{n-k}) = \{x_{\ell_a+1}, \ldots, x_{n-k}\}$$

2 Enumerate

$$L_j = \{\mathbf{y}_j \mid \mathbf{y}_j \in \mathcal{B}(k/2, p_1/2) \times 0^{k/2}\}, \quad j = 1, 3$$
$$L_j = \{\mathbf{y}_j \mid \mathbf{y}_j \in \mathcal{B}(k/2, p_1/2) \times 0^{k/2}\}, \quad j = 2, 4$$

3 **repeat**

4 $\quad$ choose random permutation matrix $\mathbf{P}$

5 $\quad$ $\mathbf{H}' \leftarrow \mathbf{Q}\mathbf{H}\mathbf{P} = (\mathbf{I}_{n-k} \ \mathbf{H}_1), \mathbf{s} \leftarrow \mathbf{Q}\mathbf{s}'$

6 $\quad$ Compute via nearest neighbor

$$L_1^{(1)} = \{\mathbf{z}_1 \mid \mathbf{z}_1 = \mathbf{y}_1 + \mathbf{y}_2, \ \mathbf{y}_i \in L_i, \ \mathrm{wt}(\pi(H_1\mathbf{z}_1)) = \omega_a^{(1)}\}$$
$$L_2^{(1)} = \{\mathbf{z}_2 \mid \mathbf{z}_2 = \mathbf{y}_3 + \mathbf{y}_4, \ \mathbf{y}_i \in L_i, \ \mathrm{wt}(\pi(H_1\mathbf{z}_2 + \mathbf{s})) = \omega_a^{(1)}\}$$
$$L = \{\mathbf{e}_2 \mid \mathbf{e}_2 = \mathbf{z}_1 + \mathbf{z}_2, \ \mathbf{z}_i \in L_i^{(1)}, \ \mathrm{wt}(\bar{\pi}(H_1\mathbf{e}_2 + \mathbf{s})) = \omega - \omega_a - p\}$$

7 $\quad$ **if** $\exists \mathbf{e}_2 \in L \colon \mathrm{wt}(\mathbf{e}_2) = p \wedge \mathrm{wt}(\mathbf{H}_1\mathbf{e}_2 + \mathbf{s}) = \omega - p$ **then**

8 $\quad\quad$ $\lfloor$ **return** $\mathbf{P}(\mathbf{H}_1\mathbf{e}_2 + \mathbf{s}, \mathbf{e}_2)$

---

[1] This term corresponds to the number of representations of one weight-ω_a vector of length ℓ_a as sum of two weight-$\omega_a^{(1)}$ vectors.

Complexity of the Algorithm. The probability for the permutation distributing the weight as desired is

$$P = \frac{\binom{\ell_a}{\omega_a}\binom{k}{p}\binom{n'}{\omega'}}{\binom{n}{\omega}},$$

where $n' := n - k - \ell_a$ and $\omega' := \omega - p - \omega_a$. Hence, after P^{-1} iterations we expect to have chosen one permutation that distributes the weight as desired.

Next we investigate the time per iteration of the loop of Algorithm 1, which is dominated by the nearest neighbor search. Therefore, let us first calculate the (expected) list sizes. The base lists L_i are of size

$$\mathcal{L}_0 = \binom{k/2}{p_1/2},$$

while we expect the level-1 lists to be of size

$$\mathcal{L}_1 := \mathbb{E}[L_i^{(1)}] = (\mathcal{L}_1)^2 \cdot \frac{\binom{\ell_a}{\omega_a^{(1)}}}{2^{\ell_a}} = \tilde{\mathcal{O}}\left(\frac{\binom{k}{p_1}\binom{\ell_a}{\omega_a^{(1)}}}{2^{\ell_a}}\right),$$

since by the randomness of $\mathbf{H}$ the probability that $\mathbf{H}_1\mathbf{x}$ for any $\mathbf{x} \neq \mathbf{0}$ has weight $\omega_a^{(1)}$ on a projection to ℓ_a coordinates is $\frac{\binom{\ell_a}{\omega_a^{(1)}}}{2^{\ell_a}}$.

For the construction of the lists $L_i^{(1)}$ and L we use the May-Ozerov nearest neighbor search algorithm. The complexity of this algorithm to find all ε close pairs on lists of size $\mathcal{L}$ containing length-ℓ vectors is given by Corollary 2.1 and we denote it as $\mathcal{N}_{\mathcal{L},\ell,\varepsilon}$. Therefore the overall time complexity of the algorithm is

$$T = P^{-1} \cdot \max(\mathcal{N}_{\mathcal{L}_1,\ell_a,\omega_a^{(1)}}, \mathcal{N}_{\mathcal{L}_2,n',\omega'}),$$

while the memory complexity is $\max(\mathcal{L}_1, \mathcal{L}_2)$. Note that the final list does not affect the memory complexity, as its elements can be checked on-the-fly for being a solution. Furthermore the construction of this list is at least as expensive as its size, which is why it does not appear in the time complexity.

Complexity exponent. In our optimizations we approximate the binomial coefficients in the analysis using Eq. 1. Then for each optimization parameter o_i we let $o_i = \hat{o}_i \cdot n$, where $\hat{o}_i \in [\![0, 1]\!]$. Furthermore, we similarly let $k = \hat{k}n$, where $\hat{k} = \frac{k}{n}$ is the rate of the code. We then minimize the running time over the choices of the $\hat{o}_i$ under the correctness constraint $q\mathcal{R}_1 \geq 1$. Finally we maximize over all possible choices for the rate $\hat{k}$ with corresponding weight $\omega = \hat{\omega}n = H^{-1}(1 - \hat{k})n$ (full distance setting). This results in a complexity of the form 2^{cn} with constant c.

To actually find the values of the $\hat{o}_i, \hat{k}$ and eventually c we use a numerical optimization tool provided by the *python* library *scipy*. The way we access this library is inspired by a code of Bonnetain et al. [3].[2] In general it is possible that such optimizers do not output a global minimum but instead run into some local minimum. However, to increase the confidence in the found optimum we ran the optimization thousands of times with random starting points, until no further improvement could be made.

This process leads to a running time of $T = 2^{cn} = 2^{0.0982n}$ with memory complexity $M = 2^{0.716n}$ at worst-case rate $\hat{k} = 0.422$ and, hence, $\omega = H^{-1}(1 - 0.422)n \approx 0.1373n$.

We stress that these results essentially match those given in the original work of Both and May [5]. The reason is that in contrast to higher search tree depth variants the depth-2 variant does not make use of a filtering step, which introduced the flaw in the analysis of [5] as we describe in the following section.

3.2 Depth-4 Variant

Both and May obtain their best result for a tree in depth four. Here the splitting of $\mathbf{e}_2$ is continued recursively, i.e. $\mathbf{y}_i = \mathbf{x}_{2i-1} + \mathbf{x}_{2i}$, $i = 1, 2, 3, 4$ and $\mathbf{x}_j = \mathbf{w}_{2j-1} + \mathbf{w}_{2j}$, $j = 1, \ldots, 8$. The algorithm then recursively makes a bet on the smallness of $\mathbf{Hy}_i$ (respectively $\mathbf{Hy}_4 + \mathbf{s}$) and $\mathbf{Hx}_j$ (respectively $\mathbf{Hx}_8 + \mathbf{s}$) on some projections to obtain nearest neighbor identities for each level. Also it enforces a specific weight on the vectors $\mathbf{y}_i$ and $\mathbf{z}_i$ itself. Eventually, all possible $\mathbf{w}_j$ are enumerated in the base lists L_j, $j = 1, \ldots, 16$.

Similar to before the $\mathbf{w}_i$ form a meet-in-the-middle split of the $\mathbf{x}_j$, i.e., $\mathbf{w}_{2i-1} \in \mathcal{B}(k/2, p_1/2) \times 0^{k/2}$ and $\mathbf{w}_{2i} \in 0^{k/2} \times \mathcal{B}(k/2, p_1/2)$, where p_1 is subject to optimization.

Additionally, a filtering step is introduced after the construction of the level-2 and level-3 lists. This filtering step discards all vectors which do not sum to predefined weights or which do not sum to predefined weights on projections that already have fixed weights, i.e., those already used for nearest neighbor search on previous levels (compare to Fig. 2).

The pseudocode of the algorithm is given by Algorithm 2 and an illustration in Fig. 2. For simplification we choose the projections on each level to be the next ℓ_a, ℓ_b and ℓ_c coordinates respectively. More precisely, we define

$$
\begin{aligned}
&\pi_a \colon \mathbb{F}_2^{n-k} \to \mathbb{F}_2^{\ell_a}, \ \pi_a(x_1, \ldots, x_{n-k}) = \{x_1, \ldots, x_{\ell_a}\} \\
&\pi_b \colon \mathbb{F}_2^{n-k} \to \mathbb{F}_2^{\ell_b}, \ \pi_b(x_1, \ldots, x_{n-k}) = (x_{\ell_a+1}, \ldots, x_{\ell_a+\ell_b}) \\
&\pi_c \colon \mathbb{F}_2^{n-k} \to \mathbb{F}_2^{\ell_c}, \ \pi_c(x_1, \ldots, x_{n-k}) = \{x_{\ell_a+\ell_b+1}, \ldots, x_{\ell_a+\ell_b+\ell_c}\}
\end{aligned}
\tag{6}
$$

Analogously to the depth-2 case, we let

$$
\bar{\pi} \colon \mathbb{F}_2^{n-k} \to \mathbb{F}_2^{n-k-\ell'}, \ \ell' := \ell_a + \ell_b + \ell_c \text{ with } \bar{\pi}(\mathbf{x}) = (x_{\ell'+1}, \ldots, x_{n-k})
\tag{7}
$$

be the projection to the remaining coordinates.

---

[2] This code is accessible at https://github.com/xbonnetain/optimization-subset-sum.

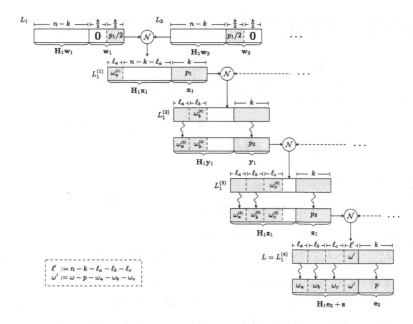

Fig. 2. Leftmost path of depth-4 algorithm from leaves (base lists) to root (final list). Gray areas indicate regions where weight differs from weight of uniformly random vectors. Numbers inside gray areas indicate regions of fixed weight. Curly arrows illustrate filtering process, $\mathcal{N}$ indicates nearest neighbor search. (Color figure online)

Remark 3.1 (Block notation). We use letters to refer to different projections (or blocks) of coordinates while we use numbers to indicate different levels of the tree. For instance, $\omega_b^{(3)}$ is the predefined weight of block b on level 3.

Finding a Representation of the Solution. Let us assume the permutation $\mathbf{P}$ distributes the weight on $\mathbf{P}^{-1}\mathbf{e} = (\mathbf{e}_1, \mathbf{e}_2)$ such that

$$\mathrm{wt}(\mathbf{e}_2) = p \text{ and } \mathrm{wt}(\pi_\delta(\mathbf{e}_1)) = \omega_\delta \text{ for } \delta \in \{a, b, c\},$$

which implies $\mathrm{wt}(\bar{\pi}(\mathbf{e}_1)) = \omega - \omega_a - \omega_b - \omega_c - p$.

The algorithm constructs on each level $i = 1, 2, 3$ vectors of weight p_i that should sum to weight-p_{i+1} vectors, where $p_4 := p$. Note that each such weight-p_{i+1} vector has $\mathcal{R}_i$ representations as sum of weight-p_i vectors, where

$$\mathcal{R}_i = \binom{p_{i+1}}{p_{i+1}/2}\binom{k - p_{i+1}}{p_i - p_{i+1}/2}.$$

Algorithm 2: BOTH-MAY DEPTH-4

Input : $\mathbf{H} \in \mathbb{F}_2^{(n-k) \times n}, \mathbf{s}' \in \mathbb{F}_2^{n-k}, \omega \in \mathbb{N}$

Output: $\mathbf{e} \in \mathbb{F}_2^n, \mathbf{He} = \mathbf{s}'$ with $\text{wt}(e) = \omega$

1 Choose optimal $p, p_1, p_2, p_3, \ell_a, \ell_b, \ell_c, \omega_a, \omega_b, \omega_c, \omega_a^{(1)}, \omega_a^{(2)}, \omega_a^{(3)}, \omega_b^{(2)}, \omega_b^{(3)}, \omega_c^{(3)}$

2 Let $\pi_a, \pi_b, \pi_c, \bar{\pi}$ be defined as in Equations (6) and (7)

3 Enumerate

$$L_j = \{\mathbf{w}_j \mid \mathbf{w}_j \in \mathcal{B}(k/2, p_1/2) \times 0^{k/2}\}, \quad j = 1, 3, \ldots, 15$$

$$L_j = \{\mathbf{w}_j \mid \mathbf{w}_j \in \mathcal{B}(k/2, p_1/2) \times 0^{k/2}\}, \quad j = 2, 4, \ldots, 16$$

4 **repeat**

5 | choose random permutation matrix $\mathbf{P}$

6 | $\mathbf{H}' \leftarrow \mathbf{QHP} = (\mathbf{I}_{n-k} \ \mathbf{H}_1), \mathbf{s} \leftarrow \mathbf{Qs}'$ and define $\mathbf{s}_{j,i} := \begin{cases} \mathbf{s} & , i = j \\ 0^{n-k} & , \text{else} \end{cases}$

7 | Compute level-1 lists via nearest neighbor for $i = 1, \ldots, 8$

$$L_i^{(1)} = \{ \quad \mathbf{x}_i \quad \mid \mathbf{x}_i = \mathbf{w}_{2i-1} + \mathbf{w}_{2i}, \ \mathbf{w}_j \in L_j, \ \text{wt}(\pi_a(H_1\mathbf{x}_i + \mathbf{s}_{8,i})) = \omega_a^{(1)}\}$$

8 | Compute via nearest neighbor then filter level-2 lists for $i = 1, \ldots, 4$

$$L_i^{(2)} = \{ \quad \mathbf{y}_i \quad \mid \mathbf{y}_i = \mathbf{x}_{2i-1} + \mathbf{x}_{2i}, \ \mathbf{x}_j \in L_j^{(1)}, \ \text{wt}(\pi_b(H_1\mathbf{y}_i + \mathbf{s}_{4,i})) = \omega_b^{(2)}\}$$

$$L_i^{(2)} \leftarrow \{\mathbf{y} \in L_i^{(2)} \mid \text{wt}(\pi_a(\mathbf{H}_1\mathbf{y} + \mathbf{s}_{4,i})) = \omega_a^{(2)} \wedge \text{wt}(\mathbf{y}) = p_2\}$$

9 | Compute via nearest neighbor then filter level-3 lists for $i = 1, 2$

$$L_i^{(3)} = \{ \quad \mathbf{z}_i \quad \mid \mathbf{z}_i = \mathbf{y}_{2i-1} + \mathbf{y}_{2i}, \ \mathbf{y}_j \in L_j^{(2)}, \ \text{wt}(\pi_c(H_1\mathbf{z}_i + \mathbf{s}_{2,i})) = \omega_c^{(3)}\}$$

$$L_i^{(3)} \leftarrow \{\mathbf{z} \in L_i^{(3)} \mid \text{wt}(\pi_a(\mathbf{v}_i)) = \omega_a^{(3)} \wedge \text{wt}(\pi_b(\mathbf{v}_i)) = \omega_b^{(3)} \wedge \text{wt}(\mathbf{z}) = p_3\}$$

$$\text{, with } \mathbf{v}_i := \mathbf{H}_1\mathbf{z} + \mathbf{s}_{2,i}$$

10 | Compute final (level-4) list via nearest neighbor, $\omega' := \omega - \omega_a - \omega_b - \omega_c - p$

$$L = \{ \quad \mathbf{e}_2 \quad \mid \mathbf{e}_2 = \mathbf{z}_{2i-1} + \mathbf{z}_{2i}, \ \mathbf{z}_j \in L_j^{(3)}, \ \text{wt}(\bar{\pi}(\mathbf{H}_1\mathbf{e}_2 + \mathbf{s}')) = \omega'\}$$

11 | **if** $\exists \mathbf{e}_2 \in L \colon \text{wt}(\mathbf{e}_2) = p \wedge \text{wt}(\mathbf{H}_1\mathbf{e}_2 + \mathbf{s}') = \omega - p$ **then**

12 | | **return** $\mathbf{P}(\mathbf{H}_1\mathbf{e}_2 + \mathbf{s}', \mathbf{e}_2)$

Therefore, we intend again to enumerate an $1/\mathcal{R}_i$-fraction of all possible representations to ensure that there is one representation on expectation of each weight-p_{i+1} vector contained on level i. Let us analyze the constraint imposed on each level introduced by restricting to a specific weight on the projections π_a, π_b and π_c. We have already seen in Sect. 3.1 that the probability that any representation of a level-2 element survives the level-1 constraint is (see Eq. (5))

$$q_1 = \frac{\binom{\omega_a^{(2)}}{\omega_a^{(2)}/2}\binom{\ell_a - \omega_a^{(2)}}{\omega_a^{(1)} - \omega_a^{(2)}/2}}{2^{\ell_a}}.$$

By the same reasoning if we now on level-2 impose weight restrictions on both projections π_a and π_b, we obtain

$$q_2 := \prod_{\delta \in \{a,b\}} \Pr \left[\mathrm{wt}(\pi_\delta(\mathbf{Hy}_1)) = \mathrm{wt}(\pi_\delta(\mathbf{Hy}_2)) = \omega_\delta^{(2)} \mid \mathrm{wt}(\pi_\delta(\mathbf{H}(\mathbf{y}_1 + \mathbf{y}_2))) = \omega_\delta^{(3)} \right]$$

$$= \prod_{\delta \in \{a,b\}} \Pr_{\mathbf{a}_i \in \mathbb{F}_2^{\ell_\delta}} \left[\mathrm{wt}(\pi_\delta(\mathbf{a}_1)) = \mathrm{wt}(\pi_\delta(\mathbf{a}_2)) = \omega_\delta^{(2)} \mid \mathrm{wt}(\pi_\delta(\mathbf{a}_1 + \mathbf{a}_2)) = \omega_\delta^{(3)} \right]$$

$$= \frac{\binom{\omega_a^{(3)}}{\omega_a^{(3)}/2} \binom{\ell_a - \omega_a^{(3)}}{\omega_a^{(2)} - \omega_a^{(3)}/2}}{2^{\ell_a}} \cdot \frac{\binom{\omega_b^{(3)}}{\omega_b^{(3)}/2} \binom{\ell_b - \omega_b^{(3)}}{\omega_b^{(2)} - \omega_b^{(3)}/2}}{2^{\ell_b}}.$$

Eventually for the last level we obtain analogously

$$q_3 := \prod_{\delta \in \{a,b,c\}} \Pr \left[\mathrm{wt}(\pi_\delta(\mathbf{Hz}_1)) = \mathrm{wt}(\pi_\delta(\mathbf{Hz}_2)) = \omega_\delta^{(3)} \mid \mathrm{wt}(\pi_\delta(\mathbf{H}(\mathbf{z}_1 + \mathbf{z}_2))) = \omega_\delta \right]$$

$$= \prod_{\delta \in \{a,b,c\}} \frac{\binom{\omega_\delta}{\omega_\delta/2} \binom{\ell_\delta - \omega_\delta}{\omega_\delta^{(3)} - \omega_\delta/2}}{2^{\ell_\delta}}.$$

Now as long as we have $q_i \cdot \mathcal{R}_i \geq 1$ we ensure that in expectation on each level i at least one representation of each possible level-$(i+1)$ element, i.e., of each $\mathbf{x} \in \mathbb{F}_2^k$ with $\mathrm{wt}(\mathbf{x}) = p_{i+1}$ is present. This implies in turn that on level 3 there is a representation of the searched weight-p vector $\mathbf{e}_2$. Since we conditioned on $\mathrm{wt}(\bar{\pi}(\mathbf{e}_1)) = \omega - p - \omega_a - \omega_b - \omega_c$ this representation is found by the level-4 list construction.

Note that to avoid duplicates in the lists we will also optimize parameters according to the constraint $q_i \cdot \mathcal{R}_i \leq 1$, which implies $q_i \cdot \mathcal{R}_i = 1$.

Complexity of the Algorithm. The probability for the permutation distributing the weight as desired is

$$P = \frac{\binom{\ell_a}{\omega_a} \binom{\ell_b}{\omega_b} \binom{\ell_c}{\omega_c} \binom{\ell'}{\omega'} \binom{k}{p}}{\binom{n}{\omega}},$$

where $\ell' := n - k - \ell_a - \ell_b - \ell_c$ and $\omega' := \omega - p - \omega_a - \omega_b - \omega_c$. Therefore after P^{-1} iterations we expect one to distribute the weight as desired.

Now let us analyze the cost to construct the tree. First, we argue about the expected list size on each level after filtering, which is exactly where the analysis of [5] goes wrong. The base lists are analogously to the depth-2 variant of size

$$\mathcal{L}_0 = \binom{k/2}{p_1/2}.$$

Now, we have already shown that for suitable parameters, satisfying $q_i \mathcal{R}_i = 1$, on level $i = 1, 2, 3$ there exists exactly one representation of each possible level-$(i+1)$ element, i.e., of each $\mathbf{x} \in \mathbb{F}_2^k$ with $\mathrm{wt}(\mathbf{x}) = p_{i+1}$. Therefore the expected list size on level-i after filtering is

$$\mathcal{L}_i = \binom{k}{p_i} \cdot \rho_i,$$

where ρ_i is the probability that a vector $\mathbf{x} \in \mathbb{F}_2^k$ fulfills the level-i restriction. Since level i imposes a weight restriction on a total of i blocks, we have

$$\rho_1 = \frac{\binom{\ell_a}{\omega_a^{(1)}}}{2^{\ell_a}}, \quad \rho_2 = \frac{\binom{\ell_a}{\omega_a^{(2)}}\binom{\ell_b}{\omega_b^{(2)}}}{2^{\ell_a+\ell_b}} \quad \text{and} \quad \rho_3 = \frac{\binom{\ell_a}{\omega_a^{(3)}}\binom{\ell_b}{\omega_b^{(3)}}\binom{\ell_c}{\omega_c^{(3)}}}{2^{\ell_a+\ell_b+\ell_c}}.$$

In Appendix A we outline the difference to the original analysis of [5].

The time complexity per iteration of the loop is again given by the time it takes to construct all lists. The level-i lists, $i = 1, 2, 3$ are constructed via a nearest neighbor search on lists of size $\mathcal{L}_{i-1}$ including vectors of length ℓ_δ with target weight $\omega_\delta^{(i)}$, $\delta \in \{a, b, c\}$. The final list is then constructed via nearest neighbor search on the remaining ℓ' coordinates for target weight ω'. Therefore the cost for each level i is T_i, where

$$T_1 = \mathcal{N}_{\mathcal{L}_0, \ell_a, \omega_a^{(1)}}, \quad T_2 = \mathcal{N}_{\mathcal{L}_1, \ell_b, \omega_b^{(2)}}, \quad T_3 = \mathcal{N}_{\mathcal{L}_2, \ell_c, \omega_c^{(3)}} \quad \text{and} \quad T_4 = \mathcal{N}_{\mathcal{L}_3, \ell', \omega'},$$

Eventually the total time complexity of Algorithm 2 is given as the number of iterations times the cost for one iteration, giving

$$T = P^{-1} \max_i(T_i).$$

Numerical Optimization of Algorithm 2. We follow the same optimization methodology as for the depth-2 case, under correctness constraints $q_i \mathcal{R}_i = 1$, to obtain the asymptotic running time and memory exponents. We find a worst case rate for the algorithm of $\hat{k} = 0.42$ with $\hat{\omega} = H^{-1}(1 - \hat{k}) \approx 0.1384$, leading to a time and memory complexity of

$$T = 2^{0.0951n} \quad \text{and} \quad M = 2^{0.076n},$$

for optimal parameters[3]

$$\hat{p} = 0.05180, \quad \hat{p}_3 = 0.04719, \quad \hat{p}_2 = 0.03371, \quad \hat{p}_1 = 0.01783,$$
$$\hat{\ell}_a = 0.05280, \quad \hat{\ell}_b = 0.10178, \quad \hat{\ell}_c = 0.12367,$$
$$\hat{\omega}_a = 0.00651, \quad \hat{\omega}_a^{(3)} = 0.00593, \quad \hat{\omega}_a^{(2)} = 0.00428, \quad \hat{\omega}_a^{(1)} = 0.05,$$
$$\hat{\omega}_b = 0.01220, \quad \hat{\omega}_b^{(3)} = 0.01091, \quad \hat{\omega}_b^{(2)} = 0.09414,$$
$$\hat{\omega}_c = 0.01504, \quad \hat{\omega}_c^{(3)} = 0.01354.$$

While this running time is far greater than the initially claimed $2^{0.0885n}$ [5], it still slightly improves on the previously best running time of $2^{0.0953n}$ reported in [4]. Further, the memory complexity is drastically improved by a factor of $2^{0.0161n}$ from previously $2^{0.0915n}$ to $2^{0.0754n}$.

In Fig. 3 we compare the time and memory exponents of the latest three ISD improvements, which are in chronological order(old to new): May-Ozerov [20], BJMM-MO [4], Both-May [5] (Sect. 3.2).

---

[3] Due to rounding to a precision of 10^{-5} there might be a certain deviation in satisfying the correctness constraints. For the exact numbers we refer to our optimization scripts.

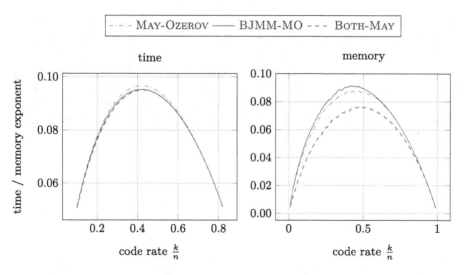

Fig. 3. Comparison between the time (left) and memory (right) exponent of the Both-May, May-Ozerov and BJMM-MO algorithm in the full distance setting.

4   A Strategy for Future Improvements

In the following we outline a possible strategy for further improvements of the Both-May algorithm on a high level. For an in-depth technical description the reader is referred to the full version of this article [10].

Note that the Both-May algorithm works on each level in two steps. First it combines two lists of the previous level to obtain vectors which fulfill a weight restriction on a subset of the coordinates. Then in a second step it filters the vectors for the weight restriction on the remaining coordinates. We propose to improve this process by embedding the filter process into the nearest neighbor search algorithm, to directly obtain vectors that satisfy the weight restriction on all or at least more coordinates.

Therefore we adapt the May-Ozerov nearest neighbor algorithm to also perform the filtering step and then use this adaptation within the Both-May algorithm. This adaptation requires to solve a specific variant of a nearest neighbor problem, which we call *fixed-weight nearest neighbor problem* as a subroutine. In the full version of this article we then develop a first algorithm to solve this variant and upper bound its complexity to finally obtain a complexity estimate for the whole decoding procedure. While we obtain no direct improvement of the asymptotic exponent, we outline several future directions to further improve the approach.

4.1   Combining Nearest Neighbor Search and Filtering

Let us first briefly recall how the May-Ozerov nearest neighbor search algorithm finds all ε-close pairs between two same-sized input lists L_1, L_2 containing uniformly random vectors from $\mathbb{F}_2^m$ and how its complexity is composed. For an in-depth explanation and analysis the reader is referred to [6,12,20]. First, the algorithm computes an exponential number of list pairs L_1', L_2' from the initial lists. For optimal parameter choices it is guaranteed that L_1', L_2' each have only polynomial size, while simultaneously any distance-ε pair between L_1 and L_2 is still contained in at least one of the constructed pairs L_1', L_2'. In a final step the algorithm then finds the ε-close pairs by computing $L_1' \times L_2'$ for every list pair L_1', L_2' naively.

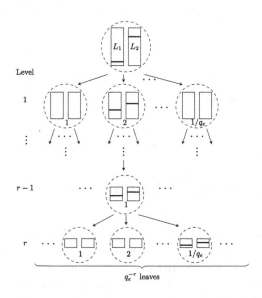

Fig. 4. Illustration of the May-Ozerov nearest neighbor search algorithm. Arrows indicate the application of a locality sensitive filter. Each node branches q_ε^{-1} times. Bold stripes in lists indicate pair of distance ε progressing through all r applied filters.

The list pairs are computed in a tree-like fashion, where the input pair L_1, L_2 forms the root of the tree (compare to Fig. 4). This tree is constructed iteratively, level by level. In every step of the algorithm each leaf of the tree is branched $1/q_\varepsilon$ times. A child-node is computed by traversing both lists of the parent node — individually, no pairs between lists are considered — and applying a locality-sensitive filter to each element. This filter discards elements that do not match the filter criterion and, hence, reduces the lists' sizes. Furthermore, it has the property, that an arbitrary element passes the filter with probability q_f, while for an ε-close pair $(\mathbf{x}, \mathbf{y})$ between the lists, $\mathbf{x}$ and $\mathbf{y}$ pass the filter at the same time with probability $q_\varepsilon > q_f^2$. Therefore close pairs are more likely to pass the same filter than non-close pairs. The branching factor of q_ε^{-1} ensures that if there is an element of distance ε contained in the current node, it progresses to the next level through at least one of the filters. This procedure is repeated r times to construct a tree of depth r containing q_ε^{-r} leaves. It is important to note that the algorithm up to the leaf-level only operates on each list individually, i.e., no pairs between the lists are examined. Therefore, lists L'_1, L'_2 contained in any leaf are subsets of the initial lists L_1, L_2. Once all leaf nodes have been constructed, the algorithm proceeds by computing the Cartesian product $L'_1 \times L'_2$ for all pairs of lists contained in any leaf.

Embedding the Filtering. In Algorithm 2 the May-Ozerov algorithm operates only on a projection π to m out of n coordinates, e.g., on projection $\pi := \pi_b$ to construct the level-2 lists. However, for some of remaining coordinates there are also weight restrictions, e.g. on projection π_a on level two, which are imposed via the filtering step. We now exchange the naive search for ε-close pairs on projection π at the leaf-level of the May-Ozerov algorithm by an algorithm that finds vectors that match the weight restriction on the remaining coordinates. Finally, we then keep only those pairs attaining distance ε on the projection π.

Note that vectors that are filtered for a certain weight on a given projection are guaranteed to have fixed weight on this same projection on the previous level. For example level-2 lists are filtered on projection π_a, which implies that elements in level-1 lists have already fixed weight on projection π_a, namely weight $\omega_a^{(1)}$.

Therefore, given any pair of leaf lists in the May-Ozerov algorithm finding elements matching the additional weight restriction on one projection can be seen as nearest neighbor problem, where the input vectors have fixed weight. More formally, we give the following definition.

Definition 4.1 (Fixed Weight Nearest Neighbor Problem). *Let ℓ, ω_1, ω_2 be integers with $\omega_1, \omega_2 \leq \ell$. Given two lists L_1, L_2 of same size containing uniformly at random drawn elements from $\mathcal{B}(\ell, \omega_1)$ the* fixed weight nearest neighbor *problem asks to find all pairs $(\mathbf{x}_1, \mathbf{x}_2), \mathbf{x}_i \in L_i$ with $\mathrm{wt}(\mathbf{x}_1 + \mathbf{x}_2) = \omega_2$*

In the full version of this article we describe an adaptation an LSH algorithm by Indyk and Motwani [17] to solve this problem. We then incorporate this algorithm into the May-Ozerov algorithm at the leaf-level, and finally embed this adapted May-Ozerov algorithm into the Both-May algorithm.

4.2 Further Improving the Approach

The current version of the algorithm does not yet yield a gain in the time or memory complexity of the decoding procedure. However, there are several ways to improve the current algorithm that have the potential to lead to an improved decoding routine.

First of all, the current algorithm does not yet eliminate the need for the filtering step completely. That is because the fixed-weight nearest neighbor problem we give in Definition 4.1 only covers the case of vectors of fixed-weight on the full length, corresponding to the filtering step on a single projection. However, the filtering has to enforce the correct weight on the vectors $\mathbf{v} \in \mathbb{F}_2^k$ themselves, and on the corresponding projections $\pi_\delta(\mathbf{Hv}), \delta \in \{a, b, c\}$. Therefore, the algorithm could clearly be improved by constructing the fully filtered lists directly via the adapted nearest neighbor routine. However, this introduces a variant of the fixed-weight nearest neighbor problem with multiple stripes of different given input and output weights. The analysis in that case clearly complicates, and it is not clear if straightforward adaptations of algorithms to that problem variant are efficient.

Another direction for improvements are improved algorithms for the fixed-weight nearest neighbor problem. The algorithm we detail in the full version of this article [10] for solving the problem is an adaptation of an early LSH algorithm by Indyk and Motwani. Improvements from the general nearest neighbor case are likely to translate to the fixed-weight setting. Also there might exist different strategies for the fixed-weight setting, such as the approach recently detailed in [16].

Acknowledgements. We thank the anonymous reviewers of Crypto '23 for pointing out a flaw in the analysis of a previous version of this work.

Furthermore, we are grateful to the whole team of authors around the publication [7] for insightful comments and remarks that led to this improved revision. Especially, we would like to express our sincere gratitude to Charles Meyer-Hilfiger for his proactive approach and thoughtful insights which greatly influenced the refinement of our work.

A   Details on flaw in original Both-May analysis

In [5] Both and May decide to calculate the expected list size on level i based on the probability that a pair of level-$(i-1)$ elements advances to level i. Let us denote this probability by ϕ_i. Then the expected list size on level i is equal to $L_i = (L_{i-1})^2 \cdot \phi_i$. However, instead Both and May take $L_i = \binom{k}{p_i} \cdot \phi_i$. Note that the square of level-$(i-1)$ lists is usually larger than the number of possible elements with weight p_i, as only an exponential small fraction sums to weight-p_i vectors (making the filtering step effective). In turn, the expected list size is underestimated in the original work.

References

1. Becker, A., Joux, A., May, A., Meurer, A.: Decoding random binary linear codes in $2^{n/20}$: how $1 + 1 = 0$ improves information set decoding. In: Pointcheval, D., Johansson, T. (eds.) EUROCRYPT 2012. LNCS, vol. 7237, pp. 520–536. Springer, Heidelberg (2012). https://doi.org/10.1007/978-3-642-29011-4_31
2. Bernstein, D.J., Lange, T., Peters, C.: Smaller decoding exponents: ball-collision decoding. In: Rogaway, P. (ed.) CRYPTO 2011. LNCS, vol. 6841, pp. 743–760. Springer, Heidelberg (2011). https://doi.org/10.1007/978-3-642-22792-9_42
3. Bonnetain, X., Bricout, R., Schrottenloher, A., Shen, Y.: Improved classical and quantum algorithms for subset-sum. In: Moriai, S., Wang, H. (eds.) ASIACRYPT 2020, Part II. LNCS, vol. 12492, pp. 633–666. Springer, Heidelberg (2020). https://doi.org/10.1007/978-3-030-64834-3_22
4. Both, L., May, A.: Optimizing BJMM with nearest neighbors: full decoding in 22/21n and mceliece security. In: WCC Workshop on Coding and Cryptography, p. 214 (2017)

5. Both, L., May, A.: Decoding linear codes with high error rate and its impact for LPN security. In: Lange, T., Steinwandt, R. (eds.) PQCrypto 2018. LNCS, vol. 10786, pp. 25–46. Springer, Cham (2018). https://doi.org/10.1007/978-3-319-79063-3_2

6. Carrier, K.: Recherche de presque-collisions pour le décodage et la reconnaissance de codes correcteurs. Ph.D. thesis, Sorbonne Université (2020)

7. Carrier, K., Debris-Alazard, T., Meyer-Hilfiger, C., Tillich, J.P.: Statistical decoding 2.0: reducing decoding to LPN. In: Agrawal, S., Lin, D. (eds.) ASIACRYPT 2022, Part IV. LNCS, vol. 13794, pp. 477–507. Springer, Heidelberg (2022). https://doi.org/10.1007/978-3-031-22972-5_17

8. Chou, T., et al.: Classic McEliece: conservative code-based cryptography 10 October 2020 (2020)

9. Dumer, I.: On minimum distance decoding of linear codes. In: Proceedings of the 5th Joint Soviet-Swedish International Workshop Information Theory, pp. 50–52 (1991)

10. Esser, A.: Revisiting nearest-neighbor-based information set decoding. Cryptology ePrint Archive, Report 2022/1328 (2022). https://eprint.iacr.org/2022/1328

11. Esser, A., Bellini, E.: Syndrome decoding estimator. In: Public-Key Cryptography - PKC 2022–25th IACR International Conference on Practice and Theory of Public-Key Cryptography. LNCS, vol. 13177, pp. 112–141. Springer, Cham (2022). https://doi.org/10.1007/978-3-030-97121-2_5

12. Esser, A., Kübler, R., Zweydinger, F.: A faster algorithm for finding closest pairs in Hamming metric. In: 41st IARCS Annual Conference on Foundations of Software Technology and Theoretical Computer Science (FSTTCS 2021). Schloss Dagstuhl-Leibniz-Zentrum für Informatik (2021)

13. Esser, A., May, A., Zweydinger, F.: McEliece needs a break - solving McEliece-1284 and quasi-cyclic-2918 with modern ISD. In: Dunkelman, O., Dziembowski, S. (eds.) EUROCRYPT 2022, Part III. LNCS, vol. 13277, pp. 433–457. Springer, Heidelberg (2022). https://doi.org/10.1007/978-3-031-07082-2_16

14. Esser, A., Zweydinger, F.: New time-memory trade-offs for subset sum-improving ISD in theory and practice. Cryptology ePrint Archive (2022)

15. Gilbert, E.N.: A comparison of signalling alphabets. Bell Syst. Tech. J. **31**(3), 504–522 (1952)

16. Guo, Q., Johansson, T., Nguyen, V.: A new sieving-style information-set decoding algorithm. Cryptology ePrint Archive (2023)

17. Indyk, P., Motwani, R.: Approximate nearest neighbors: towards removing the curse of dimensionality. In: 30th ACM STOC, pp. 604–613. ACM Press (1998). https://doi.org/10.1145/276698.276876

18. Leon, J.S.: A probabilistic algorithm for computing minimum weights of large error-correcting codes. IEEE Trans. Inf. Theory **34**(5), 1354–1359 (1988)

19. May, A., Meurer, A., Thomae, E.: Decoding random linear codes in $\tilde{\mathcal{O}}(2^{0.054n})$. In: Lee, D.H., Wang, X. (eds.) ASIACRYPT 2011. LNCS, vol. 7073, pp. 107–124. Springer, Heidelberg (2011). https://doi.org/10.1007/978-3-642-25385-0_6

20. May, A., Ozerov, I.: On computing nearest neighbors with applications to decoding of binary linear codes. In: Oswald, E., Fischlin, M. (eds.) EUROCRYPT 2015, Part I. LNCS, vol. 9056, pp. 203–228. Springer, Heidelberg (2015). https://doi.org/10.1007/978-3-662-46800-5_9

21. Prange, E.: The use of information sets in decoding cyclic codes. IRE Trans. Inf. Theory **8**(5), 5–9 (1962)

22. Stern, J.: A method for finding codewords of small weight. In: Cohen, G., Wolfmann, J. (eds.) Coding Theory 1988. LNCS, vol. 388, pp. 106–113. Springer, Heidelberg (1989). https://doi.org/10.1007/BFb0019850

23. Canto Torres, R., Sendrier, N.: Analysis of information set decoding for a sub-linear error weight. In: Takagi, T. (ed.) PQCrypto 2016. LNCS, vol. 9606, pp. 144–161. Springer, Cham (2016). https://doi.org/10.1007/978-3-319-29360-8_10

24. Varshamov, R.R.: Estimate of the number of signals in error correcting codes. Docklady Akad. Nauk SSSR **117**, 739–741 (1957)

Symmetric Cryptography:
Constructions and Attacks

Feistel Ciphers Based on a Single Primitive

Kento Tsuji and Tetsu Iwata[(✉)]

Nagoya University, Nagoya, Japan
tsuji.kento.y1@s.mail.nagoya-u.ac.jp, tetsu.iwata@nagoya-u.jp

Abstract. We consider Feistel ciphers instantiated with tweakable block ciphers (TBCs) and ideal ciphers (ICs). The indistinguishability security of the TBC-based Feistel cipher is known, and the indifferentiability security of the IC-based Feistel cipher is also known, where independently keyed TBCs and independent ICs are assumed. In this paper, we analyze the security of a single-keyed TBC-based Feistel cipher and a single IC-based Feistel cipher. We characterize the security depending on the number of rounds. More precisely, we cover the case of contracting Feistel ciphers that have $d \geq 2$ lines, and the results on Feistel ciphers are obtained as a special case by setting $d = 2$. Our indistinguishability security analysis shows that it is provably secure with $d+1$ rounds. Our indifferentiability result shows that, regardless of the number of rounds, it cannot be secure. Our attacks are a type of a slide attack, and we consider a structure that uses a round constant, which is a well-known counter measure against slide attacks. We show an indifferentiability attack for the case $d = 2$ and 3 rounds.

Keywords: Feistel cipher · Tweakable block cipher · Ideal cipher · Provable security

1 Introduction

Background. A Feistel structure is one of the widely used structures of a block cipher, and its security proof was given by Luby and Rackoff [LR88]. It is shown that the 3-round Feistel structure instantiated with 3 independent pseudorandom functions (PRFs), which we call the Feistel cipher, is a pseudorandom permutation (PRP), a block cipher that is indistinguishable from a random permutation against adversaries in a chosen plaintext attack (CPA) setting. Similarly, the 4-round Feistel cipher is a strong PRP (SPRP), where the adversary is in a chosen ciphertext attack (CCA) setting.

A question of whether one can securely reduce the number of independent PRFs has been studied, as reducing the number of PRFs implies the reduction of the key length, and hence it reduces the cost for maintaining, exchanging, and updating the secret key. Let $\Phi[F_1, F_2, \ldots, F_r]$ be the r-round Feistel cipher, where the PRF F_i is used in the i-th round. The structure that simply replaces all the PRFs with a single-keyed PRF F, i.e., $\Phi[F, F, \ldots, F]$, is easily distinguishable from a random permutation regardless of the number of rounds [ZMI89]. Pieprzyk showed that $\Phi[F_1, F_1, F_1, F_2]$ and $\Phi[F_1, F_1, F_1, F_1 \circ F_1]$

© The Author(s), under exclusive license to Springer Nature Switzerland AG 2024
E. A. Quaglia (Ed.): IMACC 2023, LNCS 14421, pp. 57–79, 2024.
https://doi.org/10.1007/978-3-031-47818-5_4

are PRPs [Pie90]. Patarin showed that $\Phi[F_1, F_2, F_1, F_2]$ is an SPRP [Pat92]. Additionally, Patarin pointed out that $\Phi[F, F, F, F \circ \zeta \circ F]$ is an SPRP, where it uses 1-bit cyclic rotation ζ. Nandi proved that $\Phi[\zeta \circ F, F, F, F]$ is an SPRP and has the optimal number of PRF calls [Nan10]. See also [Nan15] for a related result that uses a mask.

A tweakable block cipher (TBC), formalized by Liskov et al. [LRW11], is the generalization of a block cipher to take an additional input called a tweak. Minematsu pointed out that TBCs can be used as a primitive for constructing block ciphers, and instantiated a concrete structure by combining TBCs and universal hash functions [Min09]. By replacing the PRFs and XORs in the Feistel cipher with TBCs, Coron et al. formalized a TBC-based Feistel cipher and proved its indistinguishability security [CDMS10].

Indifferentiability, formalized by Maurer et al. [MRH04], is one of the security definitions for cryptographic permutations, a key-less permutation. This definition captures the hardness to distinguish a cryptographic permutation from a random permutation, where the cryptographic permutation makes oracle calls to an ideal primitive. Some instances of random oracle (RO) based Feistel ciphers are analyzed with the indifferentiability notion. See [CHK+16, DKT16, DS16] for the results on this line of research. The TBC-based Feistel cipher [CDMS10] can be seen as a cryptographic permutation by regarding the TBC as the ideal cipher (IC), which models an ideally secure block cipher, and its indifferentiability analysis is presented in [CDMS10], where independent ICs are used in the construction. Bhaumik et al. later improved the security bound [BNR21].

Contracting Feistel structures are derivations of the Feistel structure, and we consider the TBC-based counterpart [Min15]. These structures have d lines, where $d \geq 2$, and $d - 1$ lines are used as the tweak of the TBC to update the remaining line. See Fig. 1 for the structure. The security of the structure is known in the indistinguishability notion [Min15, NI19], and in the indifferentiability notion [GL15, NI20], where we consider the IC with key length of $d - 1$ lines instead of a TBC.

Our Contributions. The indistinguishability results on the TBC-based Feistel ciphers [CDMS10] and on the TBC-based contracting Feistel ciphers [Min15, NI19] assume independent TBCs, and the indifferentiability results on the IC-based Feistel ciphers [CDMS10, BNR21] and on the IC-based contracting Feistel ciphers [GL15, NI20] assume independent ICs. In this paper, we investigate the security of the single primitive-based counterparts, which replace the TBCs or the ICs with a single primitive, i.e., a single-keyed TBC or a single IC. Our target is the n-bit block and $(d - 1)n$-bit tweak single-keyed TBC-based Feistel cipher for indistinguishability, and the n-bit block, $(d - 1)n$-bit key single IC-based Feistel cipher for indifferentiability. We remark that by setting $d = 2$, our results cover the case of regular Feistel ciphers of 2 lines. We present the following results:

Indistinguishability Results. Let Φ_r be the r-round single-keyed TBC-based Feistel cipher with d lines. We show that for any $r \leq d$, Φ_r can be distinguished from a random permutation with $O(1)$ queries. We then show that Φ_{d+1} is secure in the indistinguishability notion, where the security bound is $O(q^2/2^n)$ for adversaries making q queries. This makes a sharp difference to the PRF-based Feistel cipher, which is insecure regardless of the number of rounds. Next, for any $r \geq d+1$, we show that Φ_r can be distinguished from a random permutation with $O(2^{n/2})$ queries, with a type of slide attack [BW99]. On one hand, this shows the tightness of the security bound of the case $r = d + 1$, i.e., it is impossible to show a better security bound for this case. This also shows that, even if we increase the number of rounds beyond $d + 1$ rounds, the security of Φ_r does not improve, showing an impossibility of improving the security by increasing the number of rounds.

These results show that the d-round structure can be practically used in applications that are sufficient with $O(2^{n/2})$ security, however, it cannot be used if higher security is needed, regardless of the number of rounds.

Indifferentiability Results. Let $\widehat{\Phi}_r$ be the r-round single IC-based Feistel cipher with d lines. We show that for any r, $\widehat{\Phi}_r$ is not secure in the indifferentiability notion. The attack is the straightforward application of the attacks against Φ_r, and they work with $O(1)$ queries. The attack can be seen as a type of slide attack [BW99]. Using a round constant is a well-known countermeasure, and one may hope that a round constant can prevent the attack. We consider a variant of $\widehat{\Phi}_r$ that uses a round constant, and demonstrate that the round constant cannot prevent the indifferentiability attack for the case $d = 2$ and $r = 3$.

These results show that single IC based structures should not be used in practice.

Table 1 and Table 2 summarize the previous results and our results. Table 1 shows the results for $d = 2$ and Table 2 shows the results for $d \geq 2$ except for $d > 2$ in [GL15].

Further Related Works. A problem of whether one can securely reduce the number of independent keys/primitives has been studied in various other constructions. See, e.g., [ABD+13, CLL+14, DDKS14, CS15, XDG22, XDG23]. With respect to slide attacks, key-reduced Feistel ciphers have been actively analysed. See, e.g., [DKR97, BS10, DDS12, IS13, BBDK18]. Compared to these results, our attacks follow a fundamentally similar approach, while our targets employ stronger primitives, TBCs/ICs, instead of PRFs/ROs.

2 Preliminaries

2.1 Notation

For a positive integer n, let $\{0,1\}^n$ be the set of all n-bit strings. For two strings X and Y, let $X \parallel Y$ denote their concatenation. For d string $X^1, X^2, \ldots, X^d$, we denote their concatenation $X^1 \parallel X^2 \parallel \ldots \parallel X^d$ by $X^{[1..d]}$. For a finite set S, $s \xleftarrow{\$} S$ is the operation of a uniformly random selection of an element from S and assigning it to s.

Table 1. Summary of previous results and our results ($d = 2$) on Feistel ciphers. In the "Key" column, "ind." is the abbreviation of "independent".

(a) Results based on indistinguishability. "Model" shows the model of the adversary. "Key" indicates the relation between the keys for each round. In the results of [Pie90, Pat92, Nan10], the number of PRF calls is additionally noted, and ϕ means that an additional function (e.g., a 1-bit rotation) is required for the structure.

Primitive	Key	Model	# of rounds	Security	Reference
PRF	ind.	PRP	3	$O(q^2/2^n)$	[LR88]
		SPRP	4	$O(q^2/2^n)$	
	single	PRP	any	$O(1)$ attack	[ZMI89]
			4 (5 calls)	$O(q^2/2^n)$	[Pie90]
		SPRP	4 (5 calls + ϕ)	$O(q^2/2^n)$	[Pat92]
			4 (4 calls + ϕ)	$O(q^2/2^n)$	[Nan10]
TBC	ind.	SPRP	2	$O(q^2/2^n)$	[CDMS10]
			3	$O(q^2/2^{2n})$	
	single	SPRP	2	$O(1)$ attack	Theorem 1
			3	$O(q^2/2^n)$	Theorem 2
			≥ 3	$O(2^{n/2})$ attack	Theorem 3

(b) Results based on indifferentiability. "Instance" indicates the relation between the ROs/ICs for each round.

Primitive	Instance	# of rounds	Security	Reference
RO	ind.	5	$O(1)$ attack	[CHK+16]
		8	$O(q^8/2^n)$	[DS16]
		10	$O(q^{12}/2^n)$	[DKT16]
		14	$O(q^{16}/2^{2n})$	[CHK+16]
IC	ind.	2	$O(1)$ attack	[CDMS10]
		3	$O(q^2/2^n)$	
			$O(n^2 q/2^n)$	[BNR21]
	single	any	$O(1)$ attack	Theorem 4

Table 2. Summary of previous results and our results on contracting Feistel ciphers. $d \geq 2$ denotes the number of lines, l is a constant value s.t. $1 \leq l \leq d-1$. In "Security", the maximum number of queries is additionally noted if exists.

(a) Results based on indistinguishability.

Primitive	Key	Model	# of rounds	Security	Reference
TBC	ind.	SPRP	$3d$	$O(q^2/2^{dn})$	[Min15]
			$3d-2$	$O(q^2/2^{dn})$	[NI19]
			$d+l$	$O(q^2/2^{(1+l)n})$ $(q \leq 2^n)$	
			d	$O(q^2/2^n)$	
	single	SPRP	$\leq d$	$O(1)$ attack	Theorem 1
			$d+1$	$O(q^2/2^n)$	Theorem 2
			$\geq d+1$	$O(2^{n/2})$ attack	Theorem 3

(b) Results based on indifferentiability. In [GL15], $d > 2$.

Primitive	Instance	# of rounds	Security	Reference
IC	ind.	$\leq 2d-2$	$O(1)$ attack	[GL15] $(d > 2)$
		$2d-1$	$O(q^2/2^n)$	
		$2d+1$	$O(q^2/2^{2n})$	[NI20]
		$2d+2l-1$	$O(q^2/2^{(1+l)n})$ $(q \leq 2^n)$	
	single	any	$O(1)$ attack	Theorem 4

2.2   (Tweakable) Block Cipher

A block cipher $E : \mathcal{M} \times \mathcal{K} \to \mathcal{M}$ is a keyed permutation. For plaintext $M \in \mathcal{M}$, key $K \in \mathcal{K}$, and ciphertext $C \in \mathcal{M}$, we write the encryption as $C = E_K(M)$ and the decryption as $M = E_K^{-1}(C)$. If $\mathcal{M} = \{0,1\}^n$, we say that it is an n-bit block cipher. Let Perm(n) be the set of all n-bit permutations, and a random permutation is an element selected from Perm(n) uniformly at random.

A tweakable block cipher $\widetilde{E} : \mathcal{M} \times \mathcal{K} \times \mathcal{T} \to \mathcal{M}$ is a keyed permutation that takes additional input called a tweak [LRW11]. For plaintext $M \in \mathcal{M}$, key $K \in \mathcal{K}$, tweak $T \in \mathcal{T}$, and ciphertext $C \in \mathcal{M}$, we write the encryption as $C = \widetilde{E}_K(T, M)$ and the decryption as $M = \widetilde{E}_K^{-1}(T, C)$. If $\mathcal{M} = \{0,1\}^n$

and $\mathcal{T} = \{0,1\}^t$, we say that it is an (n,t)-bit TBC. Let $\widetilde{\mathrm{Perm}}(n,t)$ be the set of all the functions $\widetilde{P} : \{0,1\}^n \times \{0,1\}^t \to \{0,1\}^n$ s.t. for any $T \in \{0,1\}^t$, $\widetilde{P}(\cdot, T) \in \mathrm{Perm}(n)$, and a tweakable random permutation (TRP) is an element selected from $\widetilde{\mathrm{Perm}}(n,t)$ uniformly at random, which we call an (n,t)-bit TRP.

The ideal cipher $\widehat{E} : \mathcal{M} \times \mathcal{K} \to \mathcal{M}$ is the set of random permutations that idealizes a block cipher. For each K, $\widehat{E}(K,\cdot)$ is a random permutation over $\mathcal{M}$. For plaintext $M \in \mathcal{M}$, key $K \in \mathcal{K}$, and ciphertext $C \in \mathcal{M}$, we write the encryption as $C = \widehat{E}(K,M)$ and the decryption as $M = \widehat{E}^{-1}(K,C)$. If $\mathcal{M} = \{0,1\}^n$ and $\mathcal{K} = \{0,1\}^k$, we say that it is an (n,k)-bit IC.

2.3   Security Definitions

We consider the security of block cipher E as a keyed primitive and as a cryptographic permutation. As a keyed primitive, we consider the indistinguishability notion [LR88], i.e., the notion of a pseudorandom permutation (PRP) and a strong pseudorandom permutation (SPRP). A PRP-adversary has oracle access to a cryptographic permutation oracle E_K in the real world, and random permutation π in the ideal world. For an adversary $\mathcal{A}$ that makes a maximum of q oracle queries, we define the PRP-advantage and SPRP-advantage as follows:

$$\mathbf{Adv}_E^{\mathrm{prp}}(\mathcal{A}) = |\Pr[\mathcal{A}^{E_K(\cdot)} \Rightarrow 1] - \Pr[\mathcal{A}^{\pi(\cdot)} \Rightarrow 1]|$$

$$\mathbf{Adv}_E^{\mathrm{sprp}}(\mathcal{A}) = |\Pr[\mathcal{A}^{E_K(\cdot),E_K^{-1}(\cdot)} \Rightarrow 1] - \Pr[\mathcal{A}^{\pi(\cdot),\pi^{-1}(\cdot)} \Rightarrow 1]|$$

Next, as a cryptographic permutation, we consider the indifferentiability notion [MRH04]. Let C be a cryptographic permutation that is built on the ideal cipher $\widehat{E}$, i.e., C makes oracle calls to $\widehat{E}$ to compute its output, and we write $C^{\widehat{E}}$ for this. In the real world, an adversary $\mathcal{A}$ has oracle access to $\widehat{E}$ and $C^{\widehat{E}}$. In the ideal world, $\mathcal{A}$ makes queries to a random permutation π and a simulator Sim^π, where the simulator Sim has oracle access to π. We call a query to $C^{\widehat{E}}$ or π as a construction query, and a query to E or Sim^π as a primitive query. For an adversary $\mathcal{A}$ that makes a maximum of q oracle queries in total, we define the advantage as follows:

$$\mathbf{Adv}_{C,\mathrm{Sim}}^{\mathrm{indiff}}(\mathcal{A}) = |\Pr[\mathcal{A}^{C^{\widehat{E}}(\cdot),\widehat{E}(\cdot)} \Rightarrow 1] - \Pr[\mathcal{A}^{\pi(\cdot),\mathrm{Sim}^\pi(\cdot)} \Rightarrow 1]|$$

2.4   Coefficient-H Technique [Pat08, CS14]

Our security proof is based on the coefficient-H technique. Let $\mathcal{R}$ and $\mathcal{R}^{-1}$ be the real world oracles that internally call a block cipher E_K and its inverse E_K^{-1}. Similarly, let $\mathcal{I}$ and $\mathcal{I}^{-1}$ be the ideal world oracles that internally call a random permutation π and its inverse π^{-1}. For an adversary $\mathcal{A}$ that makes a maximum of q oracle queries, a transcript θ denotes a tuple that records all the interactions between $\mathcal{A}$ and the oracles. Let $\Theta_\mathcal{R}$ be the random variable of θ when $\mathcal{A}$ interacts with $\mathcal{R}$ and $\mathcal{R}^{-1}$, and $\Theta_\mathcal{I}$ be the random variable of θ when $\mathcal{A}$ interacts with $\mathcal{I}$ and $\mathcal{I}^{-1}$. An attainable transcript is a transcript θ such that $\Pr[\Theta_\mathcal{I} = \theta] > 0$. Then, the coefficient-H technique states the following result:

Lemma 1. *Consider a deterministic adversary $\mathcal{A}$. Partition all the attainable transcripts into two disjoint sets $\mathcal{T}_{\mathrm{good}}$ and $\mathcal{T}_{\mathrm{bad}}$. Suppose that there exists ϵ_1 such that $\Pr[\Theta_{\mathcal{I}} \in \mathcal{T}_{\mathrm{bad}}] \leq \epsilon_1$, and there exists ϵ_2 such that, for all $\theta \in \mathcal{T}_{\mathrm{good}}$, $\Pr[\Theta_{\mathcal{R}} = \theta]/\Pr[\Theta_{\mathcal{I}} = \theta] \geq 1 - \epsilon_2$. Then we have $\mathbf{Adv}_E^{\mathrm{sprp}}(\mathcal{A}) \leq \epsilon_1 + \epsilon_2$.*

We remark that although Lemma 1 is modified specifically for an SPRP adversary, the coefficient-H technique can be applied to general security definitions. See e.g., [Pat08, CS14].

3 Constructions

3.1 Block Ciphers

Fix $d \geq 2$. Let $\widetilde{E}$ be an $(n, (d-1)n)$-bit TBC and K be a key of $\widetilde{E}$. First, we define an encryption round function ϕ as

$$\phi[\widetilde{E}_K](X^{[1..d]}) = X^{[2..d]} \parallel \widetilde{E}_K(X^{[2..d]}, X^1),$$

where $X^{[1..d]} \in \{0,1\}^{dn}$ is the input. See Fig. 1a. Then, the r-round single-keyed TBC-based Feistel cipher Φ_r is defined by iterating the round function ϕ for r times as follows:

$$\Phi_r[\widetilde{E}_K](M^{[1..d]}) = \underbrace{\phi[\widetilde{E}_K] \circ \phi[\widetilde{E}_K] \circ \cdots \circ \phi[\widetilde{E}_K]}_{r \text{ times}}(M^{[1..d]})$$

It takes $M^{[1..d]} \in \{0,1\}^{dn}$ as input.

Likewise, we define a decryption round function ϕ^{-1} as

$$\phi^{-1}[\widetilde{E}_K](X^{[1..d]}) = \widetilde{E}_K^{-1}(X^{[1..d-1]}, X^d) \parallel X^{[1..d-1]},$$

where $X^{[1..d]} \in \{0,1\}^{dn}$ is the input. Next, the decryption of Φ_r, which we write Φ_r^{-1}, is defined by repeating ϕ^{-1} for r times as follows:

$$\Phi_r^{-1}[\widetilde{E}_K](C^{[1..d]}) = \underbrace{\phi^{-1}[\widetilde{E}_K] \circ \phi^{-1}[\widetilde{E}_K] \circ \cdots \circ \phi^{-1}[\widetilde{E}_K]}_{r \text{ times}}(C^{[1..d]})$$

It takes $C^{[1..d]} \in \{0,1\}^{dn}$ as input.

3.2 Cryptographic Permutations

Let $\widehat{E}$ be an $(n, (d-1)n)$-bit IC. Cryptographic permutations can be defined from an ideal cipher similarly to block ciphers.

With round functions $\phi[\widehat{E}]$ and $\phi^{-1}[\widehat{E}]$ shown in Fig. 1b, where the key of $\widehat{E}$ is regarded as a tweak of $\widehat{E}_K$ in $\phi[\widetilde{E}_K]$, the r-round single IC-based Feistel cipher, which we write $\widehat{\Phi}_r$, is defined as follows:

$$\widehat{\Phi}_r[\widehat{E}](M^{[1..d]}) = \underbrace{\phi[\widehat{E}] \circ \phi[\widehat{E}] \circ \cdots \circ \phi[\widehat{E}]}_{r \text{ times}}(M^{[1..d]})$$

$$\widehat{\Phi}_r^{-1}[\widehat{E}](C^{[1..d]}) = \underbrace{\phi^{-1}[\widehat{E}] \circ \phi^{-1}[\widehat{E}] \circ \cdots \circ \phi^{-1}[\widehat{E}]}_{r \text{ times}}(C^{[1..d]})$$

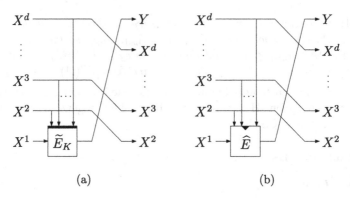

Fig. 1. (a) $\phi[\widetilde{E}_K](X^{[1..d]}) = X^{[2..d]} \| Y$, where $Y = \widetilde{E}_K(X^{[2..d]}, X^1)$ and (b) $\phi[\widehat{E}](X^{[1..d]}) = X^{[2..d]} \| Y$, where $Y = \widehat{E}(X^{[2..d]}, X^1)$

4   Security of Φ_r

We present three results on Φ_r. In Theorem 1, we first show an efficient distinguisher on Φ_r with $r \leq d$. Next, with an additional round, in Theorem 2, we prove that Φ_r with $r = d+1$ is provably secure up to $O(2^{n/2})$ queries. Finally, in Theorem 3, we present a distinguisher that makes $O(2^{n/2})$ queries against Φ_r for any $r \geq d+1$. This shows the tightness of Theorem 2, and this also shows that increasing the number of rounds beyond $r = d+1$ does not increase the security.

We remark that we use a TRP $\widetilde{E}$ as the underlying TBC, and we thus omit writing the key K, while $\widetilde{E}$ and $\Phi_r = \Phi_r[\widetilde{E}]$ are still keyed primitives.

4.1   Attack on Φ_r for $r \leq d$

We have the following theorem for Φ_r for $r \leq d$.

Theorem 1. *Fix $d \geq 2$. Let $\widetilde{E}$ be the $(n, (d-1)n)$-bit TRP, and $\Phi_r = \Phi_r[\widetilde{E}]$ be the r-round single-keyed TBC-based Feistel cipher. Then there exists an adversary $\mathcal{A}$ against Φ_r with $r \leq d$ such that $\mathbf{Adv}_{\Phi_r}^{\mathrm{prp}}(\mathcal{A}) = O(1)$, where $\mathcal{A}$ makes $O(1)$ queries.*

Proof. Let O be the oracle, which is either the block cipher Φ_r or the random permutation π.

The Attack on Φ_r for $r \leq d-1$. We first introduce $\mathcal{A}$ on Φ_r for $r \leq d-1$.

$\mathcal{A}$ makes an encryption query using an arbitrary plaintext $M^{[1..d]} \in \{0,1\}^{dn}$ to obtain the corresponding ciphertext $C^{[1..d]} \in \{0,1\}^{dn}$, and returns 1 iff $C^{d-r} = M^d$. In Φ_r, M^d never goes through $\widetilde{E}$, and it directly appears as C^{d-r}. In π, C^{d-r} is a part of a uniformly random output of π, thus $\mathcal{A}$ outputs 0 except for a negligible probability of an n-bit collision. Therefore $\mathcal{A}$ can distinguish Φ_r from π with 1 query.

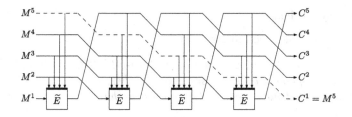

Fig. 2. Structure of Φ_4 for $d = 5$. M^5 directly appears as C^1.

An example of Φ_4 with $d = 5$ is shown in Fig. 2.

The Attack on Φ_d. We introduce our adversary $\mathcal{A}$ on Φ_d.

$\mathcal{A}$ first makes an encryption query M to obtain C, and then makes an encryption query M' to obtain C', where $M' = M^{[1..d-1]} \| C'^1$. Then $\mathcal{A}$ outputs 1 iff $C^{[2..d]} = C'^{[1..d-1]}$. In Φ_d, the first round of the second query reproduces the second round of the first query. This state collision continues in the subsequent rounds, and eventually, $C^{[2..d]} = C'^{[1..d-1]}$ always holds. In π, $C^{[2..d]}$ and $C'^{[1..d-1]}$ are the outputs of random permutation π, and hence $\mathcal{A}$ outputs 0 except for a negligible probability of a $(d-1)n$-bit collision. Therefore, $\mathcal{A}$ can distinguish Φ_d from π with $O(1)$ queries.

An example of Φ_5 with $d = 5$ is shown in Fig. 3. □

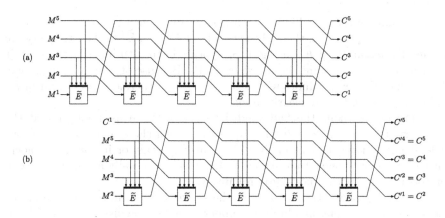

Fig. 3. Structure of Φ_5 for $d = 5$. (a) step 1, (b) step 2.

4.2 Security of Φ_{d+1}

We have the following theorem for Φ_{d+1}.

Theorem 2. *Fix $d \geq 2$. Let $\widetilde{E}$ be the $(n, (d-1)n)$-bit TRP, and $\Phi_{d+1} = \Phi_{d+1}[\widetilde{E}]$ be the r-round single-keyed TBC-based Feistel cipher, where $r = d + 1$. Then for any adversary $\mathcal{A}$ that makes at most q queries, we have*

$$\mathbf{Adv}_{\Phi_{d+1}}^{\mathrm{sprp}}(\mathcal{A}) \leq \frac{(4d+1)q^2}{2^n} + \frac{0.5q^2}{2^{dn}} \ .$$

We present the outline of the proof. The detailed proof is given in Appendix A.

Outline of Proof. In $\Phi_{d+1} = \Phi_{d+1}[\widetilde{E}]$, we use a single TRP $\widetilde{E}$, and we write $\widetilde{E}^i$ to indicate $\widetilde{E}$ in the i-th round. Note that $\widetilde{E}^i = \widetilde{E}$ for all i.

Let $S = \widetilde{E}^1(M^{[2..d]}, M^1)$, an output of the TRP in the 1st round. We regard S as the internal state, and we see that, for each of the TRP calls, S appears as the output block of the TRP (as $\widetilde{E}^1$), or as a tweak (as $\widetilde{E}^2, \dots, \widetilde{E}^d$), or as the input block (as $\widetilde{E}^{d+1}$). See Fig. 4 for an example of Φ_6 for $d = 5$.

Our proof is based on the coefficient-H technique. Let $M_i^{[1..d]}$, S_i, and $C_i^{[1..d]}$ be the plaintext, internal state, and the ciphertext of the i-th query, respectively. We define the bad conditions as follows:

1. $\{M_1^1, \dots, M_1^d, \dots, M_q^1, \dots, M_q^d\} \cap \{S_1, \dots, S_q\} \neq \emptyset$
2. $\{C_1^1, \dots, C_1^d, \dots, C_q^1, \dots, C_q^d\} \cap \{S_1, \dots, S_q\} \neq \emptyset$
3. $|\{S_1, \dots, S_q\}| < q$

Namely, if any of the S_i collides with other variables, then the transcript is bad.

If S_i is a unique value, then all the tweaks of $\widetilde{E}^2, \dots, \widetilde{E}^d$ in the i-th query are unique. For example, in $\widetilde{E}^2$ in Fig. 4, S_i appears in the 4th line of the tweak. It never appears on the same line in other TRPs. Because of this, if S_i is unique, the tweak of $\widetilde{E}^2$ never collides with other tweaks. Furthermore, an output of $\widetilde{E}^1$ and an input of $\widetilde{E}^{d+1}$ are clearly unique.

Intuitively, without the bad conditions and with an assumption that the adversary does not make redundant queries, we can show that every TRP has at least one unique element in the output block, tweak, or in the input block. This is sufficient to show that all the TRPs, which is actually a single TRP, can interpolate them with a non-zero probability.

The good probabilities are almost the same in Φ_{d+1} and π, and from the coefficient-H technique, we obtain the upper bound of the distinguishing advantage.

4.3 Attack on Φ_r for $r \geq d + 1$

We have the following theorem for Φ_r for $r \geq d + 1$.

Theorem 3. *Fix $d \geq 2$. Let $\widetilde{E}$ be the $(n, (d-1)n)$-bit TRP, and $\Phi_r = \Phi_r[\widetilde{E}]$ be the r-round single-keyed TBC-based Feistel cipher. Then there exists an adversary $\mathcal{A}$ against Φ_r with $r \geq d+1$ such that $\mathbf{Adv}_{\Phi_r}^{\mathrm{prp}}(\mathcal{A}) = O(1)$, where $\mathcal{A}$ makes $O(2^{n/2})$ queries.*

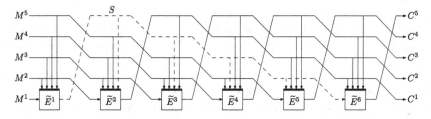

Fig. 4. Structure of Φ_6 for $d = 5$. S appears in all the tweaks from $\widetilde{E}^2$ to $\widetilde{E}^5$, and is used as an output in $\widetilde{E}^1$ and an input in $\widetilde{E}^6$.

Proof. We present our adversary $\mathcal{A}$ for $d \geq 3$ and $r \geq d+1$. We later cover the case $d = 2$.

1. Fix $M^{[2..d]} \in \{0,1\}^{(d-1)n}$ arbitrarily.
2. For $i = 1, \ldots, 2^{n/2}$, choose M_i^1 uniformly at random without overlaps, i.e., $M_i^1 \neq M_{i'}^1$ holds for any $1 \leq i < i' \leq 2^{n/2}$. Then make $2^{n/2}$ encryption queries $C_i^{[1..d]} \leftarrow O(M_i^1 \parallel M^{[2..d]})$ for $i = 1, \ldots, 2^{n/2}$.
3. For $j = 1, \ldots, 2^{n/2}$, choose S_j' uniformly at random without overlaps. Then make $2^{n/2}$ encryption queries $C_j'^{[1..d]} \leftarrow O(M^{[2..d]} \parallel S_j')$ for $j = 1, \ldots, 2^{n/2}$.
4. If there exists (i, j) s.t. $C_i^{[2..d]} = C_j'^{[1..d-1]}$, then output 1, else output 0.

This algorithm adopts the same approach as the one for Φ_d. However, the internal states $S_i = \widetilde{E}(M^{[2..d]}, M_i)$ cannot be directly observed. We make $O(2^{n/2})$ queries so that we have the dn-bit state collision with a high probability. Let $q = 2^{n/2}$. The collision probability among the q values of S_i and q values of S_j' can be evaluated as follows:

$$\Pr[\{S_1, \ldots, S_q\} \cap \{S_1', \ldots, S_q'\} \neq \emptyset] \geq \left(1 - \frac{1}{e}\right)\frac{q(q-1)}{2^n} \approx 0.632$$

Here, e is the base of the natural logarithm and the last approximation follows from $q = 2^{n/2}$.

As for the random permutation, the probability of the collision among $C_i^{[2..d]}$ and $C_j'^{[1..d-1]}$ can be evaluated in a similar way by regarded them as $(d-1)n$-bit random values. We obtain

$$\Pr[\{C_1^{[2..d]}, \ldots, C_q^{[2..d]}\} \cap \{C_1'^{[1..d-1]}, \ldots, C_q'^{[1..d-1]}\} = \emptyset] \leq \frac{0.5q^2}{2^{(d-1)n}} = \frac{0.5}{2^{(d-2)n}},$$

where we used $q = 2^{n/2}$ for the last equality.

From the discussion above, we obtain the lower bound of the distinguishing advantage as

$$\mathbf{Adv}_{\Phi_r}^{\mathrm{prp}}(\mathcal{A}) \gtrsim 0.5 \left(1 - \frac{1}{2^{(d-2)n}}\right).$$

An example of Φ_6 for $d = 5$ is shown in Fig. 5.

If $d = 2$, this algorithm does not work because in π, we have an n-bit output collision in step 4 with a high probability. To deal with this problem, we modify the algorithm as follows:

4′. If there exists no (i, j) satisfying $C_i^2 = C_j'^1$, then output 0.

5′. For (i, j) s.t. $C_i^2 = C_j'^1$, make encryption queries $X^{[1..2]} \leftarrow O(C_i^{[1..2]})$ and $X'^{[1..2]} \leftarrow O(C_j'^{[1..2]})$.

6′. If $X^2 = X'^1$ holds, then output 1, else output 0.

Steps with a prime symbol are modified or added for $d = 2$. In both Φ_r and π, this algorithm aborts in step 4 with almost the same probability, and we see that the algorithm proceeds to steps 5′ and 6′ with a high probability.

Extra steps (steps 5′ and 6′) are based on the distinguisher on Φ_d. If $S_i = S_j'$ holds for some (i, j) in Φ_r, then we see that $C_i^{[1..2]}$ and $C_j'^{[1..2]}$ in step 5′ are the input and output of the r-th round of the encryption of (M^2, S_j'). Therefore, this algorithm outputs 1 with a high probability in Φ_r and outputs 0 in π with a similar discussion for Φ_d. □

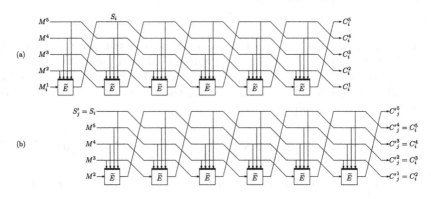

Fig. 5. Structure of Φ_6 for $d = 5$. (a): i-th query, (b) j-th query satisfying $S_j' = S_i$.

5   Security of $\widehat{\Phi}_r$

We have the following theorem for $\widehat{\Phi}_r$.

Theorem 4. *Fix $d \geq 2$. Let $\widehat{E}$ be the $(n, (d-1)n)$-bit IC, and $\widehat{\Phi}_r = \widehat{\Phi}_r[\widehat{E}]$ be the r-round single IC-based Feistel cipher. Then for any $r \geq 1$, $\widehat{\Phi}_r$ is not indifferentiable from a random permutation.*

Proof. We first consider the case $r \leq d$. Now we see that the same adversary against Φ_r for $r \leq d$ in Sect. 4.1 works as the adversary against $\widehat{\Phi}_r$, since the adversary against Φ_r can be regraded as the adversary against $\widehat{\Phi}_r$ in the indifferentiability notion that makes only construction queries without making any primitive queries. Although the simulator can make queries to a random permutation π, the simulator cannot control π's entries at all, so that any simulator does not affect the success probability of the adversary.

Next, we consider the case $r \geq d+1$. We take the approach of the adversary against Φ_r with $r \geq d+1$ presented in Sect. 4.3. For an arbitrary plaintext $M^{[1..d]} \in \{0,1\}^{dn}$, $\mathcal{A}$ first obtains the output of the 1st round IC by using a primitive query $S \leftarrow \widehat{E}(M^{[2..d]}, M_1)$. Next, $\mathcal{A}$ makes two construction queries with plaintexts $M^{[1..d]}$ and $M^{[2..d]} \parallel S$ to obtain ciphertexts $C^{[1..d]}$ and $C'^{[1..d]}$. Then $\mathcal{A}$ outputs 1 if $C^{[2..d]} = C'^{[1..d-1]}$. Otherwise, $\mathcal{A}$ outputs 0.

In $\widehat{\Phi}_r$, the ciphertexts $C^{[1..d]}$ and $C'^{[1..d]}$ always satisfy $C^{[2..d]} = C'^{[1..d-1]}$. Observe that the complexity to search for the internal state S is replaced with a primitive query, and hence $\mathcal{A}$ runs with $O(1)$ queries. On the other hand, in π, the simulator has to find S such that the last $(d-1)n$ bits of $\pi(M^{[1..d]})$ collides with the first $(d-1)n$ bits of $\pi(M^{[2..d]} \parallel S)$. However, finding such S needs approximately $O(2^{(d-1)n})$ queries, or there does not exist such S. Therefore, $\mathcal{A}$ can distinguish $\widehat{\Phi}_r$ from π with a high probability. □

6 Indifferentiability of Feistel Cipher with Constants

We have seen in the previous section that for any $r \geq 1$, $\widehat{\Phi}_r[\widehat{E}]$ cannot be secure in the indifferentiability notion. The attack can be seen as a type of slide attacks [BW99], and introducing a round constant is a well-known countermeasure against the attack. In this section, we consider a variant of $\widehat{\Phi}_r$ that uses a round constant. One may hope that the round constant prevents the slide attacks. However, we show that this is not the case for $d = 2$ and $r = 3$ in the indifferentiability notion.

We consider a 3-round structure that we write $\widehat{\Phi}'_3$ within the indifferentiability notion. A round function ϕ'_i used in $\widehat{\Phi}'_3$ is defined as

$$\phi'_i[\widehat{E}](X^{[1..2]}) = X^2 \parallel \widehat{E}(X^2 \oplus c_i, X^1),$$

where c_i is the n-bit round constant. Then $\widehat{\Phi}'_3$ is defined with ϕ'_i as

$$\widehat{\Phi}'_3[\widehat{E}](M^{[1..2]}) = \phi'_3[\widehat{E}] \circ \phi'_2[\widehat{E}] \circ \phi'_1[\widehat{E}](M^{[1..2]}).$$

We show that $\widehat{\Phi}'_3$ can be distinguished from π with $O(1)$ queries.

1. Fix $M_1^{[1..2]} \in \{0,1\}^{2n}$ arbitrarily.
2. Make a primitive query $S_1 \leftarrow \widehat{E}(M_1^2 \oplus c_1, M_1^1)$.
3. Make a construction query $C_1^{[1..2]} \leftarrow O(M_1^{[1..2]})$.
4. Make a construction query $C_2^{[1..2]} \leftarrow O(M_1^2 \parallel S_1 \oplus c_1 \oplus c_2)$.

5. Make a construction query $M_3^{[1..2]} \leftarrow O^{-1}(C_1^1 \oplus c_2 \oplus c_3 \parallel C_2^1)$.
6. Make a construction query $C_4^{[1..2]} \leftarrow O(M_3^2 \parallel S_1)$.
7. If $C_4^1 = C_1^2$ holds, then output 1, else output 0.

Figure 6 visualizes how the algorithm works.

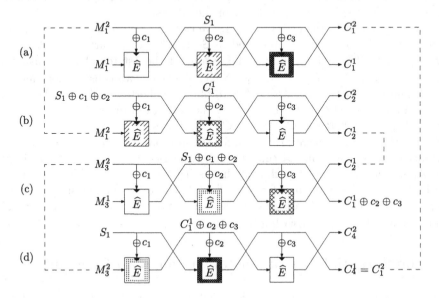

Fig. 6. Structure of $\widehat{\Phi}'_3$. ICs of the same background except for white ones have the same input block, key, and output block. (a) step 3, (b) step 4, (c) step 5, (d) step 6.

The 2nd and succeeding construction queries reproduce inputs and outputs of an adjacent IC in the previous query. As shown in Fig. 6, in the final query in step 6, we have two reproductions, one from step 3 and the other one from step 5, and we always observe the previous value of C_1^2 as a part of the output.

Now we observe that a loop is formed if we focus on the input and output of the construction, which is shown with dotted lines in Fig. 6. We see that finding such a loop in π is not possible if we consider efficient simulators. Therefore, the probability of $C_4^1 = C_1^2$ is negligible in π.

As a remark, this algorithm never makes primitive queries once a construction query is made. This implies that $\widehat{\Phi}'_3[\widehat{E}]$ does not achieve the sequential indifferentiability notion [MPS12] which is a weaker notion of indifferentiability.

7   Conclusions

In this paper, we analyzed the security of the single-keyed TBC-based Feistel ciphers in the indistinguishability notion, and the single IC-based Feistel ciphers in the indifferentiability notion. We completed the security characterization depending on the number of rounds. We also considered a structure that employs a round constant, and showed that this does not work for the case $d = 2$ and $r = 3$ in the indifferentiability notion.

As open problems, there have been various proposals to modify the PRF-based Feistel cipher so that the security is maintained [Pie90, Pat92, Nan10, Nan15], and it would be interesting to see how one can modify the single-keyed TBC-based/single IC-based Feistel ciphers to improve the security. With respect to the construction with a round constant, we have only covered the indifferentiability notion of the case $d = 2$ and $r = 3$, and it would be interesting to see the security with other parameters and/or in the indistinguishability notion.

Acknowledgements. The authors would like to thank the anonymous reviewers of IMACC 2023 for their constructive comments. This work was supported by JSPS KAKENHI JP20K11675.

A   Security Proof of Φ_{d+1}

We show the detailed proof of Theorem 2. We recall the theorem.

Theorem 2. *Fix $d \geq 2$. Let $\widetilde{E}$ be the $(n, (d-1)n)$-bit TRP, and $\Phi_{d+1} = \Phi_{d+1}[\widetilde{E}]$ be the r-round single-keyed TBC-based Feistel cipher, where $r = d + 1$. Then for any adversary $\mathcal{A}$ that makes at most q queries, we have*

$$\mathbf{Adv}^{\mathrm{sprp}}_{\Phi_{d+1}}(\mathcal{A}) \leq \frac{(4d+1)q^2}{2^n} + \frac{0.5q^2}{2^{dn}} .$$

We first define the transcripts followed by two oracles, the real world oracle based on Φ_{d+1} and the ideal world oracle based on the random permutation π, and the bad conditions. Next, we compute the bad probability in Lemma 2 and the good probability ratio in Lemma 3. The security bound is obtained from these lemmas and the coefficient-H technique in Lemma 1.

Transcripts. The adversary $\mathcal{A}$ is given access to the encryption and decryption oracles. If the i-th query is an encryption query $M_i^{[1..d]}$, then $\mathcal{A}$ obtains the corresponding ciphertext $C_i^{[1..d]}$. If the i-th query is a decryption query $C_i^{[1..d]}$, then $\mathcal{A}$ obtains $M_i^{[1..d]}$. Without loss of generality, we assume that $\mathcal{A}$ makes exactly q queries, does not repeat a query, and does not make a redundant query, i.e., if $\mathcal{A}$ obtains $C_i^{[1..d]}$ for an encryption query $M_i^{[1..d]}$, then it does not use $C_i^{[1..d]}$ in the subsequent decryption queries, and vice versa. As we detail below, after making q queries and before returning the decision bit, $\mathcal{A}$ is given all the internal state values $S_1, \ldots, S_q$. Since it is only beneficial to $\mathcal{A}$, there is no loss of generality of giving the additional input to $\mathcal{A}$. Then the transcript is defined as follows:

$$((M_1^{[1..d]}, C_1^{[1..d]}), \ldots, (M_q^{[1..d]}, C_q^{[1..d]}), S_1, \ldots, S_q) \qquad (1)$$

Definition of the Oracles. The real world oracles $\mathcal{R}, \mathcal{R}^{-1}$ internally make use of the block cipher Φ_{d+1} and its inverse Φ_{d+1}^{-1}. After making q queries, the oracles $\mathcal{R}, \mathcal{R}^{-1}$ give $\mathcal{A}$ all the internal states $S_1, \ldots, S_q$. Figure 7 shows the algorithms of $\mathcal{R}, \mathcal{R}^{-1}$.

Algorithm 1 Procedure of $\mathcal{R}$ for the i-th query (encryption)

Input: $M_i^{[1..d]} \in \{0,1\}^{dn}$
Output: $C_i^{[1..d]} \in \{0,1\}^{dn}$
1: $X_i^{[1..d]} \leftarrow M_i^{[1..d]}$
2: **for** $j = 1$ to $d + 1$ **do**
3:     $X_i^{d+j} \leftarrow \widetilde{E}(X_i^{[1+j..d-1+j]}, X_i^j)$
4: $S_i \parallel C_i^{[1..d]} \leftarrow X_i^{[d+1..2d+1]}$
5: **return** $C^{[1..d]}$

Algorithm 2 Procedure of $\mathcal{R}^{-1}$ for the i-th query (decryption)

Input: $C^{[1..d]} \in \{0,1\}^{dn}$
Output: $M^{[1..d]} \in \{0,1\}^{dn}$
1: $X_i^{[d+2..2d+1]} \leftarrow C_i^{[1..d]}$
2: **for** $j = d + 1$ to 1 **do**
3:     $X_i^j \leftarrow \widetilde{E}(X_i^{[2+j..d+j]}, X_i^{1+j})$
4: $M_i^{[1..d]} \parallel S_i \leftarrow X_i^{[1..d+1]}$
5: **return** $M^{[1..d]}$

Fig. 7. Algorithm of $\mathcal{R}$ and $\mathcal{R}^{-1}$

The ideal world oracles $\mathcal{I}, \mathcal{I}^{-1}$ internally make use of the random permutation π and its inverse π^{-1}. After q queries, $\mathcal{I}, \mathcal{I}^{-1}$ generate dummy internal states $S_1, \ldots, S_q$ with the same probability distribution as TRP $\widetilde{E}$. For this, for an encryption query, the oracle simulates the 1st round TRP. For a decryption query, the oracle simulates the $(d + 1)$-st round TRP. After completing the simulation, $S_1, \ldots, S_q$ are given to $\mathcal{A}$. Figure 8 shows the algorithms of $\mathcal{I}, \mathcal{I}^{-1}$.

Bad Conditions. For the TRP $\widetilde{E}$ in the real world, the tweak determines the permutation between the input and output of the TRP. Accordingly, if the tweaks are the same, the TRP does not output distinct outputs from the same inputs or distinct inputs from the same outputs. By applying this to all the combinations of the TRPs in Φ_{d+1}, we obtain the bad conditions of the whole structure of Φ_{d+1} as follows:

1. $\{M_1^1, \ldots, M_1^d, \ldots, M_q^1, \ldots, M_q^d\} \cap \{S_1, \ldots, S_q\} \neq \emptyset$

Algorithm 3 Procedure of $\mathcal{I}$ for the i-th query (encryption)

Input: $M_i^{[1..d]} \in \{0,1\}^{dn}$
Output: $C_i^{[1..d]} \in \{0,1\}^{dn}$
  1: $C_i^{[1..d]} \leftarrow \pi(M_i^{[1..d]})$
  2: **return** $C_i^{[1..d]}$

Algorithm 4 Procedure of $\mathcal{I}^{-1}$ for i-th query (decryption)

Input: $C_i^{[1..d]} \in \{0,1\}^{dn}$
Output: $M_i^{[1..d]} \in \{0,1\}^{dn}$
  1: $M_i^{[1..d]} \leftarrow \pi^{-1}(C_i^{[1..d]})$
  2: **return** $M_i^{[1..d]}$

Algorithm 5 Generation of dummy internal states $S_1,\ldots,S_q$

Input: $(M_1^{[1..d]}, C_1^{[1..d]}),\ldots,(M_q^{[1..d]}, M_q^{[1..d]}) \in (\{0,1\}^{dn} \times \{0,1\}^{dn})^q$
Output: $S_1,\ldots,S_q \in (\{0,1\}^n)^q$
  1: **for** $i = 1$ to q **do**
  2:   **if** the i-th query is encryption **then**
  3:     **if** $\widetilde{E}(M_i^{[2..d]}, M_i^1)$ is defined **then**
  4:       $S_i \leftarrow \widetilde{E}(M_i^{[2..d]}, M_i^1)$
  5:     **else**
  6:       $S_i \xleftarrow{\$} \{0,1\}^n \setminus \mathrm{Ran}(M_i^{[2..d]})$
  7:   **else**   ▷ *the i-th query is decryption*
  8:     **if** $\widetilde{E}^{-1}(C_i^{[1..d-1]}, C_i^d)$ is defined **then**
  9:       $S_i \leftarrow \widetilde{E}^{-1}(C_i^{[1..d-1]}, C_i^d)$
 10:     **else**
 11:       $S_i \xleftarrow{\$} \{0,1\}^n \setminus \mathrm{Dom}(C_i^{[1..d-1]})$
 12:   $X_i^{[1..2d+1]} \leftarrow M_i^{[1..d]} \| S_i \| C_i^{[1..d]}$
 13:   **for** $j = 1$ to $d+1$ **do**
 14:     $\widetilde{E}(X_i^{[1+j..d-1+j]}, X_i^j) \leftarrow X_i^{d+j}$
 15: **return** $S_1,\ldots,S_q$

Fig. 8. Algorithm of $\mathcal{I}$ and $\mathcal{I}^{-1}$, where $\mathrm{Dom}(T)$ and $\mathrm{Ran}(T)$ are defined as $\mathrm{Dom}(T) = \{x \mid \widetilde{E}(T,x) = y \text{ is defined for some } y\}$ and $\mathrm{Ran}(T) = \{y \mid \widetilde{E}(T,x) = y \text{ is defined for some } x\}$

2. $\{C_1^1, \ldots, C_1^d, \ldots, C_q^1, \ldots, C_q^d\} \cap \{S_1, \ldots, S_q\} \neq \emptyset$
3. $|\{S_1, \ldots, S_q\}| < q$

Recall that a transcript is defined as (1), and let $\mathcal{T}_{\text{bad}}$ be the set of all the transcripts that satisfy at least one of the conditions above. Let $\mathcal{T}_{\text{good}}$ be the set of all the transcripts that does not satisfy any of the conditions above.

In what follows, we discuss the correctness of the above bad conditions, i.e., without the bad conditions, we show that the underlying TRP $\widetilde{E}$ can interpolate all the relevant inputs, tweaks, and the outputs with a non-zero probability.

First, observe that the absence of the above three conditions guarantees that all the tweaks in $\widetilde{E}^2, \ldots, \widetilde{E}^d$ are distinct. That is, there are q tweaks for each of $\widetilde{E}^2, \ldots, \widetilde{E}^d$, and we thus have $q(d-1)$ values of the tweak in total for $\widetilde{E}^2, \ldots, \widetilde{E}^d$. It can be verified that all these $q(d-1)$ values are distinct, and they are also different from the q tweaks of $\widetilde{E}^1$ and the q tweaks of $\widetilde{E}^{d+1}$.

Next, let $\mathcal{T}^1 = \{M_1^{[2..d]}, \ldots, M_q^{[2..d]}\}$ be the set of the q tweaks of $\widetilde{E}^1$ and $\mathcal{T}^{d+1} = \{C_1^{[1..d-1]}, \ldots, C_q^{[1..d-1]}\}$ be the set of the q tweaks of $\widetilde{E}^{d+1}$. From the discussion above, all these $2q$ tweaks are different from those of $\widetilde{E}^2, \ldots, \widetilde{E}^d$, while we may have $|\mathcal{T}^1| < q$, $\mathcal{T}^1 \cap \mathcal{T}^{d+1} \neq \emptyset$, or $|\mathcal{T}^{d+1}| < q$.

- If $|\mathcal{T}^1| < q$, i.e., if $M_i^{[2..d]} = M_j^{[2..d]}$ holds for some $1 \leq i < j \leq q$, we necessary have $M_i^1 \neq M_j^1$ since the adversary does not repeat a query, and from $S_i \neq S_j$, this case does not yield inconsistency in $\widetilde{E}$.
- If $\mathcal{T}^1 \cap \mathcal{T}^{d+1} \neq \emptyset$, there are two cases to consider.
  The first case is $M_i^{[2..d]} = C_j^{[2..d]}$ for some $1 \leq i < j \leq q$. In this case, $\widetilde{E}^1$ and $\widetilde{E}^{d+1}$ have to satisfy $S_i = \widetilde{E}^1(M_i^{[2..d]}, M_i^1)$ and $C_j^d = \widetilde{E}^{d+1}(C_j^{[1..d-1]}, S_j)$, which is possible since $S_i \neq C_j^d$ and $M_i^1 \neq S_j$.
  The second case is $M_i^{[2..d]} = C_i^{[2..d]}$ for some $1 \leq i \leq q$. In this case, $\widetilde{E}^1$ and $\widetilde{E}^{d+1}$ have to satisfy $S_i = \widetilde{E}^1(M_i^{[2..d]}, M_i^1)$ and $C_i^d = \widetilde{E}^{d+1}(C_i^{[1..d-1]}, S_i)$, which is again possible since $S_i \neq C_i^d$ and $M_i^1 \neq S_i$.
- The analysis of the case $|\mathcal{T}^{d+1}| < q$ is similar to the case $|\mathcal{T}^1| < q$.

Therefore, the absence of the bad conditions implies that the TRP $\widetilde{E}$ can interpolate all the relevant inputs, tweaks, and the outputs with a non-zero probability. We next compute the probability of the bad conditions and the ratio of the good probabilities to use the coefficient-H technique.

Probability of the Bad Conditions. We have the following lemma.

Lemma 2. *We have* $\Pr[\Theta_{\mathcal{I}} \in \mathcal{T}_{\text{bad}}] \leq \dfrac{(4d+1)q^2}{2^n}$.

Proof. We compute the probability of the bad conditions based on the randomness of $S_1, \ldots, S_q$. Assume that $\mathcal{A}$ has completed making q queries to the oracles, and hence $(M_1^{[1..d]}, C_1^{[1..d]}), \ldots, (M_q^{[1..d]}, C_q^{[1..d]})$ are fixed. We further assume that we do not have the bad conditions for $S_1, \ldots, S_{i-1}$, and we compute the probability that S_i causes one of the bad conditions, which we write "S_i is bad." We then have

$$\Pr[S_i \text{ is bad}] \leq \frac{2dq + (i-1)}{2^n - 2q}.$$

The term $2q$ of the denominator indicates the maximum value of $|\mathrm{Ran}(M_i^{[2..d]})|$ or $|\mathrm{Dom}(C_i^{[1..d-1]})|$. Due to the uniqueness of $S_1, \ldots, S_{i-1}$, the tweaks of TRPs other than $\widetilde{E}^1$ and $\widetilde{E}^{d+1}$ also have unique values. Therefore, $|\mathrm{Ran}(M_i^{[2..d]})|$ or $|\mathrm{Dom}(C_i^{[1..d-1]})|$ takes the maximum value of $2q$ when $M_j^{[2..d]}$ and $C_j^{[1..d-1]}$ take the same value for all $j = 1, \ldots, i-1$. Besides, from the uniqueness of $S_1, \ldots, S_{i-1}$ and the assumption that no queries are repeated, it is guaranteed that the corresponding entry, i.e., $(M_i^{[2..d]}, M_i^1)$ for encryption or $(C_i^{[1..d-1]}, C_i^d)$ for decryption, does not exist at the generation of S_i. That is, S_i has randomness when generating it.

Now, by taking the summation of $\Pr[S_i \text{ is bad}]$, we have

$$\Pr[\Theta_{\mathcal{I}} \in \mathcal{T}_{\mathrm{bad}}] \leq \sum_{i=1}^{q} \frac{2dq + (i-1)}{2^n - 2q}$$
$$\leq \frac{(2d + 0.5)q^2}{2^n - 2q}$$
$$\leq \frac{(4d + 1)q^2}{2^n},$$

where the third inequality follows from $2q < 2^{n-1}$.

Ratio of the Good Probabilities. We have the following lemma.

Lemma 3. *For any* $\theta \in \mathcal{T}_{\mathrm{good}}$, *we have* $\dfrac{\Pr[\Theta_{\mathcal{R}} = \theta]}{\Pr[\Theta_{\mathcal{I}} = \theta]} \geq 1 - \dfrac{0.5q^2}{2^{dn}}$.

Proof. First, we define the following two sets:

$$Q_e = \{i \mid \text{the } i\text{-th query is encryption}\}$$
$$Q_d = \{i \mid \text{the } i\text{-th query is decryption}\}$$

In the real world, we additionally define two sets as follows:

$$S_i^{\mathrm{enc},x} = \{(j, k) \mid ((j < i \land 1 \leq k \leq d+1) \lor (j = i \land 1 \leq k < x))$$
$$\land \ (\text{the } j\text{-th tweak of } \widetilde{E}^k) = (\text{the } i\text{-th tweak of } \widetilde{E}^x)\}$$
$$S_i^{\mathrm{dec},x} = \{(j, k) \mid ((j < i \land 1 \leq k \leq d+1) \lor (j = i \land x < k \leq d+1))$$
$$\land \ (\text{the } j\text{-th tweak of } \widetilde{E}^k) = (\text{the } i\text{-th tweak of } \widetilde{E}^x)\}$$

Intuitively, $S_i^{\mathrm{enc},x}$ is the set of (j,k) that shares the same tweak as the i-th tweak of $\widetilde{E}^x$ when the i-th query is encryption, and $S_i^{\mathrm{dec},x}$ is that when the i-th query is decryption. That is, for the i-th tweak of $\widetilde{E}^x$, these sets indicate the indices that share the same tweak in the previous TRP calls. Then, the probability can be evaluated as follows:

$$\Pr[\Theta_{\mathcal{R}} = \theta] = \prod_{x=1}^{d+1}\left(\prod_{i \in Q_e} \frac{1}{2^n - |S_i^{\mathrm{enc},x}|} \times \prod_{i \in Q_d} \frac{1}{2^n - |S_i^{\mathrm{dec},x}|}\right)$$

$$\geq \frac{1}{(2^n)^{dq}} \times \prod_{i \in Q_e} \frac{1}{2^n - |S_i^{\mathrm{enc},1}|} \times \prod_{i \in Q_d} \frac{1}{2^n - |S_i^{\mathrm{dec},d+1}|}.$$

The last inequality is obtained by assuming $|S_i^{\mathrm{enc},x}| = |S_i^{\mathrm{dec},x}| = 0$ except for $|S_i^{\mathrm{enc},1}|$ and $|S_i^{\mathrm{dec},d+1}|$.

In the ideal world, as with the real world, we define two sets as follows:

$$T_i^{\mathrm{enc},x} = \{(j,k) \mid ((j < i \wedge 1 \leq k \leq d+1) \vee (j = i \wedge 1 \leq k < x))$$
$$\wedge \, (\text{the } j\text{-th tweak of } \widetilde{E}^k) = (\text{the } i\text{-th tweak of } \widetilde{E}^x)\}$$

$$T_i^{\mathrm{dec},x} = \{(j,k) \mid ((j < i \wedge 1 \leq k \leq d+1) \vee (j = i \wedge x < k \leq d+1))$$
$$\wedge \, (\text{the } j\text{-th tweak of } \widetilde{E}^k) = (\text{the } i\text{-th tweak of } \widetilde{E}^x)\}.$$

Here, in the definitions above, we abuse the notation to write $\widetilde{E}^k$ for the TRP $\widetilde{E}$ used in the k-th round in Algorithm 5. Then, the probability can be evaluated as follows:

$$\Pr[\Theta_{\mathcal{I}} = \theta] = \frac{1}{(2^{dn})_q} \times \prod_{i \in Q_e} \frac{1}{2^n - |T_i^{\mathrm{enc},1}|} \times \prod_{i \in Q_d} \frac{1}{2^n - |T_i^{\mathrm{dec},d+1}|}.$$

Finally, we compute the ratio of the two possibilities. We have

$$\frac{\Pr[\Theta_{\mathcal{R}} = \theta]}{\Pr[\Theta_{\mathcal{I}} = \theta]} \geq \frac{(2^{dn})_q}{(2^n)^{dq}} \times \prod_{i \in Q_e} \frac{2^n - |S_i^{\mathrm{enc},1}|}{2^n - |T_i^{\mathrm{enc},1}|} \times \prod_{i \in Q_d} \frac{2^n - |S_i^{\mathrm{dec},d+1}|}{2^n - |T_i^{\mathrm{dec},d+1}|}$$

$$\geq 1 - \frac{0.5q^2}{2^{dn}},$$

where the last inequality follows since $S_i^{\mathrm{enc},x} = T_i^{\mathrm{enc},x}$ and $S_i^{\mathrm{dec},x} = T_i^{\mathrm{dec},x}$ are always satisfied from the definitions of the oracles.

From Lemma 2, Lemma 3, and the coefficient-H technique, we obtain Theorem 2.

References

[ABD+13] Andreeva, E., Bogdanov, A., Dodis, Y., Mennink, B., Steinberger, J.P.: On the indifferentiability of key-alternating ciphers. In: Canetti, R., Garay, J.A. (eds.) CRYPTO 2013. LNCS, vol. 8042, pp. 531–550. Springer, Heidelberg (2013). https://doi.org/10.1007/978-3-642-40041-4_29

[BBDK18]   Bar-On, A., Biham, E., Dunkelman, O., Keller, N.: Efficient slide attacks. J. Cryptol. **31**(3), 641–670 (2018)

[BNR21]   Bhaumik, R., Nandi, M., Raychaudhuri, A.: Improved indifferentiability security proof for 3-round tweakable Luby-Rackoff. Des. Codes Cryptogr. **89**(10), 2255–2281 (2021)

[BS10]   Biryukov, A., Shamir, A.: Structural cryptanalysis of SASAS. J. Cryptol. **23**(4), 505–518 (2010)

[BW99]   Biryukov, A., Wagner, D.: Slide attacks. In: Knudsen, L. (ed.) FSE 1999. LNCS, vol. 1636, pp. 245–259. Springer, Heidelberg (1999). https://doi.org/10.1007/3-540-48519-8_18

[CDMS10]   Coron, J.-S., Dodis, Y., Mandal, A., Seurin, Y.: A domain extender for the ideal cipher. In: Micciancio, D. (ed.) TCC 2010. LNCS, vol. 5978, pp. 273–289. Springer, Heidelberg (2010). https://doi.org/10.1007/978-3-642-11799-2_17

[CHK+16]   Coron, J.-S., Holenstein, T., Künzler, R., Patarin, J., Seurin, Y., Tessaro, S.: How to build an ideal cipher: the indifferentiability of the feistel construction. J. Cryptol. **29**(1), 61–114 (2016)

[CLL+14]   Chen, S., Lampe, R., Lee, J., Seurin, Y., Steinberger, J.: Minimizing the two-round even-mansour cipher. In: Garay, J.A., Gennaro, R. (eds.) CRYPTO 2014. LNCS, vol. 8616, pp. 39–56. Springer, Heidelberg (2014). https://doi.org/10.1007/978-3-662-44371-2_3

[CS14]   Chen, S., Steinberger, J.: Tight security bounds for key-alternating ciphers. In: Nguyen, P.Q., Oswald, E. (eds.) EUROCRYPT 2014. LNCS, vol. 8441, pp. 327–350. Springer, Heidelberg (2014). https://doi.org/10.1007/978-3-642-55220-5_19

[CS15]   Cogliati, B., Seurin, Y.: On the provable security of the iterated even-mansour cipher against related-key and chosen-key attacks. In: Oswald, E., Fischlin, M. (eds.) EUROCRYPT 2015. LNCS, vol. 9056, pp. 584–613. Springer, Heidelberg (2015). https://doi.org/10.1007/978-3-662-46800-5_23

[DDKS14]   Dinur, I., Dunkelman, O., Keller, N., Shamir, A.: Cryptanalysis of iterated even-mansour schemes with two keys. In: Sarkar, P., Iwata, T. (eds.) ASIACRYPT 2014. LNCS, vol. 8873, pp. 439–457. Springer, Heidelberg (2014). https://doi.org/10.1007/978-3-662-45611-8_23

[DDS12]   Dinur, I., Dunkelman, O., Shamir, A.: Improved attacks on full GOST. In: Canteaut, A. (ed.) FSE 2012. LNCS, vol. 7549, pp. 9–28. Springer, Heidelberg (2012). https://doi.org/10.1007/978-3-642-34047-5_2

[DKR97]   Daemen, J., Knudsen, L., Rijmen, V.: The block cipher square. In: Biham, E. (ed.) FSE 1997. LNCS, vol. 1267, pp. 149–165. Springer, Heidelberg (1997). https://doi.org/10.1007/BFb0052343

[DKT16]   Dachman-Soled, D. Katz, J., Thiruvengadam, A.: 10-Round feistel is indifferentiable from an ideal cipher. In: Fischlin, M., Coron, J.-S. (eds.) EUROCRYPT 2016. LNCS, vol. 9666, pp. 649–678. Springer, Heidelberg (2016). https://doi.org/10.1007/978-3-662-49896-5_23

[DS16]   Dai, Y., Steinberger, J.: Indifferentiability of 8-round feistel networks. In: Robshaw, M., Katz, J. (eds.) CRYPTO 2016. LNCS, vol. 9814, pp. 95–120. Springer, Heidelberg (2016). https://doi.org/10.1007/978-3-662-53018-4_4

[GL15]   Guo, C., Lin, D.: Improved domain extender for the ideal cipher. Cryptogr. Commun. **7**(4), 509–533 (2015)

[IS13]   Isobe, T., Shibutani, K.: Generic key recovery attack on feistel scheme. In: Sako, K., Sarkar, P. (eds.) ASIACRYPT 2013. LNCS, vol. 8269, pp. 464–485. Springer, Heidelberg (2013). https://doi.org/10.1007/978-3-642-42033-7_24

[LR88]   Luby, M., Rackoff, C.: How to construct pseudorandom permutations from pseudorandom functions. SIAM J. Comput. 17(2), 373–386 (1988)

[LRW11]   Liskov, M.D., Rivest, R.L., Wagner, D.A.: Tweakable block ciphers. J. Cryptol. 24(3), 588–613 (2011)

[Min09]   Minematsu, K.: Beyond-birthday-bound security based on tweakable block cipher. In: Dunkelman, O. (ed.) FSE 2009. LNCS, vol. 5665, pp. 308–326. Springer, Heidelberg (2009). https://doi.org/10.1007/978-3-642-03317-9_19

[Min15]   Minematsu, K.: Building blockcipher from small-block tweakable blockcipher. Des. Codes Cryptogr. 74(3), 645–663 (2015)

[MPS12]   Mandal, A., Patarin, J., Seurin, Y.: On the public indifferentiability and correlation intractability of the 6-round feistel construction. In: Cramer, R. (ed.) TCC 2012. LNCS, vol. 7194, pp. 285–302. Springer, Heidelberg (2012). https://doi.org/10.1007/978-3-642-28914-9_16

[MRH04]   Maurer, U., Renner, R., Holenstein, C.: Indifferentiability, impossibility results on reductions, and applications to the random oracle methodology. In: Naor, M. (ed.) TCC 2004. LNCS, vol. 2951, pp. 21–39. Springer, Heidelberg (2004). https://doi.org/10.1007/978-3-540-24638-1_2

[Nan10]   Nandi, M.: The characterization of Luby-Rackoff and its optimum single-key variants. In: Gong, G., Gupta, K.C. (eds.) INDOCRYPT 2010. LNCS, vol. 6498, pp. 82–97. Springer, Heidelberg (2010). https://doi.org/10.1007/978-3-642-17401-8_7

[Nan15]   Nandi, M.: On the optimality of non-linear computations of length-preserving encryption schemes. In: Iwata, T., Cheon, J.H. (eds.) ASIACRYPT 2015. LNCS, vol. 9453, pp. 113–133. Springer, Heidelberg (2015). https://doi.org/10.1007/978-3-662-48800-3_5

[NI19]   Nakamichi, R., Iwata, T.: Iterative block ciphers from tweakable block ciphers with long tweaks. IACR Trans. Symmetric Cryptol. 2019(4), 54–80 (2019)

[NI20]   Nakamichi, R., Iwata, T.: Beyond-birthday-bound secure cryptographic permutations from ideal ciphers with long keys. IACR Trans. Symmetric Cryptol. 2020(2), 68–92 (2020)

[Pat92]   Patarin, J.: How to construct pseudorandom and super pseudorandom permutations from one single pseudorandom function. In: Rueppel, R.A. (ed.) EUROCRYPT 1992. LNCS, vol. 658, pp. 256–266. Springer, Heidelberg (1993). https://doi.org/10.1007/3-540-47555-9_22

[Pat08]   Patarin, J.: The "coefficients H" technique. In: Avanzi, R.M., Keliher, L., Sica, F. (eds.) SAC 2008. LNCS, vol. 5381, pp. 328–345. Springer, Heidelberg (2009). https://doi.org/10.1007/978-3-642-04159-4_21

[Pie90]   Pieprzyk, J.: How to construct pseudorandom permutations from single pseudorandom functions. In: Damgård, I.B. (ed.) EUROCRYPT 1990. LNCS, vol. 473, pp. 140–150. Springer, Heidelberg (1991). https://doi.org/10.1007/3-540-46877-3_12

[XDG22]   Xu, S., Da, Q., Guo, C.: Minimizing Even-Mansour ciphers for sequential indifferentiability (without key schedules). In: Isobe, T., Sarkar, S. (eds.) INDOCRYPT 2022. LNCS, vol. 13774, pp. 125–145. Springer, Cham (2022). https://doi.org/10.1007/978-3-031-22912-1_6

[XDG23] Shanjie, X., Da, Q., Guo, C.: Chosen-key secure even-mansour cipher from a single permutation. IACR Trans. Symmetric Cryptol. **2023**(1), 244–287 (2023)

[ZMI89] Zheng, Y., Matsumoto, T., Imai, H.: Impossibility and optimality results on constructing pseudorandom permutations. In: Quisquater, J.-J., Vandewalle, J. (eds.) EUROCRYPT 1989. LNCS, vol. 434, pp. 412–422. Springer, Heidelberg (1990). https://doi.org/10.1007/3-540-46885-4_41

Rectangle Attacks on Reduced Versions of the FBC Block Cipher

Wenchang Zhou[1,2,3] and Jiqiang Lu[1,2,3(✉)]

[1] School of Cyber Science and Technology, Beihang University, Beijing 100083, China
{wenchangzhou,lvjiqiang}@buaa.edu.cn
[2] State Key Laboratory of Cryptology, P. O. Box 5159, Beijing 100878, China
[3] Hangzhou Innovation Institute, Beihang University, Hangzhou 310051, China

Abstract. The FBC block cipher is an award-winning algorithm of the recent Cryptographic Algorithm Design Competition in China, which has three versions: FBC128-128 with a 128-bit block size and a 128-bit key size, FBC128-256 with a 128-bit block size and a 256-bit key size, and FBC256 with a 256-bit block size and a 256-bit key size. The best previously published cryptanalysis results on FBC are an impossible differential attack on 13-round FBC128-128 and a boomerang attack on 13-round FBC128-256. In this paper, we exploit a 12-round rectangle distinguisher with probability 2^{-234} of FBC128 and a 16-round rectangle distinguisher with probability 2^{-448} of FBC256, and observe that preliminary satisfying ciphertext quartets can be efficiently filtered out by sorting plaintext pairs according to some nibble positions at the ciphertext side during key-recovery phase, and finally we mount rectangle attacks on 14-round FBC128-128, 15-round FBC128-256 and 19-round FBC256 to recover their respective user key. Our attacks break more rounds than any previously published attacks on FBC.

Keywords: Cryptology · Block cipher · FBC · Rectangle attack

1 Introduction

Aiming to select block cipher and public-key encryption algorithms, the Cryptographic Algorithm Design Competition in China, organised by the Chinese Association of Cryptologic Research under the guidance of State Cryptography Administration Office, started in 2018, and finished in 2020. The FBC block cipher, designed by Feng et al. [5], is an award-winning algorithm of the competition. FBC employs a generalized Feistel structure and has three versions: FBC128-128 with a 128-bit block size and a 128-bit key size, FBC128-256 with a 128-bit block size and a 256-bit key size, and FBC256 with a 256-bit block size and a 256-bit key size, which have a total of 48, 64 and 80 rounds, respectively.

The main published cryptanalytic results on FBC are as follows. In 2019, Ren et al. [13] described an 11-round differential [2] with probability 2^{-122} and

E. A. Quaglia (Ed.): IMACC 2023, LNCS 14421, pp. 80–95, 2024.
https://doi.org/10.1007/978-3-031-47818-5_5

Table 1. Main cryptanalytic results on FBC

Cipher	Attack Type	Rounds	Data	Memory	Time	Source
FBC128-128	Linear	11	2^{84}KP	2^{32} Bytes	$2^{112.54}$Enc.	[13]
	Differential	12	2^{122}CP	2^{64} Bytes	$2^{93.41}$Enc.	[13]
	Impossible differential	11	2^{127}CP	2^{160} Bytes	$2^{94.54}$Enc.	[13]
		13	2^{126}CP	2^{52} Bytes	$2^{122.96}$Enc.	[16]
	Rectangle	14	$2^{126.17}$CP	$2^{133.17}$ Bytes	$2^{126.59}$Enc.	Sect. 3.2
FBC128-256	Rectangle	13	$2^{117.67}$CP	$2^{118.67}$ Bytes	$2^{243.97}$Enc.	[13]
		15	$2^{126.17}$CP	$2^{133.17}$ Bytes	$2^{252.29}$Enc	Sect. 3.3
FBC256	Rectangle	19	$2^{231.75}$CP	$2^{239.75}$ Bytes	$2^{231.83}$Enc	Sect. 4.2

KP: Known plaintexts; CP: Chosen plaintexts.

a 12-round differential attack on FBC128-128, a 10-round linear approximation [11] with bias 2^{-42} and an 11-round linear attack on FBC128-128, a 7-round impossible differential [3,8] and an 11-round impossible differential attack on FBC128-128, and a 12-round boomerang [15] distinguisher with probability $2^{-235.34}$ (more specifically, an amplified boomerang [6] or rectangle [1] distinguisher) and a 13-round boomerang attack on FBC128-256. In 2022, Zhang et al. [16] described 7-round impossible differentials of FBC128 and an impossible differential attack on 13-round FBC128-128.

Being an extension to differential cryptanalysis [2], the boomerang attack [15] treats a block cipher as a cascade of two sub-ciphers and is based on the idea of using two short differentials with larger probabilities instead of a long differential with a smaller probability, under an adaptive chosen plaintext or ciphertext attack scenario. The amplified boomerang attack [6] and the rectangle attack [1] simplify the attack scenario of the boomerang attack to a chosen plaintext or ciphertext attack scenario under a uniformity assumption. The boomerang-style attacks can use more than two differentials, some for the first sub-cipher and the others for the other sub-cipher, and generally assume that the differentials for the sub-ciphers behave independently [7,12], although boomerang connectivity table tools [4,14] have recently been proposed for use under certain circumstances.

In this paper, we further analyse the security of the FBC block cipher against rectangle attack. First, we exploit a 12-round rectangle distinguisher with probability 2^{-234} on FBC128, and observe that during key-recovery phase the output difference of the 12-round distinguisher enables us to obtain preliminary satisfying ciphertext quartets efficiently by sorting the plaintext pairs according to the values of some nibble positions with a zero difference at the ciphertext side, and finally we can use the 12-round rectangle distinguisher to make key-recovery attacks on 14-round FBC128-128 and 15-round FBC128-256, breaking one or two more rounds than the best previously published cryptanalytic results on FBC128-128 and FBC128-256, respectively. Similarly, we exploit a 16-round rectangle distinguisher with probability 2^{-448} on FBC256 and use it to mount a key-recovery attack on 19-round FBC256. Table 1 summarises previous and our main cryptanalytic results on FBC. Our attacks are better than any previously published attacks on FBC in terms of the numbers of attacked rounds.

The remainder of the paper is organized as follows. In the next section, we give the notion used throughout this paper and briefly describe the FBC block cipher and Ren et al.'s 13-round FBC128-256 attack. We present our rectangle attacks on FBC128 and FBC256 in Sects. 3 and 4, respectively. Section 5 concludes this paper.

2 Preliminaries

In this section, we give the notation and briefly describe the FBC block cipher and Ren et al.'s boomerang attack on 13-round FBC128-256.

2.1 Notation

In all descriptions we assume that the bits of an n-bit value are numbered from 0 to $n-1$ from left to right, a number without a prefix represents a decimal number, a number with prefix $0x$ represents a hexadecimal number, and we use the following notation throughout this paper.

$\oplus$ bitwise logical exclusive XOR
$\lll$ left rotation of a bit string
$\star$ an arbitrary value of some length, where two values represented by the $\star$ symbol may be different
e   the base of the natural logarithm (e $= 2.71828\cdots$)

2.2 The FBC Block Cipher

The FBC block cipher employs a 4-branch generalised Feistel structure and has three versions: FBC128-128 with a 128-bit block size and key size, FBC128-256 with a 128-bit block size and a 256-bit key size, and FBC256 with a 256-bit block size and key size, and they have a total of 48, 64 and 80 rounds, respectively. Denote the input and output of the i-th round ($i \geq 0$) by $(X_i^0, X_i^1, X_i^2, X_i^3) \in (\mathbb{F}_2^b)^4$ and $(X_{i+1}^0, X_{i+1}^1, X_{i+1}^2, X_{i+1}^3) \in (\mathbb{F}_2^b)^4$ respectively, then the encryption process of the i-th round, as illustrated in Fig. 1, is as follows,

$$X_{i+1}^0 = \mathbf{F}(X_i^0, K_{2i}) \oplus X_i^1,$$
$$X_{i+1}^1 = \mathbf{F}(X_i^3, K_{2i+1}) \oplus X_i^2 \oplus X_i^0,$$
$$X_{i+1}^2 = \mathbf{F}(X_i^0, K_{2i}) \oplus X_i^1 \oplus X_i^3,$$
$$X_{i+1}^3 = \mathbf{F}(X_i^3, K_{2i+1}) \oplus X_i^2,$$

where b is 32 for FBC128 and 64 for FBC256, $\mathbf{F}$ is the round function, and K_{2i+1} and K_{2i} are round keys.

The round function $\mathbf{F}$ consists of the following three operations:

– Key Addition: Input is XORed with a round key to produce output u.

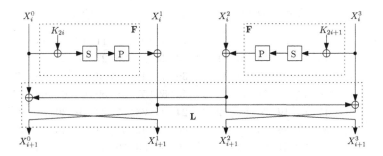

Fig. 1. One-round encryption of FBC

Table 2. The S-box of FBC

x	0	1	2	3	4	5	6	7	8	9	10	11	12	13	14	15
$S(x)$	5	10	15	4	9	14	11	8	2	7	12	13	3	6	1	0

– Column Transform S: Representing u as $u = (u_0\|u_1\|u_2\|u_3)$, apply the same 4×4-bit bijective S-box S 8 or 16 times in parallel to u to produce output $v = (v_0\|v_1\|v_2\|v_3)$ as $(v_{0,j}\|v_{1,j}\|v_{2,j}\|v_{3,j}) = S(u_{0,j}\|u_{1,j}\|u_{2,j}\|u_{3,j})$, where u_i and v_i are 8-bit for FBC128 and 16-bit for FBC256, and $u_{i,j}$ and $v_{i,j}$ are respectively the j-th bit of u_i and v_i ($0 \le i \le 3$, $0 \le j \le 7$ for FBC128 and $0 \le j \le 15$ for FBC256). The S-box specification is given in Table 2.
– Row Transform P: Given input v, the output z is computed as $z = v \oplus (v \lll 3) \oplus (v \lll 10)$ for FBC128, and $z = v \oplus (v \lll 17) \oplus (v \lll 58)$ for FBC256.

At last, to simplify our subsequent descriptions and cryptanalysis, we denote by **L** the linear operation except the F layer in a round, as shown in Fig. 1, and give the details of the Row Transform of FBC128 and FBC256 in Tables 3 and 4, respectively.

Table 3. Details of row transform of FBC128

v	0	1	2	3	4	5	6	7
	8	9	10	11	12	13	14	15
	16	17	18	19	20	21	22	23
	24	25	26	27	28	29	30	31
$v \lll 3$	3	4	5	6	7	8	9	10
	11	12	13	14	15	16	17	18
	19	20	21	22	23	24	25	26
	27	28	29	30	31	0	1	2
$v \lll 10$	10	11	12	13	14	15	16	17
	18	19	20	21	22	23	24	25
	26	27	28	29	30	31	0	1
	2	3	4	5	6	7	8	9

Table 4. Details of row transform of FBC256

v	0	1	2	3	4	5	6	7	8	9	10	11	12	13	14	15
	16	17	18	19	20	21	22	23	24	25	26	27	28	29	30	31
	32	33	34	35	36	37	38	39	40	41	42	43	44	45	46	47
	48	49	50	51	52	53	54	55	56	57	58	59	60	61	62	63
$v \lll 17$	17	18	19	20	21	22	23	24	25	26	27	28	29	30	31	32
	33	34	35	36	37	38	39	40	41	42	43	44	45	46	47	48
	49	50	51	52	53	54	55	56	57	58	59	60	61	62	63	0
	1	2	3	4	5	6	7	8	9	10	11	12	13	14	15	16
$v \lll 58$	58	59	60	61	62	63	0	1	2	3	4	5	6	7	8	9
	10	11	12	13	14	15	16	17	18	19	20	21	22	23	24	25
	26	27	28	29	30	31	32	33	34	35	36	37	38	39	40	41
	42	43	44	45	46	47	48	49	50	51	52	53	54	55	56	57

2.3   Ren et al.'s Boomerang Attack on 13-Round FBC128-256

Ren et al.'s boomerang attack on 13-round FBC128-256 [13] is actually an amplified boomerang or rectangle attack, which is based on a 12-round (amplified boomerang or rectangle) distinguisher with $2^{-235.34}$. The 12-round distinguisher is made up of two groups of 6-round differentials, where the group of 6-round differentials $\Delta\alpha \to \Delta\beta'$ for Rounds 0–5 have the same input difference $\alpha = 0x00000000000000000100020801000000$ but different output differences β': 4096 β' with probability 2^{-34}, 204800 β' with probability 2^{-36} and 966656 β' with probability 2^{-38}, and the group of 6-round differentials $\Delta\gamma' \to \Delta\delta$ for Rounds 6–11 have the same output difference δ but different input differences γ', which are similar to the 6-round differentials $\Delta\alpha \to \Delta\beta'$ in the decryption direction. As a result, they obtained a 12-round distinguisher with probability $[4096 \times (2^{-34})^2 + 204800 \times (2^{-36})^2 + 966656 \times (2^{-38})^2] \times [4096 \times (2^{-34})^2 + 204800 \times (2^{-36})^2 + 966656 \times (2^{-38})^2] \times 2^{-128} \approx 2^{-107.34} \times 2^{-128} = 2^{-235.34}$ by Biham et al.'s probability formula $\left(\sqrt{\sum_{\beta'} Pr^2[\alpha \to \beta']} \cdot \sqrt{\sum_{\gamma'} Pr^2[\gamma' \to \delta]}\right)^2 \times 2^{-n}$ of [1] (n is block size), and finally they appended one round at the end of this 12-round distinguisher to attack 13-round FBC128-256 in the following procedure:

1. Choose $2^{117.67}$ plaintext pairs with difference α, and get the corresponding ciphertext pairs.
2. Guess the round key in Round 12, partially decrypt every ciphertext pair to get the corresponding intermediate values immediately after Round 11, XOR each of them with δ, and store the resulting pair in a table.
3. Partially decrypt every ciphertext pair with the round key guessed in Step 2 to get the corresponding intermediate values immediately after Round 11, and check whether the resulting pair is in the table of Step 2. If there is a match, the guessed round key may be correct, since it is expected that there is $(2^{117.67})^2 \times 2^{-235.34} = 1$ satisfying quartet under the correct key.

3   Rectangle Attacks on 14-Round FBC128-128 and 15-Round FBC128-256

In this section, we describe a 12-round rectangle distinguisher with probability 2^{-234} of FBC128, and present rectangle attacks on 14-round FBC128-128 and 15-round FBC128-256.

3.1   A 12-Round Rectangle Distinguisher with Probability 2^{-234} of FBC128

We exploit a 12-round rectangle distinguisher with probability 2^{-234} for FBC128, which has a slightly larger probability than Ren et al.'s. Our 12-round distinguisher is made up of a group of 6-round differentials $\Delta\alpha \rightarrow \Delta\beta'$ for the first 6 rounds and a group of 6-round differentials $\Delta\gamma' \rightarrow \Delta\delta$ for the last 6 rounds, here the 6-round differentials $\Delta\alpha \rightarrow \Delta\beta'$ have the same input difference $\alpha = 0x0000000000000000008000042080000000$ but different output differences β': 256 β' with probability 2^{-32} and $7 \times 2^{10} = 7168$ β' with probability 2^{-33}, and the 6-round differentials $\Delta\gamma' \rightarrow \Delta\delta$ have the same output difference $\delta = 0x0800000008000042000000008000042$ but different input differences γ', which are similar to the 6-round differentials $\Delta\alpha \rightarrow \Delta\beta'$ in the decryption direction. Table 5 gives a 6-round differential $\Delta\alpha \rightarrow \Delta\beta'$ with probability 2^{-32}, and Table 6 gives a 6-round differential $\Delta\alpha \rightarrow \Delta\beta'$ with probability 2^{-33}. The other 6-round differentials $\Delta\alpha \rightarrow \Delta\beta'$ can be easily obtained by changing the output difference of the last round of one of the two 6-round differentials of Tables 5 and 6. The difference distribution table (DDT) of the FBC S-box is given as Table 7 in the appendix.

Hence, the 12-round rectangle distinguisher has a probability of $[256 \times (2^{-32})^2 + 7168 \times (2^{-33})^2] \times [256 \times (2^{-32})^2 + 7168 \times (2^{-33})^2] \times 2^{-128} = 2^{-106} \times 2^{-128} = 2^{-234}$.

3.2   Attacking 14-Round FBC128-128

We can attack 14-round FBC128-128 by appending one round respectively at the beginning and end of the above 12-round rectangle distinguisher. We assume the attacked 14 rounds are Rounds 0–13, and the 12-round distinguisher is used from Rounds 1–12, as illustrated in Fig. 2. The attack procedure is as follows.

1. By the S-box DDT in Table 7, we have $DDT(0x8, 0x8) = DDT(0x8, 0xA) = DDT(0x2, 0x2) = DDT(0x2, 0x6) = DDT(0x2, 0xA) = DDT(0x2, 0xE) = DDT(0x4, 0x1) = DDT(0x4, 0x4) = DDT(0x4, 0xC) = DDT(0x4, 0xD) = 4$ and $DDT(0x8, 0x3) = DDT(0x8, 0x7) = DDT(0x8, 0x9) = DDT(0x8, 0xD) = 2$ under the notation $DDT(\Delta a, \Delta b) = \#\{x | S(x) \oplus S(x \oplus a) = b\}$. Thus, given the input difference α to Round 1 from the 12-round distinguisher, there are $6 \times 4 \times 4 \times 6 \approx 2^{9.17}$ possible input differences to Round 0, which we denote by Δ_j ($j = 0, 1, \cdots, 2^{9.17} - 1$). We choose $2^{117} \times 2^{9.17} = 2^{126.17}$ plaintext pairs $(P_i, P_{i,j})$ such that $P_{i,j} = P_i \oplus \Delta_j$, and obtain their ciphertext

Table 5. A 6-round differential with probability 2^{-32} of FBC128

Round	ΔX^0	ΔX^1	Prob	ΔX^2	ΔX^3	Prob
Round 1	$0x00000000$	$0x00000000$		$0x08000042$	$0x08000000$	
→ S box	$0x00000000$		1		$0x08000000$	2^{-2}
→ P	$0x00000000$				$0x08000042$	
Round 2	$0x00000000$	$0x00000000$		$0x08000000$	$0x00000000$	
→ S box	$0x00000000$		1		$0x00000000$	1
→ P	$0x00000000$				$0x00000000$	
Round 3	$0x00000000$	$0x08000000$		$0x00000000$	$0x08000000$	
→ S box	$0x00000000$				$0x08000000$	2^{-2}
→ P	$0x00000000$				$0x08000042$	
Round 4	$0x08000000$	$0x08000042$		$0x00000000$	$0x08000042$	
→ S box	$0x01000000$		2^{-2}		$0x01000024$	2^{-6}
→ P	$0x08000042$				$0x08040100$	
Round 5	$0x00000000$	$0x00040100$		$0x08000042$	$0x08040100$	
→ S box	$0x00000000$				$0x08010100$	2^{-6}
→ P	$0x00000000$				$0x10190142$	
Round 6	$0x00040100$	$0x18190100$		$0x08000000$	$0x18190100$	
→S box	$0x00020800$		2^{-4}		$0x18120100$	2^{-10}
→ P	$0x421C0100$				$0xB90A090A$	
Output difference	$0x5A050000$	$0xB10E080A$		$0x421C0100$	$0xB10A090A$	

Table 6. A 6-round differential with probability 2^{-33} of FBC128

Round	ΔX^0	ΔX^1	Prob	ΔX^2	ΔX^3	Prob
Round 1	$0x00000000$	$0x00000000$		$0x08000042$	$0x08000000$	
→ S box	$0x00000000$		1		$0x08000000$	2^{-2}
→ P	$0x00000000$				$0x08000042$	
Round 2	$0x00000000$	$0x00000000$		$0x08000000$	$0x00000000$	
→ S box	$0x00000000$		1		$0x00000000$	1
→ P	$0x00000000$				$0x00000000$	
Round 3	$0x00000000$	$0x08000000$		$0x00000000$	$0x08000000$	
→ S box	$0x00000000$				$0x08000000$	2^{-2}
→ P	$0x00000000$				$0x08000042$	
Round 4	$0x08000000$	$0x08000042$		$0x00000000$	$0x08000042$	
→ S box	$0x01000000$		2^{-2}		$0x01000024$	2^{-6}
→ P	$0x08000042$				$0x08040100$	
Round 5	$0x00000000$	$0x00040100$		$0x08000042$	$0x08040100$	
→ S box	$0x00000000$				$0x08040100$	2^{-6}
→ P	$0x00000000$				$0x4A1C0142$	
Round 6	$0x00040100$	$0x421C0100$		$0x08000000$	$0x421C0100$	
→S box	$0x00020800$		2^{-4}		$0x18120100$	2^{-11}
→ P	$0x421C0100$				$0xB90A090A$	
Output difference	$0x00000000$	$0x88008288$		$0x421C0100$	$0x88048388$	

pairs $(C_i, C_{i,j})$, where $i = 0, 1, \cdots, 2^{117}-1$. Clearly, $P_i \oplus P_{i,j} = (0x080000000\star 0000 \star \star 0 \star 0 \star \star \star \star \star 08000042)$.

2. Store $(C_i, C_{i,j})$ into a hash table indexed by $(\mathbf{L}^{-1}(C_i)[0, 2-8, 10-13, 16, 18, 24, 26-29], \mathbf{L}^{-1}(C_{i,j})[0, 2-8, 10-13, 16, 18, 24, 26-29])$, that is, nibbles $(0, 2-8, 10-13, 16, 18, 24, 26-29)$ of $\mathbf{L}^{-1}(C_i)$ and $\mathbf{L}^{-1}(C_{i,j})$, store also

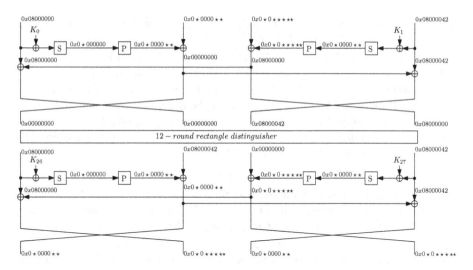

Fig. 2. Rectangle attack on 14-round FBC128-128

$(C_{i,j}, C_i)$ into this hash table indexed by $(\mathbf{L}^{-1}(C_{i,j})[0, 2-8, 10-13, 16, 18, 24, 26-29], \mathbf{L}^{-1}(C_i)[0, 2-8, 10-13, 16, 18, 24, 26-29])$, and obtain preliminary satisfying ciphertext quartets $((C_a, C_b), (C_c, C_d))$ such that $\mathbf{L}^{-1}(C_a)[0, 2-8, 10-13, 16, 18, 24, 26-29] = \mathbf{L}^{-1}(C_c)[0, 2-8, 10-13, 16, 18, 24, 26-29]$ and $\mathbf{L}^{-1}(C_b)[0, 2-8, 10-13, 16, 18, 24, 26-29] = \mathbf{L}^{-1}(C_d)[0, 2-8, 10-13, 16, 18, 24, 26-29]$, by accessing every table entry to get the preliminary satisfying ciphertext quartets and removing their actually identical counterparts at the corresponding entries. (Note that $((C_{i_0}, C_{i_0, j_0}), (C_{i_1}, C_{i_1, j_1}))$ and $((C_{i_0}, C_{i_0, j_0}), (C_{i_1, j_1}, C_{i_1}))$ are different quartets, but $((C_{i_0, j_0}, C_{i_0}), (C_{i_1, j_1}, C_{i_1}))$ and $((C_{i_0}, C_{i_0, j_0}), (C_{i_1}, C_{i_1, j_1}))$ are actually identical quartets, more specifically, two ciphertext pairs (C_a, C_b) and (C_c, C_d) under a table index constitute a preliminary satisfying ciphertext quartet $((C_a, C_b), (C_c, C_d))$, but this quartet appears pairwise with its actually identical counterpart $((C_b, C_a), (C_d, C_c))$ in the whole table, and the entry of the quartet $((C_b, C_a), (C_d, C_c))$ can be immediately determined from the entry of the quartet $((C_a, C_b), (C_c, C_d))$, so it takes only an access to remove a counterpart.) As a result, it is expected that there are approximately $(2^{126.17})^2 \times (2^{-19 \times 4})^2 = 2^{100.34}$ preliminary satisfying ciphertext quartets $((C_a, C_b), (C_c, C_d))$.

3. Check whether the $2^{100.34}$ preliminary quartets $((C_a, C_b), (C_c, C_d))$ meet $\mathbf{L}^{-1}(C_a) \oplus \mathbf{L}^{-1}(C_c) = 0x080000000 \star 0000 \star \star 0 \star 0 \star \star \star \star \star 08000042$ and $\mathbf{L}^{-1}(C_b) \oplus \mathbf{L}^{-1}(C_d) = 0x080000000 \star 0000 \star \star 0 \star 0 \star \star \star \star 08000042$, and keep only the satisfying quartets. It is expected that there remain $2^{100.34} \times (2^{-4 \times 4})^2 = 2^{68.34}$ satisfying quartets $((C_a, C_b), (C_c, C_d))$.

4. Guess $(K_{26}[1], K_{27}[1, 6, 7])$, and do as follows.
   (a) Partially decrypt every remaining quartet $((C_a, C_b), (C_c, C_d))$ to check whether both (C_a, C_c) and $(C_b, C_d))$ produce the difference δ immediately before Round 13. It is expected that there remains $2^{68.34} \times (2^{-9 \times 4})^2 =$

$2^{-3.66} < 1$ satisfying quartet $((C_a, C_b), (C_c, C_d))$ for every key guess, and $2^{16} \times [1 - \binom{2^{68.34}}{0}(2^{-9 \times 4 \times 2})^0(1 - 2^{-9 \times 4 \times 2})^{2^{68.34}}] \approx 2^{16} \times 2^{-3.71} = 2^{12.29}$ guesses of $(K_{26}[1], K_{27}[1, 6, 7])$ have at least one remaining quartet.

(b) For every remaining quartet $((C_a, C_b), (C_c, C_d))$ (if any), get the corresponding $((P_a, P_b), (P_c, P_d))$ and extract the subkeys $(K_0[1], K_1[1, 6, 7])$ such that $((P_a, P_b), (P_c, P_d))$ produces the difference α immediately after Round 0. (Skip this quartet if there is no satisfying $(K_0[1], K_1[1, 6, 7])$.)

5. For every remaining $(K_0[1], K_1[1, 6, 7])$, exhaustively search the remaining 112 key bits to determine the 128-bit user key.

The attack requires $2^{126.17} + 2^{117} \approx 2^{126.17}$ chosen plaintexts. The memory complexity of the attack is dominated by Step 2, which is $2^{126.17} \times 4 \times 16 \times 2 = 2^{133.17}$ bytes. The time complexity of the attack is dominated by the encryptions of the $2^{126.17}$ chosen plaintexts and Steps 2 and 5, Step 2 has a time complexity of $2^{126.17} \times 2 = 2^{127.17}$ memory accesses, which is equivalent to $\frac{2^{127.17}}{14 \times 2} \approx 2^{122.36}$ 14-round FBC128-128 encryptions under an extreme approximation that a one-round FBC128-128 encryption is approximated as two table lookups, Step 5 has a time complexity of $2^{12.29} \times 2^{112} = 2^{124.29}$ 14-round FBC128-128 encryptions, and thus the attack has a total time complexity of $2^{126.17} + 2^{122.36} + 2^{124.29} \approx 2^{126.59}$ 14-round FBC128-128 encryptions. The attack has an expected success probability of approximately $1 - (1 - 2^{-234})^{2^{234}} \approx 1 - e^{-1} \approx 63\%$.

Notice that an usual process for rectangle attack is to check whether the two ciphertext pairs (C_{i_0}, C_{i_1}) and $(C_{i_0, j_0}, C_{i_1, j_1})$ out of a ciphertext quartet $((C_{i_0}, C_{i_1}), (C_{i_0, j_0}, C_{i_1, j_1}))$ could produce the expected δ difference, but in this 14-round FBC128-128 attack, some nibble positions immediately before the **L** operation of Round 13 have a determinate zero difference, so $\mathbf{L}^{-1}(C_{i_0})[0, 2 - 8, 10 - 13, 16, 18, 24, 26 - 29] \oplus \mathbf{L}^{-1}(C_{i_1})[0, 2 - 8, 10 - 13, 16, 18, 24, 26 - 29] = \mathbf{L}^{-1}(C_{i_0, j_0})[0, 2 - 8, 10 - 13, 16, 18, 24, 26 - 29] \oplus \mathbf{L}^{-1}(C_{i_1, j_1})[0, 2 - 8, 10 - 13, 16, 18, 24, 26 - 29] = 0$ leads to $(\mathbf{L}^{-1}(C_{i_0})[0, 2 - 8, 10 - 13, 16, 18, 24, 26 - 29], \mathbf{L}^{-1}(C_{i_0, j_0})[0, 2 - 8, 10 - 13, 16, 18, 24, 26 - 29]) = (\mathbf{L}^{-1}(C_{i_1})[0, 2 - 8, 10 - 13, 16, 18, 24, 26 - 29], \mathbf{L}^{-1}(C_{i_1, j_1})[0, 2 - 8, 10 - 13, 16, 18, 24, 26 - 29])$. This is why we can filter out preliminary satisfying ciphertext quartets efficiently by sorting the ciphertext pairs of the chosen plaintext pairs as described in Step 2.

Note that in Step 2 we can make a more refined filtering by further sorting the plaintext pairs according to the values of some nibble positions with a non-zero difference at the ciphertext side, but this is not necessary from the perspective of time complexity.

3.3 Attacking 15-Round FBC128-256

We can attack 15-round FBC128-256, by appending one round at the end of the above 14-round FBC128-128 attack. As illustrated in Fig. 3, we assume the attacked 15 rounds are Rounds 0–14, the 12-round distinguisher is used from Rounds 1–12, and the attack procedure is as follows.

1. Same as Step 1 of the above 14-round FBC128-128 attack.
2. Store $(C_i, C_{i,j})$ into a hash table indexed by $(\mathbf{L}^{-1}(C_i)[0, 2-5, 8, 10, 24, 26]$, $\mathbf{L}^{-1}(C_{i,j})[0, 2-5, 8, 10, 24, 26])$, that is, nibbles $(0, 2-5, 8, 10, 24, 26)$ of $\mathbf{L}^{-1}(C_i)$ and $\mathbf{L}^{-1}(C_{i,j})$, store also $(C_{i,j}, C_i)$ into this hash table indexed by $(\mathbf{L}^{-1}(C_{i,j})[0, 2-5, 8, 10, 24, 26], \mathbf{L}^{-1}(C_i)[0, 2-5, 8, 10, 24, 26])$, and obtain preliminary satisfying ciphertext quartets $((C_a, C_b), (C_c, C_d))$ such that $\mathbf{L}^{-1}(C_a)[0, 2-5, 8, 10, 24, 26] = \mathbf{L}^{-1}(C_c)[0, 2-5, 8, 10, 24, 26]$ and $\mathbf{L}^{-1}(C_b)[0, 2-5, 8, 10, 24, 26] = \mathbf{L}^{-1}(C_d)[0, 2-5, 8, 10, 24, 26]$. It is expected that there are $(2^{126.17})^2 \times (2^{-9 \times 4})^2 = 2^{180.34}$ preliminary satisfying ciphertext quartets $((C_a, C_b), (C_c, C_d))$.
3. Guess $(K_{28}[1, 6, 7], K_{29}[1, 3-7])$, and do as follows.
   (a) Partially decrypt each of the $2^{180.34}$ preliminary quartets $((C_a, C_b), (C_a, C_b))$ to check whether both (C_a, C_c) and (C_b, C_d) produce the difference $0x080000000\star0000\star\star0\star0\star\star\star\star\star08000042$ immediately before the $\mathbf{L}$ operation of Round 13. It is expected that there remain $2^{180.34} \times (2^{-14 \times 4})^2 = 2^{68.34}$ satisfying quartets $((C_a, C_b), (C_c, C_d))$ for every key guess.
   (b) Guess $(K_{26}[1], K_{27}[1, 6, 7], K_{28}[3, 4], K_{29}[0, 2])$, partially decrypt every remaining quartet $((C_a, C_b), (C_c, C_d))$ to check whether both (C_a, C_c) and $(C_b, C_d))$ produce the difference δ immediately before Round 13. It is expected that there are $2^{68.34} \times (2^{-9 \times 4})^2 = 2^{-3.66} < 1$ satisfying quartet $((C_a, C_b), (C_c, C_d))$ for every key guess and $2^{68} \times [1 - \binom{2^{68.34}}{0} (2^{-9 \times 4 \times 2})^0 (1 - 2^{-9 \times 4 \times 2})^{2^{68.34}}] \approx 2^{16} \times 2^{-3.71} = 2^{64.29}$ guesses of $(K_{26}[1], K_{27}[1, 6, 7], K_{28}[1, 3, 4, 6, 7], K_{29})$ have at least one remaining quartet.
   (c) For every remaining quartet $((C_a, C_b), (C_c, C_d))$ (if any), get the corresponding $((P_a, P_b), (P_c, P_d))$ and extract the subkeys $(K_0[1], K_1[1, 6, 7])$ such that $((P_a, P_b), (P_c, P_d))$ produces the difference α immediately after Round 0. (Skip this quartet if there is no satisfying $(K_0[1], K_1[1, 6, 7])$.)
4. For every remaining $(K_{26}[1], K_{27}[1, 6, 7], K_{28}[1, 3, 4, 6, 7], K_{29})$, exhaustively search the remaining 188 key bits to determine the 256-bit user key.

The attack has a data complexity of approximately $2^{126.17}$ chosen plaintexts, a memory complexity of approximately $2^{126.17} \times 4 \times 16 \times 2 = 2^{133.17}$ bytes and a success probability of 63%. The time complexity of the attack is dominated by Step 4, which is $2^{64.29} \times 2^{188} = 2^{252.29}$ 15-round FBC128-256 encryptions.

4 Rectangle Attack on 19-Round FBC256

In this section, we describe a 16-round rectangle distinguisher with probability 2^{-448} of FBC256, and present a rectangle attack on 19-round FBC256.

4.1 A 16-Round Rectangle Distinguisher with Probability 2^{-448} of FBC256

The 16-round distinguisher is made up of two groups of 8-round differentials $\Delta\alpha \rightarrow \Delta\beta'$ for the first 8 rounds and a group of 8-round differentials $\Delta\gamma' \rightarrow \Delta\delta$ for the last 8 rounds, here the 8-round differentials $\Delta\alpha \rightarrow \Delta\beta'$

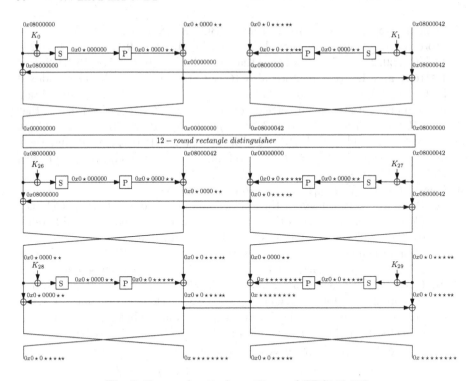

Fig. 3. Rectangle attack on 15-round FBC128-256

have the same input difference $\alpha = 0x08000000000000004800000800000000000$ 00000000008014800000800000000 but 2^6 different output differences β' with probability 2^{-51}, and the 8-round differentials $\Delta\gamma' \rightarrow \Delta\delta$ have the same output difference $\delta = 0x00000000000000000000000000000080148000$ 008000000000080000000000801 but 2^6 different input differences γ' with probability 2^{-51}, which are similar to the 8-round differentials $\Delta\alpha \rightarrow \Delta\beta'$ in the decryption direction. Hence, the 16-round rectangle distinguisher has a probability of $[2^6 \times (2^{-51})^2] \times [2^6 \times (2^{-51})^2] \times 2^{-256} = 2^{-448}$.

An 8-round differential $\Delta\alpha \rightarrow \Delta\beta'$ is described in detail in Table 8 in the appendix. The other 8-round differentials can be easily obtained by changing the output difference of the last round of the 8-round differential of Table 8.

4.2   Attacking 19-Round FBC256

We can attack 19-round FBC256 by appending one round at the beginning and two rounds at the end of the above 15-round rectangle distinguisher, and we assume the attacked 19 rounds are Rounds 0–18 and the 16-round distinguisher is used from Rounds 1–16, as illustrated in Fig. 4. Slightly different from the above 14-round FBC128-128 attack and 15-round FBC128-256 attack, here we use the early abort technique [9,10] for a reduced time complexity, by guessing

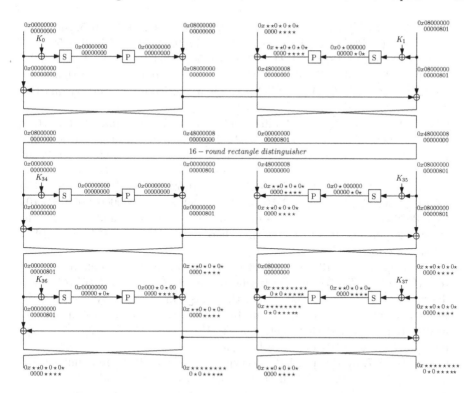

Fig. 4. Rectangle attack on 19-round FBC256

only a small fraction of the unknown required subkey bits at a time in Round 18, instead of guessing all of them at once.

1. By the S-box DDT in Table 7, we have $DDT(0x1, 0x1) = DDT(0x1, 0x5) = DDT(0x8, 0x8) = DDT(0x8, 0xA) = 4$ and $DDT(0x8, 0x3) = DDT(0x8, 0x7) = DDT(0x8, 0x9) = DDT(0x8, 0xD) = DDT(0x1, 0x3) = DDT(0x1, 0x7) = DDT(0x1, 0xB) = DDT(0x1, 0xF) = 2$. Thus, given the input difference α to Round 1 from the 16-round distinguisher, there are $6 \times 6 \times 6 \approx 2^{7.75}$ possible input differences to Round 0, which we denote by Δ_j ($j = 0, 1, \cdots, 2^{7.75} - 1$). We choose $2^{224} \times 2^{7.75} = 2^{231.75}$ plaintext pairs $(P_i, P_{i,j})$ such that $P_{i,j} = P_i \oplus \Delta_j$, and obtain their ciphertext pairs $(C_i, C_{i,j})$, where $i = 0, 1, \cdots, 2^{224} - 1$. Clearly, $P_i \oplus P_{i,j} = (0x000000000000000000080000000000$ $0000 \star \star 0 \star 0 \star 0 \star 0000 \star \star \star \star 0800000000000801)$.

2. Store $(C_i, C_{i,j})$ into a hash table indexed by $(\mathbf{L}^{-1}(C_i)[0 - 12, 14, 18, 20, 22, 24 - 27, 40, 42, 50, 52, 54, 56 - 59], \mathbf{L}^{-1}(C_{i,j})[0 - 12, 14, 18, 20, 22, 24 - 27, 40, 42, 50, 52, 54, 56 - 59])$, that is, nibbles $(0 - 12, 14, 18, 20, 22, 24 - 27, 40, 42, 50, 52, 54, 56 - 59)$ of $\mathbf{L}^{-1}(C_i)$ and $\mathbf{L}^{-1}(C_{i,j})$, store also $(C_{i,j}, C_i)$ into this table indexed by $(\mathbf{L}^{-1}(C_{i,j})[0 - 12, 14, 18, 20, 22, 24 - 27, 40, 42, 50, 52, 54, 56 - 59], \mathbf{L}^{-1}(C_i)[0 - 12, 14, 18, 20, 22, 24 - 27, 40, 42, 50, 52, 54, 56 - 59])$, and obtain preliminary quartets $((C_a, C_b), (C_c, C_d))$

such that $\mathbf{L}^{-1}(C_a)[0 - 12, 14, \; 18, 20, 22, 24 \; - \; 27, 40, 42, 50, 52, 54, 56 \; - 59] = \mathbf{L}^{-1}(C_c)[0 - 12, 14, 18, 20, 22, 24 - 27, 40, 42, 50, 52, 54, 56 - 59]$ and $\mathbf{L}^{-1}(C_b)[0-12, 14, 18, 20, 22, 24-27, 40, 42, \; 50, 52, 54, 56-59] = \mathbf{L}^{-1}(C_d)[0-12, 14, 18, 20, 22, 24 - 27, 40, 42, 50, 52, 54, 56 - 59]$. It is expected that there are $(2^{231.75})^2 \times (2^{-30 \times 4})^2 = 2^{223.5}$ preliminary satisfying ciphertext quartets $((C_a, C_b), (C_c, C_d))$.

3. Check whether the $2^{223.5}$ preliminary satisfying ciphertext quartets $((C_a, C_b), (C_c, C_d))$ meet $\mathbf{L}^{-1}(C_a)[0-12, 14, 18, 20, 22, 24-27, 40, 42, 50, 52, 54, 56-59] \oplus \mathbf{L}^{-1}(C_c)[0 - 12, 14, 18, 20, 22, 24 - 27, 40, 42, 50, 52, 54, 56 - 59] = 0x000000 0000000801\star\star0\star0\star0\star0000\star\star\star\star\star\star\star\star\star\star\star\star\star0\star0\star\star\star\star\star\star\star0\star0\star0\star0000\star\star\star\star$ and $\mathbf{L}^{-1}(C_b)[0 - 12, 14, 18, 20, 22, 24 - 27, 40, 42, 50, 52, 54, 56 - 59] \oplus \mathbf{L}^{-1}(C_b)[0 - 12, 14, 18, 20, 22, 24-27, 40, 42, 50, 52, 54, 56-59] = 0x0000000000000801\star\star0\star 0\star0\star0000\star\star\star\star\star\star\star\star\star\star\star\star\star0\star0\star\star\star\star\star\star\star0\star0\star0\star0000\star\star\star\star$, and keep only the satisfying quartets. It is expected that there remain $2^{223.5} \times (2^{-2 \times 4})^2 = 2^{207.5}$ satisfying quartets $((C_a, C_b), (C_c, C_d))$.

4. Guess $K_{37}[0, 1, 3, 12, 13]$, partially decrypt each of the $2^{207.5}$ remaining quartets $((C_a, C_b), (C_c, C_d))$ to check whether both (C_a, C_c) and (C_b, C_d) produce $\Delta X_{18}^2[0 - 3] = 0x0800$. (Note that this can be done by checking the two ciphertext pairs out of a quartet one after the other as introduced in [9].) It is expected that there remain $2^{207.5} \times (2^{-4 \times 4})^2 = 2^{175.5}$ satisfying $((C_a, C_b), (C_c, C_d))$ for every key guess.

5. Guess $K_{37}[5, 7, 14, 15]$, partially decrypt each of the $2^{175.5}$ remaining quartets $((C_a, C_b), (C_c, C_d))$ to check whether both (C_a, C_c) and (C_b, C_d) produce $\Delta X_{18}^2[4 - 7, 9, 11 - 15] = 0$. It is expected that there remain $2^{175.5} \times (2^{-10 \times 4})^2 = 2^{95.5}$ satisfying $((C_a, C_b), (C_c, C_d))$ for every key guess.

6. Guess $K_{36}[13, 15]$, partially decrypt each of the $2^{95.5}$ remaining quartets $((C_a, C_b), (C_c, C_d))$ to check whether both (C_a, C_c) and (C_b, C_d) produce $\Delta X_{18}^1 = \Delta X_{18}^3$. It is expected that there remain $2^{95.5} \times (2^{-9 \times 4})^2 = 2^{23.5}$ satisfying $((C_a, C_b), (C_c, C_d))$ for every key guess.

7. Guess $(K_{37}[2, 9, 11], K_{35}[1, 13, 15])$, partially decrypt each of the $2^{23.5}$ remaining quartets $((C_a, C_b), (C_c, C_d))$ to check whether both (C_a, C_c) and (C_b, C_d) produce $\Delta X_{17}^2 = 0x4800000800000000$. It is expected that there remains $2^{23.5} \times (2^{-9 \times 4})^2 = 2^{-48.5} < 1$ satisfying quartets for every key guess, and $2^{68} \times [1 - \binom{2^{23.5}}{0}(2^{-9 \times 4 \times 2})^0(1 - 2^{-9 \times 4 \times 2})^{2^{23.5}}] \approx 2^{68} \times 2^{-48.5} = 2^{19.5}$ guesses of $(K_{37}[0 - 3, 5, 7, 9, 11 - 15], K_{36}[13, 15], K_{35}[1, 13, 15])$ have at least one remaining quartet. For every remaining quartet $((C_a, C_b), (C_c, C_d))$ (if any), get the corresponding $((P_a, P_b), (P_c, P_d))$ and extract the subkeys $K_1[1, 13, 15]$ such that $((P_a, P_b), (P_c, P_d))$ produces the difference α immediately after Round 0. (Skip this quartet if there is no satisfying $K_1[1, 13, 15]$.)

8. For every remaining $(K_{37}[0 - 3, 5, 7, 9, 11 - 15], K_{36}[13, 15], K_{35}[1, 13, 15])$, exhaustively search the remaining 188 key bits to determine the 256-bit user key.

The attack has a data complexity of approximately $2^{231.75} + 2^{224} \approx 2^{231.75}$ chosen plaintexts, a memory complexity of approximately $2^{231.75} \times 4 \times 32 \times 2 = 2^{239.75}$ bytes and a success probability of $1 - (1 - 2^{-448})^{2^{448}} \approx 1 - e^{-1} \approx 63\%$.

The time complexity of the attack is dominated by the encryptions of the $2^{231.75}$ chosen plaintexts and Step 2, and Step 2 has a time complexity of $2^{231.75} \times 2 = 2^{232.75}$ memory accesses, which is equivalent to $\frac{2^{232.75}}{19 \times 2} \approx 2^{227.51}$ 19-round FBC256 encryptions under an extreme approximation that a one-round FBC256 encryption is approximated as two table lookups. Therefore, the attack has a total time complexity of $2^{231.75} + 2^{227.51} \approx 2^{231.83}$ 19-round FBC256 encryptions. Note that there are different data-memory-time tradeoffs and we can increase the success probability by using more chosen plaintexts.

5   Conclusion

The FBC block cipher is an award-winning algorithm of the recent Cryptographic Algorithm Design Competition in China. In this paper, we have presented rectangle attacks on 14-round FBC128-128, 15-round FBC128-256 and 19-round FBC256 to recover their respective user key. These are better than any previously published cryptanalytic results on FBC in terms of the numbers of attacked rounds. Like most cryptanalytic results on block ciphers, our attacks are theoretical in the sense of the independence and uniformity assumptions of rectangle attack, and they do not endanger the security of the full FBC cipher.

Acknowledgements. This work was supported by State Key Laboratory of Cryptology (No. MMKFKT202114). Jiqiang Lu was Qianjiang Special Expert of Hangzhou.

Appendix

Table 7. Difference distribution table of the FBC S-box

Input difference	0x0	0x1	0x2	0x3	0x4	0x5	0x6	0x7	0x8	0x9	0xA	0xB	0xC	0xD	0xE	0xF
0x0	16	0	0	0	0	0	0	0	0	0	0	0	0	0	0	0
0x1	0	4	0	2	0	4	0	2	0	0	0	2	0	0	0	2
0x2	0	0	4	0	0	0	4	0	0	0	4	0	0	0	4	0
0x3	0	4	0	2	0	4	0	2	0	0	0	2	0	0	0	2
0x4	0	4	0	0	4	0	0	0	0	0	0	0	4	4	0	0
0x5	0	0	0	2	4	0	0	2	0	0	0	2	4	0	0	2
0x6	0	0	2	2	0	0	2	2	0	0	2	2	0	0	2	2
0x7	0	4	2	0	0	0	2	0	0	0	2	0	0	4	2	0
0x8	0	0	0	2	0	0	0	2	4	2	4	0	0	2	0	0
0x9	0	0	4	0	0	0	0	0	4	2	0	2	0	2	0	2
0xA	0	0	0	2	0	0	0	2	4	2	0	0	0	2	4	0
0xB	0	0	0	0	0	0	4	0	4	2	0	2	0	2	0	2
0xC	0	0	0	0	2	2	2	2	0	2	0	2	2	0	2	0
0xD	0	0	0	2	2	2	2	0	0	2	0	0	2	0	2	2
0xE	0	0	2	2	2	2	0	0	0	2	2	0	2	0	0	2
0xF	0	0	2	0	2	2	0	2	0	2	2	2	2	0	0	0

Table 8. An 8-round differential with probability 2^{-51} of FBC256

Round	ΔX^0	ΔX^1	Pro	ΔX^2	ΔX^3	Prob
Round 1	0x08000000	0x48000008		0x00000000	0x48000008	
	00000000	00000000		00000801	00000000	
→S box	0x08000000		2^{-2}		0x48000008	2^{-6}
	00000000		1		00000000	1
→ P	0x48000008				0x08000000	
	00000000				00000801	
Round 2	0x00000000	0x00000000		0x48000008	0x08000000	
	00000000	00000000		00000000	00000000	
→S box	0x00000000		1		0x08000000	2^{-2}
	00000000		1		00000000	1
→ P	0x00000000				0x48000008	
	00000000				00000000	
Round 3	0x00000000	0x00000000		0x08000000	0x00000000	
	00000000	00000000		00000000	00000000	
→S box	0x00000000		1		0x00000000	1
	00000000		1		00000000	1
→ P	0x00000000				0x00000000	
	00000000				00000000	
Round 4	0x00000000	0x08000000		0x00000000	0x08000000	
	00000000	00000000		00000000	00000000	
→ S box	0x00000000		1		0x08000000	2^{-2}
	00000000		1		00000000	1
→ P	0x00000000				0x48000008	
	00000000				00000000	
Round 5	0x08000000	0x48000008		0x00000000	0x48000008	
	00000000	00000000		00000000	00000000	
→ S box	0x08000000		2^{-2}		0x48000008	2^{-6}
	00000000		1		00000000	1
→ P	0x48000008				0x08000000	
	00000000				00000801	
Round 6	0x00000000	0x00000000		0x48000008	0x08000000	
	00000000	00000801		00000000	00000801	
→ S box	0x00000000		1		0x08000000	2^{-2}
	00000000		1		00000801	2^{-4}
→ P	0x00000000				0x48010208	
	00000000				00004881	
Round 7	0x00000000	0x00010100		0x08000000	0x00010200	
	000000801	00004848		00000009	00004881	
→ S box	0x00000000		1		0x00010200	2^{-4}
	00000801		2^{-4}		00004881	2^{-8}
→ P	0x00010200				0x00000000	
	00004881				01000C01	
Round 8	0x00000000	0x08000000		0x00010200	0x08000000	
	00000000	01000400		00004881	01000C01	
→ S box	0x00000000		1		0x08000000	2^{-2}
	00000000		1		01000401	2^{-7}
→ P	0x00000000				0x48080208	
	00000000				81002480	
Output	0x08000000	0x48090008		0x00000000	0x48090008	
difference	01000400	81006C01		00000801	81006C01	

References

1. Biham, E., Dunkelman, O., Keller, N.: The rectangle attack rectangling the serpent. In: Pfitzmann, B. (ed.) EUROCRYPT 2001. LNCS, vol. 2045, pp. 340–357. Springer, Heidelberg (2001). https://doi.org/10.1007/3-540-44987-6_21
2. Biham, E., Shamir, A.: Differential Cryptanalysis of the Data Encryption Standard. Springer, New York (1993). https://doi.org/10.1007/978-1-4613-9314-6
3. Biham, E., Biryukov, A., Shamir, A.: Cryptanalysis of skipjack reduced to 31 rounds using impossible differentials. In: Stern, J. (ed.) EUROCRYPT 1999. LNCS, vol. 1592, pp. 12–23. Springer, Heidelberg (1999). https://doi.org/10.1007/3-540-48910-X_2
4. Cid, C., Huang, T., Peyrin, T., Sasaki, Y., Song, L.: Boomerang connectivity table: a new cryptanalysis tool. In: Nielsen, J.B., Rijmen, V. (eds.) EUROCRYPT 2018. LNCS, vol. 10821, pp. 683–714. Springer, Cham (2018). https://doi.org/10.1007/978-3-319-78375-8_22
5. Feng, X., et al.: On the lightweight block cipher FBC. J. Cryptol. Res. 6, 768–785 (2019)
6. Kelsey, J., Kohno, T., Schneier, B.: Amplified boomerang attacks against reduced-round MARS and serpent. In: Goos, G., Hartmanis, J., van Leeuwen, J., Schneier, B. (eds.) FSE 2000. LNCS, vol. 1978, pp. 75–93. Springer, Heidelberg (2001). https://doi.org/10.1007/3-540-44706-7_6
7. Kim, J., Hong, S., Preneel, B., Biham, E., Dunkelman, O., Keller, N.: Related-key boomerang and rectangle attacks: theory and experimental analysis. In: IEEE Transactions on Information Theory, vol. 4948–4966. IEEE (2012)
8. Knudsen, L.R.: DEAL–a 128-bit block cipher. Technical report, Department of Informatics, University of Bergen, Norway (1998)
9. Lu, J., Kim, J.: Attacking 44 rounds of the SHACAL-2 block cipher using related-key rectangle cryptanalysis. IEICE Trans. Fundam. Electron. Commun. Comput. Sci. 91-A(9), 2588–2596 (2008)
10. Lu, J., Kim, J., Keller, N., Dunkelman, O.: Improving the efficiency of impossible differential cryptanalysis of reduced Camellia and MISTY1. In: Malkin, T. (ed.) CT-RSA 2008. LNCS, vol. 4964, pp. 370–386. Springer, Heidelberg (2008). https://doi.org/10.1007/978-3-540-79263-5_24
11. Matsui, M.: Linear cryptanalysis method for DES cipher. In: Helleseth, T. (ed.) EUROCRYPT 1993. LNCS, vol. 765, pp. 386–397. Springer, Heidelberg (1994). https://doi.org/10.1007/3-540-48285-7_33
12. Murphy, S.: The return of the cryptographic boomerang. In: IEEE Transactions on Information Theory, vol. 57, no. 4, pp. 2517–2521. IEEE (2011)
13. Ren, B., Chen, J., Zhou, S., Jin, X., Xia, Z., Liang, K.: Cryptanalysis of raindrop and FBC. In: Liu, J.K., Huang, X. (eds.) NSS 2019. LNCS, vol. 11928, pp. 536–551. Springer, Cham (2019). https://doi.org/10.1007/978-3-030-36938-5_33
14. Song, L., Qin, X., Hu, L.: Boomerang connectivity table revisited. In: Application to SKINNY and AES. IACR Transactions on Symmetric Cryptology, vol. 2019, no. 1, pp. 118–141. Spring (2019)
15. Wagner, D.: The boomerang attack. In: Knudsen, L. (ed.) FSE 1999. LNCS, vol. 1636, pp. 156–170. Springer, Heidelberg (1999). https://doi.org/10.1007/3-540-48519-8_12
16. Zhang, Y., Liu, G., Li, C., Shen, X.: Impossible differential cryptanalysis of FBC-128. J. Inf. Secur. Appl. 69, 103279 (2022). Elsevier

Zero-Knowledge Protocols

zk-SNARKs from Codes with Rank Metrics

Xuan-Thanh Do[1]($\boxtimes$)(iD), Dang-Truong Mac[1,2](iD), and Quoc-Huy Vu[2](iD)

[1] Institute of Cryptography Science and Technology, Hanoi, Vietnam
`dxthanh@bcy.gov.vn`
[2] Léonard de Vinci Pôle Universitaire, Research Center, Paris-La Défense, France

Abstract. Succinct non-interactive zero-knowledge arguments of knowledge (zk-SNARKs) are a type of non-interactive proof system enabling efficient privacy-preserving proofs of membership for NP languages. A great deal of works has studied candidate constructions that are secure against quantum attackers, which are based on either lattice assumptions, or post-quantum collision-resistant hash functions. In this paper, we propose a code-based zk-SNARK scheme, whose security is based on the rank support learning (RSL) problem, a variant of the random linear code decoding problem in the rank metric. Our construction follows the general framework of Gennaro *et al.* (CCS'18), which is based on square span programs (SSPs). Due to the fundamental differences between the hardness assumptions, our proof of security cannot apply the techniques from the lattice-based constructions, and indeed, it distinguishes itself by the use of techniques from coding theory. We also provide the scheme with a set of concrete parameters.

Keywords: Code-based Cryptography · Rank support learning problem · Square span programs · zk-SNARKs

1 Introduction

Zero-knowledge proof systems [25], since its first appearance in 1985, have been become the cornerstone of cryptography. They are an essential component of many privacy-preserving cryptographic systems, including credentials and digital currencies [3,4,12,13,20] as well as group signatures [8,9,15,19] and verifiable computation [10,22,23]. In a zero-knowledge proof of knowledge system for an NP relation $\mathcal{R}$, a prover can convince a verifier that a statement is true without revealing anything more about the statement to the verifier. For practical applications, succinct non-interactive zero-knowledge arguments of knowledge (zk-SNARKs) [28,31] are more desirable: we additionally require that (*i*) the proof should consist of a single message from the prover to the verifier (non-interactivity); (*ii*) the length of the proof and the verification complexity is sublinear (ideally, polylogarithmic) in the size of the circuit computing $\mathcal{R}$ (succinctness); and (*iii*) the proof also guarantees that the prover knows the witness (argument of knowledge).

E. A. Quaglia (Ed.): IMACC 2023, LNCS 14421, pp. 99–119, 2024.
https://doi.org/10.1007/978-3-031-47818-5_6

Constructions of succinct non-interactive zero-knowledge can be based on numerous different assumptions, of which one may name collision-resistant hash functions [5,16], the discrete logarithm assumption [11], various pairing-based assumptions [26], and lattice-based assumptions [24,27]. On the other hand, the advancing threat of quantum computers has given tremendous stimulant to the cryptographic community to put more effort into cryptographic constructions that would plausibly withstand the power of quantum attacks. However, present post-quantum zk-SNARKs are only known from hash functions and lattice-based assumptions.

Our Result. In this work, following the method of [24], we introduce the first (designated-verifier) zk-SNARK scheme in the rank metric context. Prior to this work, there has been no construction in the code-based cryptography realm, so the construction herein could be viewed as the first. Furthermore, being based on code-based assumptions with rank metrics, our scheme is plausibly considered to be secure under quantum attacks. We note that the work of Lipmaa [29] makes use of error-correcting codes to improve the performance of span programs and does not concern with code-based assumptions.

Overview of Our Technique. Our starting point is the framework of Gennaro *et al.* [24]. Conceptually, based on the techniques of [17] and [23], the framework of [24] uses square span programs to characterize the complexity class NP, leading to a simpler and faster designated-verifier zk-SNARK. The main technical challenge in the framework of [24] is the growth of noise of the lattice-based homomorphic operations. As mentioned there, this growth might leak information of the witness to the verifier, thus violate the zero-knowledge property. Fortunately, in the asset of lattice-based techniques, the so-called noise-smudging technique can be used to overcome this leakage problem. The idea is that after doing homomorphic addition, a noise with much larger weight is added to the computed one, thus, the final noise is dominated by that of the adding noise. (One might think of this technique as hiding "leaves" in "forest.") This technical challenge, resolved by smudging, also causes the setting of the common reference string to become involved, that is, the natures of encodings are not the same: some having small noise while others requiring much larger one. The reason underlying this setting is to guarantee success of the reduction.

The naive scheme obtained when one carries out the construction to the rank metric context is even worse since the noise grows linearly with respect to the number of homomorphic operations. And in order to be able to decrypt these ciphertexts, the length of the public code in used must be very large (and thus, the degree of extension field as well) causing parameters of the whole system to be out of concern. (We assume one uses the rank-quasi cyclic (RQC) encryption scheme to design the underlying encoding scheme). Out of this situation, a natural question arises:

Can we design a SNARK in code-based cryptography (and even in lattice-based cryptography) without using the smudging technique?

We put forth effort to resolve this question in code-based cryptography by making use of the rank support learning problem. We now recall the main technical ingredients of [24]'s framework, which lie in the way the common reference string (CRS) is constructed. In particular, the CRS in the construction of Gennaro *et al.* consists of encoding elements together with the description of a square span program which computes the statement and public parameters of some additively homomorphic "noisy" encoding scheme. In [24], their encoding scheme is instantiated from lattice-based assumption. Let E denote this encoding scheme. By examining the form of the CRS, we make the observation that the encodings therein could be divided into three groups. The first group consists of encodings of powers of a hidden element, say, $\mathsf{E}(1), \mathsf{E}(s), \ldots, \mathsf{E}(s^d)$, where s is kept secret. The second group consists of encodings of elements which are resulted from the first group by a common mask, *i.e.*, $\mathsf{E}(\alpha), \mathsf{E}(\alpha s), \ldots, \mathsf{E}(\alpha s^d)$, where α plays the role of a mask. The third group consists of encodings of elements which are values of polynomials at s masked by a common element, *i.e.*, $\mathsf{E}\big(\beta t(s)\big), \mathsf{E}\big(\beta v_{\ell_u+1}(s)\big), \ldots, \mathsf{E}\big(\beta v_m(s)\big)$. The crucial point is that the error for each of these encodings has to be chosen carefully, so that addition of encodings computationally hides the witness. This is needed when showing the zero-knowledge property of the scheme, whose security proof is based on the smudging technique. Furthermore, when paying closer attention to the way a proof is generated, we observe that homomorphic evaluations (or rather additions) are always performed between elements of each group together with a set of coefficients in the prescribed finite field.

In rank metric code-based cryptography, it seems difficult to do so due to the aforementioned reasons. However, these two observations lead us to the idea of using one and the same vector space of noises for each group. More precisely, let V_1, V_2, V_3 be randomly chosen subspaces of prescribed dimensions, then for $i = 1, 2, 3$, all elements of the ith group are produced by using noises coming from V_i. The effect is that after doing homomorphic additions with coefficients *in the base field,* the noise of the obtained ciphertext has the same magnitude as that of its components. Furthermore, the magnitude of noises in the three groups are slightly different, *i.e.*, the one in the first group is of the smallest value while the other two groups have the same magnitude of noises, and allow "truly" homomorphic addition of order two, that is, any linear combination of two independent encodings/ciphertexts is again a valid encoding/ciphertext. The reason for this requirement will become clear in the proof of security. By further adding another encoding, *i.e.*, a mask, whose noises belong essentially to the same vector space as that of each group, we can argue from this property that the resulted ciphertext does not leak any potential information of the witness.

We also note that though the concrete parameters of our scheme do not compete well with those of [24], we emphasize that the novelty of our work lies in the way the encoding elements are divided and treated. We believe this method may be of independent interest for other applications.

Organization of the Paper. The rest of this work is organized as follows. Section 2 recalls some basic matters needed; Sects. 3 and 4 describe an encoding scheme and the corresponding zk-SNARK construction. The efficiency and some examples of parameter are the content of Sect. 6.

2 Preliminaries

2.1 Notations

Vectors are denoted by bold low-case letters, $e.g.$, vector $\mathbf{v}$. Bold capital letters are used to denote matrices, $e.g.$, matrix $\mathbf{A}$. The notation S_r^n is defined to be the sphere of radius r in $\mathbb{F}_{q^{m_0}}^n$ for some positive integer m_0. We use the notation $[n]$ to denote the set $\{0, 1, \ldots, n\}$ for a positive integer n, $\lfloor x \rfloor$ to denote the greatest integer less than or equal to x, and $a \mid b$ to denote a divides b. Negligible functions are denoted by $\mathsf{neg}(\cdot)$.

2.2 Background on Code-Based Cryptography

This section recalls some basic code-based notions as well as ingredients needed, all of which could be found in [7]. Let m_0, n be two positive integers and q a power of a prime number. Let $\{\alpha_1, \ldots, \alpha_{m_0}\}$ be a basis of $\mathbb{F}_{q^{m_0}}$ over $\mathbb{F}_q$. This basis can be used to associate any vector $\mathbf{x} := (x_1, \ldots, x_n) \in \mathbb{F}_{q^{m_0}}^n$ to the corresponding matrix $\mathbf{A_x} \in \mathbb{F}_q^{n \times m_0}$ as

$$\begin{pmatrix} x_1 \\ \vdots \\ x_n \end{pmatrix} = \begin{pmatrix} a_{11} & \cdots & a_{1m_0} \\ \vdots & \vdots & \vdots \\ a_{n1} & \cdots & a_{nm_0} \end{pmatrix} \cdot \begin{pmatrix} \alpha_1 \\ \vdots \\ \alpha_{m_0} \end{pmatrix}.$$

The rank weight of $\mathbf{x}$ is defined to be the rank of matrix $\mathbf{A_x}$, that is, $\|\mathbf{x}\| := \text{rank}(\mathbf{A_x})$. In this metric, the distance between two vectors $\mathbf{x}$ and $\mathbf{y}$, denoted by $d(\mathbf{x}, \mathbf{y})$, is defined to be equal the rank weight of $\mathbf{x} - \mathbf{y}$, $i.e.$, $d(\mathbf{x}, \mathbf{y}) := \|\mathbf{x} - \mathbf{y}\|$.

Now, let $f(x) \in \mathbb{F}_{q^{m_0}}[x]$ be a polynomial of degree n and $\mathcal{R}_f := \mathbb{F}_{q^{m_0}}[x]/\langle f \rangle$. Consider the following mapping:

$$\phi \colon \mathbb{F}_{q^{m_0}}^n \longrightarrow \mathcal{R}_f$$
$$(a_0, \ldots, a_{n-1}) \longmapsto a_0 + \cdots + a_{n-1}x^{n-1}.$$

The inverse mapping, denoted by ϕ^{-1}, simply maps a polynomial to the vector formed by its coefficients. For the sake of simplicity, if $\mathbf{a} := (a_0, \ldots, a_{n-1}) \in \mathbb{F}_{q^{m_0}}^n$, we let $\phi(\mathbf{a}) = a_0 + \cdots + a_{n-1}x^{n-1} = a(x)$. For $\mathbf{a}, \mathbf{b} \in \mathbb{F}_{q^{m_0}}^n$, their product $\mathbf{a} \cdot \mathbf{b}$ is defined as

$$\mathbf{a} \cdot \mathbf{b} := \phi^{-1}\big(a(x) \cdot b(x)\big).$$

Clearly, we have $\mathbf{a} \cdot \mathbf{b} = \mathbf{b} \cdot \mathbf{a}$. It is also not hard to see that

$$\mathbf{a} \cdot \mathbf{b} = (a_0, \ldots, a_{n-1}) \cdot \begin{pmatrix} \phi^{-1}\big(b(x)\big) \\ \vdots \\ \phi^{-1}\big(x^{n-1}b(x)\big) \end{pmatrix}. \qquad (1)$$

The right-most expression on the right-hand side of Eq. 1 is usually referred to as the ideal matrix generated by $b(x)$ with respect to $f(x)$. For ease of notation, vectors are identified with their corresponding polynomials, *i.e.*, $x^k\mathbf{b}$ is understood to be $\phi^{-1}(x^k b(x))$. Thus, the ideal matrix of a vector $\mathbf{b}$ with respect to f is written as

$$b = \begin{pmatrix} \mathbf{b} \\ x \cdot \mathbf{b} \\ \vdots \\ x^{n-1} \cdot \mathbf{b} \end{pmatrix}.$$

In our construction, we will use 2- and 3-ideal codes. A 2-ideal code of length $2n$ with respect to a polynomial $f(x)$ of degree n over $\mathbb{F}_{q^{m_0}}$ is a code whose parity-check matrix is of the form

$$\mathbf{H} = \begin{bmatrix} \mathbf{I}_n \mid h^T \end{bmatrix}, \tag{2}$$

where h is the ideal matrix of a vector $\mathbf{h}$ with respect to $f(x)$ in $\mathbb{F}_{q^{m_0}}^n$. Similarly, a 3-ideal code of length $3n$ with respect to a polynomial $f(x)$ of degree n over $\mathbb{F}_{q^{m_0}}$ is a code whose parity matrix is of the form

$$\mathbf{H} = \begin{pmatrix} \mathbf{I}_n & \mathbf{0} & h_1^T \\ \mathbf{0} & \mathbf{I}_n & h_2^T \end{pmatrix}. \tag{3}$$

For a given vector $\mathbf{x} \in \mathbb{F}_{q^{m_0}}^n$, it is usually associated with the vector space generated by its coordinates.

Definition 1. *Let* $\mathbf{x} := (x_1, \ldots, x_n) \in \mathbb{F}_{q^{m_0}}^n$. *The vector space over* $\mathbb{F}_q$ *defined by* $x_1, \ldots, x_n$ *is called the support of* $\mathbf{x}$, *and denoted by* $\mathrm{supp}(\mathbf{x})$. *That is,*

$$\mathrm{supp}(\mathbf{x}) := \mathrm{Span}_{\mathbb{F}_q}(x_1, \ldots, x_n).$$

Next, we recall some definitions concerning code-based hardness assumptions.

Definition 2 (Rank Syndrome Decoding Problem). *Let* n, k, *and* w *be positive integers,* $\mathbf{H}$ *a random matrix over* $\mathbb{F}_{q^{m_0}}^{(n-k) \times n}$, *and* $\mathbf{y}$ *a random vector in* $\mathbb{F}_{q^{m_0}}^{n-k}$. *The rank syndrome decoding problem,* $\mathrm{RSD}(n, k, w)$, *asks to find a vector* $\mathbf{x} \in S_w^n$ *such that* $\mathbf{H}\mathbf{x}^T = \mathbf{y}^T$.

In the following definitions, for $\nu \in \{2, 3\}$, let $S_P(n, \nu)$ be the set of all parity matrices of ν-ideal codes with respect to a polynomial $P(x)$ of degree n over $\mathbb{F}_{q^{m_0}}$, as defined in Eqs. 2 or 3, respectively.

Definition 3 (ν-IRSD Distribution). *Let* n, w *be positive integers,* $P(x) \in \mathbb{F}_q[x]$ *an irreducible polynomial of degree* n. *The* ν-$\mathrm{IRSD}(n, w)$ *distribution chooses uniformly at random a matrix* $\mathbf{H} \in S_P(n, \nu)$ *together with a vector* $\mathbf{x} \in \mathbb{F}_{q^{m_0}}^{\nu n}$ *such that* $\|\mathbf{x}\| = w$ *and outputs* $(\mathbf{H}, \mathbf{H} \cdot \mathbf{x}^T)$.

Definition 4 (Computational ν-IRSD Problem). *Let n, w be positive integers, $P(x) \in \mathbb{F}_q[x]$ an irreducible polynomial of degree n, $\mathbf{H} \in S_P(n, \nu)$ a random matrix, and $\mathbf{y} \leftarrow \mathbb{F}_{q^{m_0}}^n$. The computational ν-IRSD(n, w) problem asks to find a vector $\mathbf{x} \in \mathbb{F}_{q^{m_0}}^{\nu n}$ such that $\|\mathbf{x}\| = w$ and $\mathbf{H} \cdot \mathbf{x}^T = \mathbf{y}^T$.*

Definition 5 (Decisional ν-IRSD Problem). *The decisional ν-IRSD(n, w) problem asks to decide with non-negligible advantage whether $(\mathbf{H}, \mathbf{y}^T)$ came from the ν-IRSD(n, w) distribution or the uniform distribution over $S_P(n, \nu) \times \mathbb{F}_{q^{m_0}}^n$.*

Next, we recall the rank support learning problem. It made its first appearance in [21], in the construction of a rank-metric based public-key encryption scheme, and recently, in [6]. This problem can be viewed as a relaxation of the RSD problem in which, instead of giving one syndrome instance as in the RSD case, it gives a certain number of syndromes, all produced from the very same support of errors. Its definition reads.

Definition 6 (Rank Support Learning Problem). *Let n, k, r, N be positive integers. Given a matrix $\mathbf{H} \in \mathbb{F}_{q^{m_0}}^{(n-k) \times n}$ and N syndromes $\mathbf{s}_i^T = \mathbf{H}\mathbf{e}_i^T$, where $\mathbf{e}_i \leftarrow V$ for all $i = 1, 2, \ldots, N$, and V is a subspace of $\mathbb{F}_{q^{m_0}}^n$ of dimension r, the RSL(n, k, r, N) problem asks to find V.*

When the number N increases, the problem becomes easier to solve. The attack in [18] suggests that parameters should be chosen satisfying $N < kr$. The decisional version of this problem is as follows.

Definition 7 (Decisional RSL Problem). *Given an instance either from $(\mathbf{H}, \mathbf{HE})$ or $(\mathbf{H}, \mathbf{U})$, where $\mathbf{H}$ is a full rank matrix of size $(n-k) \times n$, $\mathbf{U}$ is a random matrix in $\mathbb{F}_{q^{m_0}}^{(n-k) \times N}$, and $\mathbf{E}$ is a matrix formed from N randomly chosen vectors $\mathbf{e}_i$'s in a vector space of dimension r, the decisional rank support learning DRSL(n, k, r, N) asks to decide which is the case.*

For our purpose, we also need another variant of this problem. In addition to a set of N vectors, either produced from preimages of the same support or from the uniform distribution, two additional vectors are also given, which are $\mathbb{F}_q$-linearly random combinations of these N vectors. The problem now still asks to decide which is the case.

Definition 8 (Variant RSL Problem-vRSL). *Given an instance either from $(\mathbf{H}, \mathbf{HE}, \mathbf{HE} \cdot \mathbf{a}^T, \mathbf{HE} \cdot \mathbf{b}^T)$ or $(\mathbf{H}, \mathbf{U}, \mathbf{U} \cdot \mathbf{a}^T, \mathbf{U} \cdot \mathbf{b}^T)$, where $\mathbf{H} \in \mathbb{F}_{q^{m_0}}^{(n-k) \times n}$ is a full rank matrix, $\mathbf{U}$ is a random matrix in $\mathbb{F}_{q^{m_0}}^{(n-k) \times N}$, $\mathbf{a}, \mathbf{b}$ are randomly chosen vectors in $\mathbb{F}_q^N$, and $\mathbf{E}$ is a matrix formed from N randomly chosen vectors $\mathbf{e}_i$'s in a vector space of dimension r, the vRSL(n, k, r, N) problem asks to decide which is the case.*

The rationale behind this formulation is that what really affects the hardness of the problem is the information of V given in the form of $\mathbf{HE}$ or, equivalently, $\{\mathbf{He}_i^T\}_{i=1}^N$. Adding one or two random $\mathbb{F}_q$-linearly combinations of these vectors does not leak more information about V. In fact, this problem is not easier than the RSL problem. Given an RSL instance, one could create a vRSL instance by randomly picking two vectors $\mathbf{a}, \mathbf{b} \in \mathbb{F}_q^N$, computing the corresponding linearly combinations; these combinations together with the provided RSL instance then form an instance of the vRSL problem. Therefore, if we can solve the vRSL problem, then we can also solve the RSL problem. The hardness of this problem is used to argue the zero-knowledge property of our scheme. Furthermore, the hardness of this problem also guarantees the zero-knowledge property of the linear coefficients, *i.e.*, the random vectors $\mathbf{a}$ and $\mathbf{b}$. An adversary, if being asked for such a set of coefficients, has either to solve the RSL problem or to make a guess, both of which succeed with negligible probability.

Remark 1. We remark that the problem in the above definition could be generalized to the case in which, in addition to the syndromes (either chosen uniformly or not), a polynomial number of random $\mathbb{F}_q$-linearly combinations of these syndromes are also given. The reduction could be carried in the same manner.

In the above definitions, the matrix $\mathbf{H}$ can be assumed to have ideal structures, and we also make the assumption that the problems corresponding to this situation, namely, the ideal rank support learning (IRSL) problem and its variant (vIRSL), are hard.

2.3   Succinct Non-interactive Arguments

We recall the definition of (designated-verifier) succinct non-interactive arguments of knowledge (SNARKs) below. We specialize our definitions to the problem of Boolean circuit satisfiability.

Definition 9. *Let $\mathcal{C} := \{C_n\}_{n \in \mathbb{N}}$ be a family of Boolean circuits. A designated-verifier non-interactive argument system for an NP relation $\mathcal{R}_\mathcal{C}$ is a triple of algorithms $\Pi = (\mathsf{G}, \mathsf{P}, \mathsf{V})$ such that*

- *$\mathsf{G}(1^\lambda, 1^n)$: On input the security parameter λ and the circuit family parameter n, the setup algorithm G generates a common reference string crs and a verification key vrs.*
- *$\mathsf{P}(\mathsf{crs}, u, w)$: On input the common reference string crs, a statement u, and its witness w, the prover algorithm P generates a proof π.*
- *$\mathsf{V}(\mathsf{vrs}, u, \pi)$: On input the verification key vrs, a statement u and a proof π, the verification algorithm V outputs 1 if the proof π is valid, and 0 otherwise.*

An argument of knowledge system is required to be complete and to have knowledge soundness.

Definition 10 (Completeness). *An argument of knowledge system Π for a relation $\mathcal{R}_\mathcal{C}$ is complete if for all $n \in \mathbb{N}$ and for any pair $(u, w) \in \mathcal{R}_{C_n}$, we have*

$$\Pr\left[\begin{array}{c} (\mathsf{crs}, \mathsf{vrs}) \leftarrow \mathsf{G}(1^\lambda, 1^n) \\ \pi \leftarrow \mathsf{P}(\mathsf{crs}, u, w) \\ s.t.\ \mathsf{V}(\mathsf{vrs}, u, \pi) = 1 \end{array}\right] \geq 1 - \mathsf{neg}(\lambda).$$

Definition 11 (Knowledge Soundness). *An argument of knowledge system Π for the relation $\mathcal{R}_\mathcal{C}$ is knowledge-sound if for any PPT adversary $\mathcal{A}$, there exists an extractor $\mathrm{Ext}_\mathcal{A}$, given access to $\mathcal{A}$'s inputs, such that*

$$\Pr \left[\begin{array}{c} (\mathsf{crs}, \mathsf{vrs}) \leftarrow \mathsf{G}(1^\lambda, \mathcal{R}) \\ (u, \pi; w) \leftarrow (\mathcal{A} \parallel \mathrm{Ext}_\mathcal{A})^{\mathsf{V}(\mathsf{vrs}, \cdot)}(\mathsf{crs}) \\ s.t.\ (u, w) \notin \mathcal{R} \wedge \mathsf{V}(\mathsf{vrs}, u, \pi) = 1 \end{array} \right] \leq \mathsf{neg}(\lambda),$$

where $(y; z) \leftarrow (\mathcal{A} \parallel \mathrm{Ext}_\mathcal{A})(x)$ signifies that on input $x, \mathcal{A}$ outputs y, and that $\mathrm{Ext}_\mathcal{A}$, given the same input x and $\mathcal{A}$'s random tape, produces z.

Additionally, a system is said to be *succinct* if it satisfies the following property.

Definition 12 (Succinctness). *There exists a fixed polynomial $p(\cdot)$ independent of $\mathcal{C}$ such that for every large enough security parameter $\lambda \in \mathbb{N}$, we have that*

- **Fully Succinct:** G *runs in time* $p(\lambda + \log |C_n|)$, V *runs in time* $p(\lambda + |x| + \log |C_n|)$, *and the length of the proof output by* P *is bounded by* $p(\lambda + \log |C_n|)$.
- **Preprocessing:** G *runs in time* $p(\lambda + |C_n|)$, V *runs in time* $p(\lambda + |x| + \log |C_n|)$, *and the length of the proof output by* P *is bounded by* $p(\lambda + \log |C_n|)$.

If an argument system has the property that the witness(es) is (computationally) hiding, then it is said to be zero-knowledge. This notion is captured by the simulation paradigm: there exists a PPT algorithm $\mathcal{S}$, called simulator, such that given a statement u, it generates a valid proof whose distribution is indistinguishable from that generated in the real protocol.

Definition 13 (Zero-knowledge). *An argument of knowledge system Π is zero-knowledge if there exists a PPT simulator $\mathcal{S} = (\mathcal{S}_1, \mathcal{S}_2)$ such that for any PPT adversary $\mathcal{A}$ given access to an oracle $\mathcal{O}$ defined as*

> *Oracle $\mathcal{O}_b(u, w)$:*
> *If $R(u, w) = \mathsf{false}$, return $\bot$.*
> *If $b = 1$, then $\pi \leftarrow \mathsf{P}(\mathsf{crs}, u, w)$,*
> *else $\pi \leftarrow \mathcal{S}_2(\mathsf{td}, u)$,*
> *return π,*

we have

$$\Pr \left[\begin{array}{c} (\mathsf{crs}, \mathsf{vrs}, \mathsf{td}) \leftarrow \mathcal{S}_1(1^\lambda, 1^n) \\ b \leftarrow \{0, 1\} \\ b' \leftarrow \mathcal{A}^{\mathcal{O}_b}(\mathsf{vrs}) \\ s.t.\ b = b' \end{array} \right] \leq \frac{1}{2} + \mathsf{neg}(\lambda).$$

Definition 14 (zk-SNARK). *A succinct non-interactive zero-knowledge argument of knowledge (zk-SNARK) is a non-interactive argument system that is complete, succinct, knowledge-sound and zero-knowledge.*

2.4   Encoding Schemes

We recall the definition of encoding schemes with noise from [24], adapted to our secret-key setting.

Definition 15. *An encoding scheme* Enc *over a finite field* $\mathbb{F}_q$ *is a tuple of PPT algorithms* $(\mathsf{K}, \mathsf{E}, \mathsf{D})$ *such that:*

- $\mathsf{K}(1^\lambda)$: *The key generating algorithm takes as input the security parameter* λ *and outputs a public information* pk *and a secret state* sk.
- $\mathsf{E}(\mathsf{sk}, m)$: *The non-deterministic encoding algorithm maps an element* $m \in \mathbb{F}_q$ *into some encoding space* S *using the secret state* sk, *such that* $\{\{\mathsf{E}(a)\} \mid a \in \mathbb{F}_q\}$ *partitions* S, *where* $\{\mathsf{E}(a)\}$ *denotes the set of the possible evaluations of the algorithm* E *on* a.
- $\mathsf{D}(\mathsf{sk}, \mathbf{c})$: *The decoding algorithm takes as input the secret state* sk, *an encoding* $\mathbf{c}$ *and outputs an element* $m \in \mathbb{F}_q$.

An encoding scheme Enc must have the following properties:

- ∂**-linearly homomorphic:** there exists a PPT algorithm Eval which takes pk, ∂ encodings $\mathsf{E}(m_1), \ldots, \mathsf{E}(m_\partial)$, and coefficients $(a_1, \ldots, a_\partial) \in \mathbb{F}_q^\partial$ as input and outputs a valid encoding of $\sum_{i=1}^\partial a_i m_i$ with overwhelming probability in λ.
- **Quadratic root detection:** there exists a PPT algorithm which takes the public key pk, a set of encodings $\{\mathsf{E}(m_1), \ldots, \mathsf{E}(m_t)\}$, and a quadratic polynomial $P \in \mathbb{F}_q[x_1, \ldots, x_t]$ as input and checks for the correctness of the equality $P(m_1, \ldots, m_t) = 0$.
- **Image verification:** there exists a PPT algorithm which takes the public key pk and an element $\mathbf{c}$ as input and decides whether $\mathbf{c}$ is a valid encoding of a field element or not.

2.5   Assumptions

The following assumptions are the adaptations of q-PDH and q-PKE assumptions (cf. [23,24]) to the code-based context together with the application of the rank support learning problem. In the following, all the encodings are produced by using *a common vector space* of noise.

Assumption 1 (q-PDH)**.** *Let* Enc $= (\mathsf{K}, \mathsf{E}, \mathsf{D})$ *be an encoding scheme over a finite field* $\mathbb{F}_q$. *The q-power Diffie-Hellman assumption, q-PDH, holds for* Enc *if for all PPT adversary* $\mathcal{A}$, *we have*

$$\Pr\left[\begin{array}{c} (\mathsf{pk}, \mathsf{sk}) \leftarrow \mathsf{K}(1^\lambda),\, s \leftarrow \mathbb{F}_q \\ y \leftarrow \mathcal{A}\left(\mathsf{pk}, \mathsf{E}(1), \mathsf{E}(s), \ldots, \mathsf{E}(s^q), \mathsf{E}(s^{q+2}), \ldots, \mathsf{E}(s^{2q})\right) \\ s.t.\ y = \mathsf{E}(s^{q+1}) \end{array} \right] \leq \mathsf{neg}(\lambda).$$

Assumption 2 (q-PKE). *Let* $\mathsf{Enc} = (\mathsf{K}, \mathsf{E}, \mathsf{D})$ *be an encoding scheme over a finite field* $\mathbb{F}_q$. *The* q-*power of knowledge of exponent assumption,* q-PKE, *holds for* Enc *if for all PPT adversary* $\mathcal{A}$, *there exists a non-uniform knowledge extractor* $\mathsf{Ext}_{\mathcal{A}}$, *given access to* $\mathcal{A}$'s *input, such that*

$$\Pr \left[\begin{array}{c} (\mathsf{pk}, \mathsf{sk}) \leftarrow \mathsf{K}(1^\lambda), \alpha, s \leftarrow \mathbb{F}_q \\ \sigma \leftarrow (\mathsf{pk}, \mathsf{E}(s), \dots, \mathsf{E}(s^q), \mathsf{E}(\alpha), \mathsf{E}(\alpha s), \dots, \mathsf{E}(\alpha s^q)) \\ (c, \hat{c}; (a_0, \dots, a_q)) \leftarrow (\mathcal{A} \parallel \mathsf{Ext}_{\mathcal{A}})(\sigma, z) \\ s.t. \ \hat{c} = \alpha c \wedge c \notin \{\mathsf{E}(\sum_{i=0}^q a_i s^i)\} \end{array} \right] \le \mathrm{neg}(\lambda),$$

for any auxiliary input $z \in \{0,1\}^{\mathrm{poly}(\lambda)}$ *that is generated independently of* α.

2.6   Square Span Programs

We briefly recall here the definition of a square span program [17].

Definition 16. *A square span program over a finite field* $\mathbb{F}_q$ *consists in a tuple of* $m + 1$ *polynomials* $v_0(x), v_1(x), \dots, v_m(x) \in \mathbb{F}_q[x]$ *and a target polynomial* $t(x)$ *such that* $\deg v_i \le \deg t$ *for all* $0 \le i \le m$. *We say that the square span program* ssp *has size* m *and degree* $d = \deg t$. *We say that* ssp *accepts an input* $a_1, \dots, a_\ell \in \{0,1\}$ *if and only if there exist* $a_{\ell+1}, \dots, a_m \in \{0,1\}$ *satisfying*

$$t(x) \mid \left(v_0(x) + \sum_{i=1}^m a_i v_i(x) \right)^2 - 1.$$

We say that ssp *verifies a boolean circuit* $\mathsf{C} \colon \{0,1\}^\ell \to \{0,1\}$ *if it accepts exactly those inputs* $(a_1, \dots, a_\ell) \in \{0,1\}^\ell$ *satisfying*

$$\mathsf{C}(a_1, \dots, a_\ell) = 1.$$

We follow [24]'s approach for the SSP generation. That is, on a boolean circuit C of size d, it generates a finite field $\mathbb{F}_q$ of q elements such that $q \ge \max\{d, 8\}$. Next, it randomly picks d elements $r_0, \dots, r_{d-1}$ and defines $t(x) := (x - r_0) \cdots (x - r_{d-1})$. It outputs ssp as

$$\big(v_0(x), \dots, v_m(x), t(x) \big) \leftarrow \mathsf{SSP}(\mathsf{C}),$$

where $v_0, \dots, v_m$ are $m + 1$ polynomials of degree at most d as in the above definition.

3   Our Code-Based Encoding Scheme

In this section, we describe our instantiation of an encoding scheme from coding theory, which is based on the RQC cryptosystem. The description of the RQC encryption scheme was originally published in [1], and can be found in [2] with little changes. In this work, it is turned into a secret-key and used as an encoding scheme in the following manner.

1. Setup(1^λ): Generate parameters $n := n(\lambda), k := k(\lambda), \delta := \delta(\lambda), w := w(\lambda), w_e := w_e(\lambda), w_r := w_r(\lambda)$. The plaintext space is $\mathbb{F}_{q^{m_0}}^k$. Output param $:= \big(n, k, \delta, w, w_e, w_r, P(x)\big)$, where $P(x) \in \mathbb{F}_q[x]$ is an irreducible polynomial of degree n which remains irreducible over $\mathbb{F}_{q^{m_0}}[x]$.

2. KeyGen(param): Generate $\mathbf{h} \leftarrow \mathbb{F}_{q^{m_0}}^n, \mathbf{x}, \mathbf{y} \leftarrow \mathcal{S}_w^n$, a generator matrix $\mathbf{G} \in \mathbb{F}_{q^{m_0}}^{k \times n}$ of a public code $\mathcal{C}$, which is capable of correcting up to δ errors. Output the public parameters pp $:= (\text{param}, \mathbf{h}, \mathbf{G})$ and sk $:= (\mathbf{x}, \mathbf{y})$.

3. Enc(pp, sk, $\mathbf{m}$): To encrypt a message $\mathbf{m} \in \mathbb{F}_{q^{m_0}}^k$, randomly choose $\mathbf{r}_1, \mathbf{r}_2 \leftarrow \mathcal{S}_{w_r}^n$ and $\mathbf{e} \leftarrow \mathcal{S}_{w_e}^n$. Compute

$$\begin{cases} \mathbf{c}_1 \leftarrow \mathbf{r}_1 + \mathbf{h} \cdot \mathbf{r}_2, \\ \mathbf{c}_2 \leftarrow (\mathbf{x} + \mathbf{h} \cdot \mathbf{y}) \cdot \mathbf{r}_2 + \mathbf{e} + \mathbf{m} \cdot \mathbf{G}. \end{cases}$$

Return $\mathbf{c} := (\mathbf{c}_1, \mathbf{c}_2)$.

We note that the noises vectors $\mathbf{r}_1, \mathbf{r}_2, \mathbf{e}$ are chosen from a common vector space. Therefore, we also have $w_r = w_e$.

4. Dec(sk, $\mathbf{c}$): To decrypt, first compute $\mathbf{c}_2 - \mathbf{y} \cdot \mathbf{c}_1$, and then use the decoding algorithm of the code $\mathcal{C}$ to recover $\mathbf{m}$.

From the RQC encryption scheme describe above, our encoding scheme (K, E, D) is defined in which K consists of Setup and KeyGen algorithms, the encoding algorithm E is the encryption algorithm Enc, the decoding algorithm D is the decryption algorithm Dec.

We aim at encoding of elements of the finite field $\mathbb{F}_q$, we do it as follows. For an element $s \in \mathbb{F}_q$, define $\mathbf{s} = (s, 0, \ldots, 0) \in \mathbb{F}_q^k$, i.e., the vector $\mathbf{s}$ is formed by placing s in the first entry and 0 elsewhere. An encoding of s is defined to be an encryption of $\mathbf{s}$, i.e., E(s) := Enc($\mathbf{s}$). For two elements $s_1, s_2 \in \mathbb{F}_q$, if we denote $t = s_1 s_2$, then we have $\mathbf{t} = \mathbf{s}_1 \cdot \mathbf{s}_2 = (s_1 s_2, 0, \ldots, 0)$, and hence, E($s_1 s_2$) = Enc($\mathbf{s}_1 \cdot \mathbf{s}_2$). Therefore, this mapping (from $\mathbb{F}_q$ to $\mathbb{F}_{q^{m_0}}^k$) is well-defined.

To complete the description of our encoding scheme, its properties are defined below.

- Eval(pk, $\mathbf{c}_1, \ldots, \mathbf{c}_{\mathfrak{d}}; a_1, \ldots, a_{\mathfrak{d}}$) computes and outputs $\tilde{\mathbf{c}} = (\tilde{\mathbf{c}}_1, \tilde{\mathbf{c}}_2)$, where $\tilde{\mathbf{c}}_b = \sum_{i=1}^{\mathfrak{d}} a_i \mathbf{c}_{b,i}$, for some prescribed positive integer $\mathfrak{d}$ describing the number of desired homomorphic additions and $b \in \{1, 2\}$.
- Quadratic root detection uses the decryption algorithm to invert ciphertexts and evaluates value of the polynomial at the obtained messages.
- Image verification uses the decryption algorithm of RQC to test whether a given vector $\mathbf{c}$ is a valid encoding of some plaintext or not.

By the hardness of IRSL problem, a random vector space of noise can be used a couple of times, which is described in the problem. Our zk-SNARK construction will exploit this variation in subsequent sections. Furthermore, similar to previous work [24], we will assume that our encoding scheme satisfies the q-PDH and q-PKE assumptions as described in Sect. 2.5.

3.1   Bound of Noise

The main point of this section is to give a feature of the sum of noises in a particular case, that is, when the sum of noise's weight is much smaller than either the vector length or the degree of the field extension. Simply stated, the weight of the sum is upper-bounded by the sum of every single noise's weight.

Proposition 1. *Let $\ell, m_0, n, w_1, \ldots, w_\ell$ be positive integers such that $m_0, n > d_w$, where $d_w = w_1 + \cdots + w_\ell$. Let t_i be randomly chosen from $S_{w_i}^n$ for $i = 1, \ldots, \ell$, and $U = \mathrm{supp}\left(\sum_{i=1}^{\ell} t_i\right)$. Then, we have $\dim U \leq d_w$.*

Proof. The proof is quite straightforwards, since we have

$$U \subseteq \mathrm{supp}\, t_1 \oplus \cdots \oplus \mathrm{supp}\, t_\ell.$$

□

As mentioned earlier, for our construction, noises used in the encodings (in each group) share a common vector space and the linear coefficient would be in the based field. Therefore, the noise of the resulted encoding would also belong to the prescribed vector space. The above proposition proves to be helpful in the security proof of our zk-SNARK later, and in fact, the equality holds with overwhelming probability [30].

3.2   Additive Homomorphism

The purpose of this section is to show the additive homomorphism of the RQC scheme. Intuitively, by the result of the previous section, the noise of the homomorphic ciphertext grows linearly with respect to the number of additive components. However, as long as the magnitude of the homomorphic noise is within the decoding capability of the public code $\mathcal{C}$, the decoding algorithm will always succeed.

Proposition 2. *Let $\eth$ be the number of additive operations, w, w_e, w_r be magnitudes of the secret key and noises from an RQC scheme whose public code can decode errors of rank weight up to δ. If $\eth(2ww_r + w_e) \leq \delta$, then $\tilde{c}$, which is the output of* Eval *is a correct encoding.*

Proof. Observe that $\tilde{c} = (\tilde{c}_1, \tilde{c}_2)$, where

$$\begin{cases} \tilde{c}_1 = \sum_{i=1}^{\eth} a_i r_i^{(1)} + h \cdot \left(\sum_{i=1}^{\eth} a_i r_i^{(2)}\right), \\ \tilde{c}_2 = s \cdot \left(\sum_{i=1}^{\eth} a_i r_i^{(2)}\right) + \sum_{i=1}^{\eth} a_i e_i + \left(\sum_{i=1}^{\eth} a_i m_i\right) \cdot G. \end{cases}$$

Since a_i's are elements of $\mathbb{F}_{q^{m_0}}$, so $\|a_i r_i^{(j)}\| = \|r_i^{(j)}\|$ and $\|a_i e_i\| = \|e_i\|$ for all $1 \leq i \leq \eth$ and $j = 1, 2$. By Proposition 1, we get

$$\begin{cases} w_r \eth \leq \sum_{i=1}^{\eth} a_i r_i^{(1)}, \\ w_r \eth \leq \sum_{i=1}^{\eth} a_i r_i^{(2)}, \\ w_e \eth \leq \sum_{i=1}^{\eth} a_i e_i. \end{cases}$$

Thus,

$$\left\| \mathbf{x} \cdot \sum_{i=1}^{\eth} a_i \mathbf{r}_i^{(2)} - \mathbf{y} \cdot \sum_{i=1}^{\eth} a_i \mathbf{r}_i^{(1)} + \sum_{i=1}^{\eth} a_i \mathbf{e}_i \right\|$$
$$\leq w \cdot w_r \eth + w \cdot w_r \eth + w_e \eth$$
$$\leq \delta,$$

which allows successful decryption.   □

4   Our Code-Based Zk-SNARK Scheme

In the following, let $(\mathsf{K}, \mathsf{E}, \mathsf{D})$ be the encoding scheme described in Sect. 3. We assume Our zk-SNARK scheme Π is detailed as:

– **Setup.** The setup algorithm takes as input the security parameter 1^λ in the unary form and the circuit C. It generates a square span program of degree d over the field $\mathbb{F}_q$ of size $q \geq d$ that verifies C by running:

$$\mathsf{ssp} = \big(v_0(x), \ldots, v_m(x), t(x)\big) \leftarrow \mathsf{SSP}(\mathsf{C}).$$

Then, it runs $(\mathsf{pp}, \mathsf{sk}) \leftarrow \mathsf{K}(1^\lambda)$ using our encoding scheme. It samples $\alpha, \beta, s \leftarrow \mathbb{F}_q$ such that $t(s) \neq 0$, and returns the crs:

$$\mathsf{crs} := \big(\mathsf{ssp}, \mathsf{pp}, \mathfrak{G}_1, \mathfrak{G}_2, \mathfrak{G}_3\big),$$

where

$$\mathfrak{G}_1 := \big\{\mathsf{E}(1), \mathsf{E}(s), \ldots, \mathsf{E}(s^d)\big\},$$
$$\mathfrak{G}_2 := \big\{\mathsf{E}(\alpha), \mathsf{E}(\alpha s), \ldots, \mathsf{E}(\alpha s^d)\big\},$$
$$\mathfrak{G}_3 := \big\{\mathsf{E}(\beta t(s)), \{\mathsf{E}(\beta v_i(s))\}_{i=\ell_u+1}^m\big\},$$

and ℓ_u denotes the size of input u of circuit C. Elements in each group are formed from the encoding scheme which uses three vector spaces of noises V_1, V_2, V_3, respectively. Furthermore, $\dim V_1 = r$, $\dim V_2 = \dim V_3 = \mathfrak{r}$, where $0 < \mathfrak{r} - r$.

Finally, it sets $\mathsf{vrs} = \mathsf{sk}$ and $\mathsf{td} = (\alpha, \beta, s)$ as the verification key and the trapdoor, respectively.

– **Prover.** The prover algorithm, on input some statement $u := (a_1, \ldots, a_{\ell_u})$, and its witness $w = (a_{\ell_u+1}, \ldots, a_m)$ such that $(a_1, \ldots, a_m)$ is a satisfying assignment for the circuit C. The $\{a_i\}_i$ also satisfies

$$t(x) \mid \left(v_0(x) + \sum_{i=1}^m a_i v_i(x)\right)^2 - 1.$$

The prover samples $\gamma \leftarrow \mathbb{F}_q$, sets $v(x) = v_0(x) + \sum_{i=1}^m a_i v_i(x) + \gamma t(x)$ and

$$h(x) = \frac{v(x)^2 - 1}{t(x)} \in \mathbb{F}_q[x].$$

It computes

$$H = \mathsf{E}(h(s)), \quad \widehat{H} = \mathsf{E}(\alpha \cdot h(s)), \quad \widehat{V} = \mathsf{E}(\alpha \cdot v(s)),$$

$$V_w = \mathsf{E}\left(\sum_{i=\ell_u+1}^{m} a_i v_i(s) + \gamma t(s)\right),$$

$$B_w = \mathsf{E}\left(\beta \cdot \left(\sum_{i=\ell_u+1}^{m} a_i v_i(s) + \gamma t(s)\right)\right).$$

The prover returns $\pi := (H, \widehat{H}, \widehat{V}, V_w, B_w)$.

We note that the prover computes H and V_w from the first encoding group $\mathfrak{G}_1$, $\widehat{H}$ and $\widehat{V}$ from the second group $\mathfrak{G}_2$, and B_w from the third group $\mathfrak{G}_3$ in the following manners. Assume that $h(x) = h_0 + h_1 x + \cdots + h_d x^d$, then

1. $H = \mathsf{Eval}(\{\mathsf{E}(s^i)\}_{i=0}^{d}; \{h_i\}_{i=0}^{d})$; the same kind of computation is used for V_w;
2. $\widehat{H} = \mathsf{Eval}(\{\mathsf{E}(\alpha s^i)\}_{i=0}^{d}; \{h_i\}_{i=0}^{d})$; this is also applied for $\widehat{V}$;
3. $B_w = \mathsf{Eval}(\mathsf{E}(\beta t(s)), \{\mathsf{E}(v_i(s))\}_{i=\ell_u+1}^{m}; \gamma, 1, \ldots, 1)$ with the observation that

$$\gamma\mathsf{E}(\beta t(s)) = \mathsf{E}(\gamma \beta t(s)).$$

– **Verifier.** Upon receiving a proof π and a statement $u = (a_1, \ldots, a_{\ell_u})$, the verifier, in possession of the verification key vrs first checks that

$$\widehat{h}_s - \alpha \cdot h_s = 0, \quad \widehat{v}_s - \alpha \cdot v_s = 0,$$

$$v_s^2 - 1 - h_s \cdot t_s = 0,$$

$$b_s - \beta \cdot \mathfrak{v}_s = 0,$$

where $(h_s, \widehat{h}_s, \widehat{v}_s, \mathfrak{v}_s, b_s)$ are the values encoded in $\pi = (H, \widehat{H}, \widehat{V}, V_w, B_w)$, and t_s, v_s are computed as $t_s := t(s)$ and $v_s := v_0 + \sum_{i=1}^{\ell_u} a_i v_i(s) + \mathfrak{v}_s$. (Recall that $t(s)$ and $v_i(s)$ are obtained from the CRS.)

The verifier checks that whether it is possible to perform one more homomorphic operation. (Thus, in our scheme, essentially $\mathfrak{d}$ takes the value 2.) If these checks pass, it outputs 1; otherwise, it outputs 0.

Theorem 1. *If the q-PKE and q-PDH assumptions hold for the encoding scheme $(\mathsf{K}, \mathsf{E}, \mathsf{D})$ then the protocol above is a zk-SNARK with perfect completeness, computational soundness and computational zero-knowledge.*

The perfectness of the scheme is guaranteed by the fact that the decryption step succeeds with probability 1. Therefore, we only need to concern ourselves with the zero-knowledge and soundness property.

5   Security Analysis of Our Zk-SNARK Scheme

5.1   Zero-Knowledge

The idea behind this property is that the distributions of the elements in a proof does not differ from that of its components. The description of the simulator $\mathcal{S}$ is as follows. On input $\mathsf{td} = (\alpha, \beta, s)$ and $u = (a_1, \ldots, a_{\ell_u})$,

1. $\mathcal{S}$ randomly picks an element $\gamma \in \mathbb{F}_q$ and computes

$$h = \frac{\left(v_0(s) + \sum_{i=1}^{\ell_u} a_i v_i(s) + \gamma\right)^2 - 1}{t(s)}.$$

2. It computes

$$\begin{cases} H = \mathsf{E}(h), \quad \widehat{H} = \mathsf{E}(\alpha h), \\ \widehat{V} = \mathsf{E}\big(\alpha(v_0(s) + \sum_{i=1}^{\ell_u} a_i v_i(s) + \gamma)\big), \quad V_\gamma = \mathsf{E}(\gamma), \\ B_\gamma = \mathsf{E}(\beta\gamma). \end{cases}$$

3. It outputs $(H, \widehat{H}, \widehat{V}, V_\gamma, B_\gamma)$.

Proof. Since the encodings in each group $\mathfrak{G}_i$ share a same vector space V_i for $i = 1, 2, 3$, and all the polynomials in consideration are in $\mathbb{F}_q[x]$, therefore, after homomorphically adding, the noises in the new encodings belong to the same vector spaces as that of its component encodings.

Observe that in the real protocol, H and V_w are resulted from adding encodings of $\mathfrak{G}_1$, $\widehat{H}$ and $\widehat{V}$ from $\mathfrak{G}_2$, and B_w from $\mathfrak{G}_3$, respectively. By the vIRSL$(2n, n, \mathfrak{r}, N)$ problem (for each group), these outputs are computationally indistinguishable from truly random ones.

On the other hand, by the decisional IRSL$(2n, n, \mathfrak{r}, N)$ problem, the distribution of the outputs of the simulated protocol are computationally indistinguishable from the uniformly random. Therefore, by hybrid argument, we conclude that the outputs distribution of the real execution and that of the simulation are computationally indistinguishable.   □

We note also that the role of $\gamma t(s)$ in the scheme is to hide the witness and is indispensable. Indeed, since the homomorphic linear coefficients are elements of $\mathbb{F}_q$, so they form a vector which can be viewed as a rank-1 vector over $\mathbb{F}_{q^{m_0}}^N$. In this particular situation, finding these low rank vectors can be performed as follows. From the encodings of $\mathfrak{G}_3$, except the first, form an $n \times (m - \ell_u)$ matrix whose columns are the first parts of these encodings. Note that, without adding $\gamma t(s)$, the last term of the proof becomes

$$B_w = \mathsf{E}\left(\beta \cdot \left(\sum_{i=\ell_u+1}^{m} a_i v_i(s)\right)\right) = \mathsf{Eval}\left(\{\mathsf{E}(\beta v_i(s))\}_{i=\ell_u+1}^{m}; \{a_i\}_{i=\ell_u+1}^{m}\right).$$

Regarding as a rank decoding problem and by applying algorithm in [14], $(a_{\ell_u+1}, \ldots, a_m)$ could be recovered in polynomial time. Thus, witness must be concealed by the necessary use of the term $\gamma t(s)$.

One may hide the witness by further repeating one more time exactly the encryption step of the RQC scheme, *i.e.*, re-randomizing the resulted encoding before outputting it (thus modifying the evaluation algorithm). By the hardness of the IRSL problem, we can argue the (computational) indistinguishability of the output. This is somewhat similar to the technique of [27].

5.2 Soundness

The idea of the proof follows the frame of [32] and [24] with some adaptations to rank-code hardness assumptions.

Proof. Assume that there is an adversary $\mathcal{A}$ who can break the scheme Π with non-negligible probability, we construct an algorithm $\mathcal{B}$ to solve q-PDH or q-PKE problems. First, we show how $\mathcal{B}$ can use $\mathcal{A}$ for this purpose.

Let π be a proof produced by $\mathcal{A}$ which is accepted. Using an extractor of the d-PKE assumption, $\mathcal{B}$ can recover the coefficients of the polynomials $v(x), h(x)$. Define

$$v_{\text{mid}}(x) = v(x) - v_0(x) - \sum_{i=1}^{\ell_u} a_i v_i(x).$$

Since the proof is accepted but the statement is false, so by the same arguments as in the proof in [32], there are only two possibilities

(i) $t(x)h(x) \neq v^2(x) - 1$ but $t(s)h(s) = v^2(s) - 1$, or
(ii) B_w is an encoding of $\beta v_{\text{mid}}(s)$ but v_{mid} is not in the linear span of $\{v_{\ell_u+1}, \dots, v_m, t\}$

□

Claim. If (i) holds, then $\mathcal{B}$ can break the q-PDH assumption with $q = 2d - 1$.

Proof. Let $p(x) = v^2(x) - 1 - t(x)h(x)$. In this case, $p(x)$ is a polynomial of degree at most $2d$ having s as a root. Assume that p_k is the leading coefficient of $p(x)$, define

$$\widehat{p}(x) = x^k - p_k^{-1} p(x).$$

We see that s is a root of $x^k - \widehat{p}(x)$, therefore, it also is a root of $x^{q+1} - x^{q+1-k}\widehat{p}(x)$. Observe that for $q = 2d - 1$, $x^{q+1-k}\widehat{p}(x)$ is a polynomial of degree at most $2d - 1$. Therefore, $\mathsf{E}(s^{q+1-k}\widehat{p}(s))$ can be computed from $\mathsf{E}(1), \mathsf{E}(s), \dots, \mathsf{E}(s^{2d-1})$, which form a challenge of the q-PDH assumption for $q = 2d - 1$. This means that $\mathcal{B}$ can compute $\mathsf{E}(s^{q+1}) = \mathsf{E}(s^{q+1-k}\widehat{p}(s))$ and break the q-PDH assumption for $q = 2d - 1$.

□

Claim. If (ii) holds, then $\mathcal{B}$ can break the q-PDH assumption with $q = d$.

Proof. First, $\mathcal{B}$ generates a uniformly random polynomial $a(x)$ of degree $q = d$ subject to the constraint that all the polynomials $a(x)t(x)$ and $\{a(x)v_i(x)\}_{i=\ell_u+1}^{m}$ do not contain the term x^q. Since $\deg a(x) = d$, so $\mathcal{B}$ can compute the value $a(s)$ from the challenge of the d-PDH assumption, namely, $\mathsf{E}(1), \mathsf{E}(s), \dots, \mathsf{E}(s^d), \mathsf{E}(s^{d+2}), \dots, \mathsf{E}(s^{2d})$. Thus, when preparing inputs for adversary $\mathcal{A}$, $\mathcal{B}$ sets $\beta = a(s)$. The proof is accepted, so the term B_w must be an encoding of a known polynomial in s, *i.e.*, the polynomial

$$a(s)v_{\text{mid}}(s) = b_0 + b_1 s + \dots + b_{2q} s^{2q}.$$

Since v_{mid} is not in the linear span of $\{v_{\ell_u+1},\ldots,v_m,t\}$, so the above polynomial has the term s^{q+1} with overwhelming probability (cf. [23]). $\mathcal{B}$ performs an evaluation as

$$h = \mathsf{Eval}\Big(\{\mathsf{E}(s^i)\}_{i\in[q+d]\setminus\{q+1\}}, \{-b_i\}_{i\in[q+d]\setminus\{q+1\}} \Big).$$

Then $b_{q+1}^{-1}(h + B_w)$ is an encoding of s^{q+1}, which is a solution to the q-PDH assumption for $q = d$. □

From these above analyses, $\mathcal{B}$ proceeds as follows.

- Target at the q-PDH problem with $q = 2d - 1$. ($\mathcal{B}$ can equally target the q-PDH assumption with $q = d$, and follow the case (ii).)
- $\mathcal{B}$, from its challenge $\mathsf{E}(1), \mathsf{E}(s),\ldots,\mathsf{E}(s^q),\mathsf{E}(s^{q+2}),\ldots,\mathsf{E}(s^{2q})$, prepares inputs for adversary $\mathcal{A}$, i.e., the crs. That is, $\mathcal{B}$ randomly picks $\alpha,\beta \in \mathbb{F}_q$ and computes the corresponding terms in the crs from $\mathsf{E}(1),\mathsf{E}(s),\ldots,\mathsf{E}(s^d)$ (depending on which problem $\mathcal{B}$ would target) which form a subset of the set of elements of the challenge. The elements of the first group come directly from the challenge while the elements of the second and third groups are produced by a further step of re-randomization, i.e., by adding some noises from a common vector space to each encoding. (This operation could be viewed as re-randomization.) The preparation for a value β is shown as in (ii). All the encodings of the so-generated crs are ciphertexts sharing a common vector space of noise, however, by the $\mathrm{IRSL}(2n,n,\mathbf{r},N)$ problem, the view of $\mathcal{A}$ on this input is computationally indistinguishable from input of the real protocol.
- By the contradictory assumption, $\mathcal{A}$ outputs a proof which is accepted, however, the statement is false.
- By using the extractor of the d-PKE assumption, $\mathcal{B}$ obtains the coefficients of polynomial $v(x)$ and $h(x)$.
- If (i) holds, $\mathcal{B}$ would find a solution for the q-PDH assumption as described above and break the q-PDH assumption for $q = 2d - 1$.
- If (ii) holds, $\mathcal{B}$ aborts.

We note that the distribution of the input for $\mathcal{A}$ prepared by $\mathcal{B}$ is computationally indistinguishable from that of the real scheme. Therefore, (i) and (ii) happen with equal chance. Thus, $\mathcal{B}$ can break the targeted assumption with non-negligible probability.

6 Efficiency and Parameters

6.1 Efficiency

- A proof consists of 5 encodings, each of which is a ciphertext of the underlying RQC scheme. Therefore, the size of proof is $|\pi| = 10m_0n\log\mathfrak{q}$.
- A crs contains $m+1$ polynomials v_i's, a polynomial $t(x)$, the public parameters pp, and $(m-\ell_u+2d+3)$ encodings. Each polynomial is of degree at most d, hence needs $(d+1)m_0\log\mathfrak{q}$ bits for its description. The size of pp is dominated by $(k+1)m_0n\log\mathfrak{q}$. Thus, the size of crs is

$$(2d+4+k+m-\ell_u)m_0n\log\mathfrak{q} + (m+2)(d+1)m_0\log\mathfrak{q} = O(mm_0d\log\mathfrak{q}).$$

6.2 Parameters

This section provides an example of parameters for the scheme. These parameters are selected to target the security level of 128 bits and soundness error of the same level.

Taking attacks in [6,18] into consideration, for the $\mathrm{IRSL}(2n, n, \mathfrak{r}, N)$ problem to be at the 128 bit-level of security, m_0, n, and $\mathfrak{r}$ are chosen such that

$$m_0 > \left\lfloor \frac{m_0 n - N}{2n - \lfloor \frac{N}{\mathfrak{r}} \rfloor} \right\rfloor .$$

And to guarantee the success of decoding, $n, r, \mathfrak{r}, w$, and k are chosen such that $w(r+\mathfrak{r}) \leq \frac{n-k}{2}$. (We use the RQC version in which 1 belongs to the vector space of the secret keys.) Also, the relation between m_0 and n is always $m_0 \geq n$, since a Gabidulin code is employed. To sum up, parameters are chosen to satisfy that

$$\begin{cases} m_0 > \left\lfloor \frac{m_0 n - N}{2n - \lfloor \frac{N}{\mathfrak{r}} \rfloor} \right\rfloor, \\ w(r+\mathfrak{r}) \leq \frac{n-k}{2}, \\ n \leq m_0. \end{cases}$$

The parameter d is fixed to be $d = 2^{13}$, and $N = 4d$ is the number of given "syndromes." Recall that the size of a proof is $|\pi| = 10m_0 n \log \mathfrak{q}$, so we get the result.

N	$\mathfrak{q} = |\mathbb{F}|$	m_0	n	k	r	$\mathfrak{r}$	w	$|\pi|$ (kB)
2^{15}	$\approx 2^{143}$	503	491	3	59	61	2	44147

Acknowledgement. The authors would like to thank Vietnam Institute for Advanced Study in Mathematics (VIASM) for providing a fruitful research environment and working condition. XTD was supported by the KHMM-2022-C07 project. QHV was supported in part by the French ANR projects CryptiQ (ANR-18-CE39-0015), SecNISQ (ANR-21-CE47-0014), TCS-NISQ (ANR-22-CE47-0004), and by the PEPR integrated project EPiQ ANR-22-PETQ-0007 part of Plan France 2030.

References

1. Aguilar, C., Blazy, O., Deneuville, J.C., Gaborit, P., Zémor, G.: Efficient encryption from random quasi-cyclic codes. Cryptology ePrint Archive, Report 2016/1194 (2016). https://eprint.iacr.org/2016/1194
2. Aguilar Melchor, C., et al.: RQC. Technical report, National Institute of Standards and Technology (2019). https://csrc.nist.gov/projects/post-quantum-cryptography/post-quantum-cryptography-standardization/round-2-submissions

3. Belenkiy, M., Camenisch, J., Chase, M., Kohlweiss, M., Lysyanskaya, A., Shacham, H.: Randomizable proofs and delegatable anonymous credentials. In: Halevi, S. (ed.) CRYPTO 2009. LNCS, vol. 5677, pp. 108–125. Springer, Heidelberg (2009). https://doi.org/10.1007/978-3-642-03356-8_7

4. Bellare, M., Goldwasser, S.: New paradigms for digital signatures and message authentication based on non-interactive zero knowledge proofs. In: Brassard, G. (ed.) CRYPTO 1989. LNCS, vol. 435, pp. 194–211. Springer, Heidelberg (1990). https://doi.org/10.1007/0-387-34805-0_19

5. Ben-Sasson, E., Bentov, I., Horesh, Y., Riabzev, M.: Scalable zero knowledge with no trusted setup. In: Boldyreva, A., Micciancio, D. (eds.) CRYPTO 2019, Part III. LNCS, vol. 11694, pp. 701–732. Springer, Heidelberg (2019). https://doi.org/10.1007/978-3-030-26954-8_23

6. Bidoux, L., Briaud, P., Bros, M., Gaborit, P.: RQC revisited and more cryptanalysis for rank-based cryptography. arXiv preprint arXiv:2207.01410 (2022)

7. Blazy, O., Gaborit, P., Mac, D.T.: A rank metric code-based group signature scheme. In: Wachter-Zeh, A., Bartz, H., Liva, G. (eds.) Code-Based Cryptography, pp. 1–21. Springer, Cham (2022)

8. Boneh, D., Boyen, X., Shacham, H.: Short group signatures. In: Franklin, M. (ed.) CRYPTO 2004. LNCS, vol. 3152, pp. 41–55. Springer, Heidelberg (2004). https://doi.org/10.1007/978-3-540-28628-8_3

9. Bootle, J., Cerulli, A., Chaidos, P., Ghadafi, E., Groth, J.: Foundations of fully dynamic group signatures. In: Manulis, M., Sadeghi, A.R., Schneider, S. (eds.) ACNS 2016. LNCS, vol. 9696, pp. 117–136. Springer, Heidelberg (2016). https://doi.org/10.1007/978-3-319-39555-5_7

10. Bootle, J., Cerulli, A., Groth, J., Jakobsen, S.K., Maller, M.: Arya: nearly linear-time zero-knowledge proofs for correct program execution. In: Peyrin, T., Galbraith, S. (eds.) ASIACRYPT 2018, Part I. LNCS, vol. 11272, pp. 595–626. Springer, Heidelberg (2018). https://doi.org/10.1007/978-3-030-03326-2_20

11. Bünz, B., Bootle, J., Boneh, D., Poelstra, A., Wuille, P., Maxwell, G.: Bulletproofs: short proofs for confidential transactions and more. In: 2018 IEEE Symposium on Security and Privacy, pp. 315–334. IEEE Computer Society Press, May 2018. https://doi.org/10.1109/SP.2018.00020

12. Camenisch, J., Krenn, S., Lehmann, A., Mikkelsen, G.L., Neven, G., Pedersen, M.Ø.: Formal treatment of privacy-enhancing credential systems. In: Dunkelman, O., Keliher, L. (eds.) SAC 2015. LNCS, vol. 9566, pp. 3–24. Springer, Heidelberg (2016). https://doi.org/10.1007/978-3-319-31301-6_1

13. Camenisch, J., Lysyanskaya, A.: An efficient system for non-transferable anonymous credentials with optional anonymity revocation. In: Pfitzmann, B. (ed.) EUROCRYPT 2001. LNCS, vol. 2045, pp. 93–118. Springer, Heidelberg (2001). https://doi.org/10.1007/3-540-44987-6_7

14. Chabaud, F., Stern, J.: The cryptographic security of the syndrome decoding problem for rank distance codes. In: Kim, K., Matsumoto, T. (eds.) ASIACRYPT 1996. LNCS, vol. 1163, pp. 368–381. Springer, Heidelberg (1996). https://doi.org/10.1007/BFb0034862

15. Chaum, D., van Heyst, E.: Group signatures. In: Davies, D.W. (ed.) EUROCRYPT 1991. LNCS, vol. 547, pp. 257–265. Springer, Heidelberg (1991). https://doi.org/10.1007/3-540-46416-6_22

16. Chiesa, A., Manohar, P., Spooner, N.: Succinct arguments in the quantum random oracle model. In: Hofheinz, D., Rosen, A. (eds.) TCC 2019, Part II. LNCS, vol. 11892, pp. 1–29. Springer, Heidelberg (2019). https://doi.org/10.1007/978-3-030-36033-7_1

17. Danezis, G., Fournet, C., Groth, J., Kohlweiss, M.: Square span programs with applications to succinct NIZK arguments. In: Sarkar, P., Iwata, T. (eds.) ASIACRYPT 2014, Part I. LNCS, vol. 8873, pp. 532–550. Springer, Heidelberg (2014). https://doi.org/10.1007/978-3-662-45611-8_28

18. Debris-Alazard, T., Tillich, J.P.: Two attacks on rank metric code-based schemes: RankSign and an IBE scheme. In: Peyrin, T., Galbraith, S. (eds.) ASIACRYPT 2018, Part I. LNCS, vol. 11272, pp. 62–92. Springer, Heidelberg (2018). https://doi.org/10.1007/978-3-030-03326-2_3

19. Delerablée, C., Pointcheval, D.: Dynamic fully anonymous short group signatures. In: Nguyen, P.Q. (ed.) Progress in Cryptology - VIETCRYPT 2006. LNCS, vol. 4341, pp. 193–210. Springer, Heidelberg (2006)

20. Fuchsbauer, G., Hanser, C., Slamanig, D.: Structure-preserving signatures on equivalence classes and constant-size anonymous credentials. J. Cryptol. 32(2), 498–546 (2019). https://doi.org/10.1007/s00145-018-9281-4

21. Gaborit, P., Hauteville, A., Phan, D.H., Tillich, J.P.: Identity-based encryption from codes with rank metric. In: Katz, J., Shacham, H. (eds.) CRYPTO 2017, Part III. LNCS, vol. 10403, pp. 194–224. Springer, Heidelberg (2017). https://doi.org/10.1007/978-3-319-63697-9_7

22. Gennaro, R., Gentry, C., Parno, B.: Non-interactive verifiable computing: outsourcing computation to untrusted workers. In: Rabin, T. (ed.) CRYPTO 2010. LNCS, vol. 6223, pp. 465–482. Springer, Heidelberg (2010). https://doi.org/10.1007/978-3-642-14623-7_25

23. Gennaro, R., Gentry, C., Parno, B., Raykova, M.: Quadratic span programs and succinct NIZKs without PCPs. In: Johansson, T., Nguyen, P.Q. (eds.) EUROCRYPT 2013. LNCS, vol. 7881, pp. 626–645. Springer, Heidelberg (2013). https://doi.org/10.1007/978-3-642-38348-9_37

24. Gennaro, R., Minelli, M., Nitulescu, A., Orrù, M.: Lattice-based zk-SNARKs from square span programs. In: Lie, D., Mannan, M., Backes, M., Wang, X. (eds.) ACM CCS 2018, pp. 556–573. ACM Press, October 2018. https://doi.org/10.1145/3243734.3243845

25. Goldwasser, S., Micali, S., Rackoff, C.: The knowledge complexity of interactive proof-systems (extended abstract). In: 17th ACM STOC, pp. 291–304. ACM Press, May 1985. https://doi.org/10.1145/22145.22178

26. Groth, J.: On the size of pairing-based non-interactive arguments. In: Fischlin, M., Coron, J.S. (eds.) EUROCRYPT 2016, Part II. LNCS, vol. 9666, pp. 305–326. Springer, Heidelberg (2016). https://doi.org/10.1007/978-3-662-49896-5_11

27. Ishai, Y., Su, H., Wu, D.J.: Shorter and faster post-quantum designated-verifier zkSNARKs from lattices. In: Vigna, G., Shi, E. (eds.) ACM CCS 2021, pp. 212–234. ACM Press, November 2021. https://doi.org/10.1145/3460120.3484572

28. Kilian, J.: A note on efficient zero-knowledge proofs and arguments (extended abstract). In: 24th ACM STOC. pp. 723–732. ACM Press, May 1992. https://doi.org/10.1145/129712.129782

29. Lipmaa, H.: Succinct non-interactive zero knowledge arguments from span programs and linear error-correcting codes. Cryptology ePrint Archive, Report 2013/121 (2013). https://eprint.iacr.org/2013/121

30. Mac, D.T.: On certain types of code-based signatures. Ph.D. thesis, University of Limoges (2021)

31. Micali, S.: CS proofs (extended abstracts). In: 35th FOCS, pp. 436–453. IEEE Computer Society Press, November 1994. https://doi.org/10.1109/SFCS.1994.365746
32. Parno, B., Gentry, C., Howell, J., Raykova, M.: Pinocchio: nearly practical verifiable computation. Cryptology ePrint Archive, Report 2013/279 (2013). https://eprint.iacr.org/2013/279

Zero-Knowledge Systems from MPC-in-the-Head and Oblivious Transfer

Cyprien Delpech de Saint Guilhem[1]([✉])[ID], Ehsan Ebrahimi[2][ID], and Barry van Leeuwen[1][ID]

[1] COSIC, KU Leuven, Leuven, Belgium
{cyprien.delpechdesaintguilhem,barry.vanleeuwen}@kuleuven.be
[2] Department of Computer Science, University of Luxembourg,
Esch-sur-Alzette, Luxembourg
ehsan.ebrahimi@uni.lu

Abstract. Zero-knowledge proof or argument systems for generic NP statements (such as circuit satisfiability) have typically been instantiated with cryptographic commitment schemes; this implies that the security of the proof system (e.g., computational or statistical) depends on that of the chosen commitment scheme. The MPC-in-the-Head paradigm (Ishai et al., JoC 2009) uses the same approach to construct zero-knowledge systems from the simulated execution of secure multiparty computation protocols.

This paper presents a novel method to construct zero-knowledge protocols which takes advantage of the unique properties of MPC-in-the-Head and replaces commitments with an oblivious transfer protocol. The security of the new construction is proven in the Universal Composability framework of security and suitable choices of oblivious transfer protocols are discussed together with their implications on the security properties and computational efficiency of the zero-knowledge system.

Keywords: Zero-Knowledge · Oblivious Transfer · MPC-in-the-Head

1   Introduction

An *interactive proof system* [24] is a two-party protocol for an unbounded prover and a verifier with the goal of convincing the verifier that a certain statement is true. Such a proof system must fulfill two properties: (1) *completeness*, if the statement is true, an honest prover is able to convince the verifier; and (2) *soundness*, if the statement is not true, no (malicious) prover is able to convince the verifier. A relaxation of an interactive proof system is an *interactive argument system* in which the prover is computationally bounded [10].

The notion of *zero-knowledge* for a proof or argument system, introduced by Goldwasser, Micali and Rackoff [24], ensures that a malicious verifier interacting with an honest prover is not able to learn any information beyond the veracity of

© The Author(s), under exclusive license to Springer Nature Switzerland AG 2024
E. A. Quaglia (Ed.): IMACC 2023, LNCS 14421, pp. 120–136, 2024.
https://doi.org/10.1007/978-3-031-47818-5_7

the statement. Generally, such a construction allows for two inputs: the receiver holds a statement x belonging to some NP Language while the prover holds a witness w with the intent of proving some relation $\mathcal{R}$ about x and w.

Most of the existing zero-knowledge protocols are constructed from *commitment schemes*, relying on their hiding and binding properties. Furthermore, there is some evidence that such commitment schemes may be necessary to construct a zero-knowledge proof system [34]. In this work, we show that a zero-knowledge protocol can alternatively be constructed from an *oblivious transfer protocol*.

To obtain a zero-knowledge protocol using oblivious transfers we use the MPC-in-the-Head (MPCitH) paradigm [27]. In this framework, the prover simulates a secure n-party *multi-party computation (MPC) protocol* which *verifies* that w is a correct witness for x. To do this the prover creates an additive sharing of its witness w, which means that the prover samples w_i, for $i \in [n]$, uniformly at random under the condition that $w = w_1 + w_2 + \ldots + w_n$. The execution of this protocol assumes n parties, P_i, with each party's private input defined as w_i. The result of the simulation of this protocol is n views $\{\text{view}_i\}_{i \in [n]}$. The prover then commits to these views by sending them to the verifier. The verifier responds with some randomly chosen indices $I \subset [n]$ for which the prover opens the commitments $(\text{view}_i)_{i \in I}$, thus demonstrating the correct verification of w by the MPC protocol.

We show, however, that the commitment scheme is unnecessary and one can obtain a zero-knowledge protocol in the MPCitH paradigm by using an oblivious transfer protocol instead. Instead of committing to n views $\{\text{view}_i\}_{i \in [n]}$, the prover, in this OT-hybrid paradigm, engages in an oblivious transfer protocol which has inputs $\{\text{view}_i\}_{i \in [n]}$ submitted by the prover and $I \subset [n]$ submitted by the verifier. At the end of the Oblivious Transfer protocol, the verifier has a subset of views, which it can then check for consistency. Below, we show how this gives us a zero-knowledge protocol in the *Universal Composability* framework [12].

1.1 Technical Overview

In Fig. 3 we describe an MPC-in-the-Head protocol which realises the zero-knowledge proof functionality described in Fig. 1 in the $\mathcal{F}_{\text{OT}}$-hybrid model (see Fig. 2). Due to the arbitrary number of parties that the verifier can choose to open (as long as it does not break the secrecy of the MPC protocol) we use an arbitrary k-out-of-n OT functionality.

We prove the UC-security of our protocol and show that its security holds in the $\mathcal{F}_{\text{OT}}$-hybrid model. First, the completeness of the proof follows from the *correctness* of the MPC protocol; if the latter is perfectly correct, then so is the resulting proof system, in the $\mathcal{F}_{\text{OT}}$-hybrid model.

Secondly, the soundness of the proof system holds unconditionally in the $\mathcal{F}_{\text{OT}}$-hybrid model since a malicious prover is caught whenever its cheating behaviour is observed in the MPC protocol by the verifier; here, the *robustness* of the MPC protocol matters, since a robust MPC protocol will still output a correct rejection of an invalid witness despite a certain number of cheating parties. The property we prove is in fact *knowledge soundness* since the definition of the ZK functionality requires a valid witness to be provided in order to inform the verifier of a valid proof. The UC simulator of our security proof is therefore able to extract a valid witness (with some soundness error) in cases where a malicious prover is able to make an honest verifier accept.

Finally, the zero-knowledge property of the proof system follows from the *privacy* property of the MPC protocol which guarantees that no information is learnt about a secret-shared witness when too few shares are known. Since the OT functionality guarantees that exactly k views out of a possible n will be opened, even for malicious verifiers, the k-privacy of the MPC protocol guarantees malicious-verifier zero-knowledge for the proof system.

When instantiating our protocol with a specific oblivious transfer protocol to realise $\mathcal{F}_{OT}$, the security type (perfect, statistical or computational) of the OT protocol must then also be taken into account to establish the final security guarantees of the proof (or argument) system.

To this effect, in Sect. 4 we list several OT protocols that could be suitable to instantiate our protocol. Given that generic k-out-of-n OT protocols are more difficult to come by in practice, we discuss several options to use simpler 1-out-of-n and even 1-out-of-2 OT protocols based on existing efficient MPCitH protocols from the literature.

1.2 Comparison and Theoretical Value

We discuss how our work differs from the existing zero-knowledge constructions and how it contributes to the theoretical research regarding the round complexity of zero-knowledge protocols.

1. While the construction we present is similar to the compiler proposed in [28], the latter is only a generic protocol which could realize, in the OT-hybrid model, the zero-knowledge proof functionality as a special case. However, due to its generic nature, this compiler carries several inefficiencies, especially due to the fact it is designed so that clients play symmetric roles in the compiled protocol.
   In our construction, only the Prover client will simulate the MPC servers that compute the circuit, rather than this being joint work with the Verifier in an expensive distributed way as propose by Ishai et al. This assymmetry in the role of the Prover and the Verifier is also advantageous for security against malicious Verifiers, since the latter cannnot influence the execution of the MPC protocol to maliciously obtain information about the Prover's secret input. In short, specialising the task of MPC in the hybrid model to the case of zero-knowledge proofs enables us to present a simpler and more optimised protocol than a direct instantiation of the IPS compiler would yield. Additionally, this MPC-in-the-Head construction provides a detailed presentation of how to instantiate this framework with oblivious transfer.
2. Given that the *rewinding* proof technique is troublesome in the quantum setting [2], our work benefits from *straight-line* extraction, especially since

using rewinding of the adversary to prove UC-security of OT protocols is also not allowed. This would be beneficial to construct post-quantum zero-knowledge protocols.

3. The round complexity of a zero-knowledge protocol has been a topic of research since the introduction of the zero-knowledge notion in 1989 (see Appendix A for a brief survey). However, the round complexity of post-quantum zero-knowledge protocols is a recent research direction and it is not as developed as in the classical case.[1] We emphasize that our approach in this paper would be valuable to construct a constant-round post-quantum zero-knowledge protocol since the round complexity of our protocol depends on the (post-quantum) implementation of the OT functionality and it benefits from a *straight-line* extraction.

4. We prove the zero-knowledge in the *Universal Composability* framework [12].

2   Preliminaries

This section introduces notations and recalls standard definitions.

2.1   Notation

We denote by λ the security parameter. For elements $n \in \mathbb{Z}$ we denote by $[n]$ the set of integers $\{1, \ldots, n\}$. We say that a function $f : \mathbb{N} \to \mathbb{N}$ is negligible if, for every positive polynomial $p(\cdot)$ and all sufficiently large integers k it holds that $f(k) < \frac{1}{p(k)}$. We abbreviate a probabilistic polynomial time machine by PPT.

For any element $a \in \mathbb{K}$, we will denote a random sampling of a from a distribution D_α as $a \leftarrow D_\alpha$. Furthermore, we shall denote by U_α the uniform distribution with variance α. If an element a is drawn uniformly random from a set, or according to a protocol, A, where the distribution used to sample from A is known, we may abbreviate by writing $a \leftarrow D_A$.

2.2   Zero-Knowledge Proof and Argument Systems

For an NP language $\mathcal{L}$, we denote by $\mathcal{R}$ the relation consisting of pairs (x, w) such that x is an instance in $\mathcal{L}$ and w is a corresponding candidate witness. In an interactive proof or argument protocol, a prover wishes to demonstrate that some NP statement $x \in \mathcal{L}$ is true using a valid witness w such that $(x, w) \in \mathcal{R}$.

The proof or argument protocol is *correct* if an honest prover always successfully convinces an honest verifier of the veracity of a true statement. The protocol is *sound* if a malicious prover cannot convince an honest verifier that a false statement $x^* \notin \mathcal{L}$ is in fact true; it is additionally *knowledge sound* if a malicious prover cannot convince a verifier even of a true statement $x \in \mathcal{L}$ without knowing at least one valid witness w such that $(x, w) \in \mathcal{R}$.

---

[1] Even with some (apparently) contradictory results: the impossibility [13] and the possibility [32] of constructing constant-round post-quantum black-box zero-knowledge.

For both notions of soundness, it is tolerated that a malicious prover can successfully convince an honest verifier with a negligible probability called the *soundness error*. If this error is negligible even for computationally unbounded malicious provers, then the protocol is called a *proof system*; if the soundness error is negligible only for PPT malicious provers, then the protocol is called an *argument* system.

A proof or argument system can also be *zero-knowledge* (ZK) if the interaction of an honest prover with a verifier reveals no information about the witness w other than its validity. This property can hold against either honest verifiers or fully malicious ones.

UC-secure ZK systems for circuit satisfiability. This work focuses on UC-secure protocols for proving in zero-knowledge the satisfiability of an arbitrary circuit C. We assume that the reader is familiar with the terminology of UC security and proofs [12]. In Fig. 1 we recall the zero-knowledge functionality [16].

The ZK Functionality: $\mathcal{F}_{\mathsf{ZK}}$

The functionality runs with a prover $\mathcal{P}$, a verifier $\mathcal{V}$, and an adversary $\mathcal{A}$.
It is parameterized by $\mathsf{ty} = \{\mathsf{Boolean}, \mathsf{Arithmetic}\}$

Proof: On input of $(\mathsf{sid}, \mathsf{prove}, \mathcal{P}, \mathcal{V}, C, \mathsf{ty}, w)$ from the prover, compute $y = C(w) \in \{0, 1\}$, send (prove, C) to $\mathcal{V}$ and $\mathcal{A}$, and store (C, y).
Verify: On receiving $(\mathsf{sid}, \mathsf{verify}, C, \mathsf{ty})$ from $\mathcal{V}$, query $\mathcal{A}$; If $\mathcal{A}$ returns fail, or if (C, y) has not been stored, send $(\mathsf{sid}, C, 0)$ to $\mathcal{V}$. Otherwise, send (sid, C, y) to $\mathcal{V}$.

Fig. 1. Ideal functionality for circuit-based ZK proofs

In this figure, C is a circuit, with format depending on ty, such that for a given x, $C_x(w) = 1 \Leftrightarrow \mathcal{R}(x, w) = 1$. At the end of the protocol, the verifier then accepts or rejects the proof. We denote by $(\mathcal{P}(x, w), \mathcal{V}(x)) = b$, $b \in \mathbb{F}_2$, the verifier's decision such that $b = 1$ means the verifier accepts and otherwise rejects.

While not explicitly defined in the functionality, the knowledge soundness and zero-knowledge properties of a protocol that securely UC-realizes $\mathcal{F}_{\mathsf{ZK}}$ follow from the different proof cases. Namely, knowledge soundness follows from security against a malicious prover: the UC simulator must input (C, w) to $\mathcal{F}_{\mathsf{ZK}}$ acting as the ideal-world malicious prover such that $\mathcal{F}_{\mathsf{ZK}}$ then induces the ideal-world verifier to accept or reject the proof with the same distribution as the real-world verifier. The simulator must then extract the witness (valid or not) from the real-world malicious prover and this simulation will fail (i.e., the ideal-world verifier will reject a false statement when the real-world verified will incorrectly accept it) exactly with the knowledge soundness error of the protocol.

Similarly, zero-knowledge follows from the security against a dishonest verifier: the UC simulator must produce a protocol transcript, without knowledge of the witness (only of its validity), that cannot be distinguished as a simulation.

2.3   Oblivious Transfer Protocols

Oblivious Transfer (OT) is a well known primitive within cryptography, which has been extensively researched since its introduction by Rabin [36]. In an OT Protocol a sender, S, and a receiver, R, execute the transfer of a subset of messages, $m = \{m_0, \ldots, m_{k-1}\}$, out of a total set of n messages. Depending on the protocol these messages could be bits or strings. Generally OT protocols are divided, broadly, into three different categories depending on k and n: $(k, n) = (1, 2)$, $(k, n) = (1, n)$, and $k, n \in \mathbb{N}, k < n$. For an Oblivious Transfer protocol to be secure the following two properties have to be obtained:

- Sender Security: Upon committing to n messages, $m_1, \ldots, m_n$, the sender is assured that R receives no more than k messages and will only learn the contents of these k messages.
- Receiver Security: Upon committing to the k indices I, $I \subset [n]$, the receiver is assured that S does not learn which messages the receiver has learnt.

In [14] they define a 1-out-of-n OT protocol which is easily adapted to the k-out-of-n variant. We describe this adapted variant in Fig. 2. As you can see this is exactly what we would expect from an OT protocol.

The k-out-of-n OT functionality $\mathcal{F}_{\mathrm{OT}}$

The functionality runs with a sender S, a receiver R, and an adversary $\mathcal{A}$.

Commit: On input of $(\mathsf{sid}, \mathsf{commit}, S, R, (c_1, \ldots, c_n))$ by S, store $(\mathsf{sid}, c_1, \ldots, c_n)$ and send $(\mathsf{sid}, \mathsf{ready})$ to $\mathcal{A}$

Abort: On receipt of $(\mathsf{sid}, \mathsf{ready})$ $\mathcal{A}$ sends (sid, b) to $\mathcal{F}_{\mathrm{OT}}$ where $b \in \{0, 1\}$. If $b = 1$ abort the functionality, else proceed.

Query: On input of $(\mathsf{sid}, \mathsf{query}, S, R, I)$ by R, check if for every $i, j \in I : i \neq j$ and $|I| = k$, moreover check if $(c_1, \ldots, c_n)$ are stored. Then do one of the following:

- If I does not fulfill the requirements return $\perp$ to R.
- If no values are stored, do nothing.
- Else send $(\{c_i\}_{i \in I})$ to R

Fig. 2. Ideal functionality for k-out-of-n OT.

2.4   MPC

In this paper the standard definitions of MPC from the literature will be followed, [11,20,27]. To this extent let n be the number of parties and let $\mathcal{P} = \{P_1, \ldots, P_n\}$ be the set of identified parties. A public input x is known to all parties, while each party individually supplies their private input w_i. To securely realize an n-party functionality f, f takes as input $(x, w_1, \ldots, w_n)$ and produces n outputs. Any protocol, Π, takes as input the party that wishes to execute the protocol, P_i, their private input, w_i, their random input, r_i, and the public parameter x, and possibly a security parameter k in the case of statistical or computational security. Moreover, for the protocol called in round $j + 1$, the protocol will additionally require the messages that P_i received in the previous j rounds. The protocol will then output n messages, and, if required, a broadcast message. Specifically, if the broadcast message of Π is abort then the protocol terminates immediately, only outputting P_i's local output. Throughout the execution of a protocol the view of a player P_i, denoted view_i, is constructed. This view includes w_i, r_i, and the messages that P_i received during the execution of Π. The following definition follows naturally:

Definition 1. *Let view_i and view_j be produced by protocol Π with respect to some public input x. Then two views can be called consistent if the outgoing messages implicit in view_i are identical to the incoming messages reported in view_j and vice versa.*

Note that this is a natural definition as we can take view_i, Π, and x and reconstruct the local output for P_i and the messages sent. In [27] it is shown that there is no difference between consistency of the views from a global perspective and a local perspective.

Lemma 1 (Lemma 2.3, [27]). *Let Π be an n-party protocol with public input x. Let $\{\mathsf{view}_1, \ldots, \mathsf{view}_n\}$ be the set of (not necessarily correct) views. Then for any $i, j \in [n]$, it holds that view_i and view_j are consistent with respect to Π and x if and only if there exists and honest execution of Π with public input x in which view_i is the view of P_i for every $i \in [n]$.*

For our MPC constructions we will consider both the semi-honest and the malicious models. For the semi-honest model, also known as "Honest, but curious", the parties will execute a protocol Π as is prescribed, however the parties will attempt to learn more information from the protocol than is intended to. In the malicious model such restrictions are lifted and the parties are allowed to act arbitrarily in regards to the protocols and each other.

In the semi-honest case security can be broken into the following two properties:

Definition 2 (Correctness [27, Definition 2.4]). *We say that Π realize a deterministic n-party functionality $f(x, w_1, \ldots, w_n)$ with perfect (resp., statistical) correctness if for all inputs $x, w_1, \ldots, w_n$ the probability that the output of some player is different from the output of f is 0 (resp., negligible in λ), where the probability is over the independent choices of the random inputs $r_1, \ldots, r_n$.*

Definition 3 (t-Privacy [27, Definition 2.5]). *Let $1 \leq t < n$. We say that Π realizes f with perfect t-privacy if there is a PPT simulator Sim such that for any inputs $x, w_1, \ldots, w_n$ and every set of corrupted players $T \subseteq [n]$, where $|T| \leq t$,* the joint view $\mathsf{View}_T(x, w_1, \ldots, w_n)$ of players in T is distributed identically to $\mathsf{Sim}(T, x, (w_i)_{i \in T}, f_T(x, w_1, \ldots, w_n))$, where $f_T(\cdot)$ denotes the view of the output of f of the parties in T.

For relaxations to statistical (resp., computational) t-privacy, we require that for every distinguisher D (resp., D with circuit size $\mathsf{poly}(\lambda)$), there is a negligible function $\delta(\cdot)$ such that

$$|\Pr[D(\mathsf{View}_T(\lambda, x, w_1, \ldots, w_n)) = 1]$$
$$- \Pr[D(\mathsf{Sim}(\lambda, T, x, (w_i)_{i \in T}, f_T(x, w_1, \ldots, w_n))) = 1]| \leq \delta(\lambda)$$

For the malicious model, however, correctness is not sufficient. Instead we adopt notion that Π is secure if and only if the protocol is t-private, as defined above, and r-robust.

Definition 4 (r-Robustness [27, Definition 2.6]). *We say that Π realizes f with* perfect *(resp., statistical) r-robustness if it is perfectly (resp,. statistically) correct in the presence of a semi-honest adversary as in Definition 2, and furthermore for any computationally unbounded malicious adversary corrupting a set R of at most r players, and for any inputs $(x, w_1, \ldots, w_n)$, the following robustness property holds. If there is no $(w_1', \ldots, w_n')$ such that $f(x, w_1', \ldots, w_n') = 1$, then the probability that some uncorrupted players outputs 1 in an execution of Π in which the inputs of the honest players are consistent with $(x, w_1, \ldots, w_n)$ is 0 (resp., negligible in λ).*

3 Zero-Knowledge from MPCitH and Oblivious Transfer

It were these definitions that led to MPC-in-the-Head (MPCitH) paradigm, as introduced in [27], where any honest-majority MPC protocol, i.e. $t < \frac{n}{2}$ corruptions, can be used to obtain a zero-knowledge proof for an arbitrary relation $\mathcal{R}$.

The idea is as follows: Let $\mathcal{P}$ be the prover and let $\mathcal{V}$ be the verifier. Given a public parameter x, $\mathcal{P}$ submits a witness w, which upon computation of $\mathcal{R}(x, w)$ shows that x belongs to a language $\mathcal{L}$ or not, specifically: $\mathcal{R}(x, w) \in \mathbb{F}_2$ such that, for a valid witness, if $x \in \mathcal{L}$, $\mathcal{R}(x, w) = 1$, otherwise $\mathcal{R}(x, w) = 0$.

Now assume that $\mathcal{P}$ generates a sharing, $\langle w \rangle = (w_1, \ldots, w_n)$, and computes $\mathcal{R}(x, \langle w \rangle)$ by choosing random coins r_i uniformly at random. By regarding each pair (w_i, r_i) as parties in an n-party MPC protocol, as described in Sect. 2.4, we then obtain a set of views, view_i, corresponding to the output of the MPC protocol.

Having obtained the views, the $\mathcal{P}$ submits the views to an oracle $\mathcal{O}$, which the verifier, $\mathcal{V}$, then queries a set of indices, I, to obtain $\{\mathsf{view}_i\}_{i \in I}$. By Lemma 1 we then obtain that the verifier can conclude if the computation was done correctly by checking that the opened views are all consistent with each other and that the protocol outputs a positive result.

One way to realize such an oracle is by implementing an oblivious transfer protocol. Figure 3 presents an MPCitH-based ZK proof system in the $\mathcal{F}_{\mathsf{OT}}$-hybrid model.

The MPCitH-based protocol: Π_{ZK}

This protocol is parametrized by an n-party MPC protocol Π_{MPC} which computes an arithmetic or Boolean circuit C and is t-private and s-robust.

Prove: On input of $(\mathsf{sid}, \mathsf{prove}, \mathcal{P}, \mathcal{V}, C, w)$,

1. $\mathcal{P}$ secret-shares $\langle w \rangle$ such that $\sum_{i=1}^{n} w_i = w$;
2. $\mathcal{P}$ generates the random coins r_i for each player P_i, for $i \in [n]$;
3. $\mathcal{P}$ simulates an execution of Π_{MPC} between $P_1, \ldots, P_n$ and records $\mathsf{view}_i = (w_i, r_i, \{m_j^i\})$ where $\{m_j^i\}$ is the set of messages received by P_i during the execution of Π_{MPC};
4. $\mathcal{P}$ sends $(\mathsf{sid}, \mathsf{send}, \mathcal{S}, \mathcal{R}, (\mathsf{view}_1, \ldots, \mathsf{view}_n))$ to $\mathcal{F}_{\mathsf{OT}}$.

Verify: On input of $(\mathsf{sid}, \mathsf{verify}, \mathcal{P}, \mathcal{V}, C)$,

1. $\mathcal{V}$ samples at random a subset $I \subset [n]$ of size t;
2. $\mathcal{V}$ sends $(\mathsf{sid}, \mathsf{receive}, \mathcal{S}, \mathcal{R}, I)$ to $\mathcal{F}_{\mathsf{OT}}$ and obtains $\{\mathsf{view}_i\}_{i \in I}$;
3. $\mathcal{V}$ outputs $(\mathsf{sid}, C, 1)$ if (1) the messages contained in and implied by the received views are consistent with each other, and (2) the opened views are consistent with the MPC protocol outputting $C(\langle w \rangle) = 1$ to each party; otherwise $\mathcal{V}$ outputs $(\mathsf{sid}, C, 0)$.

Fig. 3. MPC-in-the-head ZK protocol in the $\mathcal{F}_{\mathsf{OT}}$-hybrid model.

This protocol, Π_{ZK}, proceeds exactly as described when instantiated with $\mathcal{F}_{\mathsf{OT}}$. In the $\mathcal{F}_{\mathsf{OT}}$-hybrid model, Π_{ZK} can be shown to UC-securely realize $\mathcal{F}_{\mathsf{ZK}}$.

Theorem 1. *Let Π_{MPC} be an n-party protocol with perfect correctness, t-privacy and perfect r-robustness, with $t = \Omega(\lambda)$ and $n = c \cdot t$ for some constant $c > 1$. Π_{ZK} of Fig. 3 UC-realises $\mathcal{F}_{\mathsf{ZK}}$ of Fig. 1 with soundness error $\epsilon = \max\{p_1(n, t, r), p_2(n, t, r)\}$, where*

$$p_1(n, t, r) = \binom{r}{t}\binom{n}{t}^{-1}, \quad and$$

$$p_2(n, t, r) = \begin{cases} 0 & otherwise \\ \left(\sum_{j=0}^{k} \binom{k}{j}\binom{n-2k}{t-j}\right)\binom{n}{t}^{-1} & if\ n - 2k > 0 \end{cases}$$

and $k = \lfloor r/2 \rfloor + 1$.

Proof. We design a simulator Sim to act as adversary in the ideal-world execution. We consider in turn the four cases of the real-world where: both parties are honest, only the verifier is honest, only the prover is honest, and both parties are corrupt.

1. Both Parties Are Honest: Upon receiving the query from $\mathcal{F}_{\mathsf{ZK}}$, the simulator Sim sends $(\mathsf{sid}, \mathsf{ready})$ to $\mathcal{A}$ on behalf of $\mathcal{F}_{\mathsf{OT}}$. If $\mathcal{A}$ responds with abort, then Sim responds abort to $\mathcal{F}_{\mathsf{ZK}}$, otherwise it responds with continue.

2. *Only the Prover Is Corrupt:* Upon receiving $\mathsf{view}^* = (\mathsf{view}_1^*, \dots, \mathsf{view}_n^*)$ from the corrupt prover $\mathcal{P}^*$, the simulator reconstructs a witness $w^* = w_1^* + \dots + w_n^*$ and sends $(\mathsf{sid}, \mathsf{prove}, \mathcal{P}, \mathcal{V}, C, w^*)$ to $\mathcal{F}_{\mathsf{ZK}}$. It also sends $(\mathsf{sid}, \mathsf{ready})$ to $\mathcal{A}$.

When $\mathcal{F}_{\mathsf{ZK}}$ queries Sim, the simulator first checks $\mathcal{A}$'s response. If $\mathcal{A}$ replied $(\mathsf{sid}, \mathsf{abort})$ to $\mathcal{F}_{\mathsf{OT}}$, then Sim also sends abort to $\mathcal{F}_{\mathsf{ZK}}$. Otherwise, Sim responds with continue.

3. *Only the Verifier Is Corrupt:* Upon receiving (prove, C) from $\mathcal{F}_{\mathsf{ZK}}$, the simulator sends $(\mathsf{sid}, \mathsf{ready})$ to $\mathcal{A}$ on behalf of $\mathcal{F}_{\mathsf{OT}}$. When $\mathcal{A}$ sends $(\mathsf{sid}, \mathsf{receive}, \mathcal{S}, \mathcal{R}, I)$ to $\mathcal{F}_{\mathsf{OT}}$, Sim sends $(\mathsf{sid}, \mathsf{verify}, C)$ to $\mathcal{F}_{\mathsf{ZK}}$. If $\mathcal{A}$ responded with $(\mathsf{sid}, \mathsf{abort})$ to $\mathcal{F}_{\mathsf{OT}}$, then Sim responds abort to $\mathcal{F}_{\mathsf{ZK}}$ when queried, otherwise it responds continue, and receives (sid, C, y).

The simulator invokes the t-privacy simulator $\mathsf{Sim}_{\mathsf{MPC}}$ of the MPC protocol on corruption set I by sampling $\{w_i\}_{i \in I}$ uniformly at random as in the protocol and inputting $(I, x, \{w_i\}_{i \in I}, y)$. From $\mathsf{Sim}_{\mathsf{MPC}}$ it then receives a set of consistent views $\{\mathsf{view}_i\}_{i \in I}$ which will agree with the required outcome, y. Finally, Sim sends these views to $\mathcal{A}$ as the response from $\mathcal{F}_{\mathsf{OT}}$.

4. *Both Parties Are Corrupt:* Just like in case 2, the corrupt prover, $\mathcal{P}^*$, submits $\mathsf{view}^* = (\mathsf{view}_1^*, \dots, \mathsf{view}_n^*)$ to Sim. Upon receiving these views Sim sends $\mathsf{sid}, \mathsf{ready}$ to $\mathcal{A}$ and processes any abort instructions coming from $\mathcal{A}$ if necessary. Unless it receives an abort instruction from $\mathcal{A}$, like in case 3, the corrupt verifier, $\mathcal{V}^*$, submits a set I to Sim. Sim then sends $(\mathsf{view}_i)_{i \in I}$ to $\mathcal{V}^*$. No further simulation is necessary as both the prover and the verifier are corrupt.

Completeness [27, proof of Theorem 3.1]: If $(x, w) \in R$ and the prover is honest, then, since $\sum_{i=1}^n w_i = w$ and Π_{MPC} is perfectly correct, the views $\mathsf{view}_1, \dots, \mathsf{view}_n$ always have output 1. Since these views are honestly produced, they are always consistent with each other.

Soundness: Note that in the real world, the prover uses an MPC-in-the-Head protocol to produce a set of n views, $(\mathsf{view}_1, \dots, \mathsf{view}_n)$, from which the verifier then gets to select a t-sized set of views to open. However, in the ideal world, the prover submits the n views to Sim who then extracts the witnesses $w_1^*, \dots, w_n^*$ and recombines them to obtain $w^* = w_1^* + \dots + w_n^*$. Sim then sends the recombined witness to $\mathcal{F}_{\mathsf{ZK}}$. $\mathcal{F}_{\mathsf{ZK}}$ then evaluates if the witness received is correct and returns the outcome, abort or accept, to the verifier. Clearly there is a discrepancy here between the real world and the ideal world if, and only if, the t sized set of views opened to the verifier is consistent while there are views in the remaining $(n - t)$ views that would cause an inconsistency; this would cause the ideal world verifier to abort while the real world verifier would accept. Since we are opening t views of a t-private and perfectly r-robust MPC protocol, the soundness analysis follows exactly that of the protocol of Ishai et al. for MPC-in-the-head with MPC in the malicious model [27, Theorem 4.1]. Here we make use of the explicit probability formulae given by Giacomelli et al. [19] following the analysis of Ishai et al. We therefore have that the soundness error is equal to the value $\epsilon(n,t,r) = \max\{p_1(n,t,r), p_2(n,t,r)\}$, where

$$p_1(n,t,r) = \binom{r}{t}\binom{n}{t}^{-1}, \quad \text{and}$$

$$p_2(n,t,r) = \begin{cases} 0 & \text{otherwise} \\ \left(\sum_{j=0}^{k}\binom{k}{j}\binom{n-2k}{t-j}\right)\binom{n}{t}^{-1} & \text{if } n-2k>0 \end{cases},$$

where $k = \lfloor r/2 \rfloor + 1$. Here p_1 illustrates the case in which $\mathcal{A}$ has corrupted a set of views which do not pass the robustness threshold and therefore $t \leq r$. This means that the soundness error, which is the probability that the ideal world aborts while the real world accepts, is dictated by the probability that a set is chosen in which the t views are consistent while there is an inconsistency within the remaining $r-t$ views out of all the possible size t sets. Similarly, p_2 illustrates the case in which $\mathcal{A}$ manages to corrupt a set that breaks the r-robustness of the protocol. Note that in this case r-robustness can not be broken if $2k \geq n$. This concludes that the soundness error can be described as

$$|\Pr[\mathsf{Exec}_{Z,\Pi,\mathcal{P}^*} = 1] - \Pr[\mathsf{Exec}_{Z,\mathcal{F},\mathsf{Sim}_{\mathcal{P}^*}} = 1]| = \epsilon(n,t,r)$$

Zero-Knowledge: If Π_{MPC} is *perfectly* t-private, then the simulation returned by $\mathsf{Sim}_{\mathsf{MPC}}$ is case 3 is distributed identically to an honest execution of the protocol. Similarly, if Π_{MPC} is *statistically or computationally* t-private, then the distribution of the views returned by $\mathsf{Sim}_{\mathsf{MPC}}$ is statistically or computationally close to that of the views produced by an honest prover.

$$|\Pr[\mathsf{Exec}_{Z,\Pi,\mathcal{A}} = 1] - \Pr[\mathsf{Exec}_{Z,\mathcal{F},\mathsf{Sim}_{\mathcal{V}^*}} = 1]| = |D_{\Pi_{\mathsf{MPC}}} - D_{\mathsf{Sim}_{\mathsf{MPC}}}|$$

□

4 Suitable Oblivious Transfer Protocols

The characteristics of the MPCitH proof system in the OT-hybrid model that we propose in Sect. 3 are strongly tied to those of the chosen OT protocol. Namely, the proof system will have as many rounds as the OT protocol does, will be secure against either unbounded or computationally-bounded[2] provers depending on the OT protocol's security against malicious senders, will be honest-verifier zero-knowledge if the OT protocol is only secure against passive malicious receivers, and so on. In this section, we therefore discuss the suitability of a non-exhaustive list of UC-secure OT protocols from the literature, summarized in Table 1, to instantiate the OT functionality used by our protocol.

While the MPCitH proof system from Sect. 3 uses an arbitrary k-out-of-n OT protocol, in practice the values for k and n are fixed by the choice of the MPC protocol. As can be seen from Table 1, in fact k-out-of-n OT protocols are the least common in the literature as they are often not the initial goal of OT protocol designers.

---

[2] In this case our protocol would formally be an MPCitH argument system.

Table 1. Non-exhaustive list of UC-secure OT protocols

Reference	Format	Rounds	UC Secure	Security Level	Post Quantum	OT type
[4]	1/2	2	ROM	Statistical	Multiple	String
[35]	1/2	2	CRS	Statistical	LWE	Bit
[31]	1/2	4	ROM	Computational	Isogenies	String
[17]	1/2	2	CRS	Statistical	LPN	String
[3] Protocol-1	1/2	2	ROM	Computational	Isogenies	String
[3] Protocol-2	1/2	4	Standard	Computational	Isogenies	String
[33]	$1/n$	5	Standard	Statistical	NTRU	String
[26]	$1/n$	2	CRS	Computational	×	String
[9]	$1/n$	3	ROM	Statistical	LWE	String
[25]	k/n	3	CRS	Computational	×	String

4.1 Generic MPCitH and 1-out-of-2 Oblivious Transfer

The initial proposal for MPCitH by Ishai et al. [27] can straightforwardly be instantiated with a 2-party MPC protocol, implying $t = 1$; this enables the use of 1-out-of-2 OT to realize $\mathcal{F}_{OT}$. This is advantageous because this is the type of OT that is most often first constructed, and is the most present in the post-quantum OT literature (see Table 1).

This type of OT also tends to be the most efficient, with several constructions requiring only two rounds of communication; this yields a two-round MPCitH zero-knowledge argument system, since the security against a malicious OT sender holds with computational assumptions.

However, a drawback of this approach is that each execution of the MPCitH protocol has a soundness error of 1/2 because a new sharing of the witness is created each time. To achieve soundness errors of $O(2^{-\lambda})$ therefore requires $O(\lambda)$ independent repetitions of the MPC protocol, which is computationally expensive for the prover.

Furthermore, two-round OT protocols that are simulation-secure (let alone UC-secure) are impossible in the plain model [23] which therefore implies that any zero-knowledge proof systems based on efficient two-round oblivious transfer must necessarily rely on setup assumptions such as the random oracle model or a common reference string.

4.2 Broadcast MPCitH and 1-out-of-n Oblivious Transfer

A drawback of the previous instantiation is that creating independent 2-party secret sharings of the witness leads to computational inefficiency for the prover, since it has to simulate $O(\lambda)$ repetitions of the MPC protocol; this is also not efficient for the communication efficiency of the proof system, since each repetition of the MPC protocol needs to open the view of one party to the verifier.

To reduce the number of repetitions, and thus the amount of communication that is sent, it can be interesting to increase the value of n, and also vary the value of t. However, as Table 1 shows, t-out-of-n UC-secure OT protocols are not common—the only one we found is furthermore not post-quantum secure. Therefore it is more interesting to look at specific values for t.

When the MPC protocol used for the MPCitH construction is $(n-1)$-private, we say that is it "full-threshold" to mean that the threshold of tolerated privacy corruptions is as high as it can possibly be. In this setting, all but one of the MPC parties' views can be opened to the verifier which means that $\mathcal{F}_{OT}$ of Fig. 1 can be realized by an $(n-1)$-out-of-n OT protocol, also known as "all-but-one OT". However, efficient constructions for this type of OT have only recently been proposed [5] and their design space is not as well understood. Independently of the chosen OT protocol, such an instantiation would still require opening $n-1$ views for each repetition of the MPC protocol, which would not improve the communication efficiency.

This can be remedied by choosing an MPC protocol which exclusively uses a broadcast communication channel; that is, whenever a party sends a message, it is received identically by all other parties in the protocol. With such a communication model, much less data needs to be included in the views of each MPC party since all incoming messages from party P_i are identical for all other parties, and equal to all outgoing messages of party P_i.

Therefore, when combined with a full-threshold MPC protocol (see Sect. 4.2), when all parties except for P_i are requested by the MPCitH verifier, the prover needs to send only the list of outgoing messages of P_i, rather than the $n-1$ lists of incoming messages for the other parties.

For the $\mathcal{F}_{OT}$-hybrid version that we propose in Sect. 3, this implies that $\mathcal{F}_{OT}$ can be realized with 1-out-of-n OT protocols for the part of the views that contain the MPC protocol messages; since that is usually the biggest part of the view, this results in a factor n reduction in the amount of communication. Furthermore, 1-out-of-n OT protocols are more commonly built than $(n-1)$-out-of-n ones (see Table 1) which gives more choices for the instantiation.

4.3   Hypercube MPCitH and 1-out-of-2 Oblivious Transfer

While most recent MPCitH constructions are based on broadcast MPC [6,15], the computational cost of $(n-1)$-out-of-n and 1-out-of-n OT protocols required to instantiate our construction may be too high, and reverse the advantages gained from the use of broadcast-based MPC protocols.

The recent technique of "Hypercube MPCitH" [1] can enable the return to 2-party MPC by secret-sharing a high number of MPC parties, say $n = N^d = 32$, into $d = 5$ parallel executions of $N = 2$-party MPC computations which use a single N^d-sharing of the witness.

The advantage of this technique is to reduce the opening of the message part of the views of the MPC protocol to 1-out-of-2 OTs, instead of 1-out-of-n, while grouping the opening of $n-1$ witness share parts of the views into a single $(n-1)$-out-of-n OT.

Acknowledgments. Cyprien Delpech de Saint Guilhem is a Junior FWO Post-doctoral Fellow under project 1266123N. Ehsan Ebrahimi is supported by the Luxembourg National Research Fund under the Junior CORE project QSP (C22/IS/17272217/QSP/Ebrahimi). This work has been supported in part by the Defense Advanced Research Projects Agency (DARPA) under Contract No. HR001120C0085, by CyberSecurity Research Flanders with reference number VR20192203 and by the FWO under Odysseus project GOH9718N. Any opinions, findings and conclusions or recommendations expressed in this material are those of the authors and do not necessarily reflect the views of DARPA, Cyber Security Research Flanders, or the FWO.

A   Constant-Round Zero-Knowledge

Table 2 surveys the round complexity of computational zero-knowledge protocols. Katz [30] shows that if a language L has a 4-round, black-box, computational zero-knowledge proof system with negligible soundness error, then $\bar{L} \in \mathbf{MA}$. Particularly, assuming the polynomial hierarchy does not collapse, the five rounds computational zero-knowledge proof systems [21] is optimal.

Table 2. Constant-round Zero-knowledge Protocols.

Ref	System	Verifier coins	Black-box Sim	Round	Achievability	Assumption
[22]	Proof	Public	✓	constant	×	
[29]	Proof	Public	×	constant	×	iO
[21]	Proof	Private	✓	5	✓	Claw-free
[18]	Proof	Private	×	3	×	iO
[8]	Proof	Private	×	4	✓	certain HF^a and LWE
[22]	Arg.	Public	✓	3	×	
[8]	Arg.	Public	×	5	✓	certain HF^a and LWE
[22]	Arg.	Private	✓	3	×	
[7]	Arg.	Private	✓	4	✓	one-way function
[8]	Arg.	Private	×	3	✓	certain HF^a and LWE

^{a} keyless multi-collision-resistant hash functions.

References

1. Aguilar Melchor, C., Gama, N., Howe, J., Hülsing, A., Joseph, D., Yue, D.: The return of the SDitH. In: Hazay, C., Stam, M. (eds.) EUROCRYPT 2023, Part V. LNCS, April 2023, vol. 14008, pp. 564–596. Springer, Heidelberg (2023). https://doi.org/10.1007/978-3-031-30589-4_20
2. Ambainis, A., Rosmanis, A., Unruh, D.: Quantum attacks on classical proof systems: the hardness of quantum rewinding. In: 55th FOCS, October 2014, pp. 474–483. IEEE Computer Society Press (2014). https://doi.org/10.1109/FOCS.2014.57

3. Badrinarayanan, S., Masny, D., Mukherjee, P., Patranabis, S., Raghuraman, S., Sarkar, P.: Round-optimal oblivious transfer and MPC from computational CSIDH. In: Boldyreva, A., Kolesnikov, V. (eds.) PKC 2023, Part I. LNCS, May 2023, vol. 13940, pp. 376–405. Springer, Heidelberg (2023). https://doi.org/10.1007/978-3-031-31368-4_14

4. Barreto, P.S.L.M., David, B., Dowsley, R., Morozov, K., Nascimento, A.C.A.: A framework for efficient adaptively secure composable oblivious transfer in the ROM. Cryptology ePrint Archive, Report 2017/993 (2017). https://eprint.iacr.org/2017/993

5. Baum, C., et al.: Publicly verifiable zero-knowledge and post-quantum signatures from vole-in-the-head. In: Handschuh, H., Lysyanskaya, A. (eds.) Advances in Cryptology, CRYPTO 2023, pp. 581–615. Springer, Cham (2023). https://doi.org/10.1007/978-3-031-38554-4_19

6. Baum, C., de Saint Guilhem, C.D., Kales, D., Orsini, E., Scholl, P., Zaverucha, G.: Banquet: short and fast signatures from AES. In: Garay, J.A. (ed.) PKC 2021, Part I. LNCS, vol. 12710, pp. 266–297. Springer, Cham (2021). https://doi.org/10.1007/978-3-030-75245-3_11

7. Bellare, M., Jakobsson, M., Yung, M.: Round-optimal zero-knowledge arguments based on any one-way function. In: Fumy, W. (ed.) EUROCRYPT 1997. LNCS, vol. 1233, pp. 280–305. Springer, Heidelberg (1997). https://doi.org/10.1007/3-540-69053-0_20

8. Bitansky, N., Kalai, Y.T., Paneth, O.: Multi-collision resistance: a paradigm for keyless hash functions. In: Diakonikolas, I., Kempe, D., Henzinger, M. (eds.) Proceedings of the 50th Annual ACM SIGACT Symposium on Theory of Computing, STOC 2018, Los Angeles, CA, USA, 25–29 June 2018, pp. 671–684. ACM (2018). https://doi.org/10.1145/3188745.3188870

9. Blazy, O., Chevalier, C., Vu, Q.H.: Post-quantum UC-secure oblivious transfer in the standard model with adaptive corruptions. In: Proceedings of the 14th International Conference on Availability, Reliability and Security, ARES 2019, pp. 28:1–28:6. ACM (2019). https://doi.org/10.1145/3339252.3339280

10. Brassard, G., Chaum, D., Crépeau, C.: Minimum disclosure proofs of knowledge. J. Comput. Syst. Sci. 37(2), 156–189 (1988). https://doi.org/10.1016/0022-0000(88)90005-0

11. Canetti, R.: Security and composition of multi-party cryptographic protocols. Cryptology ePrint Archive, Report 1998/018 (1998). https://eprint.iacr.org/1998/018

12. Canetti, R.: Universally composable security: a new paradigm for cryptographic protocols. In: 42nd FOCS, October 2001, pp. 136–145. IEEE Computer Society Press (2001). https://doi.org/10.1109/SFCS.2001.959888

13. Chia, N.H., Chung, K.M., Liu, Q., Yamakawa, T.: On the impossibility of post-quantum black-box zero-knowledge in constant round. In: 62nd FOCS, February 2022, pp. 59–67. IEEE Computer Society Press (2022). https://doi.org/10.1109/FOCS52979.2021.00015

14. David, B., Dowsley, R., Nascimento, A.C.A.: Universally composable oblivious transfer based on a variant of LPN. In: Gritzalis, D., Kiayias, A., Askoxylakis, I. (eds.) CANS 2014. LNCS, vol. 8813, pp. 143–158. Springer, Cham (2014). https://doi.org/10.1007/978-3-319-12280-9_10

15. Delpech de Saint Guilhem, C., Orsini, E., Tanguy, T.: Limbo: efficient zero-knowledge MPCitH-based arguments. In: Vigna, G., Shi, E. (eds.) ACM CCS 2021, November 2021, pp. 3022–3036. ACM Press (2021). https://doi.org/10.1145/3460120.3484595

16. Delpech de Saint Guilhem, C., Orsini, E., Tanguy, T., Verbauwhede, M.: Efficient proof of RAM programs from any public-coin zero-knowledge system. Cryptology ePrint Archive, Report 2022/313 (2022). https://eprint.iacr.org/2022/313

17. Döttling, N., Garg, S., Hajiabadi, M., Masny, D., Wichs, D.: Two-round oblivious transfer from CDH or LPN. In: Canteaut, A., Ishai, Y. (eds.) EUROCRYPT 2020. LNCS, vol. 12106, pp. 768–797. Springer, Cham (2020). https://doi.org/10.1007/978-3-030-45724-2_26

18. Fleischhacker, N., Goyal, V., Jain, A.: On the existence of three round zero-knowledge proofs. In: Nielsen, J.B., Rijmen, V. (eds.) EUROCRYPT 2018. LNCS, vol. 10822, pp. 3–33. Springer, Cham (2018). https://doi.org/10.1007/978-3-319-78372-7_1

19. Giacomelli, I., Madsen, J., Orlandi, C.: ZKBoo: faster zero-knowledge for Boolean circuits. In: Holz, T., Savage, S. (eds.) USENIX Security 2016, August 2016, pp. 1069–1083. USENIX Association (2016)

20. Goldreich, O.: Foundations of Cryptography: Basic Tools, vol. 1. Cambridge University Press, Cambridge (2001)

21. Goldreich, O., Kahan, A.: How to construct constant-round zero-knowledge proof systems for NP. J. Cryptol. 9(3), 167–190 (1996)

22. Goldreich, O., Krawczyk, H.: On the composition of zero-knowledge proof systems. In: Paterson, M.S. (ed.) ICALP 1990. LNCS, vol. 443, pp. 268–282. Springer, Heidelberg (1990). https://doi.org/10.1007/BFb0032038

23. Goldreich, O., Oren, Y.: Definitions and properties of zero-knowledge proof systems. J. Cryptol. 7(1), 1–32 (1994). https://doi.org/10.1007/BF00195207

24. Goldwasser, S., Micali, S., Rackoff, C.: The knowledge complexity of interactive proof systems. SIAM J. Comput. 18(1), 186–208 (1989)

25. Green, M., Hohenberger, S.: Practical adaptive oblivious transfer from simple assumptions. In: Ishai, Y. (ed.) TCC 2011. LNCS, vol. 6597, pp. 347–363. Springer, Heidelberg (2011). https://doi.org/10.1007/978-3-642-19571-6_21

26. Hauck, E., Loss, J.: Efficient and universally composable protocols for oblivious transfer from the CDH assumption. Cryptology ePrint Archive, Report 2017/1011 (2017). https://eprint.iacr.org/2017/1011

27. Ishai, Y., Kushilevitz, E., Ostrovsky, R., Sahai, A.: Zero-knowledge proofs from secure multiparty computation. SIAM J. Comput. 39(3), 1121–1152 (2009). https://doi.org/10.1137/080725398

28. Ishai, Y., Prabhakaran, M., Sahai, A.: Founding cryptography on oblivious transfer – efficiently. In: Wagner, D. (ed.) CRYPTO 2008. LNCS, vol. 5157, pp. 572–591. Springer, Heidelberg (2008). https://doi.org/10.1007/978-3-540-85174-5_32

29. Kalai, Y.T., Rothblum, G.N., Rothblum, R.D.: From obfuscation to the security of Fiat-Shamir for proofs. In: Katz, J., Shacham, H. (eds.) CRYPTO 2017, Part II. LNCS, vol. 10402, pp. 224–251. Springer, Cham (2017). https://doi.org/10.1007/978-3-319-63715-0_8

30. Katz, J.: Which languages have 4-round zero-knowledge proofs? In: Canetti, R. (ed.) TCC 2008. LNCS, vol. 4948, pp. 73–88. Springer, Heidelberg (2008). https://doi.org/10.1007/978-3-540-78524-8_5

31. Lai, Y.-F., Galbraith, S.D., Delpech de Saint Guilhem, C.: Compact, efficient and UC-secure isogeny-based oblivious transfer. In: Canteaut, A., Standaert, F.-X. (eds.) EUROCRYPT 2021, Part I. LNCS, vol. 12696, pp. 213–241. Springer, Cham (2021). https://doi.org/10.1007/978-3-030-77870-5_8

32. Lombardi, A., Ma, F., Spooner, N.: Post-quantum zero knowledge, revisited or: how to do quantum rewinding undetectably. In: 63rd FOCS, October/November 2022, pp. 851–859. IEEE Computer Society Press (2021). https://doi.org/10.1109/FOCS54457.2022.00086

33. Mi, B., Huang, D., Wan, S., Hu, Y., Choo, K.K.R.: A post-quantum light weight 1-out-n oblivious transfer protocol. Comput. Electr. Eng. **75**, 90–100 (2019). https://doi.org/10.1016/j.compeleceng.2019.01.021

34. Ong, S.J., Vadhan, S.: An equivalence between zero knowledge and commitments. In: Canetti, R. (ed.) TCC 2008. LNCS, vol. 4948, pp. 482–500. Springer, Heidelberg (2008). https://doi.org/10.1007/978-3-540-78524-8_27

35. Peikert, C., Vaikuntanathan, V., Waters, B.: A framework for efficient and composable oblivious transfer. In: Wagner, D. (ed.) CRYPTO 2008. LNCS, vol. 5157, pp. 554–571. Springer, Heidelberg (2008). https://doi.org/10.1007/978-3-540-85174-5_31

36. Rabin, M.O.: How to exchange secrets with oblivious transfer. Cryptology ePrint Archive, Report 2005/187 (2005). https://eprint.iacr.org/2005/187

ZK-for-Z2K: MPC-in-the-Head Zero-Knowledge Proofs for $\mathbb{Z}_{2^k}$

Lennart Braun[1], Cyprien Delpech de Saint Guilhem[2], Robin Jadoul[2], Emmanuela Orsini[3], Nigel P. Smart[2,4(✉)], and Titouan Tanguy[4]

[1] Department of Computer Science, Aarhus University, Aarhus, Denmark
braun@cs.au.dk
[2] COSIC, KU Leuven, Leuven, Belgium
{cyprien.delpechdesaintguilhem,nigel.smart}@kuleuven.be,
robin.jadoul@esat.kuleuven.be
[3] Department of Computing Sciences, Bocconi University, Milan, Italy
emmanuela.orsini@unibocconi.it
[4] Zama. Inc, Paris, France
titouan.tanguy@zama.ai

Abstract. In this work, we extend the MPC-in-the-Head framework, used in recent efficient zero-knowledge protocols, to work over the ring $\mathbb{Z}_{2^k}$, which is the primary operating domain for modern CPUs. The proposed schemes are compatible with any threshold linear secret sharing scheme and draw inspiration from MPC protocols adapted for ring operations. Additionally, we explore various batching methodologies, leveraging Shamir's secret sharing schemes and Galois ring extensions, and show the applicability of our approach in RAM program verification. Finally, we analyse different options for instantiating the resulting ZK scheme over rings and compare their communication costs.

1 Introduction

Zero-knowledge (ZK) proofs [21] are a fundamental tool for numerous privacy-preserving applications. A proof system enables a prover to convince a verifier that a statement is true beyond reasonable doubt. The zero-knowledge property additionally ensures that the only information learnt from the interaction by the verifier (or any other listener) is the veracity of the statement, and nothing else.

A common method of expressing statements for proof systems is circuit satisfiability. In this approach, both the prover and verifier possess a circuit C, and the prover aims to demonstrate their knowledge of a witness w which satisfies the condition $C(w) = 0$. Usually, C is a circuit defined over a field, either binary or arithmetic. However, many use cases of ZK proof systems (such as program verification) require the statement to be expressed with arithmetic over a ring, such as $\mathbb{Z}_{2^k}$. In particular, the underlying structure of choice for modern CPUs, 64-bit integers, can be expressed over the ring $\mathbb{Z}_{2^{64}}$. Hence proof systems natively compatible with this ring arithmetic allow to preserve the semantics of a conventional CPU, without the costly need to emulate it with finite field arithmetic instead.

© The Author(s), under exclusive license to Springer Nature Switzerland AG 2024
E. A. Quaglia (Ed.): IMACC 2023, LNCS 14421, pp. 137–157, 2024.
https://doi.org/10.1007/978-3-031-47818-5_8

There are few exceptions to this approach and some ZK protocols have been extended to operate over rings. In particular, when considering highly efficient and scalable zero-knowledge protocols, some works [3,4,27] have extended protocols based on vector oblivious linear evaluation (VOLE) to work over $\mathbb{Z}_{2^k}$. These kinds of proofs are able to handle very large statements, such as proving properties of complex computer programs, but are only designated-verifier, i.e., the verifier needs to keep some state secret from the prover. This means that these proofs cannot be made non-interactive and require both parties to be online at the same time.

Publicly verifiable proofs can be generated in different ways, for example following the MPC-in-the-Head (MPCitH) paradigm introduced by Ishai, Kushilevitz, Ostrovsky and Sahai in [23]. Despite its simplicity, this technique has proven efficiency and flexibility, and found a variety of different applications. In the context of zero-knowledge, MPCitH leads to very efficient protocols [2,6,17,18,20,25,26] for proving statements that can be expressed with small to medium-size circuits, and it can be used to develop efficient post-quantum digital signature schemes [5,9].

MPC-in-the-Head. The core idea behind MPCitH is for the prover $\mathcal{P}$ to emulate an MPC protocol for the circuit C, amongst N parties, *in their head*, and commit to each of the emulated parties' view. The verifier $\mathcal{V}$ then asks to decommit a small enough subset of these views so as not to break the privacy of the MPC scheme. The soundness of the proof comes from the correctness of the underlying secure MPC protocol and the decommitment of parties' views. In this way, if the prover wants to cheat in the MPC protocol, they need to simulate some parties as acting maliciously, which in turn can be detected if the set of malicious parties overlaps the set of decommited parties. In addition, since the verifier sees fewer views than the privacy threshold of the MPC protocol, the zero-knowledge property holds.

The seminal work of Ishai et al. [23] describes a generic compiler which makes black-box use of the underlying MPC protocol, but only considers asymptotic complexity; on the other hand, recent concretely efficient protocols [2,17,18,20,26] provide different concrete instantiations for the MPC protocol used to evaluate the circuit C, based both on full-threshold [6,12,25,26] and variable t-threshold secret-sharing schemes [2,17,18,20]. In the latter case, the resulting ZK scheme can achieve better soundness and different choices of t result in different proof-size/efficiency/soundness trade-offs.

Another significant difference among these efficient MPCitH based schemes lies in the way the MPC protocol is used, i.e., whether its task consists of *computing* the circuit C or just *verifying* it. In the former approach, taken for example by [6,23,26], the prover locally emulates the MPC protocol by secret-sharing the witness w among the N simulated parties as the input of the MPC evaluation; then it evaluates in MPC the circuit C and sends to the verifier commitments to each parties' input shares, random tapes and received messages (these values constitute a party's *view*) and to all output shares. Then, the verifier randomly chooses t of the views' commitments to be opened, and verifies that the committed messages are all consistent with each other and with the output shares.

In the latter approach, used for example by [2,5,12], instead of computing the entire circuit C in MPC, the prover, that knows the witness and all the intermediate values of the circuit evaluation, inputs (or *injects*) all these values (the witness and results of non-linear operations) in a secret-shared form as input of the MPC protocol, whose role at this point is simply checking that these inputs are indeed correct. This approach usually leads to better performance for the prover. The input of this MPC protocol is also called *extended witness*, since the role of the MPC protocol is not only that of verifying that w is a valid witness, i.e., that $C(w) = 0$, but also that the non-linear operations in C have been honestly computed.

1.1 Our Contribution

This work describes how to adapt some efficient MPCitH protocols, like [6,12,18], to work over a ring of the form $\mathbb{Z}_{2^k}$. As said before, compared to VOLE-based schemes, MPCitH proofs have the advantage to be public coin, which enables public verifiability and the ability to obtain non-interactive proofs via the Fiat–Shamir transformation [19]. [1] We summarize our contributions as follows.

MPCitH over $\mathbb{Z}_{2^k}$. Our approach considers MPCitH schemes such as Limbo [12] and [18] where the MPC protocol is used to *verify* the correctness of the committed extended inputs. This type of protocols can be well suited to particular use cases, such as verifying computations or proving the correct execution of RAM programs (where an extension of existing protocols to work over $\mathbb{Z}_{2^k}$ can be practically relevant).

In recent years, MPC protocols have also been extended to work over rings; see for example [11,15] for the case of dishonest majority (i.e. $t \geq N/2$), and [1,24] for the case of honest majority (i.e. $t < N/2$). In the case of honest majority protocols, the natural secret-sharing scheme to instantiate a threshold MPC protocol, Shamir's secret sharing [28], requires the underlying algebraic structure to be suitably large. In the case of MPC over finite fields one simply extends the base field so that it contains $N + 1$ elements (where N is the number of parties). In the case of rings it requires a large enough Galois ring extension, so that the largest *exceptional sequence*[2] in the extension ring contains $N + 1$ elements. This was originally introduced in the context of secret sharing by Fehr [16].

A similar approach is also needed in our protocols, where we replace the full-threshold additive sharing scheme used in Limbo with a t-threshold secret sharing scheme to achieve better soundness. We show different options to instantiate our MPC verification procedures, and analyse their respective communication

---

[1] Many VOLE proofs can be split into an interactive, witness-independent preprocessing phase and a public-coin online phase, of which the latter can be made non-interactive. Note that this still requires the designated verifier to keep secret state.

[2] Informally, an exceptional sequence of elements in a ring R is such that their pairwise difference is invertible. (See Sect. 2.2.).

costs. While the t-threshold approach generally comes with a larger proof size than the additive sharing, it trades this for higher efficiency for the verifier, who now only needs to verify that t parties behaved honestly rather than $N-1$.

Finally, we recall that KKW [26] already works over any rings. This scheme is known for its efficiency when dealing with small to medium-sized circuits, however, as mentioned earlier, it requires an MPC evaluation of the entire circuit C, which may not be the most suitable approach for applications like program verification.

Packing Techniques. In the full version [8], we describe a methodology for *packing* within our MPCitH proofs, that is, proving multiple statements for the same circuit in parallel, in a single proof. It consists of two orthogonal approaches that could potentially be combined to achieve better packing rates. We take advantage of Shamir's threshold secret sharing scheme by embedding multiple secrets in the roots of the sharing polynomial, and we also make use of the additional coefficients provided by Galois ring extensions by placing multiple secrets within a single ring element.

Performing batch proofs in this way additionally alleviates the extra communication cost for a threshold scheme, since the extra space that was introduced to have a large enough exceptional set becomes completely utilised. In combination with the increased verifier efficiency and the better soundness guarantees, this makes the threshold setting preferable to the additive setting for batch proofs.

RAM Applications. Also in the full version, we adapt the compilation procedure of [13] to the ring structure. The techniques used there allow to *compile* a list of read and write array accesses to a *standard* arithmetic circuit for proof systems in order to enable program verification. This compilation naturally fits the MPCitH framework extended to the ring $\mathbb{Z}_{2^k}$ that we describe in this paper. This approach removes the need of any bit-decomposition operation; this is different from other recent works [22] that use MPCitH schemes based on the KKW protocol [26] for program verification and ring switching techniques based on edaBits [14].

In our work, to verify the correctness of the memory operations, the initial array is extended to a *checking circuit* C_{check} over $\mathbb{Z}_{2^k}$—with standard linear and multiplication gates and calls to a random oracle—that verifies the consistency of a list of access tuples which contains both the initial array and the accesses performed, encoded as a set of tuples. Given this list, C_{check} produces new multiplication triples that need to be verified via a checking procedure over rings. To perform these consistency checks, [13] describes three subcircuits EqCheck, BdCheck and PermCheck to verify respectively equality, upper and lower bounds and permutation of a list of values in zero-knowledge.

While our compilation follows the blueprint of [13], the main difference is that, to suit the ring structure, we require a large enough exceptional sequence and the removal of the EqCheck sub-circuit that crucially relies on every element having an inverse. Our resulting construction inherits all the properties of the scheme described in [13], leading to a public-coin constant-overhead ZK proof system for computations over $\mathbb{Z}_{2^k}$ in the RAM model.

2   Preliminaries

This section establishes notation and recalls standard results.

2.1   Notation

We denote by λ the computational security parameter and by σ the statistical security parameter. For a set S, we let $a \leftarrow S$ denote the uniform sampling a from S. If D is a probability distribution over S, we let $a \leftarrow D$ denote sampling a from S according to D. For a probabilistic algorithm A, we let $a \leftarrow A$ denote the probabilistic assigning to a of the output of algorithm A, with the distribution being determined by the random coins of A. We let $[n] \subset \mathbb{N}$ denote the set $\{1, \ldots, n\}$. We use $\mathbf{x}$ for vectors of elements, and $\mathbf{x} \circ \mathbf{y}$ for element-wise products.

Zero-knowledge proofs. We use standard definitions of zero-knowledge proofs; we construct our protocols to allow proving arbitrary NP language-membership statements. Let L be in NP and $\mathcal{R}(x, w)$ be a corresponding NP relation with statement x and witness w. That is, the statement x is a member of L if and only if a witness w exists such that $(x, w) \in \mathcal{R}$. We can then consider an arithmetic circuit C (with addition and multiplication gates) that decides (or rather confirms) membership of L when given such a witness. Concretely, the circuit satisfies $C(x, w) = 0$ if and only if $(x, w) \in \mathcal{R}$. The focus of this work are zero-knowledge proofs of knowledge for relations where C is an arithmetic circuit over the ring $\mathbb{Z}_{2^k}$.

2.2   Rings

While the circuits we use in our proof systems are defined over the ring $\mathbb{Z}_{2^k}$, we need to work over larger rings to enable threshold secret sharing and to achieve low soundness errors. In this work we consider two ways to obtain such larger rings as described below.

2-Adic Extensions. Instead of using $\mathbb{Z}_{2^k}$, we increase the modulus and work over $\mathbb{Z}_{2^{k+s}}$, where s depends on the security parameter. This methodology of extending the ring 2-adically in order to check various relations was first introduced in the SPD$\mathbb{Z}_{2^k}$ protocol [11]. While this is a well-studied technique in the MPC literature, there are some limitations inherent to our application to MPCitH. Many soundness checks that use such an extension only guarantee consistency for the k lower bits; this may therefore require iterating such extensions to $\mathbb{Z}_{2^{k+n \cdot s}}$. Moreover, since $\mathbb{Z}_{2^k}$ is not a subring of $\mathbb{Z}_{2^{k+s}}$, we cannot easily lift $\mathbb{Z}_{2^k}$ elements to $\mathbb{Z}_{2^{k+s}}$ if we also wish to retain some auxiliary algebraic relationship between the lifted values. The converse direction— truncating elements of $\mathbb{Z}_{2^{k+s}}$ to $\mathbb{Z}_{2^k}$—is a well-defined ring homomorphism.

Galois Extensions. We extend the base ring $\mathbb{Z}_{2^k}$ by forming the Galois ring $GR(2^k, d) = \mathbb{Z}_{2^k}[X]/(p(X))$, the ring of polynomials with $\mathbb{Z}_{2^k}$ coefficients reduced modulo an irreducible polynomial $p(X)$ of degree d. One advantage of this technique is that reduction modulo 2 results in the field $\mathbb{F}_{2^d}$, i.e., we have $GR(2^k, d)/(2) \simeq \mathbb{F}_{2^d}$. Also, while taking a degree-d extension increases the size of elements by a multiplicative factor d, it can be used for several different checks—unlike the 2-adic extensions. Moreover, a $\mathbb{Z}_{2^k}$ element can be easily "lifted" into a $GR(2^k, d)$ element by using zero for the coefficients of non-constant terms. This lift often retains algebraic relationships between the lifted elements.

Note that both techniques can also be combined to obtain rings of the form $GR(2^{k+s}, d)$.

Definition 1 ((Maximal) Exceptional Sequence). *Let $GR(2^k, d)$ be a degree-d Galois extension of $\mathbb{Z}_{2^k}$. A set $\{\alpha_1, \ldots, \alpha_n\}$ is an exceptional sequence (of length n emph) in $GR(2^k, d)$ if for all $i \neq j \in [n]$ we have $\alpha_i - \alpha_j \in GR(2^k, d)^*$.*

An exceptional sequence of length n is maximal *if there does not exist an exceptional sequence of length $n' > n$.*

In $GR(2^k, d)$, there exists a maximal exceptional sequence of length 2^d, see [1, Prop. 2]. We use $\mathsf{Ex}(R)$ to denote a maximal exceptional sequence of a Galois ring R and assume that we can efficiently sample uniformly random elements from it. For $\mathsf{Ex}(R)$ we can take the 2^d polynomials with $\{0, 1\}$ coefficients as an exceptional sequence.

To perform soundness checks in our proof systems, we will often reduce these to equality checks between two polynomials. While the Schwartz–Zippel Lemma is frequently used for this purpose when the polynomials are defined over finite fields, we require a generalised variant that is adapted to our ring-based setting.

Lemma 1 Generalized Schwartz–Zippel Lemma [10]). *Let R be a ring, and $f: R^n \to R$ an n-variate non-zero polynomial of total degree (the sum of degrees of each variable) D over R. Let $A \subseteq R$ be a finite exceptional sequence with $|A| \geq D$. Then, $\mathrm{Pr}_{\mathbf{x} \in_R A^n}[f(\mathbf{x}) = 0] \leq \frac{D}{|A|}$.*

For soundness checks over 2-adic extensions, we also introduce the following lemma to bound the soundness error over $\mathbb{Z}_{2^k}$ when performing computations over $\mathbb{Z}_{2^{k+s}}$. The proof is standard, and can be found in the full version.

Lemma 2 (2-adic Random Linear Combinations). *Let $\delta_1, \ldots, \delta_n$ be elements of $GR(2^{k+s}, d)$, such that at least one $\delta_i \not\equiv 0 \pmod{2^k}$. Also let $\alpha_1 = 1$ and $\alpha_2, \ldots, \alpha_n \leftarrow GR(2^{s+1}, d)$ be chosen uniformly at random. Then we have the probability bound $\Pr\left[\sum \alpha_i \cdot \delta_i \equiv 0 \pmod{2^{k+s}}\right] \leq 2^{-(s+1) \cdot d}$.*

2.3 Secret-Sharing Schemes Over Rings

We consider additive (A) as well as threshold (T) secret sharing schemes over our commutative finite rings R, e.g. $R = GR(2^k, d)$, which we denote as $[\![\cdot]\!]^A$ and $[\![\cdot]\!]^T$ respectively. Our protocols work with any *linear* secret sharing scheme.

Only the overall soundness and the communication cost depend on the instantiation. Hence, we will often drop the A or T from the notation and just write $[\![\cdot]\!]$. Both schemes allow the parties to compute linear functions on shared values such as $[\![\gamma]\!] = a \cdot [\![\alpha]\!] + b \cdot [\![\beta]\!] + c$ by performing only local computations on their individual shares.

Additive Secret-Sharing. An additive $(N-1)$-out-of-N secret sharing over R is straightforward. To share a value $v \in R$, first sample values $v_1, \ldots, v_N \leftarrow R$ and then set $\Delta_v = v - \sum_{i \in [N]} v_i$. The share of party P_i is then defined as $[\![v]\!]_i^A := (v_i; \Delta_v)$. We denote this procedure as $[\![v]\!]^A \leftarrow \mathsf{Share}^A(v)$. Reconstruction is performed by computing $v = \Delta_v + \sum_{i \in [N]} v_i$, which we denote as $v \leftarrow \mathsf{Rec}^A([\![v]\!]^A)$.

Threshold Secret-Sharing. The well-known threshold secret sharing scheme due to Shamir [28] relies on polynomial interpolation which usually requires a field structure. We follow the work of Abspoel et al. [1], who have shown how to use Galois rings to realize Shamir-style threshold secret sharing over rings in the context of MPC.

Let $\alpha_0, \ldots, \alpha_N$ be an exceptional sequence of length $N+1$ within $GR(2^k, d)$. To share a value $v \in \mathbb{Z}_{2^k}$ among parties $P_1, \ldots, P_N$ with threshold t, first sample a random degree-t polynomial f from $GR(2^k, d)[X]^{\leq t}$ with the condition that $f(\alpha_0) = v$. To then create shares, give each party P_i, for $i \in [N]$, the value $[\![v]\!]_i^T := y_i := f(\alpha_i)$. We denote such a sharing with $[\![v]\!]^T \leftarrow \mathsf{Share}^T(v)$.

To reconstruct a value v, we use Lagrange interpolation using any index set $S \subseteq [1, N]$ of at least $t+1$ shares:

$$f(X) = \sum_{i \in S} y_i \cdot \prod_{j \in S \setminus \{i\}} \frac{X - \alpha_j}{\alpha_i - \alpha_j}$$

This interpolation over $GR(2^k, d)$ is well-defined since, by definition of an exceptional sequence, all differences $\alpha_i - \alpha_j$ are invertible. Let the reconstruction procedure be denoted by $v \leftarrow \mathsf{Rec}^T(\{[\![v]\!]_i^T\}_{i \in S})$.

Note that, in general, one needs to check whether a shared value lies in the base ring $\mathbb{Z}_{2^k}$ or (strictly) in the ring extension $GR(2^k, d) \setminus \mathbb{Z}_{2^k}$. To deal with this, we describe a checking procedure $\Pi_{\mathsf{Ring-Check}}$, which ensures a set of shares corresponds to values in $\mathbb{Z}_{2^k}$ without violating t-privacy, in Sect. 4. This procedure can then be applied to the input shares. In our protocols, no other wires or shares, such as the rest of the extended witness, need be validated in this way, as either these shares are obtained through linear operations that preserve this property, or the property is guaranteed by the correctness of our subprotocol to check multiplications.

2.4   MPC-in-the-Head via Linear Secret Sharing

This section presents a general framework for MPCitH protocols based on threshold linear secret sharing schemes, built on the framework of Feneuil et al. [18] that provides a generic transformation for MPC protocols based on threshold linear secret sharing. We first describe a generic MPC protocol for circuit verification, then show how it can be used to obtain a ZK proof system, and finally analyse the resulting soundness.

MPC Protocol for MPCitH. The MPC protocol presented in Fig. 1 is generic for threshold LSSS over $\mathbb{Z}_{2^k}$, in the sense that it can be instantiated with any *multiplication checking protocol* and any suitable LSSS. It involves an *input party* who distributes secret shared values to the computing parties. Looking ahead, we refer to the totality of these input values as the *extended witness* of the resulting proof system. In addition, computing parties have access to two oracles: a *hint oracle* $\mathcal{O}_H$ which provides the parties with a sharing of an arbitrary secret value from the input party; and a *randomness oracle* $\mathcal{O}_R$ which outputs random public values.

These oracles are mainly used in the following subprotocols whose goal is to verify some properties on shares of (extended) witness values:

$\Pi_{\text{Zero-Check}}$ takes as input a value $[\![v]\!]$ (resp. a vector of values $[\![\mathbf{v}]\!]$) and returns $\top$ when $v = 0$ (resp. every entry of $\mathbf{v}$ is zero), or $\bot$ otherwise. This can be achieved similarly to share reconstruction, with the difference that the opened value is not sent.

$\Pi_{\text{Mult-Check}}$ takes a triple $([\![\mathbf{a}]\!], [\![\mathbf{b}]\!], [\![\mathbf{c}]\!])$ and returns $\top$ if and only if $\mathbf{a} \circ \mathbf{b} = \mathbf{c}$. In some cases, this equality can be checked over a different ring than that in which the input values are shared. We provide three instantiations of $\Pi_{\text{Mult-Check}}$ in Sect. 3, and these form the main contribution of this paper.

$\Pi_{\text{Ring-Check}}$ takes as input a vector of values $[\![\mathbf{v}]\!]$, shared over a 2-adic extension $GR(2^{k+s_{rc}}, d_0)$ and outputs $\top$ if and only if the truncation of $\mathbf{v}$ to $GR(2^k, d_0)$ lies in the subring $\mathbb{Z}_{2^k}$. It also truncates the elements of $\mathbf{v}$ to the ring $GR(2^{k+s}, d_0)$. (See Sect. 4.)

We write $\Pi_{\text{Mult-Check}}^{\tau}$ to denote the parallel repetition of τ instances. By *verifying* a property through one of these subprotocols, we mean that the subprotocol is run, and Reject is returned by the MPC protocol when the output differs from $\top$. Reconstructing a shared value is performed by each party P_j first broadcasting its share $[\![v]\!]_j$ and then running $v \leftarrow \text{Rec}([\![v]\!])$ In the threshold setting, only $t + 1$ shares are required since the other shares are determined by these.

In essence, this protocol does not compute the circuit C, but only checks that the values given by the input party are consistent with an honest evaluation of C. To do so, the computation parties parse C in topological order but only (locally) compute the linear gates, whereas output of non-linear gates and Rec are provided as input and hence need to be checked. This is necessary because the input party is not trusted to provide the correct values. The output of the protocol is either Accept or Reject. To decrease the false-positive rate of the multiplication checking procedure, the parties execute it τ_{in} times in parallel.

Generic MPC Protocol Π_C for Circuit Verification

Parameters: A circuit C over $\mathbb{Z}_{2^k}$ consisting of linear and multiplication gates with #inputs inputs and m multiplications Mul; a LSSS sharing scheme $[\![.]\!]$ defined over $GR(2^{k+s}, d_0)$ for parameters s and d_0. The inputs w_i are defined over $GR(2^{k+s_{rc}}, d_0)$, for parameter $s_{rc} \geq s$ which matches the parameter for $\Pi_{\text{Ring-Check}}$.

Inputs: The input party calls Share on its input w_i, $i \in [\text{#inputs}]$ and w_γ for each gate $(\alpha, \beta, \gamma, \text{Mul})_i$ for $i \in [m]$, and send $[\![w_*]\!]_j$ to the computing party P_j.

Protocol: Each P_j initializes an empty checklist $\mathcal{M}$
1. Verify the inputs are in $\mathbb{Z}_{2^k}$: $\Pi_{\text{Ring-Check}}(w_1, \ldots, w_{\text{#inputs}})$
2. For each gate $(\alpha, \beta, \gamma, T) \in C$, in topological order:
   (a) Case $T = \text{Lin}$: $[\![v_\gamma]\!] := a \cdot [\![v_\alpha]\!] + b \cdot [\![v_\beta]\!] + c$ done locally by each party.
   (b) Case $T = \text{Mul}$:
      – Party P_j retrieves $[\![w_\gamma]\!]_j$ received from the input party and sets $[\![v_\gamma]\!]_j = [\![w_\gamma]\!]_j$.
      – Each P_j adds a tuple to (their share of) the multiplication checklist $\mathcal{M}_j \leftarrow \mathcal{M}_j \cup \{([\![v_\alpha]\!]_j, [\![v_\beta]\!]_j, [\![v_\gamma]\!]_j)\}$
3. Verify circuit output: $\Pi_{\text{Zero-Check}}([\![v_o]\!])$.
4. Verify multiplications: parties parse $\mathcal{M}$ column-wise as $([\![\mathbf{x}]\!], [\![\mathbf{y}]\!], [\![\mathbf{z}]\!])$ and run $\Pi_{\text{Mult-Check}}^{\tau_{\text{in}}}([\![\mathbf{x}]\!], [\![\mathbf{y}]\!], [\![\mathbf{z}]\!])$.

Fig. 1. Generic MPC protocol for circuit verification

From MPC to ZK. The compilation technique of Ishai et al. [23], applied to this MPC protocol, provides our interactive zero-knowledge scheme between a prover $\mathcal{P}$ and a verifier $\mathcal{V}$.

The prover executes, in their head, the MPC protocol $\Pi_C(x, w)$ between N parties using an LSSS with t-privacy. To do so, $\mathcal{P}$ first evaluates $C(x, w)$ in the clear, and secret shares w as well as the intermediate values required for a local computation of C. After recording these N input views, it plays the role of the input party and distributes these shares to virtual computing parties. These parties execute $\Pi_C(x, w)$ and its checking sub-protocols. When the protocol queries $\mathcal{O}_H$, the requested shared values are provided by $\mathcal{P}$ to the virtual parties and recorded in the input views. Queries to $\mathcal{O}_R$ are replaced by an interaction with the verifier, where first $\mathcal{P}$ commits to the input views so far, and then $\mathcal{V}$ responds with a random value.

In the final interaction, after Π_C terminates, $\mathcal{V}$ asks to open t of the N views, which it checks for consistency. If the consistency check succeeds, and the output of $\Pi_C(x, w)$ is Accept, then $\mathcal{V}$ also outputs Accept.

ZK Protocol Soundness. The MPC protocol may output Accept for an invalid witness with some bounded false-positive rate p, i.e., the probability that $\Pi_C(x, w)$ outputs Accept when in fact $C(x, w) \neq 0$. When p is not sufficiently small, we increase the detection probability by performing τ_{in} parallel *inner repetitions* of the circuit check *inside* the MPC protocol. This leads to an overal false-positive rate of $\mathsf{err_{MPC}} = p^{\tau_{in}}$.

The framework of Feneuil et al. [18] provides a generic transformation for any such MPC protocol with N parties and tolerating up to t corruptions into an MPCitH proof, with a soundness error of

$$\mathsf{err_{ZK}} = \frac{1}{\binom{N}{t}} + \mathsf{err_{MPC}} \cdot \frac{t \cdot (N-t)}{t+1}. \tag{1}$$

For an additive full-threshold secret sharing scheme $(t = N - 1)$, this becomes

$$\mathsf{err_{ZK}} = \frac{1}{N} + \mathsf{err_{MPC}} \cdot \left(1 - \frac{1}{N}\right).$$

By setting N and t, we obtain a certain $\mathsf{err_{ZK}}$ for the soundness error of a *single execution* of the protocol. Since this may be too high for a given security setting, we can repeat the transformed protocol τ_{out} times (*outer repetitions*) to obtained any desired soundness error, $\mathsf{err_{ZK}^{\tau_{out}}}$.

We denote the overall proof size by $\mathsf{size_{proof}}$, which one can think of as the communication cost in bits, required to commit to the parties' views and open t of them in τ_{out} repetitions.

3   Checking Multiplications Over Rings

We now describe three instantiations for $\Pi_{\mathsf{Mult\text{-}Check}}$. The three protocols have appeared previously in the context of MPCitH over fields, but their extension to MPC over rings is mostly new, although a protocol similar to our sacrificing check can be found in [3] for VOLE-based zero-knowledge proofs over $\mathbb{Z}_{2^k}$.

We analyse their soundness in the ring-based setting, and compare their performance. For each of the checking procedures, we analyse the false-positive rate $\mathsf{err_{MPC}}$ of the resulting MPC protocol. It then suffices to use the generic transformation of Feneuil and Rivain [18] to compile our MPC protocol into an MPCitH proof system with soundness error as in Eq. (1).

Our three different checking procedures are: 1) A simple sacrifice-based check, $\Pi_{\mathsf{Sac\text{-}Check}}$ (described in Sect. 3.1), 2) an inner product multiplication check, $\Pi_{\mathsf{IP\text{-}Check}}$ (in Sect. 3.2), and 3) a compressed multiplication check, Π_{Compress} (in Sect. 3.3). For the first two of these, one can improve the soundness by utilizing either 2-adic or Galois extensions. The third, compressed multiplication check, is adapted from the methodology in [7,12], and requires a Galois ring extension.

Looking ahead, in the next section we also present a fourth procedure which checks that a set of shares (typically the input to the circuit) all correspond to values in $\mathbb{Z}_{2^k}$ (as in line 1 of Fig. 1). This procedure takes its inputs as shares in $GR(2^{k+s_{rc}}, d_0)$, has a soundness error of $\mathsf{err_{Ring\text{-}Check}}$. When the chosen multiplication checking procedure would have sufficient soundness with smaller $s < s_{rc}$, it is possible to locally truncate the input shares correspondingly before performing the procedure.

The false-positive rate of the MPC protocol becomes $\mathsf{err}_{\mathsf{MPC}} := \mathsf{err}_{\mathsf{Check}}^{\mathsf{Tin}} + \mathsf{err}_{\mathsf{Ring\text{-}Check}}$ where $\mathsf{err}_{\mathsf{Check}}$ denotes the false-positive rate of a single execution of the checking procedure. In Sect. 5, we investigate the differences in communication cost for our different multiplication checks and sharing scheme choices.

3.1 Sacrifice Based Check

Our first multiplication checking procedure is a sacrificing based check. This is based on the checking protocol of Baum and Nof [6], combined with an optimization of Kales and Zaverucha [25, Sect. 2.5, Optimization 3], transferred to the ring setting. The algorithm is presented in Fig. 2.

$\Pi_{\mathsf{Sac\text{-}Check}}$: Sacrificing Check

Parameters: Additional Galois extension size d_1.

Inputs: $(\llbracket \mathbf{x} \rrbracket, \llbracket \mathbf{y} \rrbracket, \llbracket \mathbf{z} \rrbracket)$ shared over $GR(2^{k+s}, d_0)$.

Protocol:
1. Lift $(\llbracket \mathbf{x} \rrbracket, \llbracket \mathbf{y} \rrbracket, \llbracket \mathbf{z} \rrbracket)$ to $GR(2^{k+s}, d_0 \cdot d_1)$.
2. $(\llbracket \mathbf{a} \rrbracket, \llbracket \mathbf{c} \rrbracket) \leftarrow \mathcal{O}_H$ uniformly random with $\mathbf{a} \circ \mathbf{y} = \mathbf{c}$ over $GR(2^{k+s}, d_0 \cdot d_1)$
3. $\varepsilon \leftarrow \mathcal{O}_R$ such that $\varepsilon \in GR(2^{1+s}, d_0 \cdot d_1)$
4. $\boldsymbol{\alpha} \leftarrow \mathsf{Rec}(\varepsilon \cdot \llbracket \mathbf{x} \rrbracket - \llbracket \mathbf{a} \rrbracket)$
5. Output $\Pi_{\mathsf{Zero\text{-}Check}}(\varepsilon \cdot \llbracket \mathbf{z} \rrbracket - \llbracket \mathbf{c} \rrbracket - \boldsymbol{\alpha} \circ \llbracket \mathbf{y} \rrbracket)$

Fig. 2. The sacrificing check over rings.

As inputs, it receives the vectors $(\llbracket \mathbf{x} \rrbracket, \llbracket \mathbf{y} \rrbracket, \llbracket \mathbf{z} \rrbracket)$ of multiplication input and output values, secret-shared over the "computation ring" $GR(2^{k+s}, d_0)$. In case of $d_1 > 1$, it first lifts these vectors to the "checking ring" $GR(2^{k+s}, d_0 \cdot d_1)$. Then, the hint oracle $\mathcal{O}_H$ distributes to the parties secret shares of $\llbracket \mathbf{a} \rrbracket$ and $\llbracket \mathbf{c} \rrbracket$, correlated in such a way that $\mathbf{a} \circ \mathbf{y} = \mathbf{c}$. After receiving a random coefficient ε from the randomness oracle $\mathcal{O}_R$, the parties "sacrifice" the vector $\llbracket \mathbf{a} \rrbracket$ by using it to mask the randomized vector $\varepsilon \cdot \llbracket \mathbf{x} \rrbracket$ and reconstruct the masked value as $\boldsymbol{\alpha}$. Finally, the protocol checks whether both $\mathbf{z}$ and $\mathbf{c}$ were computed correctly by $\mathcal{O}_H$ by checking that the sacrificing equation $\varepsilon \cdot \llbracket \mathbf{z} \rrbracket - \llbracket \mathbf{c} \rrbracket - \boldsymbol{\alpha} \circ \llbracket \mathbf{y} \rrbracket$ is equal to 0. The argument is that if either $\mathbf{z}$ or $\mathbf{c}$ is incorrect, then the probability that the equality holds, taken over the choice of $\varepsilon \in GR(2^{1+s}, d_0 \cdot d_1)$, is very small.

We first take a brief look at the correctness of the protocol. If the input is valid, then the protocol always outputs Accept, since

$$\varepsilon \cdot \mathbf{z} - \mathbf{c} - \boldsymbol{\alpha} \circ \mathbf{y} = \varepsilon \cdot \mathbf{x} \circ \mathbf{y} - \mathbf{a} \circ \mathbf{y} - (\varepsilon \cdot \mathbf{x} - \mathbf{a}) \circ \mathbf{y}$$
$$= \varepsilon \cdot \mathbf{x} \circ \mathbf{y} - \mathbf{a} \circ \mathbf{y} - \varepsilon \cdot \mathbf{x} \circ \mathbf{y} + \mathbf{a} \circ \mathbf{y} = 0.$$

The zero-knowledge property remains preserved by virtue of $\boldsymbol{\alpha}$ being uniformly random as a result of the mask $\mathbf{a}$ being uniformly random.

We obtain the following theorem, whose proof can be found in the full version.

Theorem 1 (Soundness of $\Pi_{\text{Sac-Check}}$). *For invalid input, i.e., $\exists i \in [m] . x_i \cdot y_i \neq z_i$, the check passes with probability at most* $\text{err}_{\text{Sac-Check}} := 2^{-(s+1) \cdot d_0 \cdot d_1}$.

3.2 Inner Product Multiplication Check

Our second checking procedure, which is based on inner product checks, is described as a precursor to the Limbo protocol [12], together with optimizations from Kales and Zaverucha [25], adapted to the ring setting. We present the algorithm in Fig. 3.

$\Pi_{\text{IP-Check}}$: Inner Product Check

Parameters: Additional Galois extension size d_1.

Inputs: $([\![\mathbf{x}]\!], [\![\mathbf{y}]\!], [\![\mathbf{z}]\!])$ shared over $GR(2^{k+s}, d_0)$.

Protocol:

1. Lift $([\![\mathbf{x}]\!], [\![\mathbf{y}]\!], [\![\mathbf{z}]\!])$ to $GR(2^{k+s}, d_0 \cdot d_1)$.
2. $([\![\mathbf{a}]\!], [\![c]\!]) \leftarrow \mathcal{O}_H$ uniformly random with $\langle \mathbf{a}, \mathbf{y} \rangle = c$ over $GR(2^{k+s}, d_0 \cdot d_1)$.
3. $\boldsymbol{\eta} \leftarrow \mathcal{O}_R$ such that $\boldsymbol{\eta} \in GR(2^{1+s}, d_0 \cdot d_1)^m$.
4. $\boldsymbol{\alpha} \leftarrow \text{Rec}(\boldsymbol{\eta} \circ [\![\mathbf{x}]\!] - [\![\mathbf{a}]\!])$
5. Output $\Pi_{\text{Zero-Check}}(\langle \boldsymbol{\eta}, [\![\mathbf{z}]\!] \rangle - [\![c]\!] - \langle \boldsymbol{\alpha}, [\![\mathbf{y}]\!] \rangle)$

Fig. 3. The inner product check over rings.

This second checking procedure $\Pi_{\text{IP-Check}}$ works very similarly to the sacrificing check $\Pi_{\text{Sac-Check}}$ of Fig. 2, the main difference is that the hint oracle $\mathcal{O}_H$ produces a single correlated inner product tuple $((\mathbf{a}, c)$ such that $\langle \mathbf{a}\mathbf{y} \rangle = c)$ rather than m correlated multiplication tuples $((\mathbf{a}, \mathbf{c})$ such that $\mathbf{a} \circ \mathbf{y} = \mathbf{c})$. This change then requires the random oracle $\mathcal{O}_R$ to produce m random values (contained in the vector $\boldsymbol{\eta}$), instead of a single one, and it also changes the checking equation so that it checks a single equality, rather than m. This time, the security rationale is that if either $\mathbf{z}$ or c is incorrect, then the single checking equation will not equal 0 except with small probability (over the choice of $\boldsymbol{\eta}$). The rationale for the zero-knowledge property is again due to the random mask $[\![\mathbf{a}]\!]$.

Here as well, the protocol is correct, since if the input is valid, then the protocol always outputs Accept as

$$\langle \boldsymbol{\eta}, \mathbf{z} \rangle - c - \langle \boldsymbol{\alpha}, \mathbf{y} \rangle = \langle \boldsymbol{\eta}, \mathbf{x} \circ \mathbf{y} \rangle - \langle \mathbf{a}, \mathbf{y} \rangle - \langle \boldsymbol{\eta} \circ \mathbf{x} - \mathbf{a}, \mathbf{y} \rangle$$
$$= \langle \boldsymbol{\eta}, \mathbf{x} \circ \mathbf{y} \rangle - \langle \mathbf{a}, \mathbf{y} \rangle - \langle \boldsymbol{\eta} \circ \mathbf{x}, \mathbf{y} \rangle + \langle \mathbf{a}, \mathbf{y} \rangle = 0.$$

We obtain the following theorem, whose proof can be found in the full version.

Theorem 2 (Soundness of $\Pi_{\text{IP-Check}}$). *For invalid input, i.e., $\exists i \in [m]$. $x_i \cdot y_i \neq z_i \pmod{2^k}$, the check passes with probability at most* $\text{err}_{\text{IP-Check}} := 2^{-(s+1)\cdot d_0 \cdot d_1}$.

3.3   Compressed Multiplication Check

Our third, and final check, is adapted from Limbo [12]. In contrast to the previous checks, we do not use 2-adic extensions here, since we would have to extend the modulus repeatedly at least $\log_\nu(m)$ times. To apply the compressed protocol with compression factor ν, the check must happen over an algebraic structure where an exceptional sequence of length at least $2\nu + 1$ exists.

We first give the subprotocol of [12] to compress a sequence of ν inner product tuples into a single inner product tuple in Fig. 4; then we present the main protocol in Fig. 5. Correctness and zero-knowledge for this checking protocol follow the same arguments as the original version over fields. Soundness follows from the following theorem, whose proof can be found in the full version.

Π_{Compress} Subroutine for Inner Product Compression

Parameters: compression factor ν, dimension ℓ, flag rand $\in \{\top, \bot\}$
Inputs: ν shared dimension-ℓ inner product tuples $(\llbracket \mathbf{x}_i \rrbracket, \llbracket \mathbf{y}_i \rrbracket, \llbracket z_i \rrbracket)_{i \in [\nu]}$ shared over $GR(2^k, d)$
Outputs: one shared dimension-ℓ inner product tuple $(\llbracket \mathbf{x} \rrbracket, \llbracket \mathbf{y} \rrbracket, \llbracket z \rrbracket)$ shared over $GR(2^k, d)$
Protocol:
Let $\{\alpha_1, \dots, \alpha_{2\nu+1}\} \subset \text{Ex}(GR(2^k, d))$.

1. If rand $= \bot$ define two shared dimension-ℓ vectors of degree-$(\nu - 1)$ polynomials $\llbracket \mathbf{f} \rrbracket, \llbracket \mathbf{g} \rrbracket$: $\mathbf{f}(\alpha_i) = (\mathbf{x}_1, \cdots, \mathbf{x}_\nu)^T$ and $\mathbf{g}(\alpha_i) = (\mathbf{y}_1, \cdots, \mathbf{y}_\nu)^T$, where $i \in [\nu]$.
   If rand $= \top$, obtain random shares $\llbracket \mathbf{v} \rrbracket, \llbracket \mathbf{w} \rrbracket \leftarrow \mathcal{O}_H$ and define $\mathbf{f}, \mathbf{g}$ instead of degree ν with the additional points $\mathbf{f}(\alpha_{\nu+1}) = \mathbf{v}$ and $\mathbf{g}(\alpha_{\nu+1}) = \mathbf{w}$.
2. Inject $\llbracket z_i \rrbracket \leftarrow \mathcal{O}_H$ for $i \in [\nu + 1, 2\nu - 1]$ such that $z_i := \langle \mathbf{f}(\alpha_i), \mathbf{g}(\alpha_i) \rangle$.
   If rand $= \top$, similarly inject $\llbracket z_i \rrbracket$ for $i \in \{2\nu, 2\nu + 1\}$.
3. If rand $= \bot$ define shared polynomial $\llbracket h \rrbracket$ of degree $2(\nu - 1)$ by $h(\alpha_i) = z_i$ for $i \in [\nu, 2\nu - 1]$.
   If rand $= \top$, instead define h of degree 2ν with the additional points $h(\alpha_i) = z_i$ for $i \in \{2\nu, 2\nu + 1\}$.
4. Obtain challenge $\varepsilon \leftarrow \mathcal{O}_R$ such that $\varepsilon \in \text{Ex}(GR(2^k, d)) \setminus \{\alpha_i\}_{i \in [\nu]}$.
5. Output $(\llbracket \mathbf{x} \rrbracket, \llbracket \mathbf{y} \rrbracket, \llbracket z \rrbracket) := (\llbracket \mathbf{f}(\varepsilon) \rrbracket, \llbracket \mathbf{g}(\varepsilon) \rrbracket, \llbracket h(\varepsilon) \rrbracket)$.

Fig. 4. The subroutine for inner product compression

Theorem 3 (Soundness of $\Pi_{\text{Comp-Check}}$). *Let $d := d_0 \cdot d_1$. For invalid input, i.e., $\exists i \in [m] \,.\, x_i \cdot y_i \neq z_i \pmod{2^k}$, the check passes with probability at most*

$$\text{err}_{\text{Comp-Check}} := 2^{-d} + (1 - 2^{-d}) \cdot \left(\left(\frac{2(\nu-1)}{2^d - \nu} \right) \cdot \sum_{j=0}^{\log_\nu(m)-2} \left(1 - \frac{2(\nu-1)}{2^d - \nu} \right)^j \right.$$

$$\left. + \left(\frac{2\nu}{2^d - \nu} \right) \cdot \left(1 - \frac{2(\nu-1)}{2^d - \nu} \right)^{\log_\nu(m)-1} \right) \leq 2^{-d} + \frac{2\nu}{2^d - \nu} \cdot \log_\nu(m).$$

4   Checking Base Ring Sharings

To ensure the prover knows and inputs a witness over the base ring $\mathbb{Z}_{2^k}$, we devise a check for the parties to ensure this in Fig. 6. We can perform a batched check that all the values we wish to inspect are simultaneously correct by taking a random linear combination with coefficients from $\mathbb{Z}_{2^{1+s_{rc}}}$, and opening that. Since this would leak a linear combination of secret values, we also allow the prover to input an additional sharing of a value in $\mathbb{Z}_{2^{k+s_{rc}}}$ to mask this relation (before receiving the random coefficients from the verifier). This is conceptually similar to the recent approach by Shoup and Smart in [29].

$\Pi_{\text{Comp-Check}}$: Compressed Multiplication Check

Parameters: number of multiplications m, compression factor ν (assume $\log_\nu(m) \in \mathbb{N}$), Galois extension degree d_1

Inputs: $([\![\mathbf{x}]\!], [\![\mathbf{y}]\!], [\![\mathbf{z}]\!])$ of length m shared over $GR(2^k, d_0)$.

Protocol:

1. Lift $([\![\mathbf{x}]\!], [\![\mathbf{y}]\!], [\![\mathbf{z}]\!])$ to $GR(2^k, d_0 \cdot d_1)$.
2. Create inner product tuple $([\![\mathbf{x}^0]\!], [\![\mathbf{y}^0]\!], [\![z^0]\!])$:
   - (a) $\boldsymbol{\eta} \leftarrow \mathcal{O}_R$ such that $\boldsymbol{\eta} \in GR(2, d_0 \cdot d_1)^m$.
   - (b) Set $[\![\mathbf{x}^0]\!] := \boldsymbol{\eta} \circ [\![\mathbf{x}]\!]$, $[\![\mathbf{y}^0]\!] := [\![\mathbf{y}]\!]$, and $[\![z^0]\!] := \langle \boldsymbol{\eta}, [\![\mathbf{z}]\!] \rangle$.
3. For each round $j \in [\log_\nu(m)]$:
   - (a) Parse $([\![\mathbf{x}^{j-1}]\!], [\![\mathbf{y}^{j-1}]\!], [\![z^{j-1}]\!])$ (of length m/ν^{j-1}) as $[\![\mathbf{x}^{j-1}]\!] = ([\![\mathbf{a}_1^j]\!], \ldots, [\![\mathbf{a}_\nu^j]\!])$ and $[\![\mathbf{y}^{j-1}]\!] = ([\![\mathbf{b}_1^j]\!], \ldots, [\![\mathbf{b}_\nu^j]\!])$ where the $\mathbf{a}_i^j, \mathbf{b}_i^j$ are of length m/ν^j.
   - (b) For $i \in [\nu]$, obtain $[\![c_i^j]\!] \leftarrow \mathcal{O}_H$ such that $c_i^j = \langle \mathbf{a}_i^j, \mathbf{b}_i^j \rangle$.
   - (c) If $j < \log_\nu(m)$, run $([\![\mathbf{x}^j]\!], [\![\mathbf{y}^j]\!], [\![z^j]\!]) \leftarrow \Pi_{\text{Compress}}(([\![\mathbf{a}_i^j]\!], [\![\mathbf{b}_i^j]\!], [\![c_i^j]\!])_{i \in [\nu]})$, else if $j = \log_\nu(m)$, run $([\![\mathbf{x}^j]\!], [\![\mathbf{y}^j]\!], [\![z^j]\!]) \leftarrow \Pi_{\text{Compress}}^{\text{Rand}}(([\![\mathbf{a}_i^j]\!], [\![\mathbf{b}_i^j]\!], [\![c_i^j]\!])_{i \in [\nu]})$. Both yield inner product tuples of length m/ν^j.
4. Open $\mathbf{x}^{\log_\nu(m)} \leftarrow \text{Rec}([\![\mathbf{x}^{\log_\nu(m)}]\!])$.
5. Output $\Pi_{\text{Zero-Check}}(\mathbf{x}^{\log_\nu(m)} \cdot [\![\mathbf{y}^{\log_\nu(m)}]\!] - [\![z^{\log_\nu(m)}]\!])$.

Fig. 5. The compressed multiplication check

$\Pi_{\text{Ring-Check}}$

Inputs: $[\![\mathbf{x}]\!] = ([\![x_1]\!], \ldots, [\![x_\ell]\!])$ shared over $GR(2^{k+s_{rc}}, d_0)$

Protocol:

1. Obtain $[\![x_0]\!]$, corresponding to a value in the ring $\mathbb{Z}_{2^{k+s_{rc}}}$ from $\mathcal{O}_H$.
2. Receive ℓ random coefficients $r_1, \ldots, r_\ell \in \mathbb{Z}_{2^{1+s_{rc}}}$ from $\mathcal{O}_R$.
3. Compute and open $[\![v]\!] = [\![x_0]\!] + r_1[\![x_1]\!] + \ldots + r_\ell[\![x_\ell]\!]$.
4. If $v \in \mathbb{Z}_{2^{k+s_{rc}}}$, return $\top$, otherwise return $\bot$.

Fig. 6. The check to ensure sharings correspond to values in the base ring.

In [1], Abspoel et al. consider a similar problem for the case of non-MPCitH MPC protocols. They solve this problem by generating random secret shared masks hiding values in the correct ring by means of hyperinvertible matrices, after which these masks can be adjusted with a public value to hide the wanted secret. In an MPCitH context however, this becomes both less convenient, since all computing parties need to contribute their own randomness, as well as requiring a higher communication cost in the final proof size. Soundness follows from the following theorem, whose proof can be found in the full version.

Theorem 4 (Soundness of $\Pi_{\text{Ring-Check}}$). *For invalid input, that is if any of $x_0, x_1, \ldots, x_\ell$ are a value in $GR(2^k, d_0) \setminus \mathbb{Z}_{2^k}$ when reduced modulo 2^k, the check passes with probability at most* $\text{err}_{\text{Ring-Check}} := 2^{-(s_{rc}+1)}$.

When dealing with additive sharings, the parties can instead simply check their own local shares to lie in the correct ring and return $\bot$ when this is not the case. For semi-honest parties, this is guaranteed to have no false positives.

Table 1. Rings and numbers of primitive operations used by the three multiplication checking protocols.

	Multiplication Check		
	$\Pi_{\text{Sac-Check}}$	$\Pi_{\text{IP-Check}}$	$\Pi_{\text{Comp-Check}}$
small ring $\mathcal{R}_{\text{small}}$	$GR(2^{k+s}, d_0)$	$GR(2^{k+s}, d_0)$	$GR(2^k, d_0)$
big ring $\mathcal{R}_{\text{large}}$	$GR(2^{k+s}, d_0 \cdot d_1)$	$GR(2^{k+s}, d_0 \cdot d_1)$	$GR(2^k, d_0 \cdot d_1)$
challenge space $\mathcal{C}$	$GR(2^{1+s}, d_0 \cdot d_1)$	$GR(2^{1+s}, d_0 \cdot d_1)$	$GR(2, d_0 \cdot d_1)$
rounds μ	1	1	$\log_\nu(m) + 1$
input over $\mathcal{R}_{\text{small}}$	#inputs $+ m$	#inputs $+ m$	#inputs $+ m$
hint over $\mathcal{R}_{\text{large}}$	m	1	$(2\nu - 1) \cdot \log_\nu(m) + 2$
uniform hint over $\mathcal{R}_{\text{large}}$	m	m	2
reconstruction over $\mathcal{R}_{\text{large}}$	m	m	1
challenge from $\mathcal{C}$	1	m	$m + \log_\nu(m)$

5   Protocol Communication Costs

The communication costs of the zero-knowledge proofs depends greatly on the used secret sharing scheme and the multiplication check protocol, as well as a large set of parameters. To simplify notation, we use $\mathcal{R}_{small}$ for the ring used to share the witness, $\mathcal{R}_{large}$ for the ring extension in which the checks are performed. Moreover, the random challenges from $\mathcal{O}_R$ live in the challenge space $\mathcal{C}$, and μ denotes the number of rounds of the MPC protocol, i.e., the number of calls to $\mathcal{O}_R$. For brevity of notation, we use $\mathcal{B}(S) = \lceil \log_2 |S| \rceil$ to denote the number of bits needed to represent an element from S.

Table 1 shows how many primitive operations we need for each checking protocol, and Table 2 gives the communication cost of each operation in both sharing types. The costs of the challenges are $\mathcal{B}(\mathcal{C}) \cdot \mu \cdot \tau_{in}$, since they can be shared across the "outer repetitions".

Table 2. Communication costs in bits of the primitive operations. Here $\mathcal{B}(\cdot)$ denotes the number of bits required to encode an element of the set passed as argument.

	Sharing Scheme	
	Additive	Threshold
input over $\mathcal{R}_{small}$	$\mathcal{B}(\mathcal{R}_{small})$	$\mathcal{B}(\mathcal{R}_{small}) \cdot t$
hint over $\mathcal{R}_{large}$	$\mathcal{B}(\mathcal{R}_{large})$	$\mathcal{B}(\mathcal{R}_{large}) \cdot t$
uniform hint over $\mathcal{R}_{large}$	0	$\mathcal{B}(\mathcal{R}_{large}) \cdot t$
reconstruction over $\mathcal{R}_{large}$	$\mathcal{B}(\mathcal{R}_{large})$	$\mathcal{B}(\mathcal{R}_{large})$
challenge from $\mathcal{C}$	$\mathcal{B}(\mathcal{C})$	$\mathcal{B}(\mathcal{C})$

Primitive Costs: The communication costs for our basic operations can be summarized as follows.

Commitments: Before each call to $\mathcal{O}_R$ the prover commits to the current state of the computation. The $\tau_{out} \cdot \mu \cdot N$ total commitments can be combined into $\tau_{out} \cdot \mu$ Merkle trees, and for each round it is sufficient to send a hash of the τ_{out} Merkle roots. Thus, committing costs $2\lambda \cdot \mu$ bits. Before the verifier selects a subset of parties whose views to open, the prover sends another hash with shares of the last reconstructed values.

To open t of the commitments in each repetition, we have to send, in addition to the committed data, λ bits of randomness per commitment as well the corresponding Merkle paths. Each path is of length $\log_2(N)$, but since we open t views and the path overlap, we pay $2\lambda \cdot \log_2(N/t)$ bits per path.

Overall, this results in

$$\mathsf{size}_{Commit} := 2\lambda \cdot (\mu + 1) + \tau_{out} \cdot \lambda \cdot \mu \cdot t \cdot (2\log_2(N/t) + 1)$$

bits of communication for committing and opening.

Opening Sharings: Since to open a sharing only the reconstructed value needs to be revealed on top of the t already decommited shares, the cost for opening a $\mathbb{Z}_{2^k}$ value is k bits (for a $GR(2^k, d)$ value this is $k \cdot d$ bits), regardless of the secret sharing scheme being used.

Providing Hints: The $\mathcal{O}_H$ oracle can be instantiated in two different ways, depending on the kind of secret sharing being used. For a threshold secret sharing scheme, both specific and uniformly random values $v \in \mathbb{Z}_{2^k}$ (or $v \in GR(2^k, d)$) can be obtained by running $\llbracket v \rrbracket \leftarrow \mathsf{Share}(v)$ and distributing the shares to the corresponding parties. This costs $t \cdot k$ (or $t \cdot k \cdot d$) bits of proof size.

For additive secret sharing, uniformly random values in $\mathbb{Z}_{2^k}$ or $GR(2^k, d)$ can be obtained at zero extra cost by having all parties individually derive their shares from a PRG seed. A uniformly random sharing $\llbracket r \rrbracket^A$ can be transformed into a sharing of a specific value $\llbracket v \rrbracket^A$ by updating the public adjustment Δ_v, at the cost of only k or $k \cdot d$ bits of proof size.

Protocol Costs: We can now summarize the communication costs per checking protocol:

$\Pi_{\mathsf{Sac\text{-}Check}}$: The sacrificing check requires

$$\mathsf{size}^A_{\mathsf{Sac\text{-}Check}} := 2 \cdot m \cdot (k + s) \cdot d_0 \cdot d_1$$
$$\mathsf{size}^T_{\mathsf{Sac\text{-}Check}} := (2 \cdot m \cdot t + m) \cdot (k + s) \cdot d_0 \cdot d_1$$

bits of additional communication for additive, resp. threshold, sharing.
$\Pi_{\mathsf{IP\text{-}Check}}$: The inner product check results requires

$$\mathsf{size}^A_{\mathsf{IP\text{-}Check}} := (m + 1) \cdot (k + s) \cdot d_0 \cdot d_1$$
$$\mathsf{size}^T_{\mathsf{IP\text{-}Check}} := ((m + 1) \cdot t + m) \cdot (k + s) \cdot d_0 \cdot d_1$$

bits of additional communication for additive, resp. threshold, sharing.
$\Pi_{\mathsf{Comp\text{-}Check}}$: The compressed multiplication check results requires

$$\mathsf{size}^A_{\mathsf{Comp\text{-}Check}} := ((2\nu - 1) \cdot \log_\nu(m) + 3) \cdot k \cdot d_0 \cdot d_1$$
$$\mathsf{size}^T_{\mathsf{Comp\text{-}Check}} := (((2\nu - 1) \cdot \log_\nu(m) + 4) \cdot t + 1) \cdot k \cdot d_0 \cdot d_1$$

bits of additional communication for additive, resp. threshold, sharing.
$\Pi_{\mathsf{Ring\text{-}Check}}$: For additive sharing, this check has no overhead. In the threshold case, this procedure requires one additional share input and one share reconstruction in $GR(2^{k+s_{rc}}, d_0)$ to the overall proof size, hence the total costs are

$$\mathsf{size}^A_{\mathsf{Ring\text{-}Check}} := 0$$
$$\mathsf{size}^T_{\mathsf{Ring\text{-}Check}} := (t + 1) \cdot (k + s_{rc}) \cdot d_0$$

bits of communication for additive, resp. threshold, sharing.

Here we do not take into account the cost of the verifier sending a challenge or a seed for outputs of the $\mathcal{O}_R$ oracle. In the non-interactive case, these are obtained from the Fiat–Shamir transform and therefore free in terms of communication; in the interactive case however, the verifier sends λ bits per "round" of dependent calls to $\mathcal{O}_R$.

Overall Costs: Finally, we can present the overall communication cost, i.e., the proof size. Note here that the cost for $\mathsf{size}_{\mathsf{Input}}$ depends on $k + s_{\mathsf{rc}}$, rather than the potentially smaller $k + s$.

$$\mathsf{size}_{\mathsf{Proof}} = \mathsf{size}_{\mathsf{Commit}} + \tau_{\mathsf{out}} \cdot (\mathsf{size}_{\mathsf{Input}} + \tau_{\mathsf{in}} \cdot \mathsf{size}_{\mathsf{Check}}) + \tau_{\mathsf{in}} \cdot \mathsf{size}_{\mathsf{Challenge}}$$

5.1 Concrete Comparison of the Three $\Pi_{\mathsf{Mult\text{-}Check}}$ Subprotocols

To compare our different protocols concretely with one another, we fix certain choices for σ, k and m and examined the per-multiplication-gate communication cost of a full proof σ bits of security. In the full version we present tables which give the communication cost of an entire proof, except for the challenges sent from the verifier. That is, we only examine the communication from the prover towards the verifier, which also gives a good idea of the proof size that would be incurred when the protocol is transformed to a non-interactive proof by the Fiat-Shamir transform.

All our experimental validations were computed with #inputs = 128 elements in $\mathbb{Z}_{2^k}$. Since the additive sharing has some optimizations for random sharings and $\Pi_{\mathsf{Ring\text{-}Check}}$ and does not require $d_0 > 1$ to enable sharing values across N parties, it generally comes out as the optimal choice for the configurations examined here.

We observe that for $\Pi_{\mathsf{Sac\text{-}Check}}$ and $\Pi_{\mathsf{IP\text{-}Check}}$, which require at least m openings each, the optimal choice for d_1 is one since the overhead for $d_0 \cdot s$ extra bits is generally smaller than $d_0 \cdot (d_1 - 1) \cdot k$ extra bits, even though the size of inputs and injected multiplications grows as well. When the communication due to the check is asymptotically smaller than the communication due to the input of the extended witness, it becomes preferable to avoid the extra $d_0 \cdot s$ bits per multiplication cost in the input already.

Since we can observe that Π_{Compress} consistently results in the smallest proof sizes, we further also look at the overhead of this protocol. That is, we investigate the ratio of proof size to the theoretical optimum of $k \cdot (\#\text{inputs} + m)$ bits for any protocol that needs to inject the results of multiplications. This rate is a constant that mostly depends on the target value of σ and decreases slightly as the number of multiplications increases. Since the choice of k doesn't influence the choice of multiplication check, it also has no further impact on the overhead.

Acknowledgements. The work was partially supported by the Defense Advanced Research Projects Agency (DARPA) under Contract No. HR001120C0085, by Cyber-Security Research Flanders with reference number VR20192203, by the FWO under an Odysseus project GOH9718N, and by the European Research Council (ERC) under the European Unions's Horizon 2020 research and innovation programme under grant agreement No. 803096 (SPEC). Cyprien Delpech de Saint Guilhem is a Junior FWO Postdoctoral Fellow under project 1266123N. The work of the last author was conducted whilst they were a PhD student at KU Leuven.

Any opinions, findings and conclusions or recommendations expressed in this material are those of the author(s) and do not necessarily reflect the views of DARPA, the US Government, Cyber Security Research Flanders or the FWO. The U.S. Government is authorized to reproduce and distribute reprints for governmental purposes notwithstanding any copyright annotation therein.

References

1. Abspoel, M., Cramer, R., Damgård, I., Escudero, D., Yuan, C.: Efficient information-theoretic secure multiparty computation over $\mathbb{Z}/p^k\mathbb{Z}$ via galois rings. In: Hofheinz, D., Rosen, A. (eds.) TCC 2019. LNCS, vol. 11891, pp. 471–501. Springer, Cham (2019). https://doi.org/10.1007/978-3-030-36030-6_19

2. Ames, S., Hazay, C., Ishai, Y., Venkitasubramaniam, M.: Ligero: lightweight sublinear arguments without a trusted setup. In: Thuraisingham, B.M., Evans, D., Malkin, T., Xu, D. (eds.) ACM CCS 2017, pp. 2087–2104. ACM Press (2017). https://doi.org/10.1145/3133956.3134104

3. Baum, C., Braun, L., Munch-Hansen, A., Razet, B., Scholl, P.: Appenzeller to brie: efficient zero-knowledge proofs for mixed-mode arithmetic and Z2k. In: Vigna, G., Shi, E. (eds.) ACM CCS 2021, pp. 192–211. ACM Press (2021). https://doi.org/10.1145/3460120.3484812

4. Baum, C., Braun, L., Munch-Hansen, A., Scholl, P.: MozZ$_{2^k}$arella: Efficient vector-OLE and zero-knowledge proofs over $\mathbb{Z}_{2^k}$. In: Dodis, Y., Shrimpton, T. (eds.) CRYPTO 2022, Part IV. LNCS, vol. 13510, pp. 329–358. Springer, Heidelberg (Aug 2022). https://doi.org/10.1007/978-3-031-15985-5_12

5. Baum, C., Delpech de Saint Guilhem, C., Kales, D., Orsini, E., Scholl, P., Zaverucha, G.: Banquet: short and fast signatures from AES. In: Garay, J. (ed.) PKC 2021, Part I. LNCS, vol. 12710, pp. 266–297. Springer, Heidelberg (2021). https://doi.org/10.1007/978-3-030-75245-3_11

6. Baum, C., Nof, A.: Concretely-efficient zero-knowledge arguments for arithmetic circuits and their application to lattice-based cryptography. In: Kiayias, A., Kohlweiss, M., Wallden, P., Zikas, V. (eds.) PKC 2020, Part I. LNCS, vol. 12110, pp. 495–526. Springer, Heidelberg (May 2020). https://doi.org/10.1007/978-3-030-45374-9_17

7. Boneh, D., Boyle, E., Corrigan-Gibbs, H., Gilboa, N., Ishai, Y.: Zero-knowledge proofs on secret-shared data via fully linear PCPs. In: Boldyreva, A., Micciancio, D. (eds.) CRYPTO 2019. LNCS, vol. 11694, pp. 67–97. Springer, Cham (2019). https://doi.org/10.1007/978-3-030-26954-8_3

8. Braun, L., Delpech de Saint Guilhem, C., Jadoul, R., Orsini, E., Smart, N.P., Tanguy, T.: ZK-for-Z2K: MPC-in-the-Head Zero-Knowledge Proofs for $\mathbb{Z}_{2^k}$. Cryptology ePrint Archive, Report 2023/1057 (2023). https://eprint.iacr.org/2023/1057

9. Chase, M., et al.: Post-quantum zero-knowledge and signatures from symmetric-key primitives. In: Thuraisingham, B.M., Evans, D., Malkin, T., Xu, D. (eds.) ACM CCS 2017, pp. 1825–1842. ACM Press (2017). https://doi.org/10.1145/3133956.3133997

10. Chen, S., Cheon, J.H., Kim, D., Park, D.: Verifiable computing for approximate computation. Cryptology ePrint Archive, Report 2019/762 (2019). https://eprint.iacr.org/2019/762

11. Cramer, R., Damgård, I., Escudero, D., Scholl, P., Xing, C.: SPD $\mathbb{Z}_{2^k}$: Efficient MPC mod 2^k for dishonest majority. In: Shacham, H., Boldyreva, A. (eds.) CRYPTO 2018, Part II. LNCS, vol. 10992, pp. 769–798. Springer, Heidelberg (2018). https://doi.org/10.1007/978-3-319-96881-0_26

12. Delpech de Saint Guilhem, C., Orsini, E., Tanguy, T.: Limbo: efficient zero-knowledge MPCitH-based arguments. In: Vigna, G., Shi, E. (eds.) ACM CCS 2021, pp. 3022–3036. ACM Press (2021). https://doi.org/10.1145/3460120.3484595

13. Delpech de Saint Guilhem, C., Orsini, E., Tanguy, T., Verbauwhede, M.: Efficient proof of RAM programs from any public-coin zero-knowledge system. In: Galdi, C., Jarecki, S. (eds.) SCN 22. LNCS, vol. 13409, pp. 615–638. Springer, Heidelberg, Amalfi, Italy (2022). https://doi.org/10.1007/978-3-031-14791-3_27

14. Escudero, D., Ghosh, S., Keller, M., Rachuri, R., Scholl, P.: Improved primitives for MPC over mixed arithmetic-binary circuits. In: Micciancio, D., Ristenpart, T. (eds.) CRYPTO 2020. LNCS, vol. 12171, pp. 823–852. Springer, Cham (2020). https://doi.org/10.1007/978-3-030-56880-1_29

15. Escudero, D., Xing, C., Yuan, C.: More efficient dishonest majority secure computation over $\mathbb{Z}_{2^k}$ via galois rings. In: Dodis, Y., Shrimpton, T. (eds.) CRYPTO 2022, Part I. LNCS, vol. 13507, pp. 383–412. Springer, Heidelberg (2022). https://doi.org/10.1007/978-3-031-15802-5_14

16. Fehr, S.: Span programs over rings and how to share a secret from a module (1998), MSc Thesis, ETH Zurich

17. Feneuil, T., Maire, J., Rivain, M., Vergnaud, D.: Zero-knowledge protocols for the subset sum problem from MPC-in-the-head with rejection. In: Agrawal, S., Lin, D. (eds.) ASIACRYPT 2022, Part II. LNCS, vol. 13792, pp. 371–402. Springer, Heidelberg (2022). https://doi.org/10.1007/978-3-031-22966-4_13

18. Feneuil, T., Rivain, M.: Threshold linear secret sharing to the rescue of MPC-in-the-head. Cryptology ePrint Archive, Report 2022/1407 (2022). https://eprint.iacr.org/2022/1407

19. Fiat, A., Shamir, A.: How to prove yourself: Practical solutions to identification and signature problems. In: Odlyzko, A.M. (ed.) CRYPTO'86. LNCS, vol. 263, pp. 186–194. Springer, Heidelberg (1987). https://doi.org/10.1007/3-540-47721-7_12

20. Giacomelli, I., Madsen, J., Orlandi, C.: ZKBoo: faster zero-knowledge for Boolean circuits. In: Holz, T., Savage, S. (eds.) USENIX Security 2016, pp. 1069–1083. USENIX Association (2016)

21. Goldwasser, S., Micali, S., Rackoff, C.: The knowledge complexity of interactive proof-systems (extended abstract). In: 17th ACM STOC, pp. 291–304. ACM Press (1985). https://doi.org/10.1145/22145.22178

22. Green, M., Hall-Andersen, M., Hennenfent, E., Kaptchuk, G., Perez, B., Laer, G.V.: Efficient proofs of software exploitability for real-world processors. PoPETs 2023(1), 627–640 (2023). https://doi.org/10.56553/popets-2023-0036

23. Ishai, Y., Kushilevitz, E., Ostrovsky, R., Sahai, A.: Zero-knowledge from secure multiparty computation. In: Johnson, D.S., Feige, U. (eds.) 39th ACM STOC, pp. 21–30. ACM Press (2007). https://doi.org/10.1145/1250790.1250794

24. Jadoul, R., Smart, N.P., Leeuwen, B.V.: MPC for Q_2 access structures over rings and fields. In: AlTawy, R., Hülsing, A. (eds.) SAC 2021. LNCS, vol. 13203, pp. 131–151. Springer, Heidelberg (2022). https://doi.org/10.1007/978-3-030-99277-4_7

25. Kales, D., Zaverucha, G.: Efficient lifting for shorter zero-knowledge proofs and post-quantum signatures. Cryptology ePrint Archive, Report 2022/588 (2022). https://eprint.iacr.org/2022/588

26. Katz, J., Kolesnikov, V., Wang, X.: Improved non-interactive zero knowledge with applications to post-quantum signatures. In: Lie, D., Mannan, M., Backes, M., Wang, X. (eds.) ACM CCS 2018, pp. 525–537. ACM Press (2018). https://doi.org/10.1145/3243734.3243805

27. Lin, F., Xing, C., Yao, Y.: More efficient zero-knowledge protocols over $\mathbb{Z}_{2^k}$ via galois rings. Cryptology ePrint Archive, Report 2023/150 (2023). https://eprint.iacr.org/2023/150

28. Shamir, A.: How to share a secret. Commun. Assoc. Comput. Mach. **22**(11), 612–613 (1979)

29. Shoup, V., Smart, N.P.: Lightweight asynchronous verifiable secret sharing with optimal resilience. Cryptology ePrint Archive, Paper 2023/536 (2023).D https://eprint.iacr.org/2023/536

Digital Signature Schemes
and Extensions

Efficient Secure Two Party ECDSA

Sermin Kocaman[1]([✉])[ID] and Younes Talibi Alaoui[2][ID]

[1] Department of Cryptology, Institute of Applied Mathematics, METU, Ankara,
Turkey
sermin.cakin@metu.edu.tr
[2] Fabric Cryptography, Santa Clara, USA
younestalibialaoui@gmail.com

Abstract. Distributing the Elliptic Curve Digital Signature Algorithm
(ECDSA) has received increased attention in past years due to the wide
range of applications that can benefit from this, particularly after the
popularity that the blockchain technology has gained. Many schemes
have been proposed in the literature to improve the efficiency of multi-
party ECDSA. Most of these schemes either require heavy homomorphic
encryption computation or multiple executions of a functionality that
transforms Multiplicative shares to Additive shares (MtA). Xue et al.
(CCS 2021) proposed a 2-party ECDSA protocol secure against malicious adversaries and only requires one execution of MtA, with an online
phase that consists of only one party sending one field element to the
other party with a computational overhead dominated by the verification step of the signature scheme. We propose a novel protocol, based
on the assumption that the Computational Diffie-Hellman problem is
hard, that offers the same online phase performance as the protocol of
Xue et al., but improves the offline phase by reducing the computational
cost by one elliptic curve multiplication and the communication cost by
two field elements. To the best of our knowledge, our protocol offers the
most efficient offline phase for a two-party ECDSA protocol with such
an efficient online phase.

Keywords: ECDSA · Two-party Protocols · Threshold Signatures

1 Introduction

Multi-party computation (MPC) is a technique from cryptography that enables
multiple parties to conduct computation on their secrets while preserving them
private. MPC was formally introduced with Yao's 2-party protocol for the Mil-
lionaires' problem [26]. Today, it became a pioneering solution for a wide variety
of real-world problems, such as cryptographic key protection, privacy-preserving
data analytics, and so forth [15].

With the rise of the blockchain technology and cryptocurrencies, multi-party
signing [7] and, in particular, threshold signing has gained significant attention

---

Y.T. Alaoui—Most of the work done while at imec-COSIC, KU Leuven, Belgium.

E. A. Quaglia (Ed.): IMACC 2023, LNCS 14421, pp. 161–180, 2024.
https://doi.org/10.1007/978-3-031-47818-5_9

in the past decade. Namely, a (t,n) signature scheme enables n parties to distribute the signing power in such a way that signing a message m requires the collaboration of at least $t+1$ of them. This is accomplished by having the n parties participate in the key generation phase to produce a private key unknown to them. At the end of this phase, each party will hold a share of the private key, together with the public key. Then the signing phase is executed as an interactive protocol as well, where at least $t+1$ parties participate with their shares so as to produce the signature, which is then checked with the verification algorithm of the signature scheme being distributed. This benefits cryptocurrencies as transactions are sent by producing a signature using the sender's private key. Thus to prevent a single point of failure while maintaining the key, one can share it among different parties placed in different locations, who need to collaborate to sign.

In this regard, thresholdizing the ECDSA algorithm has drawn most of the attention, as it is the signing algorithm used in Bitcoin. We can find in the literature many works that addressed this [2,5,6,8,9,12–14,23,25] where various schemes were constructed, either addressing the 2-party case [8,13,14,25], or more generally, the n-party case [2,5,6,9,12,23]; using generic MPC protocols [5,23], or special purpose protocols targeting ECDSA [2,6,8,9,12–14,25]. Those schemes differ particularly in the way of sharing values, namely additively or multiplicatively. That is, at the heart of the ECDSA algorithm, one needs to calculate $s = k^{-1}(H(m) + x \cdot r) \mod q$. In a threshold version of ECDSA, both the private key x and the random nonce k used for signing the message m are secretly shared among parties. In fact, to provide a threshold version of ECDSA, the main challenge consists of choosing an adequate way to secretly share k and x so that s can be computed efficiently. Note that this calculation contains inverting a secret, and multiplying it with another value obtained by evaluating linear operations over another secret (addition and multiplication with opened values).

For instance, for the 2-party case, additively secret sharing k is problematic for inversion, as in this case, party $\mathcal{P}_1$ holds k_1 and party $\mathcal{P}_2$ holds k_2 subject to $k_1 + k_2 = k \mod q$, and from this, the two parties need to calculate k^{-1}. Alternatively, one can secretly share k in a multiplicative way to overcome this obstacle, as in this case, inverting becomes a local operation; however, the resulting value still needs to be multiplied by $H(m) + x \cdot r$, which still introduces obstacles either x was additively or multiplicatively secret shared.

As a solution to these challenges, several authors in the field proposed using homomorphic encryption. This approach allows one party to transmit a secret to the other party in encrypted form so that they can execute the challenging computation and decrypt it afterward. The homomorphic encryption schemes that were used are partially homomorphic, as performing one type of operation over the ciphertexts was sufficient for the computation needed.

For the most part, homomorphic encryption was introduced to realize a Multiplicative-to-Additive (MtA) functionality which enables parties to obtain an additive version of the shares of a secret from a multiplicative one, adopting ideas from [17]. Based on this functionality, parties who hold multiplicative shares α and β, respectively, can get the corresponding additive shares a and b where $a + b = \alpha.\beta$ by querying this functionality. The need for querying this protocol arises when an additive sharing is preferable than a multiplicative one from a performance point of view. Of course, this functionality does not come for free, and it introduces a cost to the protocol whenever it is called; however, there exist many instantiations of it, such as Paillier encryption [20]-based MtA [12], El Gamal encryption [10]-based MtA [16], and Castagnos-Laguillaumie (CL) encryption [4]-based MtA [3]. Besides, one can also construct Oblivious Transfer (OT) [21]-based MtA [8], which has the advantage of decreasing the computational complexity by eliminating the need for homomorphic encryption at the expense of incurring a relatively high bandwidth. As a result, one has multiple options for MtA instantiations, each of which offers a different tradeoff between the computation and communication costs, thanks to which one can select the one that best fits the constraints faced. Also, it should be noted that Fireblocks' teams showed a Paillier key vulnerability in [12] leaking secret key or inverse nonce information [18]. These attacks occur when the MtA functionality is used without range proofs that ensure the inputs of MtA are chosen from the required domain. Thus, it is recommended to use suitable range proofs to detect maliciously formed input in Paillier-based MtA functionality.

For the 2-party case of threshold ECDSA, two works are most related to ours, namely, the one of Lindell [14] and Xue et al. [25]. Lindell has proposed a simple and efficient 2-party protocol against malicious adversaries. To briefly go over this protocol, both x and k are secretly shared in a multiplicative way, where each party $\mathcal{P}_i$ generates x_i in the key generation phase so that the private key x is equal to $x = x_1 \cdot x_2$. Party $\mathcal{P}_1$ also encrypts x_1 so as to send it to $\mathcal{P}_2$, then in the signing phase, the two parties generate their share of the nonce k, then $\mathcal{P}_2$ computes its share of s and sends it to $\mathcal{P}_1$, which involves encrypting and performing homomorphic encryption operations. Finally, $\mathcal{P}_1$ calculates the signature s, which involves decryption before the verification step.

On the other hand, Xue et al. proposed an online-friendly algorithm against malicious adversaries. That is, this protocol has a nearly optimal online phase, in the sense that the heaviest part of it consists of the verification step of the signature, which in turn consists of calculating two scalar multiplications M of elliptic curve points (scalar multiplications will be denoted as M from now on). The communication cost is also efficient, as only a single field element needs to be sent. This is opposed to [14] as one needs to send and operate over ciphertexts during the online phase. However, providing such an efficient online phase came with the cost of offloading all the heavy computation in the offline phase of the signing step. That is, while the key generation does not involve any encryption, an MtA is being executed for every signature during the signing phase, which is still a good compromise as it reduces the number of calls to the MtA functionality compared to other schemes. Thus the resulting protocol offers an efficient online phase with a good overall cost. However, this scheme can be further optimized, as we will see in the next section.

1.1 Our Contribution

We present a protocol against malicious adversaries with a nearly optimal online phase as in [25], but with reduced computation and communication costs for the offline phase. That is, our key generation is the same as in [25], where we produce additive secret sharings of x ($\mathcal{P}_i$ generates $Q_i \leftarrow [x_i] \cdot P$, where P is a generator of the curve, and the public key is $Q \leftarrow Q_1 + Q_2$), and our online phase requires two scalar multiplication M as in [25]. However, our offline phase reduces the number of EC multiplications by one and the size of data communicated by two field elements.

The cost reduction is achieved by eliminating the additional step of re-sharing the secret x in [25], and basing the security of our protocol on the 1-Weak Diffie-Hellman problem, which is equivalent to the Computational Diffie-Hellman problem. That is, at the heart of the signing phase of the protocol of [25], x was re-shared between the two parties (following obvious notation) as $x = x_1'.(k_2 + r_1) + x_2'$, where the nonce k is shared as $k = k_1(r_1 + k_2)$, then the shares x_1' and k_2 are the values forwarded to the MtA functionality.

Instead, we simplified the protocol by adopting a multiplicative sharing of k where it is unnecessary to perform a re-sharing step ($\mathcal{P}_i$ generates $R_i \leftarrow [k_i] \cdot P$ for P the generator of the curve, and the point R from which we take the x-coordinate r is $R \leftarrow [k_1 \cdot k_2] \cdot P$). We query the MtA only once on the most convenient inputs for our choices. Namely, querying the MtA on x_1 as the input of $\mathcal{P}_1$, and k_2^{-1} as the input of $\mathcal{P}_2$. This was a logical choice as holding an additive sharing as

$$x_1 \cdot k_2^{-1} = a + b \mod q$$

by the players allows them to do the online phase in only one pass, as the signature s can be written as

$$s = k_1^{-1} \cdot (k_2^{-1} \cdot (H(m) + x_2 \cdot r) + x_1 \cdot k_2^{-1} \cdot r) \mod q$$

In this case, $\mathcal{P}_2$ computes locally its signature share as

$$s_2 \leftarrow k_2^{-1} \cdot (H(m) + x_2 \cdot r) + b \cdot r \mod q$$

and sends it to $\mathcal{P}_1$ to construct the signature

$$s \leftarrow k_1^{-1} \cdot (s_2 + a \cdot r) \mod q$$

However, it is crucial to note that the protocol requires $\mathcal{P}_1$ to input x_1 for MtA. If there are no checks on this input to MtA, a malicious $\mathcal{P}_1$ can corrupt the system since $\mathcal{P}_1$ takes the partial signature s_2 and then generates the full signature s. For example, a malicious $\mathcal{P}_1$ can forge a signature on a different message m' of his choice by crafting the value to be sent to MtA as $x_1' \leftarrow -r^{-1} \cdot (H(m') - H(m) + x_1 \cdot r)$, then $\mathcal{P}_1$ will compute the full signature s as $k_1^{-1} \cdot (s_2 + a \cdot r) = k_1^{-1} \cdot (k_2^{-1} \cdot (H(m) + x_2.r) + (a + b) \cdot r) = k^{-1} \cdot (H(m') + x \cdot r)$ which is a valid signature on m' that is chosen by $\mathcal{P}_1$.

In order to prevent $\mathcal{P}_1$ from mounting such an attack and manipulating the distribution of s_2, we add a check operation on the correctness of the MtA input of $\mathcal{P}_1$. Namely after calling MtA and receiving its outputs, $\mathcal{P}_1$ computes $[a] \cdot P$ and sends it to $\mathcal{P}_2$, who computes $k_2 \cdot ([a] \cdot P + [b] \cdot P)$ and checks whether it is equal to Q_1 or not. The correctness of this equality ensures that $\mathcal{P}_1$ used the correct x_1 value as MtA input, and as we will see, $\mathcal{P}_1$ will not be able to bypass it, unless he breaks the standard assumption that the Computational Diffie-Hellman problem is hard. It is worth noting that the check we add is not concerned with the security of the underlying MtA, but rather to ensure that the parties involved are invoking the MtA with the appropriate inputs. This of course adds a round of communication to the protocol, however, it is a critical step in ensuring the protocol's security, which is analogous to the consistency check executed immediately following the MtA call in [25].

In sum, the protocol we end up with utilized an additive sharing of x and a multiplicative sharing of k, which is a similar setting of [8] for the (1, n)-ECDSA case (i.e., any two parties among the n parties can construct a valid signature). However, we only call the MtA functionality once while it is being called three times in [8]. Besides, we only perform 13M, while 16M are needed for [8].

This improvement has an impact depending on the instantiation of MtA. For instance, in the case of an OT-based MTA, where such a choice is usually made to have a low computation cost, reducing the number of EC multiplications by one will decrease the computation cost of the offline phase of [25] (Table 4 of [25]) by 5.4%. On the other hand, in the case of a CL-based MtA, which introduces a low communication cost, reducing the size of transmitted data by two field elements decreases the communication cost of the offline phase of [25] (Table 5 of [25]) for the case of the secp256k1 curve by 3.7%. While these percentages may seem modest, the potential gains are substantial, given the vast scale at which ECDSA signatures are executed, and all the applications that can benefit from a distributed version of it.

We also implemented our protocol and obtained an online phase of 0.1 ms, which is half the time required for the online phase of [25]; however, given the similarity of the online phase between the two protocols, this difference in time is most likely due to our implementation's use of the highly optimized C library secp256k1 for the operations over the curve.

1.2 Paper Organization

This paper is organized as follows: Sect. 2 provides the necessary background over the hardness assumption upon which we are basing the security of our protocol, the ECDSA scheme, and the ideal functionalities we used. Section 3 presents the proposed protocol, along with the cost analysis, comparison with related work, and its running time based on our implementation. Section 4 concludes the paper. Then in the Appendix, security proofs are given.

2   Preliminaries

2.1   Hardness Assumptions

The security of our protocol is based on the 1-Weak Diffie-Hellman problem [19], also referred to as the Inverse Diffie-Hellman problem [1]. That is, this problem is a special case of the k-Weak Diffie-Hellman problem (and can be proven to be equivalent to it), where the adversary is given a set of points $\{P, [x]\cdot P, [x^2]\cdot P, \ldots, [x^k]\cdot P\}$ for a randomly chosen x, and asked to find $[x^{-1}]\cdot P$.

Definition 1. *(Computational Diffie-Hellman Assumption.) Let $\mathbb{G}$ be a cyclic group of a large prime order, and P a generator of $\mathbb{G}$. Given a tuple $(P, [a]\cdot P, [b]\cdot P)$ for a randomly chosen a and b, it is computationally hard to compute $[a\cdot b]\cdot P$.*

Definition 2. *(1-Weak Diffie-Hellman Assumption.) Let $\mathbb{G}$ be a cyclic group of a large prime order, and P a generator of $\mathbb{G}$. Given a tuple $(P, [x]\cdot P)$ for a randomly chosen x, it is computationally hard to compute $[x^{-1}]\cdot P$.*

Theorem 1. *The 1-Weak Diffie-Hellman and the Computational Diffie-Hellman assumptions are equivalent.*

The proof of theorem 1 is given Appendix A.

2.2   The ECDSA Scheme

The ECDSA scheme is a signature algorithm that involves key generation, signing, and verification. Let $\mathbb{G}$ be an elliptic curve group of order q of size λ bits, with a generator P, and the neutral element being denoted as $\mathcal{O}$. The ECDSA scheme works as follows:

- KeyGen(1^λ) $\rightarrow (x, Q)$: set a random private key $x \leftarrow Z_q$ and compute the corresponding public key $Q = [x] \cdot P$.
- Sign(x, m) $\rightarrow (r, s)$: generate the signature (r, s) using private key x, message m, and hash function H with codomain of size λ bits. That is:
  - Set a random nonce $k \leftarrow Z_q^*$ and compute $R \leftarrow [k] \cdot P = (r_x, r_y)$, then set $r \leftarrow r_x \mod q$.
  - Compute $s \leftarrow k^{-1} \cdot (H(m) + r \cdot x) \mod q$ and output (r, s).
- Verify($m; (r, s)$) $\rightarrow b \in \{0, 1\}$: equals 1 if the signature is valid; 0 otherwise. That is:
  - Compute $R \leftarrow s^{-1} \cdot ([H(m)] \cdot P + [r] \cdot Q) = (r_x, r_y)$.
  - If $r = r_x \mod q$, output 1; otherwise output 0.

Due to the structure of elliptic curves, if (r, s) is a valid signature, then its complement $(r, -s)$ is also a valid signature. Thus, this gives rise to the malleability problem of the ECDSA scheme. To overcome this problem, one can follow the low-s rule, where the low-s is the value between 0 and $\frac{q-1}{2}$. Therefore, we assume that the output of the signing procedure is always the lower s value.

2.3   Ideal Functionalities

We describe below the ideal $\mathcal{F}_{2ECDSA}$ functionality that our protocol realizes, as well as the ideal functionalities queried by our protocol, namely, an ideal zero-knowledge proof (ZKP) functionality $\mathcal{F}_{ZKP}$ and an ideal committed non-interactive zero-knowledge functionality $\mathcal{F}_{Commit-ZK}$ which are similar to the ones used in [14], as well as an ideal Multiplicative-to-Additive (MtA) functionality $\mathcal{F}_{MtA}$. In this content, we assume that each functionality provides a fresh session identifier (sid) for each invocation of it. This can be achieved by having the parties exchange random strings between each other, which will be further concatenated then hashed so as to produce the session identifiers.

$\mathcal{F}_{2ECDSA}$ **Functionality.** The $\mathcal{F}_{2ECDSA}$ functionality is composed of a key generation phase and a signing phase. In the key generation phase, the key pair (x, Q) is generated, where x is stored internally, and Q is given to the parties. In the signing phase, the signature on the given message is constructed and given to $\mathcal{P}_1$. The functionality is introduced in Fig. 1.

2-party ECDSA functionality $\mathcal{F}_{2ECDSA}$

Given an elliptic curve group $\mathbb{G}$ of order q, a generator P of $\mathbb{G}$, and a hash function H with a codomain of size λ bits. The functionality works as follows:

KeyGen: On input init from both parties $\mathcal{P}_1$ and $\mathcal{P}_2$:
  - Run KeyGen as defined in Subsection 2.2, so as to generate a key pair (x, Q).
  - Store (x, Q) and send Q to both parties.
  - Set an internal flag ready to 1 and ignore further calls.

Sign: On input Sign(sid, m) from both parties $\mathcal{P}_1$ and $\mathcal{P}_2$. If ready $= 1$ and the session identifier sid has not been used previously:
  - Run Sign as defined in Subsection 2.2, so as to generate the signature (r, s).
  - Send (r, s) to $\mathcal{P}_1$.
  - Store internally (sid, delivered).

Fig. 1. 2-party ECDSA functionality $\mathcal{F}_{2ECDSA}$

$\mathcal{F}_{ZKP}$ **Functionality.** The $\mathcal{F}_{ZKP}$ functionality is depicted in Fig. 2. With this functionality, one party can prove the knowledge of a witness w for an element y, such that the pair (y, w) satisfies the relation $\mathcal{R}$. For our protocol, this relation is $\mathcal{R} \leftarrow \{(Q, x) \in \mathbb{G} \times Z_q | Q = [x] \cdot P\}$ for public parameters $\mathbb{G}$ and its generator P, which allows to prove knowledge of the discrete log of an elliptic curve point. The sigma protocol of Schnorr [22] can be used to instantiate this functionality, which can be made non-interactive using the Fiat-Shamir paradigm in the random-oracle model [11].

ZKPs are expected to satisfy three key properties, completeness, soundness, and zero knowledge. Completeness means that given a witness w for a statement

$$\mathcal{F}_{\mathsf{ZKP}}$$

$\mathcal{F}_{\mathsf{ZKP}}$ functionality between $\mathcal{P}_1$ and $\mathcal{P}_2$ works as follows:

Prove: On input $(prove, sid, x, w)$ from $\mathcal{P}_i$ for $i \in \{1, 2\}$, send $(proof, sid, x)$ to $\mathcal{P}_{3-i}$ if $(x, w) \in R$ and sid has not been previously used, otherwise ignore the message.

Fig. 2. $\mathcal{F}_{\mathsf{ZKP}}$

$x \in \mathcal{R}$, there is an efficient algorithm that provides a convincing $proof$, i.e. it ensures that if two parties follow the protocol, the verifier accepts the proof. Soundness means a malicious prover cannot construct a convincing $proof$ for $x \notin \mathcal{R}$, i.e. soundness prevents the verifier from accepting a false proof of the statement. Also, zero-knowledge means that $proof$ does not reveal the used witness w, i.e. it states that $proof$ does not leak any information except for the truth of the statement.

$\mathcal{F}_{\mathsf{Commit\text{-}ZK}}$ **Functionality.** The $\mathcal{F}_{\mathsf{Commit\text{-}ZK}}$ functionality is depicted in Fig. 3. Through this functionality, a party will be able to commit to its Non-interactive ZKP (NIZKP) and open it afterwards. As mentioned in [14], this functionality can be realized in the random oracle model by having the parties hash their NIZKP concatenated with a randomness r, which will be both opened in the decommitment phase.

$$\mathcal{F}_{\mathsf{Commit\text{-}ZK}}$$

$\mathcal{F}_{\mathsf{Commit\text{-}ZK}}$ functionality between $\mathcal{P}_1$ and $\mathcal{P}_2$ works as follows:

Commit: On input (com-prove, sid, x, w) from $\mathcal{P}_i$ for $i \in \{1, 2\}$, record (sid, i, x, w) if sid has not been used previously and $(x, w) \in R$, then send (proof-receipt, sid) to $\mathcal{P}_{3-i}$, otherwise ignore the message.
Decommit: On input (decom-proof, sid) to $\mathcal{P}_i$, send (decom-proof, $sid, x, 1$) to $\mathcal{P}_{3-i}$ if (sid, i, x, w) is recorded and $(x, w) \in R$, otherwise send (decom-proof, $sid, x, 0$) to $\mathcal{P}_{3-i}$

Fig. 3. $\mathcal{F}_{\mathsf{Commit\text{-}ZK}}$

$\mathcal{F}_{\mathsf{MtA}}$ **Functionality.** The $\mathcal{F}_{\mathsf{MtA}}$ functionality is depicted in Fig. 4. This functionality takes as an input the two values α and β coming from $\mathcal{P}_1$ and $\mathcal{P}_2$ respectively, and forwards to them respectively two random values a and b, subject to the relation $a + b = \alpha \cdot \beta \mod q$, i.e., it transforms a multiplicative sharing of a secret to an additive sharing. As stated earlier, one can instantiate

MtA from many constructions, such as the Paillier encryption scheme [20] or El
Gamal [10], Castagnos-Laguillaumie (CL) [4] or OT [21].

$\mathcal{F}_{\mathsf{MtA}}$

$\mathcal{F}_{\mathsf{MtA}}$ functionality between $\mathcal{P}_1$ and $\mathcal{P}_2$ works as follows:

Reshare: On input $(sid, \alpha \in Z_q)$ from $\mathcal{P}_1$ and $(sid, \beta \in Z_q)$ from $\mathcal{P}_2$. If sid has
been used before ignore this message. Otherwise:
  - Sample $a \leftarrow Z_q$ and calculate $b \leftarrow \alpha \cdot \beta - a \bmod q$
  - Send (sid, a) to $\mathcal{P}_1$ and (sid, b) to $\mathcal{P}_2$.

Fig. 4. $\mathcal{F}_{\mathsf{MtA}}$

3 Protocol

Our two party ECDSA protocol is composed of two phases; one phase for a
distributed key generation that runs once, at the end of which the parties will
hold an additive sharing of the secret x as $x = x_1 + x_2$, then the second phase
is for signing, which consists of:

- Generating the nonce k, which will be multiplicatively shared between the
  parties as $k = k_1 \cdot k_2$.
- Querying the MtA functionality, so as to convert the product of $\mathcal{P}_1$'s secret
  key x_1 and $\mathcal{P}_2$'s nonce k_2^{-1} to an additive sharing $a + b$, namely, $\mathcal{P}_1$ and $\mathcal{P}_2$
  receive a and b respectively such that $a + b = x_1 . k_2^{-1} \bmod q$. After the query,
  $\mathcal{P}_1$ computes $Z \leftarrow [a] \cdot P$ and sends it to $\mathcal{P}_2$, who computes $(Z + [b] \cdot P) \cdot k_2$
  and checks if it is equal to Q_1, so as to control the correctness of the MtA
  input against a malicious $\mathcal{P}_1$.
- Online signing, that starts by $\mathcal{P}_2$ generating locally its share of the signature
  after the MtA invocation, namely $s_2 = k_2^{-1}(H(m) + r.x_2) + b \cdot r \bmod q$,
  then sends it to $\mathcal{P}_1$ who will generate the signature by calculating locally
  $s = k_1^{-1}(s_2 + a \cdot r) \bmod q$ and verifying whether this signature is valid. Note
  that the nonce generation and the MtA invocation are message-independent,
  thus we can refer to these two steps as the offline signing.

The complete process is illustrated in Fig. 5. Also the graphical representation of the key distribution and signing phase are given in Fig. 6 and Fig. 7,
respectively.

Security of our protocol is simulation based, following the real/ideal paradigm
[24]. The type of adversary we considered is a malicious one with static corruption. This implies that the adversary $\mathcal{A}$ can deviate from the protocol, but the
party he corrupts (either $\mathcal{P}_1$ or $\mathcal{P}_2$) is set prior to the protocol execution.

2-party ECDSA Protocol

Given an elliptic curve group $\mathbb{G}$ of order q and a generator P of $\mathbb{G}$:

Key Generation: To generate a pair of keys for the ECDSA algorithm, the parties do as follows:

1. $\mathcal{P}_1$ generates $x_1 \leftarrow \mathbb{Z}_q$ and calculates $Q_1 = [x_1] \cdot P$.
2. $\mathcal{P}_1$ sends (com-prove, $1, Q_1, x_1$) to $\mathcal{F}_{\text{Commit-ZK}}$.
3. $\mathcal{P}_2$ receives (proof-receipt, 1)
4. $\mathcal{P}_2$ generates $x_2 \leftarrow \mathbb{Z}_q$ and calculates $Q_2 = [x_2] \cdot P$.
5. $\mathcal{P}_2$ sends (prove, $2, Q_2, x_2$) to $\mathcal{F}_{\text{ZKP}}$.
6. $\mathcal{P}_1$ receives (proof, $2, Q_2$) from $\mathcal{F}_{\text{ZKP}}$. If not, $\mathcal{P}_1$ aborts.
7. $\mathcal{P}_1$ sends (decom-proof, 1) to $\mathcal{F}_{\text{Commit-ZK}}$.
8. $\mathcal{P}_2$ receives (decom-proof, $1, Q_1, z$) from $\mathcal{F}_{\text{Commit-ZK}}$. If $z = 0$, $\mathcal{P}_2$ aborts.

Both parties set $Q \leftarrow Q_1 + Q_2$ to be the public key. The private key is $x \leftarrow x_1 + x_2 \mod q$ (note that no party holds x, but only an additive share of it).

Signing: To sign a message m, the parties do as follows:

1. **Generating the nonce k:**
    (a) $\mathcal{P}_1$ generates $k_1 \leftarrow \mathbb{Z}_q$ and calculates $R_1 = [k_1] \cdot P$.
    (b) $\mathcal{P}_1$ sends (com-prove, $sid\|1\ R_1, k_1$) to $\mathcal{F}_{\text{Commit-ZK}}$.
    (c) $\mathcal{P}_2$ receives (proof-receipt, $sid\|1, 1$)
    (d) $\mathcal{P}_2$ generates $k_2 \leftarrow \mathbb{Z}_q$ and calculates $R_2 = [k_2] \cdot P$.
    (e) $\mathcal{P}_2$ sends (prove, $sid\|2, R_2, k_2$) to $\mathcal{F}_{\text{ZKP}}$
    (f) $\mathcal{P}_1$ receives (proof, $sid\|2, R_2$) from $\mathcal{F}_{\text{ZKP}}$. If not, $\mathcal{P}_1$ aborts.
    (g) $\mathcal{P}_1$ sends (decom-prove, $sid\|1$) to $\mathcal{F}_{\text{Commit-ZK}}$.
    (h) $\mathcal{P}_2$ receives (decom-proof, $sid\|1, R_1, z$) from $\mathcal{F}_{\text{Commit-ZK}}$. If $z = 0$, $\mathcal{P}_2$ aborts.

    Both parties set $R \leftarrow [k_1 \cdot k_2] \cdot P = (r, y)$, corresponding to the nonce $k \leftarrow k_1 \cdot k_2$ (note that no party holds k, but only a multiplicative share of it).

2. **Querying the MtA functionality:**
    (a) $\mathcal{P}_1$ and $\mathcal{P}_2$ query $\mathcal{F}_{\text{MtA}}$ with the respective inputs x_1 and k_2^{-1}. $\mathcal{F}_{\text{MtA}}$ forwards a to $\mathcal{P}_1$ and b to $\mathcal{P}_2$.
    (b) $\mathcal{P}_1$ calculates $Z \leftarrow [a] \cdot P$ and sends it to $\mathcal{P}_2$.
    (c) $\mathcal{P}_2$ verifies if $k_2 \cdot (Z + [b] \cdot P) = Q_1$. If it is not the case $\mathcal{P}_2$ aborts.

3. **Online signing:**
    - $\mathcal{P}_2$ calculates $s_2 \leftarrow k_2^{-1} \cdot (H(m) + x_2 \cdot r) + b \cdot r \mod q$ and sends it to $\mathcal{P}_1$.
    - $\mathcal{P}_1$ calculates $s \leftarrow k_1^{-1} \cdot (s_2 + a \cdot r) \mod q$.
    - $\mathcal{P}_1$ verifies if s is a valid signature of m, if so $\mathcal{P}_1$ outputs (r, s) as the signature.

Fig. 5. 2-party ECDSA Protocol

Theorem 2. *The protocol of Fig. 5 securely implements the functionality of Fig. 1 in the $(\mathcal{F}_{\text{ZKP}}, \mathcal{F}_{\text{Commit-ZK}}, \mathcal{F}_{\text{MtA}})$-hybrid model in the presence of a malicious static adversary under the ideal/real definition of [24], assuming the Computational Diffie-Hellman problem is hard.*

The proof of theorem 2 is given in Appendix B.

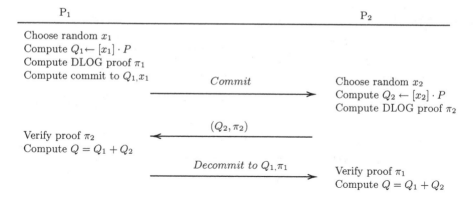

P_1		P_2
Choose random x_1		
Compute $Q_1 \leftarrow [x_1] \cdot P$		
Compute DLOG proof π_1		
Compute commit to Q_1, x_1	*Commit* $\longrightarrow$	Choose random x_2
		Compute $Q_2 \leftarrow [x_2] \cdot P$
		Compute DLOG proof π_2
Verify proof π_2	$\longleftarrow$ (Q_2, π_2)	
Compute $Q = Q_1 + Q_2$		
	Decommit to Q_1, π_1 $\longrightarrow$	Verify proof π_1
		Compute $Q = Q_1 + Q_2$

Fig. 6. The 2-Party ECDSA Key Distribution Protocol

3.1 Cost Analysis

We analyze below the theoretical complexity of our two party ECDSA protocol, and compare it with the one of [14, 25].

Theoretical Complexity - Key Distribution. The distributed key generation consists of generating keys and zero-knowledge proofs. The computation cost can be examined in terms of EC multiplications as this is the heaviest operation performed. For the keys, each party carries out 1M to produce its share of the public key. On the other hand, two zero-knowledge proofs of knowledge of discrete log need to be produced. Using the standard Schnorr proofs in non-interactive from, each party carries out 1M as a prover and 2M as a verifier. Thus the key distribution requires 8M in total. For the communication cost, each party needs to send its share of the public key and the corresponding NIZKP, and $\mathcal{P}_1$, needs to send as well a commitment to its share at the beginning of the protocol, which consists of an output of the hash function H being used (of size λ bits). Assuming one EC point can be represented in λ bits, and a NIZKP consists of two field elements and one EC point, the size of data communicated between the parties is $9 \cdot \lambda$. Note that the cost of our key distribution is the same as [25], which is a negligible cost compared to the one of Lindell [14], as the latter is dominated by the usage of homomorphic encryption.

Theoretical Complexity-Signing. The computation cost of the signing protocol can be examined in terms of EC multiplications and MtA invocations. That is, the first step of the offline phase is similar to the key generation, except that the nonce is multiplicatively shared, thus each party needs to perform an extra EC multiplication so as to obtain R. Also, the calculation needed to check $\mathcal{P}_1$'s input to MtA requires 3 EC multiplications. Thus, it results in a computation

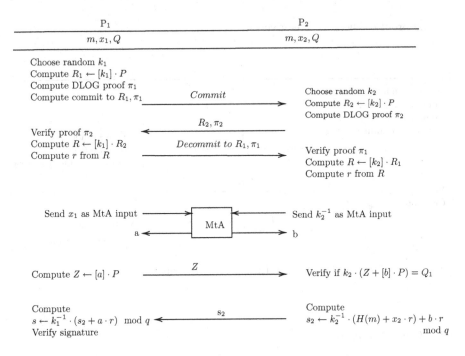

Fig. 7. The 2-Party ECDSA Signing Protocol

cost of 13M, and a communication cost of $10 \cdot \lambda$. To obtain the total cost of the offline phase, one needs to add these costs to the executing of 1 MtA. The cost of this depends on the instantiation used, which can yield different results. For instance, MtA can be instantiated from the Paillier encryption scheme, i.e., the building block upon which [14] is based. This would result in a protocol where homomorphic encryption is used in the offline phase, with an inferior performance to that of [14], however with an improved online phase performance than [14]

In fact, the online phase consists of performing operations over a field by both parties, and a verification phase of the signature, which requires from the verifier (in our case P_1) to carry out 2M. Thus neglecting the cost of operations over a field, the computation cost of the online phase if 2M. As for the communication cost, P_2 needs to send one field element to P_1, thus λ bits of data need to be communicated between the parties.

Table 1 compares these costs with the ones of [14,25]. For [14], the cost of the homomorphic operations is dominated by exponentiations modulo N^2 by numbers from Z_N. We refer to these exponentiations as E. The value N refers to the public key of Paillier, which determines the size of a Paillier encryption, which is a number from Z_{N^2}. MtA refers to the cost of invoking an instantiation of the MtA functionality.

As one can notice, the computation and communication cost of our online phase is the same as [25], which outperforms the one of [14], for which the online phase requires performing an extra exponentiation, and sending an encryption of Paillier (N is typically of size 2048 bits) instead of a field element. However, our offline phase outperforms the one of [25], as in our case the computation and communication required are reduced respectively by 1M, and $2 \cdot \lambda$.

Table 1. Cost Analysis of Signing

Protocol	Computation		Communication	
	Offline	Online	Offline	Online
Lindell [14]	10M+2E	2M+1E	$9 \cdot \lambda$	$2 \cdot log_2(N)$
Xue et al. [25]	14M+1MtA	2M	$12 \cdot \lambda + 1MtA$	λ
Ours	13M+1MtA	2M	$10 \cdot \lambda + 1MtA$	λ

3.2 Implementation

We implemented our protocol in C++, over the secp256k1 curve standardized by NIST, which is the one used by Bitcoin. The hash function we used is Sha256, and for the curve operation we used the Secp256k1[1] C library. The implementation can be found in https://github.com/YounesTall/2ecdsa

We took runtimes with an Amazon instance of "t2.xlarge" (16 GiB of memory and 4 vCPU), running with "Ubuntu 18.04.6 LTS", this instance was located in "us-east-1" (Virginia). The runtimes we obtained are given in Table 2. Note that our implementation used a single thread, and that the runtimes reflect only the computation cost of our protocol. These runtimes were obtained by calculating the average time needed for a 1000 key generation, where each key was used to sign 100 messages. Note also that the MtA implemented is a dummy one (one party receives the multiplicative share of the other party, and produces the additive shares for both parties), hence Table 2 contains the term MtA, where one can plug in the time needed to execute the MtA of their choice to obtain the overall runtime of the offline signing. As can be observed, our protocol is efficient in terms of the computation cost, for both key generation and signing. That is, the key generation only requires 1.05 ms and the offline phase (excluding the MtA call) requires 1.26ms. The difference in runtimes is mainly due to the five extra EC multiplications, namely two extra EC multiplications that need to be performed for calculating R, as the nonce is shared multiplicatively, and three extra EC multiplications that need to be performed for checking the correctness of $\mathcal{P}_1$'s input to MtA. The online phase only requires 0.1ms, as this is dominated by two EC multiplications for the signature verification.

---

[1] https://github.com/bitcoin-core/secp256k1

Table 2. Runtimes in milliseconds of our protocol. These runtimes correspond to the time needed for one key generation, one execution of the offline phase, and one execution of the online phase.

Key generation	Offline signing	Online signing
1.05	1.26 + MtA	0.10

To understand the impact of the MtA functionality on the runtimes, so as to give a comprehensive evaluation of our protocol, let us consider two cases, an OT based MtA, and a CL based MtA. For this we will base our analysis on the runtimes of [25]. That is, [25] implemented their protocol with different MtA instanciations. For the case of OT, the offline phase took 2.6ms and required 90.9 KBytes of data to be communicated (Table 4 of [25]). For the case of CL, the offline phase took 1386ms and required 1.7KB of data to be communicated (Table 5 of [25]). As for the online phase, it took 0.2ms, which is dominated by 2M operations.

As the offline phase of [25] consists of 14M+1MtA, and requires $12 \cdot \lambda$ +1MtA (see Table 1), for the case of OT, one would estimate the MtA runtime to be around 1.2ms, and the communication cost of the MtA to be 90.52 KBytes, thus based on this, our offline phase would take around 2.46ms and require 9.84 KBytes, hence a gain of 5.4% on the running time. For the case of CL, one would estimate the MtA runtime to be around 1384.6ms, and the communication cost of the MtA to be 1.32 KBytes, thus based on this, our offline phase would take around 1385.9ms and require 1.636 KBytes, hence a gain of 3.7% of the size of communicated data.

4   Conclusion

We proposed an efficient two-party ECDSA protocol secure against malicious adversaries. Our protocol has a light online phase, dominated by the verification step of ECDSA, and requires only sending one field element from one party to the other. Our offline phase uses a single call of the MtA functionality, and to the best of our knowledge, it offers the most efficient offline phase in terms of the computational and communication cost for such an online phase.

It is worth noting that the asymmetry introduced to the protocol, between what the two parties do, particularly the inputs they send to the MtA functionality, poses a challenge to generalize the protocol to the multiparty case with a low number of invocation to the MtA functionality (say at most equal to the number of parties). We leave further exploration as future work.

Acknowledgments. Authors would like to thank the anonymous reviewers for their valuable comments, as well as Muhammed Ali Bingol and Daniele Cozzo for the valuable discussions over the protocol security. This work has been supported by TUBITAK under 2244 project, and by CyberSecurity Research Flanders with reference number VR20192203. Any opinions, findings and conclusions or recommendations expressed in this material are those of the author(s) and do not necessarily reflect the views of any of the funders.

A   Proof of Theorem 1

The proof below is taken from [19].

Let us assume we can solve the Diffie-Hellman problem, then given the tuple $(P, [x] \cdot P)$ one can obtain $[x^{-1}] \cdot P = [x^{-1} \cdot x^{-1}] \cdot ([x] \cdot P)$ from solving the Diffie-Hellman problem over the tuple $([x] \cdot P, P = x^{-1} \cdot ([x] \cdot P), P = x^{-1} \cdot ([x] \cdot P))$.

Conversely, let us assume we can solve the 1-Weak Diffie-Hellman problem, then given the tuple $(P, [a] \cdot P, [b] \cdot P)$, one can obtain $([a^2] \cdot P)$ from solving the 1-Weak Diffie-Hellman problem over the tuple $([a] \cdot P, P = a^{-1} \cdot ([a] \cdot P))$. Similarly, one can obtain $([b^2] \cdot P)$ and $([(a+b)^2] \cdot P)$ from the tuples $([b] \cdot P, P)$ and $([a+b] \cdot P, P)$ respectively. Next, one can obtain $([a \cdot b] \cdot P)$ by calculating $2^{-1} \cdot [((a + b)^2 - (a)^2 - (b)^2)] \cdot P$.

B   Proof of Theorem 2

In Fig. 8, we build a simulator $\mathcal{S}$, to simulate $\mathcal{P}_1$ when $\mathcal{P}_2$ is corrupt, and to simulate $\mathcal{P}_2$ when $\mathcal{P}_1$ is corrupt. Below, we sketch a proof to demonstrate why the views in a real and a simulated execution will be indistinguishable for an adversary $\mathcal{A}$.

B.1   Corrupted $\mathcal{P}_1$

Key Generation Phase. The difference between the real execution and the simulated execution is the generation of Q_2. In the case of a real execution, Q_2 is computed as $[x_2] \cdot P$ where x_2 is randomly generated, while in the case of a simulated run, Q_2 is computed by calculating $Q_2 \leftarrow Q - Q_1$. Since Q is randomly generated by the $\mathcal{F}_{2ECDSA}$ functionality of Fig. 1 ($Q \leftarrow [x] \cdot P$ for a randomly generated x), then the distributions from which Q_2 is generated in the real and simulated executions are indistinguishable.

Signing Phase. In the nonce generation, a similar argument can be given to show that the views are indistinguishable. That is in a real execution, R_2 is computed as $[k_2] \cdot P$ where k_2 is randomly generated, while in the case of a simulated run, R_2 is computed by calculating $R_2 \leftarrow [k_1^{-1}] \cdot R$. Since R is randomly generated by $\mathcal{F}_{2ECDSA}$ ($R \leftarrow [k] \cdot P$ for a randomly generated k), then the distributions from which R_2 is generated in the real and simulated executions are indistinguishable.

In the MtA call, both in the real and simulated executions, $\mathcal{P}_1$ is intended to receive a randomly generated a, thus the views are indistinguishable. Afterwards, $\mathcal{P}_1$ sends Z to $\mathcal{P}_2$. In a simulated execution, $\mathcal{P}_2$ aborts if $\mathcal{P}_1$ has provided to the MtA functionality a different input than x_1, or if he sends a different value than

2-party ECDSA Simulator

The simulator S does as follows:

Corrupt $\mathcal{P}_1$ (i.e. simulating $\mathcal{P}_2$):

1. **Key Generation:**
   - S queries $\mathcal{F}_{\text{2ECDSA}}$ to obtain the public key Q.
   - S receives (com-prove, 1, Q_1, x_1) from $\mathcal{A}$ intended to be sent to $\mathcal{F}_{\text{Commit-ZK}}$.
   - S checks whether $Q_1 = [x_1] \cdot P$, if it is the case, S calculates $Q_2 = Q - Q_1$, and sends (proof,2 Q_2) to $\mathcal{A}$, as if $\mathcal{F}_{\text{ZKP}}$ sent it. If Q_1 is different than $[x_1] \cdot P$, S does the same with a randomly generated Q_2.
   - S receives (decom-proof, 1, Q_1, z) from $\mathcal{F}_{\text{Commit-ZK}}$. If $z = 1$, the simulator stores (x_1, Q) for further use, otherwise, S simulates $\mathcal{P}_2$ aborting.
2. **Signing:**
   (a) **Nonce generation:**
   - S queries $\mathcal{F}_{\text{2ECDSA}}$ to obtain the signature (r, s), then calculates $R \leftarrow [s^{-1} \cdot H(m)] \cdot P + [s^{-1} \cdot r] \cdot Q$ as in the verification procedure.
   - S receives (com-prove, $sid||1$, R_1, k_1) from $\mathcal{A}$ intended to be sent to $\mathcal{F}_{\text{Commit-ZK}}$.
   - S checks whether $R_1 = [k_1] \cdot P$, if it is the case, S calculates $R_2 = k_1^{-1} \cdot R$, and sends (proof, $sid||2$, R_2) to $\mathcal{A}$, as if $\mathcal{F}_{\text{ZKP}}$ sent it. If R_1 is different than $[k_1] \cdot P$, S does the same with a randomly generated R_2.
   - S receives (decom-proof, 1, R_1, z) from $\mathcal{F}_{\text{Commit-ZK}}$. If $z = 1$, the simulator stores (k_1, R) for further use, otherwise, S simulates $\mathcal{P}_2$ aborting.
   (b) **MtA:**
   - The simulator here receives x_1 from $\mathcal{A}$ intended to be sent to $\mathcal{F}_{\text{MtA}}$, then forwards a randomly generated number a to $\mathcal{P}_1$. If the x_1 received here is different from the share of the secret key of $\mathcal{P}_1$, the simulator sets an internal flag $\text{cheat}_{sid||1}$ to be 1.
   - The simulator receives Z from $\mathcal{P}_1$. If $\text{cheat}_{sid||1}$ is equal to 1, or Z is different than $[a] \cdot P$, S simulates $\mathcal{P}_2$ aborting.
   (c) **Online signing:**
   - S calculates $s_2 \leftarrow s \cdot k_1 - a \cdot r \mod q$ and sends it to $\mathcal{P}_1$.

Corrupt $\mathcal{P}_2$ (i.e. simulating $\mathcal{P}_1$):

1. **Key Generation:**
   - S queries $\mathcal{F}_{\text{2ECDSA}}$ to obtain the public key Q.
   - S sends (receipt, 1) to $\mathcal{A}$ as if it was sent by $\mathcal{F}_{\text{Commit-ZK}}$.
   - S receives (prove, 2, Q_2 , x_2) from $\mathcal{P}_2$ intended to be sent to $\mathcal{F}_{\text{ZKP}}$.
   - S checks if $Q_2 = [x_2] \cdot P$. If it is not the case, S simulates $\mathcal{P}_1$ aborting.
   - S calculates $Q_1 = Q - Q_2$, and sends (decom-proof, 1, Q_1, 1) as if $\mathcal{F}_{\text{Commit-ZK}}$ sent it. S stores (x_2, Q) for further use.
2. **Signing:**
   (a) **Nonce generation:**
   - S queries $\mathcal{F}_{\text{2ECDSA}}$ to obtain the signature (r, s), then calculates $R \leftarrow [s^{-1} \cdot H(m)] \cdot P + [s^{-1} \cdot r] \cdot Q$ as in the verification procedure.
   - S sends (receipt, $sid||1$, 1) to $\mathcal{A}$ as if it was sent by $\mathcal{F}_{\text{Commit-ZK}}$.
   - S receives (prove, $sid||2$, R_2 , k_2) from $\mathcal{P}_2$ intended to be sent to $\mathcal{F}_{\text{ZKP}}$.
   - S checks if $R_2 = [k_2] \cdot P$. If it is not the case S simulates $\mathcal{P}_1$ aborting.
   - S calculates $R_1 = k_2^{-1} \cdot R$, and sends (decom-proof, 1, R_1, 1) as if $\mathcal{F}_{\text{Commit-ZK}}$ sent it. S stores (k_2, R) for further use.
   (b) **MtA:**
   - The simulator here receives k_2^{-1} from $\mathcal{A}$ intended to be sent to $\mathcal{F}_{\text{MtA}}$, then forwards a randomly generated number b to $\mathcal{P}_2$. If the k_2^{-1} received here is different from the one stored in the nonce generation, the simulator sets an internal flag $\text{cheat}_{sid||2}$ to be 1.
   - S sends $k_2^{-1} \cdot Q_1 - [b] \cdot P$ to $\mathcal{A}$. The k_2 used by the simulator here and in the next step is the one he received in the MtA call.
   (c) **Online signing:**
   - S receives s_2 from $\mathcal{A}$. If $\text{cheat}_{sid||2} = 1$ or s_2 is different from $k_2^{-1} \cdot (H(m) + x_2 \cdot r) + b \cdot r \mod q$, S simulates $\mathcal{P}_1$ aborting. Otherwise, S outputs (r, s) as the signature.

Fig. 8. 2-party ECDSA Simulator

$[a] \cdot P$. This behaviour is equivalent to what happens in a real execution, where P_2 checks whether $k_2 \cdot (Z + [b] \cdot P) = Q_1$. That is, let us denote by ϵ_1, the additive error that P_1 can introduce to x, namely, P_1 sends to MtA the value $x' \leftarrow x + \epsilon$ mod q, and by E, the additive error that P_1 can introduce to Z, namely, P_1 sends P_2 the value $Z' \leftarrow Z + E$. To pass the check of P_2, the following equation needs to be satisfied:

$$
\begin{aligned}
Q_1 &= k_2 \cdot (Z' + [b] \cdot P) \\
&= k_2 \cdot (E + Z + [b] \cdot P) \\
&= k_2 \cdot (E + [a] \cdot P + [b] \cdot P) \\
&= k_2 \cdot (E + (x_1 + \epsilon_1) \cdot k_2^{-1} \cdot P) \\
&= k_2 \cdot (E + x_1 \cdot k_2^{-1} \cdot P + \epsilon_1 \cdot k_2^{-1} \cdot P) \\
&= Q_1 + k_2 \cdot (E + \epsilon_1 \cdot k_2^{-1} \cdot P)
\end{aligned}
$$

which implies that $k_2 \cdot E + \epsilon_1 \cdot P = 0$. If $E = \mathcal{O}$, then $\epsilon_1 = 0$ mod q. Also if $\epsilon_1 = 0$ mod q, then $E = \mathcal{O}$ as $k_2 \neq 0$ mod q. Thus $E = \mathcal{O}$ or $\epsilon_1 = 0$ mod q implies that the adversary has not cheated, as we end up with a case where he does not modify the values he is supposed to send.

Let us look at the case where $E \neq \mathcal{O}$ and $\epsilon_1 \neq 0$ mod q. The equation holds if the adversary chooses ϵ_1 in such a way that $E = \epsilon_1 \cdot [k_2^{-1}] \cdot P = \mathcal{O}$. While $R_2 = [k_2] \cdot P$ is known to the adversary, obtaining $[k_2^{-1}] \cdot P$ from it would mean breaking the 1-Weak Diffie-Hellman problem, which as we have seen is equivalent to the Computational Diffie-Hellman problem which is believed to be hard.

Thus to summarize, the adversary will not be able to make the check pass if he cheats, either in the MtA call or the step afterward.

In the online signing:

If the parties reach this stage, P_1 will be receiving in the simulated execution $s_2 = s \cdot k_1 - a \cdot r$ mod q, which is equal to

$$
\begin{aligned}
s_2 &= s \cdot k_1 - a \cdot r \\
&= k^{-1} \cdot (H(m) + r \cdot x) \cdot k_1 - a \cdot r \\
&= k_2^{-1} \cdot (H(m) + r \cdot x) - a \cdot r) \\
&= k_2^{-1} \cdot (H(m) + r \cdot x_1 + r \cdot x_2) - a \cdot r \\
&= k_2^{-1} \cdot (H(m) + r \cdot x_2) + k_2^{-1} \cdot r \cdot x_1 - a \cdot r \\
&= k_2^{-1} \cdot (H(m) + r \cdot x_2) + r \cdot (a + b) - a \cdot r \\
&= k_2^{-1} \cdot (H(m) + r \cdot x_2) + r \cdot b
\end{aligned}
$$

which is what P_1 receives in a real execution.

B.2   Corrupted $\mathcal{P}_2$

Key Generation Phase. Similarly to the case of a corrupted $\mathcal{P}_1$, the difference between the real execution and the simulated execution is the generation of Q_1. In the case of a real execution, Q_1 is computed as $[x_1] \cdot P$ where x_1 is randomly generated, while in the case of a simulated run, Q_1 is computed by calculating $Q_1 \leftarrow Q - Q_2$. Since Q is randomly generated by the $\mathcal{F}_{2\mathsf{ECDSA}}$ functionality of Fig. 1 ($Q \leftarrow [x] \cdot P$ for a randomly generated x), then the distributions from which Q_1 is generated in the real and simulated executions are indistinguishable.

Signing Phase. Similarly to the case of a corrupted $\mathcal{P}_1$, in the nonce generation, a similar argument can be given to show that the views are indistinguishable. That is in a real execution, R_1 is computed as $[k_1] \cdot P$ where k_1 is randomly generated, while in the case of a simulated run, R_1 is computed by calculating $R_1 \leftarrow [k_2^{-1}] \cdot R$. Since R is randomly generated by $\mathcal{F}_{2\mathsf{ECDSA}}$ ($R \leftarrow [k] \cdot P$ for a randomly generated k), then the distributions from which R_1 is generated in the real and simulated executions are indistinguishable.

In the MtA call, both in a real and simulated executions, $\mathcal{P}_2$ is intended to receive a randomly generated b (In the simulated execution $b = x_1 \cdot k_2^{-1} - a$ mod q for a randomly generated a. Note that the Simulator uses here and in what follows the k_2 he received at the MtA call, and not the one received during the nonce generation), thus the views are indistinguishable. In the step afterwards, in the simulated execution, $\mathcal{P}_2$ receives $[k_2^{-1}] \cdot Q_1 - [b] \cdot P$, which is the same as what he receives in a real execution, as $[k_2^{-1}] \cdot Q_1 - [b] \cdot P = [k_2^{-1} \cdot x_1] \cdot P - [b] \cdot P = [a] \cdot P$. Thus the views are indistinguishable.

In the online signing:

- if $\mathcal{P}_2$ does not cheat at all during the protocol, he will be able to calculate $s_2 = k_2^{-1} \cdot (H(m) + x_2 \cdot r) + b \cdot r$ mod q and send it to $\mathcal{P}_1$. In the real execution $\mathcal{P}_1$ will add it to its share s_1, and the sum will yield a valid signature which will be published by $\mathcal{P}_1$. In the simulated execution, s_2 will pass the check of the simulator and therefore he will publish the signature.

- if $\mathcal{P}_2$ cheated at the MtA call, or does not send the correct s_2, in the real execution, $\mathcal{P}_1$ will not find a valid signature after summing up its share with the one of $\mathcal{P}_2$, thus $\mathcal{P}_1$ will send the abort signal. In the simulated execution, either cheat flag will be equal to 1 at this stage, or s_2 will not pass the check of the simulator. In both cases the simulator will abort. That is, the only case where the views will be distinguishable, is when the adversary cheats on the MtA call, and yet manages to send the correct s_2. Let us denote by ϵ, the additive error that the adversary introduces to his input to MtA, namely he sends $k_2^{-1} + \epsilon$ instead of k_2^{-1}. In this case $a + b = x_1 \cdot (k_2^{-1} + \epsilon)$. In order to pass the check, $\mathcal{P}_2$ needs to send s_2 such that $s \cdot k_1 = s_2 + a \cdot r$ mod q. This implies that:

$$s_2 = s \cdot k_1 - a \cdot r$$
$$= k^{-1} \cdot (H(m) + r \cdot x) \cdot k_1 - a \cdot r$$
$$= k_2^{-1} \cdot (H(m) + r \cdot x_1 + r \cdot x_2) - a \cdot r$$
$$= k_2^{-1} \cdot (H(m) + r \cdot x_2) + k_2^{-1} \cdot r \cdot x_1 - a \cdot r$$
$$= k_2^{-1} \cdot (H(m) + r \cdot x_2) + r \cdot b - x_1 \cdot r \cdot \epsilon$$

As x_1 is unknown to the adversary, he can satisfy this equation only if $\epsilon = 0$, i.e., the case where he does not cheat in the MtA call. Thus the behaviour of the simulator will make the real execution and the simulated one indistinguishable.

References

1. Bao, F., Deng, R.H., Zhu, H.F.: Variations of diffie-hellman problem. In: Qing, S., Gollmann, D., Zhou, J. (eds.) ICICS 2003. LNCS, vol. 2836, pp. 301–312. Springer, Heidelberg (2003). https://doi.org/10.1007/978-3-540-39927-8_28
2. Canetti, R., Gennaro, R., Goldfeder, S., Makriyannis, N., Peled, U.: UC non-interactive, proactive, threshold ECDSA with identifiable aborts. IACR Cryptol. ePrint Arch, p. 60 (2021). https://eprint.iacr.org/2021/060
3. Castagnos, G., Catalano, D., Laguillaumie, F., Savasta, F., Tucker, I.: Two-party ECDSA from hash proof systems and efficient instantiations. In: Boldyreva, A., Micciancio, D. (eds.) Advances in Cryptology - CRYPTO 2019, pp. 191–221. Springer International Publishing, Cham (2019). https://doi.org/10.1007/978-3-030-26954-8_7
4. Castagnos, G., Laguillaumie, F.: Linearly homomorphic encryption from DDH. In: Nyberg, K. (ed.) CT-RSA 2015. LNCS, vol. 9048, pp. 487–505. Springer, Cham (2015). https://doi.org/10.1007/978-3-319-16715-2_26
5. Dalskov, A., Orlandi, C., Keller, M., Shrishak, K., Shulman, H.: Securing DNSSEC keys via threshold ECDSA from Generic MPC. In: Chen, L., Li, N., Liang, K., Schneider, S. (eds.) ESORICS 2020. LNCS, vol. 12309, pp. 654–673. Springer, Cham (2020). https://doi.org/10.1007/978-3-030-59013-0_32
6. Damgård, I., Jakobsen, T.P., Nielsen, J.B., Pagter, J.I., Østergaard, M.B.: Fast threshold ECDSA with honest majority. In: Galdi, C., Kolesnikov, V. (eds.) SCN 2020. LNCS, vol. 12238, pp. 382–400. Springer, Cham (2020). https://doi.org/10.1007/978-3-030-57990-6_19
7. Desmedt, Y.: Society and group oriented cryptography: a new concept. In: Pomerance, C. (ed.) CRYPTO 1987. LNCS, vol. 293, pp. 120–127. Springer, Heidelberg (1988). https://doi.org/10.1007/3-540-48184-2_8
8. Doerner, J., Kondi, Y., Lee, E., Shelat, A.: Secure two-party threshold ECDSA from ECDSA assumptions. In: 2018 IEEE Symposium on Security and Privacy (SP), pp. 980–997. IEEE (2018)
9. Doerner, J., Kondi, Y., Lee, E., Shelat, A.: Threshold ECDSA from ECDSA assumptions: The multiparty case. In: 2019 IEEE Symposium on Security and Privacy (SP), pp. 1051–1066 (2019)

10. ElGamal, T.: A public key cryptosystem and a signature scheme based on discrete logarithms. IEEE Trans. Inf. Theory **31**(4), 469–472 (1985)
11. Fiat, A., Shamir, A.: How to prove yourself: practical solutions to identification and signature problems. In: Odlyzko, A.M. (ed.) CRYPTO 1986. LNCS, vol. 263, pp. 186–194. Springer, Heidelberg (1987). https://doi.org/10.1007/3-540-47721-7_12
12. Gennaro, R., Goldfeder, S.: Fast multiparty threshold ECDSA with fast trustless setup. In: Proceedings of the 2018 ACM SIGSAC Conference on Computer and Communications Security, pp. 1179–1194 (2018)
13. Kondi, Y., Magri, B., Orlandi, C., Shlomovits, O.: Refresh when you wake up: proactive threshold wallets with offline devices. In: 42nd IEEE Symposium on Security and Privacy, SP 2021, San Francisco, CA, USA, 24–27 May 2021, pp. 608–625. IEEE (2021). https://doi.org/10.1109/SP40001.2021.00067, https://doi.org/10.1109/SP40001.2021.00067
14. Lindell, Y.: Fast secure two-party ECDSA signing. In: Katz, J., Shacham, H. (eds.) CRYPTO 2017. LNCS, vol. 10402, pp. 613–644. Springer, Cham (2017). https://doi.org/10.1007/978-3-319-63715-0_21
15. Lindell, Y.: Secure multiparty computation. Commun. ACM **64**(1), 86–96 (2020)
16. Lindell, Y., Nof, A.: Fast secure multiparty ECDSA with practical distributed key generation and applications to cryptocurrency custody. In: Proceedings of the 2018 ACM SIGSAC Conference on Computer and Communications Security, pp. 1837–1854 (2018)
17. MacKenzie, P., Reiter, M.K.: Two-party generation of DSA signatures. In: Kilian, J. (ed.) CRYPTO 2001. LNCS, vol. 2139, pp. 137–154. Springer, Heidelberg (2001). https://doi.org/10.1007/3-540-44647-8_8
18. Makriyannis, N., Peled, U.: A note on the security of GG18 (2021)
19. Mitsunari, S., Sakai, R., Kasahara, M.: A new traitor tracing. IEICE Trans. Fundam. Electron. Commun. Comput. Sci. **85**(2), 481–484 (2002)
20. Paillier, P.: Public-key cryptosystems based on composite degree residuosity classes. In: Stern, J. (ed.) EUROCRYPT 1999. LNCS, vol. 1592, pp. 223–238. Springer, Heidelberg (1999). https://doi.org/10.1007/3-540-48910-X_16
21. Rabin, M.O.: How to exchange secrets with oblivious transfer. Technical Report TR-81, Aiken Computation Lab (1981). https://www.iacr.org/museum/rabin-obt/obtrans-eprint187.pdf
22. Schnorr, C.: Efficient signature generation by smart cards. In: Advances in Cryptology – CRYPTO 1987, pp. 161–174 (1991)
23. Smart, N.P., Talibi Alaoui, Y.: Distributing any elliptic curve based protocol. In: Albrecht, M. (ed.) IMACC 2019. LNCS, vol. 11929, pp. 342–366. Springer, Cham (2019). https://doi.org/10.1007/978-3-030-35199-1_17
24. Wigderson, A., Goldreich, O., Micali, S.: How to play any mental game. In: Proceedings the 19th Annual ACM Symposium on the Theory of Computing, pp. 218–229 (1987)
25. Xue, H., Au, M.H., Xie, X., Yuen, T.H., Cui, H.: Efficient online-friendly two-party ECDSA signature. In: Proceedings of the 2021 ACM SIGSAC Conference on Computer and Communications Security, pp. 558–573 (2021)
26. Yao, A.C.: Protocols for secure computations. In: 23rd Annual Symposium on Foundations of Computer Science (sfcs 1982), pp. 160–164. IEEE (1982)

Selective Delegation of Attributes in Mercurial Signature Credentials

Colin Putman$^{(\boxtimes)}$ and Keith M. Martin

Royal Holloway, University of London, Egham, Surrey TW200EX, UK
{Colin.Putman.2017,Keith.Martin}@rhul.ac.uk

Abstract. Anonymous credential schemes enable service providers to verify information that a credential holder willingly discloses, without needing any further personal data to corroborate that information, and without allowing the user to be tracked from one interaction to the next. Mercurial signatures are a novel class of anonymous credentials which show good promise as a simple and efficient construction without heavy reliance on zero-knowledge proofs. However, they still require significant development in order to achieve the functionality that most existing anonymous credential schemes provide. Encoding multiple attributes of the credential holder in such a way that they can be disclosed selectively with each use of the credential is often seen as a vital feature of anonymous credentials, and is one that mercurial signatures have not yet implemented. In this paper, we show a simple way to encode attributes in a mercurial signature credential and to regulate which attributes a credential holder can issue when delegating their credential to another user. We also extend the security model associated with mercurial signatures to account for the inclusion of attributes, and prove the security of our extension with respect to the original mercurial signature construction.

Keywords: Privacy · Anonymous credentials · Delegatable credentials · Mercurial signatures · Selective disclosure

1 Introduction

Privacy in the digital world is an increasingly serious concern, with many efforts being made to minimise the use, storage, and disclosure of personal information. However, this goal is difficult to reconcile with the interests of service providers who often have a need to know that their clients are engaging in good faith and are permitted to use their services. These reasonable checks usually involve some form of identification, which makes it easy for providers to build profiles on their users.

One powerful solution to these conflicting interests is the use of anonymous credentials, which are designed to allow service providers to verify information that the credential holder willingly discloses, without needing any further personal data to corroborate that information, and without allowing the user to be

© The Author(s), under exclusive license to Springer Nature Switzerland AG 2024
E. A. Quaglia (Ed.): IMACC 2023, LNCS 14421, pp. 181–196, 2024.
https://doi.org/10.1007/978-3-031-47818-5_10

tracked from one interaction to the next. Anonymous credentials have been fully realised since 2001 [2], but their adoption has been extremely slow, due in large part to the cumbersome nature of the zero-knowledge proofs they rely on.

A recently developed type of anonymous credential, known as mercurial signatures [6], shows promise in overcoming this hurdle, as its malleable nature replaces much of the need for traditional zero-knowledge proofs. Mercurial signatures also allow for credential holders to delegate their credentials anonymously to other users, forming a chain of trust and enabling more private and versatile use of their systems.

However, the novelty of mercurial signatures means that they still lack much of the functionality that more established types of anonymous credential offer. Most notably, they do not yet offer the ability to encode detailed information about the credential holder's attributes and disclose only a subset of that information, a feature known as selective disclosure which is often viewed as necessary for an anonymous credential system.

Our contribution. This paper proposes an elegant extension to mercurial signatures which allows the selective disclosure of attributes, in a way which also remains compatible with the delegation of credentials. We also extend the security game associated with the original mercurial signatures to take account of the additional requirements that accompany credential attributes, and we prove the security of our extension with respect to the original CL19 mercurial signature construction. Although we use the CL19 construction for simplicity in our demonstration, the extension is also compatible with other credentials based on FHS-type structure-preserving signatures and set commitments, including the CL21, CLP22, and MSBM23 constructions [4,7,10].

Section 2 introduces the basic concepts that underpin this work. Section 3 gives an overview of the previous development of mercurial signatures. In Sect. 4, we detail our extension and give an overview of the associated proofs. We conclude in Sect. 5 with a brief look at the other areas in which this field can be progressed.

2   Preliminaries

A function $\epsilon : \mathbb{N} \to \mathbb{R}^+$ is called **negligible** if for all $c > 0$ there is a k_0 such that $\epsilon(k) < 1/k^c$ for all $k > k_0$. We use $a \xleftarrow{R} S$ to denote that a is chosen uniformly at random from a set S. Given a probabilistic algorithm $\mathtt{A}(a_1, ..., a_n)$, we use $\mathtt{A}(a_1, ..., a_n; r)$ to make the randomness r used by the algorithm explicit, and $[\mathtt{A}(a_1, ..., a_n)]$ to denote the set of points with positive probability of being output by A. We write groups multiplicatively throughout this paper, and given a group $\mathbb{G}$ we use $\mathbb{G}^*$ to denote $\mathbb{G} \backslash \{1_{\mathbb{G}}\}$.

2.1   Bilinear Maps

Given three cyclic groups $\mathbb{G}_1$, $\mathbb{G}_2$, and $\mathbb{G}_T$, all of prime order p, a **bilinear map** or **pairing** is an efficiently computable function $e : \mathbb{G}_1 \times \mathbb{G}_2 \to \mathbb{G}_T$ such that, given generators P and $\hat{P}$ of $\mathbb{G}_1$ and $\mathbb{G}_2$ respectively, $e(P^a, \hat{P}^b) = e(P, \hat{P})^{ab}$. The pairing is called **non-degenerate** if $e(P, \hat{P}) \neq 1_{\mathbb{G}_T}$, in which case $e(P, \hat{P})$ generates $\mathbb{G}_T$.

All of the bilinear maps used in this paper will be non-degenerate and based on cyclic groups of the same prime order. We define a **bilinear-group generator** to be a polynomial-time algorithm that takes as input a security parameter 1^κ and outputs a tuple $(p, \mathbb{G}_1, \mathbb{G}_2, \mathbb{G}_T, e, P, \hat{P})$ such that the groups $\mathbb{G}_1 = \langle P \rangle$, $\mathbb{G}_2 = \langle \hat{P} \rangle$, and $\mathbb{G}_T$ are cyclic groups of prime order p with $\lceil \log_2 p \rceil = \kappa$, and $e : \mathbb{G}_1 \times \mathbb{G}_2 \rightarrow \mathbb{G}_T$ is a non-degenerate bilinear map.

2.2 Zero-Knowledge Proofs of Knowledge

Let $L_\mathcal{R} = \{x | \exists w : (x, w) \in \mathcal{R}\} \subseteq \{0, 1\}^*$ be a formal language with a binary, polynomial-time witness relation $\mathcal{R} \subseteq \{0, 1\}^* \times \{0, 1\}^*$, so that the membership of $x \in L_\mathcal{R}$ can be decided in polynomial time when given a witness w of length polynomial in $|x|$ certifying $(x, w) \in \mathcal{R}$. Consider an interactive protocol $(\mathcal{P}, \mathcal{V})$ between a potentially unbounded prover $\mathcal{P}$ and a PPT verifier $\mathcal{V}$ with outcome $(\cdot, b) \leftarrow (\mathcal{P}(\cdot, \cdot), \mathcal{V}(\cdot))$ where $b = 0$ indicates that $\mathcal{V}$ rejects and $b = 1$ indicates that $\mathcal{V}$ accepts the conversation with $\mathcal{P}$. Such a protocol is a **zero-knowledge proof of knowledge (ZKPoK)** if it satisfies the following three properties:

- **Completeness:** We call such a protocol $(\mathcal{P}, \mathcal{V})$ complete if, for all $x \in L_\mathcal{R}$ and w such that $(x, w) \in \mathcal{R}$ we have that $(\cdot, 1) \leftarrow (\mathcal{P}(x, w), \mathcal{V}(x))$ with probability 1.
- **Zero knowledge:** We say that the protocol $(\mathcal{P}, \mathcal{V})$ is zero-knowledge if for all PPT algorithms $\mathcal{V}^*$ there exists a PPT simulator $\mathcal{S}$ such that:

$$\{\mathcal{S}^{\mathcal{V}^*}(x)\}_{x \in L_\mathcal{R}} \approx \{\langle \mathcal{P}(x, w), \mathcal{V}^*(x) \rangle\}_{(x,w) \in \mathcal{R}}$$

  where $\langle \mathcal{P}(\cdot, \cdot), \mathcal{V}^*(\cdot) \rangle$ denotes the transcript of the interaction between $\mathcal{P}$ and $\mathcal{V}$, and "$\approx$" denotes perfect indistinguishability.
- **Knowledge soundness:** We say that $(\mathcal{P}, \mathcal{V})$ is a proof of knowledge (PoK) relative to an NP relation $\mathcal{R}$ if, for any (possibly unbounded) malicious prover $\mathcal{P}^*$ such that $(\cdot, 1) \leftarrow (\mathcal{P}^*(x), \mathcal{V}(x))$ with non-negligible probability, there exists a PPT knowledge extractor $\mathcal{K}$ with rewinding black-box access to $\mathcal{P}^*$ such that $\mathcal{K}^{\mathcal{P}^*}(x)$ returns a value w satisfying $(x, w) \in \mathcal{R}$.

Zero-knowledge proofs of knowledge are used by provers to convince verifiers that they know a secret value w satisfying a specific statement x. For this work we are particularly interested in protocols to prove knowledge of a discrete logarithm, which can be efficiently instantiated using Σ-protocols as in Cramer et al. [5]. When using zero-knowledge proofs of knowledge, we denote the composite of proofs of witnesses $w_1, \ldots, w_n$ satisfying statements $x_1, \ldots, x_n$ by $\mathrm{PoK}\{(w_1, \ldots, w_n) \mid x_1 \wedge \cdots \wedge x_n\}$.

2.3   Anonymous Credentials

Anonymous credentials are a privacy-preserving system which allows a prover to obtain, from a trusted issuer, a credential on one or more **attributes** representing access rights or pieces of identifying information, which can then be used to prove their possession of these attributes to a verifier in zero knowledge. An anonymous credential system consists of the following PPT algorithms:

IssuerKeyGen($1^\kappa, 1^t$): A probabilistic algorithm which takes as input a security parameter κ and an upper bound t on the size of attribute sets, and outputs a key pair (osk, opk) for an issuer.

ProverKeyGen(opk): A probabilistic algorithm which takes as input an issuer's public key opk and outputs a key pair (usk, upk) for a prover.

(Obtain(usk, opk, A), Issue(upk, osk, A)): A pair of probabilistic algorithms run by a prover and an issuer, respectively, which interact during execution. Obtain takes as input the prover's secret key usk, the issuer's public key opk, and a non-empty attribute set A of size $|A| \leq t$, and Issue takes as input the prover's public key upk, the issuer's secret key osk, and a non-empty attribute set A of size $|A| \leq t$. At the end of the protocol, Obtain outputs a credential cred for the user on the attribute set A, or $\perp$ if the execution failed.

(Show(opk, A, D, cred), Verify(opk, D)): A pair of algorithms run by a prover and a verifier, respectively, which interact during execution. Show is a probabilistic algorithm which takes as input an issuer's public key opk, an attribute set A of size $|A| \leq t$, a non-empty set $D \subseteq A$, and a credential cred. Verify is a deterministic algorithm which takes as input an issuer's public key opk and a set D. At the end of the protocol, Verify outputs either 1 or 0, indicating whether it accepts the credential showing or not.

Informally, the security properties that an anonymous credential must satisfy are as follows:

- **Correctness:** A showing of a credential cred with respect to a non-empty set of attributes D always verifies if cred was issued honestly for some attribute set A such that $D \subseteq A$.
- **Unforgeability:** A prover cannot perform a valid showing of attributes for which they do not possess a credential, and no coalition of provers can combine their credentials to perform a valid showing of attributes for which no single prover in the coalition has a credential. This must hold even after seeing arbitrary showings of valid credentials by honest users.
- **Anonymity:** During a showing, no verifier, issuer, or coalition of multiple verifiers and/or issuers can learn anything about the prover except that they possess a valid credential on an attribute set that includes D.

We say that an anonymous credential system offers **selective disclosure** if it supports attribute sets of size greater than 1 (and therefore allows D to be a proper subset of A). Such credentials are often called **attribute-based credentials**.

We say that a credential is **multi-show** if it can be used in multiple runs of the Show algorithm and the verifier(s) to which it has been shown cannot distinguish them from protocol runs using different credentials. We can identify two distinct families of multi-show credentials: **zero-knowledge credentials**, which are not revealed to the verifier during the Show algorithm, instead using zero-knowledge proofs to convince the verifier of the valid credential's existence, and **self-blindable credentials**, which are partially or fully shown to the verifier during the Show algorithm, and subsequently altered such that they remain valid but are unrecognisable in later showings.

2.4   Delegatable Credentials

Delegatable credentials, first proposed in 2006 by Chase and Lysyanskaya [3], extend the anonymous credential model by allowing the holder of a credential to (anonymously) issue new credentials to other users. This process is called delegation, and allows credentials to form a chain of trust; each credential identifies the root authority which issued the original credential, and how many steps removed from that original credential it is, but does not uniquely identify the other delegators along the chain.

Crites and Lysyanskaya [6] provide a model for delegatable credentials, which differs from the basic anonymous credential model in a few key ways. First, they add the following PPT algorithm:

NymGen(sk, $L(\text{pk}_0)$): A probabilistic algorithm that takes as input a participant's secret key sk and a **delegation level** (i.e. number of steps removed from the root issuer) $L(\text{pk}_0)$ under the root issuer whose public key is pk_0, and generates a pseudonym and auxiliary information for that participant at that level.

The pseudonym and auxiliary information function as a fresh public key and secret key, respectively, that other participants cannot link to the underlying long-term key pair. The Issue/Obtain and Prove/Verify algorithms then become:

(Obtain($L_I(\text{pk}_0)$, pk_0, sk_R, nym_R, aux_R, nym_I), Issue($L_I(\text{pk}_0)$, pk_0, sk_I, nym_I, aux_I, cred_I, nym_R)): Obtain takes as input the issuer's delegation level, the root authority's public key, the secret key and a pseudonym and auxiliary information belonging to the recipient, and the issuer's pseudonym (not the issuer's long-term public key), and Issue takes as input the issuer's delegation level, the root authority's public key, the secret key, pseudonym, auxiliary information, and credential belonging to the issuer, and the recipient's pseudonym. The protocol outputs a new credential for the recipient, which has a (potentially equal) subset of the attributes in cred_I and delegation level $L_I(\text{pk}_0) + 1$. By convention, a root authority runs Issue with $L_I(\text{pk}_0) = 0$, $\text{nym}_I = \text{pk}_0$, and $\text{aux}_I = \text{cred}_I = \perp$.

(Prove($L_P(\text{pk}_0)$, pk_0, sk_P, nym_P, aux_P, cred_P), Verify(pp, $L_P(\text{pk}_0)$, pk_0, nym_P)): Prove takes as input the prover's delegation level, the root authority's public key, the prover's secret key, the pseudonym by which the verifier knows the prover (which should differ from the pseudonym to which the credential was issued) and its auxiliary information, and the prover's credential. Verify takes as input the system parameters pp (which were assumed in the basic model to be part of the issuer's public key), the prover's delegation level, the root authority's public key, and the prover's pseudonym. The output is unchanged from the basic anonymous credential model.

Delegatable credentials also extend the basic security goals of anonymous credentials. In particular, the Correctness and Unforgeability properties are extended such that every credential along a chain must be generated correctly and honestly in order for the credential shown at the end to be considered correct and honest. The Anonymity property is also extended to apply to delegators; this can be to protect the delegators' privacy, but it is also necessary for providing anonymity to the prover, since two credentials with the same root authority but different delegators would otherwise become distinguishable, which would reduce the prover's anonymity set.

Though there is no clear consensus on how delegatable credentials should use attributes, Blömer and Bobolz [1] propose the requirement that a delegated credential must encode a subset of the attributes in the delegator's credential, conceptually enforcing that not only the credential but the attributes themselves are delegated from one level to the next. We will refer to this as **selective delegation** (of attributes). This model is ideal for scenarios in which the attributes of delegated credentials are expected to represent strictly equal or lesser privileges than those of the credentials higher up the chain. This includes the case in which the issuing process itself is delegated, as the selective delegation model allows the root issuer to provide each sub-issuer with a credential containing all of the attributes that sub-issuer is empowered to sign.

3   Previous Work

3.1   SPS-EQ Credentials

The precursor to mercurial signatures, SPS-EQ credentials are a form of self-blindable, attribute-based credentials first proposed by Hanser and Slamanig in 2014 [9] and refined by Fuchsbauer et al. in 2019 [8]. They are based on a novel primitive called structure-preserving signatures on equivalence classes, usually abbreviated as SPS-EQ.

A structure-preserving signature scheme is one in which the message and the signature are both made up of group elements in the same bilinear pairing, as is the public key. SPS-EQ schemes further define an equivalence relation on the message and signature spaces, and allow both messages and signatures to be randomised within the resulting equivalence classes.

In addition to the usual Sign and Verify functions, SPS-EQ schemes include a function $\mathsf{ChgRep}_{\mathcal{R}}(M, \sigma, \mu, \mathsf{pk})$, parametrised by equivalence relation $\mathcal{R}$, which takes as input a message M, a signature σ, a randomising factor μ, and a public key pk, and outputs a message M' in the same equivalence class as M and a signature σ' such that:

$$\mathsf{Verify}(M', \sigma', \mathsf{pk}) = \mathsf{Verify}(M, \sigma, \mathsf{pk}).$$

The security requirements of SPS-EQ schemes include a class-hiding property, which states that an adversary given a pair of messages should not be able to tell whether they are in the same equivalence class, and an origin-hiding property, which states that the output of the $\mathsf{ChgRep}_{\mathcal{R}}$ function should be indistinguishable from a fresh message-signature pair.

Hanser and Slamanig's construction defines its message space by generating a bilinear pairing $e : \mathbb{G}_1 \times \mathbb{G}_2 \to \mathbb{G}_T$ with DDH-hard groups, and creating a vector space of elements in $(\mathbb{G}_1^*)^l$ with l greater than 1. The equivalence relation is then defined such that two messages M and M' are equivalent if and only if M' is a scalar power of M.

The secret key is a vector $(x_i)_{i \in l}$ in $(\mathbb{Z}_p^*)^l$ and the public key is the corresponding vector $(\hat{X}_i)_{i \in l} = (\hat{P}^{x_i})_{i \in l}$ where $\hat{P}$ is a generator of $\mathbb{G}_2$ included in the public parameters; the public key is therefore a vector in $(\mathbb{G}_2^*)^l$. A signature σ on a message $M \in (\mathbb{G}_1^*)^l$ is a tuple $(Z, Y, \hat{Y})$ with $Z, Y \in \mathbb{G}_1$ and $\hat{Y} \in \mathbb{G}_2$ such that:

$$Z = \prod_{i \in l} M_i^{x_i y}, \ Y = P^{\frac{1}{y}}, \ \hat{Y} = \hat{P}^{\frac{1}{y}},$$

where P and $\hat{P}$ are generators of $\mathbb{G}_1$ and $\mathbb{G}_2$, respectively, included in the public parameters, and y is chosen randomly from $\mathbb{Z}_p^*$ at the time of signing.

SPS-EQ schemes were specifically designed for use in anonymous credentials, using their randomisation as the credential blinding mechanism, with SPS-EQ's class-hiding and origin-hiding properties providing unlinkability for the resulting credentials. In order to encode attributes, they had to be combined with a commitment scheme that could be randomised in a manner consistent with the SPS-EQ construction.

3.2 Randomisable Set Commitments

In order to support attributes with selective disclosure, Hanser and Slamanig also constructed a set commitment scheme which can opened securely to a chosen subset of the committed set, and can be randomised in a similar manner to the signature scheme, allowing a set commitment to the desired attribute set A to be used as the message in the signature scheme.

The scheme works by committing to a polynomial $f_S(X)$ whose roots are the members of the committed set S; that is, $f_S(X) = \prod_{s \in S} (X - s)$. S must be a subset of $\mathbb{Z}_p$, but could encode other types of data using a hash function.

The commitment scheme is instantiated by a manager who selects the security parameter 1^κ and a maximum set cardinality 1^t and generates a bilinear pairing $e : \mathbb{G}_1 \times \mathbb{G}_2 \to \mathbb{G}_T$ which is published along with generators P and $\hat{P}$ for $\mathbb{G}_1$ and $\mathbb{G}_2$ respectively. The manager then chooses a random trapdoor $a \in \mathbb{Z}_p$ and publishes $(P^{a^i}, \hat{P}^{a^i})_{i \in [t]}$. This ensures that the trapdoor is not needed to compute $P^{f_S(a)} = \prod_{i=0}^{|S|} P^{f_i a^i}$, which is needed to generate and verify commitments, or $\hat{P}^{f_S(a)}$, which is needed to verify subsets.

In order to commit to a set, the prover chooses a random $\rho \in \mathbb{Z}_p^*$ and computes the commitment $C = P^{\rho f_S(a)}$ which is stored along with the opening information

$O = (0, \rho)$. To open this commitment to the full set S, the prover sends S, C, and O to the verifier, who is able to compute C from S and O and confirm the match.

If the prover wishes to open a subset T of the committed set S, they first generate a witness $W = P^{\rho f_{S \setminus T}(a)}$. This can be verified without revealing the full set S by using the bilinear map to check whether $e(W, \hat{P}^{f_T(a)}) = e(C, \hat{P})$.

If a commitment C is randomised using a blinding factor μ after a witness W has been generated as above, applying the same blinding factor to W produces a new witness W' which is consistent with the new commitment. This allows the set commitments to be used as messages for SPS-EQ signatures, such that it is possible to encode attributes in an SPS-EQ credential and selectively disclose them to a verifier even after the credential has been randomised.

Subsequent work by Connolly et al. [4] extended this commitment scheme with a function for opening on disjoint sets, allowing the commitment's owner to prove that certain values are not included in the committed set. They also add an optional proof of exponentiation (PoE) technique to shift computation work from the verifier to the prover during openings. These functions require no changes to the structure of the commitment, and hence incur no additional cost, while significantly expanding the expressiveness of the scheme.

3.3 Mercurial Signatures

Mercurial signatures are an extension to SPS-EQ proposed by Crites and Lysyanskaya [6] with the intention of supporting delegatable credentials. To do this, they add a set of functions to allow a key pair (pk, sk) to be randomised such that the resulting (pk', sk') is still a valid key pair, and a signature under pk to be randomised to produce a valid signature on the same message under pk'. Randomising the public key allows delegators to be anonymised, and prevents the credential chain of a delegated credential from becoming identifiable.

Given parameterised equivalence relations $\mathcal{R}_M$, $\mathcal{R}_{pk}$, and $\mathcal{R}_{sk}$, Crites and Lysyanskaya define mercurial signatures generally as consisting of the following PPT algorithms:

PPGen(1^k) $\rightarrow PP$: A probabilistic algorithm which takes as input the security parameter 1^k and outputs the public parameters PP, including parameters for $\mathcal{R}_M$, $\mathcal{R}_{pk}$, and $\mathcal{R}_{sk}$, and parameters for algorithms sample$_\rho$ and sample$_\mu$, which are used to generate converters for keys and for messages, respectively.

KeyGen(PP, l) $\rightarrow$ (pk, sk): A probabilistic algorithm which takes as input the public parameters PP and a length parameter l and outputs a key pair (pk, sk). Following the authors' example, we also write (pk, sk) $\in$ KeyGen(PP, l) to denote that there exists a set of random choices KeyGen could make on input (PP, l) that would result in (pk, sk) as the output. It is also noted that the message space $\mathcal{M}$ is well-defined from PP and l.

Sign(sk, M) $\rightarrow \sigma$: A probabilistic algorithm which takes as input a signing key sk and a message $M \in \mathcal{M}$ and outputs a signature σ.

Verify(pk, M, σ): $\rightarrow 0/1$: A deterministic algorithm which takes as input a public key pk, a message $M \in \mathcal{M}$, and a purported signature σ, and outputs 0 or 1.

ConvertSK(sk,ρ) $\rightarrow$ s̄k: A deterministic algorithm which takes as input a signing key sk and a key converter $\rho \in \mathsf{sample}_\rho$ and outputs a new signing key s̄k $\in [\mathsf{sk}]_{\mathcal{R}_{\mathsf{sk}}}$.

ConvertPK(pk,ρ) $\rightarrow$ p̄k: A deterministic algorithm which takes as input a public key pk and a key converter $\rho \in \mathsf{sample}_\rho$ and outputs a new public key p̄k $\in [\mathsf{pk}]_{\mathcal{R}_{\mathsf{pk}}}$.

ConvertSig(pk,M, σ, ρ) $\rightarrow$ $\bar{\sigma}$: A probabilistic algorithm which takes as input a public key pk, a message $M \in \mathcal{M}$, a signature σ, and a key converter $\rho \in \mathsf{sample}_\rho$, and outputs a new signature $\bar{\sigma}$.

ChangeRep(pk, M, σ, μ) $\rightarrow$ (M', σ'): A probabilistic algorithm which takes as input a public key pk, a messages $M \in \mathcal{M}$, a signature σ, and a message converter $\mu \in \mathsf{sample}_\mu$, computes a new message $M' \in [M]_{\mathcal{R}_M}$ and a new signature σ', and outputs (M', σ').

In order to define a construction for mercurial signatures, Crites and Lysyanskaya made a simple extension from Hanser and Slamanig's structure-preserving signature construction. Recalling that the secret key is a vector $(x_i)_{i \in l}$ in $(\mathbb{Z}_p^*)^l$ and the public key is the corresponding vector $(\hat{X}_i)_{i \in l} = (\hat{P}^{x_i})_{i \in l}$ in $(\mathbb{G}_2^*)^l$, Crites and Lysyanskaya's construction randomises the keys by taking an input $\rho \in \mathbb{Z}_p^*$ and setting sk$' = (\rho x_i)_{i \in l}$ and pk$' = (\hat{X}_i^\rho)_{i \in l}$. A signature $\sigma = (Z, Y, \hat{Y})$ can then be randomised by choosing a random $\psi \in \mathbb{Z}_p^*$ and setting $\sigma' = (Z^{\psi \rho}, Y^{\frac{1}{\psi}}, \hat{Y}^{\frac{1}{\psi}})$. This is identical to the signature randomisation in SPS-EQ, and ensures that if σ is a valid signature on a message M under pk, σ' is a valid signature on M under pk$'$.

One major limitation of the CL19 mercurial signature construction (and, indeed, of the SPS-EQ construction before it) is that the length of the signer's key serves as an upper bound on the length of the message to be signed. This is especially problematic in the context of delegatable credentials, where a typical message consists of the prover's public key plus a representation of at least one attribute. If the issuer has a key of length l and signs a credential with k group elements representing its attributes, the prover's key length can only be at most $l - k$. Furthermore, if that prover then wishes to delegate the credential with all of its attributes, the recipient's key length can only be up to $l - 2k$, and so on.

In a subsequent paper, Crites and Lysyanskaya proposed a method to overcome this problem [7]. The message is assumed to be of the form $(P, M_1, ..., M_n)$, where P is a generator of $\mathbb{G}_1$ and $M_i = P^{m_i}$ for all $1 \leq i \leq n$, with the values m_i being encoded information such as private key elements and attributes. The approach taken by Crites and Lysyanskaya is to transform each element of the message into its own fixed-length message which can be signed separately using the original scheme.

Later work by Connolly et al. [4] used similar techniques to obtain issuer-hiding SPS-EQ credentials which could easily be converted to mercurial signatures by adding a protocol for delegation. They also made use of the FHS randomisable set commitment scheme in Sect. 3.2 to encode attributes with selective disclosure; however, their work does not achieve selective delegation, as we will see in the next section.

The only relative of mercurial signatures to directly combine delegation with selective disclosure of attributes is the recent work by Mir et al. [10], which replaces the SPS-EQ primitive with SPS-EQ on Updatable Commitments in order to achieve an efficient construction with several desirable properties, including the ability to restrict the number of times a credential can be delegated and to prevent a delegatee from showing attributes from a higher delegation level. They also introduce a method to batch subset openings of multiple commitments for efficient verification, called cross-set commitment aggregation. However, their approach also does not consider selective delegation of attributes; in contrast to Blömer and Bobolz's model, there is no enforced relationship between the attributes on different delegation levels. A relationship could still be shown to a verifier, but only if every delegator provides the delegatee with the opening of their commitment so that the delegatee can show the relevant attributes on higher levels. Even if the delegator uses a subset witness to keep some attributes hidden, this would sacrifice the information-theoretic privacy of the delegation protocol.

4   Providing Selective Disclosure

The CL19 credential construction does not include a way to encode any information other than the holder's public key, meaning it cannot be used to prove anything other than that the holder is the genuine owner of the credential. While the mere fact of possessing a credential can be taken to certify a single, binary attribute, most existing credential schemes are built to be able to certify a multitude of attributes, along with providing a way to disclose only those that are relevant during a particular transaction.

One approach to encoding these attributes is to use the same set commitment scheme as SPS-EQ signatures. Since mercurial signatures directly extend SPS-EQ and the credential schemes are derived in a similar way, when a mercurial signature is first issued the set commitment can work identically to the commitments in SPS-EQ credentials. This also has the benefit of allowing a credential's size to be constant, rather than linear in the number of attributes.

The CLP22 scheme [4] takes this approach, but their work does not consider credential delegation. The MSBM23 scheme [10] is similar but does allow credential delegation; however, under their model the attributes in a delegated credential bear no relation to the delegator's attributes. In this paper, we are concerned with the more restrictive model of selective delegation introduced by Blömer and Bobolz [1], which adds a further challenge to overcome.

4.1 Selective Delegation

The difficulty here arises because when one user, Alice, delegates a credential to another user, Bob, Bob's attribute commitment $\hat{C}_B$ has not been signed by the root issuer, and Alice's identity is intentionally hidden from any party Bob discloses the credential to, meaning that her signature cannot be trusted in the same way.

In order to ensure that no user has issued a credential more permissive than their own, the verifier of Bob's credential must have some way of confirming that Alice was authorised to issue the attributes in Bob's attribute set B. This means that the verifier must be able to check whether or not B is a subset of Alice's attribute set A. In order to achieve this, we will design a special subset witness that can be included on the delegation chain to connect Alice and Bob's credentials, leading to a chain in which each credential except for the first has an associated witness value linking it to the one before. The difficulty in this approach lies in designing a witness value that can be computed by Alice and Bob at the time of delegation and does not leak any information about either attribute set.

In the case that A = B, the verifier can already confirm the relation with the pairing equation $e(X_1^{\rho_1 \rho_2}, \hat{C}_B^{\rho_3}) = e(C_A^{\rho_1 \rho_2}, \hat{Y}_1^{\rho_3})$ which can be verified using only the elements $X_1^{\rho_1 \rho_2}, C_A^{\rho_1 \rho_2}, \hat{Y}_1^{\rho_3}, \hat{C}_B^{\rho_3}$ within the blinded cred_B. Here X_1 is the first element of the public key in Alice's credential, $\hat{Y}_1$ is the first element of the public key in Bob's credential, C_A and $\hat{C}_B$ are Alice and Bob's attribute commitments, respectively, as formulated in the FHS19 credential scheme [8], and ρ_1, ρ_2, and ρ_3 are the blinding factors used by Alice and Bob to randomise their credentials, with Alice applying ρ_1 to her credential, and Bob applying ρ_2 to Alice's credential and ρ_3 to his own credential. Note that the assignment of $\mathbb{G}_1$ and $\mathbb{G}_2$ in this example is arbitrary and can be reversed as needed depending on the delegation level.

To support the case where B is a proper subset of A, the verifier will need to replace $X_1^{\rho_1 \rho_2}$ with $X_1^{\rho_1 \rho_2 f_{A \backslash B}(a)}$, a subset witness that can only be generated by Alice. Alice could in theory supply this witness to Bob during delegation, but if Bob subsequently delegates the credential further, that witness will need to be passed along again. Effectively, this is no different to storing the witness value as part of the credential chain.

However, formulating the witness in this way leaks whether or not A = B, since in that case $f_{A \backslash B}(a) = 1$, and so $X_1^{\rho_1 \rho_2 f_{A \backslash B}(a)} = X_1^{\rho_1 \rho_2}$. Indeed, this means anyone could attempt to guess the full attribute set of a credential they have seen and check their guess by creating a commitment $\hat{C}_Q$ and testing whether $e(X_1^{\rho_1 \rho_2}, \hat{C}_Q) = e(C_A^{\rho_1 \rho_2}, \hat{Y}_1^{\rho_3})$. This can be prevented by decoupling the commitment's opening factor from the owner's key pair, making it instead a fresh, random exponent, ψ. The pairing equation then correspondingly becomes:

$$e(P^{\rho_1 \rho_2 \psi_A f_{A \backslash B}(a)}, \hat{C}_B^{\rho_3}) = e(C_A^{\rho_1 \rho_2}, \hat{P}^{\psi_B \rho_3}).$$

Because the element $P^{\psi_A f_{A \backslash B}(a)}$ is in $\mathbb{G}_1$, it cannot be signed by Alice, and it cannot be generated in advance to gain the issuer's signature, since it requires knowledge of Bob's attribute set. With two unsigned elements in the equation, the values could be adjusted to a trivial solution, and so the result cannot be trusted by a verifier. However, Bob can include the exponent $\rho_3^{-1}\psi_B^{-1}$ and rearrange the pairing equation to:

$$e\left(P^{\rho_1\rho_2\psi_A\rho_3^{-1}\psi_B^{-1}f_{A\setminus B}(a)}, \hat{C}_B^{\rho_3}\right) = e\left(C_A^{\rho_1\rho_2}, \hat{P}\right).$$

Because $P^{\rho_1\rho_2\psi_A\rho_3^{-1}\psi_B^{-1}f_{A\setminus B}(a)}$ is a unique solution to this equation and is being compared with two signed elements and a public parameter, an adversary cannot modify it without rendering the credential useless, so it can safely be placed on the credential chain as an unsigned witness tag connecting party A's credential to party B's credential. Using this tag, any verifier can easily check that $B \subseteq A$, while the random factors mask any further information.

4.2 Construction of Mercurial Signature Credentials with Set Commitments

Applying these modifications to CL19 credentials [6], we arrive at the following construction.

Let λ be the maximum delegation level that should be permitted on a credential. This has to be specified because the keys must get shorter at each delegation level to allow signing attributes. Define $\mathsf{MS}_i = (\mathsf{PPGen}_i, \mathsf{KeyGen}_i, \mathsf{Sign}_i, \mathsf{Verify}_i, \mathsf{ConvertSK}_i, \mathsf{ConvertPK}_i, \mathsf{ConvertSig}_i, \mathsf{ChangeRep}_i)$ for all $0 \le i \le \lambda$ as instantiations of mercurial signatures as constructed by Crites and Lysyanskaya [6], such that for all $i, j \in [\lambda]$, $\mathsf{PPGen}_i = \mathsf{PPGen}_j$, MS_i is parameterised with key and message length $l_i = \lambda+1-i$, and the roles of $\mathbb{G}_1$ and $\mathbb{G}_2$ are reversed in all other algorithms of MS_i if i is odd, so that for $0 \le i < \lambda$, $(\mathcal{R}_M)_i = (\mathcal{R}_{pk})_{i+1}$. Let $\mathsf{Com}_0 = (\mathsf{Setup}_0, \mathsf{Commit}_0, \mathsf{Open}_0, \mathsf{OpenSubset}_0, \mathsf{VerifySubset}_0)$ and $\mathsf{Com}_1 = (\mathsf{Setup}_1, \mathsf{Commit}_1, \mathsf{Open}_1, \mathsf{OpenSubset}_1, \mathsf{VerifySubset}_1)$ be two instantiations of FHS randomisable set commitments [8] with the roles of $\mathbb{G}_1$ and $\mathbb{G}_2$ in Com_1 reversed.

The construction consists of the following algorithms and protocols. For simplicity, the protocols are written as if the credential chain length L is even; if L is odd, the roles of $\mathbb{G}_1$ and $\mathbb{G}_2$ must be reversed.

$\mathsf{Setup}(1^k, 1^t, 1^\lambda) \to (params)$: Given $k, t, \lambda > 0$, compute $PP \leftarrow \mathsf{PPGen}_0(1^k)$; extract $(P, \hat{P})$ from PP, choose $a \leftarrow^R \mathbb{Z}_p$, and compute $(P^{a^i}, \hat{P}^{a^i})_{i \in [t]}$; output $params = (PP, p, t, \lambda, (P^{a^i}, \hat{P}^{a^i})_{i \in [t]})$.

$\mathsf{KeyGen}(params) \to (\mathsf{pk}, \mathsf{sk})$: There are two cases. For the root authority, compute $(\mathsf{pk}_0, \mathsf{sk}_0) \leftarrow \mathsf{KeyGen}_0(PP, l_0)$ and output it. For others, compute $(\mathsf{pk}_i, \mathsf{sk}_i) \leftarrow \mathsf{KeyGen}_i(PP, l_i)$ for all $i \in [\lambda]$ and output all of the key pairs $(\mathsf{pk}_i, \mathsf{sk}_i)_{i \in [\lambda]}$.

$\mathsf{Issue}(params, L, \mathsf{pk}_0, \mathsf{sk}_I, \mathsf{pk}_I, O_I, \mathsf{cred}_I, A_I, A_R)$ $\leftrightarrow$
$\mathsf{Receive}(params, L, \mathsf{pk}_0, \mathsf{sk}_{L+1}, \mathsf{pk}_{L+1}, A_R) \to (\mathsf{cred}_R, \rho)$

  – If $L = 0$, define $\mathsf{cred}_I = \bot$ and $A_I = \mathbb{Z}_p$.

- If $L \geq \lambda$, return $\bot$.
- Receiver calculates $(C_R, O_R) \leftarrow$ Commit$(params, \mathsf{A}_R)$, extracts ρ_R from $O_R = (b, \rho_R)$, and calculates P^{ρ_R}.
- Receiver sends $C_R, P^{\rho_R}, \mathsf{pk}_{L+1}$.
- Receiver proves $\mathsf{PoK}\{\alpha_1, ..., \alpha_l, \beta | (P^{\alpha_1}, ..., P^{\alpha_l}) = \mathsf{pk}_{L+1} \wedge P^\beta = P^{\rho_R}\}$.
- If $\mathsf{A}_R \not\subseteq \mathsf{A}_I$ or $|\mathsf{A}_R| > t$ or the PoK fails, Issuer returns $\bot$.
- If $e(C_R, \hat{P}) \neq e(P^{\rho_R}, \hat{P}^{f_{A_R}(a)})$ and $\forall a' \in \mathsf{A}_R : P^{a'} \neq P^a$, Issuer returns $\bot$.
- If $L = 0$, Issuer computes $\sigma_1 \leftarrow \mathsf{Sign}_0(\mathsf{sk}_I, (\mathsf{pk}_{L+1}, C_R))$ and sends $\mathsf{cred}_R = (\mathsf{pk}_{L+1}, C_R, \sigma_1)$.
- If $L > 0$, Issuer computes $(\mathsf{cred}'_I, \mathsf{sk}'_I, \psi) \leftarrow \mathsf{RandCred}(\mathsf{cred}_I, \mathsf{sk}_I, \mathsf{pk}_0, L)$ and $\sigma_{L+1} \leftarrow \mathsf{Sign}_L(\mathsf{sk}'_I, (\mathsf{pk}_{L+1}, C_R))$.
- If $L > 0$ and $\forall a' \in \mathsf{A}_I : P^{a'} \neq P^a$, Issuer extracts ρ_I from O_I and $\hat{C}'_I$ from cred'_I, computes $\bar{W}_R \leftarrow \mathsf{OpenSubset}(params, \hat{C}'_I, \mathsf{A}_I, (0, \rho_I \psi), \mathsf{A}_R)$, and sends $\sigma_{L+1}, \bar{W}_R$, and cred'_I.
- If $L > 0$ and $\exists a' \in \mathsf{A}_I \backslash \mathsf{A}_R : P^{a'} = P^a$, Issuer calculates $f_{A_R}(a')^{-1}$, sets $\bar{W}_R \leftarrow (C'_I)^{f_{A_R}(a')^{-1}}$, and sends $\sigma_{L+1}, \bar{W}_R$, and cred'_I.
- If $L > 0$ and $\exists a' \in \mathsf{A}_R : P^{a'} = P^a$, Issuer sets $\bar{C}_R = C'_I$, $\bar{W}_R = P^{\rho_R}$, and $\sigma_{L+1} \leftarrow \mathsf{Sign}_L(\mathsf{sk}'_I, (\mathsf{pk}_{L+1}, \bar{C}_R))$, and sends $\sigma_{L+1}, \bar{C}_R, \bar{W}_R$, and cred'_I.
- If $\exists a' \in \mathsf{A}_R : P^{a'} = P^a$, Receiver sets $C_R = \bar{C}_R$.
- If $\forall 2 \leq i \leq L : \mathsf{Verify}_{i-1}(\mathsf{pk}'_{i-1}, \mathsf{nym}'_i, \sigma'_i) = 1 \wedge e(C'_i, W'_i) = e(P, C'_{i-1})$ and $\mathsf{Verify}_0(\mathsf{pk}_0, \mathsf{nym}'_1, \sigma'_1) = 1$ and $\mathsf{Verify}_L(\mathsf{pk}'_I, \mathsf{nym}_R, \sigma_{L+1}) = 1$ and $e(C_R, \bar{W}_R) = e(P^{\rho_R}, C'_I)$, Receiver calculates $W_R = \bar{W}_R^{\rho_R^{-1}}$, appends pk_{L+1}, C_R, σ_{L+1}, W_R to cred'_I to form cred_R, and stores $\mathsf{cred}_R, O_R, \mathsf{sk}_R = \mathsf{sk}_{L+1}, \mathsf{pk}_R = \mathsf{pk}_{L+1}$.

$\mathsf{RandCred}(\mathsf{cred}, \mathsf{sk}, \mathsf{pk}_0, L) \rightarrow (\mathsf{cred}', \mathsf{sk}', \rho)$: If $L > \lambda$, return $\bot$; otherwise, given cred of the form $(\mathsf{nym}_1, ..., \mathsf{nym}_L, \sigma_1, ..., \sigma_L, W_2, ..., W_L)$, where $\mathsf{nym}_i = (\mathsf{pk}_i, C_i)$, choose random $(\rho_1, ..., \rho_L) \leftarrow (\mathbb{Z}_p^*)^L$; define $\mathsf{nym}'_0 = \mathsf{pk}_0, \bar{\sigma}_1 = \sigma_1$; if $L \geq 2$, for $2 \leq i \leq L$, set $\bar{\sigma}_i = \mathsf{ConvertSig}_{i-1}(\mathsf{pk}_{i-1}, \mathsf{nym}_i, \sigma_i, \rho_{i-1})$ and $W'_i = W_i^{\rho_{i-1}\rho_i^{-1}}$; for $1 \leq i \leq L$, set $(\mathsf{nym}'_i, \sigma'_i) = \mathsf{ChangeRep}_i(\mathsf{nym}'_{i-1}, \mathsf{nym}_i, \bar{\sigma}_i, \rho_i)$; set $\mathsf{cred}' = (\mathsf{nym}'_1, ..., \mathsf{nym}'_L, \sigma'_1, ..., \sigma'_L, W'_2, ..., W'_L)$ and $\mathsf{sk}' = \rho_L(\mathsf{sk})$; output $(\mathsf{cred}', \mathsf{sk}', \rho_L)$.

$\mathsf{CredProve}(params, L_P, \mathsf{pk}_0, \mathsf{sk}_P, \mathsf{pk}_P, O_P, \mathsf{cred}_P, \mathsf{A}_P, S, D)$ $\leftrightarrow$ $\mathsf{CredVerify}$ $(params, \mathsf{pk}_0) \rightarrow \{0, 1\}$

- Prover extracts C_{L_P} from cred_P and computes $W_{L_P} \leftarrow \mathsf{OpenSubset}(params, C_{L_P}, \mathsf{A}_P, O_P, S)$, $\hat{W}_{L_P} \leftarrow \mathsf{OpenDisjoint}(params, C_{L_P}, \mathsf{A}_P, O_P, D)$.
- If $L_P \leq \lambda$, Prover computes $(\mathsf{cred}'_P, \mathsf{sk}'_P, \psi) \leftarrow \mathsf{RandCred}(\mathsf{cred}_P, \mathsf{sk}_P, \mathsf{pk}_0, L_P)$, $W'_{L_P} = W_{L_P}^\psi$, and $\hat{W}'_{L_P} = \hat{W}_{L_P}^\psi$.
- Prover sends $\mathsf{cred}'_P, W'_{L_P}, \hat{W}'_{L_P}, S, D$.
- Prover proves $\mathsf{PoK}\{\alpha_1, ..., \alpha_l | (P^{\alpha_1}, ..., P^{\alpha_l}) = \mathsf{pk}'_{L_P}\}$.
- Verifier extracts $\mathsf{nym}'_{L_P} = (\mathsf{pk}'_{L_P}, C'_{L_P})$ from cred_P and infers L_P from the length of cred'_P.
- If $L_P > \lambda$ or the PoK fails, Verifier returns 0.

- If $\forall 2 \leq i \leq L_P$: $\mathsf{Verify}_{i-1}(\mathsf{pk}'_{i-1}, \mathsf{nym}'_i, \sigma'_i) = 1 \wedge e(C'_i, W'_i) = e(P, C'_{i-1})$, $\mathsf{Verify}_0(\mathsf{pk}_0, \mathsf{nym}'_1, \sigma'_1) = 1$, $\mathsf{VerifySubset}(params, C'_{L_P}, \mathsf{S}, W'_{L_P}) = 1$, and $\mathsf{VerifyDisjoint}(params, C'_{L_P}, \mathsf{D}, \hat{W}'_{L_P}) = 1$, Verifier outputs 1; otherwise, Verifier outputs 0.

Similar adjustments can be made to add selective delegation to the variable-length CL21 scheme [7] and to the issuer-hiding CLP22 scheme [4], since all three constructions randomise message elements in the same way and are therefore compatible with the same set commitments and witness values. The witness values in Sect. 4.1 are also compatible with the MSBM23 credential scheme [10], allowing its delegation mechanism to be used with the more restrictive Blömer and Bobolz model.

In the next subsection, we give an overview of the security proofs for the above construction, which can be found in full in the appendices. Similar proofs should be obtainable for the variable-length Crites-Lysyanskaya scheme and the Connolly et al. scheme with minimal changes to the proof strategy.

4.3   Security Analysis

In order to assess the security of this scheme, we must first establish the security goals of a delegatable, attribute-based credential (DABC): namely correctness, unforgeability, and anonymity. In the context of this scheme, these can loosely be defined as follows:

- **Correctness:** The scheme is correct if, whenever Setup and KeyGen are run correctly and the Issue-Receive protocol is executed correctly on correctly generated inputs including an attribute set $\mathcal{X}$, the receiver outputs a certification chain that, when used as input to the prover in an honest execution of the CredProve-CredVerify protocol with input sets $\mathcal{S}$ and $\mathcal{D}$ such that $\mathcal{S} \subseteq \mathcal{X}$ and $\mathcal{D} \cap \mathcal{X} = \emptyset$, is accepted by the verifier with probability 1.
- **Unforgeability:** The scheme is unforgeable if:
  - a (non-root) user without a correctly-issued credential cannot perform a showing or issue a credential that would be accepted by a verifier with non-negligible probability
  - a user in possession of a credential for an attribute set $\mathcal{X}$ cannot with non-negligible probability perform a valid showing for sets $\mathcal{S}$ and $\mathcal{D}$ such that $\mathcal{S} \not\subseteq \mathcal{X}$ and $\mathcal{D} \cap \mathcal{X} \neq \emptyset$, even if colluding with other users.
  - a user in possession of a credential for an attribute set $\mathcal{X}$ cannot with non-negligible probability issue a valid delegated credential for a set $\mathcal{Y} \not\subseteq \mathcal{X}$, even if colluding with other users.
- **Anonymity:** The scheme is anonymous if, during a showing of a credential, no verifier, issuer, or coalition of verifiers and issuers can identify the user, identify past showings of the same credential, or learn anything about the user other than that they possess a valid credential for the attributes being shown.

Note that the CL19 and CL21 schemes [6,7] cannot satisfy anonymity in cases where the credential chain includes a public key (other than the root issuer) whose secret key is known by the adversary. Such cases are therefore eliminated in the security game that provides the formal criteria.

In order to formalise the security definitions, we extend the security game from Crites and Lysyanskaya's DAC model [6] to account for the addition of attributes to the credentials, and of subset and disjoint set openings to the showing protocol. The resulting security game is included in the full version of the paper.

Correctness: The correctness of the scheme in Sect. 4.2 follows by inspection. In particular, it can be seen that it matches Crites and Lysyanskaya's original mercurial signature scheme [6], expanded to make the contents of each credential explicit, and with the addition of attribute sets, attribute witnesses, and verification checks on attributes.

Unforgeability: The proof of unforgeability for the scheme in Sect. 4.2 works by enumerating the ways in which an adversary could achieve a forgery in the attribute-based security game, and shows how each reduces to either a forgery in the non-attribute-based mercurial signature model or a breaking of one of the security properties of the set commitment scheme. See the full version of the paper for further details.

Anonymity: The proof of anonymity for the scheme in Sect. 4.2 is an extension of the hybrid argument in Crites and Lysyanskaya's proof of anonymity for the original mercurial signature construction, which shows that the adversary's view when attributes are included is indistinguishable from the case in which all honest parties have identical attributes; therefore the inclusion of credential attributes and subset witnesses does not enable the adversary to distinguish between credentials. See the full version of the paper for further details.

5   Conclusion and Future Work

In this paper, we have introduced a method by which mercurial signatures can encode and delegate multiple attributes of the credential holder, in keeping with the properties of selective disclosure and restricted, selective delegation as described by Blömer and Bobolz. This is an extremely important feature for an anonymous credential system, providing far more versatility than a credential that does not encode any detailed attribute information, and so it represents a significant step toward bringing mercurial signature credentials into line with the functionality available from older credential schemes.

There are still other major avenues for improving mercurial signature credentials, however. Most notably, the CL19 mercurial signature scheme suffers from a severe reduction in its anonymity property, resulting from the fact that an adversary that has delegated a credential can subsequently recognise its own key in that credential's delegation chain. This weakness is addressed by the work of Connolly et al. [4], who use a different key structure in their scheme, but this still only solves it in the honest parameter model. In theory, a zero-knowledge proof of honest parameter generation given at the time of delegation would close this weakness, but further work is needed to accomplish this.

Mercurial signatures also have yet to be extended to a multi-authority model enabling their seamless use in systems with multiple issuing authorities, and there is interest in finding other basic constructions from which mercurial signatures could be developed, particularly any based on quantum-secure assumptions.

References

1. Blömer, J., Bobolz, J.: Delegatable attribute-based anonymous credentials from dynamically malleable signatures. In: Preneel, B., Vercauteren, F. (eds.) ACNS 2018. LNCS, vol. 10892, pp. 221–239. Springer, Cham (2018). https://doi.org/10.1007/978-3-319-93387-0_12

2. Camenisch, J., Lysyanskaya, A.: An efficient system for non-transferable anonymous credentials with optional anonymity revocation. In: Pfitzmann, B. (ed.) EUROCRYPT 2001. LNCS, vol. 2045, pp. 93–118. Springer, Heidelberg (2001). https://doi.org/10.1007/3-540-44987-6_7

3. Chase, M., Lysyanskaya, A.: On signatures of knowledge. In: Dwork, C. (ed.) CRYPTO 2006. LNCS, vol. 4117, pp. 78–96. Springer, Heidelberg (2006). https://doi.org/10.1007/11818175_5

4. Connolly, A., Lafourcade, P., Perez Kempner, O.: Improved constructions of anonymous credentials from structure-preserving signatures on equivalence classes. In: Hanaoka, G., Shikata, J., Watanabe, Y. (eds.) Public-Key Cryptography - PKC 2022, pp. 409–438. Springer International Publishing, Cham (2022). https://doi.org/10.1007/978-3-030-97121-2_15

5. Cramer, R., Damgård, I., MacKenzie, P.: Efficient zero-knowledge proofs of knowledge without intractability assumptions. In: Imai, H., Zheng, Y. (eds.) PKC 2000. LNCS, vol. 1751, pp. 354–372. Springer, Heidelberg (2000). https://doi.org/10.1007/978-3-540-46588-1_24

6. Crites, E.C., Lysyanskaya, A.: Delegatable anonymous credentials from mercurial signatures. In: Matsui, M. (ed.) CT-RSA 2019. LNCS, vol. 11405, pp. 535–555. Springer, Cham (2019). https://doi.org/10.1007/978-3-030-12612-4_27

7. Crites, E.C., Lysyanskaya, A.: Mercurial signatures for variable-length messages. In: Proceedings on Privacy Enhancing Technologies (PoPETs), pp. 441–463. de Gruyter (2021)

8. Fuchsbauer, G., Hanser, C., Slamanig, D.: Structure-preserving signatures on equivalence classes and constant-size anonymous credentials. J. Cryptol. **32**(2), 498–546 (2019)

9. Hanser, C., Slamanig, D.: Structure-preserving signatures on equivalence classes and their application to anonymous credentials. In: Sarkar, P., Iwata, T. (eds.) ASIACRYPT 2014. LNCS, vol. 8873, pp. 491–511. Springer, Heidelberg (2014). https://doi.org/10.1007/978-3-662-45611-8_26

10. Mir, O., Slamanig, D., Bauer, B., Mayrhofer, R.: Practical delegatable anonymous credentials from equivalence class signatures. In: Proceedings on Privacy Enhancing Technologies (PoPETs), pp. 488–513. PETS (2023)

Advances in Post-Quantum Cryptography

Middle-Products of Skew Polynomials and Learning with Errors

Cong Ling and Andrew Mendelsohn[(✉)]

Department of EEE, Imperial College London, London SW7 2AZ, UK
{c.ling,andrew.mendelsohn18}@imperial.ac.uk

Abstract. We extend the middle product to skew polynomials, which we use to define a skew middle-product Learning with Errors (LWE) variant. We also define a skew polynomial LWE problem, which we connect to Cyclic LWE (CLWE), a variant of LWE in cyclic division algebras. We then reduce a family of skew polynomial LWE problems to skew middle-product LWE, for a family which includes the structures found in CLWE. Finally, we give an encryption scheme and demonstrate its IND-CPA security, assuming the hardness of skew middle-product LWE.

Keywords: middle product · LWE · cyclic division algebras · skew polynomials

1 Introduction

The development of efficient quantum algorithms for cryptographic problems (e.g. [21]) has lead to the development of *post*-quantum cryptography, which relies on computationally intractable problems for both classical and quantum computers. A prime candidate for a family of such computationally intractable problems are *lattice* problems, following the pioneering work of Ajtai [1]. In particular, much post-quantum cryptographic functionality is based on the Learning with Errors (LWE) problem, introduced by Regev [18].

LWE-style problems consist of solving systems of noisy linear equations. Over the integers, LWE loosely asks a challenger to find $\mathbf{s} \in \mathbb{Z}_q^n$ from a number of samples of the form $(\mathbf{a}_i, \langle \mathbf{a}_i, \mathbf{s} \rangle + e_i \bmod q)$, where $\mathbf{a}_i \in \mathbb{Z}_q^n$ and e_i is some noise. However, cryptosystems based on LWE have sub-optimal storage requirements and computation with LWE samples is often inefficient, due to the relative inefficiency of high-dimensional matrix multiplication. For this reason, structured variants of LWE have been introduced.

These include Ring LWE (RLWE) [15], which uses multiplication in the ring of integers of a number field to create multiple correlated LWE samples. For instance, if $\mathcal{R}$ is the ring of integers of the $2n$th cyclotomic field for power-of-two n, then $\mathcal{R} = \mathbb{Z}[x]/(x^n + 1)$ and multiplication on a fixed basis by a polynomial

$a \in \mathcal{R}$ can be represented by a matrix

$$\begin{pmatrix} a_0 & -a_{n-1} & \cdots & -a_1 \\ a_1 & a_0 & \cdots & -a_2 \\ \vdots & \vdots & \ddots & \vdots \\ a_{n-1} & a_{n-2} & \cdots & a_0 \end{pmatrix}.$$

Other structured forms of LWE have been studied, such as PLWE [22], which considers $\mathcal{R} = \mathbb{Z}[x]/(f(x))$ for a broader range of $f(x)$, and CLWE [9], which developed LWE from orders in cyclic division algebras (CDAs). These variants both use algebraic objects which permit matrix representations over $\mathbb{Z}$ to rewrite multiplication by an element a as multiplication by an integral matrix.

Another variant, middle-product LWE (MPLWE) [19], replaced ring multiplication with the *middle product*, denoted $\odot$. This product takes two polynomials a, b and outputs a polynomial whose coefficients are the 'middle' coefficients of the product $a \cdot b$, discarding higher and lower order terms. In particular, given $a = \sum_{i=0}^{d_a-1} x^i a_i$, $b = \sum_{i=0}^{d_b-1} x^i b_i$ with $d_a + d_b - 1 = d + 2k$ for some d, k, we have

$$a \odot_d b = \left\lfloor \frac{(a \cdot b) \bmod x^{k+d}}{x^k} \right\rfloor.$$

The discarding of coefficients allows for fast algorithms to compute middle products [8,10] and this product has a matrix presentation such that samples of shape $(a, a \odot r + e)$ form structured instances of LWE. In particular, one can write

$$a \odot_d r = \begin{pmatrix} a_0 & a_1 & a_2 & \cdots & a_{d_a-1} & 0 & \cdots & 0 \\ 0 & a_0 & a_1 & \cdots & a_{d_a-2} & a_{d_a-1} & \cdots & 0 \\ \vdots & \ddots & \ddots & \ddots & \ddots & & \ddots & \vdots \\ 0 & \cdots & \cdots & \cdots & 0 & a_0 & \cdots & a_{d_a-1} \end{pmatrix} \cdot \begin{pmatrix} r_{d_r-1} \\ \vdots \\ r_1 \\ r_0 \end{pmatrix}$$

In [19] a reduction from a family of PLWE problems to MPLWE was given, guaranteeing that MPLWE is at least as hard as the hardest PLWE problem in the family. Notably the chosen family includes RLWE instances. They also gave a public key encryption scheme and proved its IND-CPA security, assuming hardness of MPLWE.

Our Contribution. We develop a novel form of MPLWE for skew polynomial rings, which are a noncommutative form of polynomial ring, named 'Skew MPLWE' (SMPLWE). We define the middle product for such rings and also a novel structured form of LWE for skew polynomial rings, named 'skew polynomial LWE' (SPLWE). We show that this LWE variant includes CLWE instances, reduce a family of SPLWE problems to SMPLWE, and give a PKE scheme.

We state four motivations for this work:

1. We define and make use of (to our knowledge) the first structured LWE-variant from skew polynomials. This was implicit in [9], but the connection

was never utilised other than for multiplication algorithms. This appears a promising avenue of future research, given the well-studied properties of skew polynomial rings and their profitable application by coding theorists.

2. We continue the study of LWE in CDAs. Defining SMPLWE and SPLWE and relating them to CLWE provides further indications of the precise security level of CLWE, which is believed to lie somewhere between that of RLWE and MLWE, but more precise understanding is lacking. Our reduction provides new quantitative information on CLWE.

3. SMPLWE enjoys a reduction from a family of SPLWE problems (including CLWE-style problems). This provides SMPLWE with a strong security guarantee and may be preferable in some contexts to CLWE, for this reason.

4. SMPLWE, like MPLWE, enjoys fast multiplication algorithms. Fast algorithms for skew polynomials exist [7], and it seems likely that these could be used to efficiently compute the skew middle product. This yields a cryptographic scheme which is both efficient and, as explained above, secure.

Our reduction holds for a restricted parameter set relative to [19], since it appears the noncommutative structure of our rings means that for only some parameters is SMPLWE structured LWE (in the notation of [19], when $n = m = d$). In more detail, we consider quotients of skew polynomial rings of the form $\mathcal{O}_L[u, \theta]/(u^d - \gamma)$, where L is a number field with ring of integers $\mathcal{O}_L$, K is an index d subfield of L such that $\mathrm{Gal}(L/K)$ is generated by an automorphism θ, u satisfies $ux = \theta(x)u$ for any $x \in \mathcal{O}_L$, and $\gamma \in \mathcal{O}_K$, and prove our results for middle product samples $(a, a \odot_d r + e)$, where $\deg(a) = d-1$ and $\deg(r) = 2(d-1)$. In this setting, we set $a \odot_d r = \left\lfloor \frac{(a \cdot r) \bmod u^{2d-1}}{u^{d-1}} \right\rfloor$ and can write

$$
a \odot_d r = \begin{pmatrix} a_{d-1} & \theta(a_{d-2}) & \dots & \theta^{d-1}(a_0) & 0 & \dots & 0 \\ 0 & \theta(a_{d-1}) & \dots & \theta^{d-1}(a_1) & \theta^d(a_0) & \dots & 0 \\ \vdots & \ddots & \ddots & \ddots & \ddots & \ddots & \vdots \\ 0 & 0 & \dots & \theta^{d-1}(a_{d-1}) & \dots & \theta^{d-3}(a_1) & \theta^{d-2}(a_0) \end{pmatrix} \begin{pmatrix} r_0 \\ r_1 \\ \vdots \\ r_{d_r-1} \end{pmatrix}
$$

We then define two problems: $\mathrm{SPLWE}_{q,s,f,\chi}$ is the problem of distinguishing samples of the form $(a_i, a_i s + e_i \bmod q)$ from samples uniform over the domain, and $\mathrm{SMPLWE}_{q,s,d,d,\chi'}$ is the challenge of distinguishing samples of the form $(a_i, a_i \odot_d s + e_i)$ from those uniform over the domain, where a_i and s are skew polynomials of bounded degree and e_i is added noise. We then prove

Main Reduction (Theorem 1). Let $d > 0, q \geq 2$, and χ an error distribution. Then there exists a ppt. reduction from $\mathrm{SPLWE}_{q,s,f,\chi}$ for any polynomial $f(u) = u^d - \gamma \in \mathcal{O}_L[u, \theta]$ with $\gamma \in \mathcal{O}_K \setminus \{0\}$ coprime with q, to $\mathrm{SMPLWE}_{q,s,d,d,\chi'}$. This result reduces a family of SPLWE problems to SMPLWE - a family which includes CLWE-style instances. To achieve this, new families of linear transformations on coefficients of skew polynomials are introduced. We then give a PKE scheme and demonstrate its IND-CPA security, if SMPLWE is hard.

We note here that we consider a family of SPLWE problems under the coefficient embedding. These SPLWE problems include the ones considered in CLWE, but in that setting the canonical embedding was used. It is not currently clear what the relationship between CLWE in the coefficient and in the canonical embedding is, but it seems likely that, in a similar way as holds for RLWE, CLWE under the coefficient embedding is still a 'hard' problem, although we stress that we do not have any formal proofs of the security of CLWE under the coefficient embedding. However, we note the work of [20] and consider it reasonable to suggest that CLWE in the canonical and coefficient embeddings can be related via a linear transformation with limited loss in parameter quality. We provide evidence toward this end in Appendix B.

Prior Work and Paper Organisation. MPLWE was introduced in [19] and CLWE in [9]. More on middle product-based cryptography can be found in [4,5,14,23]. In [17], MPLWE was related to a number of LWE variants, such as RLWE. We note the extensive use of skew polynomials in coding theory [3].

Preliminaries are in Sect. 2, we recollect LWE in Sect. 3, skew polynomials in Sect. 4, and CDAs in Sect. 5. We introduce the skew middle product in Sect. 6, give a reduction from SPLWE to SMPLWE in Sect. 7, provide a PKE scheme in Sect. 8, and then conclude.

2   Preliminaries

If $\mathbf{v}$ is an n-dimensional vector, we denote by $\bar{\mathbf{v}}$ the n-dimensional vector whose entries are those of $\mathbf{v}$ in reverse order; i.e. if $\mathbf{v} = (v_1, ..., v_n)^T$, then $\bar{\mathbf{v}} = (v_n, ..., v_1)^T$.

We prove IND-CPA security of our cryptosystem below. Recall:

Definition 1. ([12]) Let $\Pi = $ (Gen, Enc, Dec) be a PKE scheme, and $\mathcal{A}$ be an adversary. We say Π is *indistinguishable under chosen-plaintext attack* if any ppt. adversary in the following experiment PubK$_{\mathcal{A},\Pi}(n)$ has negligible advantage:

1. Gen is run to obtain keys (pk, sk).
2. Adversary $\mathcal{A}$ is given pk, and outputs a pair of equal-length messages m_0, m_1 in the message space.
3. A uniform bit $b \in \{0,1\}$ is chosen, and then a ciphertext $c \leftarrow \text{Enc}_{pk}(m_b)$ is computed and given to $\mathcal{A}$. We call c the challenge ciphertext.
4. $\mathcal{A}$ outputs a bit b'. The output of the experiment is 1 if $b' = b$, and 0 otherwise. If $b' = b$ we say that $\mathcal{A}$ succeeds.

That is, $\Pr[\text{PubK}_{\mathcal{A},\Pi}(n) = 1] \leq \frac{1}{2} + \text{neg}(n)$.

To complete the proof, we will rely on properties of hash functions:

Definition 2. A family $\mathcal{H}$ of hash functions $h : X \to Y$ of finite cardinality is called *universal* if $\Pr_{h \leftarrow U(\mathcal{H})}[h(x_1) = h(x_2)] = 1/|Y|, \ \forall \ x_1 \neq x_2 \in X$.

The *statistical distance* between two distributions D, D' over a discrete set S is defined $\Delta(D, D') = \frac{1}{2} \sum_{x \in S} |D(x) - D'(x)|$. The uniform distribution over a finite set S' is denoted $U(S')$.

Lemma 1. *[19, Lemma 2.1] Let X, Y, Z be finite sets. Let $\mathcal{H}$ be a universal hash function family $h : X \to Y$ and $f : X \to Z$ be arbitrary. Then for any random variable T taking values in X, and $\gamma(T) = \max_{t \in X} \Pr[T = t]$, we have:*

$$\Delta((h, h(T), f(T)), (h, U(Y), f(T))) \leq \frac{1}{2} \cdot \sqrt{\gamma(T) \cdot |Y| \cdot |Z|}$$

3 Learning with Errors and Middle Products

The Middle Product. The middle product can be thought of as the multiplication rule which takes two polynomials, multiplies them together, then discards the lower and higher coefficients, forming a polynomial whose coefficients are the 'middle' part of the product. Formally, if $\mathcal{R}$ is an arbitrary ring and $\mathcal{R}^{<d}[x]$ denote the polynomials over $\mathcal{R}$ of degree at most $d - 1$:

Definition 3. Let $d_a, d_b, d, k \in \mathbb{N}$ such that $d_a + d_b - 1 = d + 2k$. The middle-product of $a \in \mathcal{R}^{<d_a}[x]$ and $b \in \mathcal{R}^{<d_b}[x]$ is defined

$$\odot_d : \mathcal{R}^{<d_a}[x] \times \mathcal{R}^{<d_b}[x] \to \mathcal{R}^{<d}[x],$$

$$(a, b) \mapsto a \odot_d b = \left\lfloor \frac{(a \cdot b) \bmod x^{k+d}}{x^k} \right\rfloor.$$

We can now define middle product learning with errors, following [19]:

Definition 4. (MPLWE distribution) Let $n, d > 0, q \geq 2$, and χ be a distribution over $\mathbb{R}^{<d}[x]$. For $s \in \mathbb{Z}_q^{<n+d-1}[x]$, define the distribution $\mathrm{MP}_{q,n,d,\chi}(s)$ over $\mathbb{Z}_q^{<n}[x] \times \mathbb{R}_q^{<d}[x]$ as the distribution obtained by sampling $a \leftarrow U(\mathbb{Z}_q^{<n}[x]), e \leftarrow \chi$ and outputting $(a, b = a \odot_d s + e)$.

Definition 5. (decision MPLWE) Let $n, d > 0, q \geq 2$, and χ be a distribution over $\mathbb{R}^{<d}[x]$. Then the decision MPLWE problem, $\mathrm{MPLWE}_{n,d,q,\chi}$, consists in distinguishing between arbitrarily many samples from $\mathrm{MP}_{q,n,d,\chi}(s)$ and the same number of samples from $U(\mathbb{Z}_q^{<n}[x] \times \mathbb{R}_q^{<d}[x])$, with non-negligible probability over $s \leftarrow U(\mathbb{Z}_q^{<n+d-1}[x])$.

4 Skew Polynomials

A skew polynomial ring over a field is defined as follows:

Definition 6. Let $\mathbb{F}$ be a field and θ be an automorphism of $\mathbb{F}$. Then $\mathbb{F}[u, \theta] := \{\sum_{i=0}^n u^i x_i : x_i \in \mathbb{F}\}$, the set of polynomials in u with coefficients in $\mathbb{F}$ equipped with standard polynomial addition and having polynomial multiplication subject to the condition $xu = u\theta(x)$ for all $x \in \mathbb{F}$, is called a skew polynomial ring.

The multiplication rule means that for non-trivial choice of θ, $\mathbb{F}[u, \theta]$ is a non-commutative ring. If $\mathbb{F}^\theta$ is the fixed field of θ, $\mathbb{F}^\theta = \{x \in \mathbb{F} : \theta(x) = x\}$, and θ has order d, then $\mathbb{F}^\theta[u^d]$ is the largest commutative subring of $\mathbb{F}[u, \theta]$. The elements of this subring are called *central* and generate two-sided ideals of $\mathbb{F}[u, \theta]$. For more on skew polynomials, see [16], [11, Chapter 8] or Appendix A.

One may restrict the coefficients to be taken from some subring of a field, and for MPLWE in skew polynomial rings we will indeed restrict the coefficients to the ring of integers of a number field. An important construction of skew polynomial rings (other examples can be found in Appendix A) is the following:

Example 1. Let $L/\mathbb{Q}$ be a finite Galois extension, and $\theta \in \mathrm{Gal}(L/\mathbb{Q})$ with fixed field K, such that $[L : K] = d$ and $\mathrm{Gal}(L/K)$ is cyclic. Then $\mathcal{O}_L[u, \theta]$ is a skew polynomial ring with center $\mathcal{O}_K[u^d]$.

Skew Polynomial Learning with Errors. In this section we define a Learning with Errors distribution sampling skew polynomials, and state search and decision problems for that distribution. Below, $R_q := R/qR$ for a ring R.

Definition 7. Let $q \geq 2$ and $d \geq 1$. Let θ be an automorphism of L of degree d, $R := \mathcal{O}_L[u, \theta]$, $s \in R_q$, $L_{\mathbb{R}} := L \otimes \mathbb{R}$, and $f \in R$ be a monic central skew polynomial of degree n. To obtain a sample from the Skew Polynomial Learning with Errors distribution (SPLWE) $\mathrm{SP}_{q,s,f,\chi}$, sample $a \leftarrow U(R_q)$, $e \xleftarrow{\chi} L_{\mathbb{R}}[u, \theta]/fR$, and output $(a, as + e \bmod q) \in R_q \times L_{\mathbb{R}}[u, \theta]/(q, f)R$.

The decision problem is then defined as follows:

Definition 8. (decision SPLWE) Let Υ be a distribution on a family of error distributions over $L_{\mathbb{R}}[u, \theta]$, and $U(\cdot)$ be the uniform distribution. The decision SPLWE problem $\mathrm{SPLWE}_{q,s,f,\chi}$ is on input a number of independent samples from either $\mathrm{SP}_{q,s,f,\chi}$ for random $(s, \chi) \leftarrow U(R_q) \times \Upsilon$ or $U(R_q \times L_{\mathbb{R}}[u, \theta]/(q, f)R)$, to decide which is the case with non-negligible advantage.

Useful Matrices for Manipulating Skew Polynomials. In this section we will define and prove basic properties of a number of linear transformations on the coefficients of skew polynomials, which we later use in establishing the hardness of SMPLWE and a cryptosystem based off it. We define these as matrices, and specialise to the skew polynomial rings of Example 1. We begin with:

Definition 9. Let $f \in \mathcal{O}_L[u, \theta]$ be a monic central skew polynomial of degree m. Let $a \in \mathcal{O}_L[u, \theta]$. Define $\mathrm{Rot}_f^d(a)$ as the $d \times m$ matrix with ith row given by the coefficients of $a \cdot u^{i-1} \bmod f$, for $i = 1, ..., d$.

It is immediate that if $a \equiv a' \bmod f$, then $\mathrm{Rot}_f^d(a) = \mathrm{Rot}_f^d(a')$. Moreover, $\mathrm{Rot}_f^d(ab) = \mathrm{Rot}_f^d(b) \mathrm{Rot}_f^d(a)$. When $m = d$, we will write $\mathrm{Rot}_f(a)$ for $\mathrm{Rot}_f^d(a)$.

Definition 10. Let $f \in \mathcal{O}_L[u, \theta]$ be a monic central skew polynomial of degree m. Define $M_{f,\theta}$ as the $m \times m$ matrix with entries such that $M_{f,\theta} \cdot \mathbf{a}$ has ith entry

$$\left(\left(\sum_{j=1}^{m} u^{i+j-2}\theta^{i-1}(a_{j-1}) \right) \mod f \right) \mod u.$$

We introduce this matrix for the following reason:

$$\left(\sum_{j=1}^{m} u^{i+j-2}\theta^{i-1}(a_{j-1}) \mod f \right) \mod u = \left(\sum_{j=1}^{m} u^{j-1}a_{j-1}u^{i-1} \mod f \right) \mod u$$

$$= \left(\sum_{j=1}^{m} u^{j-1}a_{j-1}u^{i-1} \mod f \right) \mod u$$

$$= \left(au^{i-1} \mod f \right) \mod u,$$

which is the constant coefficient of $au^{i-1} \mod f$, and hence

$$M_{f,\theta} \cdot \mathbf{a} = \mathrm{Rot}_f(a) \cdot (1, 0, ..., 0)^T.$$

Example: Suppose $f(u) = u^d - \gamma$ for some $\gamma \in \mathcal{O}_K$ and $\deg(a) = d - 1$. Then

$$\mathrm{Rot}_f(a) = \begin{pmatrix} a_0 & a_1 & \cdots & a_{d-1} \\ \gamma\theta(a_{d-1}) & \theta(a_0) & \cdots & \theta(a_{d-2}) \\ \vdots & \vdots & \ddots & \vdots \\ \gamma\theta^{d-1}(a_1) & \gamma\theta^{d-1}(a_2) & \cdots & \theta^{d-1}(a_0) \end{pmatrix}, \quad M_{f,\theta} = \begin{pmatrix} 1 & 0 & \cdots & 0 & 0 \\ 0 & 0 & \cdots & 0 & \gamma\theta \\ 0 & 0 & \cdots & \gamma\theta^2 & 0 \\ \vdots & \vdots & \cdots & \vdots & \vdots \\ 0 & \gamma\theta^{d-1} & \cdots & 0 & 0 \end{pmatrix}$$

We introduce a kind of generalised Toeplitz matrix which we will later require:

Definition 11. Let $d, k > 0$. Let $r \in \mathcal{O}_L^{\leq k+1}[u, \theta]$. Set $\mathrm{GToep}^{d,k+1}(r)$ to be the $d \times (k + d)$ matrix whose i, jth entry is given by $\theta^{j-1}(r_{k-j+i})$.

This definition is important for writing the middle product in matrix form, as we shall see later. It also has the following property: if $f(u) = u^d - \gamma$ for some $\gamma \in K$ and $a \in \mathcal{O}_L[u, \theta]^{<d}$ is a skew polynomial, there exists a $2d - 1 \times d$ matrix N_f and skew polynomial $\tilde{a}$ such that $\mathrm{GToep}^{d,d}(a) \cdot N_f = \mathrm{Rot}_f(\tilde{a})$. Formally:

Proposition 1. Let $a \in \mathcal{O}_L[u, \theta]^{<d}$, $f(u) = u^d - \gamma$, and θ have order d. Then there exists a $2d-1 \times d$ matrix N_f and a skew polynomial $\tilde{a}$ such that $\mathrm{GToep}^{d,d}(a) \cdot N_f = \mathrm{Rot}_f(\tilde{a})$. Moreover, if $a = a_0 + ua_1 + ... + u^{d-1}a_{d-1}$, we have $\tilde{a} = a_{d-1} + u\theta(a_{d-2}) + ... + u^{d-1}\theta^{d-1}(a_0)$.

Proof. Write $a = a_0 + ua_1 + ... + u^{d-1}a_{d-1} \in \mathcal{O}_L[u, \theta]$. $\mathrm{GToep}^{d,d}(a)$ has the form

$$\mathrm{GToep}^{d,d}(a) = \begin{pmatrix} a_{d-1} & \theta(a_{d-2}) & \cdots & \theta^{d-1}(a_0) & 0 & \cdots & 0 \\ 0 & \theta(a_{d-1}) & \cdots & \theta^{d-1}(a_1) & \theta^d(a_0) & \cdots & 0 \\ & & \ddots & \ddots & \ddots & & \\ 0 & 0 & \cdots & \theta^{d-1}(a_{d-1}) & \cdots & \theta^{d-3}(a_1) & \theta^{d-2}(a_0) \end{pmatrix}$$

Note that the entries of each column of $\text{GToep}^{d,d}(\cdot)$ all feature the same power of θ. Since $\text{GToep}^{d,d}$ has size $d \times 2d-1$ and Rot_f size $d \times d$, any matrix N such that $\text{GToep}^{d,d} \cdot N = \text{Rot}_f$ must have size $2d-1 \times d$. Setting N_f to be the matrix

$$N_f = \left(\begin{array}{c} I_d \\ \hline \begin{array}{ccccc} \gamma & 0 & 0 & \dots & 0 \\ 0 & \gamma & 0 & \dots & 0 \\ \dots & \dots & \ddots & \dots & \dots \\ 0 & 0 & \dots & \gamma & 0 \end{array} \end{array}\right),$$

where I_d is the $d \times d$ identity matrix, one finds

$$\text{GToep}^{d,d}(a) \cdot N_f = \begin{pmatrix} a_{d-1} & \theta(a_{d-2}) & \dots & \theta^{d-1}(a_0) \\ \gamma\theta^d(a_0) & \theta(a_{d-1}) & \dots & \theta^{d-1}(a_1) \\ \vdots & \vdots & \dots & \vdots \\ \gamma\theta^d(a_{d-2}) & \gamma\theta(a_{d-3}) & \dots & \theta^{d-1}(a_{d-1}) \end{pmatrix},$$

which is $\text{Rot}_f(\tilde{a})$, where $\tilde{a} = a_{d-1} + u\theta(a_{d-2}) + \dots + u^{d-1}\theta^{d-1}(a_0)$.   □

5   Cyclic Division Algebras and CLWE

In this section we review Cyclic LWE. Suppose L/K is a finite Galois extension of number fields of degree d and $\langle\theta\rangle = \text{Gal}(L/K)$. Consider

$$\mathcal{A} := L + uL + \dots + u^{d-1}L,$$

where u is such that 1) $u^d = \gamma$ for some $\gamma \in K$ and 2) $ux = \theta(x)u$ for all $x \in L$. Then we call $\mathcal{A}$ a cyclic algebra over K, and write $(L/K, \theta, \gamma)$. When $\gamma \in \mathcal{O}_K$, $\mathcal{A}$ contains a discrete subring

$$\Lambda := \mathcal{O}_L + u\mathcal{O}_L + \dots + u^{d-1}\mathcal{O}_L.$$

An important property of cyclic algebras is the *division* property; we say a cyclic algebra $\mathcal{A}$ is division if every element has a multiplicative inverse. Division algebras are noncommutative equivalents of fields (and sometimes known as skew fields). The following provides a useful criterion for a cyclic algebra to be division:

Definition 12. An element α of K is *non-norm* if there does not exist an element $x \in L$ such that $\alpha^i = N_{L/K}(x)$, for $0 < i < [L : K]$.

Proposition 2. *[2] The cyclic algebra $\mathcal{A}$ is a division algebra if and only if γ is a non-norm element.*

We connect CDAs with skew polynomial rings via the following:

Lemma 2. *Let $[L : K] = d$ and $\langle\theta\rangle = \text{Gal}(L/K)$. Then $\Lambda \cong \mathcal{O}_L[u, \theta]/(u^d - \gamma)$.*

Proof. We define a map $\varphi : \mathcal{O}_L[u, \theta] \to \Lambda$ via

$$g(u) \mapsto g'(u) := g(u) \bmod (u^d - \gamma) \mapsto g',$$

where $g(u) = g_0 + ug_1 + ... + u^{k-1}g_{k-1}$ is a skew polynomial in $\mathcal{O}_L[u, \theta]$ and $g' \in \Lambda$ has coefficients g'_i, $i = 0, ..., d-1$. This map is surjective, since any element of Λ can be written $g = g_0 + ug_1 + ... + u^{d-1}g_{d-1}$ with coefficients in $\mathcal{O}_L$, so $\varphi(g_0 + ug_1 + ... + u^{d-1}g_{d-1}) = g$ trivially. Let $x \in \ker(\varphi)$, so $\varphi(x) = 0$. This means $g'(u) = 0$, since the second map sends the u^i-coefficients of the skew polynomial to the u^i-coefficients of the element of Λ, so an element of the kernel is in the ideal generated by $u^d - \gamma$ in $\mathcal{O}_L[u, \theta]$. This ideal is two-sided, as $u^d - \gamma$ is central, so $\mathcal{O}_L[u, \theta]/(u^d - \gamma)$ is a ring, and we obtain an isomorphism o rings.   □

When $K = \mathbb{Q}(\zeta_m)$ is the mth cyclotomic field, L/K is such that $\mathrm{Gal}(L/K)$ is cyclic, and $\gamma \in \mathcal{O}_K^\times$ with $\gamma \notin N_{L/K}(L^\times)$, then Λ is a maximal order in a CDA [9]. This enables us to connect SPLWE, CLWE and SMPLWE (defined below).

CLWE. In [9], an LWE problem was defined in Λ via the CLWE distribution. We state a version in which a and s are sampled from Λ. Below $L_\mathbb{R} := L \otimes \mathbb{R}$.

Definition 13. Let L/K be a Galois extension of number fields with $[L : K] = d$ and $\mathrm{Gal}(L/K)$ cyclic, generated by θ. Let $\mathcal{A} := (L/K, \theta, \gamma)$ be the resulting cyclic K-algebra with element u such that $u^d = \gamma \in \mathcal{O}_K$ and γ satisfying the non-norm condition. Let Λ be the natural order of $\mathcal{A}$. For an error distribution ψ over $\bigoplus_{i=0}^{d-1} u^i L_\mathbb{R}$, $q \geq 2$, and secret $s \in \Lambda_q$, a sample from the CLWE distribution $\Pi_{q,s,\psi}$ is obtained by sampling $a \leftarrow \Lambda_q$ uniformly at random, $e \leftarrow \psi$, and outputting $(a, b) = (a, a \cdot s + e \bmod q\Lambda) \in \left(\Lambda_q, \bigoplus_{i=0}^{d-1} u^i L_\mathbb{R}/q\Lambda\right)$.

Definition 14. Let Υ be a family of error distributions and let U_Λ be the uniform distribution on $\left(\Lambda_q, \left(\bigoplus_{i=0}^{d-1} u^i L_\mathbb{R}\right)/q\Lambda\right)$. The decision CLWE problem DCLWE$_{q,s,\psi}$ is, given a number of independent samples from $\Pi_{q,s,\psi}$ for a random pair $(s, \psi) \leftarrow U(\Lambda_q) \times \Upsilon$ or from U_Λ, to decide which with non-negligible advantage.

The hardness of DCLWE was proven in [9] under the canonical embedding[1]. Unlike in that work, here we consider CLWE under the coefficient embedding. This currently lacks a formal security proof, but as explained in the introduction, there is good reason to consider DCLWE a 'hard' problem.

6   The Middle Product for Skew Polynomials

We now define a middle product for skew polynomials. This middle product again takes two (skew) polynomials, multiplies them together, then discards the lower and higher coefficients, forming a (skew) polynomial whose coefficients are the 'middle' part of the product. Below, $\mathcal{R}$ is a ring.

---

[1] We note here that the reduction required a restriction of the secret space.

Definition 15. Let $d_a, d_b, d, k \in \mathbb{Z}_{\geq 0}$ such that $d_a + d_b - 1 = d + 2k$. The middle-product of $a \in \mathcal{R}^{<d_a}[u, \theta]$ and $b \in \mathcal{R}^{<d_b}[u, \theta]$ is defined

$$\odot_d : \mathcal{R}^{<d_a}[u, \theta] \times \mathcal{R}^{<d_b}[u, \theta] \to \mathcal{R}^{<d}[u, \theta],$$

$$(a, b) \mapsto a \odot_d b = \left\lfloor \frac{(a \cdot b) \bmod u^{k+d}}{u^k} \right\rfloor.$$

We now define skew middle product learning with errors, over $\mathcal{O}_L$:

Definition 16. (SMPLWE distribution) Let $n, d > 0, q \geq 2$, and χ be a distribution over $L_{\mathbb{R}}^{\leq d}[u, \theta]$. For $s \in \mathcal{O}_{L_q}^{<n+d-1}[u, \theta]$, define the distribution $\mathrm{SMP}_{q,s,n,d,\chi}$ over $\mathcal{O}_{L_q}^{<n}[u, \theta] \times L_{\mathbb{R}_q}^{\leq d}[u, \theta]$ as the distribution obtained from sampling $a \leftarrow U\left(\mathcal{O}_{L_q}^{<n}[u, \theta]\right)$, $e \leftarrow \chi$ and outputting $(a, b = a \odot_d s + e)$.

Definition 17. (decision SMPLWE) Let $n, d > 0, q \geq 2$, and χ be a distribution over $L_{\mathbb{R}}^{\leq d}[u, \theta]$. Then decision SMPLWE, $\mathrm{SMPLWE}_{q,s,n,d,\chi}$, consists in distinguishing between arbitrarily many samples from $\mathrm{SMP}_{q,s,n,d,\chi}$ and the same number of samples from $U\left(\mathcal{O}_{L_q}^{<n}[u, \theta] \times L_{\mathbb{R}_q}^{\leq d}[u, \theta]\right)$, with non-negligible probability over $s \leftarrow U\left(\mathcal{O}_{L_q}^{<n+d-1}[u, \theta]\right)$.

We now prove two lemmas:

Lemma 3. Let $d, k > 0$, $r \in \mathcal{O}_L^{<k+1}[u, \theta]$, $a \in \mathcal{O}_L^{<k+d}[u, \theta]$, and $b = r \odot_d a$. Let θ be an L-automorphism of order d. We have $\mathbf{b} = \mathrm{GToep}^{d,k+1}(r) \cdot \mathbf{a}$.

Proof. We can write $r \odot_d a = \sum_{i=0}^{d-1} u^i(\sum_{j+l=i+k} \theta^l(r_j)a_l)$. Thus

$$\mathbf{b} = \left(\theta^k(r_0)a_k + \theta^{k-1}(r_1)a_{k-1} + \ldots + r_k a_0,\right.$$

$$\theta^{k+1}(r_0)a_{k+1} + \theta^k(r_1)a_k + \ldots + \theta(r_k)a_1,$$

$$\ldots, \theta^{k+d-1}(r_0)a_{k+d-1} + \theta^{k+d-2}(r_1)a_{k+d-2} + \ldots + \theta^{d-1}(r_k)a_{d-1}).$$

and this is precisely $\mathrm{GToep}^{d,k+1}(r) \cdot \mathbf{a}$. and the result follows. $\square$

Lemma 4. *(associativity)* Let $d, k, n > 0$. For $r \in \mathcal{O}_L^{<k+1}[u, \theta]$, $a \in \mathcal{O}_L^{<n}[u, \theta]$, and $s \in \mathcal{O}_L^{<n+d+k-1}[u, \theta]$, we have $\theta^{n-1}(r) \odot_d (a \odot_{d+k} s) = (r \cdot a) \odot_d s$.

Proof. First, observe that the left hand side and right hand side have the same degree. Let the vector of $(r \cdot a) \odot_d s$ be denoted by $\mathbf{u}$, that of $\theta^{n-1}(r) \odot_d (a \odot_{d+k} s)$ by $\mathbf{v}$, and that of $a \odot_{d+k} s$ by $\mathbf{w}$.

For $d, k > 0$, and $r \in \mathcal{O}_L^{<k+1}[u, \theta]$, set $\mathrm{HToep}^{d,k+1}(r)$ to be the $d \times (k + d)$ matrix whose i, jth entry is given by $\theta^{k+d-j}((u^{i-1}r)_{j-1})$, where for polynomial f, $(f)_l$ denotes the lth coefficient of f, indexed from 0. This is the matrix such that $\overline{\mathbf{b}} = \mathrm{HToep}^{d,k+1}(r)\overline{\mathbf{a}}$ for $b = r \odot_d a$. We then have

$$\overline{\mathbf{v}} = \mathrm{HToep}^{d,k+1}(\theta^{n-1}(r)) \cdot \overline{\mathbf{w}} = \mathrm{HToep}^{d,k+1}(\theta^{n-1}(r)) \left(\mathrm{HToep}^{d+k,n}(a) \cdot \overline{\mathbf{s}}\right).$$

Moreover, $\bar{\mathbf{u}} = \mathrm{HToep}^{d,k+n}(r \cdot a) \cdot \bar{\mathbf{s}}$. The result follows from the property $\mathrm{HToep}^{d,k+1}(\theta^{n-1}(r))\,\mathrm{HToep}^{d+k,n}(a) = \mathrm{HToep}^{d,k+n}(r \cdot a)$. $\qquad\square$

We can view decision $\mathrm{SMPLWE}_{q,d,d,\chi}$ as a structured RLWE variant as follows: given polynomially many samples $(\mathrm{GToep}^{d,d}(a_i), \mathbf{b}_i) \in \mathcal{O}_{L_q}^{d \times (2d-1)} \times L_{\mathbb{R}_q}^d$ for uniform $a_i \leftarrow U\left(\mathcal{O}_{L_q}^{<d}[u,\theta]\right)$, decide if the $\mathbf{b}_i$ were sampled uniformly over the domain or have the form $\mathbf{b}_i = \mathrm{GToep}^{d,d}(a_i)\mathbf{s} + \mathbf{e}_i$ for some uniform $s \leftarrow U\left(\mathcal{O}_{L_q}^{<2d-1}[u,\theta]\right)$ and $e_i \leftarrow \chi$. Note the samples are correlated.

7   Reduction from SPLWE to SMPLWE

We adapt the reduction for standard MPLWE, under the coefficient embedding.

Theorem 1. *Let $d > 0, q \geq 2$, and χ a distribution over $L_{\mathbb{R}}^{<d}[u,\theta]$. Then there exists a ppt. reduction from $\mathrm{SPLWE}_{q,s,f,\chi}$ for any polynomial of the form $f(u) = u^d - \gamma \in \mathcal{O}_L[u,\theta]$ with $\gamma \in \mathcal{O}_K \setminus \{0\}$ coprime with q, to $\mathrm{SMPLWE}_{q,s,d,d,\chi'}$.*

Proof. Like in [19], we use an efficiently computable transformation ϕ that maps $(a_i, b_i) \in \mathcal{O}_{L_q}[u,\theta]/f \times L_{\mathbb{R}_q}[u,\theta]/f$ to $(a_i', b_i') \in \mathcal{O}_{L_q}^{<d}[u,\theta] \times L_{\mathbb{R}_q}^{<d}[u,\theta]$, sending $U\left(\mathcal{O}_{L_q}[u,\theta]/f \times L_{\mathbb{R}_q}[u,\theta]/f\right)$ to $U(\mathcal{O}_{L_q}^{<d}[u,\theta] \times L_{\mathbb{R}_q}^{<d}[u,\theta])$ and $\mathrm{SP}_{q,s,f,\chi}$ to $\mathrm{SMP}_{q,s',d,d,\chi'}$, for a new s' that is a function of s and a new distribution χ' that depends on χ and f. Given such a ϕ, the steps of the reduction are:

1. Sample a uniform $t \leftarrow U\left(\mathcal{O}_{L_q}^{<2d-1}[u,\theta]\right)$.
2. For each SPLWE sample (a_i, b_i), compute $(a_i, b_i') = \phi(a_i, b_i)$. Give $(a_i, b_i') + (0, \tilde{a}_i \odot_d t)$ to the SMPLWE oracle.
3. Return the output of the oracle.

For such a transformation ϕ, the reduction preserves the uniformity of uniform samples, and maps $\mathrm{SP}_{q,s,f,\chi}$ samples to $\mathrm{SMP}_{q,s'+t,d,d,M_{f,\theta}\cdot\chi}$ samples. When s is uniform, the $\mathrm{SMP}_{q,s'+t,d,d,M_{f,\theta}\cdot\chi}$ samples have a uniform $s' + t$.

To construct ϕ, let $(a_i, b_i) \in \mathcal{O}_{L_q}[u,\theta]/f \times L_{\mathbb{R}_q}[u,\theta]/f$ be a SPLWE sample. Let $\deg(f) = d$. Set $\phi(a_i, b_i) = (a_i, b_i')$ where b_i' is defined

$$\mathbf{b}_i' = M_{f,\theta} \cdot \mathbf{b}_i \in L_{\mathbb{R}_q}^{<d}[u,\theta].$$

Plainly a_i is uniform, by definition. Observe that if b_i is uniformly distributed, then so is its vector of coefficients $\mathbf{b}_i$. Moreover, since the matrix $M_{f,\theta}$ is invertible modulo q we find $M_{f,\theta} \cdot \mathbf{b}_i$ is also uniform.

Now write $b_i = a_i \cdot s + e_i$, for $s \in \mathcal{O}_{L_q}[u, \theta]/f$ and $e_i \leftarrow \chi$. Since $\mathrm{Rot}_f(b_i) = \mathrm{Rot}_f(a_i) \cdot \mathrm{Rot}_f(s) + \mathrm{Rot}_f(e_i)$, we have

$$
\begin{aligned}
M_{f,\theta} \cdot \mathbf{b}_i &= \mathrm{Rot}_f(b_i) \cdot (1, 0, .., 0)^T \\
&= (\mathrm{Rot}_f(a_i) \cdot \mathrm{Rot}_f(s) + \mathrm{Rot}_f(e_i)) \cdot (1, 0, ..., 0)^T \\
&= \mathrm{Rot}_f(a_i) \cdot \mathrm{Rot}_f(s) \cdot (1, 0, ..., 0)^T + \mathrm{Rot}_f(e_i) \cdot (1, 0, ..., 0)^T \\
&= \mathrm{Rot}_f(a_i) \cdot M_{f,\theta} \cdot \mathbf{s} + M_{f,\theta} \cdot \mathbf{e}_i \\
&= \mathrm{GToep}^{d,d}(\tilde{a}_i) \cdot N_f \cdot M_{f,\theta} \cdot \mathbf{s} + M_{f,\theta} \cdot \mathbf{e}_i \\
&= \mathrm{GToep}^{d,d}(\tilde{a}_i) \cdot \mathbf{s}' + M_{f,\theta} \cdot \mathbf{e}_i,
\end{aligned}
$$

where $\mathbf{s}' = N_f \cdot M_{f,\theta} \cdot \mathbf{s}$. Since $\mathbf{b}_i' = M_{f,\theta} \cdot \mathbf{b}_i = \mathrm{GToep}^{d,d}(\tilde{a}_i) \cdot \mathbf{s}' + M_{f,\theta} \cdot \mathbf{e}_i$, the new error is $\mathbf{e}_i' = M_{f,\theta} \cdot \mathbf{e}_i$, as required.   □

In order to remove dependence on the choice of γ, one can consider a family of polynomials $\mathcal{F}_\beta := \{f(u) = u^d - \gamma : |\gamma| \le \beta\}$. If $\chi = D_{\alpha q}$, then $\chi' = M_{f,\theta} \cdot D_{\alpha q}$. Expanding $M_{f,\theta}$ over $\mathbb{Z}$, since $M_{f,\theta}$ is invertible, we have $\chi' = D_{M_{f,\theta} \cdot (\alpha q I_{[L:\mathbb{Q}]})}$. Since the the square of the largest singular value $\|M_{f,\theta}\|^2 = |\gamma|^2$, then restricting to $f \in \mathcal{F}_\beta$, adding an error $e_i' \leftarrow D_\Sigma$ for a positive definite Σ such that $M_{f,\theta} \cdot e_i + e_i' \sim D_{\alpha q \beta}$ removes any dependence of the error on the choice of $f \in \mathcal{F}_\beta$.

8   Public Key Encryption Scheme

In this section we give an encryption scheme and prove its IND-CPA security. Let L/K be a cyclic Galois extension of degree d, $\mathrm{Gal}(L/K) = \langle \theta \rangle$, $[K : \mathbb{Q}] = n$, and q unramified in $\mathcal{O}_L$. The scheme uses the following error distribution: let $\chi = \lfloor D_{\alpha q} \rceil$ be a discretised Gaussian over $\mathcal{O}_L^{<d+k}[u, \theta]$, where coefficients are sampled from $D_{\alpha q}$, rounded to the nearest integer, and set as the $\mathbb{Z}$-coefficients of a skew polynomial in $\mathcal{O}_L^{<d+k}[u, \theta]$. Plaintexts are taken from $\mathcal{B}^{<d}[u, \theta]$, where $\mathcal{B} = \{a(x) \in \mathcal{O}_L : a_i \in \{0, 1\} \text{ for all } i\}$. We denote $\mathcal{B}^\times := \mathcal{B} \bmod q\mathcal{O}_L \cap \mathcal{O}_{L_q}^\times$. Ciphertexts will be elements of $\mathcal{O}_{L_q}^{<d+2k}[u, \theta] \times \mathcal{O}_{L_q}^{<d}[u, \theta]$.

Key Generation. To generate a key pair (pk, sk), begin by sampling $s \leftarrow U\left(\mathcal{O}_{L_q}^{<2(d+k)-1}[u, \theta]\right)$. Then for all $i \le t$, sample uniform $a_i \leftarrow U\left(\mathcal{O}_{L_q}^{<d+k}[u, \theta]\right)$ and errors $e_i \leftarrow \chi$, and set $b_i = a_i \odot_{d+k} s + 2 \cdot e_i \in \mathcal{O}_{L_q}^{<d+k}[u, \theta]$, $i = 1, ..., t$. The public key is $pk := (a_i, b_i)_{i \le t}$, and the secret key is $sk := s$.

Encryption. Given public key $pk = (a_i, b_i)_{i \le t}$ we encrypt a message $\mu \in \mathcal{B}^{<d}[u, \theta]$ as follows. We sample $r_i \leftarrow U\left(\mathcal{B}^{<k+1}[u, \theta]\right)$, $i = 1, ..., t$, replace the smallest non-zero $\mathcal{O}_L$-coefficient of each r_i with an element sampled uniformly from $\mathcal{B}^\times$, and output a ciphertext $c = (c_1, c_2) \in \mathcal{O}_{L_q}^{<d+2k}[u, \theta] \times \mathcal{O}_{L_q}^{<d}[u, \theta]$, where

$$
c_1 = \sum_{i \le t} r_i \cdot a_i, \text{ and } c_2 = \mu + \sum_{i \le t} \theta^{d+k-1}(r_i) \odot_d b_i
$$

Decryption. Given $sk = s$, to decrypt a ciphertext $c = (c_1, c_2)$, compute

$$\mu' := (c_2 - c_1 \odot_d s \bmod q) \bmod 2$$

We now show correctness.

Lemma 5. *Let* $\alpha < 1/(16\sqrt{ndt(k+1)})$ *and* $q \geq 16ndt(k+1)$. *With probability at least* $1 - nd^2 \cdot 2^{-\Omega(n)}$ *over valid key pairs* (pk, sk), *for all plaintexts* $\mu \in \mathcal{B}^{<d}[u, \theta]$ *and with probability 1 over the encryption randomness, decryption is correct.*

Proof. Suppose that $c = (c_1, c_2)$ is a ciphertext encrypting a message μ under a public key $pk = (a_i, b_i)_{i \leq t}$. Then to decrypt c we compute

$$c_2 - c_1 \odot_d s = \mu + \sum_{i \leq t} \theta^{d+k-1}(r_i) \odot_d b_i - \left(\sum_{i \leq t} r_i \cdot a_i\right) \odot_d s$$

$$= \mu + \sum_{i \leq t} \left(\theta^{d+k-1}(r_i) \odot_d (a_i \odot_{d+k} s + 2 \cdot e_i) - (r_i \cdot a_i) \odot_d s\right)$$

$$= \mu + \sum_{i \leq t} \theta^{d+k-1}(r_i) \odot_d (a_i \odot_{d+k} s) - (r_i \cdot a_i) \odot_d s + 2\theta^{d+k-1}(r_i) \odot_d e_i$$

$$= \mu + 2 \sum_{i \leq t} \theta^{d+k-1}(r_i) \odot_d e_i \bmod q$$

where the final equality holds by Lemma 4. Note that if

$$\left\| \mu + 2 \cdot \sum_{i \leq t} \theta^{d+k-1}(r_i) \odot_d e_i \right\|_\infty < q/2,$$

then $c_2 - c_1 \odot_d s \bmod q = \mu + 2 \cdot \sum_{i \leq t} \theta^{d+k-1}(r_i) \odot_d e_i$, so $c_2 - c_1 \odot_d s \bmod q \bmod 2 = \mu$. Similarly to [19, Lemma 4.1], the coefficients of $\sum_{i \leq t} \theta^{d+k-1}(r_i) \odot_d e_i$ can be written as an inner product between a binary $[\mathcal{O}_L : \mathbb{Z}]t(k+1)$-dimensional vector and a vector distributed according to $\lfloor D_{\alpha q} \rceil^{[\mathcal{O}_L : \mathbb{Z}]t(k+1)}$, so applying a (Gaussian) tail bound and the triangle inequality, the coefficients each have magnitude at most $\alpha q \sqrt{[\mathcal{O}_L : \mathbb{Z}]t(k+1)} + [\mathcal{O}_L : \mathbb{Z}]t(k+1)$ with probability at least $1 - 2^{-\Omega(n)}$. Thus $\|\mu + 2 \cdot \sum_{i \leq t} \theta^{d+k-1}(r_i) \odot_d e_i\|_\infty < 2\alpha q \sqrt{[\mathcal{O}_L : \mathbb{Z}]t(k+1)} + 2t[\mathcal{O}_L : \mathbb{Z}](k+1) + 1$ with probability at least $1 - d[\mathcal{O}_L : \mathbb{Z}]2^{-\Omega(n)}$. □

To show security of the above scheme, we demonstrate its IND-CPA security, assuming the hardness of SMPLWE, following [19]. We denote the set of r_i obtainable during the encryption procedure by $\overline{\mathcal{B}}^{<k+1}[u, \theta]$, and write $r_i \leftarrow \overline{\mathcal{B}}^{<k+1}[u, \theta]$.

Lemma 6. *Let* $q, k, d \geq 2$. *For* $b_i \in \mathcal{O}_{L_q}^{<d+k}[u, \theta]$, *let* h_{b_i} *denote the map that sends* $r_i \leftarrow \overline{\mathcal{B}}^{<k+1}[u, \theta]$ *to* $r_i \odot_d b_i \in \mathcal{O}_{L_q}^{<d}[u, \theta]$. *Then the hash function family* $\mathcal{H} = (h_{b_i})_{b_i}$ *is universal.*

Proof. Identical to [19, Lemma 4.2], included for completeness. It suffices to prove that for all $y \in \mathcal{O}_{L_q}^{<d}[u, \theta]$

$$\text{Pr}_{b_1}[r_1 \odot_d b_1 = y] = |\mathcal{O}_{L_q}|^{-d}.$$

Let j be the smallest integer such that the u^j-coefficient of r_1 is non-zero and let r_1 have ith coefficient $r_{1,i}$. Then $r_1 \odot_d b_1 = y$ restricted to entries $j, ..., j+d-1$ can be written as a triangular linear map with entries in $\{r_{1,j}, ..., r_{1,j+d-1}\}$ and $r_{1,j}$ along the diagonal, applied to the vector of d coefficients of b_1, up to application of θ. Since $r_{1,j}$ is invertible by construction, restricting the map $b_1 \mapsto r_1 \odot_d b_1$ to these d coefficients of b_1 is a bijection, which implies the result. $\square$

By linearity the hash function family $(h_{(b_i)_i})_{(b_i)_i}$ with $(b_i)_i \in \left(\mathcal{O}_{L_q}^{<d+k}[u, \theta]\right)^t$ and h_{b_i} mapping $(r_i)_{i \leq t} \leftarrow \left(\overline{\mathcal{B}}^{<k+1}[u, \theta]\right)^t$ to $\sum_i r_i \odot_d b_i$ is also universal.

Theorem 2. *Let $t \geq \frac{2+2(k+d)\log(q)}{k}$. Then the SMPLWE PKE scheme is IND-CPA secure, assuming the hardness of SMPLWE$_{q,d+k,d+k,D_{\alpha q}}$.*

Proof. We perform two hops from the IND-CPA experiment for SMPLWE to an experiment which we show to be of negligible statistical distance from our starting point. We first consider a variant of the IND-CPA experiment in which $pk = (a_i, b_i)_i$ is sampled uniformly. Assuming the hardness of decision SMPLWE, the probabilities that $\mathcal{A}$ outputs $b' = b$ in the IND-CPA experiment and in the variant experiment are negligibly close.

Now consider a second experiment. Suppose $pk = (a_i, b_i)_i$ is a valid public key, but instead of computing a valid ciphertext c encrypting μ_b under pk for $b \in \{0, 1\}$, $c = (c_1, c_2)$ is computed by the following process: sample uniform $r_i \leftarrow \overline{\mathcal{B}}^{<k+1}[u, \theta]$, $i = 1, ..., t$, sample a uniform $v \leftarrow U\left(\mathcal{O}_{L_q}^{<d}[u, \theta]\right)$, and set

$$(c_1, c_2) := \left(\sum_{i=1}^{t} r_i \cdot a_i, v\right)$$

Since v is independent of b, the probability that $\mathcal{A}$ outputs $b' = b$ is precisely $1/2$. We now show that the distributions of $((a_i, b_i)_i, c_1, c_2)$ in the two variant experiments are of negligible statistical distance from one another; that is, that

$$\Delta\left(\left((a_i, b_i)_i, \sum_{i \leq t} r_i \cdot a_i, \sum_{i \leq t} r_i \odot_d b_i\right), \left((a_i, b_i)_i, \sum_{i \leq t} r_i \cdot a_i, v\right)\right) \leq \text{neg}(n)$$

where a_i, b_i, r_i, and v are sampled uniformly from $\mathcal{O}_{L_q}^{<d+k}[u, \theta]$, $\mathcal{O}_{L_q}^{<d+k}[u, \theta]$, $\overline{\mathcal{B}}^{<k+1}[u, \theta]$ and $\mathcal{O}_{L_q}^{<d}[u, \theta]$ respectively, for $i = 1, ..., t$. Applying Lemma 1, since Lemma 6 showed the hash function family $(h_{b_i})_{b_i}$ is universal, and noting that

$\sum_{i \leq t} r_i \cdot a_i \in \mathcal{O}_{L_q}^{<d+2k}[u, \theta]$ which is of cardinality $|\mathcal{O}_{L_q}|^{d+2k}$, we find that the statistical distance above is upper bounded by $\frac{1}{2}\sqrt{\gamma(T) \cdot |Y| \cdot |Z|}$, where $X = (\overline{\mathcal{B}}^{<k+1}[u, \theta])^t$, $\gamma(T) = \max_{w \in X} \Pr[T = w] \leq |\mathcal{B}|^{-tk}$, $|Y| = |\mathcal{O}_{L_q}|^d$, and $|Z| = |\mathcal{O}_{L_q}|^{d+2k}$; so the upper bound is

$$\frac{1}{2}\left(|\mathcal{B}|^{-tk} \cdot |\mathcal{O}_{L_q}|^{2(d+k)}\right)^{1/2} = \frac{1}{2}\left(2^{-ndtk} \cdot q^{2nd(d+k)}\right)^{1/2}$$

If $t \geq \frac{2+2(k+d)\log(q)}{k}$ this becomes negligible in n. $\qquad\square$

9   Conclusion

We have introduced SMPLWE and SPLWE and reduced a family of problems based on the latter to the former. We have connected SPLWE and CLWE. We also gave a PKE scheme and proved its security under a reasonable assumption. Future work might include removing restrictions on the degrees of the polynomials involved, and obtaining greater functionality from the SMPLWE problem.

A   Skew Polynomial Rings

In this appendix we give a fuller explanation of the theory of skew polynomials.

Definition 18. Let R be a commutative ring. A polynomial in the indeterminate x with coefficients in R is an expression of the form

$$a_0 + a_1 x + ... + a_n x^n,$$

where x commutes with elements of R, $a_i \in R$ for $i = 0, ..., n$, and $n < \infty$.

We call n the degree of the polynomial, and if we label $f(x) = a_0 + a_1 x + ... + a_n x^n$, then we write $\deg(f) = n$. The set of polynomials with coefficients in R is denoted $R[x]$. This set has a ring structure, where addition is performed coefficient-wise (e.g. $a_0 + a_1 x + b_0 + b_1 x = a_0 + b_0 + (a_1 + b_1)x$) and multiplication is defined

$$(a_0 + a_1 x + ... + a_n x^n) \cdot (b_0 + b_1 x + ... + b_m x^m) = \sum_{k=0}^{n+m} \sum_{l=0}^{k} a_l b_{k-l} x^k$$

Definition 19. If R and S are two rings, we let $\mathrm{Hom}(R, S)$ denote the set of homomorphisms from R to S and $\mathrm{Iso}(R, S)$ the set of isomorphisms from R to S. If $R = S$, then we write $\mathrm{End}(R) = \mathrm{Hom}(R, R)$ for the endomorphisms of R and $\mathrm{Aut}(R) = \mathrm{Iso}(R, R)$ for the automorphisms of R.

Let $\mathbb{F}'$ be an algebraic field extension of $\mathbb{F}$. Then any $\mathbb{F}$-endomorphism of $\mathbb{F}'$ is an $\mathbb{F}$-automorphism of $\mathbb{F}'$.

The order of an endomorphism θ is the smallest integer d such that $\theta^d = \mathrm{id}$.

Examples

1. Let $\mathbb{C}$ denote the complex numbers and $\bar{\cdot}$ complex conjugation, that is, the map sending $a + ib \mapsto a - ib =: \overline{a + ib}$. Then $\bar{\cdot}$ is an automorphism of $\mathbb{C}$, and has order 2.

2. Let $\mathbb{F}_q$ be a finite extension of $\mathbb{F}_p$, the finite field of p elements. Then the map $a \mapsto a^p$ is an automorphism of $\mathbb{F}_q$, called the Frobenius map, denoted Frob_p. If $q = p^r$, Frob_p has order r.

3. Let $\mathbb{Q}(\sqrt{d})$ be a real quadratic extension of $\mathbb{Q}$ with defining polynomial $f(x) = x^2 - d$ for some $d \in \mathbb{N}$. Then the map τ sending $d \mapsto -d$ and fixing $\mathbb{Q}$ is an automorphism of $\mathbb{Q}(\sqrt{d})$ of order 2.

Definition 20. Let R be a ring and θ an endomorphism of R. Then expressions in the indeterminate x of the form

$$a_0 + a_1 x + \ldots + a_n x^n$$

where $xr = \theta(r)x$ for all $r \in R$, $a_i \in R$ for $i = 0, \ldots, n$, and $n < \infty$ are called skew polynomials.

The degree of a skew polynomial $f(x) = a_0 + a_1 x + \ldots + a_n x^n$ is n. We denote the set of skew polynomials with coefficients in R and indeterminate x defined by some endomorphism θ by $R[x, \theta]$. If θ is the identity map id, then $R[x, \mathrm{id}] = R[x]$.

Proposition 3. *Let R be a ring and $\theta \in \mathrm{End}(R)$. Then $R[x, \theta]$ is a ring.*

Proof. Addition is coefficient-wise (e.g. $a_0 + a_1 x + b_0 + b_1 x = a_0 + b_0 + (a_1 + b_1)x$). Multiplication is defined

$$(a_0 + a_1 x + \ldots + a_n x^n) \cdot (b_0 + b_1 x + \ldots + b_m x^m) = \sum_{k=0}^{n+m} \sum_{l=0}^{k} a_l \theta^l (b_{k-l}) x^k$$

The result follows from axiom checking. $\qquad\square$

Let R be an integral domain and θ be injective. Then $a_n \theta^n (b_m) \neq 0$ if $a_n, b_m \neq 0$, so the leading term of the product of $a_0 + a_1 x + \ldots + a_n x^n$ and $b_0 + b_1 x + \ldots + b_m x^m$ is non-zero. This allows us to generalise the notion of degree to skew polynomials. Thus when R is a domain and θ injective the degree of the above product is $n + m$ and the degree of the product of two skew polynomials is the sum of the degrees.

Examples

1. $\mathbb{C}[x, \bar{\cdot}]$. Write $\iota(\cdot) = \bar{\cdot}$ for convenience. We have

$$(a_0 + \ldots + a_n x^n) \cdot (b_0 + \ldots + b_m x^m) = \sum_{k=0}^{n+m} \sum_{l=0}^{k} a_l \iota^l (b_{k-l}) x^k$$

$$= \sum_{k=0}^{n+m} \left(\sum_{l \text{ even}} a_l b_{k-l} + \sum_{l \text{ odd}} a_l \overline{b_{k-l}} \right) x^k$$

2. $\mathbb{F}_{p^r}[x, \mathrm{Frob}_p]$. Then $(a_0 + \ldots + a_n x^n) \cdot (b_0 + \ldots + b_m x^m) = \sum_{k=0}^{n+m} \sum_{l=0}^{k} a_l b_{k-l}^{p^l} x^k$.

3. $\mathbb{Q}(\sqrt{d})[x, \tau]$. Then

$$(a_0 + \ldots + a_n x^n) \cdot (b_0 + \ldots + b_m x^m) = \sum_{k=0}^{n+m} \sum_{l=0}^{k} a_l \tau^l (b_{k-l}) x^k$$

$$= \sum_{k=0}^{n+m} \left(\sum_{l \text{ even}} a_l b_{k-l} + \sum_{l \text{ odd}} a_l \tau(b_{k-l}) \right) x^k$$

A left ideal $\mathcal{I}$ of a ring R is an additively closed subgroup which is closed under multiplication on the left from R, that is, $R\mathcal{I} \subset \mathcal{I}$. Right ideals are defined analogously. An ideal is principal if it is generated by a single element. We have

Proposition 4. *If R is an integral domain and θ is injective, then $R[x, \theta]$ is an integral domain. If K is a field and σ an endomorphism of K, then every left ideal of $K[x, \sigma]$ is principally generated.*

The above gives an analogous statement to the fact that a polynomial ring $K[x]$ over a (commutative) field K is a PID. A similar statement holds for right ideals.

Definition 21. Let R be a ring and $\theta \in \mathrm{End}(R)$. Then we call

$$R^\theta := \{y \in R : \theta(y) = y\}$$

the fixed ring of θ.

Note the above is a ring: $0, 1 \in R^\theta$, R^θ inherits associativity and distributivity from R, and is additively and multiplicatively closed by the properties of θ. If K is a field and $\sigma \in \mathrm{Aut}(K)$, K^σ is a subfield of K called the fixed field of σ.

Definition 22. The center $\mathcal{Z}(R)$ of a (noncommutative) ring R is the set of elements of R which commute with all other elements of R; that is,

$$\mathcal{Z}(R) := \{y \in R : yz = zy \text{ for all } z \in R\}$$

It is clear that $\mathcal{Z}(R)$ is a commutative subring of R. The following describes the center of a skew polynomial ring:

Proposition 5. *Let R be a ring and $\theta \in \mathrm{End}(R)$ have finite order d. Then the center of $R[x, \theta]$ is given by $\mathcal{Z}(R[x, \theta]) = \mathcal{Z}(R)[x^d]$. If θ has infinite order, then $\mathcal{Z}(R[x, \theta]) = \mathcal{Z}(R)$.*

A central element z generates a two-sided ideal, since $Rz = zR$ by definition.

Examples

1. $\mathcal{Z}(\mathbb{C}[x, \bar{\ }])$. The fixed field of $\bar{\ }$ is $\mathbb{R}$, since $\overline{a + i \cdot 0} = \bar{a} = a$. Since $\bar{\ }$ has order two, we find $\mathcal{Z}(\mathbb{C}[x, \bar{\ }]) = \mathbb{R}[x^2]$.

216   C. Ling and A. Mendelsohn

2. $\mathcal{Z}(\mathbb{F}_{p^r}[x,\mathrm{Frob}_p])$. The fixed field of Frob_p is $\mathbb{F}_p$ and Frob_p has order r, so we find $\mathcal{Z}(\mathbb{F}_{p^r}[x,\mathrm{Frob}_p]) = \mathbb{F}_p[x^r]$.

3. $\mathcal{Z}(\mathbb{Q}(\sqrt{d})[x,\tau])$. Since $\mathbb{Q}(\sqrt{d})^\tau = \mathbb{Q}$ and $\tau^2 = \mathrm{id}$, $\mathcal{Z}(\mathbb{Q}(\sqrt{d})[x,\tau]) = \mathbb{Q}[x^2]$.

We briefly consider some further properties of skew polynomial rings. We first note that Hilbert's basis theorem holds:

Theorem 3. *Let R be a Noetherian ring, θ an automorphism of R, and $S = R[x,\theta]$. Then S is Noetherian.*

Let K be an algebraic number field Galois over $\mathbb{Q}$ and $\mathcal{O}_K$ the ring of integers of K. The $\mathbb{Q}$-automorphisms of K restrict to endomorphisms of $\mathcal{O}_K$, so we can consider the skew polynomial ring $\mathcal{O}_K[x,\theta]$ where $\theta \in \mathrm{Gal}(K/\mathbb{Q})$. Since $\mathcal{O}_K$ is Noetherian, by the theorem so is $\mathcal{O}_K[x,\theta]$.

Let $f, g \in R[x,\theta]$. We say g is a left divisor of f if $f = gh$ for some $h \in R[x,\theta]$. A skew polynomial f is irreducible if all its left divisors are either units or skew polynomials of the same degree as f. Then

Theorem 4. *[16] Let $f_1, ..., f_n$, $g_1, ..., g_m$ be irreducible skew polynomials such that $f_1 \cdot ... \cdot f_n = g_1 \cdot ... \cdot g_m$. Then $n = m$ and $\deg(f_i) = \deg(g_{\pi(i)})$ for some permutation π and $i = 1, ..., n$.*

We can consider quotients of skew polynomial rings. If $\mathcal{I}$ is a left ideal of $R[x,\theta]$, then $R[x,\theta]/\mathcal{I}$ is a left $R[x,\theta]$-module, since if $f(x), g(x) \in R[x,\theta]$

$$f(x)(g(x) + \mathcal{I}) = f(x)g(x) + f(x)\mathcal{I} \subset f(x)g(x) + \mathcal{I}$$

If $\mathcal{I}$ is a two-sided ideal, then $R[x,\theta]/\mathcal{I}$ is a ring:

$$(f(x) + \mathcal{I})(g(x) + \mathcal{I}) = f(x)g(x) + \mathcal{I}g(x) + f(x)\mathcal{I} + \mathcal{I}^2 \subset f(x)g(x) + \mathcal{I}$$

When K is a field, every ideal is principally generated, and so if $z \in \mathcal{Z}(K[x,\sigma])$, then $K[x,\sigma]/zK[x,\sigma]$ is a ring.

Examples

1. Note that $x^2 + \pi \in \mathcal{Z}(\mathbb{C}[x,\bar{\ }])$, so $\mathbb{C}[x,\bar{\ }]/(x^2+\pi)\mathbb{C}[x,\bar{\ }]$ is a ring.

2. Since $x^{r^2}+1 \in \mathcal{Z}(\mathbb{F}_{p^r}[x,\mathrm{Frob}_p])$, $\mathbb{F}_{p^r}[x,\mathrm{Frob}_p]/(x^{r^2}+1)\mathbb{F}_{p^r}[x,\mathrm{Frob}_p]$ is a ring.

3. Note that $x^8 + 1 \in \mathcal{Z}(\mathbb{Q}(\sqrt{d})[x,\tau])$, so $\mathbb{Q}(\sqrt{d})[x,\tau]/(x^8+1)\mathbb{Q}(\sqrt{d})[x,\tau]$ is a ring.

B   On the Equivalence of Embeddings for CLWE

In [6,20] instances of number fields were given for which the distortion induced by mapping between the canonical and the coefficient embedding was polynomially bounded, impyling a polynomial-time equivalence between solving RLWE in those fields and solving the corresponding PLWE instances. They achieved this by bounding Frobenius norm of the map V_f which sends the canonical embedding of an element x to a coefficient representation of x, that is

$$\sigma_L(x) = V_f \cdot \operatorname{coeff}(x),$$

where $\operatorname{coeff}(\cdot)$ is the vector of coefficients of $x \in \mathbb{Z}[x]/f(x)$ and σ_L is the canonical embedding. In this appendix, we give examples of CDAs for which the coefficient representation of an algebra element is only polynomially distorted by mapping it into canonical space. These instances were studied in [13].

In particular, we consider CDAs obtained from quadratic extensions of power-of-two conductor cyclotomic fields $K = \mathbb{Q}(\zeta_{2^r})$, obtained by adjoining $\sqrt{\ell}$ to K, where $\ell > 2$ is prime and satisfies $\ell \equiv 1 \bmod 2^r$, $\ell \not\equiv 1 \bmod 2^{r+1}$. Then $\mathcal{A} = (L/K, \theta, \zeta_n)$ is a CDA and Λ is a maximal order in $\mathcal{A}$, with $L = \mathbb{Q}(\zeta_{2^r}, \sqrt{\ell})$.

Write $m = 2^r$ and $n = 2^{r-1}$. We then define the powerful basis of $\mathcal{O}_L$:

$$\overrightarrow{p} := (1, \zeta_m, ..., \zeta_m^{n-1}, \frac{1 + \sqrt{\ell}}{2}, \zeta_m \frac{1 + \sqrt{\ell}}{2}, ..., \zeta_m^{n-1} \frac{1 + \sqrt{\ell}}{2})$$

From this we obtain a matrix in $\mathbb{R}^{n \times n}$ by applying the canonical embedding to the entries of $\overrightarrow{p}$:

$$\sigma_L(\overrightarrow{p}) = \left(\sigma_L(1), ..., \sigma_L(\zeta_m^{n-1}), \sigma_L\left(\frac{1 + \sqrt{\ell}}{2}\right), ..., \sigma_L\left(\zeta_m^{n-1} \frac{1 + \sqrt{\ell}}{2}\right) \right)$$

It can be checked that $\sigma_L(x) = \sigma_L(\overrightarrow{p}) \cdot \operatorname{coeff}(x)$. This implies that $\|\sigma_L(x)\| \leq s_1(\sigma_L(\overrightarrow{p})) \cdot \|x\|_{\overrightarrow{p}}$, where $\| \cdot \|_{\overrightarrow{p}}$ denotes taking the ℓ_2-norm of the coefficient vector of an element expressed in the basis $\overrightarrow{p}$, and $s_1(\sigma_L(\overrightarrow{p}))$ is the largest singular value of $\sigma_L(\overrightarrow{p})$. Labelling the smallest singular value by $s_{2n}(\cdot)$, we have

Proposition 6. [13, Proposition 1] Let $n = 2^{r-1}$, $\ell \equiv 1 \bmod 2^r$ a prime, and $L = \mathbb{Q}(\zeta_{2^r}, \sqrt{\ell})$. Then, using the powerful basis of $\mathcal{O}_L$, we have

$$s_1(\overrightarrow{p}) = \frac{\sqrt{n}}{2} \sqrt{\ell + 5 + \sqrt{\ell^2 - 6\ell + 25}},$$

$$s_{2n}(\overrightarrow{p}) = \frac{\sqrt{n}}{2} \sqrt{\ell + 5 - \sqrt{\ell^2 - 6\ell + 25}}.$$

Therefore for bounded values of ℓ, say $\ell = \mathrm{poly}(n)$, the singular values are also polynomial in n. Bounding the $s_i(\sigma_L(\overrightarrow{p}))$ allows us to bound V_f.

The above can be extended to Λ: considering an element $x = x_0 + ux_1$ with $x_i \in \mathcal{O}_L$, $i = 0, 1$, we let the canonical embedding extend coefficient-wise for $\sigma_{\mathcal{A}}(x) := (\sigma_L(x_0), \sigma_L(x_1))$ and find that

$$V_\Lambda = \begin{pmatrix} \sigma_L(\overrightarrow{p}) & \mathbf{0} \\ \mathbf{0} & \sigma_L(\overrightarrow{p}) \end{pmatrix}$$

sends $\mathrm{coeff}(x) = (\mathrm{coeff}(x_0), \mathrm{coeff}(x_1))$ to $\sigma_{\mathcal{A}}(x)$. The singular values of this matrix are simply the singular values of $\sigma_L(\overrightarrow{p})$ multiplied by $\sqrt{2}$. As before, if $\ell = \mathrm{poly}(n)$, we find that the singular values of the above are polynomial in n, and similarly for V_Λ^{-1}.

References

1. Ajtai, M.: Generating hard instances of lattice problems. Electron. Colloquium Comput. Complex. TR96 (1996). https://doi.org/10.1145/237814.237838
2. Albert, A.: Structure of Algebras, AMS colloquium publications, vol. 24. American Mathematical Society (1939)
3. Augot, D., Loidreau, P., Robert, G.: Generalized gabidulin codes over fields of any characteristic. Des. Codes Cryptogr. **86**(8), 1807–1848 (2018). https://doi.org/10.1007/s10623-017-0425-6
4. Bai, S., Boudgoust, K., Das, D., Roux-Langlois, A., Wen, W., Zhang, Z.: Middle-product learning with rounding problem and its applications. In: Galbraith, S.D., Moriai, S. (eds.) ASIACRYPT 2019. LNCS, vol. 11921, pp. 55–81. Springer, Cham (2019). https://doi.org/10.1007/978-3-030-34578-5_3
5. Bai, S., et al.: MPSign: a signature from small-secret middle-product learning with errors. In: Kiayias, A., Kohlweiss, M., Wallden, P., Zikas, V. (eds.) PKC 2020. LNCS, vol. 12111, pp. 66–93. Springer, Cham (2020). https://doi.org/10.1007/978-3-030-45388-6_3
6. Blanco-Chacón, I.: On the RLWE/PLWE equivalence for cyclotomic number fields. Appl. Algebra Eng. Commun. Comput. **33**, 53–71 (2022). https://doi.org/10.1007/s00200-020-00433-z
7. Caruso, X., Le Borgne, J.: Fast multiplication for skew polynomials. In: Burr, M., Yap, C.K., Din, M.S.E. (eds.) ISSAC 2017, pp. 77–84. Association for Computing Machinery (2017). https://doi.org/10.1145/3087604.3087617
8. Giorgi, P.: A probabilistic algorithm for verifying polynomial middle product in linear time. Inf. Process. Lett. **139**, 30–34 (2018). https://doi.org/10.1016/j.ipl.2018.06.014
9. Grover, C., Mendelsohn, A., Ling, C., Vehkalahti, R.: Non-commutative ring learning with errors from cyclic algebras. J. Cryptol. **35**(3), 22 (2022). https://doi.org/10.1007/s00145-022-09430-6
10. Hanrot, G., Quercia, M., Zimmermann, P.: The middle product algorithm I. Appl. Algebra Eng. Commun. Comput. **14**(6), 415–438 (2004). https://doi.org/10.1007/s00200-003-0144-2
11. Huffman, W., Kim, J., Solé, P.: Concise Encyclopedia of Coding Theory. CRC Press, Boca Raton (2021)

12. Katz, J., Lindell, Y.: Introduction to Modern Cryptography, 2nd Edition. Chapman & Hall/CRC Cryptography and Network Security Series, Taylor & Francis (2014)

13. Ling, C., Mendelsohn, A.: NTRU in quaternion algebras of bounded discriminant. In: Johansson, T., Smith-Tone, D. (eds.) PQCrypto 2023. LNCS, vol. 14154, pp. 256–290. Springer Nature, Switzerland (2023). https://doi.org/10.1007/978-3-031-40003-2_10

14. Lombardi, A., Vaikuntanathan, V., Vuong, T.: Lattice trapdoors and IBE from middle-product LWE. In: Hofheinz, D., Rosen, A. (eds.) TCC 2019. LNCS, vol. 11891, pp. 24–54. Springer International Publishing, Cham (2019). https://doi.org/10.1007/978-3-030-36030-6_2

15. Lyubashevsky, V., Peikert, C., Regev, O.: On ideal lattices and learning with errors over rings. In: Gilbert, H. (ed.) EUROCRYPT 2010. LNCS, vol. 6110, pp. 1–23. Springer, Berlin Heidelberg (2010). https://doi.org/10.1007/978-3-642-13190-5_1

16. Ore, O.: Theory of non-commutative polynomials. Ann. Math. **34**(3), 480–508 (1933). http://www.jstor.org/stable/1968173

17. Peikert, C., Pepin, Z.: Algebraically structured LWE, revisited. In: Hofheinz, D., Rosen, A. (eds.) TCC 2019. LNCS, vol. 11891, pp. 1–23. Springer International Publishing, Cham (2019). https://doi.org/10.1007/978-3-030-36030-6_1

18. Regev, O.: On lattices, learning with errors, random linear codes, and cryptography. J. ACM. **56**, 1–40 (2009). https://doi.org/10.1145/1568318

19. Rosca, M., Sakzad, A., Stehlé, D., Steinfeld, R.: Middle-product learning with errors. In: Katz, J., Shacham, H. (eds.) CRYPTO 2017. LNCS, vol. 10403, pp. 283–297. Springer International Publishing, Cham (2017). https://doi.org/10.1007/978-3-319-63697-9_10

20. Rosca, M., Stehlé, D., Wallet, A.: On the Ring-LWE and Polynomial-LWE problems. In: Nielsen, J., Rijmen, V. (eds.) EUROCRYPT 2018. LNCS, vol. 10820, pp. 146–173. Springer International Publishing, Cham (2018). https://doi.org/10.1007/978-3-319-78381-9_6

21. Shor, P.W.: Algorithms for quantum computation: discrete logarithms and factoring. In: 35th FOCS, pp. 124–134. IEEE Computer Society Press, November 1994

22. Stehlé, D., Steinfeld, R., Tanaka, K., Xagawa, K.: Efficient public key encryption based on ideal lattices. In: Matsui, M. (ed.) ASIACRYPT 2009. LNCS, vol. 5912, pp. 617–635. Springer, Berlin, Heidelberg (2009). https://doi.org/10.1007/978-3-642-10366-7_36

23. Steinfeld, R., Sakzad, A., Zhao, R.K.: Practical MP-LWE-based encryption balancing security-risk versus efficiency. Des. Codes Cryptogr. **87**, 2847–2884 (2019). https://doi.org/10.1007/s10623-019-00654-5

Identity-Based Threshold Signatures from Isogenies

Shahla Atapoor[✉] [iD]

COSIC, KU Leuven, Leuven, Belgium
shahla.atapoor@kuleuven.be

Abstract. The identity-based signature, initially introduced by Shamir [26], plays a fundamental role in the domain of identity-based cryptography. It offers the capability to generate a signature on a message, allowing any user to verify the authenticity of the signature using the signer's identifier information (e.g., an email address), instead of relying on a public key stored in a digital certificate. Another significant concept in practical applications is the threshold signature, which serves as a valuable tool for distributing the signing authority. The notion of an identity-based threshold signature scheme pertains to the distribution of a secret key associated with a specific identity among multiple entities, rather than depending on a master secret key generated by a public key generator. This approach enables a qualified group of participants to jointly engage in the signing process. In this paper, we present two identity-based threshold signature schemes based on isogenies, each of which addresses a different aspect of security. The first scheme prioritizes efficiency but offers security with abort, while the second scheme focuses on robustness. Both schemes ensure active security in the quantum random oracle model. To build these identity-based threshold signatures, we begin by modifying the identity-based signature scheme proposed by Shaw and Dutta [27], to accommodate the CSI-SharK signature scheme. Subsequently, we leverage the resulting identity-based signature and build two threshold schemes within the CSIDH (Commutative Supersingular Isogeny Diffie-Hellman) framework. Our proposed identity-based threshold signatures are designed based on CSI-SharK and can be easily adapted with minimal adjustments to function with CSI-FiSh.

Keywords: Identity-based signature · Identity-based threshold signature · Isogeny-based cryptography · CSI-SharK · CSI-FiSh · CSIDH

1 Introduction

In recent years, there has been a notable surge of interest in identity-based cryptography, initially introduced by Shamir [26]. The rationale behind this heightened attention lies in its remarkable advantages over conventional certificate-based cryptography, primarily due to its ability to circumvent the arduous certificate management procedures inherent in the latter approach. Identity-based

© The Author(s), under exclusive license to Springer Nature Switzerland AG 2024
E. A. Quaglia (Ed.): IMACC 2023, LNCS 14421, pp. 220–240, 2024.
https://doi.org/10.1007/978-3-031-47818-5_12

identification serves as a fundamental element in identity-based cryptography, which was initially proposed in 2004 by Bellare et al. [6] and Kurosawa et al. [22] as separate endeavors. In an identification scheme based on identity, each user designates their identity, such as an email address, as their public key. The Public Key Generator (e.g., a dealer) generates the corresponding secret key for the user's identity by utilizing its master secret key. Subsequently, the user, assuming the role of a prover, can employ this secret key to establish its identity to a verifier who possesses the associated public key.

Shamir in the same work [26] introduced the concept of an IDentity-based Signature (IDS) scheme. This innovation garnered significant attention and later gained further prominence through the Fiat-Shamir transformation [17]. The advent of IDS schemes brought a fresh perspective to the field, as they enabled users to sign messages instead of merely authenticating their identities [19,20]. Consequently, the verification process became the responsibility of the verifier, who checks the validity of the signature. On the other hand, due to a wide range of applications (e.g., in blockchains), threshold signature schemes have received more attention in recent years. Such schemes allow distributing the secret key into shares among multiple parties or devices, such that only a set of authorized parties can jointly sign a message to produce a single signature. Key recovery attacks on threshold signature schemes require more effort than on the non-threshold ones, as the adversary has to attack more than one device or party simultaneously. In the realm of IDS, Baek and Zheng [4], for the first time, introduced the concept of secret sharing among multiple parties. They devised an IDentity-based THreshold Signature (IDTHS) that uses bilinear pairings.

An illustrative application of the IDTHS scheme can be envisioned in the following scenario: Let us consider Alice, who serves as the president of a company. In this capacity, she has established an identity that represents the company and possesses a private key associated with this identity. Through the utilization of this private key, Alice can affix her signature to various documents. However, she harbors concerns regarding situations where she may be physically absent. Consequently, she desires to delegate this signing authority to a set of signature-generation servers. By employing this arrangement, signatures for a given message can be collectively generated by these servers. Importantly, any user can successfully verify the resulting signature using the company's publicly accessible identity, provided that the user obtains a specific number of partial signatures from the signature-generation servers.

After Shor's quantum attack [28] on the Factoring and Discrete Logarithm (DL) problems, a new wave of investigation emerged among researchers. Their focus shifted towards the exploration of post-quantum cryptographic techniques capable of constructing protocols resilient against the formidable threat posed by quantum adversaries. One prominent avenue of inquiry in this domain revolves around isogeny-based cryptography. The concept of employing isogenies as a cryptographic foundation was initially introduced by Couveignes [12], followed by the notable works of Rostovtsev and Stolbunov [25,30]. These scholars embarked upon devising innovative methods to build cryptographic scheme based on isogenies that could achieve post-quantum security. In [24], Peng et al. introduced an IDTHS scheme based on isogenies that accounts for post-quantum security concerns. Their scheme is built based on CSI-FiSh signature [9]. In 2021, Shaw and Dutta [27] analysed Peng et al.'s scheme and uncovered vulnerabilities in both the IDS scheme itself and its underlying trapdoor samplable relation. Then, Shaw and Dutta [27] presented a fixed version of their construction.

Our Contribution. We first modify the CSI-FiSh-based IDS of Shaw and Dutta [27] to work with the CSI-SharK scheme, which was recently proposed by Atapoor et al. [2] and shown to outperform CSI-FiSh in the threshold setting. This translation allows us to leverage the properties of CSI-SharK, and obtain a new IDS from isogenies that has considerably shorter master secret key in comparison with the original scheme [27].

Next, we use the resulting IDS scheme and propose two IDTHS schemes based on isogenies, each of which addresses a different aspect of security. Both protocols are designed to achieve active security, ensuring the security of the protocol even in the scenarios where parties are malicious and deviate from honest protocol execution. In our initial threshold signature scheme, honest parties have the ability to detect any misbehaviour from malicious entities, resulting in the termination of the protocol execution. However, it is important to note that this protocol only achieves active security with abort and identification of the adversary remains unattainable.

To deal with the above concern, as the next contribution, we propose a robust scheme, which additionally guarantees the correctness of final output. The second threshold signature scheme ensures security against active adversaries and achieves robustness, thereby enabling the identification and expulsion of any malicious party responsible for protocol malfunctions or misconduct. The remaining parties then collaboratively reconstruct the compromised party's secret, facilitating the seamless continuation and completion of the protocol, ultimately yielding the final signature. Our technique to achieve robustness is inspired from the construction of ThreshER SharK signature scheme [3]. ThreshER SharK is a threshold, efficient and robust signature scheme that recently is proposed by Atapoor et al. [3] and is built on top of CSI-SharK signature scheme [2]. To achieve robustness, the distributed signing protocol needs to be run by all the parties, rather than a qualified set of them. Therefore, our second construction is less efficient in comparison with the first one, but it can achieve robustness.

Organization. Section 2 presents some preliminaries which will be used in the follow-up sections. In Sect. 3, we adapt the CSI-FiSh based IDS scheme of Shaw and Dutta [27] to work with the CSI-SharK scheme [2]. In Sect. 4, we present the first IDTHS based on isogenies with abort. In Sect. 5, we propose the first robust IDTHS scheme based on isogenies. We conclude the paper in Sect. 6.

2 Preliminaries

Next, we provide an overview of several key concepts, which are used in the follow-up sections. Some of them are provided in the full version of the paper [1].

Notation. We use the notation $x \leftarrow X$ to represent the assignment of a uniformly random value to the variable x from the set X, assuming a uniform distribution over X. If $\mathcal{D}$ is a probability distribution over a set X, we indicate the assignment $x \leftarrow \mathcal{D}$ as the process of sampling from the set X according to the distribution $\mathcal{D}$. The concatenation of strings s_1 and s_2 is represented by $s_1 \| s_2$. When referring to a probabilistic polynomial-time (PPT) algorithm as A, the notation $a \leftarrow A$ represents the assignment of the output of A, where the probability distribution is over the random tape of A. Furthermore, we denote $\mathbb{Z}_N$ as the set of integers modulo N, expressed as $\mathbb{Z}/N\mathbb{Z}$. The function $\log(x)$ is defined as the logarithm of x with base 2.

2.1 Isogeny-Based Cryptography

Isogenies are rational maps between elliptic curves that are also homomorphisms with respect to the natural group structure on these curves. Our investigation is limited to the set $\mathcal{E}$ of supersingular elliptic curves over prime fields $\mathbb{F}_p$ and separable $\mathbb{F}_p$-rational isogenies defined between them (the so-called CSIDH setting). Isogenies from an elliptic curve to itself are called endomorphisms. Under the addition and composition operations, the endomorphisms of elliptic curves form a ring. The subring of $\mathbb{F}_p$-rational endomorphism rings of curves in $\mathcal{E}$ is always isomorphic to an order $\mathcal{O}$ in the quadratic imaginary field $\mathbb{Q}(\sqrt{-p})$. Separable isogenies are uniquely defined by their kernel, which can be identified with the kernels of ideal classes in the ideal-class group $\mathsf{Cl}(\mathcal{O})$. As a result, we can see the class group as acting on the set $\mathcal{E}$ via a free and transitive group action.

To ensure efficient computation of isogenies, the prime p is usually chosen such that $p - 1 = 4\prod_i \ell_i$, where the ℓ_i are small prime factors. The factor 4 ensures that $p \equiv 3 \bmod 4$ and that the special elliptic curve $E_0 : y^2 = x^3 + x$ is supersingular. Throughout this work, we assume that the class group $\mathsf{Cl}(\mathcal{O})$ is known, enabling the transformation of arbitrary ideals into efficiently computable isogeny chains of degrees l_i using the relation lattice. We note that this is not a trivial assumption as current class group computations in reach fall short of realistic security levels [9,10,23] or lead to very slow protocols [15]. We point out, however, that there are polynomial-time quantum algorithms to this end [21]. We refer to [7,9,11,31] for more details on the explicit computations of isogenies. For a more thorough introduction to isogenies and isogeny-based cryptography, we recommend [11,15,29].

Finally, we note that class groups are generally of composite order. By working in cyclic subgroups of $\mathsf{Cl}(\mathcal{O})$ with generator $\mathfrak{g}$ and order $N \mid \#\mathsf{Cl}(\mathcal{O})$, we can redefine the group action as $[\ ] : \mathbb{Z}_N \times \mathcal{E} \to \mathcal{E}$, where ideals of the form $\mathfrak{g}^a$ for $a \in \mathbb{Z}_N$ can be reduced modulo the relation lattice and efficiently computed. To work in a subgroup $\mathbb{Z}_{N'} \subset \mathbb{Z}_N$, we can simply use the generator $\mathfrak{g}^{N/N'}$. For the rest of this work, we always assume the choice of the subgroup $\mathbb{Z}_N$ to be such that $\{1, \ldots, n\}$ defines an exceptional set modulo N, i.e. that n is smaller than the smallest divisor of N. Next, we recall some security assumptions that are used in our studied and constructed protocols.

Definition 2.1 (Group Action Inverse Problem (GAIP) [11,16]). *Given two supersingular elliptic curves $E, E' \in \mathcal{E}$ over the same finite field $\mathbb{F}_p$ and with $\mathsf{End}_{\mathbb{F}_p}(E) \simeq \mathsf{End}_{\mathbb{F}_p}(E') \simeq \mathcal{O}$, find $a \in \mathbb{Z}_N$, such that $E' = [a]E$.*

Definition 2.2 (Multi-Target-GAIP [9,16]). *Given $k + 1$ supersingular elliptic curves $E_0, E_1, \ldots, E_k \in \mathcal{E}$ over $\mathbb{F}_p$ with the same $\mathbb{F}_p$-rational endomorphism ring, find $a \in \mathbb{Z}_N$, s. t. $E_i = [a]E_j$ for some $i, j \in \{0, \ldots, k\}$ with $i \neq j$.*

Definition 2.3 $((c_0, c_1, \cdots, c_{k-1})$-Vectorization Problem with Auxiliary Inputs $(\mathbb{C}_{k-1}$-VPwAI) [5]). *Given an element $E \in \mathcal{E}$ and the pairs $(c_i, [c_i x]E)_{i=1}^{k-1}$, where $\mathbb{C}_{k-1} = \{c_0 = 0, c_1 = 1, c_2, \ldots, c_{k-1}\}$ is an exceptional set, find $x \in \mathbb{Z}_N$.*

2.2 Identity-Based Signature Schemes

Next, we recall the definition of IDS from [27], which originally were proposed by Shamir in [26].

Definition 2.4 (Identity-Based Signature Scheme). *An IDS scheme consists of four PPT algorithms* (Setup, Extract, Sign, Verify).

- $(pp, \mathsf{msk}) \leftarrow \mathsf{Setup}(1^\lambda)$: *Given the security parameter λ, it outputs public parameters pp and a master secret key* msk.
- $\mathsf{usk}_{\mathsf{id}} \leftarrow \mathsf{Extract}(pp, \mathsf{msk}, \mathsf{id})$: *Given pp, msk, and the user identity* id, *it outputs the user secret key $\mathsf{usk}_{\mathsf{id}}$ for the given* id.
- $\sigma \leftarrow \mathsf{Sign}(pp, m, \mathsf{usk}_{\mathsf{id}})$: *Given pp, $\mathsf{usk}_{\mathsf{id}}$, and a message m, it outputs σ.*
- $(1/0) \leftarrow \mathsf{Verify}(pp, \mathsf{id}, m, \sigma)$: *Given pp,* id, *m, and signature σ, it outputs 1 if σ is a valid signature on m, otherwise outputs 0.*

Definition 2.5 (Correctness). *For all $(pp, \mathsf{msk}) \leftarrow \mathsf{Setup}(1^\lambda)$, all $\mathsf{usk}_{\mathsf{id}} \leftarrow \mathsf{Extract}(pp, \mathsf{msk}, \mathsf{id})$, all m and* id, *we have* $\mathsf{Verify}(pp, \mathsf{id}, m, \mathsf{Sign}(pp, m, \mathsf{usk}_{\mathsf{id}})) = 1$.

Definition 2.6 (Security). *An IDS scheme is said to be secure against UnForgeability against chosen-identity and Chosen Message Attacks (UF-IDS-CMA) [24,27] if for all PPT adversaries $\mathcal{A}$, there exists a negligible function ϵ such that*

$$Adv_{IDS,\mathcal{A}}^{UF-IDS-CMA}(\lambda) = \Pr[\mathcal{A} \text{ wins in } Exp_{IDS,\mathcal{A}}^{UF-IDS-CMA}(\lambda)] < \epsilon,$$

where the experiment $Exp_{IDS,\mathcal{A}}^{UF-IDS-CMA}(\lambda)$ is described in Fig. 1.

Input: The challenger $\mathcal{C}$ takes input the security parameter 1^λ, and generates $(pp, \mathsf{msk}) \leftarrow \mathsf{Setup}(1^\lambda)$. It gives the public parameters pp to the adversary $\mathcal{A}$ while keeping the secret msk to itself.

Query Phase: $\mathcal{C}$ responds to polynomially many adaptive queries made by $\mathcal{A}$,

- Oracle $O_{\mathsf{Extract}(\mathsf{msk},\cdot)}$: On receiving queries on a user identity id from $\mathcal{A}$, the challenger $\mathcal{C}$ responds with her user secret key $\mathsf{usk_{id}} \leftarrow \mathsf{Extract}(pp, \mathsf{msk}, \mathsf{id})$ for the given identity id.
- Oracle $O_{\mathsf{Sign}(\mathsf{usk_{id}},\cdot)}$: On receiving queries on a message m, and a user identity id from the adversary $\mathcal{A}$, the challenger $\mathcal{C}$ responds with a signature $\sigma \leftarrow \mathsf{Sign}(pp, m, \mathsf{usk_{id}})$ where $\mathsf{usk_{id}} \leftarrow \mathsf{Extract}(pp, \mathsf{msk}, \mathsf{id})$ is the user secret key corresponding to the identity id.

Forgery: $\mathcal{A}$ eventually outputs a message $m^\star$, user identity $\mathsf{id}^\star$, and a forge signature $\sigma^\star$. $\mathcal{A}$ wins the game if $1 \leftarrow \mathsf{Verify}(pp, \mathsf{id}, m, \sigma)$, with the restriction that $\mathsf{id}^\star$ has not been queried to $O_{\mathsf{Extract}(\mathsf{msk},\cdot)}$ and $(m^\star, \mathsf{id}^\star)$ has not been queried to $O_{\mathsf{Sign}(\mathsf{usk_{id}},\cdot)}$.

Fig. 1. $Exp_{IDS,\mathcal{A}}^{UF-IDS-CMA}(\lambda)$: UnForgability against Chosen Message Attacks.

2.3 Identity-Based Threshold Signature Scheme

We use the definition of an IDTHS scheme as proposed by Baek and Zheng [4], which is outlined below:

Definition 2.7 (Identity-Based Threshold Signature Scheme). *A (t, n) IDTHS consists* (Setup, Extract, DKey, DSign, Verify)*:*

- $(pp, \mathsf{msk}) \leftarrow \mathsf{Setup}(\lambda)$: *Given a security parameter λ, the algorithm generates the master secret key msk and the public parameters pp.*
- $\mathsf{usk_{id}} \leftarrow \mathsf{Extract}(pp, \mathsf{msk}, \mathsf{id})$: *Given the public parameters pp, the master secret key msk, and a user identity id, the algorithm generates a private key $\mathsf{usk_{id}}$ associated with id.*
- $\{\mathsf{sk}_l\}_{l=1}^{n} \leftarrow \mathsf{DKey}(pp, \mathsf{usk_{id}}, n, t)$: *Given a private key $\mathsf{usk_{id}}$ associated with an identity id, a number of signers n and a threshold parameter t, the algorithm generates n shares of sk_l and provides each one to the party P_l for $l = \{1, \cdots, n\}$.*
- $\sigma \leftarrow \mathsf{DSign}(pp, m, \{\mathsf{sk}_l\}_{l \in S}, \mathsf{id})$: *Given pp, a message m, shares $\{\mathsf{sk}_l\}_{l \in S}$, where $|S| = t + 1$, and id. Signers using a robust protocol jointly generate σ. Note that partial signatures of m computed by each party may be broadcast during the execution of the DSign protocol.*
- $1/0 \leftarrow \mathsf{Verify}(pp, \mathsf{id}, m, \sigma)$: *Given a signers' identity id, a message m and σ, the algorithm outputs 1 if the signature is valid, otherwise 0.*

Note that these definitions are specifically designed for (t, n) IDTHS with abort security. It's important to distinguish between this level of security and a stronger concept known as "identifiable-abort." In the case of identifiable-abort, the system can reveal the identity of at least one malicious party in the event of an abort. Our first threshold signature, as proposed in Sect. 4, provides security with abort but does not achieve the identifiable-abort property. This limitation arises from the fact that the DKey algorithm, executed by the dealer, does not output the verification keys (equivalent to partial public keys). Consequently, during the partial opening phase, honest parties are unable to identify the malicious party based on their partial opening. While it's possible to detect cheating and trigger an abort after summing up all partial signatures, but identifying the malicious party remains a challenge.

In the case of a robust IDTHS scheme, the algorithm DKey, which is executed by a trusted dealer, not only provides the secret keys $\{sk_l\}_{l=1}^n$ but also outputs the verification keys $\{vk_l\}_{l=1}^n$. Additionally, the signing protocol DSign, which involves all n parties and uses the secret keys $\{sk_l\}_{l=1}^n$, also receives the verification keys $\{vk_l\}_{l=1}^n$. It's worth noting that in a robust IDTHS system, when $t+1$ parties involve in the DSign protocol, it can achieve the identifiable-abort property. Lastly, it's important to highlight that the IDTHS with abort only requires a single honest signer to maintain security, whereas the identifiable-abort and robust versions of the signature require an honest majority of participants.

The following will consider the security definitions of an IDTHS, which are unforgeability and robustness [4]. Note that the attacker is assumed to be static.

Definition 2.8 (Unforgeability Against Chosen Message and Identity Attack). *Let $\mathcal{A}^{IDTHS}$, be an attacker assumed to be a probabilistic Turing machine. Consider the following game G^{IDTHS} in which $\mathcal{A}^{IDTHS}$ interacts with the challenger $\mathcal{C}^{IDTHS}$.*

Phase 1. The challenger runs the Setup algorithm and gives $\mathcal{A}^{IDTHS}$ the resulting common parameters pp.

Phase 2. $\mathcal{A}^{IDTHS}$ corrupts $t-1$ signature generation servers.

Phase 3. $\mathcal{A}^{IDTHS}$ issues a number of private key extraction queries, each of which consists of usk. On receiving usk, the challenger runs the key extraction algorithm taking usk as input and obtains a corresponding private key x. The challenger gives x to $\mathcal{A}^{IDTHS}$.

Phase 4. $\mathcal{A}^{IDTHS}$ submits a target identity $usk^\star$. On receiving $usk^\star$, the challenger runs the key extraction algorithm taking $usk^\star$ as input and obtains a corresponding private key $x^\star$. Subsequently, it runs the private key distribution algorithm taking $x^\star$ as input to share it among n signature generation servers. We denote the key shares by $x^{\star,i}$ for $i=1,\cdots,n$. The challenger gives $x^{\star,i}$ for $i=1,\cdots,t-1$, (private keys for the corrupted servers) to $\mathcal{A}^{IDTHS}$.

Phase 5. $\mathcal{A}^{IDTHS}$ issues a number of signature generation queries, each of which consists of a message denoted by m. On receiving m, the challenger, on behalf of the uncorrupted servers, runs the signature generation algorithm taking $x^{\star,i}$ for $i=t,\cdots,n$ and m as input, and responds to $\mathcal{A}^{IDTHS}$ with σ output by the signature generation algorithm. Note that in this phase, $\mathcal{A}^{IDTHS}$ is allowed to issue private key extraction queries (identities) except for $usk^\star$. Note also that $\mathcal{A}^{IDTHS}$ is allowed to see partial signature broadcast during the execution.

Phase 6. $\mathcal{A}^{IDTHS}$ outputs (usk*, $\tilde{m}$, $\tilde{\sigma}$), where $\tilde{\sigma}$ is a valid signature of the identity usk* on the message $\tilde{m}$. A restriction here is that $\mathcal{A}^{IDTHS}$ must not make a private key extraction query for $x^\star$ and it must not make a signature generation query for $\tilde{m}$. We denote $\mathcal{A}^{IDTHS}$'s success by

$$Succ_{IDTHS,\mathcal{A}^{IDTHS}}^{UF-IDTHS-CMA}(k) = \Pr[\text{Verify}(pp, x^\star, \tilde{m}, \tilde{\sigma}) = 1].$$

We denote by

$$Succ_{IDTHS,\mathcal{A}^{IDTHS}}^{UF-IDTHS-CMA}(t, q_e, q_s)$$

the maximum of the attacker $\mathcal{A}^{IDTHS}$'s success over all attackers $\mathcal{A}^{IDTHS}$ having running time t_2 and making at most q_e key extraction queries and q_s signature generation queries. The ID-based threshold signature scheme is said to be (t, q_e, q_s, ϵ)-UF-IDTHS-CMA secure if

$$Succ_{IDTHS,\mathcal{A}^{IDTHS}}^{UF-IDTHS-CMA}(t, q_e, q_s) < \epsilon.$$

Definition 2.9 (Abort). *A (t, n) ID-based threshold signature scheme is said to be secure with abort if parties abort in the presence of an attacker that makes the corrupted signature generation servers deviate from the normal execution.*

Definition 2.10 (Robustness). *A (t, n) ID-based threshold signature scheme is said to be robust if it computes a correct output even in the presence of an attacker that makes the corrupted signature generation servers deviate from the normal execution.*

Note that in the case of the abort scenario, the verification process solely focuses on assessing the validity of the final signature. This final signature is acquired by combining the partial signatures generated by individual parties. It either accepts the signature as valid or aborts the process, all without singling out the malicious party. Conversely, in the robust case, the parties not only validate the final signature but also verify the individual signatures (referred to as "openings") to identify and disqualify any malicious participants. This verification process ensures the guaranteed delivery of the output.

In terms of achieving active security with either an *abort* or *robustness* approach, these definitions closely resemble the security criteria found in regular threshold signature schemes [14,18]. However, when it comes to the algorithms involved, IDTHS differ from regular threshold signatures. In identity-based schemes, a master secret key is employed to generate specific secret keys for each ID, followed by an algorithm that distributes these ID-specific secret keys to the corresponding ID holders. In contrast, regular threshold signatures utilize a single secret key that is shared among all n participating parties.

Commitment Schemes. In our protocols, we assume parties have access to a commitment functionality $\mathcal{F}_{\mathsf{Commit}}$, which allows one party to commit, and later open the value to a set of parties. We assume the opened value is only available to the targeted receivers and is sent over a secure communication channel. The description of $\mathcal{F}_{\mathsf{Commit}}$ is provided in Fig. 2, which can be easily implemented in the random oracle model.

Init: Given (Init, P_i, B) from all parties, this initializes a commitment functionality from party P_i to the parties in B. This is shown with $\mathcal{F}_{\mathsf{Commit}}^{i,B}$, if B is a singleton set $B = \{j\}$ then we write $\mathcal{F}_{\mathsf{Commit}}^{i,j}$, and if $B = \mathcal{P} \setminus \{i\}$ then we write $\mathcal{F}_{\mathsf{Commit}}^{P_i}$.

Commit: On input of $(\mathsf{Commit}, \mathsf{id}, \mathsf{data})$ from parties P_i and $(\mathsf{Commit}, \mathsf{id}, \bot)$ from all parties in B the functionality stores $(\mathsf{id}, \bot)$.

Open: On input of $(\mathsf{Commit}, \mathsf{id})$ from all players in $B \cup \{i\}$ the functionality retrieves the entry $(\mathsf{id}, \mathsf{data})$ and returns data to all parties in B.

Fig. 2. The Functionality $\mathcal{F}_{\mathsf{Commit}}$ [13].

2.4 k-MT-GAIP Distributed Key Generation

Now we recall the DKG protocol presented in the CSI-SharK framework by Atapoor et al. [2] (Fig. 3), which will be used in Sect. 4 to build our specific IDTHS scheme.

2.5 Shamir Secret Sharing

A (t,n)-Shamir secret sharing scheme allows n parties to individually hold a share s_i of a common secret s, such that any subset of fewer than $t+1$ parties are not able to learn any information about the secret s while any subset of at least $t+1$ parties are able to efficiently reconstruct the common secret s via Lagrange interpolation by computing $s = f(0) = \sum_{i \in S} s_i \cdot L_{0,i}^S$, where

$$L_{0,i}^S := \prod_{j \in S \setminus \{i\}} \frac{j}{j-i} \pmod{N},$$

are Lagrange basis polynomials evaluated at 0. Any subset of fewer than $t+1$ parties are not able to find $s = f(0)$, as this is information-theoretically hidden, even given t shares. Since we will be working over the ring $\mathbb{Z}_N$ with N composite, the difference $j - i$ of any two elements in $i, j \in S$ must be invertible modulo N. If q' is the smallest prime factor of N, it is enough to require that $n < q'$. This is indeed the case of our applications.

Input: The fixed elliptic curve E_0 and a set Q of n parties.
Output: $([s_1]E_0, \ldots, [s_{k-1}]E_0)$

1. Parties individually sample $k-1$ secrets $s_i \in \mathbb{Z}_N$ shared between the parties, where $P_j \in Q$ holds $s_{1,j}, \ldots, s_{k-1,j}$ such that $s_i = \sum_{P_j \in Q} s_{i,j}$.
2. Define an ordering the players in $Q = \{P_1, \ldots, P_n\}$.
3. Each party P_j initialises an instance of $\mathcal{F}_{\mathsf{Commit}}$; call it $\mathcal{F}_{\mathsf{Commit}}^{P_j}$.
4. For $i = 1, \ldots, k-1$, each party P_j executes
   - $E_{i,P_j} \leftarrow [s_{i,j}]E_0$.
   - $\pi_{i,j}^1 \leftarrow \mathsf{NIZK}.P((E_0, E_{i,P_j}), s_{i,j})$.   (Run the ID protocol for GAIP [9])
   - Use $\mathcal{F}_{\mathsf{Commit}}^{P_j}$ where P_j submits input $(\mathsf{Commit}, \mathsf{id}_{P_j}, (E_{i,P_j}, \pi_{i,j}^1))$ and all other parties input $(\mathsf{Commit}, \mathsf{id}_{P_j}, \perp)$.
5. For $i = 1, \ldots, k-1$
   - Parties run $\mathcal{F}_{\mathsf{Commit}}^{P_j}$ with input $(\mathsf{Open}, \mathsf{id}_{P_j})$ & abort if $\mathcal{F}_{\mathsf{Commit}}^{P_j}$ returns abort.
   - All other players execute $\mathsf{NIZK}.V((E_0, E_{i,P_j}), \pi_{i,j}^1)$ and abort if the verification algorithm fails.
6. $E_1^0 \leftarrow E_0, E_2^0 \leftarrow E_0, \cdots, E_{k-1}^0 \leftarrow E_0$.
7. For $j = 1, \ldots, n$
   - Party P_j computes $E_1^j \leftarrow [s_{1,j}]E_1^{j-1}, \cdots, E_{k-1}^j \leftarrow [s_{k-1,j}]E_{k-1}^{j-1}$.
   - For $i = 1, \ldots, k-1$, compute $\pi_{i,j}^2 \leftarrow \mathsf{NIZK}.P((E_0, E_{i,P_j}, E_i^{j-1}, E_i^j), s_{i,j})$.
     (Run the argument in the full version of the paper [1])
   - Broadcast $(E_1^j, E_2^j, \cdots, E_{k-1}^j, \pi_{1,j}^2, \ldots, \pi_{k-1,j}^2)$ to all players.
   - For $i = 1, \ldots, k-1$, all other players execute $\mathsf{NIZK}.V(E_0, E_{i,P_j}, E_i^{j-1}, E_i^j)$ and abort if the verification algorithm fails.
8. Return $(E_1^n, E_2^n, \ldots, E_{k-1}^n) = ([s_1]E_0, [s_2]E_0, \cdots, [s_{k-1}]E_0)$.

Fig. 3. Full-threshold k-MT-GAIP distributed key generation protocol [2].

3   Identity-Based Signatures from CSI-SharK

In this section, we modify the CSI-FiSh-based IDS of Shaw and Dutta [27] to work with the CSI-SharK signature scheme [2]. The primary benefit inherent in this adaptation arises from the singular nature of the secret key of CSI-SharK. The process of adapting Shaw and Dutta's signature [27] to the CSI-SharK signature is mostly alterations in the Setup and Extract algorithms. The Setup algorithm generates pp and a master secret key msk, where msk consists of S_0 different coefficients of a single secret value s. Since the soundness rate of the underlying ID protocol is $\frac{1}{1+S_0}$, one needs to amplify the soundness error rate by repeating the protocol T_0 times. The Extract algorithm gets msk $:= s$ and generates a new user secret key $\mathsf{usk}_{\mathsf{id}_{i,j}}$ for a specific id. The length of the user public key is S_1 and since the soundness rate of the protocol now is $\frac{1}{1+S_1}$, one needs to amplify the soundness error rate by repeating the protocol T_1 times. Note that both the Setup and Extract algorithms are executed by a trusted authority. Bellow, we describe the algorithms of the resulting IDS scheme:

Setup *Algorithm*. Given the security parameter 1^λ, act as follows,

1. Select the integers $T_0, T_1, S_0 = 2^{\gamma_0} - 1$ and $S_1 = 2^{\gamma_1} - 1$ where γ_0, γ_1 are integers and $T_0 < S_0, T_1 < S_1$
2. Sample a cryptographic hash function $H : \{0,1\}^\star \to [0, S_0]^{T_0 S_1}$ and a public (super) exceptional set $\varXi_{S_0} := \{c_0 = 0, c_1 = 1, c_2, \cdots, c_{S_0}\}$
3. Sample $s \leftarrow\!\!\$\ \mathbb{Z}_N$, and for $i = 1$ to S_0 set: $E_i = [c_i s] E_0$
4. Return
   $$pp = \{E_0, T_0, T_1, S_0, S_1, H, \varXi_{S_0} := \{c_0 = 0, c_1 = 1, c_2, \cdots, c_{S_0}\}, \{E_i\}_{i=1}^{S_0}\}$$
   and $\mathsf{msk} = s$.

Extract *Algorithm*. Given $(pp, \mathsf{msk}, \mathsf{id})$ act as follows,

1. Set $s_0 \leftarrow 0$ and for $i = 1$ to T_0, $j = 1$ to S_1: $r_{i,j} \leftarrow\!\!\$\ \mathbb{Z}_N$ and $R_{i,j} = [r_{i,j}] E_0$
2. Compute $u \leftarrow H(\mathsf{id}||\{R_{i,j}\}_{i=1,j=1}^{T_0,S_1})$
3. Parse u as $\{u_i \in [0, s_0]\}_{i=1}^{T_0 S_1}$ and $\varXi_{S_0}$ as $\{c_0 = 0, c_1 = 1, c_2, \cdots, c_{S_0}\}$
4. For $i = 1$ to T_0, $j = 1$ to S_1 open: $x_{i,j} = r_{i,j} - c_{u_i} s \quad \mod N$
5. Return $\mathsf{usk}_{\mathsf{id}_{i,j}} = (\{u_i\}_{i=1}^{T_0 S_1}, \{x_{i,j}\}_{i=1,j=1}^{T_0,S_1})$.

Sign *Algorithm*. Given $(pp, \mathsf{usk}_{\mathsf{id}_{i,j}}, m)$, act as follows,

1. Parse $\mathsf{usk}_{\mathsf{id}_{i,j}}$ to $(\{u_i\}_{i=1}^{T_0 S_1}, \{x_{i,j}\}_{i=1,j=1}^{T_0,S_1})$
2. For $i = 1$ to T_0 set: $x_{i,0} \leftarrow 0$
3. For $i = 1$ to T_0 do:
   (a) For $j = 1$ to S_1 compute: $X_{i,j} = [x_{i,j}] E_{u_i}$
4. For $i = 1$ to T_0 do:
   (a) For $j = 1$ to T_1 sample: $k_{i,j} \leftarrow\!\!\$\ \mathbb{Z}_N$ and compute $K_{i,j} = [k_{i,j}] E_{u_i}$
5. Compute $v \leftarrow H'(m||\{K_{i,j}\}_{i=1,j=1}^{T_0,T_1})$
6. Parse v as $\{v_{i,j} \in [0, S_1]\}_{i=1,j=1}^{T_0,T_1}$
7. For $i = 1$ to T_0 do:
   (a) For $j = 1$ to T_1 open: $z_{i,j} = k_{i,j} - x_{i,v_{i,j}} \quad \mod N$
8. Return $\sigma \leftarrow (\{z_{i,j}\}_{i=1,j=1}^{T_0,T_1}, \{X_{i,j}\}_{i=1,j=1}^{T_0,S_1}, v)$.

Verify *Algorithm*. Given $(pp, \mathsf{id}, m, \sigma)$, act as follow,

1. Retrieve $u = H(\mathsf{id}||\{X_{i,j}\}_{i=1,j=1}^{T_0,S_1})$ and parse v as $\{v_{i,j}\}_{i=1,j=1}^{T_0,T_1}$
2. For $i = 1$ to T_0 do:
   (a) For $j = 1$ to T_1 if: $v_{i,j} = 0$ then $K'_{i,j}[z_{i,j}] E_{u_i}$, else $K'_{i,j}[z_{i,j}] X_{i,v_{i,j}}$
3. Compute $v' \leftarrow H'(m||\{K'_{i,j}\}_{i=1,j=1}^{T_0,T_1})$
4. If $v' \neq v$ then return "Invalid" otherwise return "valid".

Correctness. The correctness of the resulting IDS follows from the correctness of the CSI-SharK signature and the underlying identity-based ID protocol (reviewed in the full version of the paper [1]).

Theorem 3.1. *Let IDS be the IDS scheme outlined above. Let $\mathcal{A}$ be an adversary that breaks the UF-IDS-CMA security of IDS (defined in Definition 2.6). Then we can construct an impersonator I breaking the IMP-PA security (IMPersonation under Passive Attacks, defined in [27, Definition 6.12]) of the underlying ID protocol of the signature scheme (given in the full version of the paper [1]).*

Efficiency. The efficiency of the resulting IDS scheme is close to the original version, presented by Shaw and Dutta [27] except that, in contrast to the original scheme based on CSI-FiSh, in our case the master secret key is a single element of $\mathbb{Z}_N$, rather than S_0 elements (of $\mathbb{Z}_N$).

4   Identity-Based Threshold Signature with Abort

This section presents an IDTHS scheme based on isogenies, using the CSI-SharK signature scheme [2]. The IDTHS ensures security with abort, meaning that if any issues arise and the protocol cannot be followed, the involved parties will abort and cease the procedure. In Sect. 3, we described an IDS using CSI-SharK which consists of PPT algorithms (Setup, Extract, Sign, Verify), where a *single* signer is involved. Using the mentioned IDS scheme, we build an IDTHS scheme consisting of five PPT algorithms (Setup, Extract, DKey, DSign, Verify) (described in Definition 2.7). In the resulting threshold scheme, the algorithms (Setup, Extract, Verify) are identical to the non-threshold case, where (Setup, Extract) are executed by a trusted authority. Due to this fact, to conserve space, we do not re-write the algorithms of (Setup, Extract, Verify). The threshold variant includes an additional algorithm DKey, which is responsible for sharing the user secret key returned by the Extract algorithm. Similar to the non-threshold case, in the threshold version, we assume that a trusted authority runs the algorithms (Setup, Extract, DKey). The trusted authority will employ the DKey algorithm to distribute the secret key $\mathsf{usk}_{\mathsf{id}_{i,j}}$ corresponding to id among all the parties sharing the same id. In this paper, we use the well-known Shamir's secret sharing scheme, although it's worth noting that alternative secret sharing schemes are also viable options. Next, we describe the procedures of the DKey and DSign algorithms:

DKey: The description of DKey is given in Fig. 4 which a dealer samples a random degree-t polynomial and uses Shamir's secret sharing to distribute the user's secret key $\mathsf{usk}_{\mathsf{id}_{i,j}}$ among multiple parties and sends the shares $x_{i,j,l}$ to each party via the secure channels.

DSign: Given the public parameters pp, the message m, the secret keys of each party $x_{i,j,l}$, the distributed signing algorithm DSign is employed to generate a signature. This algorithm is executed by a qualified set of parties $Q = \{1, \cdots, q\}$ and if any individual fails to adhere to the designated protocol, the honest parties will collectively abort the process and cease the ongoing computation. The description of DSign is given in Fig. 5. As it can be seen, during Step 3, the parties collaboratively compute the public key and determine $E_{i,j,L} = [x_{i,j,l}]E_{i,j,l-1}$,

Input: $(pp, \mathsf{usk}_{\mathsf{id}_{i,j}} = (\{u_i\}_{i=1}^{T_0 S_1}, \{x_{i,j}\}_{i=1,j=1}^{T_0,S_1}), n, t)$, where n is the number of parties and t is threshold parameter $(t + 1$ parties can reconstruct the secret).
Output: Private $\{x_{i,j,l}\}_{l=1,i=1,j=1}^{l=n,i=T_0,j=S_1}$ and Public $\{F_{i,j,l}\}_{l=1,i=1,j=1}^{l=n,i=T_0,j=S_1}$.

An authority acts as follows:

1. Parse $\mathsf{usk}_{\mathsf{id}_{i,j}} = (\{u_i\}_{i=1}^{T_0 S_1}, \{x_{i,j}\}_{i=1,j=1}^{T_0,S_1})$
2. For $i = 1$ to T_0, $j = 1$ to S_1 do:
    (a) Sample a degree-t polynomial $f_{i,j}(X) = x_{i,j} + c_{i,j,1}X^1 + \cdots + c_{i,j,t}X^t$.
    (b) For $l = 1$ to n: set $x_{i,j,l} = f_{i,j}(l)$ as a secret for each party.
3. For $l = 1, \cdots, n$: send $x_{i,j,l}$ to party P_l securely.

Fig. 4. DKey algorithm for the proposed IDTHS.

Input: $(pp, m, \{x_{i,j,l}\}_{l=1,i=1,j=1}^{l=q,i=T_0,j=S_1})$,
Output: $\sigma \leftarrow (\{z_{i,j}\}_{i=1,j=1}^{T_0,T_1}, \{E_{i,j}\}_{i=1,j=1}^{T_0,S_1}, v)$.

Signing Algorithm DSign: a qualified set of parties $\{P_1, \cdots, P_q\}$ act as follows,

1. For $l = 1$ to q each party for $i = 1$ to T_0: set $x_{i,0,l} \leftarrow 0$
2. For $i = 1$ to T_0 and $j = 1$ to S_1: set $E_{i,j,0} = E_0$
3. For $i = 1$ to T_0 and $j = 1$ to S_1 do:
    (a) For $l = 1$ to q do:
        i. Party P_l computes $E_{i,j,l} \leftarrow [x_{i,j,l}]E_{i,j,l-1}$
        // Parties use the NIZK argument (given in the full version of the paper [1]), to prove they are updating the curve with the secret which they got from the dealer.
        ii. Compute $\pi_{i,j,l} \leftarrow \mathsf{NIZK}.P((E_0, F_{i,j,l}, E_{i,j,l-1}, E_{i,j,l}), x_{i,j,l})$
        iii. Broadcast $(E_{i,j,l}, \pi_{i,j,l})$
        // Parties use the verifier of NIZK argument (given in the full version of the paper [1]), to verify the proof.
        iv. All players execute $\mathsf{NIZK}.V((E_0, F_{i,j,l}, E_{i,j,l-1}, E_{i,j,l}), \pi_{i,j,l})$ and abort if the verification algorithm fails.
    (b) Set $E_{i,j} = E_{i,j,q}$ and return $E_{i,j}$
4. For $i = 1$ to T_0 and $j = 1$ to T_1: given E_{u_i}, parties of the qualified set run Full-threshold 2-MT-GAIP given in Fig. 3, and generate $K_{i,j} = [k_{i,j}]E_{u_i}$
5. Compute $v \leftarrow H'(m||\{K_{i,j}\}_{i=1,j=1}^{T_0,T_1})$
6. Parse v as $\{v_{i,j} \in [0, S_1]\}_{i=1,j=1}^{T_0,T_1}$
7. For $i = 1$ to T_0, $j = 1$ to T_1, and $l = 1$ to q: party P_l opens $z_{i,j,l} = k_{i,j,l} - x_{i,v_{i,j,l}} \mod N$
8. For $i = 1$ to T_0, $j = 1$ to T_1: parties compute $z_{i,j} = \sum_{l=1}^q (z_{i,j,l})$
Return $\sigma \leftarrow (\{z_{i,j}\}_{i=1,j=1}^{T_0,T_1}, \{E_{i,j}\}_{i=1,j=1}^{T_0,S_1}, v)$.

Fig. 5. DSign algorithm for the proposed IDTHS with abort.

We let $\mathcal{A}$ denote the set of parties controlled by the adversary.

Sign: On input of a message m the functionality proceeds as follows:

1. The functionality adversary waits for an input from the adversary.
2. If the input is not abort then the functionality generates a signature σ on the message m.
3. The signature is returned to the adversary, and the functionality again waits for input. If the input is again not abort then the functionality returns σ to the honest players.

Fig. 6. Distributed signature functionality $\mathcal{F}_{\text{DSign}}$ [13].

where $E_{i,j,l}$ is shared among the parties. This computation involves updating the curve $E_{i,j,l}$ with their respective shares $x_{i,j,l}$ in a round-robin way and providing a proof, using the Non-Interactive Zero-Knowledge (NIZK) argument (summarized in the full version of the paper [1]), to demonstrate that they correctly updated E_{u_i} with the secret $x_{i,j,l}$ received from the authority. Subsequently, the parties must verify the proofs provided by all other parties using the verification process outlined in the full version of the paper [1]. Given that the process is executed in a round-robin manner, the final update is performed by the last participant in the qualified set Q. As outlined in Step 3b, the update contributed by party P_q yields the conclusive public key $E_{i,j} := E_{i,j,q}$. In Step 4, the involved parties execute the full-threshold DKG protocol (depicted in Fig. 3) for $k = 2$, and calculate the value of $K_{i,j}$. Note that when implementing this in practice, it is possible to parallelize these executions and loops. In Step 5, the challenge v is generated by hashing the concatenation of message m and $K_{i,j}$ computed in the previous step. Then, in Step 7, parties open their response $z_{i,j,l}$ and locally add them all together and achieve $z_{i,j}$. Finally, the algorithm returns the signature σ which consists of $(z_{i,j}, E_{i,j}, v)$.

Next, we argue the security of our new IDTHS scheme. To this end, in Fig. 6, we first describe the distributed signature functionality $\mathcal{F}_{\text{DSign}}$ and then simulate our proposed threshold signing protocol.

Security of DKey: We highlight that the DKey algorithm is executed by a trusted dealer and does not need to be simulate.

Theorem 4.1. *The (t, n) IDTHS protocol described in Fig. 5 is UF-IDTHS-CMA secure with abort in the quantum random oracle model (the hash functions are modelled as quantum random oracles), against a static adversary corrupting up to t parties, with $t < n/2$, if the IDS scheme proposed in Sect. 3 is EUF-IDS-CMA secure.*

Proof. In Theorem 3.1, we showed that the IDS scheme proposed in Sect. 3 is EUF-IDS-CMA secure. Next, we show that the DSign protocol presented in Fig. 5 securely implement the functionality $\mathcal{F}_{\text{DSign}}$ (given in Fig. 6) in the $\mathcal{F}_{\text{Commit}}$-hybrid model against an active adversary corrupting up to t parties.

DSign **Simulation:** The proof is analogous to that of Theorem 4.3 in Atapoor et al. [2]. One key difference is in the case of Atapoor et al. [2], parties get the commitment to $x_{i,j}$ from the distributed key generation phase, while in our case the trusted dealer publishes the commitments to $x_{i,j}$. Let P_l be the honest party. $\mathcal{A}$ and $\mathcal{S}$ engage in an execution of the DSign protocol in Fig. 5. The authority has committed to the secret shares of $x_{i,j}$. Now $\mathcal{A}$ and $\mathcal{S}$ proceed with the round-robin protocol for computing the public keys as in Step 3 of Fig. 5. All steps for honest players can be simulated exactly by following the real protocol, except for the party P_l which holds the unknown shares $x_{i,j,l}$ for $i = 1, \cdots, T_0$ and $j = 1, \cdots, S_1$. The input to this party in execution l will be $E_{i,j,l-1} = \left[\sum_{p=1}^{l-1} x_{i,j,p} \right] E_0$, while the output needs to be $E_{i,j,l} = \left[-\sum_{p=1}^{l-1} x_{i,j,p} \right] E_{i,j}$, so as to create the correct output curve $E_{i,j}$. The curve $E_{i,j,l}$ can thus be computed by $\mathcal{S}$ as $E_{i,j,l} := \left[-\sum_{p \neq l} x_{i,j,p} \right] E_{i,j}$. After computing $E_{i,j,l}$ the associated ZK proof can hence be simulated as well. If $\mathcal{A}$ deviates from the protocol in any way, this is caught by the ZK proofs and $\mathcal{S}$ will be able to abort. Thus if abort does not happen in the protocol, the simulator will output the same curve $E_{i,j}$.

Again in Step 4 of the Fig. 5, parties are running a full-threshold 2-MT-GAIP protocol from Fig. 3 to jointly compute $K_{i,j} = [k_{i,j}] E_{u_i}$. Next, w.l.o.g., we write the simulation for particular values of i, j, while it can also be extended for all $i = 1, \cdots, T_0$, and $j = 1, \cdots, T_1$. Let P_l be the honest party. $\mathcal{A}$ and $\mathcal{S}$ engage in an execution of the full-threshold 2-MT-GAIP protocol in Fig. 3. As each party needs to commit to its secret share of s, the simulator commits to a random share s_l^*, say $K_{P_l}^* = [s_l^*] E_{u_i}$, produces a simulated proof and then commits to the curve and proof using the commitment scheme. If later the simulator is asked to open this, the simulator will equivocate the commitment so that it can be opened to the correct elliptic curve and proofs. Note that, the simulator is able to compute them after extracting the adversarial shares. From the $\pi_{P_p}^1$ (in Fig. 3), given in the commit phase, $\mathcal{S}$ is able to extract the values s_p entered by $\mathcal{A}$ in the first round of proofs. The extracted values s_p are now passed to the functionality, which completes them to a valid set of shares of the secret and returns the corresponding curves E_{u_i}, K. At this point, $\mathcal{S}$ has all the adversarial shares and the curves E_{u_i}, K. The honest share s_l is unknown to $\mathcal{S}$. Even though it does not have the honest share, it can fake the commitment by setting $K_{P_l} := \left[-\sum_{p \neq l} s_p \right] K$ which it can do by using the curves it got from the functionality and the adversarial shares that it got from the proofs-of-knowledge. Having E_{u_i} and K_{P_l}, $\mathcal{S}$ can simulate the corresponding proof. It then commits to this proof using $\mathcal{F}_{\text{Commit}}^{P_l}$. The commitments can now be opened. Now $\mathcal{A}$ and $\mathcal{S}$ proceed with the round-robin protocol for computing the public keys as in Step 7 of the Fig. 3. All steps for honest players can be simulated exactly by following the real protocol, except for the party P_l which holds the unknown share s_l. The input to this party in execution l will be $K^{l-1} = \left[\sum_{p=1}^{l-1} s_p \right] E_{u_i}$ while the output needs to be $K^l = \left[-\sum_{p=1}^{l-1} s_p \right] K$, so as to create the correct output K. The curve K^l can thus be computed by $\mathcal{S}$ like it did for computing

K_{P_l} and the associated ZK proof can hence be simulated as well. If $\mathcal{A}$ deviates from the protocol in any way, this is caught by the ZK proofs and $\mathcal{S}$ will be able to abort.

In our simulation of full-threshold 2-MT-GAIP generation protocol the value $k_{i,j,l}$ is unknown and 'fixed' by the implicit equation given by the signature $(\{z_{i,j}\}_{i=1,j=1}^{T_0,T_1}, \{X_{i,j}\}_{i=1,j=1}^{T_0,S_1}, v)$ returned by the functionality which gives us $K_{i,j} = [k_{i,j}]E_{u_i} = [z_{i,j}]X_{i,v_{i,j}}$, where $v_{i,j}$ is the random challenge value obtained from the quantum random oracle, i.e., $v \leftarrow H'(m||\{K_{i,j}\}_{i=1,j=1}^{T_0,T_1})$. The final part of the signature which needs to be simulated is the output of $z_{i,j,l}$. We know what $\mathcal{A}$ *should* output and hence can define $z_{i,j,l} = z_{i,j} - \sum_{l \neq l'} z_{i,j,l'}$. If $\mathcal{A}$ deviates from the protocol in the final step and uses an invalid value of $z_{i,j,l'}$, then the adversary will learn the signature, but the honest players will abort; which realizes the ideal functionality described in Fig. 6. □

5 Robust Identity-Based Threshold Signature Scheme

Our threshold signature from the previous section does not provide a guarantee for output delivery. The protocol is susceptible to the Denial-of-Service (DoS) attack, which allows malicious parties to indefinitely deny the generation of the desired result. In this section, we extend our IDTHS from Sect. 4 to achieve robustness and assure output delivery. Our robust scheme is also build based on the CSI-SharK signature, however with some changes, at the cost of a longer master secret key, can be adapted to work with the CSI-FiSh signature as well. In the proposed robust IDTHS if any dishonest behaviour by a participant occurs, the efforts invested thus far are not rendered futile. The involved parties are able to identify the malicious parties, exclude them from the protocol, reconstruct their shares, and seamlessly continue the protocol to achieve the correct output. In the rest of section, we are highlighting the distinctions between the signature discussed in Sect. 4 and the new one, without reiterating the similarities.

DKey: In Step 2 of the new DKey protocol (given in Fig. 7), in addition to generating the polynomial $f_{i,j}(X)$ for sharing the secret $x_{i,j}$, the authority generates another polynomial $g_{i,j(Y)}$ to re-share each share of $x_{i,j,l}$ among all the parties. At the end, the authority privately sends a share of this re-sharing, denoted as $w_{i,j,l,k}$, to each party, along with their respective share of $x_{i,j,l}$. Later, we show how the parties use these values to verify the opening responses in Step 7 of DSign algorithm (described in Fig. 8). This approach originally is proposed and used in the ThreshER SharK scheme [3] to achieve robustness. However, it is not directly applicable within the context of our scheme. We will provide a detailed explanation as we proceed through the description of the DSign algorithm.

DSign: Figure 8 describes the procedure of our proposed robust DSign protocol. Compared to the DSign protocol from Fig. 5, in the robust DSign, the first key difference is that we need all the parties to be present in the signing procedure, as explained in Step 7 of Fig. 8. Steps 1-3b are the same as our previous DSign protocol. Then,

---

An authority runs DKey:

1. Parse $\mathsf{usk}_{\mathsf{id}_{i,j}} = (\{u_i\}_{i=1}^{T_0 S_1}, \{x_{i,j}\}_{i=1,j=1}^{T_0,S_1})$
2. For $i = 1$ to T_0, $j = 1$ to S_1 do:
   (a) Choose a random degree t poly $f_{i,j}(X) = x_{i,j} + c_{i,j,1}X^1 + \cdots + c_{i,j,t}X^t$
   (b) for $l = 1$ to n: set $x_{i,j,l} = f_{i,j}(l)$ as a secret for each party and create the corresponding commitment $F_{i,j,l} = [x_{i,j,l}]F_0$ for each secret $x_{i,j,l}$
      i. Choose a random degree t poly $g_{i,j,l}(Y) = x_{i,j,l} + d_{i,j,1}Y^1 + \cdots + d_{i,j,t}Y^t$ and reshare secrets $x_{i,j,l}$ obtained from the previous step
      ii. for $k = 1$ to n: set $w_{i,j,l,k} = g_{i,j,l}(k)$ as a new secret for each party's secret $x_{i,j,l}$.
3. For $p = 1, \cdots, n$: send all the related $(x_{i,j,l}, w_{i,j,l,k})_{i=1,j=1,l=1,k=1}^{i=T_0,j=S_1,l=n,k=n}$ to party P_p securely and publish $\{F_{i,j,l}\}_{i=1,j=1,l=1}^{i=T_0,j=S_1,l=n}$.

Fig. 7. DKey algorithm for the proposed robust IDTHS.

in Step 4, parties run the robust Distributed Key Generation (DKG) protocol CSI-RAShi++ from [3], to compute $K_{i,j}$. The robust DKG protocol CSI-RAShi++ works with Shamir secret sharing and is recently proposed as an improved version of the DKG protocol CSI-RAShi [8]. CSI-RAShi++ allows a set of parties to sample $[x]E$ in a fully distributed manner, such that at the end, each party gets a Shamir share of x. Using CSI-RAShi++ and our re-sharing from the DKey step allows us to achieve robustness. Creating the challenge in Step 6 remains the same as before. Step 7 is the subtle part of the protocol to achieve the robustness. In this step, we use the reshares of the shares of all parties (from the DKey step) along with the reshares generated during the execution of CSI-RAShi++ DKG protocol, and verify the partial openings of individual parties.

In this step, parties open a polynomial instead of a value. In the abort version, when the parties open a value it gives the possibility to find the misbehaviour and abort but they can not identify the malicious parties. But in this case, since we are in the honest majority setting, due to opening a polynomial, the parties can identify an adversary (using the reshares from the DKey and DKG steps) and disqualify him. Then, they can reconstruct his share and continue the computation until the end.

Finally, parties sum all the responses up and achieve the final $z_{i,j}$. The signature as before consists of $(\{z_{i,j}\}_{i=1,j=1}^{T_0,T_1}, \{E_{i,j}\}_{i=1,j=1}^{T_0,S_1}, v)$.

Theorem 5.1. *The (t,n) IDTHS described in Fig. 8, is UF-IDTHS-CMA secure and robust in the quantum random oracle model (the hash functions are modelled as quantum random oracles), against a static adversary corrupting up to t parties, with $t < n/2$, if the IDS scheme proposed in Sect. 3 is EUF-IDS-CMA secure.*

Security Proofs. The security of DKey can be argued similar to the abort construction, given in Sect. 4, and the simulation of DSign is analogous to the proof

---

Signing Algorithm DSign: All Parties $\{P_1, \cdots, P_n\}$ act as follows,

1. For $l = 1$ to n party P_l for $i = 1$ to T_0: set $x_{i,0,l} \leftarrow 0$
2. Set $E_{i,j,0} = E_0$
3. For $i = 1$ to T_0 and $j = 1$ to S_1 do:
   (a) For $l = 1$ to n do:
      i. Party P_l computes $E_{i,j,l} \leftarrow [x_{i,j,l}]E_{i,j,l-1}$
      ii. Compute $\pi_{i,j,l} \leftarrow$ NIZK.$P((E_0, F_{i,j,l}, E_{i,j,l-1}, E_{i,j,l}), x_{i,j,l})$, using the NIZK argument (given in the full version of the paper [1]),
      iii. Broadcast $(E_{i,j,l}, \pi_{i,j,l})$
      iv. All players execute NIZK.$V((E_0, F_{i,j,l}, E_{i,j,l-1}, E_{i,j,l}), \pi_{i,j,l})$ (given in the full version of the paper [1]), and abort if the verification algorithm fails.
   (b) Set $E_{i,j} = E_{i,j,n}$ and return $E_{i,j}$
4. For $i = 1$ to T_0, $j = 1$ to T_1, and For $l = 1$ to n, given E_{u_i}, parties run the DKG of CSI-RAShi++ (given in the full version of the paper [1]) and generate $K_{i,j} = [k_{i,j}]E_{u_i}$.
   // Note that $b_{i,j,l}(X)$ which is a degree t polynomial sampled by parties during the DKG protocol of CSI-RAShi++ and the degree t polynomial of $g_{i,j}$ which was sampled by a trusted dealer in the DKey algorithm for re-sharing the share of the parties, both are using for checking and robustness.
5. Compute $v \leftarrow H'(m||\{K_{i,j}\}_{i=1,j=1}^{T_0,T_1})$
6. Parse v as $\{v_{i,j} \in [0, S_1]\}_{i=1,j=1}^{T_0,T_1}$
7. For $i = 1$ to T_0, $j = 1$ to T_1, and $l = 1$ to n do:
   (a) Each party P_l computes $z_{i,j,l}(Y) = b_{i,j,l}(Y) - g_{i,v_{i,j},l}(Y)$
   (b) Using their secret value shared during the NI-VSS protocol (given in the full version of the paper [1]), namely $b_{i,j,l}(l)$ and $g_{i,j}^l(l)$ given by the authority, each party P_l' verifies
   $$z_{i,j,l}(l') \stackrel{?}{=} b_{i,j,l}(l') - g_{i,v_{i,j},l}(l')$$
   (c) Whenever one of these checks fails, P_l' broadcasts a complaint against P_l When a player P_l has $t + 1$ or more complaints against them, they are disqualified. The remaining players can then construct $z_{i,j,l}(0)$ by reconstructing both $b_{i,j,l}(0)$ and $g_{i,j,l}(0)$ using the information from the DKG and given by the authority. This is always possible when there are at least $t + 1$ honest parties (honest majority).
   (d) Using $\{z_{i,j,l}(0)\}_{i=1}^n$, parties build the responses $z_{i,j}(0) = \sum_{i \in Q} z_{i,j,l}(0)$
8. Return $\sigma \leftarrow (\{z_{i,j}\}_{i=1,j=1}^{T_0,T_1}, \{E_{i,j}\}_{i=1,j=1}^{T_0,S_1}, v)$.

Fig. 8. DSign algorithm for the proposed robust IDTHS.

of theorem 5.1, which is omitted. We highlight that, in this case, one key difference is that the security of the DSign protocol relies on the security of the robust CSI-RAShi++ DKG protocol from [3].

6 Conclusion

We initiated our work by modifying the existing identity-based signature based on isogenies, as proposed by Shaw and Dutta [27], in order to align it with the CSI-SharK signature scheme. Subsequently, we proposed two identity-based threshold signature schemes in the CSIDH setting. Both of the proposed signatures possess active security within the quantum random oracle model, with the first one offering security with abort, while the second one is characterized by robustness. Although these novel constructions represent theoretical outcomes, they can be considered as the first step towards the development of identity-based threshold protocols that are based on isogenies. It is worth noting that any advancements made in the underlying protocols, e.g., CSI-SharK signature, CSI-RAShi++ DKG protocol, or even improvements in the computations of group actions, can be applied to our identity-based threshold signatures as well.

Acknowledgments. We thank the anonymous reviewers for their valuable comments and suggestions. We would also like to extend our special thanks to Elizabeth Crites for shepherding the final version of the paper and her insightful and valuable comments. Additionally, we would like to acknowledge Karim Baghery for his helpful discussions during the initial phases of the paper.

This work has been supported in part by the FWO under an Odysseus project GOH9718N and by CyberSecurity Research Flanders with reference number VR20192203. Any opinions, findings and conclusions or recommendations expressed in this material are those of the author(s) and do not necessarily reflect the views of the Cyber Security Research Flanders or the FWO.

References

1. Atapoor, S.: Identity-based threshold signatures from isogenies. Cryptology ePrint Archive, Paper 2023/1459 (2023). https://eprint.iacr.org/2023/1459
2. Atapoor, S., Baghery, K., Cozzo, D., Pedersen, R.: CSI-SharK: CSI-FiSh with Sharing-friendly Keys. In: Simpson, L., Rezazadeh Baee, M.A. (eds.) Information Security and Privacy - 28th Australasian Conference, ACISP 2023, Brisbane, QLD, Australia, 5–7 July 2023, Proceedings. LNCS, vol. 13915, pp. 471–502. Springer, Cham (2023). https://doi.org/10.1007/978-3-031-35486-1_21
3. Atapoor, S., Baghery, K., Cozzo, D., Pedersen, R.: VSS from distributed ZK proofs and applications. In: Guo, J., Steinfeld, R. (eds.) Advances in Cryptology - ASIACRYPT 2023–29th International Conference on the Theory and Application of Cryptology and Information Security, Guangzhou, China, 4–8 December 2023, Proceedings. LNCS. Springer, Cham (2023)
4. Baek, J., Zheng, Y.: Identity-based threshold signature scheme from the bilinear pairings. In: International Conference on Information Technology: Coding and Computing (ITCC 2004), Las Vegas, Nevada, USA, 5–7 April 2004, vol. 1, pp. 124–128. IEEE Computer Society (2004)
5. Baghery, K., Cozzo, D., Pedersen, R.: An isogeny-based ID protocol using structured public keys. In: Paterson, M.B. (ed.) IMACC 2021. LNCS, vol. 13129, pp. 179–197. Springer, Cham (2021). https://doi.org/10.1007/978-3-030-92641-0_9
6. Bellare, M., Namprempre, C., Neven, G.: Security proofs for identity-based identification and signature schemes. In: Cachin, C., Camenisch, J.L. (eds.) EUROCRYPT 2004. LNCS, vol. 3027, pp. 268–286. Springer, Heidelberg (2004). https://doi.org/10.1007/978-3-540-24676-3_17
7. Bernstein, D., De Feo, L., Leroux, A., Smith, B.: Faster computation of isogenies of large prime degree. arXiv preprint arXiv:2003.10118 (2020)

8. Beullens, W., Disson, L., Pedersen, R., Vercauteren, F.: CSI-RAShi: distributed key generation for CSIDH. In: Cheon, J.H., Tillich, J.-P. (eds.) PQCrypto 2021 2021. LNCS, vol. 12841, pp. 257–276. Springer, Cham (2021). https://doi.org/10.1007/978-3-030-81293-5_14

9. Beullens, W., Kleinjung, T., Vercauteren, F.: CSI-FiSh: efficient isogeny based signatures through class group computations. In: Galbraith, S.D., Moriai, S. (eds.) ASIACRYPT 2019. LNCS, vol. 11921, pp. 227–247. Springer, Cham (2019). https://doi.org/10.1007/978-3-030-34578-5_9

10. Bonnetain, X., Schrottenloher, A.: Quantum security analysis of CSIDH. In: Canteaut, A., Ishai, Y. (eds.) EUROCRYPT 2020. LNCS, vol. 12106, pp. 493–522. Springer, Cham (2020). https://doi.org/10.1007/978-3-030-45724-2_17

11. Castryck, W., Lange, T., Martindale, C., Panny, L., Renes, J.: CSIDH: an efficient post-quantum commutative group action. In: Peyrin, T., Galbraith, S. (eds.) ASIACRYPT 2018. LNCS, vol. 11274, pp. 395–427. Springer, Cham (2018). https://doi.org/10.1007/978-3-030-03332-3_15

12. Couveignes, J.M.: Hard homogeneous spaces. IACR Cryptology ePrint Archive 2006:291 (2006)

13. Cozzo, D., Smart, N.P.: Sashimi: cutting up CSI-FiSh secret keys to produce an actively secure distributed signing protocol. In: Ding, J., Tillich, J.-P. (eds.) PQCrypto 2020. LNCS, vol. 12100, pp. 169–186. Springer, Cham (2020). https://doi.org/10.1007/978-3-030-44223-1_10

14. Crites, E.C., Komlo, C., Maller, M.: Fully adaptive Schnorr threshold signatures. In: Handschuh, H., Lysyanskaya, A. (eds.) Advances in Cryptology - CRYPTO 2023–43rd Annual International Cryptology Conference, CRYPTO 2023, Santa Barbara, CA, USA, 20–24 August 2023, Proceedings, Part I. LNCS, vol. 14081, pp. 678–709. Springer, Cham (2023). https://doi.org/10.1007/978-3-031-38557-5_22

15. De Feo, L.: Mathematics of isogeny based cryptography. arXiv preprint arXiv:1711.04062 (2017)

16. De Feo, L., Galbraith, S.D.: SeaSign: compact isogeny signatures from class group actions. In: Ishai, Y., Rijmen, V. (eds.) EUROCRYPT 2019. LNCS, vol. 11478, pp. 759–789. Springer, Cham (2019). https://doi.org/10.1007/978-3-030-17659-4_26

17. Fiat, A., Shamir, A.: How to prove yourself: practical solutions to identification and signature problems. In: Odlyzko, A.M. (ed.) CRYPTO 1986. LNCS, vol. 263, pp. 186–194. Springer, Heidelberg (1987). https://doi.org/10.1007/3-540-47721-7_12

18. Gennaro, R., Jarecki, S., Krawczyk, H., Rabin, T.: Robust threshold DSS signatures. In: Maurer, U. (ed.) EUROCRYPT 1996. LNCS, vol. 1070, pp. 354–371. Springer, Heidelberg (1996). https://doi.org/10.1007/3-540-68339-9_31

19. Hess, F.: Efficient identity based signature schemes based on pairings. In: Nyberg, K., Heys, H. (eds.) SAC 2002. LNCS, vol. 2595, pp. 310–324. Springer, Heidelberg (2003). https://doi.org/10.1007/3-540-36492-7_20

20. Kiltz, E., Neven, G.: Identity-based signatures. In: Joye, M., Neven, G. (eds.) Identity-Based Cryptography. Cryptology and Information Security Series, vol. 2, pp. 31–44. IOS Press (2009)

21. Kitaev, A.Y.: Quantum measurements and the abelian stabilizer problem. Electronic Colloquium on Computational Complexity, TR96-003 (1996)

22. Kurosawa, K., Heng, S.-H.: From digital signature to ID-based identification/signature. In: Bao, F., Deng, R., Zhou, J. (eds.) PKC 2004. LNCS, vol. 2947, pp. 248–261. Springer, Heidelberg (2004). https://doi.org/10.1007/978-3-540-24632-9_18

23. Peikert, C.: He gives C-sieves on the CSIDH. In: Canteaut, A., Ishai, Y. (eds.) EUROCRYPT 2020. LNCS, vol. 12106, pp. 463–492. Springer, Cham (2020). https://doi.org/10.1007/978-3-030-45724-2_16

24. Peng, C., Chen, J., Zhou, L., Choo, K.-K.R., He, D.: CsiiBS: a post-quantum identity-based signature scheme based on isogenies. J. Inf. Secur. Appl. **54**, 102504 (2020)

25. Rostovtsev, A., Stolbunov, A.: Public-key cryptosystem based on isogenies. IACR Cryptology ePrint Archive, 2006:145 (2006)

26. Shamir, A.: Identity-based cryptosystems and signature schemes. In: Blakley, G.R., Chaum, D. (eds.) CRYPTO 1984. LNCS, vol. 196, pp. 47–53. Springer, Heidelberg (1985). https://doi.org/10.1007/3-540-39568-7_5

27. Shaw, S., Dutta, R.: Identification scheme and forward-secure signature in identity-based setting from isogenies. In: Huang, Q., Yu, Yu. (eds.) ProvSec 2021. LNCS, vol. 13059, pp. 309–326. Springer, Cham (2021). https://doi.org/10.1007/978-3-030-90402-9_17

28. Shor, P.W.: Algorithms for quantum computation: discrete logarithms and factoring. In: Proceedings of the 35th Annual Symposium on Foundations of Computer Science, pp. 124–134 (1994)

29. Silverman, J.H.: The Arithmetic of Elliptic Curves. GTM, vol. 106. Springer, New York (2009). https://doi.org/10.1007/978-0-387-09494-6

30. Stolbunov, A.: Constructing public-key cryptographic schemes based on class group action on a set of isogenous elliptic curves. Adv. Math. Commun. **4**(2), 215 (2010)

31. Vélu, J.: Isogénies entre courbes elliptiques. CR Acad. Sci. Paris, Séries A **273**, 305–347 (1971)

Cryptography in Practice: Analyses and Constructions

Dynamic Security Aspects of Onion Routing

Alessandro Melloni$^{(\boxtimes)}$, Martijn Stam , and Øyvind Ytrehus

Simula UiB, Bergen, Norway
{alessandro,martijn,oyvindy}@simula.no

Abstract. An *anonymous communication network (ACN)* is designed to protect the identities of two parties communicating through it, even if an adversary controls or observes parts of the network. Among the ACNs, Tor represents a practical trade-off between offering a reasonable level of anonymity and, simultaneously, an acceptable transmission delay. Due to its practical impact, there is abundant literature on the performance of Tor concerning both communication and security aspects.

Recently, a static framework was suggested for evaluating and comparing, in a quantifiable way, the effect of different scenarios (attacks, defence mechanisms, and other protocol changes). Although a static model is useful, many scenarios involve parameters and stochastic variables that change or evolve over time, or that may be influenced by active and malicious adversaries. In this paper, we propose a *dynamic* framework for evaluating such scenarios. We identify several scenarios where this framework is applicable, and illustrate our framework by considering the *guard node* mechanism in Tor. We evaluate and compare variations on the guard node concept suggested in the literature with respect to relevant performance metrics and, using the framework, support our evaluation with a theoretical analysis.

Keywords: Anonymity · Onion Routing · Tor · Traffic Analysis

1 Introduction

Onion routing aims to provide anonymity by obfuscating the link between a user and their network destination [9,10,28,31]. Ideally, the link remains hidden even against adversaries who observe or influence large swaths of the network. The most widespread implementation of onion routing is Tor [7], which relies on users picking multiple nodes from the network and establishing *circuits* to relay traffic through the nodes. These nodes are referred to as *onion routers*, and their identities are collected and distributed to the users by a central authority.

The anonymity provided by a Tor circuit strongly depends on what an adversary can observe. If all routers on the circuit are adversarially controlled, no anonymity is possible. Moreover, the first and last node on a circuit play a crucial role as the first node can easily identify the user whereas the last node knows the destination. If an adversary can correlate the two, e.g., by traffic analysis,

E. A. Quaglia (Ed.): IMACC 2023, LNCS 14421, pp. 243–262, 2024.
https://doi.org/10.1007/978-3-031-47818-5_13

anonymity is lost. Furthermore, an adversary only observing the first node can still attempt website fingerprinting to infer the destination.

Indeed, since its inception, these and other attacks, as well as improvements to Tor to counter them, have been proposed (see [17] for a recent overview). Whereas some attacks, such as traffic analysis and website fingerprinting, can be cast in a static framework [25], more advanced adversaries and countermeasures require a more dynamic framework to evaluate and compare threat models and protocol modifications. To limit the length and the scope of the paper, we will focus on guard nodes as illustrative scenario.

In recognition of the importance of the entry node and its honesty in providing anonymity, *guard nodes* were introduced through a series of modifications to the original Tor design [20,23]. Based on previous research [8,12,27,32], the underlying philosophy is to improve the anonymity for the majority of users by sacrificing that of a few. Although guard nodes are initially randomly selected by a user, they become the choice of entry node for that user's circuits across an extended period of time. In this way, users who pick an honest entry node will be "guaranteed" to be safe for an extended time frame, compared to always choosing a new entry node for every circuit. In contrast, users picking a corrupted guard node will suffer from a security degradation as more of their circuits will be exposed. Hence, analysing the security trade-offs provided by guard nodes necessarily involves the modelling of circuit re-establishment, which is a dynamic feature.

Our Contribution. We provide an evaluation framework to evaluate the efficacy of attacks by adversaries observing and possibly interacting with the Tor network over time. The framework can be applied to a variety of aspects of the onion routing protocol, including for instance:

1. effects of the guard nodes feature on anonymity;
2. guarantees of dynamic unlinkability;
3. severity of tagging attacks.

In particular, we focus on the first of these to illustrate the use of the framework. The framework enables the comparison of different attacks, threat models, and metrics in the dynamic scenario, and facilitates the discovery and identification of gaps in the literature. Such gaps may occur, for example, in the cases where different attacks (or defences against them) are published and evaluated with the use of mutually incompatible metrics.

Related Work. Since its inception, several analyses of Tor's anonymity have been conducted [1–3,18,19,24] (see also [22, Section 2] for a comprehensive account of different frameworks). A common approach, inspired by cryptographic games and proofs of security, is to formally define a game, the adversary, and a challenge. A main drawback of this approach is the lack of time-dependent and dynamic features being captured in the framework, as highlighted by Backes et al. [3]. They combined the formal approach with a concept of "time" within the framework, but focused on timing as additional information available to the adversary (e.g., for traffic analysis) instead of the evolution of the network itself over time. On the other hand, simulation-based approaches [14,15] allow for more practical analyses, with the distinct challenge of isolating and analysing the impact that the many parameters have on the results of the experiment.

2   Preliminaries

Notation. We use capitalised letters $A, B, \ldots$ to refer to random variables, and we base our treatment on the relationships among them. In particular, the causal relationship, denoted $A \rightsquigarrow B$, indicates that in a real-world system random variable A will be set before B and $I(A; B) > 0$; in other words, the random process modelled by the variable A happens before the process modelled by B and the outcome of the former influences the outcome of the latter. We use $\mathcal{U}$ and $\mathcal{C}$ to indicate the sets of users and, respectively, circuits; the boldface letters **u** and **n** refer to the numbers of users and guard nodes. We will use standard concepts from information theory, as detailed in the full version [26].

2.1   The Static Framework

Melloni, Stam, and Ytrehus [25] introduced a novel framework for assessing the security of low-latency ACNs in static scenarios such as traffic analysis and website fingerprinting. This *static framework* deviates from prevailing, more rigid approaches [13,18] by incorporating security metrics beyond conventional adversarial advantages and drawing inspiration from cryptographic games.

Central to the framework are random variables that capture different aspects of the game. These variables describe general behaviour of ACNs, and their purpose is to enable the identification of potential information leakages and quantify these in terms of conditional entropy and mutual information.

At the core of the framework sits the random variable S, which models the users connecting to their chosen destinations; S represents the secret an adversary wants to uncover. The random variable G represents all information in the system that could possibly be observed. For instance, in Tor it contains the states of all proxies (users) and routers, as well as all sorts of traffic traces.

In general, the precise distribution of G is hard to pin down as it depends on a lot of factors, e.g. the length of circuits, how nodes are chosen, protocol specification, as well as general load on the ACN and its underlying infrastructure. However, G uniquely determines S in the sense that $H(S \mid G) = 0$.

The view of the adversary, V, captures the information (from G) that is actually available to the adversary: once the threat model is fixed, V is completely determined by G, so $H(V \mid G) = 0$.

The goal of the adversary is specified by a query q, that identifies partial information on S of particular interest. The adversary processes its view V into an output O that is relevant for the query q at hand. For instance, it could be the adversary's posterior best guess for the answer to q. In any case, in the literature this processing is usually referred to as an *attack* on Tor and metrics are used to measure how well the attack actually fared.

Even though the exact probability distributions of the random variables may be unknown, their relationship is clear and can be defined in terms of information-theoretic notions, in particular using conditional entropy as done above. Moreover, as O arises from data processing of V, $\mathrm{H}(O \mid V) = 0$ holds and the data-processing inequality [4, Theorem 2.8.1] implies that $\mathrm{I}(V; S) \geq \mathrm{I}(O; S)$. Note that these conditions coexist with the causality relations $S \rightsquigarrow G \rightsquigarrow V \rightsquigarrow O$.

Our description of the static framework so far contained one small simplification. Melloni et al. additionally introduce a random variable Z representing auxiliary information gathered by an adversary during an initial training phase that can subsequently be used to refine the actual attack, that is the processing of V into O. For instance, V typically includes traffic traces and their shaping may be heavily affected by the destination or network topology, irrespective of the identity or even behaviour of the user. The variable Z captures what an adversary learns about the random behaviour of the ACN independent of the secret S. Thus $\mathrm{I}(S; Z) = 0$, yet the information might be useful for the processing, in the sense that $\mathrm{H}(S \mid V, Z) \leq \mathrm{H}(S \mid V)$ or, equivalently, $\mathrm{I}(S; V, Z) \geq \mathrm{I}(S; V)$.

Melloni et al. suggest Z might also contain an estimate of how S is distributed, for instance an adversary might try to determine the rough popularity of websites prior to any attack. To capture such a scenario formally, one could take a Bayesian approach where S is distributed according to a fixed model with unknown parameters (themselves following an uninformative prior); in that case Z can contain an estimation of the parameters according to which S is distributed. As we are primarily interested in evaluation scenarios, as opposed to real-life attacks, we can always assume the distribution of S is fixed and known.

Perspectives. The static framework is especially useful to specify an experimental setup used to evaluate security. In that case, a simplified scenario may be studied in lieu of a more complicated, realistic model and identifying the simplifications and their justifications (and limitations) can be useful. Often different metrics are required depending on the perspective that is taken, for instance a user might be primarily concerned about the likelihood of being deanonymised (a worst case), whereas a designer might be more interested in the expected number of compromises (an average case). Some simplifications will be suitable for one perspective, but perhaps less so for another.

3 A Dynamic Framework

Although the static framework can model attacks that involve time, such as traffic analysis, it is ill-equipped to deal with situations where parties actively change their behaviour over time, or where the system design introduces dependencies over time. To address such scenarios, in this section we introduce a general framework for an analysis of ACNs involving dynamic behaviour. Similar to the static framework, the dynamic one is described in terms of general random variables and the relations between them, where we focus on those relations that best capture dynamic aspects of the game. When applying the framework to a concrete scenario, the random variables and their relations should be specified in sufficient detail to answer any relevant research question, for instance what spaces the various random variables are defined over and how they are distributed. Irrelevant details, not pertinent to the research question can be abstracted away or left un(der)specified.

Introducing Epochs. To enable research into the effects of active adversaries tampering with the network as well as dynamic features of the onion protocol, we allow evolution of the environment by introducing the concept of epochs. An epoch is a period of time during which we assume behaviour by the parties to be fixed, so within an epoch the static framework applies. A dynamic picture emerges by considering a sequence of epochs, effectively discretising real time. Indeed, for each epoch $t \in \mathbb{N}$ we will consider the random variables S_t, G_t, V_t, O_t, and Z_t. Additionally, we will for a given random variable X_t, let X^t denote the collection of all the previous X_i up to and including t.

In the dynamic setting, the focus of an adversary's goal with respect to the epoch t can be made explicit by writing q_t for the adversarial query and $\mu_q(t)$ for a corresponding evaluation metric. The notation $\mu_q(t)$ emphasizes the metric as a function over time; in Sects. 4 and 5 we will consider different metrics μ_i, subscripted simply by an index i, as they all relate to the same query q.

Cross-Epoch Variable Dependencies. Within a given epoch t, the way the variables S_t, G_t, V_t, O_t, and Z_t relate to each other is directly inherited from the static framework. For the dynamic framework, we are interested in plausible relationships between variables from different epochs. Here we make a further distinction between intra-variable dependencies (e.g. between S_t and S^{t-1}) and inter-variable dependencies (e.g. between S_t and G^{t-1}).

We identify several possible scenarios, mainly depending on whether and how the dependency manifests for the different random variables. Here we concentrate on the core of the dependency, for instance when considering how G_t depends on G^{t-1}, we are less interested in the logical consequences in any dependency that can be (fully) explained by S_t depending on S^{t-1}.

Intra-variable Dependencies. Consider how users select their destinations, as captured by S_t. As the boundary between two epochs is somewhat arbitrary when considering real-life Tor, some users are likely to stick to a destination, whereas others might change (or connect for the first time). Thus, a user's future behaviour might depend on the present, but arguably not on the past, so S_t satisfies the (first order) Markov property, namely that $I(S_{t+1}; S^t) = I(S_{t+1}; S_t)$.

For evaluation purposes, it can be useful to restrict to one of the two extreme cases: either the outcome is drawn once and then fixed, so $S_{t+1} = S_t$ which implies that $I(S_{t+1}; S_t)$ is maximal; or the different epochs are independent of each other, so $I(S_{t+1}; S_t) = 0$ and minimal. The former, fixed case is useful to analyse active attacks exploiting adversarially triggered circuit tear-downs (including tagging attacks), whereas the latter case can be used to analyse linkability over longer time domains. In a real-life setting, the mutual information lies somewhere between these extremes.

When considering G_t, we recall that according to Tor protocol specifications, each user and router participating in the network is stateful and maintains all relevant information about its circuits and connections in the current state [6]. Thus, for circuits that remain active from one epoch to the next, G_{t+1} will depend on G_t, without any further dependency on past epochs. Similarly, for guard nodes, any state maintained by a user regarding the identity (and usage) of guard nodes will be part of G_t. Consequently, without significant loss of applicability, we can assume that also G_t exhibits a first order Markov property, i.e. $I(G_{t+1}; G^t) = I(G_{t+1}; G_t)$.

As the adversary's view V_t is a function of G_t, it might inherit its Markov property. In the static model, the threat model ruling how V is a function of G can be deemed fixed; in the dynamic model, an adversary might corrupt different routers in different epochs, thus changing which part of G_t is visible in V_t.

For an adversary's output O_t the question of how it relates to its predecessors O_{t-1} is, to a large extent, moot. What matters is that, on the one hand, O_t may well depend on the adversary's view on all epochs so far, i.e. on V^t and not just V_t. For instance, when trying to link users' information over multiple epochs, an adversary will necessarily have to combine its view across epochs. On the other hand, we might be interested in how an adversary's success evolves as a function of time t. However, in that case the appropriate tool is a metric $\mu_q(t)$ rather than a direct statement on O_t itself.

Finally, for the auxiliary random variable Z_t, we assume the adversary to accumulate all the collected information, so $H(Z_t \mid Z_{t+1}) = 0$ for $t \in \mathbb{N}$.

Inter-variable Dependencies. We already identified one inter-variable dependency above, namely in situations where an adversary's output O_t may depend on the view V^t across all epochs so far in case the goal is epoch-spanning. Yet, even if the goal is specific to the current epoch, if S_t is partially dependent on S_{t-1}, then information collected in the previous epoch might still serve an adversary well, for instance to rule out some destinations from the pool of possible ones (improving the confidence level in the output O_t).

Another inter-variable dependency arises when an adversary uses the view in V_t to disrupt the network, which will subsequently be reflected in G_{t+1}. For instance, an adversary might block access to some routers, thereby influencing how users pick the routers for their circuits.

4   Application of the Framework to Guard Nodes

In this section we discuss how to apply the dynamic framework to the study of the performance of guard node scenarios. Due to page limitations we need to keep the discussion brief.

Context. Guard nodes were introduced in 2013 [23], recognizing that *"some circuits are going to be compromised, but it's better to increase your probability of having no compromised circuits at the expense of also increasing the proportion of your circuits that will be compromised if any of them are."* The underlying technical assumption is that a single party controlling both the first and last nodes of a circuit can link source and destination of the traffic, and a single compromised circuit may suffice to ruin a user's anonymity.

Fixing the first node over a period of time increases the probability of having no compromised circuits over that period of time when compared to randomly picking a new entry node every new circuit setup. This fixed entry node is known as a *guard node*. In practice, users will still need to change guard nodes from time to time, for instance when their guard node is overloaded or unavailable, the last referred to as the natural *churn* of the network. To balance these unpredictable events, the guard node feature employed by Tor shortlists several nodes and then selects the guard node from this list; after a while, the list is refreshed [21].

As a result of this mechanism, the guard node policy actually consists of two distinct selection parts. First, a *guard list maintenance policy* describes how to construct the list of potential guard nodes, how many to pick, and when to pick new ones: this refresh process is referred to as *guard rotation*. Second, a *guard selection policy* dictates which node to pick from the short list whenever the proxy builds a new circuit. It is noteworthy to remark that literature on the subject tends to disregard the distinction between guard list maintenance policy and guard selection policy, focusing almost exclusively on the first.

The guard list maintenance policy is influenced by two factors: the churn of the nodes happening in the network and the guard rotation defined in the policy itself. Guard rotation also allows for recovery after compromise, as unlucky users picking corrupted guard nodes will refresh them after their lifetime expires.

Several changes [5, 8, 11, 12, 20, 30] to the original guard list maintenance algorithm have been proposed and analysed. These proposals mainly investigate the effects of changing the lifetime and quantity of guard nodes, both on performance and security. The fact that fixing a single guard node maximises security has already been recognised [5], but with some caveats when considering that nodes might be unreachable [8].

Security Evaluation. When the guard node feature was announced [23], the goal stated by the Tor team was to decrease the *number of deanonymised users*, conceding a higher *number of uncovered destinations for the users that have been deanonymised*. The first two security metrics we will consider are focused at estimating these quantities.

Later, Johnson et al. [16] employed the probability distribution of the *time until first compromise* as a security metric. In this paper, for ease of presentation we will instead use the average time until first compromise as our third metric. Lastly, we will consider a fourth metric to describe the situation for a user who is among the unlucky ones. We will describe these metrics in more detail in the **Metrics** subsection, after we have discussed the dynamic framework in the context of this specific application.

Security evaluation depends also greatly on the specific definition of *compromise*: different authors employ different approaches, possibly affecting a fair comparison. For example, Hayes and Danezis [12] consider a user to be compromised the moment they choose a malicious guard node (even before using it), while for Johnson et al. [16] a user needs to actually build a circuit through a malicious node to be compromised. We discuss this further in Sect. 5.1.

Our evaluation framework allows us to reveal hidden assumptions and simplifications (Sect. 5.1), facilitating both an exploration of possible alternatives and a combinatorial analysis and comparison of various guard node policies across scenarios (Sect. 5.2). It also enables a unified comparison of approaches discussed in the literature.

Remark 1. When considering the security offered by guard nodes, the emphasis is usually on circuit compromise. In our analysis, we will follow this lead, however there are other security ramifications tied to the use of guard nodes. For instance, it might be possible to identify a user based on their chosen guards (guard node fingerprinting [5]), which could violate the privacy goal of unlinkability of sessions over an extended period of time. The above holds even if each circuit is selected with an a honest exit node. In addition to guard node fingerprinting, ingress traffic fingerprinting allows linking user across epochs. We omit a further discussion of these issues in order to bound the length and scope of the paper.

Dynamic Modelling. To model guard nodes in our framework, we start by specifying a minimal setup of the random variables that suffices to capture the various guard node policies and their intended effect on security.

System Setup. We will consider u users that each connect to a single destination $d_{u,t}$ per epoch t, where we furthermore assume that users select their destinations independently of each other and different users may select their destination with different probability distributions. These choices specify the secrets S_t, where additionally we assume S_t to be independent across epochs. From the users' perspective, each epoch is marked by the setup of their respective circuits.

The variable G_t contains the state of the system and possible observables for an adversary. We assume that during each epoch, every user establishes a new circuit to its destination, resulting in the set of circuits C. Sticking to the default Tor circuit length of 3, each circuit can be represented as $c_i = (c_{\text{ID}}, u_{\text{ID}}, g_{\text{ID}}, m_{\text{ID}}, e_{\text{ID}}, d_{\text{ID}})$, consisting of ID for the circuit itself, the user, guard, middle, exit nodes and destination. Here the circuit identity c_{ID} is simply a global identifier used *in the framework*.

Given the circuit belonging to user u in epoch t, the destination d_{ID} will match that in S_t, so equal $d_{u,t}$. The middle router m_{ID} and exit router e_{ID} are assumed to be chosen independently and uniformly at random, whereas, crucially, the guard node g_{ID} is selected according to the guard node policy.

The guard node policy itself is modelled by maintaining (in G_t) on the one hand all information that proxies require to select their guard nodes (such as bandwidth and availability) and on the other, for each proxy, that proxy's state pertaining to its guard nodes, as prescribed by the specific policy (for instance, the priority of the guard nodes, how long they have been in use by that proxy, etc.). Different guard selection proposals may require additional information, such as the mapping of guard nodes to their set in the *guard sets* proposal [12].

The guard node feature advantage starts from the second circuit setup and involves information from the previous epoch that is maintained into the current one, consistent with G_t being a Markov process. In case there is no guard node feature, G_t is memoryless and users select new entry nodes every circuit setup.

For the possible observables and for each node, operational information is maintained in G_t for all the circuits routed by that node. Here we use the model common for traffic analysis and website fingerprinting, and let guard and exit nodes observe $(u_{ID}, m_{ID}, \text{ingress trace})$ and $(m_{ID}, d_{ID}, \text{egress trace})$, respectively.

The Adversary. The view of the adversary V_t consists of a selection of the last two types of tuples. Which tuples an adversary can observe depends on the threat model, more specifically on which nodes are corrupted; we indicate the ratio of malicious entry and exit nodes with γ and ε respectively. Here one could make a distinction, as Melloni et al. [25] do, between full control where the adversary has completely corrupted the node and can see its state (including the identity of the middle router m_{ID} for every circuit through that node); and partial control where an adversary can observe the link traffic between the node and the outside world (so u_{ID} and ingress trace, respectively d_{ID} and egress trace, but not m_{ID}). The difference between these two types of adversarial views relates to the amount of information acquired by the adversary *per time unit*, so that an adversary with the weaker level of node compromise may have to observe more traffic to obtain the same results. Pragmatically, the difference between these two cases can be modelled by different ε values (where ε is changed to mean "the probability of full circuit deanonymisation given a guard compromise".)

In these minimal settings, the adversary aims to uncover as many user–destination pairs as possible, based on V_t. Since each user only has one destination per epoch, the adversary can simply output $O_t = \left\{ \widehat{d}_{u_j,t} \right\}$, indicating the guessed destination for users $u_1, \ldots, u_i$ in epoch t.

Metrics. To formalize the security metrics mentioned earlier, we introduce two auxiliary random variables: $X_{\leq t}(u)$ represents the number of correct guesses by the adversary up to epoch t for user u, defined as $X_{\leq t}(u) = \sum_{i=1}^{t} \left[\widehat{d}_{u,i} \stackrel{?}{=} d_{u,i} \right]$; and $Y_{\leq t}$ denotes the number of users that have never been deanonymised (up to epoch t), i.e. $Y_{\leq t} = |\{u | X_{\leq t}(u) = 0\}|$.

The goal of the guard nodes feature is to minimize the deanonymised users:

$$\mu_1(t) = \mathbb{E}\left[Y_{\leq t}\right], \text{ or equivalently with } \mu_1(t) = \sum_u \Pr[X_{\leq t}(u) = 0]. \quad (1)$$

Table 1. Description of the identified metrics.

Metric	Description
$\mu_1(t)$	Expected number of users that, up to epoch t, have never been deanonymised (1).
$\mu_2(t)$	Expected number of uncovered destinations for any user that has been already deanonymised (2).
μ_3	Average time until first deanonymisation (3).
$\mu_4(t)$	Average of Pr[compromise at time t + 1	compromise at time t] (4).

The "price" is an increase in deanonymised destinations for compromised users:

$$\mu_2(t) = \frac{1}{u} \sum_u \mathbb{E}[X_{\leq t}(u) \mid X_{\leq t}(u) > 0]. \tag{2}$$

We also simplify the metrics of by Johnson et al. [16], considering the average instead of the full distribution:

$$\mu_3 = \frac{1}{u} \sum_u \mathbb{E}[\min\{t | X_{\leq t}(u) > 0\}]. \tag{3}$$

Recalling that the guard node construction gains anonymity for the majority by sacrificing a few, it is also useful to have a metric that quantifies how much the few will suffer. We will use the following metric:

$$\mu_4(t) = \frac{1}{u} \sum_u \Pr[X_{\leq t+1}(u) > X_{\leq t}(u) \mid X_{\leq t}(u) > X_{\leq t-1}(u)]. \tag{4}$$

4.1 Guard Nodes Policies

The framework allows us to compare several variations of guard node policies through computation of the metrics, but we first need to identify the parameters needed to describe a guard node policy. The number of nodes picked by each proxy, according to a defined probability distribution Δ, is **n**. We also need an ordering $\preceq$ to specify the relative preference of guard nodes to use each time the user wants to setup a new circuit, and the maximum lifetime of T epochs for guard nodes before being refreshed.

No Guard Nodes. The base case is having no guard nodes feature at all: the proxy chooses a new entry node for every circuit setup, i.e. T = 1; we refer to this as no-guards policy.

Table 2. Different models of guard node policies.

Type	Policy	Description
Guard maintenance	No-guards	No guard nodes.
	1-guard	Single guard node.
	3-guards	3 guard nodes, simplified Tor current specification.
	Tor Guard Specification	The current Tor guard node specification [21].
Guard selection	Ideal uniform-use	See "Simplified policies" in Sect. 5.1.
	Greedy	See "Simplified policies" in Sect. 5.1.

Single Guard. The simplest guard based policy is the one with a single guard node, using only that for circuit setups until it expires or if it is unreachable. Formally, $n = 1$ and $T > 1$.

3-Guards. A more practical policy is represented by the 3-guards policy, where the proxy selects 3 entry nodes and uses them as guard nodes until they expire or become unreachable. This guard policy is a simplified version of the current Tor Guard Specification (see below). The introduction of multiple guard nodes prompts the need to specify the guard selection policy, ruling which guard node to select for each circuit creation.

Tor Guard Specification. The current Tor guard node specification [21] is based on a series of subsequent samplings performed by the proxies, starting from the set of all the current guard nodes according to some probability distribution and some further processing (see [26]). The proxy picks, at run-time, 3 nodes to use as guards from a persistent short list, with nodes being removed from it when they are either unreachable for some epochs or their lifetime as guards expired.

5   Analysis

In Sect. 5.1, we first explain the simplifications and assumptions we apply in order to design an analytical model *for evaluation purposes*. Subsequently, in Sect. 5.2 we derive quantitative values for the metrics in Table 1 based on the parameters already introduced. As an alternative to the analytical results, we also created a simple simulation program that is described in Sect. 5.3. Section 5.4 discusses suitable parameter ranges, and in Sect. 5.5 we provide numerical results.

5.1   Simplifications and Assumptions

Research on ACNs is seldom performed on real-world data and systems, for both practical and ethical reasons, e.g. the lack of available information, the intractable complexity of the live Tor network, the need to create reproducible results from controllable network states and parameter values, or the privacy intrusion of observing actual Tor communication. To overcome these limitations, researchers introduce simplifications and assumptions when analysing some aspects of Tor. Here we summarize the simplifications we subsequently apply in Sect. 5.2. Justifications for these simplifications can be found in the full version [26]. The simplifications we use include:

1. S_t: *Simple and uniform user behaviour.* In each epoch, each user selects a destination independently of the others and connects to it.
2. *Uniform node corruption.* Each guard node is corrupted with a fixed probability γ, and each exit node is corrupted with a fixed probability ε.
3. *Uniform guard node churn.* Each guard node experiences churn with a fixed probability φ.
4. *A "breach of anonymity" occurs iff a circuit's entry/guard node and its exit nodes are both corrupted.* Other models can be represented by adjusting ε.
5. *The analysis ignores parameters irrelevant to the computation of metrics.*
6. *Simplified policies for*
   - *Guard list selection.* Each time a guards list is renewed, guards are selected uniformly at random.
   - *Selection of guard for each circuit.* In a *greedy* policy (respectively, the *ideal uniform use* (IU) policy), the user will use a guard node that has been used *most often* (resp. *least often*) during the lifetime of the current guard list. In our context, these theoretical policies serve to obtain bounds on Tor's anonymisation performance.
   - *Churn policy.* If all **n** guard nodes are simultaneously unavailable in an epoch, an immediate renewal of the entire guard list is triggered.
7. *Guard lists are disjoint over time.*

5.2   Quantitative Formulas for Metrics

In this section, we provide formulas for the metrics introduced in Sect. 4 (see Table 1) for the guard node policies identified in Table 2 (except the Tor Guard policy, the performance of which is bounded by that of other policies). We omit the proofs and refer to the full version [26] for proofs.

Three General and Basic Lemmas. In Lemmas 1 to 3 we give general expressions for metrics $\mu_i, i \in 1, \ldots, 3$ that are valid for all guard node policies and the user behaviour that we will discuss. These expressions still rely on further calculations, specific to each policy, that will be derived further later on for some policies.

Lemma 1 (Formulas for $\mu_1(t)$ for any guard node policy). *Assume that in each epoch, each user, independent from the others, selects a destination and establishes a new Tor circuit to it. Then*

$$\mu_1(t) = \mathbb{E}\big[Y_{\leq t}\big] = \mathbf{u} \cdot \Pr[X_{\leq t}(u) = 0]. \tag{5}$$

Lemma 2 (Formulas for $\mu_2(t)$ for any guard node policy). *Let S_t be as described in Sect. 4, and assume that for each circuit setup, the exit node is selected independently of the guard node. Then, for any guard node policy,*

$$\mu_2(t) = \frac{t\gamma\varepsilon}{1 - \Pr[X_{\leq t} = 0]}. \tag{6}$$

Lemma 3 (Formulas for μ_3 for any guard node policy). *Let S_t be as described in Sect. 4. Then, for any guard node policy,*

$$\mu_3 = \sum_{\tilde{t}=1}^{t} \left(\tilde{t} \cdot \Pr[X_{\leq \tilde{t}} = 1 \mid X_{\leq \tilde{t}-1} = 0] \cdot \Pr[X_{\leq \tilde{t}-1} = 0] \right). \tag{7}$$

The No-Guards and 1-Guard Policies, Reachable Guard Nodes. In this subsection we derive results for the simple cases of the no-guards policy and the 1-guard policy, when Tor nodes are always reachable (i.e., there is no churn, so $\varphi = 0$). From Lemmas 1 to 3, we see that we need to calculate $\Pr[X_{\leq t} = 0]$ for each specific scenario. The next lemma gives the probability of no compromise when a guard node is reused for several circuits.

Lemma 4. *Consider a sequence of ℓ circuits, created with a single guard node and with random exit nodes. Then the probability of no compromise in any of the ℓ circuits is $F_{\gamma,\varepsilon}(\ell) = F(\ell)$ (dropping the subscripts for convenience), where*

$$\Pr[X_{\leq \ell} = 0] = F(\ell) \triangleq 1 - \gamma + \gamma(1 - \varepsilon)^{\ell}. \tag{8}$$

Proposition 1 (Formulas for $\Pr[X_{\leq t} = 0]$ for no guards, single guards). *Let S_t be as described. Then for the no guards policy,*

$$\Pr[X_{\leq t} = 0] = (1 - \gamma\varepsilon)^t$$

while for a single guard policy,

$$\Pr[X_{\leq t} = 0] = (F(T))^{\lfloor t/T \rfloor} F(t \bmod T). \tag{9}$$

Proposition 2 (Formulas for μ_3 for $\varphi = 0$). *Let S_t be as described in Sect. 4, and let $\mu_3 = \mathbb{E}[\min\{t|X_{\leq t} > 0\}] = \mathbb{E}[\max\{t|X_{\leq t} = 0\}]+1$. Then, without guard nodes,*

$$\mu_3 = \frac{1}{\varepsilon\gamma}. \tag{10}$$

With a single guard node,

$$\mu_3 = \frac{\gamma}{\varepsilon} \left(\frac{T\varepsilon(1 - (1 - \varepsilon)^T)F(T) + (1 - (T\varepsilon + 1)(1 - \varepsilon)^T)(1 - F(T))}{(1 - F(T))^2} \right). \tag{11}$$

With more than one guard node and the greedy guard selection policy, $\varphi = 0$ implies that only a single guard node is ever used, so that (11) is valid also for this case. Also, for $T = 1$, (11) reduces to (10).

Proposition 3 (Formulas for $\mu_4(t)$ for $\varphi = 0$). *In the no-churn case, i.e.* $\varphi = 0$,

$$\mu_4(t) = \begin{cases} \gamma\varepsilon & \text{if } t \equiv 0 \mod T, \\ \\ \varepsilon & \text{otherwise.} \end{cases} \tag{12}$$

The General Case: $\varphi \geq 0, n \geq 1, T \geq 1$. The previous subsection gives an insight into the performance when the churn probability φ is very small. The results for $\varphi = 0$ imply that choosing a *single guard* policy with T as large as possible is the best thing to do, but for practical reasons, the Tor protocol uses guard lists with more than one guard node. Hence we proceed with the case of $\varphi > 0$, with a reset policy as discussed in Sect. 5.1. In this case, over t epochs, a user will go through a random number m of consecutive guard lists. Since, due to churn, a guard list may be prematurely reset, the ith guard list will actually last for a random number T_i of epochs, where the last guard list may still be active at time t and

$$1 \leq T_i \leq T, 1 \leq i \leq m \tag{13}$$

and

$$\sum_{i=1}^{m} T_i = t. \tag{14}$$

Thus, the metrics values for a given set of parameters and a given policy depend on the probability distribution of m and the sequence $T_i, i = 1, \ldots, m$ for each t. We will return to how to calculate $\mu_1(t)$ in Proposition 4, but it is convenient to state a couple of supporting results first.

For a guard list of n guards, and for each $i = 1, \ldots, n$, let ℓ_i be the number of times guard i is used during t epochs, so that $\sum_i \ell_i = t$. By Lemma 5, γ, ε, and the distribution $\chi = (\ell_1, \ldots, \ell_n)$ completely determine $\Pr[X_{\leq t} = 0]$.

Lemma 5. *Assume that, at time $t = \ell_1 + \cdots + \ell_n \leq T$, the n different guard nodes from the guard list have been used (in any order) respectively $\ell_1, \ldots, \ell_n$ times since the last guard list renewal. Then*

$$\Pr[X_{\leq t} = 0] = \prod_{i=1}^{n} F(\ell_i) \tag{15}$$

Lemma 6 (Monotonicity of $F(\ell)$). *Assume, without loss of generality, that $\ell_i \geq \ell_{i+1}$, for $1 \leq i < n$. For positive integers $\ell_1 \geq \ell_2$,*

$$F(\ell_1 + 1) F(\ell_2 - 1) \geq F(\ell_1) F(\ell_2) \tag{16}$$

and for positive integers ℓ_1, ℓ_2,

$$F(\ell_1 + \ell_2) \geq F(\ell_1) F(\ell_2). \tag{17}$$

It follows from Lemma 5 and Lemma 6 that a *greedy* policy is optimum with respect to maximizing $\Pr[X_{\leq \ell} = 0]$, and that an *ideally uniform use* (IU) policy is the worst possible. Hence the performance of any policy (for selecting a guard from the guard list for use for the next circuit) will lie between these two extremes. Another consequence of these lemmas is that the $\mu_1(t)$-performance of the IU policy is lower bounded by that of the no-guard case (see Fig. 1).

Assume that the user has created t circuits (one circuit per epoch), and that the n guard nodes have been used respectively $\chi_1, \chi_2, \ldots, \chi_n$ times, where $\chi_1 + \chi_2 + \cdots + \chi_n = t$ and, without loss of generality, $\chi_1 \geq \chi_2 \geq \cdots \geq \chi_n$. Then let the *guard node distribution* be $\chi(t) = (\chi_1, \chi_2, \ldots, \chi_n)$. The ordering of the actual guard nodes may change over time to maintain the constraint $\chi_1 \geq \chi_2 \geq \cdots \geq \chi_n$. Finally, let $\underline{\chi}(t)$ be the set of all guard distributions at epoch t. At time $t > 0$, the current guard set has been used for a random time of b epochs, and the Markov process describing the guard use will be in a random state $\chi(b)$.

Let $P_\chi(b)$ be the probability of guard distribution $\chi = (\chi_1, \chi_2, \ldots, \chi_n)$ at epoch b, where $b = \chi_1 + \chi_2 + \cdots + \chi_n$ and $1 \leq b \leq \mathsf{T}$. Guard distributions develop over epochs through a random walk if $\varphi > 0$. Let $P_{\chi'(t-1) \to \chi(t)}$ denote the probability that a guard distribution $\chi'(t-1)$ at epoch $t-1$ develops into $\chi(t)$ at epoch t. The probability $P_{\chi'(t-1) \to \chi(t)}$ depends (only) on φ and the guard selection policy. More details can be found in the full version [26].

For $\chi' = (1, \underbrace{0, \ldots, 0}_{n-1})$, define $P_{\chi'}(1) = 1$, and for $1 < b \leq \mathsf{T}$ and $\chi \in \underline{\chi}(b)$,

$$P_\chi(b) = \sum_{\chi' \in \underline{\chi}(b-1)} P_{\chi'}(b-1) P_{\chi'(b-1) \to \chi(b)}.$$

Proposition 4 (Formula for $\Pr[X_{\leq t} = 0]$ for n-guards scenarios). *Let* $G_0(P, Z) = \sum_{b=1}^{\mathsf{T}} P_b Z^b$ *and* $G(Q, Z) = \sum_{b=1}^{\mathsf{T}} Q_b Z^b$, *where* $P_b = F(b) P_\chi(b)$ *for* $b = 1, \ldots, \mathsf{T}$ *and* $Q_b = F(b) P_\chi(b) \varphi^n$ *for* $b = 1, \ldots, \mathsf{T}-1$ *while* $Q_\mathsf{T} = F(\mathsf{T}) P_\chi(\mathsf{T})$. *Then, for* $\forall t > 1, \forall t' \geq t - 1$, *the probability* $\Pr[X_{\leq t} = 0]$ *is the coefficient of* Z^t *in the polynomial*

$$G_0(P, Z) \sum_{\ell=0}^{t'} G(Q, Z)^\ell. \tag{18}$$

5.3 Simulation Program

The analytical approach in Sect. 5.2 offers expressions that, at least for some metrics, give "exact" numerical results. However, some expressions are complicated and offer little in terms of intuitive understanding. A simulation process may be easier to apply to most of the metrics we consider, and gives sufficiently precise results. Since *tornettools* does not support the guard node feature [15, Section 3.2.2] and *shadow* [14] would require adapting Tor's source code for each of the various policies, we wrote a program to simulate a Tor scenario simplified as discussed in Sect. 5.1. To check the correctness of the simulation program, we have verified that the results coincide exactly with our theoretical results where applicable.

For each simulation sample, a set of parameter values is applied to a random process in which guard lists are selected, guards and exit nodes are compromised according to probabilities γ and ε, guard nodes are selected according to a given policy and based on availability according to the churn parameter φ, and a guard list is completely renewed when it has been used for T epochs or all guards are simultaneously unavailable. Each sample is run for a preselectable number of epochs, and data for the metrics are collected for each sample. For each set of parameters, the simulation is run for as many $(10^6 - 10^7)$ samples as needed.

Lemma 7 (Formulas for μ_4 for $\varphi > 0$). *For the case of $\varphi > 0$, the asymptotic value of $\mu_4 = \lim_{t \to \infty} \mu_4(t)$ is given by*

$$\mu_4 = (\pi_{change}(\gamma - 1) + 1)\varepsilon, \tag{19}$$

where π_{change} is the probability that the guard node used at time $t + 1$ is different from the one used at time t.

Remark 2 (Regarding Lemma 7). It can be seen that (with equality for $n = 1$),

$$\pi_{change} \geq \frac{1}{\sum_{i=1}^{T}(1 - \varphi^n)^i}.$$

For $n > 1$, π_{change} is a lower bound on π_{change}, since guard changes can occur also due to other reasons. For $n > 1$, π_{change} can be estimated by simulation. A direct estimator for $\mu_4(t)$ can naïvely be obtained by counting pairs of compromised circuits in a simulation and dividing this number by $\gamma\varepsilon$, but using (19) gives a more precise way of estimating $\mu_4(t)$.

5.4 Discussion: Relevant Parameter Ranges

To provide further insight into the practical ramifications of our work, we next discuss suitable parameter ranges, followed by an interpretation of the results from our analytical model for these parameters.

Network Characteristics n and φ. Natural churn rate φ in the Tor network can be computed by collecting and comparing subsequent consensus files. We observe from previous research [29, Section 5.2] that φ is typically in the range $[0.001, 0.003]$. For an n-guard policy, the probability that all n guard nodes are simultaneously unavailable in an epoch is φ^n. This observation is an argument for using lists with at least three guard nodes. Conversely, it suggests robustness and small downtime as criteria for selecting guard nodes.

Epoch Granularity T. In our experiments, we have used both small (to shed light on the mechanisms) and large values of T. Our model is simplified with respect to real users, who will not be continuously connected. However, it seems reasonable that a real user can create some hundred circuits, one epoch per circuit, during a normal Tor guard list lifetime.

Compromise Levels γ and ε. We can model different scenarios through careful choice of γ and ε:

- $\varepsilon = 1$: The case when guard compromise is considered equivalent to circuit compromise.
- $0 < \varepsilon < 1$: guard compromise combined with a probability ε of the union of events {*website fingerprinting is successful, exit node is compromised*}.
- $0 < \varepsilon = \gamma < 1$: The case where both ends need to be compromised for a circuit to be compromised; we are concerned with *one single adversary* that controls the fraction $\varepsilon = \gamma$ of Tor node bandwidth.
- $0 < \varepsilon \ll \gamma < 1$: The case where both ends need to be compromised for a circuit to be compromised; we are concerned by compromise by *any* of these. Each adversary controls a fraction ε of Tor node bandwidth. Thus, the effective guard node compromise ratio γ is $\varepsilon \times$ (number of adversaries).

5.5 Results

Figure 1 shows results for $\mu_1(t)$ and $\mu_2(t)$ for selected sets of parameters. From the results, different patterns emerge:

- The value of $\mu_1(t)$ for the greedy policy quickly converges to its expected value of $(1 - \gamma)$, until the guard list is renewed.
- The value of $\mu_1(t)$ for the IU policy is sometimes close to the greedy policy (curves C and D), and always lower bounded by the no-guard policy (curve E). For the parameter set corresponding to curve B, the IU policy curve (not explicitly shown) coincides almost exactly with curve E. In general, for large n and T and small φ, the guard selection policy influences $\mu_1(t)$ heavily.
- The value of $\mu_2(t)$ for the greedy policy quickly converges to (6).
- For the realistic $\varphi \in [0, 0.003]$ there is no significant impact of φ on any of our metrics. Thus our results for all four metrics conditioned on $\varphi = 0$ are good approximations.
- In general, the two other metrics (not shown due to lack of space) seem to vary less dramatically.

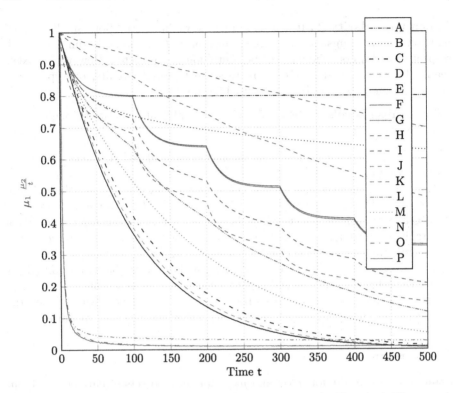

Fig. 1. Simulation results for 500 epochs and parameter sets $(\mathbf{n}, \mathsf{T}, \varphi, \gamma, \varepsilon)$. The parameter sets as listed in the figure legend are A: (1, 1000, 0, 0.2, 0.05), B: (100, 1000, 0.1, 0.2, 0.05), C: (3, 10, 0.1, 0.2, 0.05), D: (3, 10, 0.1, 0.2, 0.05, IU), E: (1, 1, 0, 0.2, 0.05), F: (3, 100, 0), G: (3, 100, 0.003, 0.2, 0.05), H: (3, 100, 0.1, 0.2, 0.05), I: (3, 100, 0.1, 0.2, 0.01), J: (3, 100, 0.1, 0.1, 0.01), K: (3, 100, 0.1, 0.2, 0.1), L: (3, 100, 0.2, 0.2, 0.05), M: (3, 100, 0.3, 0.2, 0.05), N: (100, 1000, 0.1, 0.2, 0.05), O: (3, 10, 0.1, 0.2, 0.05), P: (1, 1, 0, 0.2, 0.05). Unless explicitly stated as IU (ideally uniform), the policy is the greedy one. Black, blue, green, and orange curves show $\mu_1(t)$. The "waves" of the blue and green curves show the effect of changing stable guard sets. The red curves passing through the lower left corner show $\mu_2(t)/t$. (Color figure online)

6 Conclusion

We have presented a general evaluation framework to evaluate the security performance of Tor network protocol policies and the efficacy of attacks carried out by adversaries observing and possibly interacting with the Tor network over time. As an example, we have used the framework to develop an analysis of the guard node feature, shedding new insights on the guard node selection as distinct from the guard list maintenance and the effects that various parameters have on the examined metrics.

References

1. Backes, M., Kate, A., Manoharan, P., Meiser, S., Mohammadi, E.: AnoA: a framework for analyzing anonymous communication protocols. In: Cortier, V., Datta, A. (eds.) CSF 2013 Computer Security Foundations Symposium, pp. 163–178. IEEE Computer Society Press (2013). https://doi.org/10.1109/CSF.2013.18

2. Backes, M., Kate, A., Meiser, S., Mohammadi, E.: (Nothing else) MATor(s): monitoring the anonymity of tor's path selection. In: Ahn, G.J., Yung, M., Li, N. (eds.) ACM CCS 2014, pp. 513–524. ACM Press (2014). https://doi.org/10.1145/2660267.2660371

3. Backes, M., Manoharan, P., Mohammadi, E.: TUC: time-sensitive and modular analysis of anonymous communication. In: Datta, A., Fournet, C. (eds.) CSF 2014 Computer Security Foundations Symposium, pp. 383–397. IEEE Computer Society Press (2014). https://doi.org/10.1109/CSF.2014.34

4. Cover, T.M., Thomas, J.A.: Elements of Information Theory. Wiley, Hoboken (2006). https://doi.org/10.1002/047174882X

5. Dingledine, R., Hopper, N., Kadianakis, G., Mathewson, N.: One fast guard for life (or 9 months) (2014)

6. Dingledine, R., Mathewson, N.: Tor protocol specification (2021). https://github.com/torproject/torspec/blob/main/tor-spec.txt. Commit 48ab890

7. Dingledine, R., Mathewson, N., Syverson, P.F.: Tor: the second-generation onion router. In: Blaze, M. (ed.) USENIX Security 2004, pp. 303–320. USENIX Association (2004)

8. Elahi, T., Bauer, K.S., AlSabah, M., Dingledine, R., Goldberg, I.: Changing of the guards: a framework for understanding and improving entry guard selection in Tor. In: Yu, T., Borisov, N. (eds.) WPES 2012, pp. 43–54. ACM (2012). https://doi.org/10.1145/2381966.2381973

9. Goldschlag, D.M., Reed, M.G., Syverson, P.F.: Hiding routing information. In: Anderson, R. (ed.) IH 1996. LNCS, vol. 1174, pp. 137–150. Springer, Heidelberg (1996). https://doi.org/10.1007/3-540-61996-8_37

10. Goldschlag, D.M., Reed, M.G., Syverson, P.F.: Onion routing. Commun. ACM **42**(2), 39–41 (1999). https://doi.org/10.1145/293411.293443

11. Hanley, H., Sun, Y., Wagh, S., Mittal, P.: DPSelect: a differential privacy based guard relay selection algorithm for tor. PoPETs **2019**(2), 166–186 (2019). https://doi.org/10.2478/popets-2019-0025

12. Hayes, J., Danezis, G.: Guard sets for onion routing. PoPETs **2015**(2), 65–80 (2015). https://doi.org/10.1515/popets-2015-0017

13. Hevia, A., Micciancio, D.: An indistinguishability-based characterization of anonymous channels. In: Borisov, N., Goldberg, I. (eds.) PETS 2008. LNCS, vol. 5134, pp. 24–43. Springer, Heidelberg (2008). https://doi.org/10.1007/978-3-540-70630-4_3

14. Jansen, R., Hopper, N.: Shadow: running Tor in a box for accurate and efficient experimentation. In: NDSS 2012. The Internet Society (2012)

15. Jansen, R., Tracey, J., Goldberg, I.: Once is never enough: foundations for sound statistical inference in tor network experimentation. In: Bailey, M., Greenstadt, R. (eds.) USENIX Security 2021, pp. 3415–3432. USENIX Association (2021)

16. Johnson, A., Wacek, C., Jansen, R., Sherr, M., Syverson, P.F.: Users get routed: traffic correlation on Tor by realistic adversaries. In: Sadeghi, A.R., Gligor, V.D., Yung, M. (eds.) ACM CCS 2013, pp. 337–348. ACM Press (2013). https://doi.org/10.1145/2508859.2516651

17. Karunanayake, I., Ahmed, N., Malaney, R., Islam, R., Jha, S.K.: De-anonymisation attacks on Tor: a survey. IEEE Commun. Surv. Tutor. **23**(4), 2324–2350 (2021). https://doi.org/10.1109/COMST.2021.3093615

18. Kuhn, C., Beck, M., Schiffner, S., Jorswieck, E.A., Strufe, T.: On privacy notions in anonymous communication. PoPETs **2019**(2), 105–125 (2019). https://doi.org/10.2478/popets-2019-0022

19. Kuhn, C., Beck, M., Strufe, T.: Breaking and (partially) fixing provably secure onion routing. In: 2020 IEEE Symposium on Security and Privacy, pp. 168–185. IEEE Computer Society Press (2020). https://doi.org/10.1109/SP40000.2020.00039

20. Lovecruft, I., Kadianakis, G., Bini, O., Mathewson, N.: Another algorithm for guard selection (2017). https://github.com/torproject/torspec/blob/main/proposals/271-another-guard-selection.txt. Commit db17344

21. Lovecruft, I., Kadianakis, G., Bini, O., Mathewson, N.: Tor guard specification (2021). https://github.com/torproject/torspec/blob/main/guard-spec.txt. Commit 29245fd

22. Lu, T., Du, Z., Wang, Z.J.: A survey on measuring anonymity in anonymous communication systems. IEEE Access **7**, 70584–70609 (2019). https://doi.org/10.1109/ACCESS.2019.2919322

23. Mathewson, N., Murdoch, S.: Top changes in Tor since the 2004 design paper (part 2) (2012). https://blog.torproject.org/top-changes-tor-2004-design-paper-part-2/

24. Mauw, S., Verschuren, J.H.S., de Vink, E.P.: A formalization of anonymity and onion routing. In: Samarati, P., Ryan, P., Gollmann, D., Molva, R. (eds.) ESORICS 2004. LNCS, vol. 3193, pp. 109–124. Springer, Heidelberg (2004). https://doi.org/10.1007/978-3-540-30108-0_7

25. Melloni, A., Stam, M., Ytrehus, Ø.: On evaluating anonymity of onion routing. In: AlTawy, R., Hülsing, A. (eds.) SAC 2021. LNCS, vol. 13203, pp. 3–24. Springer, Cham (2022). https://doi.org/10.1007/978-3-030-99277-4_1

26. Melloni, A., Stam, M., Ytrehus, Ø.: Dynamic security aspects of onion routing. Cryptology ePrint Archive, Paper 2023/1439 (2023). https://eprint.iacr.org/2023/1439

27. Øverlier, L., Syverson, P.: Locating hidden servers. In: 2006 IEEE Symposium on Security and Privacy, pp. 100–114. IEEE Computer Society Press (2006). https://doi.org/10.1109/SP.2006.24

28. Reed, M.G., Syverson, P.F., Goldschlag, D.M.: Proxies for anonymous routing. In: ACSAC 1996, pp. 95–104. IEEE Computer Society (1996). https://doi.org/10.1109/CSAC.1996.569678

29. Sharma, P.K., Chaudhary, S., Hassija, N., Maity, M., Chakravarty, S.: The road not taken: re-thinking the feasibility of voice calling over tor. PoPETs **2020**(4), 69–88 (2020). https://doi.org/10.2478/popets-2020-0063

30. Sun, Y., Edmundson, A., Feamster, N., Chiang, M., Mittal, P.: Counter-RAPTOR: safeguarding tor against active routing attacks. In: 2017 IEEE Symposium on Security and Privacy, pp. 977–992. IEEE Computer Society Press (2017). https://doi.org/10.1109/SP.2017.34

31. Syverson, P.F., Goldschlag, D.M., Reed, M.G.: Anonymous connections and onion routing. In: 1997 IEEE Symposium on Security and Privacy, pp. 44–54. IEEE Computer Society Press (1997). https://doi.org/10.1109/SECPRI.1997.601314

32. Wright, M.K., Adler, M., Levine, B.N., Shields, C.: Defending anonymous communications against passive logging attack. In: 2003 IEEE Symposium on Security and Privacy, pp. 28–43. IEEE Computer Society Press (2003). https://doi.org/10.1109/SECPRI.2003.1199325

Practical and Efficient FHE-Based MPC

Nigel P. Smart[1,2]([⊠]) [iD]

[1] COSIC, KU Leuven, Leuven, Belgium
nigel.smart@kuleuven.be,nigel@zama.ai
[2] Zama Inc., Paris, France

Abstract. We present a *reactive* MPC protocol built from FHE which is *robust* in the presence of active adversaries. In addition the protocol enables reduced bandwidth via means of transciphering, and also enables more expressive/efficient programs via means of a Declassify operation. All sub-components of the protocol can be efficiently realised using existing technology. We prove our protocol secure in the UC framework.

1 Introduction

Multi-Party Computation (MPC) and Fully Homomorphic Encryption (FHE) are often seen as competing technologies in the cryptographic goal of Computing on Encrypted Data. However, this is a rather naive view. One can base MPC on various different cryptographic building blocks, for example traditionally one based MPC on Linear Secret Sharing Schemes (LSSSs) or Garbled Circuits (GCs). However, one can also base MPC on FHE, as was originally pointed out in Gentry's thesis [29]. Gentry provides a simple Secure-Function Evaluation (SFE) protocol in which parties use an FHE algorithm to encrypt their inputs to each other, the parties then compute independently the function output homomorphically, and then the (public) output is obtained via a distributed decryption protocol.

Since its creation by Gentry, the development of FHE has been rapid. There are now a plethora of schemes to choose from: BGV [10], BFV [9,25], CKKS [15], GSW [30], FHEW [24], and TFHE [16], to name but a few. Each scheme comes with its own advantages and disadvantages, and particular applications for which it is well suited.

One can view the distributed decryption protocol in Gentry's SFE protocol above as a mini-MPC protocol, thus we have (in some sense) built an SFE protocol from an FHE scheme and a mini-MPC protocol, with the key generation itself performed by another mini-MPC protocol (such as that in [34]). There are a few drawbacks with Gentry's blueprint. Firstly, it only provides secure function evaluation (i.e. evaluation of a single function, with a public output, in a one-shot manner), therefore it does not provide full reactive MPC. Secondly, the protocol only provides semi-honest (a.k.a. passive) security. On the other hand the communication complexity is a (admittedly large) function of the input size, i.e. the communication complexity does not depend on the function complexity.

E. A. Quaglia (Ed.): IMACC 2023, LNCS 14421, pp. 263–283, 2024.
https://doi.org/10.1007/978-3-031-47818-5_14

MPC and FHE have been combined in other ways. For example the SPDZ protocol [21] produces an actively-secure MPC protocol based on LSSS technology, but one which uses an FHE scheme supporting circuits of multiplicative depth one (so called Somewhat Homomorphic Encryption (SHE) schemes of depth one) as a means of providing an efficient offline phase. Indeed one can view the offline phase of SPDZ as a variant of Gentry's FHE-based MPC protocol for the functionality of producing Beaver multiplication triples. To obtain active security in SPDZ one needs to augment the FHE ciphertexts with Zero-Knowledge Proofs of Knowledge (ZKPoKs). There are ZKPoKs which have been specifically designed for this usage in the SPDZ protocol [5].

In a different direction, [18] provides a *robust* MPC protocol, in the honest majority setting, which utilizes an SHE scheme of a specified depth, which follows Gentry's blueprint for SFE. The extension from SHE to supporting any function is enabled by replacing the bootstrapping in FHE by a special protocol based on distributed decryption; namely bootstrapping is performed by interaction.

Another combination of MPC and FHE technologies has been the work on Multi-Key FHE (MK-FHE), see [1,2,33] amongst many other works. In these works, instead of parties generating a global single FHE key in an initialization phase (as in the works above), the parties take their existing individual (multiple) FHE key pairs and combine them in order to perform an MPC-like computation. Whilst this provides a simpler operational setup, the practical implementations of MK-FHE are not as efficient as single key FHE. Another variant of MK-FHE is that of Multi-Party FHE (MP-FHE). The work on MP-FHE is much like our own application; namely there is a distributed key generation protocol and a distributed decryption protocol. However in MP-FHE, the key derivation is created directly from the underlying mathematics, as opposed to applying generic MPC technology. Thus the resulting FHE schemes obtained are slightly different, or have slightly larger parameters, than those proposed in single party FHE. We emphasise that in our work we envisage the use of standard FHE scheme's with the same parameter sets for the single user case; but we use them in a multi-user environment. To distinguish this from MK-FHE and MP-FHE, we call our usage simply Threshold-FHE. In the full version we outline some of the related work in this area in more detail.

In a separate line of work, stretching over the last twenty years, a major performance improvement in practical LSSS-based MPC protocols has been seen to come from "opening", or "declassifying" secret information during an MPC computation. This use of Declassify as a basic operation has been exploited in many MPC systems to enable efficient fixed point, floating point and other advanced operations, see for example [12–14,20] amongst other works. Whilst the above works on applying FHE to SFE/MPC protocols utilize a method to declassify data, via the distributed decryption protocol inherent in the output operation, they have not exploited the ability to perform distributed decryption as a means of declassifying data during a computation; and thus enabling a richer set of basic operations than just Add and Mult.

In a final line of work, researchers have been investigating transciphering as a means of reducing the huge ciphertexts seen in FHE computations. For example in the above works, the parties need to encrypt via FHE, and so the input (whilst independent of the function size) is still very large (as the FHE ciphertexts are large). In addition an MPC protocol may wish to store data for a long period of time. By transciphering from the FHE cipher to a more compact cipher (for example a simple encryption scheme based on a stream cipher) and back again, one can reduce input bandwidth and storage quite considerably. The paper [23] considers transciphering for BGV/BFV style FHE schemes, and presents a specialized cipher tuned for these two schemes, called Pasta. They show that with levelled BGV/BFV style FHE such a transciphering, from an encryption under Pasta to an encryption under the FHE scheme, can be done in about 120 s for plaintext spaces of 17 and 33 bits. For TFHE style FHE, it would appear that utilizing a standard bit-oriented stream cipher with low multiplicative depth (for example Trivium [22]) would be more efficient, or even a small modification of Trivium such as Kreyvium [11]. In [23], the authors report on a homomorphic implementation of Kreyvium using TFHE which outputs one encrypted bit of output every 237 ms. In [4] this is improved to roughly 4 ms per bit.

1.1 Our Contribution

We start by the observation that current FHE schemes are now fast enough that they can be deployed in real life scenarios. In particular bootstrapping is no longer a bottleneck, for example bootstrapping for the TFHE encryption scheme [16] can be done in under 20 ms [17]. In addition distributed decryption can be done (depending on the type of FHE scheme, the parameters and the number of parties) in either a few milli-seconds or around half a second [19][1]. Thus one can reasonably imagine implementing, in the real world, an MPC protocol which utilizes a Threshold-FHE scheme.

Our second observation is that such (practical) protocols need to be fully general and fully secure. By this we mean that the MPC protocol should be *robust*, i.e. it should be maliciously secure and should provide guaranteed output delivery for honest parties, and the input and output parties may be distinct from the parties executing the MPC operation. In addition the protocol should be *composable*, so any security proof needs to be given in the UC framework.

Our third observation is that one wants a protocol that supports fully reactive computation, with both public and private outputs to parties. In particular the "programs" executed by the MPC system should support useful features such as the Declassify operation discussed above.

Our final observation is that one does not want the communication complexity of the input, output and storage of data to depend on the relatively

---

[1] These are timings using standard processors, if FPGA or ASIC acceleration is applied then these run-times for distributed decryption could be reduced by at least two orders of magnitude.

large FHE ciphertexts (and any associated zero-knowledge proofs which need to accompany them for active security considerations). For example, one may want to support clients entering data which are on a resource bound mobile device. Thus our MPC protocol should support transciphering as a basic primitive.

Thus we provide an FHE based MPC protocol which implements the four main points above. We provide a full UC proof of security for the protocol. We believe this is the first time both transciphering and Declassify operations have been shown to the secure within an FHE-based MPC protocol, as opposed to being secure in a stand-alone manner. We pay particular attention to ensure that *all* building blocks used by our protocol are efficiently implementable with current technology. Thus our protocol can be implemented, and utilized today, to enable low-bandwidth, FHE-based MPC computations.

1.2 System Overview

We work in an MPC model in which we separate the parties into three sets; the parties who provide input $\mathbb{I} = (\mathcal{I}_1, \ldots, \mathcal{I}_I)$, the parties who obtain output $\mathbb{O} = (\mathcal{O}_1, \ldots, \mathcal{O}_O)$, and the parties who perform the computation $\mathbb{C} = (\mathcal{C}_1, \ldots, \mathcal{C}_C)$. This distinguishing of roles between the parties seems to have first been introduced in the FairplayMP system [6], a generalization to secret sharing based MPC was presented in the Cybernetica research report [7], with a full presentation being given in [8].

We assume a monolithic adversary that can *statically* corrupt any number of input parties, any number of output parties, and a specified fraction of the computing parties. The number of computing parties which are corruptible is given by a threshold t, where we assume $t < C/3$ in order to ensure that our distributed decryption protocol is robust[2]. Obviously if all input parties are corrupted then there is little point in performing a secure computation at all, so we can assume that at least one input party is honest.

We present our model in the synchronous communication model, but we believe it can be easily adapted to the asynchronous model (assuming an asynchronous protocol for our Declassify operation, and assuming a standard synchronization point for obtaining parties inputs). Parties are assumed to be connected by authentic channels, except in specific instances where we require private channels (these will be explicitly mentioned when we require them).

1.3 Discussion

Our protocol is essentially an MPC protocol realised via FHE, and not via Yao- or LSSS-based, constructions. We are using this MPC formalisation of an FHE-enabled protocol to capture various use cases of FHE all in one go.

---

[2] One can theoretically push this to $t < C/2$, but then the distributed decryption protocol is much less efficient given current technology.

Standard MPC: In the standard MPC definition we have $\mathbb{I} = \mathbb{O} = \mathbb{C}$. This captures standard MPC use cases of secure data collaboration, and collaborative computing. As already remarked, an initial (passively secure) SFE protocol based on FHE was originally given in Gentry's PhD thesis [29].

The advantage of using our FHE-based MPC protocol, over a standard LSSS- or GC-based MPC protocol, is that the communication costs can be reduced considerably. Indeed our consideration of transciphering within our model is key to reducing communication costs.

In practice network performance improves at a slower rate than computing performance; this is inherent in technology as network latency is bound by the speed-of-light, and network bandwidth is also bound by physical limitations. On the other hand, methods of improving computational efficiency seem to have no limits[3]. Thus it is expected in the long run that computation intensive FHE-based MPC will outperform communication intensive LSSS- or GC-based MPC.

Outsourcing FHE: In the standard outsourcing scenario, considered in many FHE papers, we have $\mathbb{I} = \mathbb{O} = \{\mathcal{I}\}$, i.e. a single identical input and output party. Then the computation is performed by a single server, $\mathbb{C} = \{\mathcal{C}\}$, with the result returned to the user. That there is only one input party, who must therefore be honest, can simplify the input protocols considered in our paper (as we can assume all inputs are honestly created). Of course some outsourcing examples have that the server also has some private input. In which case one has $\mathbb{I} = \{\mathcal{I}, \mathcal{C}\}$, $\mathbb{O} = \{\mathcal{I}\}$ and $\mathbb{C} = \{\mathcal{C}\}$; in which case one cannot assume that all inputs are validly created.

If we restricted our programs to not have any Declassify instructions then this becomes the standard FHE outsourcing scenario and we can obtain semi-honest security if $\mathbb{C}$ contains just one server[4]. However, to obtain robust security (i.e. to protect against a dishonest server) one needs a form of Verifiable Computation (VC). A simple way to obtain VC, and hence active robust security, is to ensure that $\mathbb{C}$ has at least three parties and the set $\mathbb{C}$ contains an honest majority. This ensures that the function has been computed correctly homomorphically.

The obvious disadvantage of not having a Declassify instruction is that every function needs to be represented as an arithmetic circuit over any underlying ring $\mathcal{R}$, which is a not so expressive a representation. Without the Declassify instruction one is (often) led to more complex representations of the same input program. Thus in practice, for outsourced FHE computation one might still want to use an MPC-like situation where one has multiple servers with at most $t < C/3$ bad servers.

---

[3] Despite many people predicting the end of Moore's Law for over two decades, there seems no evidence that the improvement in compute performance is slowing down.

[4] Although we need a slightly different method for the Output command than what we will use, and also a different FHE key setup, for example so that the single party in $\mathbb{O}$ knows the decryption key. These are all minor changes, which simplify the discussion and so we ignore them going forward.

Blockchain Scenario: In a blockchain scenario one can imagine the parties $\mathbb{I}$ and $\mathbb{O}$ being users of the blockchain, with data stored on the blockchain in encrypted form (when the data is sensitive). The computing parties then become an analogue of network validators, which process a smart contract over this encrypted data. That the input parties must agree on the smart contract in this scenario, implies that the input parties and computing parties automatically have consensus on the program $\mathcal{P}$. The blockchain is simply the data store used by the validators to store the variables and the program. Thus our methodology of transciphering to reduce the cost of data storage will be key to such applications.

In the blockchain scenario one can also imagine a situation in which one actually has two sets of parties making up the computing parties $\mathbb{C}$. The first set $\mathbb{C}^1$ just computes the deterministic operations which require no interaction. We require of these operations that they are executed correctly, thus the consensus mechanism of the blockchain can ensure that the specific deterministic values are computed correctly, i.e. we have that $\mathbb{C}^1$ must contain an honest majority.

When an interactive operation needs to be performed on the FHE ciphertexts, one now passes to a different set of parties $\mathbb{C}^2$ of size C where one can tolerate only $t < C/3$ adversarial parties[5]. In the blockchain situation one can image the set $\mathbb{C}^2$ being the set of blockchain validators.

Finally, in blockchains it is often important to enable bad actors to be identified, since, for example, they can then be "slashed" in Proof-of-Stake style blockchains. This additional systems security requirement is orthogonal to our work, but is enabled since we utilize robust MPC components which enable the honest parties to detect which adversarial parties are misbehaving.

2   Homomorphic Building Blocks

Our protocol relies on same basic building blocks arising from developments in Fully Homomorphic Encryption (FHE); namely FHE itself, Threshold-FHE, FHE transciphering, and ZKPoKs of plaintext knowledge for FHE ciphertexts. We present all these objects generically, with pointers to specific instantiations. All our building blocks can be realised in practical applications today.

2.1   Fully Homomorphic Encryption

We consider an FHE scheme with plaintext space a ring $\mathcal{R}$, which one can think of either as a finite field $\mathbb{F}$ or as a finite ring such as $\mathbb{Z}/(p^k)$ (with $\mathbb{Z}/(2^k)$ being a ring of particular interest). An FHE scheme, with plaintext space a ring $\mathcal{R}$, is a tuple of algorithms (KeyGen, Enc, Dec, Add, Mult) and a space $\mathcal{E}$ of "valid" encryptions. The set $\mathcal{E}$ is a subset of a larger set $\mathbb{E}$. These algorithms have the following signatures:

- KeyGen(1^κ): On input of the security parameter κ, this randomized algorithm produces a public/private key pair $(\mathfrak{pk}, \mathfrak{sk})$.

---

[5] Again $t < C/3$ is chosen as opposed to $t < C/2$ for efficiency reasons with current technology.

- Enc(m, $\mathfrak{pk}$; r): On input of $m \in \mathcal{R}$, a public key, and randomness from a space of random coins Coins, this produces a ciphertext $\mathfrak{ct} \in \mathcal{E}$.
- Dec($\mathfrak{ct}$, $\mathfrak{sk}$): On input of an element $\mathfrak{ct} \in \mathcal{E}$ and a secret key $\mathfrak{sk}$ this outputs the corresponding plaintext $m \in \mathcal{R}$.
- Add($\mathfrak{ct}_1$, $\mathfrak{ct}_2$, $\mathfrak{pk}$): On input of two elements $\mathfrak{ct}_1$, $\mathfrak{ct}_2 \in \mathcal{E}$ which decrypt to $m_1, m_2 \in \mathcal{R}$ this deterministically produces a ciphertext $\mathfrak{ct}_3 \in \mathcal{E}$ which decrypts to $m_1 + m_2$.
- Mult($\mathfrak{ct}_1$, $\mathfrak{ct}_2$, $\mathfrak{pk}$): On input of two elements $\mathfrak{ct}_1$, $\mathfrak{ct}_2 \in \mathcal{E}$ which decrypt to $m_1, m_2 \in \mathcal{R}$ this deterministically produces a ciphertext $\mathfrak{ct}_3 \in \mathcal{E}$ which decrypts to $m_1 \cdot m_2$.

The correctness conditions of an FHE scheme are obvious; i.e. every element in $\mathcal{E}$ should be decryptable to the correct value.

To ease notation we write Add($\mathfrak{ct}_1$, $\mathfrak{ct}_2$, $\mathfrak{pk}$) as $\mathfrak{ct}_1 + \mathfrak{ct}_2$ and Mult($\mathfrak{ct}_1$, $\mathfrak{ct}_2$, $\mathfrak{pk}$) as $\mathfrak{ct}_1 \cdot \mathfrak{ct}_2$. We also assume that scalars (i.e. non-encrypted values in $\mathcal{R}$) can be added and multiplied into ciphertexts at will. Thus one can form arbitrary arithmetic expressions combining ciphertexts and plaintexts, with the output being a ciphertext if any of the input variables are valid ciphertexts.

A key issue with existing FHE techniques, unlike many traditional public key ciphers, is that it is not possibly to efficiently test whether a supposed ciphertext $\mathfrak{ct}$ lies in $\mathcal{E}$ or in $\mathbb{E}$. In fact the IND-CPA security of the scheme is often reduced to the hard problem of distinguishing elements of $\mathcal{E}$ from elements of $\mathbb{E}$. This causes a problem in protocols as we need to ensure that all ciphertexts which are attempted to be decrypted, are indeed decryptable (i.e. valid ciphertexts). This is, one of the reasons, why we will require zero-knowledge proofs of knowledge (ZKPoKs) below. In addition, not all elements in $\mathcal{E}$ may arise from applications of the Enc function, i.e. $\mathcal{E}$ is not the image of $\mathcal{R}$ under Enc. This is because valid ciphertexts also arise from the application of the homomorphic operations Add and Mult.

There are a plethora of FHE schemes available; each with different properties.

- BGV/BFV: These schemes [9,10,25] usually utilize a plaintext ring of $\mathcal{R} = \mathbb{F}_p$, or more generally $\mathcal{R} = \mathbb{F}_p^r$ if r slots are used, where p is a large prime. For such schemes bootstrapping (needed to ensure the output of a series of homomorphic operations lies in $\mathcal{E}$) is very slow.
- CKKS: This scheme [15] enables a plaintext ring of an approximation to $\mathbb{R}$, i.e. $\mathcal{R} \approx \mathbb{R}$, or an approximation to $\mathbb{R}^r$ if r slots are used. Here bootstrapping is relatively fast, but it only allows a smoothing out of the approximation to the real numbers being used.
- TFHE: This scheme [16], in its most common implementation, enables a plaintext space of $\mathcal{R} = \mathbb{Z}/(2^k)$ (for a small value of k, say $k = 1$ or $k = 4$). However, bootstrapping is highly efficient, and one can extend the homomorphic operations to arbitrary look up tables on $\mathcal{R}$.

FHE Security: We assume a slightly different notion of FHE security than perhaps is sometimes used (although this notion was used previously in for example [21]); a notion which we dub IND-KEY security.

Definition 1 (IND-KEY). *We assume there is a "fake" key generation algo-rithm denoted* $\mathsf{KeyGen}^*(1^\kappa)$, *which only outputs public keys, which are indistin-guishable from standard public keys. In addition we require that applying the non-fake encryption algorithm with the fake public key, produces a ciphertext which is statistically indistinguishable from an encryption of zero with the fake public key. Thus we assume the following relationships between distributions:*

$$\left\{ \mathfrak{pk} : (\mathfrak{pk}, \mathfrak{sk}) \leftarrow \mathsf{KeyGen}(1^\kappa) \right\} \cong_c \left\{ \widetilde{\mathfrak{pk}} : \widetilde{\mathfrak{pk}} \leftarrow \mathsf{KeyGen}^*(1^\kappa) \right\}. \tag{1}$$

$$\left\{ \mathsf{Enc}(m, \widetilde{\mathfrak{pk}}; r) : \widetilde{\mathfrak{pk}} \leftarrow \mathsf{KeyGen}^*(1^\kappa), \quad m \leftarrow \mathcal{R}, \quad r \leftarrow \mathcal{R} \right\}$$

$$\cong_s \left\{ \mathsf{Enc}(0, \widetilde{\mathfrak{pk}}; r) : \widetilde{\mathfrak{pk}} \leftarrow \mathsf{KeyGen}^*(1^\kappa), \quad r \leftarrow \mathcal{R} \right\}. \tag{2}$$

A scheme which satisfies Eqs. (1) and (2) is said to be IND-KEY secure.

All the above FHE schemes satisfy this security requirement as their public keys, and ciphertexts, consist of a collection of LWE/Ring-LWE pairs. By the LWE assumption these are indistinguishable from random pairs of elements from the appropriate sets.

FHE security is usually defined via an IND-CPA notion; namely that an adversary, on input of $\mathfrak{pk}$, who selects two messages m_1 and m_2 of his choosing, cannot, on being given a ciphertext $\mathfrak{ct}^*$ encrypting either m_1 or m_2, decide whether $\mathfrak{ct}^*$ encrypts m_1 or m_2. Our IND-KEY notion, however, implies the standard IND-CPA security notion via the following sequence of hybrids: Take the experiment in the standard IND-CPA game in which the encrypted message is the adversarially chosen message m_0, now switch to the using a fake public key $\widetilde{\mathfrak{pk}}$. By our first security assumption (in Eq. (1)) this hop is indistinguishable. Now hop to encrypting an encryption of zero, again this hop is indistinguishable by our second security assumption (in Eq. (2)). Now hop to encrypting m_1, and finally hop from the fake public key $\widetilde{\mathfrak{pk}}$ to the real one $\mathfrak{pk}$. These last two hops are indistinguishable for the same reason.

2.2   Threshold-FHE

Formally we define the threshold decryption via two ideal functionalities. The first $\mathcal{F}_{\mathsf{KeyGen}}$, in Fig. 1, acts as a set-up assumption for our protocol, needed for the UC proof we provide. It generates a key pair, and secret shares the secret key among the computing parties $\mathbb{C}$ using a linear secret sharing scheme $\langle \cdot \rangle$ which tolerates up to t adversaries. Party $\mathcal{C}_i$'s share of a secret shared value x is denoted by $\langle x \rangle_i$.

One can realise this functionality using a generic MPC protocol. Note, despite wanting active security we do not "complete" adversarial input shares into a complete sharing (as is often done in such situations), as we can assume the implementing MPC protocol for $\mathcal{F}_{\mathsf{KeyGen}}$ does not actually need to do this.

The key functionality we want to implement is $\mathcal{F}_{\mathsf{KeyGenDec}}$ given in Fig. 2. Note, that this functionality always returns the correct result, irrespective of

$\mathcal{F}_{\mathsf{KeyGen}}$

Init(sid):
1. Execute $(\mathfrak{pk}, \mathfrak{sk}) \leftarrow \mathsf{KeyGen}(1^\kappa)$ for the underlying FHE encryption scheme.
2. Generate a secret sharing $\langle \mathfrak{sk} \rangle$ of the secret key amongst the C players in $\mathbb{C}$.
3. Send $(\mathsf{sid}, \mathfrak{pk})$ to all players (including the adversary), and send $(\mathsf{sid}, \langle \mathfrak{sk} \rangle_i)$ to player C_i (including adversarially controlled players).

Fig. 1. The ideal functionality for distributed key generation

$\mathcal{F}_{\mathsf{KeyGenDec}}$

Init(sid):
1. Execute $(\mathfrak{pk}, \mathfrak{sk}) \leftarrow \mathsf{KeyGen}(1^\kappa)$ for the underlying FHE encryption scheme.
2. Send $(\mathsf{sid}, \mathfrak{pk})$ to all players, including the adversary and store the value $\mathfrak{sk}$.

DistDecrypt(sid, $\mathfrak{ct}, \mathcal{U}$): For a ciphertext $\mathfrak{ct} \in \mathcal{E}$ and a set of players $\mathcal{U}$.
1. Compute $m \leftarrow \mathsf{Dec}(\mathfrak{ct}, \mathfrak{sk})$.
2. Output $(\mathsf{sid}, \mathfrak{ct}, m)$ to all players in $\mathcal{U}$, and $(\mathsf{sid}, \mathfrak{ct})$ to the adversary (if the adversary controls no party in $\mathcal{U}$).

Fig. 2. The ideal functionality for distributed key generation and decryption

what the adversary does. A protocol which realises $\mathcal{F}_{\mathsf{KeyGenDec}}$ in the $\mathcal{F}_{\mathsf{KeyGen}}$-hybrid model is given in [19] when $t < C/3$, for all the FHE schemes above.

The functionality implies that if the target set of players $\mathcal{U}$ in the DistDecrypt cannot be adversarially corrupted by definition, then the functionality is connected to the players in $\mathcal{U}$ via private channels. When the players in $\mathbb{C}$ implement such a functionality, this implies (for such sets $\mathcal{U}$) that the communication between the sets of players in $\mathbb{C}$ and those in $\mathcal{U}$ is over private channels.

In our protocol the functionality is used in two situations:

– $\mathcal{U}$ contains a single output player, this is when DistDecrypt is used for private output to an output player. We do not know if the player is adversarially corrupted, thus we need private channels between the functionality and the player in $\mathcal{U}$.
– $\mathcal{U}$ is the set of computing parties $\mathbb{C}$. Here $\mathbb{C}$ could contain an adversarial player, and thus the output can be made in the clear by definition. So we only need authentic channels.

2.3   FHE Transciphering

A big problem with FHE ciphertexts is that they are large, i.e. the bits needed to represent an element in $\mathcal{E}$ is large. Hence, a common proposal to avoid this is to enable a form of homomorphic transciphering via another cipher (usually symmetric). We define the underlying symmetric cipher with the following syntax,

$$\mathsf{Sym}: \begin{array}{c} \mathcal{R} \times \mathcal{R}^\rho \times \{0,1\}^* \times \mathbb{N} \longrightarrow \mathbb{S}, \\ (m, \mathbf{k}; \mathsf{nonce}, \mathsf{cnt}) \longmapsto \mathbf{c} \end{array}$$

Note, the key is an element of $\mathcal{R}^\rho$ as eventually we will be evaluating the symmetric cipher given a homomorphic encryption of the key. We will also require the inverse operation

$$\mathsf{Sym}^{-1}: \begin{array}{c} \mathbb{S} \times \mathcal{R}^\rho \times \{0,1\}^* \times \mathbb{N} \longrightarrow \mathcal{R}, \\ (\mathbf{c}, \mathbf{k}; \mathsf{nonce}, \mathsf{cnt}) \longmapsto m \end{array}$$

with an obvious correctness requirement

$$\mathsf{Sym}^{-1}\Big(\mathsf{Sym}(\ m, \mathbf{k};\ \mathsf{nonce}, \mathsf{cnt}\ ), \mathbf{k};\ \mathsf{nonce}, \mathsf{cnt} \Big) = m.$$

In what follows, for simplicity, we assume that $\mathbb{S} \subset \mathcal{R}^\sigma$ for some value of σ (so we can also evaluate Sym^{-1} homomorphically). We also assume that every element of $\mathbb{S}$ corresponds to a valid encryption of some message under Sym[6]. We require the cipher to be IND-CPA secure, which our two constructions below (from a secure PRG and a secure PRF) satisfy.

The cipher Sym is said to be FHE-friendly if there is an efficient way to implement the algorithm homomorphically (with no distributed decryption interactions) within the FHE scheme[7] given a homomorphic encryption of the key, and possibly a homomorphic encryption of the message and/or ciphertext.

Being FHE friendly means that, given a homomorphic encryption of the key

$$\mathsf{Enc}(\mathbf{k}, \mathfrak{pk}) = (\mathfrak{ct}_1, \dots, \mathfrak{ct}_\rho) = (\ \mathsf{Enc}(k_1, \mathfrak{pk}), \dots, \mathsf{Enc}(k_\rho, \mathfrak{pk})\ ),$$

and a (plaintext) nonce nonce/counter cnt, one can homomorphically compute

$$\mathsf{Enc}(\ \mathsf{Sym}(\ m, \mathbf{k};\ \mathsf{nonce}, \mathsf{cnt}\ ),\ \mathfrak{pk}\ ) \tag{3}$$

efficiently from $\mathsf{Enc}(\mathbf{k}, \mathfrak{pk})$ and either m or $\mathsf{Enc}(m, \mathfrak{pk})$. In addition one can also compute efficiently

$$\mathsf{Enc}(\ \mathsf{Sym}^{-1}(\ \mathbf{c}, \mathbf{k};\ \mathsf{nonce}, \mathsf{cnt}\ ),\ \mathfrak{pk}\ ) \tag{4}$$

efficiently from $\mathsf{Enc}(\mathbf{k}, \mathfrak{pk})$ and either $\mathbf{c}$ or $\mathsf{Enc}(\mathbf{c}, \mathfrak{pk})$.

---

[6] This can be relaxed, but that would require further zero-knowledge proofs, and complications, in our protocol, in order to prove that ciphertexts where actually valid encryptions.

[7] Obviously it also has to be efficiently computable in the clear.

In particular a vector plaintext message $\mathbf{m}$ can be encrypted, by someone who knows the secret key $\mathbf{k}$, into a compact ciphertext $\mathbf{c}$. Then given $\mathbf{c}$, someone who holds the homomorphically encrypted secret key, $\mathsf{Enc}(\mathbf{k}, \mathfrak{pk})$, can transcipher $\mathbf{c}$ into the encryption of the message $\mathbf{m}$ under the FHE cipher Enc by evaluating Eq. (4). With access to a distributed decryption functionality one can also transcipher a ciphertext encrypted under Enc to a ciphertext encrypted under Sym, by evaluating Eq. (3), followed by applying the distributed decryption functionality.

Such a symmetric encryption scheme can be easily derived from an FHE-friendly stream or block cipher;

- If we are given an FHE-friendly stream cipher

$$\mathsf{PRG} : \begin{array}{rcl} \mathcal{R}^\rho \times \{0,1\}^* & \longrightarrow & \mathcal{R}^*, \\ (\mathbf{k}, \mathsf{IV}) & \longmapsto & \mathsf{PRG}(\mathbf{k}, \mathsf{IV}). \end{array}$$

then we can define Sym by the operation, with $\mathbb{S} = \mathcal{R}$,

$$\mathsf{Sym}(\, m, \mathbf{k};\, \mathsf{nonce}, \mathsf{cnt}\,) := m + \mathsf{PRG}(\mathbf{k}, \mathsf{nonce})^{(\mathsf{cnt})},$$

using the nonce as the stream cipher IV, and the counter cnt to index into the resulting keystream.
- If we are given an FHE-friendly block cipher

$$\mathsf{PRF} : \begin{array}{rcl} \mathcal{R}^\rho \times \{0,1\}^* & \longrightarrow & \mathcal{R}, \\ (\mathbf{k}, \mathsf{IV}) & \longmapsto & \mathsf{PRF}(\mathbf{k}, \mathsf{IV}). \end{array}$$

then we can define Sym by essentially using the block cipher in CTR-mode

$$\mathsf{Sym}(\, m, \mathbf{k};\, \mathsf{nonce}, \mathsf{cnt}\,) := m + \mathsf{PRF}(\mathbf{k}, \mathsf{nonce}\|\mathsf{cnt}),$$

using the IV as the nonce concatenated with the counter and $\mathbb{S} = \mathcal{R}$.

Note, the key difference between the block and the stream cipher is that in the block cipher one has a potentially high cost on every invocation, whereas in the stream cipher each invocation (a different increasing value of cnt for the same value of nonce) can be cheap, but the initialization phase (processing the key and nonce) can be expensive.

2.4   Zero-Knowledge Proofs of Plaintext Knowledge

The zero-knowledge proofs we use will always be called with a prover being a party in $\mathbb{I} \cup \mathbb{O} \cup \mathbb{C}$ and the verifiers being the set $\mathbb{C}$. We will apply the ZKPoKs to prove the specific NP-relation R_{enc} given by

$$R_{\mathsf{enc}} = \Big\{ (\mathfrak{ct}, (m, r)) \;:\; m \in \mathcal{R}, \quad r \in \mathsf{Coins}, \quad \mathfrak{ct} = \mathsf{Enc}(m, \mathfrak{pk}; r) \Big\}.$$

The zero-knowledge proofs will be defined by four algorithms, which make use of a random oracle:

- Prv(ct, (m, r)): A prover algorithm which, on input of a ciphertext ct and a witness (m, r) for the relation R_{enc}, will produce a proof π.
- Ver(ct, π): A verifier algorithm which, on input of a ciphertext ct and a proof, will output true or false.
- Sim(ct): A simulator algorithm which, on input of a ciphertext ct, will produce a simulated proof π; it does so by programming the underlying random oracle.
- Ext(ct): This knowledge extraction algorithm, which has black box (potentially rewindable) access to the proving algorithm will extract the underlying witness for the ciphertext ct from a prover which holds this witness.

For all of the FHE schemes mentioned earlier (BGV,BFV,CKKS and TFHE) the encryption algorithm Enc is of the following form: It generates some "small" random integer values (which one can consider as sums of bits, where the bits are part of the random coins in r), then two values $(\mathbf{a}, \mathbf{b})$ are constructed which are *linear combinations* of the random bits, the message, and the values in the public key $\mathfrak{pk}$. The final ciphertext is the pair $(\mathbf{a}, \mathbf{b})$. One can therefore interpret the NP-relation R_{enc} as a (multiple) subset-sum relation over the hidden bits in the random coins r and the bits making up the message m.

Many proof systems for subset-sum/lattice like relations exhibit a form of *soundness slack*. This means that the statement, which we can guarantee a dishonest prover actually commits to, is a slightly modified version of the one which an honest prover is using. Use of such proof systems in FHE-based protocols result in us having to increase parameters in order to deal with the *slack* introduced by such proofs[8]. To ensure simpler protocols, and optimal parameters for our underlying FHE scheme, we require our zero-knowledge proofs to exhibit no such soundness slack. With this requirement in mind there appears two forms of (efficient) zero-knowledge proofs one could use.

Proofs Based on MPC-in-the-Head: If post-quantum secure proofs are required then one technique to prove such subset sum NP-relations is to use MPC-in-the-Head based zero-knowledge proofs. For example the techniques of [26] and [27] can be applied directly to this situation resulting in a very simple proof technique. Both these papers are based on specializations of the general KKW [31] method for MPC-in-the-Head. At heart these are interactive proof systems (essentially Σ-protocols), but they are made non-interactive using the Fiat–Shamir heuristic in the standard way. In these proofs the simulation algorithm Sim works by programming the random oracle challenges, and the extraction algorithm Ext works (again by programming the random oracle) by rewinding the prover and issuing the prover different responses to it's random oracle queries.

Proofs Based on Vector Commitments: If one is prepared to accept pre-quantum security assumptions (in particular hardness assumptions in elliptic

---

[8] Effectively the FHE noise in fresh ciphertexts is increased, resulting in larger parameters, or more bootstrapping, or both.

curve groups which support pairings) one can utilize proofs based on a vector commitment scheme, [32]. These proofs are proven secure in the Algebraic Group Model (AGM) [28]. The prover, verifier and simulator work roughly (from a very high level) just as in the previous case; with the simulator also needing to program the underlying random oracle. However, the extraction algorithm works in the AGM and does not need to rewind the prover. The extraction algorithm simply "observes" the group operations performed by the prover, and from these is able to extract the underlying witness.

In both cases the knowledge extraction via rewinding or via the use of the AGM, causes the underlying ZKPoK to not be UC secure. However, this does not cause an issue in our main protocol security proof. We can still prove UC security of our underlying MPC-FHE protocol. The reason for this is as follows: Our UC protocol simulator will know the secret key of the underlying cryptosystem and so can extract the important part of the witness, i.e. m, by simply decrypting. In our security proof that the simulator is valid, where we do not know the secret key, we can extract the witness at that point by either rewinding the environment or using the AGM. In particular the rewinding/AGM execution is required only for the security reduction that the protocol simulator is correct, and not for actually implementing the protocol simulator. Thus the proof will ensure we have a UC-secure protocol.

3   Ideal Functionality

The ideal functionality, in Fig. 3 below, represents a generic MPC functionality, which captures the ability to transcipher between two secure domains; one which allows arithmetic (i.e. homomorphic) operations and one which does not. It also captures the ability of computing parties to execute programs which include a Declassify operation. The basic programming model we envision is described in the full version, which is a simple extension of the M-Circuit MPC model of [3] to the case of FHE (which we therefore call an F-Circuit). With the ideal functionality being a functionality which ideally realises this programming model.

We assume a register bank $\mathbb{V} = \{\text{varid}_i\}$, which (for simplicity) we assume is a flat single file of registers, i.e. no stacks or index-able memory. The ideal functionality keeps track of registers which are in the clear, as well as registers which are meant to be held securely within the functionality.

For simplicity of exposition we allow this ideal functionality to output an abort, but this only happens for a badly typed program; which should be caught by the compiler. Thus the reader should treat the abort's as purely syntactic sugar for their reading, and not as actual abort's by the functionality.

Note the ideal functionality assumes that all players agree on each instruction sent to it, thus this implies consensus on the input F-Circuit program.

4   The MPC-FHE Protocol

Here, we combine all the components together into one protocol which executes the F-Circuit functionality.

$\mathcal{F}_{F-Circuit}$

Init: On input (sid, Init, $\mathcal{R}$) from all parties store $\mathcal{R}$.

Input: On input of (sid, Input, $\mathcal{I}_i$, varid, x), for $\mathcal{I}_i \in \mathbb{I}$, from $\mathcal{I}_i$ and (sid, Input, $\mathcal{I}_i$, varid) from all other parties:

1. If $\text{type}^2(\text{varid}) \notin \{s, -\}$ then abort.
2. If $\text{type}^1(\text{varid}) = \mathcal{R}$ and $x \in \mathcal{R}$ then store x in varid.
3. If $\text{type}^1(\text{varid}) = -$ and $x \in \mathbb{Z}$ then store x in varid.
4. If $\text{type}^2(\text{varid}) = -$ then send x to the adversary.
5. If $x = \perp$ then store the value zero in varid.
   This last case corresponds to an adversarial input x which is mistyped.

Output: On input of (sid, Output, $\mathcal{O}_i$, varid) for $\mathcal{O}_i \in \mathbb{I}$ from all parties:

1. If $\text{type}^2(\text{varid}) \notin \{s, -\}$ then abort.
2. Send the value x stored in varid to $\mathcal{O}_i$.
3. If $\text{type}^2(\text{varid}) = -$ then also send x to the adversary.

Add: On input of (sid, Add, varid_z, varid_x, varid_y) from all parties:

1. If $\text{type}^1(\text{varid}_x) \neq \text{type}^1(\text{varid}_y)$ or $\text{type}^1(\text{varid}_x) \neq \text{type}^1(\text{varid}_z)$ then abort.
   With a caveat here in relation to the implicit coercions mentioned earlier.
2. If $\text{type}^2(\text{varid}_x) \notin \{s, -\}$ then abort.
3. If $(\text{type}^2(\text{varid}_x) = s$ or $\text{type}^2(\text{varid}_y) = s)$ and $\text{type}^2(\text{varid}_z) \neq s$ then abort.
4. Retrieve x from varid_x and y from varid_y and store $z = x + y$ in varid_z.

Mult: On input of (sid, Mult, varid_z, varid_x, varid_y) from all parties:

1. If $\text{type}^1(\text{varid}_x) \neq \text{type}^1(\text{varid}_y)$ or $\text{type}^1(\text{varid}_x) \neq \text{type}^1(\text{varid}_z)$ then abort.
   Again, with a caveat here in relation to the implicit coercions mentioned earlier.
2. If $\text{type}^2(\text{varid}_x) \notin \{s, -\}$ then abort.
3. If $(\text{type}^2(\text{varid}_x) = s$ or $\text{type}^2(\text{varid}_y) = s)$ and $\text{type}^2(\text{varid}_z) \neq s$ then abort.
4. Retrieve x from varid_x and y from varid_y and store $z = x \cdot y$ in varid_z.

Declassify: On input of (sid, Declassify, varid_y, varid_x) from all parties:

1. If $\text{type}(\text{varid}_x) \neq (\mathcal{R}, s)$ or $\text{type}(\text{varid}_y) \neq (\mathcal{R}, -)$ then abort.
2. Assign the contents x of varid_x to varid_y and send x to the adversary if $\mathbb{C}$ contains a corrupt party.

$\text{Trans}^{s \to t}$: On input of (sid, $\text{Trans}^{s \to t}$, varid_y, varid_x) from all parties:

1. If $\text{type}(\text{varid}_x) \neq (\mathcal{R}, s)$ or $\text{type}(\text{varid}_y) \neq (\mathcal{R}, t)$ then abort.
2. Assign the contents x of varid_x to varid_y.

$\text{Trans}^{t \to s}$: On input of (sid, $\text{Trans}^{t \to s}$, varid_y, varid_x) from all parties:

1. If $\text{type}(\text{varid}_x) \neq (\mathcal{R}, t)$ or $\text{type}(\text{varid}_y) \neq (\mathcal{R}, s)$ then abort.
2. Assign the contents x of varid_x to varid_y.

Fig. 3. The ideal functionality for executing a program represented by a F-Circuit

The protocol is given in Figs. 4, 5, 6 and 7, where we assume the input F-Circuit is validly typed. The protocol is given in the $\{\mathcal{F}_{\text{KeyGenDec}}\}$-hybrid model, and works in the fully robust/malicious setting; i.e. the protocol should not abort. All players are assumed to be connected by authentic channels. However, if the output routine with variant = Enc is used then the servers $\mathbb{C}$ need to be connected to the parties in $\mathbb{O}$ via **private** channels.

$\Pi_{F-Circuit}$ (Part I)

Init(sid):

1. The players call Init on $\mathcal{F}_{\mathsf{KeyGenDec}}$ so that all players obtain $\mathfrak{pk}$.
2. All players $\mathcal{I}_i \in \mathbb{I}$ generate a random symmetric key $\mathbf{k}_{i,i} \in \mathcal{R}^\rho$, encrypt it using $\mathsf{Enc}(\mathbf{k}_{i,i}, \mathfrak{pk}; r_{i,i})$ to obtain $\mathfrak{ct}_{i,i} \in \mathcal{E}^\rho$. The ciphertext $\mathfrak{ct}_{i,i}$ is *broadcast* to all players in $\mathbb{C}$.
3. All players $\mathcal{O}_i \in \mathbb{O}$ generate a random symmetric key $\mathbf{k}_{o,i} \in \mathcal{R}^\rho$, encrypt it using $\mathsf{Enc}(\mathbf{k}_{o,i}, \mathfrak{pk}; r_{o,i})$ to obtain $\mathfrak{ct}_{o,i} \in \mathcal{E}^\rho$. The ciphertext $\mathfrak{ct}_{o,i}$ is *broadcast* to all players in $\mathbb{C}$.
4. All players $\mathcal{C}_i \in \mathbb{C}$ generate a random symmetric key $\mathbf{k}_{c,i} \in \mathcal{R}^\rho$, encrypt it using $\mathsf{Enc}(\mathbf{k}_{c,i}, \mathfrak{pk}; r_{c,i})$ to obtain $\mathfrak{ct}_{c,i} \in \mathcal{E}^\rho$. The ciphertext $\mathfrak{ct}_{c,i}$ is *broadcast* to all players in $\mathbb{C}$.
5. The players in $\mathbb{I}$, $\mathbb{O}$ and $\mathbb{C}$ call the prover $\pi \leftarrow \mathsf{Prv}(\mathfrak{ct}(m, r))$ with input the respective ciphertexts ($\mathfrak{ct}_{i,i}$, $\mathfrak{ct}_{o,i}$ and $\mathfrak{ct}_{c,i}$), the respective plaintexts ($\mathbf{k}_{i,i}$, $\mathbf{k}_{o,i}$ and $\mathbf{k}_{c,i}$), and the respective randomness ($r_{i,i}$, $r_{o,i}$ and $r_{c,i}$), in order to obtain proofs $\pi_{i,i}$, $\pi_{o,i}$ and $\pi_{c,i}$.
6. The proofs are broadcast to the players in $\mathbb{C}$. The players in $\mathbb{C}$ verify the proofs using $\mathsf{Ver}(\mathfrak{ct}, \pi)$. If any proof fails then the parties in $\mathbb{C}$ replace the associated ciphertext with a default encryption of zero.
7. Set $\mathfrak{ct}_0 \leftarrow \mathfrak{ct}_{c,1} + \cdots + \mathfrak{ct}_{c,C}$, this is an encryption of $\mathbf{k}_0 = \mathbf{k}_{c,1} + \cdots + \mathbf{k}_{c,C}$.
8. Set $\mathsf{cnt}_{i,i} \leftarrow 0$ for all $\mathcal{I}_i \in \mathbb{I}$.
9. Set $\mathsf{cnt}_{o,i} \leftarrow 0$ for all $\mathcal{O}_i \in \mathbb{O}$.
10. Set $\mathsf{cnt}_c \leftarrow 0$.

Fig. 4. The protocol for executing a program represented by a F-Circuit – Part I

The connections between the players in $\mathbb{I}$ and the players in $\mathbb{C}$ are assumed to be by *reliable broadcast channels*, which are reliable in the presence of byzantine faults, including by the sender. This can be ensured by the players in $\mathbb{C}$ executing an echo-broadcast upon receiving data from a player in $\mathbb{I}$, to ensure the value has indeed been broadcast correctly. As $\mathbb{C}$ contains an honest majority, the players in $\mathbb{C}$ can take a majority vote on what the precise input is, or declare the parties input to be invalid.

For the Input and Output commands we provide two different implementations when $\mathsf{type}^2(\mathsf{varid}) = s$. We refer to the type of input/output as the variant, which is an element of $\{\mathsf{Enc}, \mathsf{Sym}, -\}$. When the input/output value is in the clear then we assume that variant $= -$.

- The first, indexed by Enc, utilizes, for input, an FHE ciphertext plus a zero knowledge proof (it therefore requires rather a large amount of data transfer),

---

$\Pi_{F-Circuit}$ **(Part II)**

Input(sid, $\mathcal{I}_i$, varid, x; variant): When player $\mathcal{I}_i$ wishes to input a value x of valid type type(varid) we execute:

1. If $\text{type}^2(\text{varid}) = -$ then player $\mathcal{P}_i$ *broadcasts* x, in the clear, to all players in $\mathbb{C}$.

2. If $\text{type}^2(\text{varid}) = s$ and variant = Enc then
   (a) Player $\mathcal{P}_i$ encrypts x using $\mathfrak{ct}_x \leftarrow \text{Enc}(x, \mathfrak{pt}; r_x)$, with randomness r_x.
   (b) Player $\mathcal{P}_i$ *broadcasts* $\mathfrak{ct}_x$ to all players in $\mathbb{C}$.
   (c) Player $\mathcal{P}_i$ invokes the prover $\pi_x \leftarrow \text{Prv}(\mathfrak{ct}_x, (x, r_x))$ with input the ciphertext $\mathfrak{ct}_x$, the message x and the associated randomness r_x, and broadcasts the resulting proof π_x to all players in $\mathbb{C}$.
   (d) If the proof verifies when calling $\text{Ver}(\mathfrak{ct}_x, \pi_x)$, then the players in $\mathbb{C}$ store $\mathfrak{ct}_x$ in register varid, otherwise they store a default encryption of zero in register varid.

3. If $\text{type}^2(\text{varid}) = s$ and variant = Sym then
   (a) Player $\mathcal{P}_i$ encrypts x using

   $$\mathbf{c}_x \leftarrow \text{Sym}(\ x, \mathbf{k}_{i,i};\ \text{sid}, \text{cnt}_{i,i}\ ).$$

   (b) Player $\mathcal{P}_i$ *broadcasts* $\mathbf{c}_x$ to all players in $\mathbb{C}$.
   (c) The players in $\mathbb{C}$ transcipher $\mathbf{c}_x$ from an encryption under Sym to an encryption under Enc by computing

   $$\mathfrak{ct}_x \leftarrow \text{Sym}^{-1}(\ \mathbf{c}_x, \mathfrak{ct}_{i,i};\ \text{sid}, \text{cnt}_{i,i}\ ).$$

   (d) Incremement $\text{cnt}_{i,i}$.
   Note, if any of the proofs do not verify, or the broadcasts are invalid then the players in $\mathbb{C}$ store a deterministic default value, say zero (resp. a homomorphic encryption of zero) in the register varid.

Fig. 5. The protocol for executing a program represented by a F-Circuit – Part II

whilst for output requires the outputting party to be connected by private channels to the parties in $\mathbb{C}$ (which execute the distributed decryption functionality). Realising so many private channels may be problematic in some situations.

– The second variant, indexed by Sym, utilizes for both input and output the transciphering methodology into a ciphertext encrypted by a key which only the input (resp. output) party knows. It requires no such private channels, and enables minimal bandwidth consumption.

$\Pi_{F-Circuit}$ (Part III)

Output(sid, $\mathcal{O}_i$, varid; variant): When player $\mathcal{O}_i$ is expecting an output value x of valid type type(varid) we execute:

1. If $\text{type}^2(\text{varid}) = -$ then
   (a) The contents of register varid is sent to player $\mathcal{O}_i$ by all players in $\mathbb{C}$.
   (b) Player $\mathcal{O}_i$ takes the majority verdict as the value of the register sent.
   (c) The value sent is the output value.

2. If $\text{type}^2(\text{varid}) = s$ and varid = Enc then
   (a) All players in $\mathbb{C} \cup \{\mathcal{O}_i\}$ invoke DistDecrypt(sid, $\mathfrak{ct}_x$, $\{\mathcal{O}_i\}$) on $\mathcal{F}_{\text{KeyGenDec}}$ where $\mathfrak{ct}_x$ is the contents of register varid.
   (b) The party $\mathcal{O}_i$ receives the output plaintext value, and takes this as the output value. *Note, that $\mathcal{O}_i$ only receives the value implies* **private channels** *between the entities in $\mathbb{C}$ and the entities in $\mathbb{O}$.*

3. If $\text{type}^2(\text{varid}) = s$ and varid = Sym then
   (a) All players in $\mathbb{C}$ take the contents $\mathfrak{ct}_x$ of register varid and computes homomorphically

   $$\mathfrak{ct}'_x \leftarrow \text{Sym}(\ \mathfrak{ct}_x, \mathfrak{ct}_{o,i};\ \text{sid}, \text{cnt}_{o,i}\ ).$$

   (b) All players in $\mathbb{C}$ invoke $\mathbf{c} \leftarrow$ DistDecrypt(sid, $\mathfrak{ct}'_x$, $\mathbb{C}$) on $\mathcal{F}_{\text{KeyGenDec}}$.
   (c) The value $\mathbf{c}$ is sent to player $\mathcal{O}_i$ by the players in $\mathbb{C}$, with $\mathcal{O}_i$ taking the majority verdict as the value of the ciphertext sent.
   (d) Player $\mathcal{O}_i$ decrypts $\mathbf{c}$ to obtain x by computing

   $$x \leftarrow \text{Sym}^{-1}(\ \mathbf{c}, \mathbf{k}_{o,i};\ \text{sid}, \text{cnt}_{o,i}\ ).$$

   (e) Incremement $\text{cnt}_{o,i}$.

Fig. 6. The protocol for executing a program represented by a F-Circuit – Part III

We see that for private output to parties we have a trade-off; either we require private channels between the output party and the parties in $\mathbb{C}$, or we only require authenticated channels, but we require the computing parties to execute a transciphering operation. Both options require a distributed decryption operation; one with private output and one with public output.

$\Pi_{F-Circuit}$ **(Part IV)**

Add(sid, varid$_z$, varid$_x$, varid$_y$):
1. The players in $\mathbb{C}$ retrieve x from varid$_x$ and y from varid$_y$ and store $z = x + y$ in varid$_z$.

Mult(sid, varid$_z$, varid$_x$, varid$_y$):
1. The players in $\mathbb{C}$ retrieve x from varid$_x$ and y from varid$_y$ and store $z = x \cdot y$ in varid$_z$.

Declassify(sid, varid$_y$, varid$_x$):
1. The players in $\mathbb{C}$ retreive $\mathfrak{ct}_x$ from varid$_x$ and execute DistDecrypt(sid, $\mathfrak{ct}_x$, $\mathbb{C}$) on $\mathcal{F}_{\mathsf{KeyGenDec}}$.
2. The output y they receive is assigned to the register varid$_y$.

Trans$^{s \to t}$(sid, varid$_y$, varid$_x$):
1. The players in $\mathbb{C}$ retrieve $\mathfrak{ct}_x$ from varid$_x$, recall this is an FHE-encrypted ciphertext.
2. The players in $\mathbb{C}$ homomorphically compute

$$\mathfrak{ct}'_x \leftarrow \mathsf{Sym}(\ \mathfrak{ct}_x, \mathfrak{ct}_0;\ \mathsf{sid}, \mathsf{cnt}_{\mathfrak{c}}\ ).$$

3. The players in $\mathbb{C}$ execute $\mathbf{c} \leftarrow$ DistDecrypt(sid, $\mathfrak{ct}'_x$, $\mathbb{C}$) on $\mathcal{F}_{\mathsf{KeyGenDec}}$.
4. The output $\mathbf{c}$ they receive (along with the counter $\mathsf{cnt}_{\mathfrak{c}}$) is assigned to the register varid$_y$.
5. Incremement $\mathsf{cnt}_{\mathfrak{c}}$.

Trans$^{t \to s}$(sid, varid$_y$, varid$_x$):
1. The players in $\mathbb{C}$ retrieve $\mathsf{cnt}'_{\mathfrak{c}} \| \mathbf{c}_x$ from varid$_x$, recall this is a Sym-encrypted ciphertext with index $\mathsf{cnt}'_{\mathfrak{c}}$.
2. The players in $\mathbb{C}$ homomorphically compute

$$\mathfrak{ct}_y \leftarrow \mathsf{Sym}^{-1}(\ \mathbf{c}_x, \mathfrak{ct}_0;\ \mathsf{sid}, \mathsf{cnt}'_{\mathfrak{c}}\ ).$$

3. The output $\mathfrak{ct}_y$ is assigned to the register varid$_y$.

Fig. 7. The protocol for executing a program represented by a F-Circuit – Part IV

In the full version we prove the following theorem

Theorem 1. *In the random oracle model the protocol $\Pi_{F-Circuit}$ (in Figs. 4, 5, 6 and 7) UC realizes the functionality $\mathcal{F}_{F-Circuit}$ from Fig. 3 in the $\{\ \mathcal{F}_{\mathsf{KeyGenDec}}\ \}$-hybrid model, assuming the underlying FHE encryption scheme is IND-KEY secure, and the cipher Sym is IND-CPA.*

Acknowledgements. The author would like to thank Benoit Libert, Cyprien Delpech de Saint Guilhem, Emmanuela Orsini, and Titouan Tanguy for helpful conversations during the work on this paper. The work of the author was supported by CyberSecurity Research Flanders with reference number VR20192203, and by the FWO under an Odysseus project GOH9718N.

References

1. Asharov, G., Jain, A., López-Alt, A., Tromer, E., Vaikuntanathan, V., Wichs, D.: Multiparty computation with low communication, computation and interaction via threshold FHE. In: Pointcheval, D., Johansson, T. (eds.) EUROCRYPT 2012. LNCS, vol. 7237, pp. 483–501. Springer, Heidelberg (2012). https://doi.org/10.1007/978-3-642-29011-4_29

2. Asharov, G., Jain, A., Wichs, D.: Multiparty computation with low communication, computation and interaction via threshold FHE. Cryptology ePrint Archive, Report 2011/613 (2011). https://eprint.iacr.org/2011/613

3. Baghery, K., Guilhem, C.D.S., Orsini, E., Smart, N.P., Tanguy, T.: Compilation of function representations for secure computing paradigms. In: Paterson, K.G. (ed.) CT-RSA 2021. LNCS, vol. 12704, pp. 26–50. Springer, Cham (2021). https://doi.org/10.1007/978-3-030-75539-3_2

4. Balenbois, T., Orfila, J.B., Smart, N.P.: Trivial transciphering with Trivium and TFHE. Cryptology ePrint Archive, Paper 2023/980 (2023). https://eprint.iacr.org/2023/980

5. Baum, C., Cozzo, D., Smart, N.P.: Using TopGear in overdrive: a more efficient ZKPoK for SPDZ. In: Paterson, K.G., Stebila, D. (eds.) SAC 2019. LNCS, vol. 11959, pp. 274–302. Springer, Cham (2020). https://doi.org/10.1007/978-3-030-38471-5_12

6. Ben-David, A., Nisan, N., Pinkas, B.: FairplayMP: a system for secure multi-party computation. In: Ning, P., Syverson, P.F., Jha, S. (eds.) ACM CCS 2008: 15th Conference on Computer and Communications Security, Alexandria, Virginia, USA, 27–31 October 2008, pp. 257–266. ACM Press (2008). https://doi.org/10.1145/1455770.1455804

7. Bogdanov, D., Kamm, L.: Constructing privacy-preserving information systems using secure multiparty computation. Cybernetica Research Report T-4-13 (2011)

8. Bogdanov, D., Kamm, L., Laur, S., Pruulmann-Vengerfeldt, P., Talviste, R., Willemson, J.: Privacy-preserving statistical data analysis on federated databases. In: Preneel, B., Ikonomou, D. (eds.) APF 2014. LNCS, vol. 8450, pp. 30–55. Springer, Cham (2014). https://doi.org/10.1007/978-3-319-06749-0_3

9. Brakerski, Z.: Fully homomorphic encryption without modulus switching from classical GapSVP. In: Safavi-Naini, R., Canetti, R. (eds.) CRYPTO 2012. LNCS, vol. 7417, pp. 868–886. Springer, Heidelberg (2012). https://doi.org/10.1007/978-3-642-32009-5_50

10. Brakerski, Z., Gentry, C., Vaikuntanathan, V.: (Leveled) fully homomorphic encryption without bootstrapping. In: Goldwasser, S. (ed.) ITCS 2012: 3rd Innovations in Theoretical Computer Science, Cambridge, MA, USA, 8–10 January 2012, pp. 309–325. Association for Computing Machinery (2012). https://doi.org/10.1145/2090236.2090262

11. Canteaut, A., et al.: Stream ciphers: a practical solution for efficient homomorphic-ciphertext compression. In: Peyrin, T. (ed.) FSE 2016. LNCS, vol. 9783, pp. 313–333. Springer, Heidelberg (2016). https://doi.org/10.1007/978-3-662-52993-5_16

12. Catrina, O.: Complexity and performance of secure floating-point polynomial evaluation protocols. In: Bertino, E., Shulman, H., Waidner, M. (eds.) ESORICS 2021. LNCS, vol. 12973, pp. 352–369. Springer, Cham (2021). https://doi.org/10.1007/978-3-030-88428-4_18

13. Catrina, O., de Hoogh, S.: Improved primitives for secure multiparty integer computation. In: Garay, J.A., De Prisco, R. (eds.) SCN 2010. LNCS, vol. 6280, pp.

182–199. Springer, Heidelberg (2010). https://doi.org/10.1007/978-3-642-15317-4_13

14. Catrina, O., Saxena, A.: Secure computation with fixed-point numbers. In: Sion, R. (ed.) FC 2010. LNCS, vol. 6052, pp. 35–50. Springer, Heidelberg (2010). https://doi.org/10.1007/978-3-642-14577-3_6

15. Cheon, J.H., Kim, A., Kim, M., Song, Y.: Homomorphic encryption for arithmetic of approximate numbers. In: Takagi, T., Peyrin, T. (eds.) ASIACRYPT 2017. LNCS, vol. 10624, pp. 409–437. Springer, Cham (2017). https://doi.org/10.1007/978-3-319-70694-8_15

16. Chillotti, I., Gama, N., Georgieva, M., Izabachène, M.: TFHE: fast fully homomorphic encryption over the torus. J. Cryptol. **33**(1), 34–91 (2020). https://doi.org/10.1007/s00145-019-09319-x

17. Chillotti, I., Joye, M., Ligier, D., Orfila, J.B., Tap, S.: CONCRETE: concrete operates on ciphertexts rapidly by extending TFHE. In: 8th Workshop on Encrypted Computing and Applied Homomorphic Cryptography (WAHC 2020), pp. 57–63. Leibniz Universität IT Services (2020)

18. Choudhury, A., Loftus, J., Orsini, E., Patra, A., Smart, N.P.: Between a rock and a hard place: interpolating between MPC and FHE. In: Sako, K., Sarkar, P. (eds.) ASIACRYPT 2013. LNCS, vol. 8270, pp. 221–240. Springer, Heidelberg (2013). https://doi.org/10.1007/978-3-642-42045-0_12

19. Dahl, M., et al.: Noah's ark: efficient threshold-FHE using noise flooding. Cryptology ePrint Archive, Paper 2023/815 (2023). https://eprint.iacr.org/2023/815

20. Damgård, I., Fitzi, M., Kiltz, E., Nielsen, J.B., Toft, T.: Unconditionally secure constant-rounds multi-party computation for equality, comparison, bits and exponentiation. In: Halevi, S., Rabin, T. (eds.) TCC 2006. LNCS, vol. 3876, pp. 285–304. Springer, Heidelberg (2006). https://doi.org/10.1007/11681878_15

21. Damgård, I., Pastro, V., Smart, N., Zakarias, S.: Multiparty computation from somewhat homomorphic encryption. In: Safavi-Naini, R., Canetti, R. (eds.) CRYPTO 2012. LNCS, vol. 7417, pp. 643–662. Springer, Heidelberg (2012). https://doi.org/10.1007/978-3-642-32009-5_38

22. Cannière, C.: TRIVIUM: a stream cipher construction inspired by block cipher design principles. In: Katsikas, S.K., López, J., Backes, M., Gritzalis, S., Preneel, B. (eds.) ISC 2006. LNCS, vol. 4176, pp. 171–186. Springer, Heidelberg (2006). https://doi.org/10.1007/11836810_13

23. Dobraunig, C., Grassi, L., Helminger, L., Rechberger, C., Schofnegger, M., Walch, R.: Pasta: A case for hybrid homomorphic encryption. Cryptology ePrint Archive, Report 2021/731 (2021). https://eprint.iacr.org/2021/731

24. Ducas, L., Micciancio, D.: FHEW: bootstrapping homomorphic encryption in less than a second. In: Oswald, E., Fischlin, M. (eds.) EUROCRYPT 2015. LNCS, vol. 9056, pp. 617–640. Springer, Heidelberg (2015). https://doi.org/10.1007/978-3-662-46800-5_24

25. Fan, J., Vercauteren, F.: Somewhat practical fully homomorphic encryption. Cryptology ePrint Archive, Report 2012/144 (2012). https://eprint.iacr.org/2012/144

26. Feneuil, T., Maire, J., Rivain, M., Vergnaud, D.: Zero-knowledge protocols for the subset sum problem from MPC-in-the-head with rejection. In: Agrawal, S., Lin, D. (eds.) ASIACRYPT 2022. LNCS, vol. 13792, pp. 371–402. Springer, Heidelberg (2022). https://doi.org/10.1007/978-3-031-22966-4_13

27. Feneuil, T., Rivain, M.: Threshold linear secret sharing to the rescue of MPC-in-the-head. Cryptology ePrint Archive, Report 2022/1407 (2022). https://eprint.iacr.org/2022/1407

28. Fuchsbauer, G., Kiltz, E., Loss, J.: The algebraic group model and its applications. In: Shacham, H., Boldyreva, A. (eds.) CRYPTO 2018. LNCS, vol. 10992, pp. 33–62. Springer, Cham (2018). https://doi.org/10.1007/978-3-319-96881-0_2
29. Gentry, C.: A fully homomorphic encryption scheme. Ph.D. thesis, Stanford University (2009). https://crypto.stanford.edu/craig
30. Gentry, C., Sahai, A., Waters, B.: Homomorphic encryption from learning with errors: conceptually-simpler, asymptotically-faster, attribute-based. In: Canetti, R., Garay, J.A. (eds.) CRYPTO 2013. LNCS, vol. 8042, pp. 75–92. Springer, Heidelberg (2013). https://doi.org/10.1007/978-3-642-40041-4_5
31. Katz, J., Kolesnikov, V., Wang, X.: Improved non-interactive zero knowledge with applications to post-quantum signatures. In: Lie, D., Mannan, M., Backes, M., Wang, X. (eds.) ACM CCS 2018: 25th Conference on Computer and Communications Security, Toronto, ON, Canada, 15–19 October 2018, pp. 525–537. ACM Press (2018). https://doi.org/10.1145/3243734.3243805
32. Libert, B.: Vector commitments with short proofs of smallness. Cryptology ePrint Archive, Paper 2023/800 (2023). https://eprint.iacr.org/2023/800
33. López-Alt, A., Tromer, E., Vaikuntanathan, V.: On-the-fly multiparty computation on the cloud via multikey fully homomorphic encryption. In: Karloff, H.J., Pitassi, T. (eds.) 44th Annual ACM Symposium on Theory of Computing, New York, NY, USA, 19–22 May 2012, pp. 1219–1234. ACM Press (2012). https://doi.org/10.1145/2213977.2214086
34. Rotaru, D., Smart, N.P., Tanguy, T., Vercauteren, F., Wood, T.: Actively secure setup for SPDZ. J. Cryptol. 35(1), 5 (2022). https://doi.org/10.1007/s00145-021-09416-w

Author Index

E. A. Quaglia (Ed.): IMACC 2023, LNCS 14421, p. 285, 2024.
https://doi.org/10.1007/978-3-031-47818-5

Printed in the United States
by Baker & Taylor Publisher Services